Encyclopedia of
Classical Philosophy

D0209787

Encyclopedia of Classical Philosophy

Edited by Donald J. Zeyl

Associate Editors:
Daniel T. Devereux and Phillip T. Mitsis

GREENWOOD PRESS
Westport, Connecticut

Library of Congress Cataloging-in-Publication Data

Encyclopedia of classical philosophy / edited by Donald J. Zeyl ;
   associate editors, Daniel T. Devereux and Phillip T. Mitsis.
      p.   cm.
   Includes bibliographical references and index.
   ISBN 0–313–28775–9 (alk. paper)
    1. Philosophy, Ancient—Encyclopedias. 2. Philosophers, Ancient—
Biography—Encyclopedias. I. Zeyl, Donald J., 1944–
II. Devereux, Daniel. III. Mitsis, Phillip.
B163.E53   1997
180′.3—dc20   96–2562

British Library Cataloguing in Publication Data is available.

Library of Congress Catalog Card Number: 96–2562
ISBN: 0–313–28775–9

First published in 1997

Greenwood Press, 88 Post Road West, Westport, CT 06881
An imprint of Greenwood Publishing Group, Inc.

Printed in the United States of America

The paper used in this book complies with the
Permanent Paper Standard issued by the National
Information Standards Organization (Z39.48–1984).

10 9 8 7 6 5 4 3 2

Contents

Preface

The Encyclopedia of Classical Philosophy is a reference work in the philosophy of Greek and Roman antiquity. As such, its subject matter comprises subjects and figures from the dawn of philosophy in Ionia (on the west coast of modern Turkey) in the sixth century B.C.E. to the decline of the Academy in Athens in the sixth century C.E. The scholarly study of the texts and the philosophical thought of this period during the last half of the twentieth century has been amazingly productive and has become increasingly more sophisticated. Classical philologists have reexamined and reconstructed ancient papyri and collated manuscripts to determine with ever greater accuracy the contents of the original documents. Methods of source criticism have been refined, enabling a more accurate reconstruction of texts now lost to us. And philosophers have successfully applied contemporary methods of philosophical criticism to rediscover the profound originality and importance of these ancient thinkers and their relevance to contemporary philosophical inquiry and debate. British and North American scholars in particular, inspired by the scholarly rigor and brilliance of classicist-philosophers like G. E. L. Owen (1922–1982) and Gregory Vlastos (1907–1991), have transformed our view of Plato and Aristotle, their predecessors and successors, from that of being initiators of philosophical traditions that command mere historical interest to that of being participants in contemporary philosophical debates. The current discussion of "virtue ethics," for example, is inconceivable except against the background of Greek accounts of morality. Furthermore, it is widely recognized that the clarification of concepts and commitment to rigorous argument, hallmarks of contemporary philosophical method, are a vital legacy passed on to us by the ancients. As a result of these developments, the field of Classical Philosophy has moved from the periphery of humanistic studies to a place of central importance. Conferences and colloquia on subjects in Classical Philosophy abound, and professional organizations like the Society for Ancient Greek Philosophy, the International Plato Society, the *Symposium Aristotelicum*, the *Symposium Hellenisticum*, and the International Society for Neoplatonic Studies, to name a few of the more prominent ones, provide forums for scholarly discussion. Periodicals like *Phronesis*, *Apeiron*, *Ancient Philosophy*, and *Oxford Studies in Ancient Philosophy* feature articles exclusively devoted to work in Classical Philosophy.

The more than 270 articles in the encyclopedia reflect much of this recent work. Many of the articles are thematic. These include sketches of ancient thought in broad areas now considered central to philosophy, such as epistemology, ethics, and political thought. Some articles focus on particular concepts that evoked significant philosophical treatment by the ancients, which has proved foundational to later thought. Some articles treat fields that are now no longer considered part of philosophy proper, though they were considered an integral part of it in antiquity. These include mathematics and science, particularly medical science. Other articles treat other fields of intellectual or cultural endeavor, such as poetry or rhetoric, or genres of philosophical expression, such as dialogue or diatribe, important for the historical study of Classical Philosophy. Still others describe the historical developments of various philosophical schools and traditions in the ancient world. The bulk of the articles, however, is devoted to individual figures, major and minor.

The list of articles included in this work is by no means exhaustive. At various stages of its development, contributors were invited to propose modifications to the entry list. Many but not all of their suggestions were accepted, given constraints of space. In the final analysis, the choice of entries reflects the considered judgment of the editors.

Since the titles of almost all ancient texts are commonly rendered either in Latin or in the vernacular, we have not pressed for consistency in the use of either Latin or English titles. Readers will readily recognize that, for example, *On the Soul* and *De Anima* may refer to one and the same ancient work. Latin titles are used in abbreviations (see table of abbreviations).

In very many cases individuals and subjects mentioned in any one article have separate articles devoted to them. Asterisks indicate whenever this is the case; readers are encouraged to refer to these separate articles for more discussion. There is also a frequent and unavoidable overlap, particularly between the topical articles and the separate articles on individual figures mentioned in them. It has seemed best not to eliminate such overlap entirely; doing so would interrupt the flow and coherence of the articles in question. Finally, it should be remembered that the contributors to the encyclopedia often hold to divergent views about the same subjects. We have not attempted to impose consistency; all authors speaks for themselves.

We wish to express our thanks to each of the ninety scholars who contributed articles to this work. In addition, A. A. Long and A. D. P. Mourelatos gave valuable advice. David Konstan provided help by translating some of the articles. André Laks served as editorial consultant at an earlier stage of the project. His input, particularly in the area of Presocratic philosophy, has proved invaluable.

It is our sincere hope that *The Encyclopedia of Classical Philosophy* will serve as a useful tool for all who have a serious interest in the subject, whether as professional scholar, as student or as layperson, and that it will help kindle new interest in the field for generations to come.

The Editors
May 1997

Abbreviations

AGP		*Archiv für Geschichte der Philosophie*
AJP		*American Journal of Philology*
ANRW		W. Haase and H. Temporini, eds., *Aufstieg und Niedergang der römischen Welt*, Berlin
AP		*Ancient Philosophy*
Ar.		Aristotle
	APo.	*Posterior Analytics*
	APri.	*Prior Analytics*
	Ath. Pol.	*Constitution of Athens*
	Cat.	*Categories*
	DC	*De Caelo (On the Heavens)*
	DA	*De Anima (On the Soul)*
	EE	*Eudemian Ethics*
	fr.	*fragments*
	GA	*De Generatione Animalium (On the Generation of Animals)*
	GC	*De Generatione et Corruptione (On Coming to Be and Passing Away)*
	HA	*Historia Animalium (Inquiry into Animals)*
	Int.	*De Interpretatione (On Interpretation)*
	MA	*De Motu Animalium (On the Motion of Animals)*
	MM	*Magna Moralia*
	Met.	*Metaphysics*

NE	*Nicomachean Ethics*
PA	*De Partibus Animalium* (*On the Parts of Animals*)
Phys.	*Physics*
Poet.	*Poetics*
Pol.	*Politics*
Rh.	*Rhetoric*
Soph. El.	*De Sophisticis Elenchis* (*On Sophistical Refutations*)
Top.	*Topics*
CAG	var. eds., *Commentaria in Aristotelem Graeca*, Berlin, 1882–1909
Cic.	Cicero
Acad.	*Academica* (*Academic Questions*)
Att.	*Epistolae ad Atticum* (*Letters to Atticus*)
Fat.	*De Fato* (*On Fate*)
Fin.	*De Finibus* (*On Ends*)
Leg.	*De Legibus* (*On Laws*)
ND	*De Natura Deorum* (*On the Nature of the Gods*)
Or.	*De Oratore* (*On the Orator*)
Off.	*De Officiis* (*On Duties*)
Rep.	*De Republica* (*On Government*)
TD	*Tusculan Disputations*
CP	*Classical Philology*
CQ	*Classical Quarterly*
CronErc	*Cronache Ercolanesi*, Naples, 1971–
DK	H. Diels and W. Kranz, eds., *Fragmente der Vorsokratiker*, 6th ed., Berlin, 1951
D.L.	Diogenes Laertius, *Lives of Eminent Philosophers*
DPA	R. Goulet, ed., *Dictionnaire des philosophes antiques*, 2 vols., Paris, 1989, 1994
Eus.	Eusebius
HE	*Historia Ecclesiastica* (*History of the Church*)
PE	*Praeparatio Evangelica* (*Preparation for the Gospel*)
FDS	K. Hülser, ed., *Die Fragmente zur Dialektik der Stoiker*, Stuttgart, 1987–1988

FGH	F. Jacoby, ed., *Die Fragmente der griechischen Historiker*, Berlin/Leiden, 1923–1957
FHS&G	W. Fortenbaugh, P. Huby, R. Sharples and D. Gutas, eds., *Theophrastus of Eresus: Sources for His Life, Writings, Thought and Influence*, 2 vols., Leiden, 1992, repr. w. corr. 1993
GRBS	*Greek, Roman and Byzantine Studies*
Hipp.	Hippolytus
Ref.	*Refutation of All Heresies*
HSCP	*Harvard Studies in Classical Philology*
JHP	*Journal of the History of Philosophy*
JHS	*Journal of Hellenic Studies*
JRS	*Journal of Roman Studies*
KRS	G. S. Kirk, J. E. Raven, and M. Schofield, *The Presocratic Philosophers*, 2nd ed., Cambridge, 1983
LS	A. A. Long and D. N Sedley, eds. and trs., *The Hellenistic Philosophers*, 2 vols., Cambridge, 1987
LSJ	H. G. Liddell, R. Scott, and H. S. Jones, *A Greek–English Lexicon*, 9th ed., Oxford, 1940
Mus. Helv.	*Museum Helveticum*
OSAP	J. Annas et al., eds., *Oxford Studies in Ancient Philosophy*, 1983–
Ox. Pap.	B. P. Grenfell and A. S. Hunt, eds., *Oxyrhynchus Papyri*, 1898–
PAS	*Proceedings of the Aristotelian Society*
PBACAP	*Proceedings of the Boston Area Colloquium in Ancient Philosophy*
PCPS	*Proceedings of the Cambridge Philological Society*
PHerc.	Herculaneum papyri (numbered)
Philod.	Philodemus
Hist. Acad.	*History of the Academy*
Philos.	Philostratus
VS	*Vitae Sophistarum* (*Lives of the Sophists*)
Pl.	Plato
Alc.	*Alcibiades*
Ap.	*Apology*

Chrm.	*Charmides*
Cra.	*Cratylus*
Cri.	*Crito*
Criti.	*Critias*
Epin.	*Epinomis*
Euth.	*Euthyphro*
Euthyd.	*Euthydemus*
Grg.	*Gorgias*
Hipparch.	*Hipparchus*
Hp. Maj.	*Hippias Major*
Hp. Mi.	*Hippias Minor*
La.	*Laches*
Menex.	*Menexenus*
Phd.	*Phaedo*
Phdr.	*Phaedrus*
Phil.	*Philebus*
Pol.	*Politicus (Statesman)*
Prm.	*Parmenides*
Prt.	*Protagoras*
Rep.	*Republic*
Symp.	*Symposium*
Soph.	*Sophist*
Tht.	*Theaetetus*
Tim.	*Timaeus*
Plot.	Plotinus
Enn.	*Enneads*
Plut.	Plutarch
Mor.	*Moralia*
SR	*De Stoicorum Repugnantiis*
PR	*Philosophical Review*
RE	A. Pauly, G. Wissowa, and W. Kroll, eds., *Real-Encyclopädie der klassischen Altertumswissenschaft*, 83 vols., 1894–1980
Rev. Met.	*Review of Metaphysics*
Rh. Mus.	*Rheinisches Museum für Philologie*
RUSCH	*Rutgers University Studies in Classical Humanities*, New Brunswick, NJ, 1983–
SSR	G. Giannantoni, ed., *Socratis et Socraticorum Reliquiae*, 4 vols., 2nd ed., Naples, 1990
S.E.	Sextus Empiricus
HP	*Outlines of Pyrrhonism*

M	*Adversus Mathematicos* (*Against the Mathematicians*)
P	*Adversus Physicos* (*Against the Natural Philosophers*)
SVF	H. von Arnim, ed., *Stoicorum Veterum Fragmenta*, 3 vols., Leipzig, 1903–1905; vol. 4, indexes by M. Adler, Leipzig, 1924
TAPA	*Transactions of the American Philological Association*
Theophr.	Theophrastus
Ign.	*De Igne* (*On Fire*)
Vent.	*De Ventis* (*On Winds*)
Met.	*Metaphysics*
Sens.	*De Sensu* (*On Sense Perception*)
see also FHS&G above	
Usener	H. Usener, ed., *Epicurea*, Leipzig, 1887, repr. Stuttgart, 1966
Wehrli	F. Wehrli, ed., *Die Schule des Aristoteles: Texte und Kommentar*, 10 vols. and 2 suppl., 2nd ed., Basel, 1969
Xen.	Xenophon
Ap.	*Apology of Socrates*
Mem.	*Memorabilia*
Symp.	*Symposium*
YCS	*Yale Classical Studies*
ZPE	*Zeitschrift für Papyrologie und Epigraphik*

A

ACADEMY. The Athenian "school" of philosophy founded by *Plato. Until recently, the standard account has had the Academy founded by Plato and in continuous existence thereafter until Justinian closed the schools of Athens in 529 C.E. Lynch and especially Glucker have completely altered our picture of developments from the first century B.C.E. on. In the second century C.E., *Sextus Empiricus writes (*HP* 1.220): "There have been, so most say, three Academies: one, and (the) most ancient, that of Plato and his circle, second, the middle (Academy), that of *Arcesilaus, the student of *Polemo, third, the new (Academy), that of *Carneades, *Clitomachus, and their circle; but some add as a fourth that of *Philo (of Larissa), Charmidas, and their circle, and some even count as a fifth that of *Antiochus and his circle." The existence of the "fourth" and "fifth" Academies is doubtful enough, but the situation is far worse thereafter. This article divides the story into five pieces: the Old Academy, the Middle Academy, the New Academy (the latter two labels should not be taken too seriously; see below), Philo and Antiochus, and the Revival of *Platonism.

The Old Academy. In the mid-380s, Plato returned from Sicily to Athens and, in a publicly owned suburban grove sacred to the hero Akademos (or Hekademos) began some sort of teaching activity. He attracted a number of leading intellectuals, including *Eudoxus, *Speusippus, *Xenocrates, *Heraclides of Pontus, and *Aristotle. There were also apparently at least two women associated with the early Academy, Lastheneia and Axiothea (who is supposed to have taken herself, disguised as a man, to the Academy after reading the *Republic*). Unfortunately, nothing whatever is known about them.

In spite of the twentieth-century connotation of the name, the Academy was no ivory tower: One of the main enterprises of the Old Academy was the training of politicians and advisors to politicians. Although this was accompanied by a lot of theorizing, many of those associated with the early Academy were men of action, of whom Dion, killed (by another Academic, Callippus) in an attempt to overthrow Dionysius II of Syracuse, is only the most famous. The Academy was best known, however, for its theorizing, in the areas of philosophy, mathematics, astronomy, biology, and just about everything else; and after the Old Academy we hear no more of the training of politicians.

The nature of Plato's teaching activity is unclear; all we have is reports of uncertain reliability to the effect that he conversed with his associates while walking, that he gave a public lecture, "On the Good," and that symposia marked by simple fare and decorous behavior were common. But it looks as if *dialectic, in the form of question-and-answer competitions as Aristotle describes them in *Topics* 7, was employed as a teaching device.

In such matches, one sooner or later had to argue on both sides of any given question. It is not surprising, then, that the views ascribable to the earliest associates of the Academy show wide variation: hedonism (Eudoxus) alongside an almost puritanical anti-hedonism (Speusippus), acceptance of the "theory of Forms" (for which see PLATO; see also XENOCRATES) and its wholesale rejection (Speusippus, Aristotle). The Academy was not a school concerned to propagate a doctrine, and Plato appears to have set problems (e.g., that of describing the motions of the heavenly bodies in terms of circles: see EUDOXUS) without attempting to establish anything as orthodoxy. Still, however much they might disagree, the members of the Old Academy supposed that there was some way of answering the sorts of problems posed by Plato; this contrasts the Old Academy with its successors.

Plato was the Academy's first head or "scholarch" (the term later used); he was succeeded after his death in 348/347 by Speusippus, and then by Xenocrates (339), Polemo (314), and *Crates of Athens (c. 276; d. c. 273). During the lifetimes of the last two, *Crantor would have been active in the school, and at least a part of its activity was devoted to commenting on the dialogues of Plato.

The Middle Academy. Crates was succeeded as head of the Academy by Arcesilaus, who in turn was succeeded by *Lacydes (in c. 242), Evander, and Hegesinus (these two are only names to us). Under Arcesilaus, the Academy ceased to show the variety of doctrines that had characterized it before; from here on through the New Academy, Academics were *skeptics. "Skeptic" is a later but convenient label; the Academics from Arcesilaus on referred to their view as "suspension" (*epochē*), that is, suspension of judgment. A number of factors may have been influential in this turn to skepticism: (i) It could be that the very tolerance of variety that prevailed in the Old Academy lent itself to skepticism. In particular, the same tendencies that kept the Old Academy from adopting an orthodox doctrine may have pointed the way: Arcesilaus was noted for his ability to argue on both sides of a question (cf. Cic. *Fin.* 5.10; D.L. 4.28: the latter needs corrective interpretation), and this was the hallmark of the Academy down to Carneades and Clitomachus. (ii) One of the first of Plato's views to come under attack in the Old Academy was the metaphysics of his middle period, the theory of Forms, but rejection of this seems to have gone along with an acceptance of the extremely high demands placed on knowledge in connection with that theory; hence, the problem surfaces in Aristotle of how we can be said to know anything if knowledge is rooted in universals but reality is composed of particulars (*Met.* 3.4). (iii) The *Stoics (see STOA, ZENO of Citium, and CHRYSIPPUS) were putting out a positive theory of knowledge, and the evidence (see, e.g., Cic. *Acad.* 2.77–78) points toward the conclusion that the skeptical Academy's views were formed in interaction with this theory, by way of criticism of it. (iv) There is evidence of a direct influence of *Pyrrho on Arcesilaus (D.L. 3.33; *Numenius, cited in Eus. *PE* 14.6.4), which cannot be simply discounted. (v) Perhaps most important, the adherents of the skeptical Academy thought they could trace their skepticism back to Plato himself: They read Plato's dialogues as espousing suspension of judgment (cf. Cic. *Acad.* 1.46, 2.74, *Or.* 3.67, D.L. 4.32). This is easy enough to understand in the case of the Socratic dialogues; the later dialogues might be more resistant to this interpretation, but even there the *Parmenides* is critical of the theory of Forms and the *Theaetetus* fails to provide an analysis of the concept of knowledge.

The skepticism of the Middle and New Academies was regarded as a distinct form of skepticism from that of Pyrrho and Pyrrhonism (see SKEPTICISM, Ancient). Agreement on what the difference is has yet to be found: Sextus, who counts himself as a Pyrrhonist, seems to think of the Academics as professing their skepticism as a positive claim to the effect that things are not knowable, whereas he himself "continues to investigate" (*HP* 1.3; cf. 232–233), while *Cicero tells us that Arcesilaus denied that anything could be known, including the claim that one knows nothing, and that he convinced people of this by arguing against every positive opinion offered (*Acad.* 1.45). This latter technique is fairly consistently associated with the Middle and New Academies.

The New Academy. Hegesinus was succeeded by Carneades (d. 129/128) and Clitomachus (d. 110/109); other philosophers mentioned in this connection are Charmadas (who perhaps is the same as the Charmidas mentioned by Sextus), Aeschines, and *Metrodorus of Stratonicea (Cic. *Or.* 1.45).

Cicero in fact labels the Academy from Arcesilaus on through Carneades "New," and that may suggest that it is only the fame of Carneades that marks Sextus' "New" off from the "Middle" Academy. But there may be a substantive difference: Carneades introduces as "a rule both for the conduct of life and for inquiry," what is plausible or truth-like (Cic. *Acad.* 2.32). "Plausible" (*probabile*, often translated, perhaps wrongly, as "probable") and "truth-like" (*veri simile*) are Cicero's attempts to Latinize the Greek *pithanon*, "persuasive"; Sextus even refers to the *pithanon* as a "criterion" (*M* 7.166–175). How precisely this differentiates Carneades and the New Academy from Arcesilaus and the Middle Academy is a matter of dispute (see CARNEADES).

Another suggestion is that a technique of arguing, not just against every positive opinion as it arises, but pro and con every thesis, was characteristic of the New Academy as opposed to the Middle Academy (cf. Plut. *SR* 1035f–1036a with Lactantius *Institutiones Divinae* 5.14.3–5); but since this technique goes back to the practice of dialectic in the Old Academy, it would be surprising if this suggestion were right.

Philo and Antiochus. Clitomachus was succeeded by Philo of Larissa, who seems to have been a skeptic when he studied under Clitomachus; his most notable students included Antiochus of Ascalon and Cicero. It looks as if it was at this point in time that the Academy fell apart, or at least began to fall apart. In 86 B.C.E., Sulla conquered Athens; Philo was already in Rome. The dispute between Philo and Antiochus appears to stem from this Roman period; it concerned skepticism and the history of the Academy itself and is the main subject of Cicero's *Academica*, in which Cicero sided with Philo. Philo now wanted to defend the possibility of knowledge, as did Antiochus; both wanted to claim that their positions were those of the Old Academy. However, it looks as if, while Antiochus accepted the Stoic idea of a "cognitive impression" (*phantasia kataleptikê*) as the basis for knowledge, Philo redefined the notion of knowledge so that knowledge could be had for less. The result in both cases, but vastly more so in the case of Antiochus, was an assimilation of the Old Academy to Stoicism, and it was this that led *Aenesidemus to defect from the Academy, saying that "those from the Academy ... are plainly Stoics fighting with Stoics" (Photius *Bibliotheca* 170ab).

Antiochus is said by Numenius (Eus. *PE* 739cd) to "have started another Academy." But it appears that the school Antiochus founded was one he called "the Old Academy": It was not a continuation of the Academy at Athens.

In 44 B.C.E. Brutus heard one "Theomnestus the Academic" in Athens (Plut. *Brutus* 24.1). About him nothing else is known (he may be the same as Theomnestus of Naucratis, mentioned by *Philostratus as a bombastic orator and philosopher in *VS* 486).

In 63 C.E., *Seneca (*Quaestiones Naturales* 7.32.2) wrote, "The Academics, both old and new, have no teacher left." There were Platonists in the intervening period, and there were Platonists afterward. But they were not associated with an institution that could be called "the Academy." The following philosophers used to be cited as "scholarchs of the Academy." (i) Ammonius the Egyptian, the teacher of *Plutarch of Chaeronea, taught in Athens and seems to have been a Platonist of sorts, but there is no reason to associate him with the Academy (see Jones). (ii) Calvisius or Calvenus Taurus was Plutarch's student and the teacher of the Roman author Aulus Gellius (c. 130–c. 180); Gellius refers to him as "a man of living memory renowned in the Platonic discipline" (7.10.1) and implies that he taught in his own house (2.2.2). (iii) One Atticus is referred to by *Proclus as a Platonist (*In Tim.* 1.276.31–277.1), but no ancient source associates him with Athens. (iv) Theodotus and Eubulus (3rd cent. C.E.) are referred to by *Porphyry as "Platonic successors at Athens" (*diadochoi*, *Life of Plotinus* 20.39–40, with 15.18–19). But this is after the institution by the emperor *Marcus Aurelius of chairs of Platonic, Stoic, *Peripatetic, and *Epicurean philosophy at Athens (Philos. *VS* 566): Theodotus and Eubulus were presumably holders of such chairs, not successors to the scholarchate of the Academy.

Revival of Platonism. In the third century *Plotinus lent new life to Platonism by creating the movement referred to as "Neoplatonism" (see PLATONISM); it was carried on by Porphyry and *Iamblichus. None of these had anything much to do with Athens. But in the fifth and sixth centuries C.E. a number of philosophers participated in the great revival of Platonism in Athens; although some of them are described as "Platonic successors," they do not pretend that their school is in any literal sense a continuation of the Academy. They include *Plutarch of Athens (d. c. 431/432), *Syrianus, Domninus, Proclus, Marinus, Isidore, Zenodotus, *Damascius, and *Simplicius. The last few of these are those affected by Justinian's decree in 529. But it is not clear that this decree had much effect: The activity of these philosophers, after a brief trip to Persia, appears to have resumed at Athens (see Cameron).

But then we hear no more.

BIBLIOGRAPHY: Cameron, A., *PCPS* 195 (n.s. 15), 1969, 7–29; Glucker, J., *Antiochus and the Late Academy* [*Hypomnemata* 56], Göttingen, 1978; Jones, C. P., *HSCP* 71, 1966, 205–213; Lynch, J. P., *Aristotle's School: A Study of a Greek Educational Institution*, Berkeley/Los Angeles, 1972.—R. M. DANCY

AELIAN, Claudius (c. 170–235 C.E.), of Praeneste. Rhetorician and anthologer. Aelian, an Italian who worked much of his life in Rome under imperial patronage, taught *rhetoric and compiled anthologies in Greek for popular reading and moral instruction. *On the Characteristics of Animals* was a collection of descriptions of the behavior of animals with special attention to quasi-human behavior, "marvelous" phenomena, and evidence of morality and providential order in nature. *Miscellanies* (*Varia Historia*) contained a collection of ethnographic information and anecdotes about famous people with moralizing comments. Though the latter survives only in abridged form, it contains a wealth of otherwise unknown historical and biographical information, some relating to the Greek philosophers. Aelian also wrote *On Providence* and *On Evidences of Divinity*, two anthologies that have been lost except for a few quotations. Aelian's works illustrate the extensive influence of *Stoicism on popular culture in the late second century C.E. and remain important sources for lost authors and writings.

BIBLIOGRAPHY: Texts in A. F. Scholfield, ed. and tr., *Aelian: On the Characteristics of Animals*, 3 vols. (Loeb), Cambridge, MA/London, 1958–59 and M. R. Dilts, ed., *Claudius Aelianus, Varia Historia*, Leipzig, 1974. Wellmann, M., "Claudius Aelianus (11)," *RE* 1, 1893, 486–88.—*DAVID E. HAHM*

AENESIDEMUS (1st cent. B.C.E.), of Cnossus. Second founder of *Pyrrhonian *skepticism. Though this has been disputed, it seems that Aenesidemus was active in the first century B.C.E. He was an Academic who became dissatisfied with the increasingly dogmatic character of the *Academy of his time and left it to become a Pyrrhonist. Though the evidence does not permit us to speak with certainty on this matter, this seems to have been more a matter of creating or reviving a Pyrrhonian school than joining an already-established one. His writings survive only in fragments. We know of eight books of *Pyrrhonian Discourses*, an *Outline Introduction to Pyrrhonian Matters*, and books entitled *Against Wisdom* and *Concerning Inquiry*. An important summary of the first of these by Photius, the ninth-century Byzantine Patriarch, has survived. It is probable that these works exerted a significant influence on the form and content of the books of subsequent Pyrrhonists, including *Sextus Empiricus, whose work has survived in bulk and who is, in consequence, our principal source of information about the later Pyrrhonism that begins with Aenesidemus.

To Aenesidemus his fellow Academics seemed to be little better than *Stoics fighting Stoics, disagreeing only about the cognitive impression, the Stoics' criterion of truth. This characterization seems to apply best to the views of *Philo of Larissa, who was the head of the Academy in the first part of the first century B.C.E. Matters are made more complicated, however, by the fact that Philo seems to have changed his views. Roughly speaking, basing himself on the arguments first developed by *Arcesilaus against the cognitive impression, he first held that knowledge was impossible. At this time he conceived knowledge pretty much as the Stoics did, but unlike them he was able to view his skeptical conclusion with equanimity because he held a very robust view of probability. Indeed he gave up the skeptical commitment to suspension of judgment and held that the wise person could and should form opinions about matters of practical and theoretical import by assenting to highly probable impressions while remaining aware that they were not completely certain. This is the position called mitigated skepticism by Hume, who knew of it through *Cicero. Later, however, Philo came to think that knowledge, properly understood, was possible; he now took the Academy's skeptical arguments to imply that knowledge was impossible only according to the Stoic conception, with its demand for a foundation of absolutely certain perceptual impressions. Neither position is likely to have found favor with Aenesidemus. The first, which enjoyed more support within the Academy, may well already have seemed enough of a betrayal of the Academy's skeptical heritage to induce Aenesidemus to break with it. In any case, he vehemently disapproved of the Academy's appeal to probability.

Thus Aenesidemus's turn to *Pyrrho marked a self-conscious return to radical skepticism. Attempts to trace a continuous line of succession back to Pyrrho were already regarded as constructions by Aenesidemus's successors, however. Rather, it seems that Pyrrho appealed to Aenesidemus primarily as an inspiring figure whose life vividly attested to the power of the skeptical attitude to produce tranquillity. Presumably, Aenesidemus drew on ancient traditions about Pyrrho. For example, the ten tropes—or argumentative strategies—for the suspension of judgment that he put together, are often thought to owe something to such traditions. Together with the eight tropes to be employed against causal explanation, the ten tropes are the Pyrrhonian teaching that can be most securely attributed to Aenesidemus. They were widely known in antiquity, making an appearance, for example, in *Philo of Alexandria, who was active in the early first century C.E.

It is also likely that Aenesidemus had some contact with and learned from medical Empiricism (see MEDICINE, Ancient theories of). There was certainly a strong affinity between Pyrrhonism and the medical Empiricists after Aenesidemus's time; six of the eight figures after him on our list of Pyrrhonists were also medical Empiricists. And though it is not clear how the figures preceding him on the list should be regarded, the fact that his two immediate predecessors were Empiricists is probably significant.

In view of Aenesidemus's insistence on the radical character of his skepticism, it comes as a surprise to find Sextus Empiricus speaking of his interest in Heracliteanism and, in particular, making frequent use of the expression "*Heraclitus according to Aenesidemus" in contexts in which he goes on to relate views that cannot be reconciled with skepticism. This has always puzzled interpreters, and there have been attempts to resolve the difficulty by postulating Heraclitean and skeptical stages in Aenesidemus's career. More recently and more plausibly an attempt has been made to show how Aenesidemus's Heraclitean interests were part of his Pyrrhonism. According to this approach, Aenesidemus was not an adherent but an interpreter of Heraclitus, who advanced his interpretations to further legitimate skeptical aims, as by showing the Stoics that Heraclitus lent himself to interpretations different from their own.

BIBLIOGRAPHY: Annas, J., and J. Barnes, *The Modes of Skepticism*, Cambridge, 1985; Burkhard, U., *Die angebliche Heraklit-Nachfolge des Skeptikers Aenesidem*, Bonn, 1973; Striker, G., in M. Burnyeat, ed., *The Skeptical Tradition*, Berkeley, 1983, 95–115.—JAMES ALLEN

AESCHINES (fl. 390 B.C.E.), of Sphettus, a deme in Athens. Also known as Aeschines Socraticus, close companion of *Socrates and writer of Socratic *dialogues. Little is known of his life; he is said to have spent some time in Syracuse at the court of Dionysius and to have written speeches in the style of *Gorgias for delivery in the Athenian courts. *Plato lists him among those present at Socrates' trial (*Ap.* 33e) and death (*Phd.* 59b).

Aeschines was often listed by ancient critics among the most important writers of Socratic dialogues, along with Plato, *Xenophon, and *Antisthenes. Praised for their lifelike portrait of Socrates and their vivid prose style, Aeschines' dialogues seem to have concentrated more on Socrates' character and influence than on the development of Socratic doctrines. Enough fragments survive of two dialogues, *Alcibiades* and *Aspasia*, for plausible reconstruction. Following the work of Ehlers, recent scholarship sees in both dialogues the characteristic Socratic idea that eros plays an indispensable role in moral pedagogy. Aeschines may well have initiated the literary exploration of this theme.

Though there is no sure way to disentangle the lines of influence between Aeschines' dialogues and the writings of the other *Socratics, he was clearly an important figure in the literary competition among Socrates' heirs in the early fourth century, and the fragments of his dialogues are precious eyewitness testimony to the personality of Socrates.

BIBLIOGRAPHY: Texts in *SSR* 2, 593–629. Dittmar, H., *Aischines von Sphettos* (= *Philologische Untersuchungen* 21), Berlin, 1912; Döring, K., *Hermes* 1984, 16–30; Ehlers, B., *Eine vorplatonische Deutung des sokratischen Eros. Der Dialog Aspasia des sokratikers Aischines* (= *Zetemata* 41), Munich, 1966; Kahn, C., in P. A. Vander Waerdt, ed., *The Socratic Movement*, Ithaca, 1995, 87–106.—DAVID K. O'CONNOR

AESCHYLUS. See POETS, TRAGIC.

AESTHETICS, Classical. The ancients never developed an autonomous branch of philosophy devoted to the experience of beauty as a distinct faculty or attitude of mind. But if aesthetics be defined broadly as philosophizing about the nature of beauty or the arts, Greco-Roman antiquity clearly contributed many key terms and lines of inquiry that inform even post-Kantian aesthetics. In surveying this contribution, however, it is useful to bear in mind some of the major respects in which ancient and modern aesthetics differ: (i) Beauty was generally conceived by the ancients as a property wholly inherent in objects, constituted independently of any mode of perception. (ii) The Greek word that comes closest to "beautiful" or "fine" (*kalos*) carried with it notions of goodness and utility so that questions of aesthetic value are very rarely treated apart from ethics, politics, or metaphysics. (iii) From earliest times, ancient discussions of artifacts value those that resemble (*eoike*) reality or truth (rather than, for example, artistic expression); hence art was thought to invite cognition at least as much as sensory appreciation. The following very selective survey will aim to touch especially on these issues.

Pre-Platonic Aesthetic Speculation. The earliest extensive discussions of aesthetic questions we have are *Plato's, although a tradition of Greek attitudes toward works of art is discernible among the remains of earlier poets and philosophers. *Homer's admiring description of Achilles' shield in *Iliad* 18 is often claimed as proto-aesthetics, but the qualities for which he and others praise artifacts range from verisimilitude and fine craftsmanship to the richness of materials employed or the social distinction of the object's owner. Equally difficult to interpret, though also relevant, are statements by poets about the functions of their art and the sources of their powers. Homer and his followers claim for song an intense and god-sent pleasurableness; copresent with this idea, but not clearly articulated with it, are claims that poetry tells the truth and disseminates social values through praise and blame. By the time of Pindar, such ideas are complicated with an awareness that natural talent and technique may contribute to success in poetry and a heightened sense that appropriateness (*to prepon*) and "sweetness" of language can be more affecting in poetry than truth. These ideas were significantly elaborated in *Sophistic explorations of *rhetoric as the art of overcoming reason with semblance (often invoking analogies with poetry and artifacts, as in *Gorgias' *Helen* and *Dissoi Logoi*, DK90.2, 3).

Pre-Platonic philosophy provided a broad conceptual context for aesthetic discussion with such notions as the universe as an ordered whole (*kosmos*) or the sundering of appearance from truth. But in the treatment of specific arts a clear landmark is the attack on Homer and *Hesiod on moral and metaphysical grounds by *Xenophanes who for the first time explicitly opposes the truth or wisdom available from reasoning (*logos*) to the "fictions" (*plasmata*) that poets or sculptors purvey (DK21B1.22). At the same time, allegorizing defenders of the poets discovered profound cosmic truths hidden beneath the literal surface of the words. Early *Pythagoreans apparently contributed a significant positive account of one of the arts: Their mathematical researches not only rendered music fully intelligible in abstract, formal terms but also linked it intimately with the underlying design of nature. Perhaps equally important was the polymathic *Democritus, as is suggested by attested works on rhythm, harmony, poetry, singing, painting, and the beauty of language (or verses). Unfortunately, we usually lack the context of his numerous striking pronouncements about such topics as imitation, inspiration, and the evolution of the arts. Notice should also be taken of the many lost treatises on individual arts composed by renowned practitioners in fifth-century Athens, such as Polycleitus' *Canon* on proportion in sculpture. Such literature is a salutary reminder that notions of art and beauty often have much to do with the social positions open to artisans and the uses to which artifacts are put in a given culture.

Plato. If on the whole Plato's views are hostile to aesthetics—in disparaging mere phenomenal beauty and in denying any valuable knowledge to art—yet aesthetics owes it to him that defining the nature of beauty is a topic of philosophy and that a certain class of artifacts has been isolated as eliciting a particular kind of response. It is mildly paradoxical but not accidental that defenses of the arts, from the Neoplatonist through the Renaissance, often keep most of Plato's terms while reversing his key judgments.

Throughout his corpus, in a variety of contexts and without perfect consistency, Plato sought to discern what properties might be shared by the many things called *kalos* by the Greeks (*Hp. Maj.* 286cff.), in this possibly continuing concerns of *Socrates (Xen. *Mem.* 3.8; 3.10). Plato conceded that sensory beauties may lead to the rapt contemplation of the Form of beauty (*Symp.* 210–12); but the Form of beauty, objectively real and invariable (*Rep.* 479a), is grasped with the mind and not the senses (*Phd.* 65). Among perceptible objects, certain (simple) sounds, shapes and colors are defined as "intrinsically" beautiful, invariably yielding "pure" or "true" pleasures (*Phil.* 50e–52b). Their beauty depends on, probably without being constituted by, objective and measurable properties of the object, especially those hallmarks of classical aesthetics, measure (*metron*), proportion (*summetron*), and unity (64e, 66b). But "imitative arts" like painting and drama provide by definition complex or "mixed" pleasures and so do not provide this distinctively aesthetic enjoyment (50). In the end, *Philebus* seems to give sensory pleasures little value in comparison with those of intellection as constituents of a happy human life (66a–c). Thus if Plato sometimes allows certain kinds of beauty and pleasure a sphere of autonomous activity and value, imitative arts have no special connection with, and indeed are often excluded from, the possibility of embodying the higher forms of beauty.

One way to indicate the aesthetic significance of the multivalent term "imitation" for Plato is to show how he combined it with the notion of "art" to collocate a class of objects that comes close to the Enlightenment category of *Beaux Arts*. The traditional Greek sense of *technê* was very wide, comprising virtually any "art," "craft," or "skill" in production or action. Among the *technai*, poetry, music, and dance had long been closely associated in practice, and by the fifth century had acquired a distinct name as the "Muses' arts"—*mousikê*. But there are no explicit comparisons between these "Musical" arts and others we would call "fine" before the classical period. In Plato this collocation occurs via a particular word for "copying," *mimêsis*. First attested in the late sixth century (*Homeric Hymn to Apollo* 163) with the sense of "mimicking" the voices or gestures of men or animals, in the fifth century *mimêsis* was extended to statues and dramatic poems. It may have been Plato's achievement to use *mimêsis* to combine the "Musical" arts with a select group of the "productive" skills (painting, sculpture, sometimes architecture) as all essentially "imitative." To make this new class of interest coherent, Plato seems to have relied on the Pythagorean notion (*Rep.* 400) that music can "imitate" states of the soul, that is, that it has content.

In the *Sophist*, Plato's most elaborate classification of the *technai*, the "imitative art" by which painters and poets produce images (*eidôla*) of existent things, is suggestively distinguished from the "productive arts" by which artisans produce actual objects (265–266c). But the imitative arts also include such "low" skills as mimicry and sophistry; they are defined metaphysically rather than aesthetically as united by the similar (and inferior) ontological status of their productions. Although the gods may be said to practice imitative art in fashioning dreams (e.g., *Soph.* 265 ff.), mortal imitators are condemned to copy or to represent appearances and not eternal Forms (*Rep.* 597). Artistic knowledge *stricto sensu* is only a "knack" (*tribê*) for producing effects, or pseudo-craft based on opinion (*doxa, Grg.* 463–465). Accordingly, the ladder by which the soul ascends to the apprehension of absolute Beauty in the *Symposium* begins with perceptions of beautiful bodies but has no rung reserved for artistic imitations of Beauty.

Plato's low estimation of the imitative arts is made more complex by his high opinion of their influence for good or ill. Plato allowed that a great poet was "inspired" in the sense (already in Democritus) of creating in a divine frenzy (*Phdr.* 245a), and that poets in their *mania* may chance to utter valuable truths (*Laws* 682a) but do so unconsciously, like diviners, and require knowledgeable interpreters (*Tim.* 71e–72b; *Ion* 534).

Because poets, painters, and sculptors can imitate the ethical character of human souls and thereby powerfully shape character (*Rep.* 400–401b), the statesman, whose art is supreme over theirs (*Rep.* 342c), is obliged to "judge" what sort of *mousikê* and art is beneficial to the state (*Rep.* 377ff.; *Laws* 653ff.). This judging involves knowing the true nature of the original so as to estimate the correctness of the copy and so judge the excellence with which the copy is executed (*Laws* 669a–b). Plato's political critique is thus based on a psychology of art in which aesthetic experience bypasses intellection while refusing what we call aesthetic distance: Poets appeal to a low part of the soul which identifies unreflectively with what is represented and demands immediate satisfaction (*Rep.* 605–6). He finally objects to art's encouraging the better parts of the soul to weaken their command over the lower.

Although neither Plato nor the Greeks ever defined art as a set of certain objects that demand to be experienced with a certain attitude of mind, Plato did come close in reflecting on the various arts (*technai*) to establishing a group like the fine arts in that they elicit a particular kind of pleasurable experience, which (to their loss) is not to be equated with philosophical knowledge.

Aristotle. The loss of *Aristotle's treatise(s) on beauty (Rose, frs. 1.69, 2.63) can partly be recuperated from his extant writings (e.g., *Met.* 13, 1078a31–b6), but the single most influential document in the history of Western art theory and criticism has been his *Poetics*, despite the fact that it is incompletely preserved (a second book on comedy seems to be lost) and often terse to the point of unclarity.

The *Poetics* begins by collecting under the term *mimêsis* roughly the same kinds of arts as Plato, but Aristotle makes their object characters and actions rather than phenomenal appearances, and he allows for idealizing or satiric as well as realistic "representations" (1460b9–11, 33–35). Poetry is wholly natural, arising from human propensities to imitate and to take pleasure in imitations, the latter due to a concomitant kind of learning (ch. 4). The natural pleasure in imitations enables Aristotle to explain the paradox that tragedies arouse pleasure by exciting painful emotions (1448b13; 10–15; cf. *Rhet.* 2.5.8), for even painful or distasteful objects may be pleasant to contemplate *in imitation* (cf. *PA* 1.5; *Rhet.* 1.11).

Each genre or mode of imitation has the *dunamis* (1447a9) to produce particular kinds of pleasure, and the "pleasure peculiar to the form" (*oikeia hêdonê*, 1453a36, etc.) yields the criteria for its evaluation. The "finest" (*kallistê*, 1452b30–33) tragedy will be the one in which final and formal causes converge, as each element (from diction to costume) contributes teleologically "to produce the pleasure of pity and fear through imitation" (1453b11–13; 1452b32–33). Hence tragedy should have a clearly unified plot "so that, like a whole, unified animal, it may produce its proper pleasure" (1459a20; cf. Pl. *Phdr.* 264c for the analogy). Judging particular works *in terms of the art* then is not a matter of evaluating their truth or moral effect but of deciding how well their component parts promote or inhibit the appropriate pleasure (1460b). In this vein Aristotle is sometimes heralded as the first formalist critic, prescribing that it is the artist's task to impose, and the recipient's to perceive, significant form on the work. But formal structures are always for Aristotle structured contents, the contents ("plots") of tragedy being ethical actions and their results. Aristotle never suggests that the fine arts are a free and independent activity of the mind. But precisely what ends he assigned to art as a whole are bound up with the vexed question of *katharsis*.

Aristotle's definition of tragedy implies that its end is "through pity and fear effecting the *katharsis* of such emotions" (1449b26–28). Different conceptions of the function of tragedy, and of art, follow from whether *katharsis* is given its medical sense, "purgation," implying elimination of harmful emotions as by a physic, or its other uses, such as ritual "purification," which might suggest some subtly improving function. A basis for the latter course has been associating the pleasant learning we derive from imitations (ch. 4) with Aristotle's declaration (ch. 9) that poetry is more philosophical than history because it relates "the kinds of thing a certain kind of person will say or do in accordance with probability or necessity" rather than the discrete and sometimes random particulars of real events. It may then be inferred that tragic *katharsis* is the pleasure of learning general patterns of moral action. But (i) "learning from imitations" in ch. 4 is illustrated at the low level of learning that a picture of Socrates represents Socrates (cf. *Rhet.* 1.11); (ii) ch. 9 as a whole seems concerned with making plots plausible rather than instructive (though it was often misread in neoclassical criticism as enjoining the poet to paint "Universals" or "Characteristicks").

Recent commentators have taken a different approach, beginning with the doctrine of the emotions in the *Nicomachean Ethics*. This shows that Aristotelian emotions are not per se in need of purging, and suggests that tragedy may be conducive to *virtue by habituating the audience to respond appropriately to proper objects. *Katharsis* may thus be seen as a "clarification" or "refinement" of the emotions in the sense that the audience gains a well-balanced disposition to react with appropriate emotions in life. On this interpretation Aristotle would be answering Plato by saying that poetry does not "water the emotions" but disciplines them by exciting them within a morally coherent structure. Still, it is not clear how, or whether, this view of *katharsis* should be reconciled with *Politics* 8, and especially 1341b32ff., where Aristotle (cross-referring to "the work on poetry") says certain kinds of music have a function, distinct from edification, of "purging" their auditors by giving their emotions harmless but pleasurable release. It is after all sufficient to respond to Plato by saying that the effects of tragedy are not harmful.

Aristotle nowhere explicitly describes the *Poetics* as a response to Plato, but, whatever view one takes of *katharsis*, it clearly offers an alternative to ontological or moralizing critiques of art. Merely by writing a *Poetics* (apparently on the model of rhetorical treatises), Aristotle elevated at least some imitative arts to the status of *technai*, which work according to generalizable principles that determine their distinct forms and functions and predict the best procedures for achieving their ends.

Hellenistic and Later Philosophers. The three centuries that separate the *Poetics* from that most influential epitome of classical aesthetic doctrines, Horace's *Ars Poetica*, saw a vast profusion of new positions on aesthetic questions and new branches of inquiry: theories of rhetoric and poetic tested Platonic and Aristotelian views and found alternative positions; the Pythagorean view of music as an ethical and cosmic entity is increasingly, from *Aristoxenus and the Stoic *Diogenes of Babylon on, threatened by an alternative that sees it in materialistic terms as irrationally pleasing sound with no deeper implications. Systematic treatments on architecture joined technique and theory, as in Vitruvius' *On Architecture* (1st cent. C.E.). Although most of this material, beginning with *Theophrastus' works on poetics and music, is lost, it is clear that the often-repeated characterization of Hellenistic aesthetics as essentially unoriginal elaboration and systematization of earlier achievements is inadequate and is unlikely to survive a renewed interest in the topic bolstered especially by a long-overdue reexamination of the papyri of *Philodemus of Gadara. This ongoing project will certainly lead to a greater appreciation of the fertility of this period as well as a finer discrimination of individual positions, but some lines in the theory of poetry may exemplify main trends.

The Hellenistic theory of poetry was conducted within the Platonic-rhetorical antithesis of thought (*dianoia*) and expression (*lexis, sunthesis lexeôs*). The strong separation of form and content led both to new attempts to synthesize them as each contributing to "good" poetry and to claims that one or the other was all important. Thus renewed canvassing of poetry for such moral truth or utility as it might convey brought more attention to purely formal qualities such as may produce "good sound" (*euphônia*) independently of moral force. Some went so far as to suggest that criticism was impossible, since poetry reduces to euphony, which is judged by the unreflective ear and not by the mind (cf. Philod. *On Poems* 5.27 Mangoni).

Early *Stoics such as *Zeno of Citium, *Cleanthes, and *Chrysippus wrote treatises on Homer, and it is usually held that they valued poets for expressing Stoic truths *allegorically; but it may be that they regarded

Homer and Hesiod simply as repositories of early ideas about the cosmos. For Stoics, the moral benefit of poetry was its chief justification: Poetry of the right sort could afford not only irrational pleasure (*hêdonê*) but a rational elevation of the soul (*chara*) in keeping with tranquillity. Their theory of beauty (for the first time extended to the world and its parts) was also linked with ethics: *Panaetius (2nd cent. B.C.E.) seems to have connected beauty defined as an arrangement of parts with virtue, itself expressed in orderly, decorous living.

*Epicurus appears to have had little use for poetry and music, especially as these were traditionally taught and expounded (e.g., 5, 163, 229 Usener), but later *Epicureans seem to have allowed that poetry could entertain a fortified soul by offering a combination of emotive words with worthwhile content. A most valuable source is Philodemus (in Italy c. 75–40 B.C.E.), whose polemics against Stoics and *Peripatetics in *On Poems* 5 betray a determination to isolate the workings of poetry qua poetry. He was hostile to the euphonists because only the intellect can judge good and bad, and purely sonic effects can blunt discrimination (he argued in *On Music* that music by itself is incapable of effecting ethical transformations in the soul); but he also rejected notions that good poetry must be scientifically true (rejecting allegorizing along the way). For Philodemus a poem must be judged whole and not in its separate aspects or particular formal qualities, such as brevity, much praised by Stoics. He thus has been taken as a prescient formalist or even Crocean aestheticist, but he is better understood as a polemical Epicurean, holding both that language is sound dedicated to conveying meaning and that poetry qua poetry cannot perform the tasks of philosophic discourse.

In the Roman period the main lines of reflection about literature seem to have been practical and pedagogical, as in the immensely influential *Cicero and *Seneca. The eighteenth century seized on the (probably 1st cent. C.E.) *On the Sublime*, which describes the quality of great writing in affective terms as that which transports, rather than persuades, the soul. Although full of rhetorical analysis, its focus on sublimity as the "echo of a great soul" makes this work the nearest ancient approximation of an expressionist aesthetic.

*Plotinus, especially in *Enneads* 1.6, 5.8 and 6.7, developed an original idealist theory of beauty that was strongly antiformalist and a spiritualist metaphysics that allowed for artistic *creation* to the extent that the human artist participated in divine reason. If, in his ontology, the divine and beautiful "One" is communicated with ever diminishing beauty to ever more inferior beings, the soul can rise to contemplation of absolute beauty via its dim manifestations in works of art, in contrast to Plato's *Symposium*. For the painting, no less than its subject, imitates ideal-form, and the artist may even improve on natural objects, "adding where na-

ture is lacking" (5.8.1). Yet Plotinus retains a Platonic suspicion of artifacts, since mimetic art dissipates true, invisible beauty by introducing it
into matter. Despite seeds of a mysticism of art in the theory, Plotinus finally aims at an ascetic, introspective contemplation of spiritual beauty.

Plotinus' beauty is a dynamic cosmic force and so not to be identified
with any merely formal property. (In yet another response to the Stoics:
A dead face may be perfectly symmetrical, but only a living face moves
us and can be called beautiful.) This critique of formalism casts doubt on
the possibility of finding either the necessary conditions of beauty or the
set of shared properties uniting the various objects—whether natural,
representational, or mathematical—that are called beautiful. The effort to
enunciate a set of conditions for beauty continued, of course, and
reached its apogee in the neoclassical period, when Aristotelian, Horatian and Stoic ideas were combined to outline the natural, universal, and
knowable rules that should infallibly guide artistic production and harmonize it with social life and scientific truth. Once the classical ideal of a
synthesis of art, ethics, and philosophy was divided into separate
spheres of inquiry, modern aesthetics had begun.

BIBLIOGRAPHY: Beardsley, M. C., *Aesthetics: From Ancient Greece to the Present*, New
York, 1966; Halliwell, S., *Aristotle's Poetics*, Chapel Hill, 1986; Janko, R., *Aristotle
on Comedy: Towards a Reconstruction of Poetics II*, Berkeley/Los Angeles, 1984;
Long, A. A., in R. Lamberton and J. Keaney, eds., *Homer's Ancient Readers*,
Princeton, 1992, 41–66; Mangoni, C., *Filodemo: Il Quinto Libro della Poetica*, Naples,
1993; Mazzucchi, C. M., *Del sublime. Dionisio Longino*, Milan, 1992; Moravcsik, J.
and P. Temko, eds., *Plato on Beauty, Wisdom and the Arts*, Totowa, NJ, 1982; Most,
G. W., "Schöne, I. Antike," in J. Ritter and K. Gründer, eds., *Historisches
Wörterbuch der Philosophie*, Basel, 1992; Müller, E., *Geschichte der Theorie der Kunst
bei den Alten*, 2 vols., Breslau, 1834–1837; Obbink, D., ed., *Philodemus on Poetry:
Poetic Theory and Practice in Lucretius, Philodemus and Horace*, Oxford, 1995; A. O.
Rorty, ed., *Essays on Aristotle's Poetics*, Princeton, 1992.—ANDREW FORD

AËTIUS. The name of an otherwise unknown writer of a survey of philosophical opinions (often called *Placita*), whose dates must fall between
the middle of the first century B.C.E. and the end of the first century C.E.
Since the famous work of Hermann Diels, *Doxographi Graeci* (1879),
Aëtius has been considered the source of the two extant main specimens
of ancient *doxography, ps.-Plutarch's *Placita Philosophorum* (2nd cent.
C.E.) and Johannes *Stobaeus' *Eclogae Physicae* (c. 470 C.E.). This identification is based on three passages in bishop Theodoretus of Cyrrhus (c.
393–460), in which he refers to Aëtius' *Placita* next to ps.-Plutarch and
*Porphyry. Aëtius presented the views of the various philosophers in
short thematic entries that purport to be answers to questions raised by
*Aristotle and Hellenistic philosophers; hence, the setting of the philo-
sophical opinions that he presents is often anachronistic. Since Aëtius

refers to philosophers and doctors of the first century B.C.E., Diels assumed that his source is another doxographical work of this period (*Vetusta Placita*) that ultimately derives from *Theophrastus. Diels' reconstruction of Aëtius has come under attack in recent times because his rearrangement of the texts sometimes seems unwarranted. Aëtius seems to have been an important source for many philosophers in late antiquity and has even been used by medieval Arabic philosophers; one Arabic translation of ps.-Plutarch from c. 900 C.E. is extant. See further under DOXOGRAPHY.

BIBLIOGRAPHY: Alt, K., *Hermes* 101, 1973, 129–164; Daiber, H., *Aëtius Arabus. Die Vorsokratiker in arabischer Überlieferung*, Wiesbaden, 1980; Diels, H., *Doxographi Graeci*, Berlin, 1879, 45ff.; Mansfeld, J., and D. T. Runia, *Aëtiana: The Method and Intellectual Context of a Doxographer*, forthcoming in multiple volumes in *Philosophia Antiqua*, Leiden, 1996–. —*JØRGEN MEJER*

AGRIPPA (possibly 1st cent. B.C.E.). *Pyrrhonian *skeptic. Agrippa is a shadowy figure to whom five modes for the suspension of judgment are ascribed by *Diogenes Laertius in his account of Pyrrhonian skepticism. *Sextus Empiricus treats the five modes more fully in his *Outlines of Pyrrhonism* but nowhere mentions Agrippa. Instead, he attributes them to the younger or more recent skeptics. Diogenes Laertius does not include Agrippa in his list of leaders of the Pyrrhonian school, but he does mention a book entitled *Agrippa* by a certain Apelles. It is not impossible that Agrippa existed only as a fictional character. In any case, the five Agrippan modes, as they have come to be called, are based respectively on (i) disagreement, (ii) regress to infinity, (iii) relativity, (iv) hypothesis, and (v) circularity. The five modes are set apart from the older scheme of ten modes by their systematic unity. With the exception of the mode of relativity, they are organized with a view to successively thwarting every possible justification a dogmatic opponent might bring in support of a disputed thesis.

BIBLIOGRAPHY: Barnes, J., *The Toils of Scepticism*, Cambridge, 1990; Caujolle-Zaslawsky, F., "Agrippa," in *DPA*, 71–72.—*JAMES ALLEN*

ALBINUS (fl. c. 150 C.E.). *Platonist philosopher, probably pupil of Gaius. Albinus taught *Galen (*De Libris Propriis* 97.6ff.) at Smyrna and possibly inspired *Lucian's *Nigrinus*. A brief *Prologue* or *Eisagôgê* to *Plato's dialogues survives. *Codex Parisinus Graecus* 1962 refers to eleven volumes on Gaius' lectures, and *Proclus mentions him in his *Republic* and *Timaeus* commentaries. For the *Didascalicus* see ALCINOUS; its *doxographic approach to Plato is far removed from Albinus' dialogue-based approach.

The *Prologue* shares material with other work on corpus arrangement, but breaks from the *Thrasyllan tradition in demanding no fixed reading order for Plato's works. It suggests *Alcibiades* I, *Phaedo, Republic,* and *Timaeus*—this last because it clarifies the Middle Platonist *telos* of assimilation to god (*Tim.* 90a–d). Proclus mentions Albinus' explanation of the "generation" of the ungenerated universe together with his text of *Timaeus* 27c5. He also mentions Albinus' willingness to regard the irrational soul as mortal and his distinction between two levels of teaching in Plato, the scientific and the probabilistic.

BIBLIOGRAPHY: Göransson, T., *Albinus, Alcinous, Arius Didymus*, Göteborg, 1995; Nüsser, O., *Albins Prolog und die Dialogtheorie des Platonismus*, Stuttgart, 1991; Tarrant, H., *Thrasyllan Platonism*, Ithaca, 1993; Whittaker, J., *Phoenix* 28, 1974, 325–330.—*HAROLD A. S. TARRANT*

ALCINOUS (2nd cent. C.E.?). Author of the *Didascalicus*, a *Platonic handbook. *Philostratus mentions a *Stoic, and Photius a Platonist, of that name. The author has been unjustifiably identified with *Albinus. Alcinous gives a concise but wide-ranging account of the doctrines that a Platonist would hold. Platonism is treated as a doctrinal system, underpinned by a complex *epistemology. While influenced by contemporary exegesis, the work is not exegetical. It discusses criteria of truth, *logic, *mathematics, *metaphysics, physics, *psychology, *ethics, and *politics. A substantial passage of the physical section, on Idea-paradigms, resembles a passage ascribed to the Stoic *Arius Didymus. It may be a reworking of Arius' handbook, with updating that involves later metaphysics; this may account for inconsistency in terminology.

The handbook's chief interest concerns metaphysics. There are five types of objects of cognition: the primary and secondary intelligibles (Ideas, immanent forms), the primary and secondary sensibles (qualities, things qualified), and the composites (e.g., fire, honey). They are each judged by some combination of intelligence, sensation, and *logos* (of which there are two types, epistemonic and doxastic). There are three principles: *matter, Ideas, and god. Ideas are thoughts of god, and paradigms. The cosmic *soul is ruled by a heavenly intellect, which always actively thinks all things; its thought is in turn a response to a higher divinity. The world soul is thus awoken and given structure through contemplation of god, who is known through the *via negativa, via analogiae,* and *via eminentiae.* The physics uses the creator of the *Timaeus,* but does not understand creation literally. The good for humankind is found in the contemplation of the first god; the *telos* is assimiliation to god, that is, the immanent heavenly god, the divinity that contemplates the transcendent god.

BIBLIOGRAPHY: Dillon, J, tr. etc., *Alcinous: the Handbook of Platonism*, Oxford, 1993; Göransson, T., *Albinus, Alcinous, Arius Didymus*, Göteborg, 1995; Whittaker, J., ed., *Alkinoos, Enseignement des doctrines de Platon*, Paris, 1990.—*HAROLD A. S. TARRANT*

ALCMAEON (c. 570–490 B.C.E.?), of Croton. Natural philosopher and physician. Some ancient sources associate him with *Pythagoras, but the area of his agreement with the Pythagoreans is limited. Only a few allusions to his doctrines in later ancient authors and a few fragments of his work *On Nature* survive.

Alcmaeon's account of knowledge correlates a scale of cognitive capacities with a scale of being. Gods alone have clarity (*saphêneia*) concerning invisible things. Humans, by contrast, using experience as the starting point of learning, have an understanding that allows mere conjecture from signs (*tekmairesthai*). The rest of living beings have sense perception (*aisthanesthai*) but do not understand. Alcmaeon thus is one of the earliest philosophers to draw a sharp distinction between perception and higher cognitive functions, including thought, and to coordinate this distinction with biological differentiae. It is unclear whether Alcmaeon's dictum that humans perish because they are incapable of connecting the beginning (*archê*) with the end (*telos*) belongs in this context; if so, it might be an early statement of a human inability to grasp direct connections between causality and finality. Other interpretations are, however, also possible (e.g., linearity is characteristic of mortality, but circularity or sphericity of immortality).

Alcmaeon claims that pairs of contraries are the first principles of all things that exist. Unlike some Pythagoreans, he did not offer a definitive, systematic enumeration of these polarities, but the extant examples tend to be qualities: white–black, sweet–bitter, good–evil, large–small, wet–dry, cold–hot, and so on. Exactly how the qualitative contraries function as "principles" is not clear, but Alcmaeon apparently understood them to possess, and to act through, "capacities" or "powers" (*dunameis*). The soul is immortal because, by virtue of always being in continuous motion, it resembles immortal divine entities such as the moon, sun (which is flat), and stars. Planetary motion and lunar eclipses are among the astronomical phenomena investigated by Alcmaeon.

In a medical application of his general principles, Alcmaeon claims that equipollence or equilibrium (*isonomia*) among the "powers" of the contrary qualities preserves health, whereas the "monarchy" of one qualitative power over others, for example, an excess of hot or cold, can cause disease. Diseases can, however, also be occasioned by an excess or deficiency of food or by external factors, such as qualities of waters, localities, exertion, or violence.

Alcmaeon apparently was the first Greek to assign central cognitive and biological functions to the brain. All the sense-organs are connected with the brain by means of ducts (*poroi*); and if the brain shifts, the ducts become blocked and the senses become impaired. Vision, hearing, smell, and taste are further explained in terms of the structures, qualities, and activities of their sense-organs. Alcmaeon's detailed anatomical account of the optic tract may have been based on excision of the eye.

In his encephalogenetic model of reproduction, seed (*sperma*) is "a part of the brain" and proceeds by ducts to the genital parts in both parents. The fetus has the gender of whichever parent produces more abundant seed in intercourse, but about the articulation of the embryo, Alcmaeon says, nothing can be discerned with certainty.

Alcmaeon's epistemologically reserved and methodologically alert exploration of animal and human biology (in part by means of analogies between plants and animals) renders him one of the more influential philosopher-scientists of the late archaic age, as the *Peripatos recognized.

BIBLIOGRAPHY: Texts in DK24; Cardini, M. Timpanaro, *Pitagorici*, fasc. I, Florence, 1958, 118–153. Lloyd, G. E. R., *Sudhoffs Archiv für Geschichte der Medizin* 59, 1975, 113–147.—*HEINRICH VON STADEN*

ALEXANDER (2nd–early 3rd cent. C.E.), of Aphrodisias, son of Hermias (probably in Caria) in Asia Minor. *Peripatetic philosopher and *commentator, traditionally taken to be student of *Aristocles of Messene (though perhaps more plausibly of Aristoteles of Mytilene). Student also of Herminus (the pupil of the commentator *Aspasius) and of Sosigenes. The only direct information about his dates and his life is the dedication of his *On Fate* to the emperors Septimius Severus and Caracalla in gratitude for his appointment to an endowed chair (whether in Athens is not certain), to be dated between 198 and 209 C.E. His main opponents were the *Stoics, but there is also some evidence of a controversy with *Galen.

Alexander wrote both commentaries on the works of *Aristotle and several systematic treatises of his own. Of the commentaries, the following are extant: on *Prior Analytics* 1, *Topics*, *Metaphysics*, *Meteorologica*, and *On Sense*. The commentary on the *Sophistic Refutations*, attributed to him in some manuscripts, is considered spurious. Among the extant systematic writings attributed to him, the following are considered genuine: *On the Soul*, *Problems and Solutions*, *Ethical Problems*, *On Fate*, and *On Mixture and Increase*. The rest, *Medical Questions*, *Physical Problems*, and *On Fevers* are considered spurious.

Throughout antiquity and the Middle Ages, Alexander was regarded as the exemplary commentator (often he is referred to simply as "the commentator"). Hence many of his works now lost were incorporated in those of his successors. There are also Arabic and Latin translations, as well as numerous quotations from his lost commentaries. Nothing certain is known about the relative chronology of his writings, but this is not an issue of much importance, since his commentaries may well incorporate the results of many years of teaching. His commentaries thus mirror the state of Aristotle's own systematic writings by the incorporation of countless alterations. This may explain the lack of any attempt at elegance and the occurrence of unmitigated inconsistencies.

Alexander concludes the series of purely "Peripatetic" commentators (starting with *Andronicus of Rhodes in the first century B.C.E.), who try to explain "Aristotle by Aristotle" (Moraux, 1942, 16). The *Neoplatonists' approach to Aristotle that succeeded them started with *Porphyry and prevailed throughout late antiquity. In commenting, Alexander usually refrains from giving comprehensive surveys. Instead he takes up individual passages in succession by citing a line or two ("*lemma*") and explains what he considers as problematic (by explanatory paraphrases, clarifications of expressions, or refutations of the views of others), often in view of what Aristotle says about the issue elsewhere. In general, he goes on the assumption that Aristotelian philosophy is a unitary whole, but where there is no clear, single, Aristotelian point of view, he leaves the matter open, citing several possibilities. Sometimes he tries to force an interpretation that does not obviously agree with the text, but he avoids stating that Aristotle contradicts himself or that he himself is not in agreement with Aristotle. Readers will not always be convinced by his suggestions but will often find them helpful and informative where Aristotle is overly compressed and obscure.

As a philosopher, Alexander presents in his writings an Aristotelian point of view that reflects in many ways the conditions of his own time, providing Aristotelian answers to questions not discussed by Aristotle himself. A good example is his construal of an Aristotelian interpretation of the concept of "fate," which he identifies with nature, viz. the natural order, that is determined by a divine providence only in so far as it depends on the regular motion of the heavenly bodies. He thus criticizes the Stoics for adopting a much stronger sense of determinism (cf. *On Fate, Quaestiones* 2.4, 5). This attempt at "naturalizing" crucial concepts is typical of his philosophical stance in general. He regards universals as inseparable from particulars and as secondary to them and stresses the unity of *matter and form. Similarly, he treats the human *soul as the perishable form of the bodily elements and argues that the intellect develops from an embodied, material intellect to a form that eventually contains forms no longer embodied. He rules out personal immortality by identifying the active intellect at the same time with pure form and with God, the Unmoved Mover (cf. *On the Soul*). In his emphasis of a naturalist point of view he appears remarkably free from the increasingly spiritualistic and mystical tendencies of his own time.

BIBLIOGRAPHY: Texts of the commentaries in *CAG.*; of the treatises considered genuine, in I. Bruns, ed., *Scripta Minora*, vols. 1 and 2, Berlin, 1887, 1892. Translations (with notes) of the "minor works": Sharples, R. M., *Ethical Problems*, London and

Ithaca, 1990; also *Quaestiones 1.2–2.15; Quaestiones 2.16–3.5*, London, 1994 (with extensive bibliography). Translations (with notes) of the commentaries: Sorabji, R., and R. M. Sharples, eds., *Alexander of Aphrodisias on Aristotle Metaphysics* (Bk. 1, tr. W. E. Dooley, London, 1989; Bks. 2 and 3, tr. Dooley, 1992; Bk 4., tr. A. Madigan, 1993; Bk. 5, tr. Dooley, 1993). *Alexander of Aphrodisias on Aristotle Prior Analytics 1.1–7*, (tr. J. Barnes et al., 1991). Moraux, P., *Der Aristotelismus bei den Griechen*, vol. 3, Berlin. See further R. M. Sharples, *ANRW* 2, 36.1, 1987, 1226–1243.—*DOROTHEA FREDE*

ALEXINUS (fl. late 4th–early 3rd cent. B.C.E.), of Elis. *Dialectician, placed by *Diogenes Laertius in the "succession" of *Eubulides (2.109). His name often figures in anecdotes and the like with that of *Menedemus the Eretrian. He attacked a variety of targets in his writings, including *rhetoric and the *sophistic interpretation of *Homer, but above all the syllogisms of *Zeno of Citium, where he deployed a form of *reductio ad absurdum* called by *Sextus *parabolē* (an example at *M* 9.108–9).
BIBLIOGRAPHY: Texts in *SSR* 2 C or (with commentary) K. Döring, *Die Megariker*, Amsterdam, 1972. Schofield, M., *Phronesis* 28, 1983, 31–58.—*MALCOLM SCHOFIELD*

ALLEGORY, Classical. The term "allegory"(*allēgoria*) in Greek is used to designate a trope of *rhetoric in which the speaker says one thing, but means another; that is, he "says other things"(*alla agoreuei*) than his language, understood in the most obvious way, would designate. Thus there occurs a radical disjunction between the "thing said" (*legomenon*) and the "thing intended" (*nooumenon*), from which a hermeneutic dilemma frequently results (Heraclitus *Quaestiones Homericae* 5). This trope is often in practice difficult to separate from those of irony, sarcasm, and emphasis; and it must be admitted that, from the perspective of modern semiotics, all are at best crude terms for related, poorly differentiated categories of allusive or obscure language. Allegory was recognized as a strategy frequently used by the poets, though in oratory its use posed the immediate risk of obscurity (*to asaphes*). The term is not attested before *Philodemus and *Cicero, but shortly thereafter we have the testimony of *Plutarch (*De Audiendis Poetis* 19) that what were "in the old days called allusions (*huponoiai*) but today, allegories" are in fact the same thing. (It should be noted that what the modern world has called "personification allegory," present from the very beginnings of Greek literature [e.g., the figure of Strife (*Eris*) at *Iliad* 4.440–445] and highly developed from the fourth century C.E. [e.g., Prudentius], has nothing to do with the rhetorical trope and that the term "allegory" is not associated with such procedures in antiquity.)

It is the hermeneutic dilemma posed by allegory that is of philosophical (as opposed to poetic or rhetorical) interest. From a date too early to recover, obscure texts, and in particular obscure poetic texts, were explained by interpreters as characterized by allusions (*huponoiai*) that these interpreters claimed to be able to decipher. This procedure has sometimes been called "allegorical reading" as distinguished from "allegorical writing," but the term is a dubious one, given that readers who understood texts before them as allegories to be deciphered did not in general clearly distinguish their own mode of reading from those of others. Still, as early as Plutarch the verb *allêgoreô* could mean "interpret allegorically as"; and in Christian Greek this verb and the nearly synonymous *tropologeô* frequently designate the allegorical interpretation of scriptural texts.

The background of such interpretation is no doubt preliterate. Many popular oral genres of verbal art—riddles, beast fables, and so on—are intrinsically allegorical and demand interpretation. Some archaic hexameter poetry, including perhaps the Orphic poems, may well have been created explicitly for this sort of exegesis by specialized practitioners (as an interpretive text recovered from a papyrus from Derveni in Greek Macedonia suggests). Some analysts have found it helpful to distinguish subcategories, such as "physical allegories" (where through a deity or other entity in a poem reference is made to an element or some other feature of the natural world), "ethical allegories" (where the text is found to contain some unstated ethical precept) and "mystical allegories" (where the text is typically discovered to contain an obscure reference to the relationship of soul and matter, or to some other metaphysical or soteriological issue). There is no period in the history of Greek thought for which we can confidently say that "allegorical" interpretation was absent, though a late, probably *Porphyrian, scholion dubiously attributes to a scholar named Theagenes of Rhegium (c. 525 B.C.E.?) the invention of both physical and ethical allegory.

*Socrates'contemporaries made generous use of this sort of hermeneutic exercise (in pedagogic or otherwise subliterary contexts), so much so that Socrates is made to specify that he rejects the *Homeric poems as educational tools, "whether they're composed in allegories or not" (*Rep.* 2, 378d). It is generally claimed that *Plato rejected allegorical interpretation, which does not figure prominently in the dialogues; he has Socrates (in the *Protagoras*) reject discussion of the meaning of poetry in general as an unpromising procedure for reaching the truth.

The thinkers of the *Stoa were frequently represented by their opponents as irresponsible readers who foisted their ideas off on the early poets and tried to show that Homer and *Hesiod were Stoics before the fact (e.g., Cic. *ND* 1.41). While much of this polemic may be discounted (along with the modern scholarship that has wanted to find Stoics wherever allegory is mentioned, and the reverse), it is nevertheless true that the Stoa seems to have taken seriously the notion that early Greek poetry contains certain truths, often in veiled form (as for example in the etymologies of divine names). These concerns go hand in hand with a new seriousness in the fields of hermeneutics and semiotics. Contemporary with the early Stoa we find a few idiosyncratic and unclassifiable allegorical systems, notably that of *Metrodorus of Lampsacus, who read the human characters of the *Iliad* as representations of parts of the physical cosmos, while the divine characters represented the constituent parts of the human body.

From the first or second century C.E. through the end of the polytheist tradition we find a great proliferation of allegorical interpretation, directed in particular toward the early hexameter poets. The collection of *Homeric Questions* assembled by one Heraclitus at the beginning of this period is composed almost entirely of allegorical decipherments, starting with a systematic treatise on Homeric allegory. His contention is that Homer in his theology (under attack since Xenophanes in the sixth century B.C.E.) "unless he was in some sense allegorizing, was utterly impious" (1.1). Such elucidation of more acceptable hidden meanings in offensive passages has often been called "defensive allegory." The *Pythagorean *Numenius in the second century addressed himself to both Homeric and Platonic myths and discovered similar secrets lurking behind both. His influence on the *Neoplatonist Porphyry (232–ca. 305) can be seen in the latter's essay *On the Cave of the Nymphs in the Odyssey*, the most attractive example of early Neoplatonic allegorical exegesis of Homer. It is to the later Neoplatonists, and particularly *Proclus (410–485) in his *Commentary on the Republic*, that we owe the richest surviving ancient collections of allegorical readings, some no doubt originating in Neoplatonic circles, but others much older. It is with Proclus, finally, that we first find a serious attempt to provide a poetics of the polysemous text to serve as a basis for the interpretation of early poetry.

The history of allegory in the Roman world is an outgrowth of the theory and practice of the Greek allegorists. *Cornutus wrote a surviving allegorical compendium of Greco-Roman religion in the mid-first century C.E. Virgil's *Aeneid*, quickly elevated, in the context of Roman education, to the role long enjoyed in Greek education by Homer, was soon subjected to allegorical interpretation, one of the modes of commentary known to Servius in the fourth century. The tradition was extended by Fulgentius (c. 467–532), whose influence in the Middle Ages was widespread.

The allegorical traditions of commentary in antiquity concerned themselves primarily with texts endowed with authority that had survived the cultural context that generated them. The interpreters who performed the required acts of accommodation often made the claim that such texts hinted at things other than those they expressed on the surface. Though the process is easily criticized (as was often the case in antiquity), there is no reason to believe that most such interpreters were not in fact simply trying to bridge the gap between their own preconceptions and the difficult texts they explained.

BIBLIOGRAPHY: Buffière, F., *Les Mythes d'Homère et la pensée grecque*, Paris, 1956; Lamberton, R., and J. J. Keaney, eds., *Homer's Ancient Readers*, Princeton, 1992; Whitman, J., *Allegory: The Dynamics of an Ancient and Medieval Technique*, Cambridge, MA, 1987.—*ROBERT LAMBERTON*

AMELIUS (3rd cent. C.E.), of Etruria in Italy. *Platonist philosopher. Amelius was *Plotinus' devoted student and assistant in Rome in 246–269, moving then to Apamea in Syria. He copied *Numenius' works and compiled a hundred volumes of notes taken from Plotinus' lectures. He also wrote in defence of Plotinus' views against *Porphyry (on the relation between intellect and the intelligibles), against Longinus (on justice in *Plato), against the *Gnostic Zostrianus, and on the doctrinal differences between Numenius and Plotinus. These works do not survive. His readings of passages in Plato's *Timaeus, Republic, Parmenides* and *Philebus* are reported in later *Neoplatonic sources. Faithful in general, it seems, to Plotinus, Amelius sometimes differed from him, perhaps in part under Numenius' influence, introducing three levels of intellect in the intelligible, allowing for participation among intelligibles, an infinity of Forms, and Forms of what is bad. In contrast to Plotinus, Amelius took an interest in religious rites, commented on St. John's gospel, and seems to have used the *Chaldaean Oracles*. Influential on Theodore of Asine, he was criticized by Porphyry and *Iamblichus.

BIBLIOGRAPHY: Brisson, L., *ANRW* 2, 36.2, 1987, 793–860; Zoumpos, A., *Amelius von Etrurien: Sein Leben und seine Philosophie*, Athens, 1956.—*DOMINIC J. O'MEARA*

AMMONIUS (b. c. 440, d. after 517 C.E.). *Neoplatonist, head of the philosophical school at Alexandria. Son of Hermeias, student of *Proclus, and teacher of Asclepius, *Damascius, *Philoponus and *Simplicius. Ammonius was responsible for the Alexandrians' concentration on the exposition of *Aristotle. This is often claimed to have been the result of a deal made with the *Christian authorities not to teach *Plato. In fact, we do not know what was agreed. Evidence for his alleged conversion to Christianity is also at best inconclusive.

Under Ammonius' own name we have *commentaries on the *Categories* and *Porphyry's *Eisagôgê*, the *De Interpretatione* and *Prior Analytics*. In additon Asclepius' commentary on the *Metaphysics* and those of Philoponus on the *Prior* and *Posterior Analytics, De Generatione et Corrup-

tione and *De Anima* are based on Ammonius' teaching. There are no direct records of his Plato teaching.

Since Ammonius' own works are commentaries on Aristotle's *logic, it is often difficult to determine clearly what his other philosophical views were. The "editions" by Asclepius and Philoponus contain some of their own ideas as well, and will refer to Ammonius as someone other than the author. But in general Ammonius subscribed to the main outlines of the type of late Neoplatonism which was common to Athens and Alexandria, and believed in a highly structured and differentiated intelligible world, ultimately derived from the One, and a sensible world that was eternal at both ends. One of the major projects of the commentaries was to show that in all important matters Aristotle agreed with Plato and could be read Neoplatonically.

BIBLIOGRAPHY: Texts in *CAG* vols. 4.4, 4.4, 4.5, 4.6. Blumenthal, H. J., *Aristotle and Neoplatonism in Late Antiquity*, London/Ithaca, 1996, 21–71; Verrycken, K., in R. Sorabji, ed., *Aristotle Transformed*, London/Ithaca, 1990, 199–231 and 233-64.—*H. J. BLUMENTHAL*

AMMONIUS SACCAS (3rd cent. C.E.) taught *Platonic philosophy in Alexandria (Egypt). Among his students were *Origen (the pagan), Longinus, and *Plotinus, who studied with him in 232–242. He published nothing, and his three close pupils (Erennius, Origen, and Plotinus) agreed not to "reveal" (i.e., publish?) his teachings, a pact Plotinus was the last to break. His teaching was decisive for Plotinus; even later, in Rome, Plotinus taught in the "spirit of Ammonius" (Porphyry *Life of Plotinus*, 14, 15–16). What this last phrase means is unclear: Did Plotinus follow Ammonius' "style" of philosophizing? Did Plotinus' principal metaphysical positions come from Ammonius? The importance Ammonius had for Plotinus has inspired ambitious and questionable efforts to reconstruct his teaching, for example, by finding what is believed to be common to Plotinus and to the *Christian *Origen of Alexandria, who is thought by some scholars also to have studied with Ammonius. Explicit testimony concerning Ammonius' philosophy in late antique sources goes back to *Porphyry, who, if able to inform himself through Longinus and Plotinus, also tends to assimilate his own ideas to those of Plotinus, which he believes go back to Ammonius. Thus the testimony that Ammonius sought to harmonize *Aristotle with *Plato corresponds to Porphyry's efforts; however, it does not fit well with Plotinus' approach. Other reports on Ammonius concern standard school arguments against the (*Stoic) idea that *soul is corporeal and include an explanation (Porphyrian in character) of how soul is united to the body. *Proclus, also depending on Porphyry, attributes to Ammonius Plotinus' fundamental thesis that the first principle of reality, the One, transcends intelligible

being. A reference in *Priscian to a collection of Ammonius' *scholia* probably concerns the fifth century *Ammonius of Alexandria, pupil of Proclus.
BIBLIOGRAPHY: Schroeder, F., *ANRW* 2, 36.1, 1987, 493–526; Schwyzer, H., *Ammo-
nios Sakkas, der Lehrer Plotins*, Opladen, 1983.—DOMINIC J. O'MEARA

ANAXAGORAS (probably 500–428 B.C.E.), of Clazomenae. The first
philosopher known to have taken up residence in Athens. The evidence
for Anaxagoras' biography, though relatively ample, is confused and
confusing. He probably arrived in Athens in 456/5 (see the excellent critical study by Mansfeld), where he philosophized for about twenty years,
until his prosecution and trial (dated by Mansfeld to 437/6) on a charge
of impiety. Probably assisted by his patron Pericles, he resettled in Lampsacus, where he died. He was buried with high honors. His name became
associated with the fall of a large meteorite at Aegospotami in Thrace (c.
467), and his explanations of other physical phenomena are already alluded to in *Aeschylus' *Supplices* (c. 463) and *Eumenides* (458).

Extensive fragments of Anaxagoras' one book are preserved by *Simplicius. It began, famously, with the words: "All things were together"
(DK59B1). Its longest and most eloquent surviving passage explains how
our diversified *kosmos* originated from the original mixture by the action
of *mind, a principle entirely distinct from and unmixed with any other
substances, though capable of ordering and controlling them (B12). The
book's most striking and paradoxical thesis is the claim that, despite the
consequent separation of hot from cold, dense from rare, and the like, "as
things were in the beginning, so now they are all together" (B6); "in everything—except mind—a portion of everything" (B11). Ancient commentators (e.g., Ar. *Phys.* 187a36–b7) provided examples: What we call
black contains a predominance of portions of black (cf. B12 *ad fin.*), but
also portions of white, for how else could water turn into snow? In the
same way sperm contains hair, flesh, and indeed everything else, for hair
cannot come from not-hair, flesh from not-flesh (B10), and so on.

Would it not be possible, after thoroughgoing analysis or division, to
arrive at particles of pure flesh or pure black? Anaxagoras explicitly rejects this idea: "the small is unlimited" (theoretical minima do not
actually exist), and as complex as the large (B3 and 6). The ultimate constituents of the world do not exist as discrete physical entities, but only
as what such entities consist of: hence the designation "portions." When
Anaxagoras speaks of an infinity as "seeds" both in the beginning and in
our world as well (B4), we should probably think of the potentiality of
latent portions to become manifest, rather than of particles.

The thesis that everything contains a portion of everything has
proved baffling. Is it even coherent? If, to count as gold, a substance has

to contain a predominance of gold, must not the predominant gold itself contain a predominance of gold, and so ad infinitum? This puzzle succumbs to the distinction between composite discrete substances and the portions or proportions of the pure elements of which they are composed. But others remain. For example, does a man somehow contain every other species of mammal as well as birds, fish, and plants, like a Leibnitzian monad? Seeds or portions of such organisms are never explicitly mentioned, and it is usually assumed that Anaxagoras intended the scope of "everything" in his thesis to be restricted to opposites and homoeomerous stuffs. An oak or a dolphin is then understood as a particular sort of higher-order mixture of such opposites and stuffs, destined in due course for dissolution back into them (cf. B17). Anaxagoras talks as if every item to which the "everything is everything" formula applies contains, for example, *both* some earth *and* the cold and the dense that are ordinarily features of earth. Yet opposites seem to have a different status from stuffs: they are powers actively effecting change, as in the conversion of earth into stones or in the operations of perception. This is a different kind of process from the separation or emergence and combining or reabsorption to which stuffs are subject and probably indicates a different sort of "in": Opposites must be actual properties rather than something present merely as a potentiality (such as the water in clouds, B16).

Anaxagoras is credited with the maxim: "The appearances are a sight of what is not apparent" (B21a). Infinite variety in phenomena reflects infinite variety in seeds, even if the dimness of our senses prevents us discerning it there (B21). And if it is apparent that virtually anything can come *from* virtually anything, it is an economical hypothesis that although this is not apparent, everything is *in* everything. But Anaxagoras' decision to express the "everything in everything" idea as "all things together," now as in the beginning, signals—alternatively or additionally— another motivation for his theory. Far removed as it is from *Parmenides' *metaphysics and *epistemology, the echo of his "all together" (DK28 B8.5) expresses a debt to the *Eleatic vision of the homogeneity of reality. It is harder to gauge any clear sign of a reaction to *Zeno of Elea, whose book of paradoxes may or may not antedate Anaxagoras' work. The proposition that of the small there is no smallest (B3) is the best evidence of possible Zenonian influence, but a crucial difference is that for Anaxagoras there is nothing paradoxical in the notion of *infinite divisibility.

Anaxagoras' *cosmology is by comparison with his ontology unoriginal, even if the claim that the sun is a huge incandescent stone larger than the entire Peloponnese shocked contemporary opinion (D.L. 2.12). The fragments speak mostly as though mind generates a single universe. At one point, however, Anaxagoras talks about a universe "elsewhere," and claims that it must have the same system of celestial bodies and an inhabited earth with the same natural environment as our own (B4). Our universe is formed by a rotary movement that separates the hot, dry, rare, and bright from the cold, wet, dense, and murky (B12 and15). The outcome is a flat central earth floating on a surrounding expanse of air and aither (i.e., clearer, fiery air), in which fragments of ignited heavier matter constituting what we know as the heavenly bodies are whirled around, with more and more of the surrounding cosmic envelope gradually drawn into the process of separation. Meteorological and mineralogical change is accounted for within this overall explanatory framework, which derives in its essentials from *Anaximenes—although the detail is sometimes more impressive. Anaxagoras knows, for example, that the moon has plains and ravines, borrows its light from the sun, and is eclipsed when screened by the earth. His explanation of the rising of the Nile in summer as due to snows melting to the south is eminently reasonable, albeit probably wholly speculative (Hipp. *Ref.* 1.8.3–10).

We hear rather less of Anaxagoras' views on the nature of man and the other animals. He has an evolutionary account of the origins of life reminiscent of *Anaximander (Hipp. *Ref.* 1.8.12.). More interesting is his claim that "it is his possession of hands that makes man the wisest of living things" (Ar. *PA* 687a7–8). *Theophrastus tells us at some length about Anaxagoras' theory of sensation. The main idea is that like is not affected by like: Something that is warm or cold as we are does not warm or cool us. We are aware of warmth because we are cold, or rather because the warmth within us is deficient relative to the cold (*Sens.* 27–8).

*Plato and *Aristotle were most of all impressed, but also disappointed, by Anaxagoras' theory of mind (Pl. *Phd.* 97bff.; Ar. *Met.* 984b 15ff., 985a18ff.). By comparison with his Presocratic predecessors Aristotle reckoned him a paragon of sobriety among the incoherent in his perception that the origin of order in the *kosmos* requires identification of an efficient cause quite distinct from the material causes of things. Like Plato, however, he thought Anaxagoras put mind to far too little appropriate—that is, teleological—work: causation in his system was mostly mechanistic, with mind invoked only as a sort of "god of the gaps" in explanation. Post-Darwinian readers will perhaps be less harsh on this feature of the theory. Order in the *kosmos* as an entire system may be thought less questionable than claims to find widespread evidence of specific teleological structures in the natural world. Anaxagoras' idea that mind will have brought about this ordering by initiating a mechanical process of rotation is undoubtedly mysterious, but conceivably no more so than our modern belief that mind gives effect to its intentions by means of impulses initiated in the brain and transmitted through the nervous system.

Anaxagoras' physical system presents an alternative, clear at least in general character, to the atomism of *Leucippus and *Democritus, within a broadly *Eleatic conceptual framework. They are thoroughgoing materialists while he—to put it anachronistically—is a mind-matter dualist. Where they posit atoms, discrete indivisible quanta in eternal motion, he sees matter as an inert, infinitely divisible, homogenous texture and construes the elements of things in qualitive terms: partly as stuffs, partly as powers, but powers that remain in ineffectual equilibrium unless disturbed by a purposive act of mind.

BIBLIOGRAPHY: Texts in DK 59 and D. Lanza, *Anassagora - testimonianze e frammenti*, Florence, 1966. Allen, R. E., & D. J. Furley, eds., *Studies in Presocratic Philosophy* vol. 2 (articles by Cornford, Vlastos, and Strang), London, 1975; Furth, M., *OSAP* 9, 1991, 95–129; Guthrie, W. K. C., *A History of Greek Philosophy*, vol. 2, Cambridge, 1965; Mansfeld, J., *Mnemosyne* 32, 1979, 39ff., and 33, 1980, 17ff.; Schofield, M., *An Essay on Anaxagoras*, Cambridge, 1980.—*MALCOLM SCHOFIELD*

ANAXARCHUS (c. 380–320 B.C.E.), of Abdera. *Democritean philosopher, teacher of *Pyrrho. Anaxarchus followed Alexander on his campaign in the East. Once, during a banquet, Anaxarchus made an enemy of Nicocreon, the tyrant of Salamis, thanks to a joke. After the death of Alexander, he was obliged to land at Cyprus and was captured and condemned by Nicocreon to be pounded in a mortar. The words he uttered in despite of Nicocreon prior to dying are famous: "Pound, pound the pouch containing Anaxarchus; ye pound not Anaxarchus."

The tradition concerning his relations with Alexander is inconsistent. Some of the sources present him as a flatterer of the king, committed to justifying his pretentions to being divinized and to consoling him after the murder of Callisthenes, while others rather highlight his ironic attitude.

Anaxarchus was the author of a treatise *On Kingship*, of which only fragments survive: The limit (*horos*) of wisdom is to know the measure of the right moment (*kairos*); it is more difficult to preserve wealth than to accumulate it.

The information concerning his philosophical position is likewise conflicting. Some ancient authors place him among the representatives of the eudaimonistic sect, which located the true goal in the achievement of *happiness (*eudaimonia*); others, however, associate him with Democritus, by way of the teachings of Diogenes of Smyrna and *Metrodorus of Chios, and make him the teacher of Pyrrho. Democritean influences are apparent in the remains of his work *On Kingship*. Traces of *skeptical doctrines surface in two fragments (Fr. 64AB Dorandi), where Anaxarchus is listed among those who deny the *kritêrion*. Nor can *Cynic influence be ruled out.

BIBLIOGRAPHY: Texts in DK72; Dorandi, T., ed., *Atti e Memorie Accademia Toscana "La Colombaria"* 59, 1994, 9–59. Bernard, P., *Journal des Savants* 1984, 3–48; Brunschwig, J., *Proceedings of the British Academy* 82, 1993, 59–88.—*TIZIANO DORANDI*

ANAXIMANDER (c. 610–540 B.C.E.), of Miletus in Asia Minor. Presocratic philosopher, after *Thales. A (suspiciously?) precise testimony mentions that Anaximander was sixty-four years old in 547/46 and died soon after. The biographers, however, imply also other, impossible dates: Anaximander was in his prime under Polycrates (tyrant of Samos after 540) or led a colony to Apollonia on the Black Sea, which had already been settled a century earlier.

Anaximander was the first to produce a philosophical book (later conventionally titled *On Nature*), if not the first to produce a book at all: Only *Pherecydes' book could have been earlier. Anaximander's innovative book contained a comprehensive, nonmythological description of the world. In addition, Anaximander drew a map and drew (or constructed) a *sphaira*, a visual representation of the heavens. He is also credited with the invention of the *gnômôn* (pointer of a sundial, presumably taken over from the Babylonians), and with the discovery of the chief astronomical reference points. He is reported to have constructed a sundial in Sparta (although another source attributes this to *Anaximenes). Even an outline of geometry is added to his credits. Some of this no doubt reflects the stock exaggerations of the *doxographic tradition. The map and the book, however, are beyond doubt.

Following Thales' lead, Anaximander specified the *archê* (first principle). His choice was the *apeiron*, an unbounded and further unspecified stuff (see INFINITE) that, being endowed with eternal motion, encompasses and steers the world. The *apeiron* is not a part of the world, although the existence of everything else is dependent on and subordinate to it. By introducing a principle that falls outside the range of the opposites, Anaximander wards off the hazard posed by a principle whose overwhelming preponderance is detrimental to entities with incompatible characteristics.

The world begins with the emergence of what is productive (*gonimon*) of hot and cold. From this point on, the history of the world is a continuous interchange of opposites. Whether the world forms a closed system through the cosmic evolution or draws in and consumes further draughts of *apeiron* is not clear from the testimonies.

When earth, air, and (surrounding it like the bark of a tree) fire have appeared, the fire begins to dry up the earth's moisture. As a result, the continuous layer of fire is torn into circles or wheels (*kukloi*) of fire, each surrounded by a misty envelope of air. These tubes have holes, through which the fire shines, and this creates the illusion of freely wandering celestial luminaries. Our sources mention the arrangement and particular sizes of these rings: Sun 27/28, Moon (18)/19, (stars 9/10) Earth measures (the values in parentheses are conjectural, and a double series of sizes is thought to allow for the thickness of the celestial wheels). As these figures are unlikely to be valid for the entire history of the cosmic evolutionary process (otherwise the bark would not have needed to be *torn* into bands), they apparently indicate that the world had already reached stable size and proportions. It is remarkable that here the heavens are much vaster compared to the Earth than in the traditional epic account (see Hesiod *Theogony* 126–8 and 722f.).

In its present layout the world is a balanced and symmetrical system, where at the center of these rings a drum-shaped Earth (breadth to height 3:1) remains at rest because of its "similarity," that is, as it is in similar relationship in every direction with the huge celestial masses, it has no inclination to move in one direction rather than in another.

In his only surviving fragment Anaximander speaks—rather poetically, as *Simplicius notes—about the things "paying penalty and retribution to one another for their injustice according to the arrangement of *time." This should refer to an ongoing process, and not just to the final settling of accounts at the end of the world, when the transgressors would no longer be able to pay penalties "to one another." The arrangement of time makes it possible that the transgression and the ensuing retribution are not simultaneous. Without this, a dynamic equilibrium of cyclical changes would be impossible. How the arrangement of time is dependent on the *apeiron*, that is, whether the world is a self-regulating, immanent order, or a natural order that has to be upheld by external factors, cannot be decided from the testimonies. The latter would emphasize the frailty of the world to the extent that interventions of a plenipotentiary or divine principle would be indispensable to keep it permanently or only temporarily in shape. Similarly, it is unclear whether the world will be dissolved in the end or whether the processes constituting its dynamic equilibrium are capable of constantly rejuvenating the cosmos. Some testimonies, as well as Anaximander's "historical" account of the emergence of the world order, favor an irreversible—and hence terminal—process.

A related unsettled issue is whether the world is unique or whether there are simultaneous or successive multiple worlds. An unlimited pool of raw material should imply unbounded generation, but the emergence of the *gonimon* might have been an exceptional process—what today we should call a "singularity."

In addition to cosmic issues, Anaximander's book covered meteorological phenomena, in which *pneuma* played a vital part, as well as zoogony. The origins of the species, as with the generation of the world, presuppose the interaction of wet and hot, and the tender "fetus" gets encapsulated in a thorny protective bark. At the end of "gestation" animals make headway to land and shed this bark. As human infants cannot survive without extended nurturing, the first humans are protected and fed inside fish until their adolescence.

Much of the agenda, and indeed many of the clichés of natural philosophy, must have originated with Anaximander. Because of the deplorable state of our sources, we are not in a position to appreciate fully his impact on his contemporaries and successors. The notion of a balanced and articulate order present in the development and layout of the world is a major innovation. Here the legacy of Anaximander to subsequent enquiry is unmistakable.

BIBLIOGRAPHY: Texts in DK12. Dancy, R. M., *Apeiron* 22, 1989, 149–190; Freudenthal, G., *Phronesis* 31,1986, 197–228; Kahn, C. H., *Anaximander and the Origins of Greek Cosmology*, New York, 1960; Rescher, N., in Rescher, ed., *Essays in Philosophical Analysis*, Pittsburgh, 1969, 3–32; Vlastos, G., in D. Furley and R. E. Allen, eds., *Studies in Presocratic Philosophy*, vol. 1, Atlantic Highlands, 1975, 56–91.—ISTVÁN BODNÁR

ANAXIMENES (c. 585–525 B.C.E.), of Miletus in Asia Minor. Presocratic philosopher, a student of *Anaximander. The biographical tradition is especially slippery: The dates of Anaximenes rest on a conjecture. Without the conjecture his birth would have to be dated no later than 525, and he should have died in 498. Confusion about the dates explains why some sources would even want to make Anaximenes a student of *Parmenides, but chronology rules this out.

Anaximenes wrote a book "in simple and plain Ionic" (DK13A1), in which he continued the program of inquiry set by Anaximander: Specifying an *archê* of his own, he went on to account for the formation, the structure, and the variegated celestial, meteorological, and other phenomena of the world. His main innovation is the novel relationship between the *archê* and its derivatives.

Although Anaximenes' principle is, like Anaximander's, unbounded and endowed with eternal motion, it is specified as *air*. Not only does this air encompass the world, but a portion of it is an integral part of the world. Processes of condensation (*puknôsis*) and rarefaction (*manôsis*, or *araiôsis*) transform air and the different stuffs into one another, in the following order: fire—[AIR]—wind—cloud—water—earth—stones. These basic components can then make up everything else in the world. Only a single world is reported as emerging from the unbounded air. This is all the more remarkable as condensation and rarefaction are ordinary, everyday processes, and so there is no need for a special generative entity or process like Anaximander's *gonimon* at the beginning of the world.

Things do not originate in a linear order according to their density. Instead, the first thing to form is the Earth; then the Sun, the Moon, and the stars originate from the Earth. These are fiery bodies; the stars, however, do not provide heat, because—unlike in Anaximander's cosmos—they are farther off than the Sun.

The Earth, Moon, Sun, and other stars, being flat, ride on air: The Earth is presumably stationary, whereas the others circle the Earth, borne along by a special whirlwind. The vortex (dinê) theories of later thinkers postulate an overall circular motion; Anaximenes, by contrast, proposes that the celestial bodies do not pass *under* the Earth when we do not see them, but pass *around* the Earth like a cap surrounding a head and are screened off by the greater distance and by the higher northern parts of the Earth.

An apparently conflicting testimony claims that stars are nailed to a crystalline periphery. This testimony would imply a distinction between literally fixed stars and freely floating luminaries, which may consist of the Sun and the Moon only or may include also (some of) the planets.

Our testimonies quote Anaximenes' concern with meteorological phenomena. These include winds, different forms of precipitation, thunder, lightning, and rainbows. In most of these explanations, air plays a crucial role. A striking exception is earthquakes, which are caused by the drying and by the excessive moistening of the interior of the Earth.

*Thales had already used a principle that was an indispensable ingredient of anything producing life. Anaximenes—probably with respiration in mind—could claim that his principle not only supported life, but was *identical* with *soul.

Anaximenes' principle is bland and neutral enough not to overrun and extinguish the other constituents of the world. On the other hand, the strength and power of gushes of air is unmistakable. Air is a sufficiently flexible and powerful constituent to exercise control over the world and is a suitable link between inorganic nature and the living world. The influence of Anaximenes is most obvious on *Diogenes of Apollonia and later on the *Stoics' doctrine of *pneuma*. By introducing the dual processes of condensation and rarefaction, Anaximenes framed the first, still rudimentary, theory of change.

BIBLIOGRAPHY: Texts in DK13. Classen, C. J., *Phronesis* 22, 1977, 89–102.—*ISTVÁN BODNÁR*

ANDRONICUS (fl. 1st cent. B.C.E.), of Rhodes. *Peripatetic philosopher commonly credited with producing the first "critical" edition of *Aristotle's esoteric writings, thereby ushering in a revival of Peripatetic philosophy. He is said to have been the eleventh Peripatetic scholarch (Ammonius *In De Int.* 5.24), although the evidence is questionable. The two main sources for information concerning the fate of Aristotle's library and Andronicus' eventual work on the texts of Aristotle are *Strabo (13.1, 54, 608) and *Plutarch (*Sulla* 26). These texts suggest that Sulla, after capturing Athens in 86 B.C.E., took the library back to Rome, where sometime after 71 B.C.E. the grammarian and Peripatetic Tyrannio of Amisus started working on the Aristotelian texts it contained. He passed on this work to Andronicus, who then completed an edition of Aristotle's esoteric writings, along with some writings of *Theophrastus. Many of the details concerning the library and Andronicus' access to it, however, are open to speculation.

Andronicus' works included (i) the edition of Aristotle comprising the main school treatises as we have them today, except for *De Interpretatione*, which he thought was spurious (see Ammonius *In De Int.* 5.28ff., Philoponus *In De Anima* 27.21f.), and *Metaphysics* 2; (ii) *commentaries on some of the works; (iii) a catalogue of the writings of Aristotle and Theophrastus, with biographical information on both Aristotle and Theophrastus; (iv) a collection of letters of Aristotle; and (v) at least one original treatise titled *On Division*. Whether the edition was produced independently of the other material (which is sometimes said to have comprised his book on Aristotle) is uncertain.

An important clue as to what Andronicus did with the works of Aristotle is supplied by *Porphyry (*Life of Plotinus*, 24), who claims that his own arrangement of the treatises of *Plotinus into ordered, topically related groups follows the methods of Andronicus and *Apollodorus of Athens. It is clear that Andronicus was not the first to attempt to arrange the works of Aristotle, since he himself refers to earlier attempts to arrange the *Postpraedicamenta* and the logical works in general (Simplicius *In Cat.* 379.8f.). There is some evidence that he may have studied assorted manuscripts of the same work (see Dexippus *In Cat.* 21.18f.). Andronicus is responsible for grouping short treatises into *pragmateiai* and for the sequence of these *pragmateiai*, which are preserved to this day. Many of his editorial decisions are undoubtedly based on his views concerning the correct order in which one should study philosophy. For instance, we know that he thought one should begin with the study of logic (Philoponus *In Cat.* 5.18f.; Elias *In Cat.* 117.24), which may well mean that the Organon stood at the beginning of his edition (as it does in modern editions). It does head the list of *pragmateiai* in the catalogue of Aristotle's works by Ptolemy-al-Garib, who seems to have used Andronicus' catalogue, perhaps indirectly.

The precise date of Andronicus' edition is open to debate. Opinions concerning this are related to the question of the degree to which there was already underway a revival of Aristotelianism by the time Andronicus was producing his edition. Often it is placed between 40 and 20

B.C.E., mainly because of *Cicero's silence concerning the esoteric works of Aristotle. Yet there is evidence of a revival of interest in Aristotelian philosophy prior to this period, which could be partially explained if Andronicus' edition had been completed earlier. Aristo of Alexandria and Cratippus of Pergamum, both members of the *Academy, changed allegiance to the Peripatos, most likely some time circa 55 B.C.E. In addition, *Eudorus and *Athenodorus wrote commentaries on the *Categories* in the middle of the first century B.C.E. One explanation would be to push back the date of Andronicus' edition to about 60 B.C.E. Yet it is also the case that, whenever Andronicus began work on his edition, there was already underway a revived interest in the works of Aristotle. Tyrannio himself seems to have produced (perhaps inadequate) editions of some of the esoteric works, and Apellicon before him seems to have written a book on Aristotle (see Aristocles, cited in Eus. *PE* 15, 2, 13) and to have shown interest in an edition of Aristotle (Strabo 13.1, 54, 609). Even earlier *Posidonius and *Panaetius clearly were influenced by the works of Aristotle. All this suggests that interest in Aristotle's more technical esoteric writing may have blossomed prior to Andronicus' edition and, indeed, that the desire to produce an accurate edition may have been generated by this renewed interest instead of producing it.

BIBLIOGRAPHY: Düring, I., *Aristotle in the Ancient Biographical Tradition*, Göteborg, 1957; Gottschalk, H. B., in *ANRW*, Principat, 36.2; Lynch, J. P., *Aristotle's School*, Berkeley/Los Angeles, 1972; Moraux, P., *Der Aristotelismus bei den Griechen, von Andronikos bis Alexander von Aphrodisias*, Peripatoi 5, Berlin/New York, 1973.—*ERIC LEWIS*

ANNICERIS. See CYRENAIC PHILOSOPHY.

ANONYMUS IAMBLICHI (late 5th or early 4th cent. B.C.E.), unknown author of a brief *sophistic treatise that survives because it is embedded in the *Protrepticus* (*Exhortation to Philosophy*) of *Iamblichus. The treatise argues that one should attain a fine reputation by cultivating *excellence (*aretê*) throughout one's life, and that one should maintain justice and good law (*eunomia*) in society. By "good law" the author implies (as often in the period) the preservation of tradition and government by an elite. Lawlessness causes people to waste time in public affairs and is liable to bring on war or tyranny.

BIBLIOGRAPHY: Text in DK98; des Place, E., *Iamblichus: Protrepticus*, Paris, 1989. Tr. in R. K. Sprague, *The Older Sophists*, Columbia, SC, 1972, and M. Gagarin and P. Woodruff, eds., *Early Greek Political Thought from Homer to the Sophists*, Cambridge, 1995. Cole, A. T., *HSCP* 55, 1961, 127–63; Guthrie, W. K. C., *The Sophists*, Cambridge, 1971.—*PAUL WOODRUFF*

ANTIOCHUS (c. 130–c. 68 B.C.E.), of Ascalon in Palestine. Antiochus was trained by the *Stoic *Mnesarchus as well as in the *Academy under

*Philo of Larissa, where he studied for many years and wrote works defending the nondogmatists (Cic. *Acad*. 2.69). He acquired his own pupils and seceded from the Academy, perhaps before the political crisis in Athens in 88 B.C.E. He acquired a patron in Lucullus and broke openly with Philo after reading, in Alexandria in 87, the latter's "Roman Books." He set up an "Academy" of his own in the Ptolemaeum at Athens, where he impressed *Cicero in 79 B.C.E. His own school, advertised as being an Old Academy, was inherited by his brother Aristus. Antiochus' doctrine is presented by Cicero as *Peripatetic in *De Finibus* 5; two of his most distinguished pupils, Aristo and Cratippus, came to call themselves Peripatetics. We know a little of two works, the *Canonica*, used directly or indirectly by *Sextus in his *doxography on the criterion of truth (*M* 7.89ff.), and the *Sosus*, his indignant reply to Philo's "Roman Books" (Cic. *Acad*. 2.12). Tarrant (ch. 5) argues that the *Canonica* is an early work, adopting an orthodox Academic view of the history of philosophy. Other titles also are known.

Antiochus is marked as the source for the dogmatist case in Cicero's *Academica* and for the "Peripatetic" *ethics in *De Finibus* 5; the criticism of Stoic ethics in *De Finibus* 4 is also written from Antiochus' perspective, leading naturally towards the position espoused in Book 5. There has been doubt as to whether the basic natural law theory of *De Legibus* 1 comes from Antiochus, but see Vander Waerdt. Other passages in Cicero are written under Antiochus' influence, but we cannot expect to separate Cicero from Antiochus with confidence; and since Antiochus reconciled his beliefs with other schools, his influence is hard to isolate, particularly from that of recent non-*Chrysippean Stoics. His history of post-Platonic philosophy was distinctive and usually is the clearest indicator of his influence.

Antiochus is known principally for his ethics and *epistemology, since he made the end of goods and the criterion of truth the two principal issues of philosophy (Cic. *Acad*. 2.29). He detected virtual agreement between *Platonism, *Aristotelianism, and Stoicism on the *telos* and the centrality of *virtue in the good life and saw all three philosophies as agreeing that knowledge was possible, though only *Zeno of Citium had demanded a *katalêptikê phantasia*. He saw no real gulf between these philosophies and emphasized Zeno's studies with the Academic *Polemo as ensuring philosophic continuity. *De Finibus* 4 tauntingly regards Zeno's novelties in ethics as a matter of mere terminology.

Three main questions arise in relation to Antiochus' philosophic standing. Was he really a near-orthodox Stoic, as Cicero (*Acad*. 2.132, 137) implies? Or an "eclectic"? Did he significantly influence the revival of Platonism as a doctrine? Clearly he did not see himself as a Stoic, and Cicero treated his moral philosophy separately from that of the Stoics; nor as "eclectic," for he saw his philosophic predecessors as propounding a single, coherent system united in his own vision. *Middle Platonism does not acknowledge Antiochus' influence, and recent studies (Glucker, Tarrant) have questioned that he played some key role. While use may have been made of Platonic Ideas (e.g., Cic. *Or.* 8–10, *Acad.* 1.30) and the theory of Recollection (*Leg.* 1.25; *TD* 1.57–58), this indicates that Antiochus was able to accommodate such doctrine rather than that he required it. For Antiochus, philosophy reached its peak with Polemo rather than with Plato.

Texts on physical matters influenced by Antiochus habitually emphasize the natural aptitude of humankind for all that philosophy values: pursuit of *happiness, reason, cognition, and law. The divine gift of reason is thus of paramount importance to Antiochus, as is his conception of the rational power within nature itself. In conformity with his Stoicizing sympathies, he recognizes an active rational power immanent within the universe, contrasted with passive matter, able to be described as god or as World Soul. Its providential power is strongest in the heavens and next-most strong in human affairs.

In epistemology, Antiochus' contribution became notorious. Ultimately he became a committed defender of the Stoic criterion, the *kataléptikê phantasia*. For anything to become known, the *mind had to receive a *phantasia* in such a way that its truth was recognized alongside its content; the clarity of the cognitive experience had to be such that its content could not fail to be true. Cooperation between mind and senses is emphasized, as is the concept of evidence (*enargeia*).

In ethics, Antiochus made use of the *Carneadea Divisio* to demonstrate that Zeno had agreed with Academics and Peripatetics in making the ethical goal consist un the acquisition of all or most of nature's primary gifts along with virtue. A human being is part soul, part body; and the latter's comforts (necessarily sought by the young) should not be forgotten when humans achieve rationality. Virtue, because of its importance, is sufficient for happiness, but not for the happiest life. The view that all crimes are equal is forcefully rejected.

BIBLIOGRAPHY: Barnes, J., in M. Griffin and J. Barnes, eds., *Philosophia Togata*, Oxford, 1989, 51–96; Dillon, J., *The Middle Platonists*, London/Ithaca, 1977; Glucker, J., *Antiochus and the late Academy* (*Hypomnemata* 56), Göttingen, 1978; Mette, H., *Lustrum*, 28-29, 1986–87, 9–63; Tarrant, H., *Scepticism or Platonism? Cambridge Classical Studies*, Cambridge, 1985; Vander Waerdt, P. A., *The Stoic Theory of Natural Law*, Diss. Princeton, 1989.—*HAROLD A. S. TARRANT*

ANTIPATER (c. 200–c. 130 B.C.E.), of Tarsus. Head of the *Stoic school in Athens after *Diogenes of Babylon; succeeded by *Panaetius. Other associates were *Apollodorus of Seleucia and *Archedemus. Antipater's many students (called "Antipatrists") included Blossius, an Italian Greek who advised Roman senators on agrarian reforms and joined a major revolt against Roman rule in Asia Minor. Antipater shouldered the main burden of defending Stoic doctrines against the *skeptical arguments of *Carneades, who dubbed him "the shouting pen" for writing numerous rejoinders but shunning spontaneous debate. He ended a long life by drinking hemlock. His works were widely used and many titles are attested; but not many fragments survive, and some (those on *cosmology and perhaps others) concern *Antipater of Tyre.

Highly versatile, Antipater covered fields as varied as *grammar (he was the first to count adverbs as a distinct part of speech), *theology (he argued that beneficence is an essential attribute of god), and zoology (he discussed cases of interdependence among species, probably to show that nature is organized providentially). But his most significant contributions were to basic problems in *logic, *epistemology, and *ethics. (i) In logic, he simplified the rules of inference for analyzing arguments, refined the theory of definition, wrote on modality, and followed *Cleanthes in defusing *Diodorus Cronus' "Master Argument" by denying that everything past is necessary. He reportedly counted sentences of the form "p, therefore q" as single-premise arguments. Hostile sources claim he meant to deflect charges that the primary Stoic syllogism ("if p then q, p, therefore q") is invalid because its first premise is redundant, hence violates Stoic criteria for validity. More likely, he avoided conflating implication with inference and sought rather to analyze informal arguments, as Crinis did for so-called paraconditionals ("since p, q"). (ii) In epistemology, Antipater charged *Academic *skeptics with incoherence on two counts: To claim that nothing can be known implies that something can be known; and suspending judgment induces inactivity, since it withholds the assent necessary for any action. He also wrote on divination, which he treated as an empirical *science and defended in part by appeal to divine providence; among cases he discussed was *Socrates' *daimonion*. (iii) In ethics, he refined the Stoic theory of value, explored the relation between legal and moral obligation, and devoted three books to arguing that *Plato shared many Stoic doctrines, principally that *virtue is the only good and sufficient for *happiness. Antipater also tried to rebut Carneades' charge that it is incoherent for the Stoics to define the goal of human life as "reasonable selection of natural things" when they insist that obtaining such things is "indifferent" to the goal. To defend this distinction between goal and intended outcome, Antipater used an analogy: every skill has its objectives, but some skills (he cited archery and dancing) are "stochastic" and often act correctly without achieving their objectives; like these, the reasonable selection that constitutes virtue is designed to obtain natural things but actually consists only in acting according to rational rules and principles, whether or not this achieves those objectives.

BIBLIOGRAPHY: Texts in *SVF* 3, 244–58. Striker, G., in M. Schofield and G. Striker, eds., *The Norms of Nature*, Cambridge/Paris, 1986, 185–204.—*STEPHEN A. WHITE*

ANTIPATER (1st cent. B.C.E.), of Tyre. *Stoic philosopher. Taught by students of *Panaetius, he came to Rome where he introduced Cato to Stoicism. Two works are securely attested: *On Duty* discussed health and wealth, not without criticizing Panaetius; *On the Cosmos* presented a largely orthodox account of the universe as finite, spherical, animate, and periodically destroyed and regenerated. He may have written on marriage (two excerpts survive); but confusion with *Antipater of Tarsus makes evidence for this and other works highly problematic.

BIBLIOGRAPHY: Texts listed in *RE* 1, 2516.—*STEPHEN A. WHITE*

ANTIPHON. Any discussion of Antiphon must commence with what has come to be known as "the Antiphon question," namely, the problem of the relationship (identity or otherwise) between up to four persons named Antiphon who all were active at Athens in the latter part of the fifth century B.C.E. These may be conveniently referred to as Antiphon the *sophist, Antiphon the orator, Antiphon the tragic poet, and the oligarch Antiphon who was put to death in 411. Scholars are divided above all as to the relationship between the sophist and the orator. In the case of the latter, we have fifteen surviving speeches together with fragments from a further eighteen. Antiphon the sophist was credited with at least three works, *On Truth*, *On Concord*, and *Politicus*. The following discussion assumes that the two are not identical. Three further works sometimes attributed to the orator should probably be assigned to the sophist, namely, *On the Interpretation of Dreams*, *The Art of Avoiding Distress*, and *Invective against Alcibiades*.

The importance of Antiphon the sophist as a thinker first became apparent in 1915 with the first publication of substantial papyrus fragments of the two treatises, *On Truth* and *On Concord*. A further very brief fragment was first published in 1984 and is of considerable importance in that it invalidates a series of conjectural supplements made by scholars to the treatise *On Truth* between 1915 and 1984. The title of the treatise suggest comparison both with the writings of *Parmenides and also of *Protagoras. It clearly included a detailed epistemological argument and an attempt to assess the importance of phenomena and perception in relation to *knowledge. The first surviving fragment (DK87B44) opens with the challenging statement that justice consists in not transgressing the laws and customs of the city of which one is a citizen. But the demands of the laws are impositions, and it is the demands of nature that are of greater importance. The opposition here developed between law (*nomos*) and nature (*phusis*) has often been said to have constituted the most distinctive doctrine of the sophistic movement as a whole. Some have concluded that Antiphon is recommending a form of immoralism involving a complete rejection of all moral and legal obligations and so a rejection of society and all its works as a whole. Others have supposed that despite his criticisms of conventional justice Antiphon does allow some place for genuinely ethical considerations. Certainly the fragments of *On Concord* seem clearly to show that the concept of concord is associated with the need for policies of self-restraint and that it is to be valued as opposed to anarchy, which is the worst of evils among men. It is then possible that the appeal to nature, as against conventional justice, is to be understood as the search for a kind of natural justice that is more real and so more advantageous to men in human societies and so involving the improvement rather than the simple destruction of such societies.

*Aristotle preserves a statement of considerable philosophical interest and importance when he says (*Phys.* 193a9ff. = B15) that according to Antiphon, if one were to bury a wooden bed that subsequently sent out a shoot, what would come up would not be a bed but simply wood. This seems to argue for the priority of basic *matter in nature, in contrast with transitory qualities that may come to be related to matter in the process of perception. It is of interest in establishing a position against which *Plato and possibly *Socrates also were concerned to argue in their expositions of the theory of Forms.

Finally, there is evidence that at least one Athenian, most probably Antiphon the sophist, showed a technical interest in the working of the human mind. This is indicated by two treatises, named *On Interpretation of Dreams* and *The Art of Avoiding Distress*. In the manner of physicians who treat those who are ill, we are told, Antiphon set up a kind of clinic or citizens' advice bureau in a room near the marketplace at Corinth. Here he claimed to be able to treat those who were in psychological distress by asking questions and so finding out the causes of his patients' distress. He was then able "by the use of words," that is, by talking to them, to encourage and so to heal those in trouble. He can thus be regarded as one of the first known practitioners of psychiatry. Associated with this may well be the statement attributed to him that "illness is a holiday for those who lack courage, for they then do not go out to do things" (B57).

BIBLIOGRAPHY: Texts in DK87 and *Ox. Pap.* 51, 1984, 1–5; also in *corpus dei Papiri filosofici greci e latini*, Parte 1, Autori noti, vol. 1, Florence, 1989; see J. Barnes, *Polis* 8, 1987, 2–5. Tr. in R. K. Sprague, *The Older Sophists*, Columbia, SC, 1972, and M. Gagarin and P. Woodruff, eds., *Early Greek Political Thought from Homer to the Sophists*, Cambridge, 1995. Bignone, E., *Studi sul pensiero antico*, Naples, 1938; Kerferd, G. B., *PCPS* 184, 1956, 26–32; Morrison, J. S., *PCPS* 187, 1961, 49–58.—*G. B. KERFERD*

ANTISTHENES (c. 445–365 B.C.E.), of Athens, of noncitizen (perhaps Thracian) lineage on his mother's side. Antisthenes fought with distinction at Tanagra in 424 B.C.E. and perhaps was rewarded with citizenship at some later date. He was regarded in antiquity as the teacher of *Diogenes of Sinope and thus as the founder of the *Cynic school, but modern scholarship rejects this claim as a product of the systematizing tendencies of Hellenistic *doxography. A close companion of *Socrates, Antisthenes is named by *Plato among those present at Socrates' death (*Phd.* 59b), and *Xenophon presents him as one of Socrates' most devoted followers (*Mem.* 3.11.17, *Symp.* 8.4). He was some two decades older than Plato and Xenophon; and for a decade or more after Socrates' death he may have been the most prominent *Socratic, to judge from *Isocrates' attacks on him. Reputed to have been very sharp with his students, Antisthenes had more in common with the abrasive philosophical style of the Cynics than with the urbane irony of Socrates. He is also said to have been a student of *Gorgias, which is consistent with the literary and *rhetorical topics of some of his writings.

We know the titles of sixty-two works of Antisthenes but have substantial verbatim fragments only of two rhetorical set pieces, *Ajax* and *Odysseus*. The rest of his literary remains consist mostly of brief anecdotes and aphorisms that testify more to Antisthenes' defense of an ideal of Socratic hardiness, frankness, and independence of mind and body than to the content of his philosophical teachings. Scholars have often tried to supplement these rather meager direct quotations by identifying allusions to Antisthenes' doctrines in Plato, Aristotle, and especially Xenophon, but with limited success.

Antisthenes' most important works seem to have had a protreptic intention. Thus he wrote a number of accounts of Heracles and of Cyrus the Great, both of whom he presented as examples of self-sufficient *virtue grounded in the capacity for hard work and endurance. He claimed that virtue is teachable and sufficient by itself for *happiness, but not dependent on arguments or specialized learning. He seems also to have argued that virtue is the same for Greeks and barbarians and for men and women, perhaps as part of a larger attack on convention.

Beyond this narrowly moral interest, Antisthenes also wrote works on *epistemology and *logic. His best attested doctrine claims that basic entities cannot be defined in terms of other entities, but only named, so that everything said about basic entities is either tautological or merely analogical (see especially Ar. *Met.* 1024b and 1043b, and Burnyeat). He also wrote literary studies, including a series on episodes in the *Odyssey*.

Whatever his contributions to logic, epistemology, and literary criticism, Antisthenes is most important as an imitator and literary heir of Socrates. More like Xenophon than Plato, he seems to have emphasized Socrates' self-sufficiency and hardiness more than his wisdom and *dialectical skill. His picture of the Socratic sage as a philosophic ideal had a formative influence on Cynicism and *Stoicism, though this influence is impossible to trace in detail.

BIBLIOGRAPHY: Texts in *SSR* 2, 137–225; F. Caizzi, *Antisthenis Fragmenta*, Milan, 1966. Burnyeat, M., *Phronesis*, 1970, 101–146; Caizzi, F., *Studi Urbinati*, 1964, 48–99; Rankin, H., *Antisthenes Sokratikos*, Amsterdam, 1986; von Fritz, K., *Rh. Mus.* 1935, 19–45.—*DAVID K. O'CONNOR*

ANTISTHENES (fl. late 3rd–early 2nd cent. B.C.E.?), of Rhodes. *Peripatetic historian and *doxographer. A plethora of vague references to authors named Antisthenes makes identification speculative. The received opinion, still vigorously defended, holds that a single author named Antisthenes (i) hailed from Rhodes and wrote a *History of Rhodes* to the beginning of the second century B.C.E., (ii) was a Peripatetic philosopher who described a series of oracles that allegedly occurred in 191 B.C.E., and (iii) authored *Successions (Diadochai) of the Philosophers.* On this view Antisthenes was one of the earliest authors of what was to become a popular philosophical genre of the last two centuries B.C.E., the history of philosophy told in the form of biographies of philosophers and organized by school affiliation or general philosophical position. An alternative interpretation holds that the author of the *Successions* was not the historian from Rhodes, but a later (Peripatetic?) writer of the first century B.C.E., perhaps to be identified with the author of an account of the Egyptian pyramids.

BIBLIOGRAPHY: Texts in *FGH*, vol. 3B, no. 508, 485–87; Andria, R. G, *I frammenti delle "Successioni dei filosofi,"* Naples, 1989. Janda, J., *Listy Filologické* 89, 1966, 341–64.—*DAVID E. HAHM*

APOLLODORUS (c. 180–after 120 B.C.E.), of Athens. Author of literary, mythological, and chronological writings. A student of the *Stoic *Diogenes of Seleucia (in Athens) and *Aristarchus of Samos, Apollodorus lived in Alexandria until 145/44 B.C.E., and then again in Athens.

Of importance to the history of philosophy is his poem *Chronica*, a synopsis of the main events of the history of Greece from the Fall of Troy (1184/83 B.C.E.) to 144/43 B.C.E. (Books 1–3), later followed up with a fourth book down to 120/19 B.C.E. Many of the dates of Greek philosophers go back to Apollodorus' poem, as he seems to be one of the main biographical sources of *Diogenes Laertius and *Philodemus. His chronology was based on that of *Eratosthenes; since, however, it was rare that any documentary evidence on a particular personality's dates and life survived after his death, Apollodorus was in many cases forced to give approximate dates. His main method was to identify the *floruit* (Gr. *acmê*), that is, the fortieth year of a person's life, with a major event that took place in the middle of his life; thus, since the sophist *Protagoras was said to have given the laws of the Athenian colony, Thurii, which was established in southern Italy in 444/43 B.C.E., Apollodorus identified this year as Protagoras' *floruit*. *Empedocles' *floruit* was placed in this year as well, even though both men seem to have been somewhat older. The relationship between two philosophers who were supposed to be connected as teacher/student or who succeeded one another was also described within this framework: A student was usually considered forty years younger than his teacher, though other intervals also occur; thus *Anaximander seems to have been considered sixty-four years old when his successor *Anaximenes was forty and *Pythagoras was twenty-five years old.

These synchronisms must always be accepted with some skepticism, and alternative dates in ancient sources should only be rejected after careful examination. Apollodorus seems, however, to have taken advantage of whatever evidence he could find, and we are in many cases in no position to correct him. In addition to dates, Apollodorus offered brief biographical sketches. His dates were given according to the year of the Athenian archons, and when, for example, Diogenes Laertius refers to Olympiads, he must have been using a revised edition of Apollodorus or an intermediate source.

BIBLIOGRAPHY: Jacoby, F., *Apollodors Chronik*, Berlin, 1902; Mosshammer, A. A., *The Chronicle of Eusebius and the Greek Chronographic Tradition*, Lewisburg/London, 1979, 113–27.—*JØRGEN MEJER*

APOLLODORUS (2nd cent. B.C.E.), of Seleucia on the Tigris. *Stoic systematizer, compatriot and student of *Diogenes of Babylon. Nicknamed *Ephêlos* (apparently from cataracts), Apollodorus worked with *Antipater of Tarsus and *Panaetius. His *Introductions to the Doctrines* provided a comprehensive treatment of Stoicism and long remained a standard text; two other attested titles—"Ethics" and "Physics"—probably refer to sections of it. Originality is hard to estimate because he is cited mostly for standard doctrines; but his methodical arrangement of "topics" probably underlies the Stoic *doxographies in *Diogenes Laertius and the catalogue of *Chrysippus' works preserved there.

Apollodorus defended orthodox positions in *logic and *epistemology. In *ethics, he endorsed *Cynic asceticism as a shortcut to virtue. Best attested is his work in *cosmology, where he is cited for several basic theses: The cosmos is unique, entirely material, continuous throughout, finite but *infinitely divisible, surrounded by infinite *void, alive, and both sensate and rational. Widely influential and apparently original was his use of geometry to define fundamental physical concepts: Bodies have threefold extension (sources do not mention resistance); surfaces are limits of bodies and have twofold extension; lines are limits of surfaces and have length only; and points are limits of lines, or "minimal signs." He also analyzed motion and rest as *change and continuity in place or shape; and, defining *time as "the extension of cosmic motion," he argued that time extends infinitely like number and that the whole of time is "broadly" present but no time "exactly" present. Explanations are lacking, but he probably sought to make Stoic materialism more systematic, perhaps also to provide an empiricist account of geometry.

BIBLIOGRAPHY: Texts in *SVF* 3, 259–61.—*STEPHEN A. WHITE*

APOLLONIUS (early 1st cent. B.C.E.), of Tyre. *Stoic biographer and historian. Apollonius' biography of *Zeno of Citium and his catalogue of members of the Stoic school with their bibliographies played a major role in preserving the history of the school. It was used by *Diogenes Laertius and may have served as his principal source for Book 7. Though Apollonius probably preserved a wide range of traditions, he seems to have given priority to the tradition that portrayed Stoicism as a development from and improvement upon *Cynicism and that sought to define Stoic orthodoxy, while marginalizing some of the variants that flourished earlier in its history.

BIBLIOGRAPHY: Hahm, D. E., *ANRW* 2, 36.6, 1992, 4076–4128.—*DAVID E. HAHM*

APULEIUS (born c. 125 C.E.), of Madaura in North Africa. Apuleius was a professional *rhetorician and is best known as the author of a novel, *Metamorphoses* (or *The Golden Ass*). His surviving philosophical writings are composed in Latin. Five philosophical treatises have come down under his name, *De Deo Socratis, De Platone et eius Dogmate, De Mundo, Peri Hermeneias*, and *Asclepius*. The authenticity of all of these has been doubted at one time or another, though the current consensus favors the authenticity of at least the first three.

De Deo Socratis is the only systematic demonological treatise extant from antiquity. According to its account, *daimones* mediate between men and gods, and their intermediary position is explained in terms of the four elements. The bodies of the (visible) gods are constituted from fire, of *daimones* from air, and of mortal animals from earth and water. Like the gods, *daimones* are immortal, whereas they share the human characteristic of susceptibility to the emotions.

De Platone et eius Dogmate is a handbook-style exposition of *Plato's philosophy under the headings of physics (Book 1) and *ethics (Book 2). In physics he begins from the three principles, god–matter–forms, and then discusses in turn the creation of the world, the World Soul, and the division of living things into kinds according to the four elements. The rest of Book 1 treats man's psychic and bodily composition. In ethics he identitifes the supreme good with god and intellect (*nous*), and defines the virtues as absolute goods, distinguishing them from lesser "human" goods, such as bodily excellences and material advantages. Apuleius attributes to Plato the view that humans at birth are neither good nor evil, but have a natural proclivity toward one or the other. As a corollary to this view he develops a theory of moral progress that shows *Peripatetic influence. Characters are grouped into three categories: virtuous, vicious, and median. The third kind of character provides the primary audience for moral education and may in itself be either good or bad, as, for example, opinion may be either true or false. Other ethical topics treated include rhetoric, friendship, god's activity through providence, the sage, and *politics.

The *De Mundo* is a translation and adaptation of the pseudo-Aristotelian *Peri Kosmou*; *Peri Hermeneias*, an introduction to logic on Peripatetic lines; and *Asclepius*, a *Hermetic treatise.

Apuleian scholarship this century has focused on his sources, and for a long time he was generally accepted, with *Albinus, as a follower of the "School of Gaius." More recent work tends to the view that the points of commonality between Apuleius and Albinus are not strong enough to prove Gaius as a common influence.

BIBLIOGRAPHY: Texts, French. tr. and comm. in J. Beaujeu, *Apulée. Opuscules Philosophiques et Fragments, Texte Établi, Traduit et Commenté*, Paris, 1973. Dillon, J., *The Middle Platonists*, London/Ithaca, NY, 1977; Gersh, S., *Middle Platonism and Neoplatonism: The Latin Tradition*, vol. 1, Notre Dame, 1986.—*JOSEPH G. DeFILIPPO*

ARCESILAUS (316/15–241/40 B.C.E.), of Pitane. Scholarch of the *Academy and father of Academic *skepticism. Arcesilaus studied with the astronomer Autolycus before leaving his native Pitane. In Athens he studied with *Theophrastus, Aristotle's successor at the *Peripatos, before being won over to the Academy by *Crantor. The Academy was led at that time by *Polemo. There Arcesilaus was a student of Polemo and his successor *Crates of Athens. Upon Crates' death, Arcesilaus succeeded to the scholarchate when another candidate, Socratides, withdrew in his favor. Reports that *Zeno of Citium—the founder of *Stoicism, against whose theories Arcesilaus later argued—was a fellow student of his under Polemo and that *Chrysippus, the third head of the Stoa, studied under Arcesilaus before embracing Stoicism give a sense of the lively philosophical interaction characteristic of the period. Though he tried his hand at poetry, Arcesilaus wrote no philosophical works. It is not clear what kind of instruction he received from his Academic masters, but he was viewed in antiquity as the initiator of the Academy's skeptical turn, which was itself regarded as a decisive break in the history of the Academy.

The skepticism for which Arcesilaus was known is best approached via the other ground of his ancient fame, his reputation as a master *dialectician. Arcesilaus did not expound Academic positions. Rather, he invited those with whom he spoke to adopt positions of their choice, which he then subjected to dialectical examination. That is, through questioning his interlocutor, he constructed an argument for a conclusion at odds with that interlocutor's stated position. This approach revealed weaknesses in an interlocutor's position or his defense of that position, without committing the questioner to a position of his own. This was of course one of *Socrates' methods, and it is reasonable to suppose that Arcesilaus emphasized the Socratic roots of the Academy.

Arcesilaus' most important application of the dialectical method was to the epistemological theory of Zeno of Citium. According to Zeno, it lies within our power as human beings to reach a condition of wisdom entirely free from opinion, that is, false or insecure belief. This condition is identical with *virtue, the sole necessary and sufficient condition for *happiness. A crucial part in the explanation of how wisdom is possible is played by the Stoic criterion of truth, the cognitive impression, a perceptual impression that affords a perfectly accurate grasp of its object in such a way that one can infallibly discriminate in favor of the impression. A wise person differs from those who are not wise, in the first instance, by exercising this discrimination, confining his assent to cognitive impressions and other impressions appropriately related to them. Arcesilaus first argued that there are no cognitive impressions, that is, that there are no perceptual impressions whose intrinsic character excludes the possibility of their being false. This is roughly equivalent to maintaining that nothing can be known with certainty. From this conclusion, taken together with the Stoic dogma that wisdom is incompatible with opinion, he then argued that the wise person is duty-bound to suspend judgment on all matters. To the obvious objection that this renders the wise person completely inactive, Arcesilaus, again drawing on resources furnished by Stoic theory itself, responded that it was possible not only to act, but to act wisely and well without assent and in the absence of cognitive impressions by relying instead on the criterion of the reasonable.

The Academy and later *Pyrrhonists conceived their skeptical stance in terms drawn from these arguments. But they are, in the first instance, dialectical arguments that need do no more than indicate various implications of the Stoics' positions with a view to revealing the weaknesses in those positions. As such they are compatible with the maintenance by the Academics who used them of nonskeptical positions not implicated with the Stoic theory under attack, and there are ancient testimonies asserting that some form of dogmatic *Platonism lay hidden behind Arcesilaus' arguments. Against this speaks the view of his Academic successors that he was a skeptic. In any case, to the extent that Arcesilaus and succeeding generations of Academics who built on the foundations he laid were skeptics of some kind, it cannot be because they followed their arguments through to and embraced their conclusions. For the conclusions that nothing is known and that judgment ought in consequence be suspended on all matters undermine themselves and the premises from which they are deduced no less than anything else. Rather, the Academy's skepticism must have been a reaction to the repeated experience that its inquiries open questions that they are unable to resolve, leading instead to a deadlock between opposed considerations on either side of the issue.

This is the experience that suggests to the Academic that he lacks knowledge and to which the appropriate response seemed to be suspension of judgment. This also is the attitude attributed to Arcesilaus by *Cicero and by *Sextus Empiricus, who acknowledges that it is essentially the same as the attitude recommended by Pyrrhonism. It was a skepticism of this kind for which the Academy was known from the time of Arcesilaus to that of *Carneades, though it was a matter of dispute among Carneades' students whether his so-called probabilism was a departure from Arcesilaus' attitude or a refinement of it.

The Academic skepticism inaugurated by Arcesilaus was widely known and much discussed in antiquity. It exerted an important influence on early modern philosophers like Descartes and Hume, who knew of it through Cicero.

BIBLIOGRAPHY: Texts in H. J. Mette, *Lustrum* 26, 1984, 7–94, 41f. Couissin, P., in M. Burnyeat, ed., *The Skeptical Tradition*, Berkeley, 1983, 31–63; *Revue des Études Grecques* 47, 1929, 373–97; Long, A. A., *Elenchos* 7, 1986, 431–449; Striker, G., in M. Schofield, M. Burnyeat, and J. Barnes, eds., *Doubt and Dogmatism: Studies in Hellenistic Epistemology*, Oxford, 1980, 54–83.—*JAMES ALLEN*

ARCHEDEMUS (c. 2nd cent. B.C.E.), of Tarsus in Cilicia. *Stoic philosopher, student of *Diogenes of Seleucia. A native of Tarsus, Archedemus went to Athens, where he studied philosophy in the school of the Stoics Diogenes of Seleucia and *Zeno of Tarsus. He subsequently opened a philosophical school in Babylon, before it was conquered by the Parthians in 145 B.C.E. Crinis may have been his student.

Archedemus had the reputation of being a subtle dialectician, superior to his fellow student *Antipater of Tarsus. His writings were still being read and commented upon in the time of *Epictetus.

Ancient sources mention the following works: *On Voice*, where "voice" was defined as "body" (*sôma*); *On Elements*, where the existence of two principles—an active and a passive—was recognized; and a work *On the Master Argument* (?), probably in opposition to the views of *Diodorus Cronus. Other fragments are *ethical in content (on the "end," which is understood as the realization of those things that are "fitting," and on "pleasure"). It is debated whether two of the fragments (7 and 11) should be assigned to him or to an orator of the same name.

BIBLIOGRAPHY: Texts in *SVF* 3, Arched. frs. 1–22. Schmidt, E. G., in *RE* Supp. 12, 1970, 1356–1392.—*TIZIANO DORANDI*

ARCHELAUS (5th cent. B.C.E.), an Athenian. Various accounts make him a pupil of *Anaxagoras and a mentor of *Socrates. Nothing of his work survives, except perhaps a single phrase: "coldness is the bond" that compacts the earth (DK60B1a). *Doxographical evidence indicates a physical treatise in the familiar Ionian manner. Reports of its contents (deriving ultimately from *Theophrastus) represent Archelaus as accepting the main principles of Anaxagoras' ontology—notably *mind and the primordial mixture—but attempting innovations elsewhere, especially in his geocentric cosmogony.

Mind, then, contains a mixture like everything else and apparently has no cosmic role. The ultimate origin of *change is (as in *Anaximander) separation of the hot from the cold. The motion of the hot made water flow to "the middle" and then burn up, so that it became either earth below or air above—which, if itself ignited, turned into the material of the heavenly bodies (cf. *Xenophanes and especially *Heraclitus). Life on earth began in a primeval slime. The development of civilization was due to mind, which as in Anaxagoras governs the behavior of the other animals as well as humans. Man's distinctive achievement is to have introduced "leaders, laws, crafts, cities and so on." Right and wrong exist only by convention, not by nature. This is the earliest evidence—and in a derivative thinker—for the key ingredients of the anthropology found, for example, in *Plato's *Protagoras*.

BIBLIOGRAPHY: Texts in DK60. Translations in KRS, ch. 13. Guthrie, W. K. C., *A History of Greek Philosophy*, vol. 2, Cambridge, 1965, 339–344; Kahn, C. H., in G. B. Kerferd, ed., *The Sophists and Their Legacy*, Wiesbaden, 1981.—*MALCOLM SCHOFIELD*

ARCHIMEDES (d. 212 B.C.E.), of Syracuse. Mathematician, physicist, and mechanician. For Archimedes alone, among prominent figures from ancient *mathematical *science, a partial biographical sketch is possible, thanks to accounts in the historians Polybius, Livy, and *Plutarch. Famous for designing powerful lifting engines, catapults, and other weaponry, Archimedes received patronage from the royal court at Syracuse. As an old man, he directed the defense of the city against the Roman army in the Second Punic War and died as the Romans eventually occupied and sacked the city. From his own writings, we learn that Archimedes was the son of an astronomer and that he exchanged correspondence with leading scientists at Alexandria, such as Conon of Samos, Dositheus, and *Eratosthenes of Cyrene. In his works, he offers no hints of specific philosophical commitments, training, or even interests, apart from those that are naturally entailed by inquiry into theoretical science.

The corpus of known works, both extant and lost, comprising over a dozen medium-length treatises, is devoted almost exclusively to pure geometry and its applications in mechanics. The principal works, in their probable order of composition, are the *Dimension of the Circle* (its extant version, however, being an edition from the schools of late antiquity), the two books on *Plane Equilibria*, the *Quadrature of the Parabola*, the two books *On the Sphere and Cylinder*, *Spirals*, *Conoids and Spheroids*, the lost *Equilibria* (on centers of gravity of conics of revolution), the two books *On Floating Bodies*, and the *Method*. The *Sand Reckoner*, a lecture on measuring the cosmos, is probably an early effort, while the arithmetic epigram on the *Cattle Problem* is late. The geometric game called *loculus Archimedis* exists in a fragment, a tract on the thirteen semiregular solids is described by Pappus, and a few additional items exist through Arabic translations: a construction of the regular heptagon, a tract on mutually tangent circles, and measurements of certain figures bounded by circular arcs. Pappus and Hero draw from other tracts, now lost, on statics, including one *On Balances* (which would probably be the earliest of Archimedes' studies of static equilibrium) and another on centers of gravity. These may relate to the medieval tradition of balances in Arabic and Latin, but the Greek originals are lost. Among devices invented by Archimedes are a hydrostatic balance (reported in Arabic from Greek sources) and a construction of a form of planetarium (described in a lost writing, the *Sphaeropoeia*, and apparently seen by *Cicero). The Arabic tradition of the Archimedean waterclock is dubious.

Archimedes' work lays to rest two oft-repeated stereotypes about ancient mathematical science: (i) *Horror infiniti*. In the *Method*, Archimedes describes the heuristic procedure he followed in discovering some of his results on the measurement of geometric figures and their centers of gravity. The figures are dissected into parallel slices of lower dimension (e.g., a cone or sphere is sectioned into its component parallel circles); one then conceives of a balance in which these are weighed individually against the correlated sections of other figures. From the equilibrium that obtains for the sections *separatim* he infers equilibrium for the sections *en ensemble*, that is, for the given figures themselves. However, these sections would be indivisibly thin elements, a type of atomic magnitude, and thus excluded from the formal exposition of geometric theorems, as in the "exhaustion method" that Archimedes inherited and extended from *Eudoxus (cf. Book 12 of *Euclid's *Elements*). But, as Archimedes' treatments in the *Method* make clear, that exclusion is an aspect of formal methodology, not of heuristic conception. Moreover, although Archimedes recognizes that the treatments by his "mechanical method" do not qualify as demonstrations, the invalidating feature here is the supposition of mechanical properties (sc. weight and equilibrium). By contrast, the assumption of indivisibles, readily modified in accordance with the Eudoxean method of limits, seems to be taken as a familiar aspect of geometric inquiry.

(ii) *Learned disdain for the practical.* Plutarch, echoing the attitude of a *Neoplatonist gentleman, describes Archimedes as too preoccupied with the life of the mind to sully its pursuit by writing on his practical inventions. Whether or not such a view holds for the ancient aristocracy in general, it has nothing to do with Archimedes. His activities as inventor of mechanical devices and supervisor of their actual construction and operation, his detailed account of the construction and use of a diopter for measuring the apparent diameter of the sun (in the *Sand Reckoner*), and the knowledge that later authorities had of his inventions through his writings (as on the hydrostatic balance and on the planetarium) reveal no signs of such a prejudice. To the contrary, Archimedes' works on mechanical theory (in *Plane Equilibria* and *Floating Bodies*) manifest complete empirical understanding of the associated phenomena of static and hydrostatic equilibrium. Indeed, the same mechanical intuition enriches his explorations in pure theory, as he explains in the *Method*.

In later times, the Archimedean works that happened still to be available for study in the schools provided the paradigm of geometric precision. The writings on the circle, on the sphere, and on statics, for instance, were expounded by the Alexandrian commentator Eutocius of Ascalon (early 6th cent.), not only for their technical results, but also for their subtlety of reasoning. If the Arabic teachers took greater note of grasping and extending the technical results, the Latin scholastics rather more emphasized the logical forms. In the Renaissance, the preparation of complete editions and translations of the corpus for a while stimulated the most advanced geometric researches until that level was matched and surpassed. Galileo self-consciously modelled his physics on Archimedes' mechanical writings; Kepler drew explicitly on Archimedes' measurements of the circle, sphere and conoids for his own innovations in geometry; and the epithet of "the new Archimedes" was coveted by both of them and by others in their generation.

BIBLIOGRAPHY: Texts in J. L. Heiberg, ed., *Archimedis Opera Omnia*,[2] 3 vols. (Teubner), Leipzig, 1910–15. Clagett, M., *Archimedes in the Middle Ages*, vol. 1, Madison, 1964; vols. 2–5, Philadelphia, 1976–1984; Dijksterhuis, E. J., *Archimedes*,[2]

Princeton, 1987, with bibl. supp. by W. R. Knorr; Schneider, I., *Archimedes*, Darmstadt, 1979.—*WILBUR R. KNORR*

ARCHYTAS (fl. 400–350 B.C.E.), of Tarentum, in southern Italy. *Pythagorean philosopher and *mathematician. Archytas was a leading political figure in Tarentum and was chosen general seven times, perhaps during the 360s. He was a prominent figure in the pseudo-Pythagorean tradition, and two complete short works and a large number of fragments ascribed to him have survived (Thesleff, pp. 2–48). However, almost all of them are surely spurious. Only three fragments are likely to be from authentic works (DK47B1–3).

The evidence for his philosophy is meager, although *Aristotle wrote three books (now lost) on Archytas alone, which suggests that he saw him as an important philosopher. Archytas expected definitions to combine *matter and form (Ar. *Met.* 1043a22), he apparently regarded the "irregular" or the "indefinite" as the cause of motion, and he is reported to have argued that the universe was unlimited by asking whether someone standing at the edge of a limited universe would be able to extend his hand into what is outside. In B1 he defines a canonical set of "sister *sciences" (astronomy, geometry, arithmetic, and music; cf. Pl. *Rep.* 530d) as the basis for the rest of philosophy. The fragment goes on to articulate a theory of sound according to which swift impacts produce high sounds while slow ones produce low. B3 distinguishes between learning and discovery and then praises reasoning or calculation (*logismos*) for its role in producing harmony in society.

There is more evidence for his technical mathematical work, and reports of two important proofs have been preserved. *Proclus (*in Eucl.* prol. 2) says that Archytas was one of those responsible for expanding the number of proofs in geometry and for giving it a more scientific organization. *Diogenes Laertius asserts that he was the first to give method to mechanics by employing mathematical principles. Geometry and mechanics were brought together in his method of finding the two mean proportionals necessary in order to solve the famous problem of duplicating the cube (Eutocius *in Archim. Sphaer. et Cyl.* 2). Most of all, Archytas excelled in the mathematics related to music theory. B2 defines three means that are important to music (arithmetic, geometric, and harmonic). He was perhaps the first to work out a coherent system of ratios for the tetrachordal divisions in all three genera (enharmonic, chromatic, and diatonic—Ptolemy *Harmonics* 1.13). His proof that there can be no mean between numbers in a superparticular ratio $(n+1/n)$ is important in music theory as showing that the tone $(9/8)$ cannot be bisected (Boethius *De Musica* 3.11).

Archytas is famous for his friendship with *Plato, although he is never mentioned in the dialogues; and Plato's controversial Letter 7, which attests to a close personal tie with Plato, is the primary source for the connection. It indicates that Plato, having first met Archytas on his visit to Italy in 389-8(?), established friendly relations between Archytas and the Tarentines and Dionysius II on his visit to Sicily in 367. When Dionysius II later tried to persuade Plato to return, Archytas sent letters mistakenly assuring Plato of Dionysius' progress in philosophy. After this second visit with Dionysius II turned out badly, Archytas and the Tarentines intervened diplomatically and sent a ship to take Plato away. Despite this close personal tie between Plato and Archytas, the evidence for and the nature of any philosophical connection is meager (Pl. *Rep.* 530d) and problematic.

This friendship with Plato may have been elaborated in the tradition as a paradigm case of Pythagorean friendship. A number of moralizing stories about Archytas similarly portray him as living the philosophical life. He supposedly refused to punish negligent servants because he did not want to act in anger. One anecdote has him arguing that reason is our greatest possession and bodily pleasure the greatest curse, since it keeps us from using reason. He is presented as liking children and inventing mechanical toys such as "the rattle of Archytas" (Ar. *Pol.* 1340b26).

While Pythagoras established the way of life that made him famous and *Philolaus was the first Pythagorean to promulgate a coherent system of first principles, Archytas is crucial as a representative of the later Pythagoreanism of the fourth century and even more important as the first and only Pythagorean who we can confidently say made important contributions to serious mathematics.

BIBLIOGRAPHY: Texts in DK47. Tr. in K. Freeman, *Ancilla to the PreSocratic Philosophers*, Cambridge, 1971. Barker, A., *Greek Musical Writings*, vol. 2, Cambridge, 1989; Heath, T., *A History of Greek Mathematics*, Oxford, 1921; Huffman, C., *CQ* 35, 1985, 344–8; Lloyd, G. E. R., *Phronesis* 35, 1990, 159–74; Thesleff, H., *Pythagorean Texts of the Hellenistic Period*, Abo, 1965.—CARL A. HUFFMAN

ARETÊ **(VIRTUE, EXCELLENCE).** See ETHICAL THOUGHT, Classical.

ARISTARCHUS (1st half 3rd cent. B.C.E.), of Samos. Astronomer, student of *Strato of Lampsacus. Aristarchus wrote an extraordinary treatise (Archimedes *Sand Reckoner* 1.4–7), now lost, hypothesizing a rotating earth revolving around a fixed sun in a universe large enough to avoid observable parallax of the stars, where the movement of the earth will not produce a noticeable change in stellar positions, a problem already known to *Aristotle. His treatise, *On the Sizes and Distances of the Sun and Moon*, survives. The source of a citation of Aristarchus in Oxyrhynchus papyrus 3710 on *Thales on eclipses and possibly *Heraclitus on the month is unknown. *Ptolemy credits him with a crude observation of the summer solstice in 280 B.C.E. He also invented a hemispherical sundial. His lunar/solar cycle or exeligmos was 2434 years, whence he added 1/1623 day to the 365 1/4 day solar year of Callippus.

The extant treatise, which assumes, nonessentially, a geocentric universe (only in props. 6–8), is a valid geometrical exercise in theoretical measurement by finding upper and lower bounds. Absent from the initial values, the boundaries arise from numerical treatment of the geometry (as later in *Archimedes). In common with other Hellenistic measuring exercises, the initial values come from theory and casual observation for providing clean computation and pleasing results, and not from careful measurement. Archimedes gives as Aristarchus' reasonable value for the size of the sun 1/2°, yet the value here is 2°. Decisive error comes from his assumed elongation of a half moon from the sun (87°; actually 89°50'), which was not observable with any precision; yet he proves in prop. 6 that it is less than 90°. These sources of error do not appear in his geometrical constructions, and those that do, such as the diameter of the shadow of the earth on the moon (2 moons; actually 2.6), the equal angular widths of the sun and moon (argued from alleged observation), or their constant distances (common in contemporary Greek astronomy), prove comparatively insignificant. The principal results are the following: The sun's distance from the earth and diameter are respectively between eighteen and twenty times the moon's distance and diameter, the ratio of the sun's diameter to the earth's diameter is between 19:3 and 43:6, and the earth's to the moon's is between 108:43 and 60:19.

BIBLIOGRAPHY: Text of *On the Sizes and Distances of the Sun and Moon* in T. L. Heath, *Aristarchus of Samos*, Oxford, 1913; text of P. Oxyrhynchus 3710 in A. C. Bowen and B. Goldstein, *Physis* n.s. 31, 1994, 689–729. Neugebauer, O., *A History of Ancient Mathematical Astronomy*, Berlin, 1975; Noack, B., *Aristarch von Samos: Untersuchungen zur Überlieferungsgeschichte*, Wiesbaden, 1992.—HENRY MENDELL

ARISTIPPUS (c. 435–355 B.C.E.), of Cyrene. While still young, Aristippus moved to Athens, where he joined the *Socratic circle and attended lectures of *sophists. His numerous travels and the fact that he taught for considerable fees gained him the reputation of being a sophist. During the last years of his life he probably returned to Cyrene, where he may have founded the *Cyrenaic school.

The evidence about Aristippus' writings is divided. Some sources maintain that he wrote nothing at all, whereas others attribute to him several dialogues and a work in three volumes. The titles of his works, if genuine, testify that he was primarily interested in practical *ethics. But he also showed a theoretical interest in ethics, as indicated by his argument that every object is related to a moral end and that, therefore, no morally neutral object exists. He dismissed the study of *mathematics and physics, but he probably recognized some usefulness in *logic. He also discussed *rhetoric, linguistic morphology, semantics, and history.

It is hard to assess Aristippus' philosophy, for few philosophical tenets can be ascribed to him with certainty. Regarding ethics, there are two distinct *doxographical traditions. The first presents him as a hedonist positing the momentary pleasure of the body as the moral end and distinguishing it from *happiness. However, this testimony lacks persuasiveness. For Aristippus atributed instrinsic value to *virtue and emphasized the importance of unpleasurable means, such as exercise and self-control, to a happy life. On the other hand, according to a second tradition, Aristippus was not a hedonist but only gave that impression, both because of his numerous lectures on pleasure and because of his voluptuous life; in fact, Aristippus was a eudaemonist who considered individual pleasures a major component of happiness, but who recommended the enjoyment of bodily pleasures only if it did not endanger one's mastery over oneself. This latter picture of Aristippus agrees with his tendency to look at his life as a whole and with the importance he attributed to the long-lasting activity of philosophy. Also, it is compatible with Aristippus' identity as a close associate of *Socrates and a philosopher who developed themes occurring in Socratic ethics.

Aristippus probably did not have detailed *epistemological views. The Cyrenaic theory of knowledge was probably formulated not by him, but by his grandson. However, he laid the *psychological and physiological foundations of that doctrine. For he emphasized the status of pleasure and pain as *pathê* and described them in terms of motions of the flesh or of the soul resulting in sensation. In these respects, Aristippus' views prefigure Cyrenaic subjectivism, which postulates that the *pathê* experienced at the present moment are related to motions, self-evident and incorrigibly apprehended.

Aristippus' social and *political attitudes were dictated by a strict individualism. He rejected the political condition of citizenship together with the civic roles of ruling and being ruled, and he held an apolitical stance "that leads ... through freedom" to happiness (Xen. *Mem.* 2.1.11). BIBLIOGRAPHY: Texts in *SSR* 2. Classen, C. J., *Hermes* 86, 1958, 182–192; Döring, K., *Die Sokratesschüler Aristipp und die Kyrenaiker*, Stuttgart, 1988; Giannantoni, G., *Rivista Critica di Storia della Filosofia* 15, 1960, 63–70.—*VOULA TSOUNA-McKIRAHAN*

ARISTIPPUS (the Younger). See CYRENAIC PHILOSOPHY.

ARISTO (fl. c. 225–200 B.C.E.), of Iulis on Ceos. *Peripatetic philosopher; probably *Lyco's successor as head of the School. In antiquity, Aristo was confused with the like-named *Stoic of Chios. *Diogenes Laertius reports a book list for the Stoic but adds that *Panaetius and Sosicrates attribute all the works except the epistles to the Peripatetic. Works with Peripatetic precedents, such as *Exhortations* and *Erotic Dissertations*, can be plausibly attributed to the Peripatetic. Other sources report additional titles: *Lyco* (perhaps part of *Dialogues* mentioned in Diogenes' list), *On Old Age,* and *On Relieving Arrogance.* Whether part of the last-named work or from a separate treatise, Aristo's descriptions of persons exhibiting inconsiderateness, self-will, and other unattractive traits (preserved in *Philodemus) relate closely to the *Characters* of *Theophrastus. In addition, Aristo wrote biographies of *Heraclitus, *Socrates, and *Epicurus. We may be sure that he did the same for the leaders of the Peripatos. Diogenes cites Aristo as his source for the will of *Strato; the wills of *Aristotle, Theophrastus, and Lyco probably also derive from Aristo.

BIBLIOGRAPHY: Texts in Wehrli 6, 27–44, with commentary 45–67.—*WILLIAM W. FORTENBAUGH*

ARISTO (fl. mid-3rd cent. B.C.E.), of Chios. Pupil of *Zeno of Citium. *Eratosthenes judged him and *Arcesilaus the leading figures among the philosophers of his time (Strabo 1.2.2). Although some scholars in antiquity held that most of the items in *Diogenes Laertius' catalogue of his writings were by the *Peripatetic *Aristo of Ceos (D.L. 7.163), the best modern research rejects this assessment. Nevertheless, the only book to which specific surviving testimonies are attributed, *Similes*, is not mentioned in the catalogue. This work may also be the source of his influential comparison of the wise man to an actor, able to play the part of Agamemnon or Thersites as circumstances dictate (D.L. 7.160).

Aristo was perceived as giving *Stoicism a *Cynic turn (D.L. 6.103, 105), successfully resisted by *Cleanthes (e.g., Seneca *Letters* 94.4) and *Chrysippus (e.g., Plutarch *SR* 1034d). What motivated most of Aristo's key positions was apparently a sense that Zeno was compromising the *Socratic inheritance that the Stoics were committed to maintaining. Thus, contrary to Zeno but like *Plato's Socrates, Aristo restricted philosophy to *ethics, on the ground that physics is beyond us and *dialectic irrelevant: like a spider's web—artistic, but of no use (e.g. D.L. 7.160–1). He "introduced indifference" (D.L. 7.37) as the goal of life, that is, the thesis that nothing but *virtue (as the *good) and vice (as evil) have any intrinsic value whatever and that we should therefore endeavor to be indifferent to everything else; compare Socrates in Plato *Euthyd.* 281d–e. Zeno had taken another view, holding some things, though indifferent for happiness, to be naturally preferable, others to be naturally nonpreferable. Again, Aristo insisted—contrary to Zeno's advocacy of a plurality of virtues—on the Socratic view that virtue is one thing only, practical wisdom, and that courage, justice, and the like are simply different contextual applications of it (e.g., Plutarch *Vir. Mor.* 440f.). Finally, Aristo could see no room within ethics for precepts or moral advice: Either a person understands the fundamental principles of ethics, in which case advice is superfluous, or not, in which case it will be ineffectual (Seneca *Letters* 94.5ff).

Aristo has sometimes been regarded as an unorthodox and indeed schismatic Stoic. But in his day the question of whether Stoics must be Zenonians, even if asked, was not yet definitively settled.

BIBLIOGRAPHY: Texts in *SVF* 1, 333–403. Ioppolo, A. M., *Aristone di Chio e lo Stoicismo antico*, Rome, 1980; Long, A. A., *CQ* 38, 1988, 150ff.; Schofield, M., *AP* 4, 1984, 83–96.—*MALCOLM SCHOFIELD*

ARISTOCLES (1st and 2nd cent. C.E.), of Messene in Sicily. *Peripatetic philosopher. No biographical details are known about Aristocles. Tradition regarded him as a teacher of *Alexander of Aphrodisias, his name misspelled "Aristoteles," but that teacher has recently been plausibly identified as Aristoteles of Mytilene.

The *Suda* (s.v. "Aristocles") lists the following works: *On Philosophy* (10 books), *Whether Homer Was Nobler than Plato*, *Handbook in Rhetoric*, *On Sarapis*, and *Ethics* (9 books). Long excerpts from *On Philosophy* are quoted in Eusebius' *Praeparatio Evangelica*. They show that his history of philosophy was much more penetrating than that of *Diogenes Laertius, but its exact nature cannot be recontructed. He may have followed a systematic division of philosophy (*logic, *ethics, physics), but a biographical procedure is more likely. It is impossible to say whether he used original texts or depended entirely on compendia, such as that of *Theophrastus.

BIBLIOGRAPHY: Texts in F. W. A Mullach, *Fragmenta Philosophorum Graecorum*, vol. 3, 206–221 (incomplete), and H. Heiland, *Aristoclis Messanii Reliquiae*, Paris, 1881. Moraux, P., *Der Aristotelismus bei den Griechen*, vol. 2, Berlin, 1984, 83–207; Trabucco, F., *Acme* 11, 1958, 97–150.—*DOROTHEA FREDE*

ARISTOPHANES. See POETS, COMIC.

ARISTOTELIAN COMMENTATORS. The term "Aristotelian Commentators" as used here includes Greek commentators from the first century B.C.E. to the seventh century C.E., the bulk of whose extant commentaries appears in the *Commentaria in Aristotelem Graeca* (*CAG*); those Byzantine Greek commentators of the eleventh and twelfth centuries C.E. who appear in the *CAG*; and Latin commentators of the fourth to sixth centuries C.E. This article prescinds from Byzantine commentators not in the *CAG*, from Arabic commentators, and from medieval Latin and Renaissance commentators.

Classification of Commentators. The Aristotelian commentators may be classified as follows:

(i) *Peripatetic Commentators.* *Andronicus edited the works of Aristotle in mid–first century B.C.E. *Aspasius and Adrastus were active in early-to-middle second century C.E. Aspasius' commentaries on *Nicomachean Ethics* 1–4, 7–8 survive; other commentaries on *Nicomachean Ethics* 2–5 may go back to Adrastus. (Authorship and dating of commentaries are sometimes difficult to fix.) *Alexander of Aphrodisias was active c. 200 C.E.; extant are his commentaries on *Prior Analytics* 1, *Posterior Analytics* (fragmentary), *Topics, Meteorologica, De Anima* (fragmentary), *De Sensu,* and *Metaphysics* 1–5. Also extant are Alexander's *Physical Problems, Ethical Problems,* the anti-*Stoic tracts *On Fate* and *On Mixture,* the essay *De Anima,* and the *Mantissa.* *Themistius (c. 317–c. 388), a *Peripatetic with some *Neoplatonic sympathies, wrote paraphrasing commentaries on *Posterior Analytics, Physics, De Caelo, De Anima,* extant in Greek, and *Metaphysics* 12, extant in Hebrew.

(ii) *Neoplatonic Aristotelian Commentators.* (a) *Early Neoplatonists:* *Plotinus (205–270 C.E.) used commentaries on the *Metaphysics* by Adrastus, Aspasius, Alexander, and others, and criticized the Aristotelian categories (*Enneads* 6.1–3). His student *Porphyry (232–305) composed the *Isagôgê* or *Introduction* to Aristotle's Organon, two commentaries on *Categories,* and other philosophical and religious works. *Iamblichus (c. 240–c. 325) composed a commentary, now lost, on *Categories,* as well as a *Protrepticus* from which Aristotle's *Protrepticus* has been reconstructed. His follower *Dexippus (active early 4th cent.) composed a commentary on *Categories.* (b) *The Athenian School:* *Plutarch of Athens (d. c. 432), teacher of *Syrianus and *Proclus, is not known to have written commentaries on Aristotle. Syrianus (d. c. 437), is represented by commentaries on *Metaphysics* 3, 4, 13, 14. Proclus (c. 412–485) is not known to have commented on Aristotle. Work by *Damascius (head of the Athenian School when it was closed by Justinian in 529) may lie behind some of *Simplicius' commentary on *De Caelo* 1. Simplicius (active after 529) composed lengthy scholarly commentaries, still extant, on *Categories, Physics, De Caelo,* and *De Anima* (doubts have lately been raised about Simplicius' authorship) and on the *Enchiridion* of *Epictetus. (c) *The Alexandrian School:* The commentaries of *Ammonius (active late 5th and early 6th cent. C.E.), son and successor of Hermeias, on *Categories, De Interpretatione,* and *Prior Analytics* (fragmentary) are extant. Ammonius' influence extends to the commentaries of his pupils, for example, the commentary on *Metaphysics* 1–7 by Asclepius (d. c. 560–570), which is also heavily dependent on Alexander. *Olympiodorus (d. after 565) wrote commentaries on *Categories* and *Meteorologica,* both extant. The *Christian John *Philoponus (c. 490–c. 565/570) commented on *Cate-*

gories, Prior and *Posterior Analytics, Physics, Meteorologica, De Generatione et Corruptione, De Generatione Animalium, De Anima,* and *Metaphysics.* Philoponus is also known for his *On the Eternity of the World Against Proclus,* to which Simplicius replied. Philoponus rejects such Aristotelian tenets as the eternity of the world and the fifth element. Later Christian Alexandrians include Elias (late 6th cent.), David (late 6th and early 7th cent., sometimes identified with the Armenian David the Invincible), and Stephanus (early 7th cent.).

(iii) *Early Latin Aristotelian Commentators.* Marius Victorinus (active in the mid-4th cent.) translated Aristotle's *De Interpretatione* and *Topics,* Porphyry's *Isagôgê* and *Categories* commentary, and probably the "books of the Platonists" read by *Augustine; a convert to Christianity in the late 350s, he also wrote against Arianism. *Boethius (480–524) translated Porphyry's *Isagôgê* and Aristotle's Organon into Latin and wrote commentaries on *Categories* and *De Interpretatione,* as well as essays on logic, theological treatises, and the *Consolation of Philosophy.*

(iv) *Byzantine Commentators.* Interest in Aristotle appears to have revived in the circle of the princess Anna Comnena (1083–after 1148); this led to the writing of commentaries on the previously neglected biological works, *Politics,* and *Rhetoric.* The commentaries of Eustratius (c. 1050/1060–c. 1120) on *Posterior Analytics* 2 and *Nicomachean Ethics* 1 and 6 are extant, as are commentaries of Michael of Ephesus (active c. 1118–1138) on various biological works and on *Nicomachean Ethics* 5, 9, and 10. Michael is commonly credited with the commentaries on *Metaphysics* 6–14 attributed to Alexander of Aphrodisias. Sophonias (13th cent.) paraphrased the *De Anima.* The all but unknown Heliodorus of Prusa paraphrased the *Nicomachean Ethics,* perhaps in the first half of the fourteenth century. Many Byzantine commentaries remain unedited.

General Characteristics. Most Aristotelian commentaries originated as lectures, though Simplicius apparently composed his commentaries to be read. Commentaries take various literary forms: paraphrase, sentence by sentence exegesis, and question-and-answer. Commentaries often discuss the authenticity of a work, its overall point, the branch of philosophy to which it belongs, and its place in Aristotle's corpus. They sometimes provide both a preliminary overview and a line-by-line analysis of the text.

The commentators are philosophers and religious thinkers as well as exegetes. Alexander is not only an interpreter of Aristotle but also a defender of *Aristotelianism, for example, in his *Ethical Questions* and *De Fato.* Porphyry is not only a commentator but also a philosopher and religious controversialist. Syrianus' *Platonism can often be detected in his commentaries on the *Metaphysics.* Simplicius and Philoponus are parties to the debate between pagan philosophy and Christianity. The line between exegesis and philosophy is sometimes difficult to draw; but it is overstatement to say that the commentaries are simply vehicles for their authors' philosophical or religious views.

Neoplatonist commentators regard study of Aristotle as preliminary (the lesser mysteries) to study of *Plato (the greater mysteries). The appearance of incompatibility between Plato and Aristotle is weakened by the assumption that Aristotle is speaking about the sensible world, not contradicting Plato's descriptions of the intelligible world. But the general tendency to harmonize Plato and Aristotle does not prevent Syrianus from criticizing Aristotle vigorously; Simplicius criticizes Philoponus for not upholding the harmony. It has been thought that the Alexandrians were more inclined than the Athenians to harmonize Plato and Aristotle and that the Alexandrians tended to stay closer to the texts while the Athenians inclined towards mysticism and theurgy. But the schools maintained close academic and family connections: Ammonius was a student of Proclus; his father and teacher Hermeias was a student of Syrianus and married Aidesia, a relative of Syrianus; Ammonius taught not only the Alexandrians Asclepius, Olympiodorus, and Philoponus but also the Athenians Damascius and Simplicius. Differences of mind and temperament are not reducible to school positions.

The commentators and commentaries represented in the *CAG* are evidence for the intellectual world of late antiquity and Byzantium. They are sources for works otherwise lost, such as Alexander on *Metaphysics* 1 for Aristotle's *On Ideas*, Simplicius on *Physics* for Parmenides DKB6 and 8. They are witnesses to the text of Aristotle, as in the case of *Categories* and *Metaphysics*. The commentators' influence is extensive but often indirect—through Plotinus on Neoplatonism, for example, or through Boethius on the Latin Middle Ages. The influence of Alexander's interpretation of Aristotle's doctrine of the intellect and the influence of Porphyry's *Isagôgê* on medieval formulations of the problem of universals have long been known. More recently the influence of Philoponus on Bonaventure and Galileo has drawn attention. While some commentators have been criticized as lacking in philosophical acumen and while Neoplatonism may at times distort their understanding of Aristotle's *psychology and *metaphysics, at their best they read Aristotle very closely.

The following incomplete list indicates the range of commentaries available today. *Categories*: Porphyry, Dexippus, Ammonius, Simplicius, Olympiodorus, Philoponus, Elias, and an anonymous commentator. *De Interpretatione*: Ammonius. *Prior Analytics*: Alexander, Ammonius, Philoponus. *Posterior Analytics*: Alexander, Ammonius, Philoponus. *Topics*: Alexander. *Physics*: Themistius, Simplicius, Philoponus. *De Caelo*: Themistius, Simplicius. *Meteorologica*: Alexander, Olympiodorus, Philoponus. *De Anima*: Alexander, Themistius, Philoponus, Sophonias. Various biological works: Sophonias, Michael of Ephesus. *Metaphysics*: Alexander, Themistius, Syrianus, Asclepius (based on Ammonius), Ps.-Alexander (probably Michael of Ephesus). *Nicomachean Ethics*: composite commentary drawn from Eustratius, Adrastus (?), Aspasius, Michael of Ephesus, and an anonymous commentator; paraphrase by Heliodorus of Prusa. *Rhetoric*: Stephanus and an anonymous commentator.

BIBLIOGRAPHY: Texts in *CAG*. Sorabji, R., ed., *Ancient Commentators on Aristotle*, Ithaca, 1987– (a series, still incomplete, of English translations currently including commentaries by Alexander, Porphyry, Dexippus, Ammonius, Simplicius and Philoponus); also Sorabji, ed., *Aristotle Transformed*, Ithaca, 1990.—*ARTHUR MADIGAN, S. J.*

ARISTOTELIANISM, the philosophy of *Aristotle in the form given it by his pupils and their successors. Aristotle died in 322 B.C.E. in Chalcis, where he had fled to escape the anti-Macedonian backlash following the death of Alexander the Great. His will, preserved by *Diogenes Laertius (5.11ff.), makes no mention of his manuscripts or his school and suggests that he had little hope of his writings being published or his teaching continued. In spite of this, some of his pupils succceeded in founding a school, the *Peripatos, to propagate and develop his doctrine. This was the beginning of a philosophical tradition that lasted until the start of the modern age. For two thousand years Aristotelianism was one of the most important factors in the philosophy of Europe and the Near East. Its development, although uneven, was never interrupted completely and can be divided into distinct periods, the first three of which fall within classical antiquity and will be described in some detail in this article.

Hellenistic period, from *Theophrastus to *Andronicus of Rhodes, c. 322–40 B.C.E. Aristotle's pupils and immediate successors took his (largely unpublished) school treatises as the starting-point of their own work and accepted his fundamental doctrines without major change: these included his doctrine of categories; his *logic, based on the categorical syllogism; teleology; the dichotomies between *matter and form and potentiality and actuality; the four basic qualities; the five simple bodies; the uniqueness, finiteness, and eternity of the world; *virtue as a mean; and so on. But they did not only pass on what they had inherited. Theophrastus studied subjects Aristotle had only touched on, such as botany, mineralogy, and comparative law. In other fields, Aristotle's conclusions were modified in order to take account of new data about natural phenomena or human behavior. Innovations in logic were the first steps on the road that was to lead from Aristotelian to "traditional" logic; some of these, such as the introduction of five "indirect" moods in the first figure of the syllogism and the *in peiorem* rule in modal logic, as well as the development of hypothetical syllogisms, are attributed to

Theophrastus and *Eudemus jointly. There is much to be said for the view that they were suggested by Aristotle himself after the completion of his extant *Analytics*. Two tendencies can be observed in the work of Aristotle's immediate pupils: on the one hand, a more systematic application of basic principles and terminology, and on the other, more stress on observation and a greater interest in particular phenomena and their immediate, that is, material and instrumental, causes. This could result in tensions between the old assumptions and the new data; for example, Theophrastus' account of heat (*Ign.* 5ff.) is not easy to reconcile with the notion that the heavens are composed of *aithêr*, which he seems to take for granted in his *Physics* (fr. 143 FHS&G), and local factors play a much larger part in his account of winds (*Vent.* 15f.) than in Aristotle's. In other areas Theophrastus questioned Aristotle's teaching, such as his definition of place and even the extent to which teleological explanations could be applied to the natural world (fr. 146 FHS&G, *Met.* 15). But in most cases he did no more than ask awkward questions. Some scholars believe that he gave up the doctrine of the unmoved mover, but the evidence is ambivalent and the only point where he certainly broke with one of Aristotle's fundamental beliefs was in assuming that matter consists of distinct particles and microvoids. He was led to this view by observing that surface contact between two bodies with opposed qualities is not always enough to cause a reaction; for example, metals are melted by dry heat, but not by steam, because their "pores" are too small to admit the relatively large particles of steam (*Ign.* 42, cf. 61). Such interplay between dynamic/formal and structural/mechanical causes is characteristic of Theophrastus' acccount of the physical world. It arose naturally out of his research into the "lower" parts of that world and continues tendencies already present in Aristotle's *Meteorologica* and zoological works (the problem is discussed by Aristotle in *PA* 1.1 and *GA* 5.1). It is quite wrong to explain Theophrastus' corpuscular theory as a weak compromise with *Atomism; if we must look for an external source, *Plato's *Timaeus* would be a more likely candidate.

Theophrastus' successor *Strato (scholarch 288/6–270/68) took this critique of Aristotle to its logical conclusion. He developed the corpuscular theory further and was even more radical in other respects. He denied teleology and the existence of the unmoved mover and the fifth element ("*aithêr*") and described nature as an unconscious principle of movement immanent in the physical world; he differed from his predecessors in his accounts of movement, *time, and place and identified the *soul of living things with their innate *pneuma*. His teaching had some influence on Boethus and perhaps *Andronicus in the first century B.C.E., but on the whole the school rejected his innovations; chs. 5 and 9 of the pesudo-Aristotelian *De Spiritu*, written in the middle of the third century B.C.E., are evidence of a reaction against his identification of the soul with *pneuma*.

Work on the central themes of Aristotle's philosophy was complemented by research in more marginal fields such as music theory (*Aristoxenus) and geography (*Dicaearchus), using a methodology influenced by Aristotle. The place of medical studies in the Peripatos is less clear. Meno compiled a history of *medicine, perhaps at Aristotle's suggestion; writings on medical topics are attributed to Theophrastus and Strato, and several sections of the pseudo-Artistotelian *Problêmata* are devoted to questions of this kind. There can be no doubt that there was some interchange of ideas between Aristotle and *Diocles of Carystus and between Aristotle's successors and *Herophilus and *Erasistratus, but the relationship was not one-sided. Diocles was probably too old to be regarded as Aristotle's pupil, and the Peripatos was not in a position to provide clinical training.

The views of the early Peripatetics are known not only from the books and fragments that have survived under their names but also from spurious writings that have come down to us under the name of Aristotle. Some of these can be connected with particular authors: *Meteorologica* 4, *De Coloribus*, and *De Lineis Insecabilibus* with Theophrastus (the first perhaps being a revised version of an Aristotelian work) and *De Audibilibus* and *Mechanica* with Strato, while *De Spiritu* belongs to the generation after Strato. The *Problemata* and other collections also contain material that can be traced back to them.

All the works mentioned so far were meant for use within the school and closely connected with its teaching. Besides them there was a large production of "exoteric" writings, mostly on *ethics, history, biography, and literary history, written for a wider audience; many were in dialogue-form. After Strato's death the energies of the school were concentrated on this kind of writing and popular teaching, while its philosophical work took second place. For two centuries the Peripatos became little more than an educational institution purveying a reasonable wordly wisdom. The reason for this decline is unclear, but probably connected with the competition for students. The numbers attracted by the Peripatos had declined during Strato's scholarchate (see Plutarch *De Tranquilitate Animi* 472a), but the school enjoyed considerable success in its new role under *Lyco (scholarch 288/6–226/4) and his successors.

But even in these years some Peripatetics took an active part in the current debates between schools. Lyco's contemporary *Hieronymus of Rhodes wrote a book, *Peri Epochês* (Wehrli fr. 24); and a doctrine of the criterion of truth that *Sextus Empiricus (*M* 2.217–26) attributes to "Aristotle and Theophrastus and the Peripatetics in general," seems to go back to an attempt to adapt Aristotle's *epistemology, as found especially in

Posterior Analytics 2.19, to the state of the question in the second century B.C.E. *Critolaus (scholarch in the middle of the century) defended the doctrine of the eternity of the world against the Hellenistic schools, although his arguments were less rigorous than those used by Aristotle. Hieronymus and others produced definitions of the "end of life" modelled on those offered by the *Stoics, and in a compendium of Peripatetic ethics summarized by *Arius Didymus (in Stobaeus *Anthology* 2.118ff.) an attempt is made to graft the Stoic concept of *oikeiôsis* onto Aristotle's teaching. The philosophical activity of the Peripatos was at a low ebb, but it had not died out altogether.

Period of Peripatetic Scholasticism, from Andronicus of Rhodes to *Alexander of Aphrodisias (c. 60 B.C.E.–230 C.E.). A revival of Aristotelianism was set in train by Andronicus with a new edition of the school-treatises of Aristotle and Theophrastus, whose purpose was to turn the attention of his contemporaries back to Aristotle's genuine philosophy. This lay in the spirit of the age: The Academy also sought renewal through a return to the classical philosophers. But the difficulty of Aristotle's *pragmateiai* and the poor quality of the available texts meant that more editorial and critical work was needed to make them accessible. This led to the development of an interpretative tradition, beginning with a *commentary on the *Categories* by Andronicus himself, which came to dominate the work of the Peripatos. It had some precedents in the lectures of Aristotle's earliest pupils, especially Eudemus, but the differences must not be underrated. The early Peripatetics wanted not only to propagate Aristotle's philosophy but to develop it further, but the later ones were on the whole satisfied with expounding and defending traditional doctrine. Such modifications as they made were presented as explanations or interpretations of Aristotle's words, and genuine innovations were attempted only where interschool controversies had raised problems that Aristotle had not considered or had treated as marginal.

The aim of this exegesis was to present Aristotelianism as a self-contained system and to interpret the texts in such a way as to eliminate any (real or apparent) contradictions; little or no account was taken of the context in which individual treatises were composed or the possibility that Aristotle's views could have changed over time. To set against this one-sided approach, many of the commentators had a wide and deep knowledge of all the writings of Aristotle and his followers and an outlook still relatively close to theirs, so that much of their work remains valuable today. It has been said that Aristotle's philosophy was distorted by being forced into a system, but a systematic tendency was at least implicit in his work from the beginning, and his successors might have claimed, with some justification, that they were only carrying out his intentions. However, if not false to the spirit of Aristotle's thought as a whole, their method could lead to a distorted view of particular works or arguments.

In spite of the limitations within which they worked, these men produced some interesting ideas, many of which can still be found in the pages of Alexander. Andronicus and Boethus seem to have favored a "naturalistic" interpretation of Aristotle. They attached great importance to the "powers" inherent in natural objects and treated the soul as a kind of second-order power subsuming all the others present in the living body. Boethus also had interesting things to say about the "impetus" of thrown bodies and the nature of time—the last, characteristically, when trying to elucidate an obscure remark in Aristotle's *Categories*. He probably owed something to Strato, and both he and Andronicus may have been influenced by Stoic views. Later the school became more conservative. In the second century *Aspasius tried to eliminate traces of Stoic notions he claimed to find in the ethics of Andronicus and Boethus, and we hear that Peripatetic logicians clung to certain conventions in the setting-out of their syllogisms that others thought outmoded. The aim was always to recover the genuine Aristotle.

During all this time the Peripatos continued to influence a wider public through popular lectures and writings. Aristotle's "exoteric" works and handbooks compiled during the Hellenistic era were widely read, and outsiders like *Philo of Alexandria, Sextus Empiricus, Diogenes Laertius, and *Clement of Alexandria gained most of their knowledge of Aristotle from such sources.

The Peripatetic writings surviving from this period are a mixed bag. From the Augustan era we have Arius Didymus' compendia of natural philosophy (fragmentary) and ethics, parts of a huge summary of Aristotle's system of the physical world by Nicolaus of Damascus and a rehash of the *Categories*, falsely ascribed to Archytas. Probably from the first century C.E. are the *De Mundo*, a rhetorical but attractive essay on the structure of the universe and its dependence on a God who is both transcendent mover and beneficent creator, and two dull ethical tracts, the *De Virtutibus et Vitiis* falsely ascribed to Aristotle and the *Peri Pathôn* falsely ascribed to Andronicus; from the second, compendia of mainly Aristotelian logic by *Apuleius and *Galen, and two commentaries on the *Nicomachean Ethics*, one by Aspasius, the other anonymous; from Alexander, commentaries on *Prior Analytics* 1, the *Topics*, *Meteorologica*, and *Metaphysics* 1–5 and several monographs, some of which may be the work of his pupils. Our knowledge is supplemented by quotations and reports in later commentaries.

Neoplatonic period, c. 230–600 C.E. The Peripatetic school as such came to an end after Alexander's death. In the following centuries *Themistius (c. 320–90) was the only prominent thinker who felt as an

Aristotelian and wrote paraphrases of Aristotle's works from this point of view; but he was an isolated figure and his known associates were *Platonists. Otherwise Aristotelianism was absorbed by Neoplatonism. The beginning of this process can be observed as early as the second century in the work of *Middle Platonists like *Alcinous, although others, like Atticus and later *Plotinus, adopted a more critical stance towards Aristotle. But the decisive impulse came from *Porphyry (c. 232–309). In his great commentary on the *Categories* he tried to overcome Plotinus' objections, and he laid down the principle that there was no substantial disagreement between Platonism and Aristotle's philosophy, rightly understood. As a result the whole of Aristotle's logic, large parts of his natural philosophy and ethics and some of his *metaphysics were incorporated in the Neoplatonic systems. However, Aristotle's philosophy was chiefly valued as a preparation for Platonism. Many of his doctrines were reinterpreted to fit in with the fundamental Platonic positions, and the relationship between the two philosophies became the subject of ongoing debate. Yet the Neoplatonist response often throws an interesting, if oblique, light on Aristotle's ideas and preserved many of his insights for later generations.

The preferred vehicle for Neoplatonic discussions of Aristotelianism were commentaries on Aristotle's works, often based on lectures; nearly all leading Neoplatonists produced at least one or two, and about thirty are still extant, ranging in date from the second half of the third century (Porphyry) to the end of the sixth.

Later History of Aristotelianism: At the end of antiquity, the Aristotelian tradition split into three streams: (i) In the Byzantine empire Aristotelianism had to face opposition from orthodox *Christianity as well as some Platonists, but the tradition continued at a rather low level, with little original work being done. In the twelfth century there was a half-hearted revival under the patronage of the ex-empress Anna Comnena. (ii) Aristotelian texts began to be translated into Syriac in the fifth, and into Arabic in the ninth century. This gave rise to a series of commentaries and monographs that led to some important developments, especially in the Arabic world. (iii) A Latin Aristotelian tradition began in the West with Marius Victorinus in the fourth, and with *Boethius at the end of the fifth century. Although limited to certain parts of the *Organon* (the so-called *Logica Vetus*), it became an important source of early mediaeval scholasticism.

These streams were reunited in the twelfth and thirteenth centuries, when new translations from Greek and Arabic into Latin made many additional works of Aristotle and his commentators available in western Europe. These formed the basis of high scholasticism.

In the late Middle Ages and the Renaissance, Aristotelianism became the basis of the "School Philosophy," but for that very reason it provoked a reaction based both on new discoveries in logic and the natural sciences and on Platonism and, later, on other, newly rediscovered ancient philosophies, notably Atomism and *Skepticism.

See also COMMENTATORS, ARISTOTELIAN; LYCEUM; PERIPATETIC SCHOOL, and individual philosophers.

BIBLIOGRAPHY: For texts, see under each author. Theophrastus' fragments are cited from FHS&G; other early Peripatetics from Wehrli. See also bibl. under COMMENTATORS, ARISTOTELIAN, and PERIPATETIC SCHOOL. General accounts: *Hellenistic period:* Wehrli, F., in F. Ueberweg, *Grundriss der Geschichte der Philosophie*, H. Flashar, ed., vol. 3, Basel, 1983, 459–599. *Period of Peripatetic Scholasticism:* Moraux, P., *Der Aristotelismus bei den Griechen*, Berlin, 1973–84; Gottschalk, H. B., *ANRW* 36.2, 1079–1174; Sharples, R. W., *ANRW* 36.2, 1176–1243. *Neoplatonic period:* Armstrong, A. H., ed., *The Cambridge History of Later Greek and Early Mediaeval Philosophy*, Cambridge, 1967; Sorabji, R., ed., *Aristotle Transformed*, London, 1990. *Later history:* Kretzmann, N. et al., eds., *The Cambridge History of Later Medieval Philosophy*, Cambridge, 1982; Schmitt, C. et al., eds., *The Cambridge History of Renaissance Philosophy*, Cambridge, 1988.—H. B. GOTTSCHALK

ARISTOTLE (384–322 B.C.E.), of Stagira. Philosopher, student of *Plato and founder of a school at the *Lyceum. Aristotle was an Ionian Greek born in Stagira, a town on the northeast coast of the peninsula of Chalcidice in Thrace. His father Nicomachus was the court physician of the Macedonian king Amyntas II, the father of Philip II and grandfather of Alexander the Great. The family of his mother, Phaestis, was from Chalcis in Euboea, where she still owned property. Both parents were from Asclepiad families, and Aristotle's interest in biology, *medicine, and natural science in general may have been influenced by his medical background. Both parents died while he was still young; and in 367, at the age of seventeen, he was sent to Athens by his guardian Proxenus of Atarneus. There he became a member of Plato's *Academy, where he remained an active participant until its founder's death some twenty years later, in 347.

Plato's nephew *Speusippus succeeded Plato as head of the Academy, and Aristotle (perhaps partially in response to anti-Macedonian feelings in Athens) traveled to the northwest coast of Asia Minor with *Xenocrates, a fellow Academic. They joined two other former students of Plato who were already living there, Erastus and Coriscus, both from Skepsis. Hermias, the ruler or tyrant of a kingdom that took as its capital the city of Atarneus near the coast of Mysia, had an interest in, and perhaps some previous contact with, Plato's Academy. He gave these philosophers the town of Assos in the Troad to use as a home.

During this time Aristotle developed a close friendship with Hermias and met a relative of the tyrant's named Pythias. She later became his wife and the mother of his daughter. Sometime after her death he lived with, but did not actually marry, a woman from Stagira named Herpyllis, thought to have been the mother of Aristotle's son Nicomachus, possibly the editor of the *Nicomachean Ethics*. Aristotle also had an adopted son, Nicanor, son of his former guardian Proxenus.

Aristotle remained in Assos or Atarneus for a period of three years and then moved to Mytiline on the island of Lesbos, where he stayed until 343. His philosophical activities during his stay in Asia Minor included a considerable amount, though not all, of his biological researches. It was also during this period that he became acquainted with a man who would later be one of his closest philosophical associates, *Theophrastus, from Eresus on Lesbos.

In 343 Aristotle was back in Macedonia, and at the invitation of Philip II became the tutor of his son Alexander, then about thirteen. During this period he developed his friendship with the Macedonian general Antipater, later named by him as the executor of his will. Aristotle's instruction lasted only about three years, until the time that Alexander was appointed regent during his father's absence on a military campaign. However, Aristotle did not return to Athens until 335/4, shortly after Alexander ascended to the throne following the death of Philip in 336. He may have spent the remaining years before his return to Athens in Stagira.

Meanwhile, in Athens, Xenocrates had assumed leadership of the Academy after Speusippus' death in 339. Upon his own return, Aristotle founded a school whose activities centered in the Lyceum, a gymnasium connected with the temple of Apollo Lyceus northeast of Athens. For the next twelve years or so he lectured, conducted research, and organized a library. As a metic, or resident foreigner, he never owned property in or around Athens and would have had to rent the buildings used for his school. According to tradition, at the Lyceum he regularly walked back and forth discussing philosophy in a *peripatos*, or covered walkway, and for this reason his school came to be referred to as *"Peripatetic." Ancient sources indicate that Alexander the Great partially financed his research during this period and had ordered hunters, fishermen, bird-catchers, beekeepers, and the like to convey to Aristotle information of scientific interest.

Shortly after Alexander's death in 323, anti-Macedonian sentiment ran high in Athens, and a legal charge of impiety, based upon his former relation with the tyrant Hermias, was lodged against Aristotle. He retreated with Herpyllis to a maternal family estate in Chalcis in Euboea, where about a year later, in 322, he died at the age of sixty-two.

Writings. Aristotle's writings included both (i) his no longer extant literary publications and (ii) the lecture notes for use within his own school. For Aristotle, philosophical investigation is directed toward the solution of puzzles that arise from phenomena or the established views, and accordingly he also composed or supervised the compilation of (iii) collections of data, observations, and previous opinions, and (iv) collections of puzzles to be solved. It is generally agreed that the bulk of the surviving corpus consists of the lecture notes, together with some of the material from (iii). However, the surviving lecture notes, in addition to putting forward philosophical theses and conclusions, often themselves incorporate surveys of data, opinions, and problems.

The present-day corpus may be traced back to a first century B.C.E. edition by *Andronicus of Rhodes, organized following the *Stoic division of philosophy into *logic, natural *science, and *ethics. The collection of fourteen treatises titled *Metaphysics* did not readily fall under these headings, and it is possible that the title indicates a decision to place it in the corpus after the treatises on natural science. The logical works are referred to collectively as the *Organon*. In the traditional ordering, the *Categories* comes first. It deals with the simple terms (subjects and predicates) that are combined to form simple statements. The *De Interpretatione*, placed second, discusses the statements that result from combining nouns and verbs. The *Prior Analytics* contains a formal theory of syllogistic reasoning and shows how statements combine to form arguments, and the *Posterior Analytics* analyzes demonstrations as explanatory syllogisms from first principles. The *Topics* is primarily a handbook on *dialectical debate, and the treatise *On Sophistical Refutations* is a treatment of fallacies of arguments that may occur in such debate.

Aristotle's most general treatment of the principles governing natural bodies is contained in the *Physics* (eight books). The *De Caelo* investigates celestial locomotion and the locomotion of the four basic elemental bodies in the sublunary sphere. The *De Generatione et Corruptione* deals with the interactions of these elements, especially mutual transformations, and gives a general account both of generation and perishing and of growth. The *Meteorologica* continues the study of the four elements by investigating a variety of sublunary phenomena for which they are the *matter and the heavens the moving cause.

The biological treatises include the *Historia Animalium* (ten books, the last of which is either inauthentic or originally an independent Aristotelian work). *De Partibus Animalium* deals with the material parts of animals and their final causes, and the *De Incessu* with those parts specifically for locomotion. The *De Generatione Animalium* (five books) is concerned with the material parts that are used for generation and an explanation of the efficient causes of animals.

There are a number of biological works that deal primarily with the *soul. The *De Anima* (three books) gives a general account of the nature of the soul and its various capacities; the *De Motu Animalium* covers the explanation of animal movement in terms of thought and desire and correlated physiological processes. A collection of short treatises known as the *Parva Naturalia* are devoted to explanations of various phenomena connected with the perceptive and nutritive faculties. They consist of *De Sensu et Sensibilibus*, *De Memoria et Reminiscentia*, *De Somno*, *De Insomniis*, *De Divinatione per Somnum*, *De Longitudine et Brevitate Vitae*, and *De Vita et Morte* (the first two chapters of which are called *De Juventute et Senectute*), and *De Respiratione*.

The extant ethical treatises are the *Nicomachean Ethics* (ten books), the *Eudemian Ethics* (eight books), and the possibly spurious *Magna Moralia*. Although its authenticity has been seriously questioned, most scholars now consider the *Eudemian Ethics* to be genuine. Recently there have been concerns as to whether it or the *NE* is later. The consensus is that the *NE* is the more mature, though their overlapping books are taken from the earlier work. (Bks. 4, 5, and 6 of the *NE* are the same as 5, 6, and 7 of the *EE*.) In addition to Aristotle's *Constitution of Athens*, there is the *Politics* (eight books), which discusses the nature of the Greek city-state and contains detailed discussions, comparisons, and classifications of constitutions.

Finally there are two treatises dealing with productive arts. The first two books of the *Rhetoric* are devoted to a systematic treatment of the modes of persuasion, and the third to the style and arrangement of a speech. The *Poetics* discusses tragedy and epic poetry. There was probably a second book, no longer extant, on comedy.

There are three ancient lists of Aristotle's writings, the oldest of which is in the *Life of Aristotle* of *Diogenes Laertius (3rd cent. C.E.). Although it exhibits a considerable amount of overlap with the topics covered in the surviving work and contains what appear to be portions of it, well over half of the material is now lost. Furthermore, much of the extant corpus is not even mentioned. The list begins with a group of works composed for a popular audience outside of the Aristotelian school. Many or most of these are in *dialogue form, including four that share their name with a Platonic dialogue: the *Statesman*, *Sophist*, *Menexenus*, and *Symposium*. These popular works are lost; although for some nothing beyond the title is known, the contents of a number are partially conveyed through fragmentary reports by later authors. The *Eudemus*, a dialogue on the soul written shortly after the death of Eudemus of Cyprus in 354 B.C.E., was apparently written with an eye to Plato's *Phaedo* and, like it, discusses the possibility of the soul's existence without the body. Around the same time Aristotle wrote his *Protrepticus*, an exhortation to the philosophical life addressed to a Cypriot ruler named Themison. There is also a three-book dialogue entitled *De Philosophia*, controversially dated by Jaeger (1923) to the period just after Plato's death, surveying previous religious and *cosmological views, criticizing Plato, and developing an alternative *theology and cosmology. In addition to the popular works, the list mentions an important work, *On Ideas*, that collected *Platonist arguments for the existence of Ideas together with a series of difficulties for their view.

*Logic. Aristotle thinks that in general we have knowledge or understanding when we grasp causes, and he distinguishes three fundamentally different types of knowledge: (i) theoretical, (ii) practical and (iii) productive. Theoretical knowledge is pursued solely for its own sake, whereas the goal of practical knowledge consists of the activities of life, and the goal of productive science is always some beautiful or useful product distinct from the exercise of the science itself (such as a statue, or health).

The theoretical sciences divide into *mathematics, natural science, and theology. The central explanatory concept involved in his treatment of these sciences is that of a *substance*. The objects of mathematics—such things as lines, numbers, and planes—do not exist separately from physical substances. Generally speaking, the mathematician studies physical substances qua indivisible units, or qua lines, or qua planes, and so on. Substances themselves are the objects of the other two kinds of science, with physics dealing with separately existing and changing perceptible substances, and theology with indestructible and unchangeable separate substance.

In the logical works something is a *primary substance* because it is a subject of predication, not itself predicable of anything further. Everything except for primary substances is predicable, either essentially or accidentally, of primary substances. The only primary substances are particulars—including the particular man, the particular horse, and so on. Being an ultimate subject of predication, only a primary substance is "some this," an individual subject of predication not itself predicable of a substance. The natural kinds to which the primary substances belong (i.e., their species and genera) are universals, and are "secondary substances." Besides these primary and secondary substances, there are no other substances.

The predicates that say of some subject *what it is* are predicated essentially of that subject. Such predications say what a subject is intrinsically, or *per se*. The "said of" relation is transitive and is connected with definition in a way that the "present in" relation is not. A universal is said of a subject if, and only if, both the name and the definition of that universal truly apply to it. It is because of this connection with definition that this relation is sometimes called "essential" predication. By way of contrast, the relation "being present in a subject" covers all types of logical predication other than essential predication, and is sometimes called "accidental" predication. The definition of a universal that is accidentally predicable of a subject can never be truly applied to that subject. The things "present in a subject" are said to be present not in the way that a part is present in a whole, and furthermore they are incapable of existing separately from some subject that they are in. This has suggested to many that what inheres in a particular substance cannot exist without being in that very substance, and hence that Aristotle is ontologically committed to particulars in nonsubstance categories. There has been a great deal of discussion as to whether this characterization involves an ontological commitment to nonsubstance particulars. Against this, Owen (1965a) and Frede (1987b) have developed interpretations intended to avoid this consequence.

Categories 4 presents a ten-fold classification of the kinds of things that may be signified by simple expressions: substances, quantities, qualities, relatives, places, times, positions, states, doings, and undergoings. This list is a classification of the kinds of things that could be said of something in response to a question asked about it. Although the ten kinds of things signified by these kinds of expressions are standardly referred to as the Aristotelian categories, Frede (1981) has shown that it is unclear whether the *Categories* itself contains a doctrine of categories of being, or a category of substance.

A theoretical science has as its subject matter either substances or mathematical entities in nonsubstance categories, and the proper attributes of its subject matter fall within the various categories. The explanatory structure of such a science is *demonstrative*. Aristotle's account of this structure is built around the concept of definition as an indemonstrable statement of essence. Scientists know things by knowing the essences signified by real definitions. Essences are the "causes" that explain the intrinsic connection between the subject and predicate in a scientific theorem, and as such they function as middle terms in demonstrations. This project has often been thought to have strong affinities with foundationalist accounts of knowledge, but may in fact be concerned with explanation and understanding rather than justification (see Burnyeat 1981).

The premises of a scientific proof both *necessitate* the conclusion and *explain* why it is true. Strictly speaking, only necessary truths can be known scientifically. The necessary truths that constitute the body of a demonstrative science are exhaustively partitioned into indemonstrable first principles and their demonstrable consequences. The principles must be true, primary, and immediate and better known than, prior to, and explanatory of those things of which they are the principles. The other necessary truths of a science are explained by tracing them back to principles and "causes" that are known through themselves. The conclusion of a demonstration is known only when one understands why it must be true.

The principles themselves are known through induction, an argumentative procedure that moves from a plurality of instances of a generalization to that generalization itself. Our *knowledge* of first principles arises out of *experience*, that experience arises out of numerous and repeated *memories,* and those memories result from numerous and repeated *perceptions.* It is perceptual knowledge that forms the ultimate inductive basis for our knowledge of first principles. The epistemic state by virtue of which we know the principles is called "*nous,*" or intelligence.

Irwin (1977 and 1988) has seriously questioned whether the *Organon* itself contains a philosophically defensible account of the knowledge of first principles. The logical works treat the principles as indemonstrable and, according to Irwin, deny the possibility of *any* general science of the principles. At best they can be reached through a dialectical examination of common beliefs. If Aristotle is concerned with justification, this is clearly inadequate. Furthermore, the *deus ex machina* of intellectual grasping by *nous* is mere pseudo-explanation (it amounts to no more than saying that we are able to grasp first principles by exercising an ability to grasp them). However, on this view, by the time he wrote the *Metaphysics,* Aristotle had devised a way of using dialectical argument from appropriately selected beliefs (what Irwin calls "strong dialectic") in a way that allows for a dialectical science that yields genuine knowledge of the first principles.

Each demonstrative science employs first principles to prove conclusions about the objects that fall under the general kind that it studies. These proofs and conclusions involve those properties that pertain *per se,* or *intrinsically,* to things of that kind. For instance, in geometry one proves the theorem that a triangle has angles equal to two right angles. Appeal to first principles explains what belongs to various kinds of figures insofar as, and because, they are figures.

Aristotle rejected the Platonic conception of a general dialectical science of all being, a science that would prove the principles of the departmental sciences. In its place he developed a rival account designed to uphold the independence or autonomy of the departmental sciences. The first principles of a science divide into axioms and theses, and the latter further divide into hypotheses and definitions. A definition is an account that states what something is, and an hypothesis is an existence postulate that states of something defined *that* it is. A definition is an account signifying an essence. If the definition of man is "biped animal," then biped animal is the essence of man. Definitions and hypotheses are proper (or unique) to a science that studies the things they define or assert to exist. Any particular set of definitions and hypotheses is employed only in that branch of knowledge and, furthermore, cannot be demonstrated by the principles of some other science. Unlike "theses," axioms are common to all sciences. They are principles from which reasoning arises, and as such must be grasped by anybody who is going to learn or scientifically understand anything at all. Examples of axioms are the principle of non-contradiction and the law of excluded middle.

A demonstration is a valid argument, or syllogism. The theory of syllogistic reasoning in the *Prior Analytics* concerns the relation between the premises and the conclusion of a syllogism. The conclusion *follows of necessity from* the premises. The account of this relation appeals to characteristics of arguments that abstract from the content of the statements involved. A few obvious (perfect) cases of this relation are identified, and the non-obvious (imperfect) cases are reduced to the obvious.

Both Aristotle's analysis of scientific reasoning and his treatment of dialectical argument rely on the notion of syllogistic inference. Scientific demonstrations prove their conclusions by showing how those conclusions necessarily follow from their explanatory principles. To know scientifically involves the ability to reason validly from indemonstrable starting points. The logical expertise exemplified by a dialectician in two person question-answer exchanges involves the production of valid inferences from credible opinions (*endoxa*). However, this does not result in knowledge, for the arguments do not reason from explanatory first principles.

Aristotle informally describes a syllogism as an account in which, certain things being posited, something other than what has been posited follows of necessity in virtue of the former's being the case. The *Prior Analytics* contains an abstract characterization of those valid arguments that contain two simple statements as premises, have a single simple statement as conclusion, and involve only three terms: the predicate of the conclusion (major term), the subject of the conclusion (minor term), and a middle term. Four "assertoric" propositional forms (forms of simple statements) are characterized in terms of their quantity (universal or particular) and quality (affirmative or negative). Three "figures" are then characterized in terms of the order of the major, middle, and minor terms in an argument. For instance, a syllogism is in the first figure if the major term is the predicate in the premise containing it and the minor term is the subject in the premise containing it. Within the three "figures" there are syllogisms, or valid arguments, which can be identified by specifying their "mood" (the propositional forms of the premises and the conclusion). For instance, a first-figure argument is a syllogism if both of the premises and the conclusion are universal affirmative: All B's are C's, all A's are B's, therefore all A's are C's. Aristotle holds that every scientific demonstration and every syllogism in the informal sense can be captured by a string of two premise syllogisms from the three figures.

Metaphysics. Substance, quality, quantity, and so on are different categories of being. Since these categories cannot be subsumed under a single genus, the various kinds of "thing that are" are not themselves species of a single genus. Nonetheless, Book 4 of the *Metaphysics* asserts the existence of a general science that studies "that which is" qua "thing which is." Like those sciences analyzed in the *Posterior Analytics*, it involves a certain subject matter and a set of items, both propositions and terms, that belong to its subject matter *per se*, in respect of itself. However, by virtue of its generality it is contrasted with those sciences that study only some part of what there is. Owen (1960) and Irwin (see above) have both argued that the *Posterior Analytics* allows no room for this kind of general science. It is part of Owen's account (1965b) of Aristotle's development that in his early stage he was committed to the view that every science must have a genus as its subject matter, but since there is no genus of "thing that is" (because there are different senses of the word "being" corresponding to the different categories), there can be no single general science of being. However, at a later stage, according to Owen, Aristotle saw a way to have a single general science despite the fact that "being" is not a genus. The fundamental explanatory principle of his general ontology is the concept of substance, and general ontology is in fact the science of substance. There is no single condition in virtue of which all "things that are" are properly called "things that are." Substances are "things that are" simply because they are substances. Other things are "things that are" because they are related in appropriate ways to substances. Qualities, for example, are "things that are" because for a quality to be just is for it to *qualify* a substance. As the first sentence of 4.2 declares, "that which is," although spoken of in a plurality of ways, is nonetheless always spoken of in relation to a single thing, that is, some single nature, and that single starting point is substance. This, according to Owen, makes room for a general dialectical science that in a sense encompasses all that there is, despite the fact that not everything falls within the same genus.

The so-called middle books, 7, 8, and 9, are concerned with sensible substance, and actuality and potentiality. This inquiry is pursued within the context of the program for general ontology. Substances are "things that are" simply because they are substances, and each substance is what it is in respect of itself, or *per se*. Book 7 presents reasons for treating the form of a sensible substance, rather than its matter or the sensible composite itself, as a primary substance. Furthermore, it presents arguments both in favor of the view that definition and essence belong primarily to substances and in support of the claim that no universals are substances. It also contains some arguments against the existence of Platonic Forms and against the idea that sensible particulars are definable.

In this book, 7.3 begins this task by listing as possible candidates for the substance of a thing four items that are familiar from Aristotelian logic: the essence, the universal, the genus, and the subject. The first three correspond to the predicate position of a statement and are items that might be invoked as an answer to the question, "What is X?" The fourth candidate for substance is the subject of which these other items are predicable. Here 7.3 states that the "subject" is thought most of all to be substance, and explains that the "subject" is that of which all other things are said, but is not itself said of anything further. Consequently, substance is that which is not said of a subject, but is that of which other things are said. This characterization of substance as the subject for predication should be compared to the claim in *Categories* 5 that the primary substances are those things of which all else is predicable, they themselves being predicable of nothing further.

In 7.3 this is found lacking as a characterization of the substance of a thing. It leads to the incorrect view that matter is the only substance. By stripping off in thought all predicables, one arrives at an ultimate subject of predication that is nothing in its own right and has whatever predicates it does only accidentally. However, matter is neither separate nor "some this," and hence cannot be the substance upon which all else is dependent. According to a traditional interpretation that has come under a variety of attacks in recent scholarship, this chapter introduces Aristotle's own concept of prime matter—a matter that has all of its determinations accidentally and, being intrinsically completely inderminate, is potentially receptive of any form. Prime matter has also traditionally been conceived of both as a principle of individuation for numerically distinct material objects and as the persisting substratum for the basic elemental transformations in his natural science. However, in Aristotle's logic, accidental predication presupposes that the subject of predication is something essentially and in its own right, which has motivated Charlton (1970) and others to resist the attribution of intrinsically featureless prime matter to Aristotle.

In connection with another candidate for substance, the essence, Aristotle argues that in a primary sense only substances have definitions and that consequently there are essences (in an unqualified sense) only for substances. He establishes the principle that all things that are primary and called what they are called intrinsically (in virtue of themselves) are one and the same as their essence. This leads to the view that a primary substance is identical with a definable form. Since Albritton

(1957), the ontological status of substantial forms has been the topic of intense scholarly debate. Some have attributed to Aristotle a doctrine of particular substantial forms; others have argued that substance forms are universals; others that form is neither particular nor universal; and still others that in the relevant texts Aristotle is employing a dialectical strategy, and not stating his own view. For representatives of these interpretations see Frede (1985), Loux (1991), Owens (1951), and Owen (1978/9), respectively. A key reason for considering them to be universals is that primary substances are first in the order of definition and knowledge, but definition is thought to be of the universal. However, when Aristotle turns to consider the claims of the other two candidates for substance—the universal and the genus—he argues in 7.13 that no universal is a substance. In any case, universals (if they exist at all) are ontologically dependent upon their particular instances, but it is thought that a substance must be separate and "some this." This provides one of the chief reasons for taking substantial forms to be particulars.

Aristotle's examination of candidates for substance leads to the view that, in the case of perceptible things, primary substance is neither the material substratum nor anything that is universal with respect to the subjects of which it is logically predicable, but rather is a definable form or essence that requires matter for its existence. He agrees with the Platonists that a substance is a logical subject, but argues against their view that it is the genus, being the logical subject for the differentia, that is substance. Their synoptic general science of being takes the highest universals to be the most substantial. By way of sharp contrast, Aristotle himself thinks that the Platonist's treatment of each item predicable in common of particulars as separate and "some this" leads to an infinite regress that he refers to as the "third man." The reasoning behind it involves something like this: If the particulars have a Form in common, and this Form is separate and "some this," then there must be an additional Form that both the particulars and the first Form have in common, and so on ad infinitum.

Aristotelian substantial forms are causes. The being of a particular material composite is explained in terms of its matter having the essence that is responsible for the fact that the matter constitutes that particular. Aristotle treats this cause as the substance of the body to which it belongs *per se*, and this in turn is identified with the form. The form is a primary substance, and as such is a primitive, irreducible cause—it is the primary cause of the being of the particular. The form of a sensible substance is separate in definition, and as such is prior in the order of definition and of knowledge. However, it cannot exist without matter; and of the trio of matter, form, and composite, in the case of perceptible things the composite is separate without qualification.

The *Metaphysics* uses the concepts of actuality and potentiality to clarify the relationship between the matter and the form of a sensible composite. The form of a composite and its matter are one and the same thing in the sense that the form of a composite is in actuality what the matter is potentially. Consequently, material composites are unities in their own right, and not merely *per accidens* unities. The matter of a substantial particular is not itself another actual substantial individual. It is "some this" in potentiality, though not in actuality. Given Aristotle's view that the soul is form and the body is the living thing in potentiality, this solution is at the heart of his treatment of the relationship between body and soul and has been the topic of much recent discussion. For an account of its meaning and place in Aristotle's metaphysics, see Kosman (1984).

The next major step in the general ontological program is to investigate suprasensible reality. The last three books of the *Metaphysics* are concerned with the various nonsensible items that have been thought to be substances. He argues that mathematical objects exist, but are not substances, and that Platonic Forms do not even exist. However, Aristotle does believe that there are suprasensible beings, and at least one of these is the unmoved mover, or god, of his metaphysics.

Book 12 presents some of Aristotle's own positive views about nonsensible substance in the form of a theology that identifies god as the unmoved mover of the outermost celestial sphere of the cosmos. This account has close affinities to Book 8 of the *Physics*. The unmoved mover is an eternal source of the motion of the outermost sphere, and it moves as an object of love does. It itself is a being the substance of which just is activity, and activity of the best sort. God is intelligent activity (*nous*), eternally engaged in the best kind of thinking, and as such is a living being. God's intelligence is not thinking of us or of the universe, but rather of thinking or intelligence itself. This activity is the good, and is the source of the order and goodness of the universe. It is for the sake of coming to an understanding of this first principle that the metaphysician initiated the study of the principles of perceptible substances—those substances that are initially most familiar to us.

Natural Science. Natural science studies natural substances, which are analyzed as compounds of matter and form. The work that we know as Aristotle's *Physics* consists of a collection of lectures that attempt a systematic treatment of the first principles, causes, and elements of natural phenomena. Drawing on previous theories according to which *change proceeds from contraries, the first book develops an analysis of the elements of change. The possibility of change requires the introduction of Aristotle's own technical innovation, the persisting substratum, in addition to the contraries. The elements of change are (i) form, (ii) the privation of that form, and (iii) their persisting substratum. If the change is qualitative, quantitative, or a locomotion, the persisting substratum is a particular substance. A particular man, for instance, becomes musical (form) from being unmusical (privation). However, if the change is the generation or passing away of a substance, it is a substantial form that is acquired or lost. Code (1976) has defended the traditional view that the persisting substratum is matter and that consequently all physical substances are hylomorphic compounds composed out of the matter from which they were generated. However, since (for example) the flesh and bones of which some blooded animal is currently composed is not the menstrual fluid from which it was generated, the persisting matter in question has been taken to be an indeterminate prime matter. Gill (1989) attempts to avoid this consequence by arguing that the four elements are not compounds and that for other substances the matter persists only as a universal but not as a subject for substantial form.

Aristotle's analysis enables him to argue, against the *Eleatics, that in a sense "that which is" does in fact come to be from "that which is not." A substance of some kind (e.g., fire) comes to be from matter that prior to the change is potentially, although not yet actually, of that kind. In general, the passing away of one substance is always the generation of another. Generation or passing away occurs when, unlike the case of alteration where a persisting perceptible substratum changes with respect to one of its qualities, no perceptible substratum persists, and the thing changes as a whole.

Each science studies some general kind and its proper attributes; in the case of natural science, the kind is "natural substance." This is what exists by nature (as opposed to some other cause such as art), and included in this classification are plants and animals, their parts, and the simple elemental bodies. A nature, or *phusis*, is an *internal* principle of change and rest in that to which it primarily and intrinsically belongs. There are specifically different kinds of natural (or "physical"—an alternative translation of the Greek) bodies, each kind with a nature that is responsible for its own characteristic natural changes—locomotions, alterations, and ways of growing or decreasing. For instance, the natural motions of the four elements of which sublunary bodies are composed (earth, water, air, and fire) are rectilinear paths to their natural places. Earth is absolutely heavy, and as such its natural place is a sphere at the center of the universe; the natural place for water is a shell surrounding the place for earth; the place for air, a shell surrounding the water; and fire, being absolutely light, occupies the outermost shell of the sublunary sphere. In addition to locomotion, the sublunary elements are subject to alteration, growth and generation, and destruction.

Each of these four elements is generated by means of a transformation from another element that perishes. The most basic powers or capacities of matter are heating and cooling and moistening and drying. These "primary opposites" not only are the basis for the other powers of inanimate matter but also serve to characterize the four elements in such a way that their mutual transformations can be explained. Earth is cold and dry; water cold and moist; air hot and moist; fire hot and dry. Each of these elements is potentially the others, and one element is changed into another by the replacement of opposites. For instance, earth becomes fire when the coldness of earth is replaced by heat. The traditional, though now controversial, view is that the elements are composites of "prime matter" and pairs of opposites. Earth is, for instance, prime matter qualified by coldness and dryness. This prime matter is the persisting substratum for these elemental transformations.

Although in the primary sense of the term, the "nature" of a thing is its form, all physical objects have both a formal and a material nature. The natural scientist, like the mathematician, studies forms that cannot exist without matter. However, unlike the mathematician, he does not define natural substances in abstraction from their material constitution, but must be concerned with both matter and form. The forms of products of art, such as houses, beds, and statues, are not internal principles of change; but, insofar as they are themselves composed of natural materials, artifacts coincidentally possess natures and hence do undergo natural changes.

The central causal concept used to demarcate and explain the class of natural substances is that of the *nature* of a thing. Aristotle's concept of *cause* (*aitia*) has a wide range of applications. It is not restricted to cases of agents or events that make something happen, but rather applies to four different types of explanatory factor. Anything that can be explained has a cause in his sense. The "cause" of something is an explanatory factor, the grasp of which constitutes knowing why something is the case.

There are four different types of cause or explanatory factor. The *material cause* is that out of which a thing is generated and which persists as a constituent (e.g., the bronze is the material cause of the statue). The *formal cause* is what is given in the definition of the being of a thing. It is what makes a thing that kind of thing it is (e.g., the ratio of two to one is what makes notes constitute an octave). The *efficient cause* is the primary principle, or origin, of change or rest. This is the agent of change (e.g., the male parent is the efficient cause in reproduction; additionally this label is applied to capacities and activities of agents as well). The *final cause* is the end, or "that for the sake of which" something comes about or is done (e.g., one takes a walk after eating for the sake of health). Although it is true that some things happen by chance, there is no other type of cause in addition to the four stated. Science does not study coincidental occurrences, but confines itself to the study of regularities that happen either always or for the most part. Chance occurrences always require the presence of something that is properly speaking the cause.

As becomes most apparent from his biological writings, although Aristotle's science makes no appeal to the intentions of a designer, it is teleological in the sense that it employs explanations that make reference to final causes. Much recent work has been devoted to clarifying the nature and basis of his commitment to teleology. For instance, Cooper (1982) has attempted to show that, with the exception of certain prescientific explanations, it is the alleged fact of the eternity of the species that underlies and justifies his natural teleology. On this view, teleological explanation would have had no place in Aristotle's science had he not accepted the permanence of the species as a basic fact underwriting explanation. For alternative treatments of the eternity of the species and of teleological explanation see Lennox (1985) and Gotthelf (1987), respectively.

Since the nature of a thing is a principle of *change*, the understanding of nature requires a definition of change. Change may take place with respect to the categories of quality, quantity, and place (and substance, if the term is extended to cover substantial change). Change itself is defined as the actuality of what is potentially so and so insofar as it is potentially so and so. Learning, for instance, is a change having knowledge as its goal. A student is one who potentially possesses knowledge, but does not yet actually have it. The process that we call "learning" is the exercise of the capacity that the student has for knowledge. Since every change requires an agent distinct from the object changed, the capacity of the student is "passive" or receptive, and its exercise requires the causal efficacy of an agent (in this case, a teacher) with the corresponding active capacity.

Aristotle's theory of change as the exercise of the powers or capacities of substances is at odds with the theory of the ancient *atomists. They hold that the universe consists of an *infinite number of indivisible bodies, or "atoms," moving around in an infinitely large *"void." Aristotle argues against the existence of a void and in favor of the view that there a single, spatially finite cosmos that is everywhere saturated with matter. Place is defined as the innermost boundary of a body containing a body, and by his definition no place can exist without a body to occupy it. Furthermore, the basic matter in Aristotle's system is not atomic, but rather uniform substances that resolve into parts that are formally the same as the whole. No bit of matter can actually be divided into an infinite number of pieces, but however far division occurs, the result can in principle always be further divided.

Since *time is infinite in the sense that there is no first or last instant of time, there must always be change. The only infinite changes are circular motions, and the only natural circular motions are those of the heavenly bodies. They are composed of ether, the natural motion of which is circular. These motions, being themselves eternal and continuous, account for the eternity and continuity of time. Every change requires an agent of change, and Aristotle appeals to this idea to argue for the existence of a single, eternal unmoved mover of the continuous, infinite circular locomotion of the sphere of fixed stars.

Biology. All living things are composites of matter and form. Their substantial form is their soul and will be treated below. As for their matter, although they are ultimately composed of inanimate elements (earth, air, fire, and water), their proximate matter is their organic body, matter that cannot exist without soul. The elements and different kinds of inorganic compounds and mixtures of the elements serve as the matter for the uniform parts of animals such as blood, marrow, semen, milk, sinew, flesh, and bone. Animals also have organic parts such as hands, heads, and bones that are nonuniform in the sense that they do not divide without limit into parts that are of the same nature of the whole (a part of a hand is not a hand), and these are in turn constituted out of the uniform substances.

In both the *Physics* and *De Partibus Animalium* Aristotle argues that the final cause, or the cause "for the sake of which," is present in nature and that in general "nature does nothing in vain." In connection with the generation of living things, he distinguishes the final cause from the efficient cause and argues that of the two the final cause is prior in that it is the essence signified or expressed by a definition of the *ousia*, or being, that will be the end result of the generation (unless something prevents its completion). The stages of such goal-directed natural processes do not occur with absolute necessity, but are rather hypothetically necessary— necessary on the hypothesis that the end result will be achieved.

An artisan, starting from an understanding of the definition of some product to be generated, can reason back to what is the best or only way for his goal to be realized. Likewise, in order for the functional, material parts of animals to be generated there must be appropriate material, and it must be worked up in the proper series of stages. Rejecting preformationist theories of reproduction, he argues that in general animal generation proceeds from uniform generative fluids. Although some lower animals are spontaneously generated without parents, in most cases there is a male parent, who is the agent of generation and as such provides the principle of form and soul, and a female parent, who is passive and provides the matter. Until recently it has been thought that Aristotle's account was "essentialist" in the sense that the offspring's growth and development is primarily directed towards a substantial form or essence that is at the same level of generality as the species. Against this, Balme (1987) and Cooper (1988) have tried to show that biological development is caused by particular powers and motions in the generative fluids and that the substantial form of the offspring is below the level of the species.

*Psychology. The properties or affections (pathê) of the soul are "enmattered accounts." They have forms that exist only in matter of an appropriate sort, and consequently their definitions must bring in both matter and form.

With the exception of the capacity for theoretical thinking, all the capacities of soul are the forms of bodily organs, and their exercise necessarily takes place in the body. De Anima 2.1 gives a general characterization of what it is to be a soul (psuchê). Every living thing in the sublunary sphere, whether plant or animal, is a composite of form and matter, its substantial form being the soul, and its matter being what is potentially alive. The kind of form that makes something an animate substance of some type is not mere shape or outward appearance, but what Aristotle calls a first actuality (entelecheia). This is a unified set of interlocking capacities, the exercise of which collectively constitutes a higher actuality— namely, the kind of life characteristic of things of that type. The soul is a first actuality in that it stands to living as, for instance, knowledge in the dispositional sense stands to its use, or the capacity to see stands to seeing. The relationship between soul and body is that of activity or actuality to what has the potential for the exercise of that activity. What is potentially living is a body having organs, and so the soul is a first actuality of an organic body. Since living things have both a formal and a material nature, the soul and body respectively, the psychological and material are both part of the natural, or "physical." As required by his metaphysical account of the unity of hylomorphic compounds, the soul and the body are not two numerically distinct things, but rather go together to constitute a composite that is itself an intrinsic unity.

On this view, the organic body's potentiality for life cannot exist without being exercised, and the material body cannot exist without its form, the soul. Since Ackrill (1972/3) raised doubts about the coherence of this kind of account, there has been much lively debate as to how this relates to contemporary philosophy of mind. For instance, Sorabji (1974), describing Aristotle's view as "sui generis," argues that he construes every psychological state as constituted by something physical. By way of contrast, Burnyeat (1992) denies that mental acts of awareness are constituted by physiological processes and urges that Aristotle's conception of the psychological is wedded to an outmoded, pre-Cartesian theory of matter and as such is no longer a viable approach to the psychological. Others, such as Nussbaum and Putnam (1992) have found it offering insights that are still valuable. Against Burnyeat, they argue that Aristotle's psychology treats mental states as "functional" states that are defined solely by reference to relations among inputs, outputs, and other functional states. These states are compositionally plastic in the sense that the same type of mental states can be realized in different types of matter and as such are not intrinsically tied to any particular theory of matter. Still others, relying on the idea that the intellect has no bodily organ, have detected in his account of the mental a form of dualism.

Nonetheless, all agree that his psychology is concerned with distinguishing and giving accounts of the various kinds of capacities that explain life. From this perspective the mental is only a part of the psychological. All living things, both plants and animals, have a *nutritive* capacity (which includes the capacity to reproduce), whereas all animals, though not plants, possess a *perceptive* capacity as well. For some animals, their perceptive capacity also involves the ability to initiate *locomotion*. Humans have all of these capacities and in addition possess *rational* soul, and hence can engage in both practical and theoretical thought.

The capacity for sense perception (*aisthêsis*), at least touch, necessarily belongs to all animals. A sense capacity is defined in terms of its objects as the capacity to receive perceptible form without matter. The sense organ in this way becomes "like" the sense object perceived. Whether the sense organ and the external object perceived possess the sense qualities in two different ways or, as Sorabji (1974) has argued, the sense organ literally takes on the perceptible quality is still a matter of considerable contention. In any case, in order for the organ to receive perceptible forms in such a way that perception occurs, the organ must possess a ratio or mean of the possible sense objects; and in a way this ratio is the sense capacity itself. Perception is caused by perceptible objects acting through a medium on the organ of sense possessed of the appropriate ratio. For instance, sight is a passive capacity of the eye, and its proper objects are colors (and phosphorescent things). A color is by nature an active capacity of physical bodies to change an actually transparent medium (such as air or water) in such a way that seeing occurs when that medium is continuous between the eye and the visible object.

Each of the five senses (touch, taste, smelling, hearing, and sight) has it own proper objects that themselves fall within a range or series. For instance, heat, cold, moistening, and drying are intrinsic objects of touch, and colors are intrinsic objects of sight. Intrinsic perception of the proper objects of the five senses is not prone to error. The special objects of one sense cannot be intrinsically perceived by another sense, but they can be *coincidentally* perceived. For instance, if by means of sight someone perceives the white thing, and the white thing is coincidentally the same as the sweet thing, she may thereby coincidentally perceive the sweet thing even though on that occasion she is not tasting it.

Although the five senses are definitionally distinct, they are in fact aspects of a single, unified perceptive capacity, which when considered in relation to activities that involve more than one of the special senses is called the "common sense." There are objects that are perceived coincidentally by the special senses (or at least, by sight and touch), which are noncoincidentally the objects of the common sense. The most important of these are change, rest, shape, magnitude, number, and unity.

Closely connected with the "common sense" is the faculty of imagination (*phantasia*) by virtue of which we are aware of images or "appearances" (*phantasmata*). The main focus of Aristotle's discussion is on images that remain after the external object of perception is no longer actually perceived. An image is a motion or change in the sense organ that is similar to perception, and it may be caused by an actual perception, but remain in the organ after perception has ceased. Among other things, such images figure into his accounts of memory, recollection, and dreams.

Images are also required for the exercise of thought or intelligence (*nous*). Aristotle divides this into practical thought and theoretical thought. The former includes as a special case our capacity to deliberate about the human good and to calculate means to ends. The latter is the exercise of the epistemic state by virtue of which we know the first principles of demonstrative sciences. The intelligible forms that serve as the objects of theoretical thought are in some sense contained in the sensible forms, and the exercise of our capacity for such thought necessarily involves the use of images derived from perceptual activity. Our passive intelligence is a capacity for receiving the intelligible forms and is analogous to the capacity to receive perceptible form without matter. Although it has no form of its own and prior to thinking is potentially each of its objects, but actually none of them, in the act of intellection it is one and the same as its object. This passive intelligence is likened to matter in that it becomes all things. Aristotle's theory also requires a productive, active intelligence, characterized as "separable, impassible, unmixed." This is likened to an efficient cause in the sense that it makes all things in the way that light, as a condition of the medium of visual perception, makes the potentially colored actually colored. His treatment of active and passive intelligence is brief and has been the subject of a great deal of controversy. Much of the discussion has focussed on whether the active intellect is immortal and, if so, if it is identical with god's thinking. One recent attempt to come to grips with these issues is provided by Wedin (1988). Building on the observation that psychological systems may be described at different levels of functioning, Wedin works out the view that active intelligence is human intelligence described at its highest level of functioning. As such it plays a crucial role in the account of the distinction between dispositional knowledge and its exercise, but has no more claim to immortality than the other capacities of soul.

*Ethics and *Politics.* Ethics is a practical science in that its goal is *praxis*, or action, and is the part of political science that deals with character and its connection with conduct, emotion, and the pursuit of goals in life. Ethics does not involve demonstrative proofs of the type required by the theoretical sciences, but does strive for the kind of accuracy that is possible concerning the understanding of just and noble actions. Its premises and conclusions hold only for the most part, and it states the truth in rough outline only. Furthermore, lectures on ethics are addressed to an audience of young, male adults who are already experienced in the actions of life and who have been brought up in good habits in such a way as to take pleasure in the noble and be pained by the disgraceful. If they already accept the common opinions *that* certain kinds of action are just or noble, without yet needing to know *why*, they will have the right kind of initial starting points for ethical discourse.

The *NE* begins by declaring that every craft, inquiry, action, and choice is thought to aim at some good, and for this reason *the good* is correctly called that at which all things aim. Most people agree that the good is *eudaimonia*—*happiness, as it is usually translated, or success in life. However, depending on the kinds of lives they lead, different people have different conceptions of happiness. Uncultured people typically take it that this good is *pleasure* (though some of them will identify it with either wealth or honor), whereas persons of refinement and good upbringing tend to conceive of it as either *honor* (as an end of political action) or perhaps as virtue. Third, there are those who identify the good with the life of theoretical *contemplation*. However, the good is not, as Plato thought, a separately existing transcendent Form of the Good Itself. It must instead be some humanly achievable good, a good for the sake of which all of our actions are performed. The good that serves as the end of human life is complete in that it is choiceworthy solely for its own sake, and never for the sake of anything else. Happiness is self-sufficient in the sense that taken by itself it makes one's life choiceworthy and lacking in nothing, and as such it is the *most* choiceworthy of all goods.

By appealing to the natural *function* of human life Aristotle provides a philosophically defensible sketch of the best good, or happiness, as activity of the soul in accordance with virtue. For a human being as a whole there is some complex activity that serves as the function of human beings. This function is not something that we have in common with plants or with the other animals, but rather is the exercise of our distinctly human capacities to obey and to apprehend *logos* or rational principle. In general a virtue, or excellence, is what enables its possessor to perform its function well. Consequently, a human virtue is either an *ethical virtue* that enables one to obey reason well or an *intellectual virtue* that enables one to apprehend reason well. The best human life, the best human activity, is the expression of these virtues throughout a complete lifetime, accompanied by a sufficient supply of external goods such as wealth, good birth, good looks, and good children.

The goal of political science is the good of the citizens who make up a state. A treatment of the nature of the *polis*, or city-state, and its principles of organization are required to complete Aristotle's account of the pursuit and attainment of the human good. A successful life is the life of virtuous activity, and laws are needed to promote the behaviors and habits that are conducive to the development and exercise of the virtues. Our distinctively human excellences are cultivated and nurtured within the kind of social and educational environment provided by the city-state, and their realization and fulfillment is possible only within this social context.

Unless we live in some kind of organized community, neither the constituents nor the necessary conditions for happiness are possible. For instance, we would be without friends and without the occasion or opportunity to acquire the ethical virtues. In general, we would be without the leisure and the resources necessary to pursue ethical and intellectual goals.

Although the city-state is not the only kind of community, for Aristotle it is the highest form of community and aims at the highest good. He assumes that both the relationship between male and female and the relationship between ruler and subject are purposeful and based on natural differences and claims that the most rudimentary natural community, the family unit, is in part based upon them. Families themselves naturally come together to form villages, and villages themselves naturally develop into complete, self-sufficient city-states. Originating in the basic necessities of life, they continue to exist for the sake of the human good. Existing for the sake of the human good and being the fully developed community of which the more primitive communities are parts, the city-state is itself natural, and humans are by nature political creatures, or *polis*-dwellers.

Justice is a bond that holds society together and a principle of order in a political society. According to Aristotle, justice requires a sense of community and friendship between the members of the city-state. Friendship is not only necessary to life, it is also noble, and without friends life would not even be worthy of choice. There are three main types of friendship, corresponding to the three objects of love: pleasure, utility, and the good. Genuine friendship is based on a goodness of character shared by the friends and obtains between those who mutually recognize that they each wish well for the sake of the other. This is friendship in the unqualified sense and is possible only for people of virtuous character. The other two types, those based on the mutual expectation of pleasure and those based on the mutual expectation of usefulness, are called "friendship" by virtue of a resemblance to this primary kind. A friend is "'another self,'" and it is through a shared life of rational activity with friends that the virtuous man is most fully able to perceive his own goodness.

The city-state is a self-governing community having as its goal the good of its citizens, those having the constitutional right to participate in both the deliberative and the judicial functions of the government. A constitution specifies the way in which the offices of power are to be distributed, and determines a sovereign or supreme civic body and the overall purpose or goal of the political association. In a good form of government the rulers rule for the sake of the common good. If there is just one ruler, it is a *monarchy*; if the sovereign body has just a few, it is *aristocracy*; and if many, it is a *polity*. A bad, or "perverted" form of government is one in which the rulers rule with an eye to their own self-interest, which undermines the unity and the stability of the organization. The three basic forms of bad government are *tyranny*, in which one person rules for his own advantage; *oligarchy*, in which a few wealthy people rule for their own benefit; and *democracy*, in which the sovereign body is composed of many competing factions. The different forms of government have different overall goals, which in turn determine the conditions of membership in the sovereign body. In an aristocracy, for instance, virtue is both the goal of and a criterion for participation in the most important political offices. Likewise, the dominant values of oligarchy and of democracy, wealth and freedom, require that property ownership and free birth, respectively, are the chief qualifications for office. It is only by sharing in the political life of a good community organized for the sake of the best and most valuable human achievements that the individual can achieve a supremely worthwhile and successful life.

NE 10 argues that the life of ethical virtue (which ultimately is a life of political action) satisfies the criteria for happiness in that it is self-sufficient and choiceworthy in itself, but the life of theoretical contemplation is the most complete happiness and the best of all lives. Nonetheless, the ethical virtues are also part of our human makeup, and the life and happiness corresponding to these is a human happiness, albeit a second best in comparison to the life of contemplation. If, as argued by Ackrill (1974), Cooper (1975), and Irwin (1978), happiness is an "inclusive end," having as its constituents the exercise of both the theoretical and ethical excellences, it is debatable whether this view is consistent with the position developed in the earlier books. Further, it seems to suggest that an amoral life of theoretical study would be supremely good, and yet the earlier books appear to take the exercise of the ethical virtues as at least partially constitutive of the good life. By itself this would show that a theoretical life devoid of ethical excellence could not be complete and self-sufficient, and hence could not be the best life possible. However, if Aristotle has a "dominant end" view according to which happiness (at least the best form) is identified with a single activity, rational contemplation, these problems can be avoided by showing how the ethical virtues are necessary conditions for happiness (see Kraut 1989).

To achieve a happy life, then, one must develop, cultivate, and exercise virtue. Intellectual virtue (which includes both practical wisdom and theoretical knowledge) is produced through learning, whereas the virtues of character result from habituation. In general, habitual behavior of a certain kind brings about the corresponding kind of character. For example, one becomes intemperate, or self-indulgent, through performing the kinds of actions characteristic of intemperate people: excessive eating or drinking. Likewise, ethical virtue is acquired by repeatedly performing the kind of noble actions typical of the possessors of that virtue. Initially this may be difficult, due to immature emotional responses. However, once one's character changes in such a way that the virtue in question has actually been acquired, the actions are performed easily and with pleasure. Noble actions may result from character states other than virtue, but they are the exercise of a virtue when they are performed knowingly, chosen for their own sake, and issue from a firm and stable character.

Aristotle defines virtue by genus and differentia. According to his definition, a virtue is a dispositional state of character that is concerned with choice, lying within a mean between excess and deficiency—a mean relative to us, as determined by the rational principle that the man of practical wisdom would employ. A virtuous person is disposed to experience *emotions* appropriately, neither excessively nor deficiently. For instance, the emotion is not felt too strongly or too weakly, towards too many or too few people, at too many or too few times. What is appropriate for one person, however, might be too much or too little for another. Consequently it is important that the mean be one that is relative to the individual in question, and not simply an arithmetic mean that is the same for all. The virtuous person is also disposed to perform *actions* that lie within an appropriate mean. What determines the mean is the rational principle that somebody with practical wisdom would employ. This is not to say that what makes an action right is that someone with practical wisdom would determine it to be so. The point is rather that the standard by which the mean is determined is the rational principle employed by the man of practical wisdom.

Thus virtues are typically opposed to pairs of vices characterized in terms of excess and deficiency. For instance, with regard to feelings of fear and confidence, courage is a mean. The coward is excessively fearful and deficiently confident; the rash are excessively confident; and there is also the nameless character defect that disposes one to excessive fearlessness. Likewise, temperance is a mean concerning those bodily pleasures pertaining to touch and tasting (and pains resulting from the desires for their pleasures); the excess is intemperance, or self-indulgence; and the defect is nameless.

It is impossible to possess a virtue, or a mean state, without the ability to determine the mean for oneself, and hence without practical wisdom. Conversely, it is impossible to be practically wise, and yet lack the virtues. Practical wisdom itself is that intellectual virtue concerned with things that are capable of being otherwise and that can serve as objects of deliberation. Both the practitioners of a craft and the man of practical wisdom are able to deliberate well about what is good and beneficial, but the latter's deliberations deal with human life in general. Practical wisdom itself may be characterized as a true and reasoned dispositional state concerned with actions that pertain to what is good and bad for humans. The deliberations of the practically wise consist of reasoning from a general understanding of what kinds of things are good or bad to the means within one's power that will bring about good results.

Deliberation is never about ends as such, but only about those things within one's power that contribute to ends that are already the objects of rational wish (*boulêsis*). Although this has been interpreted as meaning that deliberation is concerned with nothing more than instrumental means, Wiggins (1975/6) has argued that deliberation also serves to specify the constituents of ends. Since ultimately it is concerned with one's own actions, the ability to deliberate well involves a reasoned perception of particulars. For successful action it is not enough simply to know in general terms the kind of result one wants. One also needs to be able to figure out in particular circumstances what counts as getting such a result, and what particular actions can be performed to bring *that* about. It is still a matter of controversy whether deliberation, as Cooper (1975) argues, serves to clarify the components of one's general, overall end, or provides rational justification for one's moral ends (Irwin 1978).

Deliberation leads to choice, which Aristotle defines as deliberative desire for what is within one's power. The virtuous person, of course, is practically wise and hence deliberates well and makes correct choices. Furthermore, being virtuous, his emotional responses always lie within a mean between what is excessive or deficient from the perspective of correct deliberation. Thus in the case of the virtuous it is impossible for other forms of desire, in particular bodily appetite or anger, to conflict with choice. The virtuous person chooses noble action for its own sake and consistently and without internal conflict acts in accordance with rational choices.

Virtuous actions are voluntary because their source is internal to the agent and, being voluntary, are appropriate objects of praise. However, not all voluntary actions are in accordance with choice, and not all action in accordance with choice is good and praiseworthy. A wicked person performs bad actions voluntarily and in accordance with a bad choice. On the other hand, the acratic, or person with a weak character, is subject to an internal conflict between correct rational choice and bad appetitive desires. Unlike the person of strong character who with difficulty, and despite bad appetitive desires, succeeds in acting correctly, the acratic is disposed to voluntarily perform actions that are contrary to his own rational choices.

To explain what weakness of character is, Book 7 first distinguishes knowledge in the dispositional sense from its exercise and then divides the former case into (i) having knowledge and being able to exercise it and (ii) having knowledge but being unable to exercise it. The presence of appetite prevents the acratic from exercising his dispositional knowledge about what is good and beneficial. Using what has come to be called the theory of the "practical syllogism" Aristotle explains what knowledge the acratic does act on, and what knowledge he does not act on. Action requires both general knowledge or beliefs about the kinds of things that are good and desirable and particular knowledge (based on perception) of particular circumstances. When the two kinds of knowledge come together in such a way as to form a unity, straightaway the agent acts. Unlike logical syllogisms that have propositions as conclusions, the conclusion of a practical syllogism is an action. The acratic possesses the general knowledge both that one ought not taste sweet things and that sweet things are pleasant to taste. When he perceives of a particular thing that it is sweet, the presence of an appetitive desire prevents him from putting into action his knowledge that such things ought not be tasted. Putting together the opinion that sweets are pleasant to taste with the proposition that *this* is sweet, his appetitive desire moves him to act in such a way as to taste it. Thus, although action against practical wisdom is impossible, voluntary action against correct rational choice is. In this penetrating treatment of human character, Aristotle shows how to accommodate irrational behavior within a general theory of rational agency, a problem that is still of central importance in action theory (see Davidson 1970 and Charles 1984).

Rhetoric. The Platonic dialogues contain challenges to the claims of rhetoric and poetry to be arts, and the *Rhetoric* and the *Poetics* may be seen as building upon and employing tools and themes from other parts of Aristotle's philosophy to vindicate their claims to be productive arts. The *Rhetoric* combines ideas and techniques from both logic and ethics to provide a systematic treatment of the modes of persuasion. The goal of oratory is to bring an audience as close as possible to persuasion, and rhetorical skill itself is defined as the ability to discern the possible modes of persuasion concerning any given subject. It is a part of dialectic and, like dialectic, not confined to any special subject matter in the way that the sciences are. Each of its three branches is directed towards some area concerning which we deliberate or make decisions. Deliberative oratory is concerned with what is beneficial or harmful with regard to the future; forensic, with the legality or illegality of past actions; and epideictic, with events taken as though they were present and considered as the objects of praise or blame.

The technical means of persuasion provided by this art are (i) the character of the speaker, (ii) the emotional disposition of the audience, and (iii) the arguments that bring about real or apparent demonstration. Previous technical manuals focussed almost entirely on appeals to the emotions; but although in the second book Aristotle discusses the emotions and the character of the audience extensively, he considers the most effective means of persuasion to be argument either through examples (the counterpart of induction) or the enthymeme (the rhetorical counterpart of the demonstrative syllogism). The enthymeme, the most powerful tool in the orator's arsenal, typically employs premises that are true only for the most part and omits premises that the intended audience will find plausible and easily supply.

Poetics. Like rhetoric, poetry too is a productive art with its own systematic principles. The main topics of the *Poetics*, the first treatise on literary criticism, center on a definition of tragedy by genus and differentiating features. The genus that different kinds of poetry share with various other forms of art, such as dance, instrumental music, and painting is "*mimêsis*." This general concept covers representation, imitation, and impersonation; and its specific types differ from each other in (i) their medium, (ii) their object, and (iii) their means of representation.

According to Aristotle's definition, tragedy is a representation that has as its *object* action that is serious, complete, and in possession of grandeur, through the *medium* of embellished speech (that is speech having both rhythm and melody), using spoken verse separately in its different parts, by *means* of a dramatic rather than a narrative form. Additionally, the definition brings in both a final cause and an efficient cause that brings it about: by pity and fear it accomplishes a *katharsis* of such emotions. The term "catharsis," which is not explained in the extant *Poetics*, can mean either purgation or purification, and both translations have had their supporters. In any case, in a good tragedy the dramatic representation arouses pity and fear in such a way that there is either a purging or purification of these unpleasant emotions, which is the source of the distinctive pleasure of tragedy. It is tempting to argue that through *katharsis* one is conditioned to feel these unpleasant emotions within a mean, and hence that tragedy has an educational and ethical function.

Contemporary Significance. Many of Aristotle's ideas have been discredited and rejected, and yet his writings are still a source of valuable philosophical insight. Science has definitely abandoned his notion that the universe is a sphere, the outer parts of which are composed of indestructible ether that eternally realizes its nature by revolving in circles around a sublunary sphere composed of earth, water, air, and fire. Detailed study of the brain and central nervous system has forever discredited the idea that the primary function of the brain is to act, together with the lungs, as part of a cooling system to prevent the heart from overheating and hence destroying the body. Furthermore, although the idea that a body of science can be treated as an axiomatic system still has its attractions, the expressive power of his logic is too weak to formulate scientific propositions.

In light of the fact that so many of Aristotle's central claims are now seen to be wrong, it is all the more impressive that in some form or other many of his ideas are at the heart of contemporary philosophy. This is due in large part to the fact that his philosophical contributions are not exhausted by some list of doctrines, but also include penetrating insights into philosophical method. First and foremost is the way in which he changed and developed ideas on definition and dialectic inherited from Plato and *Socrates. In order to understand anything whatever, whether it be a living organism, a speech, a course of action, or an astronomical event, one needs first to understand *what it is* and then to see how its characteristic properties relate to this. Without buying into his own theory about the ontological underpinnings of definitions (ultimately, the substantial forms that constitute the natures of physical bodies), much of contemporary philosophy is devoted to clarifying our understanding of what things are. For instance, debates about abortion or about cognitive processing are led back to such Aristotelian questions as "What is life?" and "What is thought?" Many of the recent discussions in metaphysics, semantics, and philosophy of science concern the identity and individuation of individuals and its relation to the notion of natural kinds. These issues ultimately have to do with answering questions about what things are—to explain the conditions under which some future object is the same person as you, for instance, involves getting clear on what it is for something to be a person.

The focus of most contemporary philosophy consists in identifying and attempting to solve the key problems involved in reaching satisfactory analyses, and this too can be traced back to Aristotle. He thought that the resources that we have at our disposal for this task are many and diverse, including facts about how language is used, common sense, what observation has revealed, and the theories of scientists and others who have investigated the same terrain. By detecting the inconsistencies and tensions inherent in these various starting points, we are able to articulate the main problems that stand in the way of understanding. We make philosophical progress by devising solutions that avoid the problems in a manner that allows us to understand how our thinking was led astray. For instance, much interesting work in ethics has resulted from an attempt to formulate the motivations for and to examine the conflict between Kantian and Humean theories of the good; and some have even mined Aristotle's own ethical writings for a nuanced theory of the relationship between intrinsically good ends and other goods that are either ends or instrumental means.

BIBLIOGRAPHY: Texts by various editors are available in the Oxford Classical Texts, Budé, Teubner, and Loeb series. Translation in J. Barnes, ed., *The Complete Works of Aristotle*, 2 vols., Princeton, 1984. The bibliography of scholarly studies on Aristotle is immense. What follows is the bibliography of works cited in this article. For a recent extensive and authoritative, if not exhaustive, bibliography see J. Barnes, ed., *The Cambridge Companion to Aristotle*, Cambridge, 1995, 295–384.

Ackrill, J. L., "Aristotle's Definitions of *Psuchê*," PAS 73, 1972/3, 119–133, and repr. in J. Barnes et al., eds., *Articles on Aristotle* vol. 4, London, 1979; also "Aristotle on *Eudaimonia*," *Proceedings of the British Academy* 60, 1974, 339–359, and repr. in A. O. Rorty, ed., *Essays on Aristotle's Ethics*, Berkeley, 1980; Albritton, R., "Forms of Particular Substances in Aristotle's *Metaphysics*," *Journal of Philosophy* 54, 1957, 699–708; Balme, D., "Aristotle's Biology Was Not Essentialist," AGP 62, 1980, 1–12, and repr. in A. Gotthelf and J. Lennox, eds., *Philosophical Issues in Aristotle's Biology*, Cambridge, 1987; Burnyeat, M. F., "Aristotle on Understanding Knowledge," in E. Berti, ed., *Aristotle on Science: the "Posterior Analytics*," Padua, 1981, 97–139; also "Is an Aristotelian Philosophy of Mind Still Credible?" in M. C. Nussbaum and A. O. Rorty, eds., *Essays on Aristotle's De Anima*, Oxford, 1992, 15–26; Charles, D., *Aristotle's Philosophy of Action*, London, 1984; Charlton, W., *Aristotle: Physics Books I and II*, Oxford, 1970, 1992; Code, A., "The Persistence of Aristotelian Matter," *Philosophical Studies* 29, 1976, 357–367; Cooper, J. M., *Reason and Human Good in Aristotle*, Cambridge, MA, 1975; also "Aristotle on Natural Teleology," in M. Schofield and M. C. Nussbaum, eds., *Language and Logos: Studies in Ancient Philosophy Presented to G. E. L. Owen*, Cambridge, 1982, 197–222; also "Metaphysics in Aristotle's Embryology," PCPS 214, 1988, 14–41, and repr. in D. T. Devereux and P. Pellegrin, eds., *Biologie, logique et métaphysique chez Aristote*, Paris, 1990, 55–84; Davidson, D., "How Is Weakness of Will Possible?" in *Moral*

Concepts, ed. J. Feinberg, Oxford, 1970, 93–113; Frede, M., "Categories in Aristotle," in D. O'Meara, ed., *Studies in Aristotle*, Washington, DC, 1981, 1–24, and repr. in Frede, *Essays in Ancient Philosophy*, Minnesota, 1987, 29–48; also "Substance in Aristotle's *Metaphysics*," in A. Gotthelf, ed., *Aristotle on Nature and Living Things*, Bristol/Pittsburgh, 1985, 17–26, and repr. in Frede, *Essays*; also "Individuals in Aristotle," in Frede, *Essays*, 49–71; Gill, M. L., *Aristotle on Substance: The Paradox of Unity*, Princeton, 1989; Gotthelf, A., "Aristotle's Conception of Final Causality," *Rev. Met.* 30, 1976, 226–254, and repr. in Gotthelf and Lennox, eds., *Philosophical Issues*; Irwin, T. H., "Aristotle's Discovery of Metaphysics, *Rev. Met.* 31, 1977, 210–229; also "First Principles in Aristotle's Ethics," *Midwest Studies in Philosophy* 3, 1978, 252–272; also *Aristotle's First Principles*, Oxford, 1988; Jaeger, W., *Aristotle: Fundamentals of the History of his Development*,[2] English tr. by R. Robinson, Oxford, 1948; Kosman, L. A., "Substance, Being and *Energeia*," *OSAP* 2, 1984, 212–149; Kraut, R., *Aristotle on the Human Good*, Princeton, 1989; Lennox, J. G., "Are Aristotelian Species Eternal?," in Gotthelf, ed., *Aristotle on Nature and Living Things*, 67–94; Loux, M. J., *Primary Ousia: An Essay on Aristotle's Metaphysics Z and H*, Ithaca, 1991; Nussbaum, M. C. and H. Putnam, "Changing Aristotle's Mind," in Nussbaum and Rorty, eds., *Aristotle's De Anima*, 27–56; Owen, G. E. L., "Logic and Metaphysics in Some Earlier Works of Aristotle," in I. Düring and G. E. L. Owen, *Aristotle and Plato in the mid-Fourth Century*, Göteborg, 1960, 160–190, and repr. in Owen, *Logic, Science and Dialectic: Collected Papers in Greek Philosophy*, M. C. Nussbaum, ed., Ithaca, 1986; also "Inherence," *Phronesis* 10, 1965, 97–105, and repr. in Owen, *Logic, Science and Dialectic*; also "The Platonism of Aristotle," *Proceedings of the British Academy* 51, 1965, 125–150, and repr. in Owen, *Logic, Science and Dialectic*; also "Particular and General," *PAS* 79, 1978/9, 1–21, and repr. in Owen, *Logic, Science and Dialectic*; Owens, J., *The Doctrine of Being in the Aristotelian Metaphysics*, Toronto, 1951, 1978; Sorabji, R., "Body and Soul in Aristotle," *Philosophy* 49, 1974, 63–89, and repr. in *Articles on Aristotle* vol. 4; Wedin, M., *Mind and Imagination in Aristotle*, New Haven, 1988; Wiggins, D., "Deliberation and Practical Reason," *PAS* 76, 1975/6, 29–51, and repr. in Rorty, ed., *Essays on Aristotle's Ethics.—ALAN D. CODE*

ARISTOXENUS (c. 370–300 B.C.E.), of Taras. Musical theorist, biographer, essayist, and student of *Aristotle. Aristoxenus was musically trained by his father and other professionals. Reared in the twilight of Tarentine *Pythagoreanism, he later studied under Xenophilus, a pupil of *Philolaus. His intellectual outlook was apparently transformed by his move to the *Lyceum: His extant writings are thoroughly *Aristotelian.

Ancient sources assign him an enormous output (453 books, according to the *Suda*). Little survives. We have traces of his biographies of *Socrates and *Plato (rancid with scurrilous gossip), and of *Pythagoras and *Archytas (probably the basis of much of the later tradition). His importance rests on his studies in musical theory, history, and practice: We have many brief quotations and reports, substantial passages on rhythm, and the major writings transmitted as *Elementa Harmonica*. Not everything in *Elementa Harmonica* comes from the same work. Books 2–3 are probably parts of a single treatise, Book 1 an excerpt from an earlier essay (for another view see Bélis, 1986).

Elementa Harmonica pursues harmonics as an Aristotelian natural science, epistemologically grounded in the *Posterior Analytics* and conceptually indebted to the *Physics*. Book 2 extracts principles inductively from perception and refines them dialectically; Book 3 draws from the principles deductive demonstrations of the melodic or unmelodic character of specified sequences. Dismissing the mathematical approach of Pythagoreans and *Platonists as irrelevant (through an application, more rigorous than Aristotle's own, of the "same domain" rule of *APo.* 1.7), Aristoxenus also criticizes those he accepts as predecessors for a merely descriptive empiricism that neglects explanation. The explanatory task must be tackled; but the musicality of audible relations cannot be derived from necessarily nonmusical features of relations between unheard aspects of sounds—the "quicker and slower movements" to which Pythagorean quantifications applied. Aristoxenian explanation consists in displaying musical properties as coordinated aspects of a unified, essentially auditory "nature" (*phusis*), that of melody (*melos*) or "the attuned" (*to hêrmosmenon*). The result is a kind of musical phenomenology, resisting all explanatory recourse to data inaccessible to the musical ear.

Aristoxenus' philosophical acuteness appears in many details: in his treatment of the "space" of pitch and the voice's "movement" within it; of relations between quantitative and "functional" attributes of notes and intervals; of the scientific roles of trained perception, memory, and reason; of the "adjacence" of neighboring musical notes despite the necessary discreteness of pitch-points on the continuum; and much more. His *Rhythmics* presents a sophisticated account of relations among time, rhythm, and "material" rhythmized. Passages paraphrased in *Plutarch's *De Musica* suggest a reflective approach to the history of music, conceived as a narrative of the progressive discovery of potentialities permanently present in musical *phusis*. His ideas on musical ethos remain obscure; but he apparently argued, against the *Damonian and Platonist tradition, that harmonic structures have no intrinsic ethical significance. If music does have the power to edify or corrupt human character, it must arise somehow from its external relations to the circumstances of its use.

Later writers on harmonics preserved much of the content of Aristoxenus' analyses, but lost sight of his philosophical subtleties. Methodological debate degenerated into squabbling between "Aristoxenians" and "Pythagoreans" over the rival criteria of reason and perception. *Ptolemy's reflections on method are the honorable exception, but even he misunderstood Aristoxenus. In a reduced, scholastic form, Aristoxenus' doctrines were nevertheless repeated throughout the Roman period, and he remained the virtually unchallenged authority on the phenomena of musical history and practice till the end of antiquity.

BIBLIOGRAPHY: Texts in Wehrli 2 and A. Barker, *Greek Musical Writings*, vol. 2, Cambridge, 1989. Bélis, A., *Aristoxène de Tarente et Aristote*, Paris, 1986; Laloy, L., *Aristoxène de Tarente et la musique de l'Antiquité*, Paris, 1904; Pearson, L., *Aristoxenus: Elementa Rhythmica*, Oxford, 1990; da Rios, R., *Aristoxeni Elementa Harmonica*, Rome, 1954.—*ANDREW BARKER*

ARIUS DIDYMUS (before 70–after 9 B.C.E.), of Alexandria. Philosopher and Roman imperial official, tentatively identified with the author of several extant *doxographical texts. Arius' philosophical education and affiliation remain uncertain. He admired the *Academic philosopher *Eudorus, a fellow Alexandrian, and became a close friend of the *Peripatetic Xenarchus, another Alexandrian. A tradition recorded by *Diogenes Laertius labelled him a *Stoic; but it is more likely that he followed the fashion of the day in valuing a general commitment to philosophy more highly than partisan school affiliation. Arius' philosophical renown gained the attention of Augustus, who invited him to join his triumphal entry into Alexandria after the battle of Actium in 30 B.C.E. Upon his return to Rome, Augustus invited Arius and his family to join the imperial court, where he became a close personal friend and advisor to the emperor. For a time he served as procurator of Sicily. In 9 B.C.E. he wrote a *Consolation* to comfort Augustus' wife Livia on the death of her son Drusus.

In addition to the *Consolation*, Arius seems to have been the author of two major doxographical works, *On Sects* and an *Epitome* of philosophical doctrines. Neither has survived, but Eusebius and *Stobaeus have preserved substantial excerpts. The two works have usually been regarded as parts of a single work, cited under two different titles; but they may more plausibly and usefully be viewed as separate but complementary doxographies, differing in structure and purpose. In *On Sects* (traditionally regarded as the introductory part of the doxography), Arius assembled excerpts of philosophers from the Presocratics through the Hellenistic schools, arranged systematically by topic. A substantial portion from the beginning of the section on *ethics, preserved by Stobaeus, indicates that its purpose was to reveal the unity underlying the apparent diversity of philosophical opinions. Arius shows particular interest in identifying the first person to formulate a point of view. In his presentation of conflicting views, he often explicitly minimizes disagreements by interpreting some as mere verbal differences intended for rhetorical variation or philosophical clarification and others as complementary perspectives on the same subject.

In his *Epitome*, from which Stobaeus preserved surveys of Stoic and *Peripatetic ethics, Arius presents a comprehensive overview of the doctrine of each school. Here he emphasizes the complementary nature of their differing perspectives. His survey of Stoic ethics is presented as an evaluative classification of moral objects and behaviors. His survey of Peripatetic ethics is presented in terms of the process of moral development and action. Thus the two systems are made to appear complementary in highlighting the two primary elements of ancient ethics, theory and action.

The full scope and overall structure of the *Epitome* is uncertain. The fact that Eusebius quotes brief excerpts of *Platonic and Stoic physical theory from the *Epitome* indicates that it comprehended physics and perhaps *logic as well as ethics and that it treated the three principal philosophical schools of the time, Academic, Peripatetic, and Stoic. Diels has speculatively assigned to it a number of excerpts of Aristotelian and Stoic physical theory from Stobaeus Book 1.

Arius' doxographical work was not primarily a scholarly compilation of historical information, but rather an attempt to solve one of the critical issues of his time. For the preceding two centuries skeptics, including the leaders of the Academy, had been citing philosophical disagreements as evidence that there can be no certain knowledge. In Alexandria at the time of Arius, *Aenesidemus was attempting to revive *skepticism under the banner of *Pyrrhonism. Arius took up arms against the skeptical movement by attempting to reconcile the disagreements among his predecessors. His position, once misleadingly labelled eclectic, was similar to that of *Antiochus of Ascalon, though there is no evidence that he knew Antiochus or his work. In contrast to Antiochus, however, Arius' aim was not to defend the dogmatic teaching of a single school, but rather to transcend school differences by incorporating them into a higher unity. He even hoped to resolve the opposition of skeptic and dogmatic by regarding the skeptic as one who is still seeking the truth that dogmatic philosophers have already found, thereby construing skeptics and dogmatics as confronting the same truth from different temporal perspectives.

Arius' work served to transmit the teachings of the Hellenistic schools to the Imperial Age in a concise form with the doctrinal edges substantially softened. Since it was Arius' version that Stobaeus chose to excerpt, Arius also became responsible for rescuing at least a small portion of the teachings of the Hellenistic schools from the shipwreck that befell the vast majority of Hellenistic literature.

BIBLIOGRAPHY: Texts in H. Diels, *Doxographi Graeci*, Berlin, 1879, 447–72; C. Wachsmuth, ed., *Ioannis Stobaei Anthologii libri duo priores*, 2 vols., Berlin, 1884, vol. 2, 37–150. Göransson, T., *Albinus, Alcinous, Arius Didymus*, Göteborg, 1995; Hahm, D. E., *ANRW* 2, 36.4, 1990, 2935–3055; *RUSCH*, vol. 1, 1983.—*DAVID E. HAHM*

ASPASIUS (c. 125 C.E.). *Peripatetic philosopher, student of Herminus. Aspasius wrote a number of *commentaries on Aristotle's treatises. Those on *Categories, De Interpretatione, Physics, De Caelo*, and *Metaphysics* have been lost. Only books 1–4, 7, and 8 survive from his *Nicomachean Ethics* commentary (G. Heylbut, ed., *CAG* 19.1). Aspasius' works were among those used by *Plotinus as a starting point for discussion (Porphyry *Life of Plotinus* 14).
BIBLIOGRAPHY: Moraux, P., *Der Aristotelismus bei den Griechen*, vol. 2, Berlin, 1984.—*JOSEPH G. DeFILIPPO*

ASTRONOMY. See MATHEMATICS, Earlier Greek; SCIENCE, Greek.

ATHEISM. See THEISM and ATHEISM.

ATHENAEUS (1st cent. B.C.E. or C.E.?), of Attaleia in Pamphylia. Founder of the Pneumatic school of *medicine. The title of his major treatise, famous for its multitude of definitions, is unknown; but many fragments, paraphrases, and ancient criticisms of his work survive.

Drawing on *Stoics, *Peripatetics, *Plato, *Empedocles, and medical precursors, Athenaeus argues that the cold, hot, dry, and moist are the elementary constituents (*stoicheia*) of all existing things. This, he claims, is self-evident and hence requires no demonstration. The hot and cold act as active or efficient causes, the dry and moist as material causes. From these four qualitative elements are constituted the homoeomerous parts (e.g., flesh, bone, hair, fat), from which, in turn, the larger parts of the body are formed. Differences between living entities (including differences in gender, age, and health) and likewise differences between seasons and places are systematically explicable in terms of the four possible pairings of the elementary qualities (hot–moist, hot–dry, etc.)

Pneuma, composed of the hot and the moist, is connate in humans. Its movement causes friction, which continuously produces natural heat. Both connate *pneuma* and natural heat have their principal seat in the ventricles of the heart, which is the central organ of all vital and cognitive activity. *Pneuma*, distributed through the arterial system from the heart by the pulse (see ERASISTRATUS), pervades the body. All diseases are due to an imbalance among the four elementary qualities (see ALCMAEON, HIPPOCRATES), which in turn affects the *pneuma*.

In his theory of reproduction, Athenaeus accepts *Herophilus' discovery of the ovaries but, adopting *Aristotle's reproductive deployment of form and *matter, he denies that the female parent contributes any seed (*sperma*) and hence any motive cause to conception. He also accepts Aristotle's and Herophilus' view that male seed is concocted out of the blood. Athenaeus' therapeutics aim at keeping the four elementary qualities in balance by means of a regimen that is adapted to gender, season, place, and activity. Extensive excerpts of his theories concerning the properties of various kinds of food are extant.

In part through the mediation of the most famous Pneumatist, Archigenes of Apamea, Athenaeus exercised considerable influence on medical thought of the Roman Empire, as *Galen and Oribasius confirm.

BIBLIOGRAPHY: Wellmann, M., *Die pneumatische Schule bis auf Archigenes* (*Philologische Untersuchungen* 14), Berlin, 1895, 5–11, 100–104, 131–156, 201–210 (to be used with caution); Kudlien, F., *R E* Suppl. 11, 1968, 1097–1108; Schroeder, S., *Prometheus* 15, 1989, 209–239.—*HEINRICH VON STADEN*

ATHENODORUS (1st cent. B.C.E.), of Tarsus. Two figures, both *Stoic philosophers of that name, date, and city of origin, must—on the basis of biographical data—be distinguished. One, also called Athenodorus Kordylion, lived with Marcus Cato, where he died (Strabo 14.5, 14). As an old man, he was in charge of the library at Pergamum, where he expunged certain parts of Stoic texts and was disgraced because of it (D.L. 7.34). The other, known as the son of Sandon, was a teacher of Augustus who returned to Tarsus late in life to play an important political role (Strabo 14.5, 14). He collaborated with *Posidonius on a work on the tides (Strabo 1.3, 12). *Cicero (*Att.* 16.11.4; 16.14.4) refers to an Athenodorus Calvus who seems to be identical to the son of Sandon, since Cicero connects him with Posidonius.

Our information about Athenodorus' views cannot definitively be attributed to either one or the other Athenodorus of Tarsus. Athenodorus divided propositions into simple and not simple (D.L. 7.68), believed that not all sins are equal, *contra* *Chrysippus and *Zeno of Citium (D.L. 7.121), and argued that divination was real and a *technê* (D.L. 7.149). Also attributed to Athenodorus are: *On Jests and Earnest* (Athenaeus 12, 519b), a work on *Aristotle's *Categories*, and *Walks* (*peripatoi*), although it is unclear whether this last work is by Athenodorus Kordylion, Athenodorus son of Sandon, or a third figure (D.L. 5.36; 6.81, 9.41).

BIBLIOGRAPHY: Texts in C. Müller, *Fragmenta Historicorum Graeca*, 5 vols., Paris, 1841–70, vol. 3, 485.—*IAKOVOS VASILIOU*

ATOMISM. See COSMOLOGY; DEMOCRITUS; EPICURUS; INFINITE, The; MATTER, Classical Theories of.

AUGUSTINE, St. (Aurelius Augustinus—354–430 C.E.), bishop of Hippo. *Theologian, philosopher, and Father of the Church.

Life. Born in the North African town of Tagaste (modern Souk Ahras, in eastern Algeria), Augustine was educated in the local grammar school, then in a higher school in nearby Madaura, and finally, under the patronage of a local nobleman, Romanianus, at the university in Carthage. It was in Carthage as a student of *rhetoric that he read *Cicero's now lost *dialogue, *Hortensius*, which, as he later wrote in *Confessions* 3.4,7, changed his outlook on life by introducing him to philosophy. After a period as teacher of rhetoric, first in his home town and then in Carthage, Augustine set sail in 383 for Rome to continue his teaching there. From Rome he moved to Milan, where he was professor of rhetoric and joined a circle of *Neoplatonists. In Book 7 of his *Confessions* he explains how the Neoplatonic works he read in the Milanese circle helped him to turn away from the *Manicheanism he had tentatively embraced in Carthage and to think freshly about the nature of God and the problem of evil. Also, under the guidance of Ambrose, Bishop of Milan, and through the continuing influence of his mother, Monica, who had followed him to Milan, Augustine became a convert to *Christianity. The year before his baptism in 387, Augustine withdrew with several philosophically inclined relatives and friends to a villa at Cassiciacum, perhaps near Lake Como, where he wrote his earliest works, including an extremely interesting dialogue critical of the *skepticism of the New *Academy, *Against the Academicians*, as well as his *Soliloquies*, a dialogue of striking originality. Shortly after Augustine's baptism, his mother died. Following a brief stay in Rome, Augustine returned to Carthage in 388 and never left North Africa again. When he became a priest and then a bishop, he managed somehow to combine his considerable pastoral duties with extensive excursions into philosophy and theology. In response to the spread of Donatism, Pelagianism, and Manicheanism in the Christian Church, especially in North Africa, Augustine wrote letters and extensive treatises to define those movements as heretical. In response to the decline and fall of the Roman Empire, blamed by some on the Christianization of Rome, Augustine wrote *The City of God*, which, next to his *Confessions*, has been his most famous and influential work. Rome had been sacked in 410, three years before Augustine began work on *The City of God*. When Augustine died in 430, four years after having completed this last great work, Hippo itself was under seige.

Relation to Philosophers before and after Him. As the first great Christian philosopher, Augustine certainly drew on the philosophy of Greek and Roman antiquity for his models of what philosophical inquiry might be; but he also set a new agenda for philosophy and developed a new style for carrying out that agenda. The most striking feature of the new style is the prominent place it makes for reasoning from a subjective, first-person point of view. Such reasoning is particularly obvious in Augustine's *Soliloquies*, a dialogue between his soul and reason; but it is also central to his most famous work, *The Confessions*, which is a protracted monologue addressed to God. Both works make a prominent place for introspection and reasoning based on that introspection. Nothing similar is to be found in earlier philosophy.

The new philosophical agenda Augustine tackles from his first-person perspective includes a family of philosophical issues that arise from belief in the grace, providence, and foreknowledge of God, coupled with an unswerving insistence on human free will. These issues occupy philosophers throughout the Middle Ages and well into the modern period. Yet for all that is new in Augustine's philosophy, both in the topics it addresses and in the point of view from which it addresses them, there are also strong continuities with what had gone before. Thus ancient skepticism, for example, lives on in Augustine's prominent efforts to put down the taunts of the skeptic. However, even when he joins the long-established debate over skepticism, he does so from his own novel perspective. Thus his most famous attempt to answer skepticism, his *si fallor, sum* ("If I am mistaken, I am"), makes use of essentially first-person reasoning and anticipates Descartes' more famous *cogito, ergo sum* ("I think, therefore I am").

It is hard to be sure how much of classical Greek philosophy Augustine knew firsthand. He admits to a dislike of the Greek language (*Conf.* 1.14). From the available evidence it seems quite possible that *The Categories* is the only work of *Aristotle's that he ever read, even in translation. *Plato he seems to have known much better. He certainly gives evidence of being familiar with several Platonic dialogues, and he clearly felt a special affinity for Plato and the *Platonists (cf., *City of God* 8.4–5, and *On True Religion* 7).

Although Augustine did respond to classical Greek philosophy in fundamental and influential ways, one would have to add that what he responded to was classical philosophy that had already been filtered through Neoplatonism, Hellenistic skepticism, and *Stoicism. In fact, it was primarily through the writings of Cicero that Augustine became schooled in the ideas of his philosophical predecessors. And it was primarily through the works of Neoplatonists that he developed his own deep appreciation for Plato, whom he clearly regarded as the greatest of his philosophical predecessors.

Reply to Skepticism. At the beginning of his stay in Italy, Augustine grew increasingly critical of Manicheanism, which he had tentatively embraced in Carthage. In Rome he found himself attracted to the skeptical position of the "Academicians," that is, the followers of *Arcesilaus and the New Academy, who "held that everything was a matter of doubt and asserted that we can know nothing for certain" (*Conf.* 5.10,19). For his understanding of ancient skepticism and the debate between Arcesilaus and the Stoic *Zeno of Citium (335–263 B.C.E.), Augustine seems to have relied principally on Cicero's *Academica*.

Augustine's most thorough discussion of skepticism is to be found in his earliest surviving work, *Against the Academicians*. According to Augustine, the Academicians base their claim that nothing can be known on the application of a strict criterion for knowledge, one put forward by Zeno, according to which something can be known just in case it cannot even seem to be false (*Ag. Acad.* 3.9,18). Indubitability would then be both a necessary and a sufficient condition for knowledge. Augustine argues that Zeno's criterion is self-defeating; but he also goes on to offer sample knowledge claims that he considers immune to skeptical challenge. These sample knowledge claims include logical truths, mathematical truths, and such reports of immediate experiences as "That tastes pleasant to me" (*Ag. Acad.* 3.10,23–11,26).

After writing *Against the Academicians* Augustine never again devoted a whole treatise to the refutation of skepticism. Yet he did respond, again and again, to the challenge of Academic skepticism. Among the most interesting of these antiskeptical passages is this one in which he presents reasoning remarkably like Descartes's *cogito*:

> In respect of those truths I have no fear of the arguments of the Academics. They say, "what if you are mistaken?" If I am mistaken, I am (*Si fallor, sum.*). Whoever does not exist cannot be mistaken; therefore I exist, if I am mistaken. Because, then, I exist if I am mistaken, how am I mistaken in thinking that I exist, when it is certain to me that I am if I am mistaken? (*City of God* 11. 26).

An important parallel passage is to be found in Book 15 of *The Trinity* at 12.21, where Augustine uses *cogito*-like reasoning to respond to the skeptic's taunt, "What if you are dreaming?" Augustine employs his own *cogito*-like reasoning primarily to defeat universal skepticism; unlike Descartes, he does not make "I am" a foundation stone in a rational reconstruction of everything one can claim to know. Once he has demonstrated how to refute universal skepticism, moreover, he considers himself free to evaluate the epistemological credentials of belief and knowledge claims on a direct and relatively straightforward basis.

Mind-Body Dualism. Although in the very early treatise, *On the Immortality of the Soul*, Augustine presents arguments for the soul's immortality—and hence for soul-body dualism—that are recognizably Platonic in nature, his reasoning to support mind-body dualism in his mature work, *The Trinity*, is quite unlike anything to be found in earlier philosophy. In the later work, Augustine claims that all of us, from our own individual first-person perspectives, "know what a soul is, since we have a soul" (*Trin.* 8.6,9). In the next book he adds, "When the *mind knows itself, it alone is the parent of its own knowledge" (9.12,18). In the following book he surveys philosophical theories about what the *mind is, including the theory that it is blood, that it is the brain, that it is a collection of atoms, that it is air, that it is fire, that it is some "fifth body," or that it is a harmony.

Reflection on how diverse these various philosophical theses on the nature of the mind or soul are might suggest that the mind does not know what it itself is after all. Yet that must be wrong if, as Augustine has just maintained, the mind knows what a mind is, simply and directly, from its own case. How could there be any room for uncertainty when the mind's knowledge of itself is paradigmatically intimate and direct? So if the mind is uncertain whether it is blood, or the brain, or fire, or air, or indeed anything corporeal, it is really none of these things. It is therefore nothing corporeal, Augustine continues, but rather something noncorporeal (*Trin.* 10.10,16).

Augustine foreshadows Descartes in many of his ideas about minds and bodies. Thus he attributes to the mind the ability to remember, understand, will, think, know, and judge, as well as—to strike an uncartesian note—the ability to live (*Trin.* 10.10,14). And he defines "body" as "that of which a part is less than the whole in the extension of place" (*Trin.* 10,7,9). But unlike Descartes Augustine explicitly recognizes that there is a philosophical problem about how each of us can know that there are other minds. Supposing, as he does, that each of us knows what mind is by introspection, from our own case, he needs to explain, as he realizes, how it is we are justified in thinking that there are minds that go with other bodies. To satisfy this need he presents what seems to be the first statement of the argument from analogy for other minds. "Just as we move our body in living," Augustine writes, "so, we notice, those bodies are moved" (*Trin.* 8.6,9). Reflecting on this observation we come to think, he writes, that there is something present in another body "such as is present in us to move our mass in a similar way" (*Trin.* 8.6,9).

The Will. The concept of the will, so important in medieval and modern philosophy, seems to have originated with Augustine. Plato's division of the self in his *Republic* into reason, spirit, and appetite, by contrast, makes no room for the will as a distinct faculty or power. And Aristotle's subtle discussion of the voluntary in Book 3 of his *Nicomachean Ethics* seems not to presuppose the idea of any such force or power as the will.

In his *Trinity*, Augustine presents, among other mental or psychological analogies to the Divine Trinity, the trinity of memory, understanding, and will. His suggestion is that just as each of the three Divine persons, Father, Son, and Holy Spirit, is distinct from the other two, even though each is also God, and not just part of God, so memory, understanding, and will are each distinct from the other two, though each is also mind, and not just part of mind. Augustine also recognizes, of course, that the human mind, with its various trinities, is only an imperfect image of the Divine Trinity. So the mind-as-will may well operate in opposition to the mind-as-understanding. Indeed, a will that is evil does precisely that. The idea of there being such a thing as what the Greeks called *akrasia*—doing what one knows one ought not to be doing—is therefore not a conundrum for Augustine in the way it is for *Socrates and Plato, or even for Aristotle in *Nicomachean Ethics* 7.3.

Illumination. Augustine's account of knowing what, say, virtue is, or what a square is, is not based on the idea of abstraction, as Aristotle's account is said to be, but rather on what commentators call the "theory of illumination." In part, Augustine's talk of illumination is the deployment of an apt Platonic metaphor. Thus in his *Soliloquies* Augustine tells us that we could not learn anything that is not "illuminated by another sun, as it were, of its own" (1.5). Platonic resonances in such language (cf., e.g., *Rep.* 508bff.) are obvious.

Beyond the aptness of the light metaphor, however, the basic idea behind the Augustinian notion of illumination is a generalization of a problem about how we can ever learn what F-ness is by having F-things identified for us. No group of instances of F-ness will display F-ness unambiguously as the single feature those items have in common. If we ever come to understand what F-ness is, Augustine reasons, it will be only by an inner illumination that reveals something that cannot be unambiguously pointed to or displayed in its instances.

In his early dialogue, *The Teacher*, Augustine concludes from reflection on the limitations of teaching through examples that no "outward" teacher can really teach us anything. The most an "outward" teacher can do, he maintains, is to admonish or remind us to look "within," where Christ, the inner teacher, dwells. Christ is identified as "the unchangeable excellence of God and the everlasting wisdom that every rational soul does indeed consult" (11.38). Augustine's reasoning in support of this conclusion has reminded some commentators of the slave-boy passage in Plato's *Meno* (82b–86b).

More generally, Augustine, like Plato before him, insists that "intelligible realities," including what we might think of as a priori truths, cannot be learned, or even confirmed, in sense experience. Augustine, however, explicitly rejects Plato's idea that the soul was introduced to the realm of intelligible realities before birth; instead, he espouses innatism. Referring now explicitly to the Socratic interrogation of the slave boy in Plato's *Meno*, which was meant to demonstrate that there is latent knowledge of geometry, even among the untutored, Augustine protests that not all would have been geometricians in their previous life, "since there are so few of them in the human race that one can hardly be found." He goes on:

We ought rather to believe that the nature of the intellectual mind is so formed as to see those things which, according to the disposition of the creator, are subjoined to intelligible things in the natural order, in a sort of incorporeal light of its own kind (*Trin.* 12.15,24).

Thinking. Running through Augustine's mature writings is the idea that thinking is speaking inwardly, where a word of thought is a concept that mediates between what is said or written to express the thought and the thing the thought is a thought about. "For the thought formed from that thing which we know is the word which we speak in our heart," he writes at *Trinity* 15.10,19, "and it is neither Greek, nor Latin, nor of any other [natural] language; but when we have to bring it to the knowledge of those to whom we are speaking, then some sign is adopted by which it may be made known." The idea of thinking as inward speaking is as old as Plato's *Theaetetus* (189e–190a). Yet it is usually to Augustine rather than to Plato that later medieval philosophers refer for support when they develop the idea of mental language (see, for example, William of Ockham, *Summa Logicae* 1.1).

God. In *On Free Choice of the Will* 2.15,39, Augustine presents an argument for the existence of God. Having gotten his interlocutor to agree that x is God if, and only if, x is more excellent than our minds and nothing is more excellent than x, Augustine argues that Truth exists and is more excellent than our minds. From these two premises he concludes that either Truth itself is God or else something more excellent than it is God. In any case, something is God, thus God exists.

Augustine is responsible for several important contributions to the task, so important in later medieval philosophy, of making philosophical sense of the "infinite attributes" of God, for example, omnipotence and omnipresence. But perhaps his most striking contribution in this area is to insist on the idea that God is perfectly simple, that is, that God is identical with his attributes (*City of God* 11.10, and *Trin.* 6.7,8). Thus God is his goodness, his wisdom, and so forth. "The reason why a nature is called simple," Augustine writes at *City of God* 11.10, "is that it cannot lose any attribute it possesses." In this way Augustine argues for God's simplicity from his immutability.

Augustine understands *Genesis* 1:1 to mean that God created the heavens and the earth out of nothing. Accepting this claim, he explicitly rejects the classical Greek idea that creation would have had to be the formation of substances out of preexistent and uncreated matter. "You did not hold anything in your hand," he writes at *Confessions* 11.5,7, "of which you made this heaven and earth; for how could you come by what you had not made, to make something? For what is there that exists, except because you exist?"

God's Foreknowledge and Human Free Will. In *De Interpretatione* 9 Aristotle considers whether the truth of a statement about some event that is still in the future (for example, a sea fight tomorrow) is compatible with that event's being contingent. As Aristotle makes clear (19a7ff.), the idea that the prior truth of a statement about some future event makes that event necessary, and so inevitable, is a threat to the real efficacy of human deliberation. A close relative of Aristotle's problem appears in Augustine as the problem about how God can foreknow what a human agent will do in such a way as to leave the agent free to do, or not do, what God foreknows that agent will do. In Book 5 of *The City of God* Augustine represents Cicero as arguing this way: (i) If God foreknows all events, then all events happen according to a fixed, causal order; and (ii) if all events happen according to a fixed, causal order, then nothing depends on us and there is no such thing as free will. Augustine is clearly prepared to affirm the antecedent of (i). But he also affirms the reality and efficacy of human free will. So why is he not committed to affirming the consequent of (ii)?

In Chapter 10 of Book 5 of *The City of God*, Augustine writes that one's doing something of one's own free will is among the things God, who is omniscient, can foreknow will happen. When God foreknows a human being will act freely, that act of human free will is part of the causal order God knows will be efficacious. Instead of blocking human free will, then, God's foreknowledge of its occurrence can actually. on Augustine's view, underwrite it.

In another important response to the problem of foreknowledge and free will, Augustine admits that talk of God's *fore*knowledge is misleading. As an eternal being, God, in Augustine's view, is actually outside *time. Thus, although from our human perspective it may be appropriate to speak of God as already knowing what a human agent will later choose to do freely, it would be closer to the truth to say that God knows, timelessly, everything that agent has done and will do.

The Problem of Evil. The problem of how it is possible that God be perfectly good when there is evil in the world is suggested in Plato, for example, toward the end of Book 2 of the *Republic*. Plato's solution to this problem is to insist that God is not responsible for everything in the world; in particular, God is not responsible for evil in the world. On this view, God's sovereignty would be only a limited sovereignty. Augustine, supposing as he does that God created the world out of nothing and also that God's power is unlimited and his sovereignty unqualified, cannot say that some things are not even potentially under God's control. How then can it be that there is evil in the world?

In Book 7 of his *Confessions* Augustine takes up the Neoplatonic idea, which he certainly finds attractive, that evil is not anything positive, but a mere privation. That idea promises to be a solution to the problem of evil. As Augustine goes on to admit, however, even evil as privation can be feared, and the fear of even a nonentity can be an existent evil. Assuming that there is such fear, there is evil (*Conf.* 7.5). In Book 12 of *The City of God*, Augustine insists that "the nature of God cannot be deficient, at any time, anywhere, in any respect." He adds, however, that the creation, what has been created by God *ex nihilo* is deficient. In particular, there is evil that arises from free human choice, and "when an evil choice happens in any being, then what happens is dependent on the will of that being." Moreover, he adds, since the failure is "voluntary, not necessary, the punishment (of the human agent) is just" (12.8).

This solution to the problem of evil is a version of what has come to be called the "free-will defense." Augustine thus does not deny the all-goodness or all-power of God, or even the existence of evil, even though he insists that evil is not anything positive, but only a deficiency. What Augustine denies is the assumption that no all-good being who had the power to prevent evil would fail to do so. God could have prevented evil by not creating free agents. Yet God in his perfect wisdom, goodness, and power has created free agents who, in their freedom, have brought about evil (see also Book 3 of *On Free Choice of the Will*).

Time. In an often-quoted passage from *Confessions* 11.14, Augustine asks, "What then is time?" and replies: "If nobody asks me, I know; but if I am asked what it is and want to explain, I don't know how to." Augustine then develops a perplexity that Aristotle had raised in highly abbreviated form in Book 4 of his *Physics* (217b32–218a8). Noting that we speak of "a long time" and "a short time" Augustine asks how we can do that, since no period of time is ever really present. Of the present year, some months, the past ones, exist no more, whereas others, the future ones, do not yet exist. It is similar with the present month, the present day, indeed for any *period* of time that can be said to be present. Some of the period, the past part, exists no more, whereas the rest, the future part, does not yet exist. All that ever really exists, Augustine reasons, is the durationless "now." Then how can it be that there is such a thing as time, Augustine asks, if no time is ever long or short? Unlike Aristotle, who never resolved this perplexity, Augustine presents a solution. He suggests that time is the measure of something mental. Although no period of time exists "outside the mind," so to speak, periods of time can be held in the mind as events remembered, experienced, or anticipated.

In Book 11 of *The City of God* Augustine seems to revert to a more Platonic theory of time, according to which time is the motion of bodies. In Book 12 of that work, however, he makes clear that he takes the movements of the angels to be sufficient for the existence of time. There Augustine says that angels have always existed in the sense that there is no time at which they failed to exist. Nevertheless, angels are created be-ings, and time was created with them (*City of God* 12.16).

It is, of course, not Augustine's view that God's creation of time took place in time. Rather his thought is that God timelessly creates time, be-ing himself immutable and timeless. Augustine is therefore not commit-ted to the view that there is a first time, though he does have to try to make sense of the idea of timeless action—indeed, of timeless creation. "It is not in time that you are before times," he says to God at *Confessions* 11.13,16, "you precede all past times in the loftiness of your ever-present eternity."

*Ethics. (i) *Intentionalism.* Sin, for Augustine, is the most basic cate-gory of moral evaluation, rather than, as with the classical Greek philosophers, virtue or vice; and salvation, rather than *eudaimonia*, is the goal of life. Sinful actions, in his view, are those that fail to accord with the divine command to love God and love one's neighbor as oneself. Au-gustine can thus be seen to have a theological ethics. Especially striking in Augustine's ethics is his intentionalism, which can be usefully com-pared and contrasted with that of such medieval ethicists as Abelard and such modern ethicists as Kant. Thus Augustine, in his *Commentary on the Lord's Sermon on the Mount* 1.12,34, identifies three steps in the commis-sion of a sin: suggestion, pleasure, and consent. What Augustine calls "suggestion" is the mere thought of doing something that does not ac-cord with the command to love God and one's neighbor. The second step, taking pleasure, is enjoying the thought of doing the suggested evil deed. The third step, consent, is forming the intention actually to per-form the deed contemplated. Augustine makes clear that there is sin whether one's intention to perform a certain wrongful action is ever suc-cessfully carried out or not.

All this being so, there is a serious problem about dreams, since the sequence of suggestion, pleasure, and consent can also occur in a dream. Can one really sin by forming in a dream the intention to perform a sin-ful act? As *Confessions* 10.30 makes clear, Augustine wants to say "No," but finds it difficult to explain why not, given his strong intentionalism and his insistence that he is his dream self, rather than a mere observer of his dreams.

(ii) *"Ought" and "Can."* In rejecting the perfectionism of his contem-porary, the British monk Pelagius, Augustine also rejected the Pelagian maxim, which modern ethicists associate with Kant, that "ought" implies "can." Or better: Augustine gave this maxim a crucial qualification. In Augustine's view one can do anything one ought to do, but one may not be able to do it from one's own strength alone; the gratuitous assistance, or grace, of God may be required. "Sin can be avoided," Augustine writes in his treatise, *On Man's Perfection in Righteousness* 2.1, "if our corrupted nature be healed by God's grace." The belief that anything one morally ought to do is something one can do "by one's own strength alone," is branded as the heresy of "Pelagianism."

(iii) *The Virtues*. Following a tradition that goes back to Plato (see the beginning of *Republic* 2), Augustine contrasts those things that are desirable in themselves with those things that are desirable for the sake of something else. Things of the first kind, he says, are to be enjoyed (*frui*) whereas those of the second kind are merely to be used (*uti*). Vice, according to Augustine, is wanting to use what should be enjoyed or enjoy what is meant to be used; and virtue is the converse (*Eighty-three Different Questions* 30). Although Augustine points out that some things, such as food, may be enjoyed as well as used, the supreme object of enjoyment, God, is to be loved for his own sake and never to be used (*On Christian Doctrine* 1).

To the classical virtues of justice, wisdom, courage, and temperance Augustine, following Saint Ambrose, adds the Pauline virtues of faith, hope, and love. He understands each virtue to be a partial expression of the love of God, and virtue as a whole to be nothing but the perfect love of God (*Morals of the Catholic Church* 15.25). In the idea of virtue as the perfect love of God, Augustine is able to give new expression to the old Platonic idea of the unity of the virtues.

BIBLIOGRAPHY: Texts: Maurist edition in J. P. Migne, *Patrologia Latina*, vols. 32–47, Paris, 1844–64. Critical editions of many individual works in *Corpus Scriptorum Ecclesiasticorum*, Vienna, 1866–; and in *Corpus Christianorum*, Series Latina, The Hague, 1953–. Translations: Rotelle, J. A., ed., *The Complete Works of Saint Augustine*, Hyde Park, NY, 1994–. Translations of major works in P. Schaff, ed., *A Select Library of the Nicene and Post-Nicene Fathers of the Christian Church*, First Series, 1886–88, repr. Grand Rapids, 1971–80. Individual works in English translation in *Fathers of the Church*, Washington, DC, 1947–; and in *Ancient Christian Writers: The Works of the Fathers in Translation*, New York, 1946–; and available from many commercial publishers (e.g., Hackett Publishing Co., Indianapolis). Brown, P., *Augustine of Hippo*, Berkeley, 1967; Chadwick, H., *Augustine*, New York/Oxford, 1986; Gilson, E., *The Christian Philosophy of Saint Augustine*, New York, 1960; Kirwan, C., *Augustine*, London, 1989; Matthews, G. B., *Thought's Ego in Augustine and Descartes*, Ithaca, 1992; O'Daly, G., *Augustine's Philosophy of Mind*, London, 1987; Rist, J. M., *Augustine: Ancient Thought Baptized*, Cambridge, 1994; Wetzel, J., *Augustine and the Limits of Virtue*, Cambridge, 1992.—*GARETH B. MATTHEWS*

AURELIUS, Antoninus Marcus (121–180 C.E.). Roman Emperor from 161 to 180. Born at Rome, Marcus Aurelius died on campaign in Germany. Though not a professional philosopher, he was broadly *Stoic in his beliefs.

After a studious upbringing and various lesser offices Marcus succeeded Antoninus Pius, his adoptive father, as emperor at the age of forty. His death ended a period of exceptional stability and prosperity—in Gibbon's words, "the period in the history of the world during which the condition of the human race was most happy and prosperous." Narrative sources for Marcus' reign are few and brief in coverage. A great deal of information about his earlier years can be derived from the correspondence between himself and his rhetorical tutor Fronto, of which substantial parts survive. Since Fronto often comments on Marcus' severity of outlook and tries to woo him away from philosophic studies, these letters also shed some light on the emperor's Stoic tendencies. There are also many charming vignettes and humorous exchanges.

The emperor's philosophic reputation, however, rests mainly on a work his subjects never saw, the work normally referred to as the *Meditations*. This title is not original; if Marcus called the book anything, it was probably "To him (my-?) self," found at the head of our manuscripts. It is a bedside book or spiritual diary, in which the emperor recorded his own reflections on human life and the workings of the universe and urged himself to work harder at eradicating his own moral defects. It is composed in Greek, the language of philosophy, and there are many echoes of the thought and language of the Greek *Epictetus. It certainly dates from his period as emperor, and internal evidence suggests that it was composed during his later years and on campaign against rebellious German tribes; he speaks of himself as an old man, and there are many references to his impending death. The work seems to have survived almost by accident. It was unknown to the writers of his time and for long after, though it seems to have surfaced in the fourth century. The period of its greatest influence is in modern times.

Although divided by modern editors into twelve "books," each containing a series of "chapters," the work seems not to have a clear structure. The so-called chapters vary greatly, sometimes containing a sustained exposition of a point of doctrine but often taking much for granted and touching lightly on a difficult issue. Brief epigrams are juxtaposed with quotations (usually of moral tags, occasionally of longer passages: esp. 7.38–46, 11.30–9; several of these come from *Plato, Epictetus, or even *Heraclitus, whom Stoics admired) and with more developed arguments on divine providence, the brevity of human life, and the necessity for moral effort and tolerance of his fellow human beings. Frustratingly, these *pensées* are almost invariably generalized: we do not learn Marcus' secret thoughts about his family, members of the court, or military policy. We do, however, get some idea of his personality and preoccupations.

The first book of the *Meditations* is a different matter, being more coherent than the others. It may have been composed independently. Here Marcus goes through a list of his closer relatives and several teachers, recording what he owes to each—in some cases a specific lesson, but more often a general moral example. This list culminates in two long passages on what he owes to his predecessor Antoninus Pius and to the gods (1.16 and 17). Though often allusive and obscure, these give us unique access to the mind of an ancient ruler, and the whole book is a precious personal document.

Because of the fragmented quality of the remaining books, it is not easy to compile a systematic account of Marcus' thought, and the following generalizations may in places oversimplify.

For Marcus, as for all Stoics, the universe is divine and rational; all things have come into existence for a purpose; providence has organized and determined all events, and it is for the individual to respond willingly and to play his proper role. The *Epicurean alternative, that all phenomena are the product of random motions of atoms, is regularly rejected. Consequently human beings have duties and responsibilities, to the gods and to one another: Marcus' reflections on physics and *cosmology swiftly move on to their moral implications. The *Meditations* lay heavy emphasis on self-control and self-discipline. Anger, lust, ambition, envy, and other unhealthy or disruptive emotions must be purged; indignation at what others say or do is pointless. Better understanding of their natures will lead to greater tolerance. What matters is to lead a moral life oneself. Perhaps surprisingly in a monarch, Marcus seems to hold out little hope of convincing others of their error and changing those who are set in misguided ways. As for the problem of evil, Marcus sometimes maintains that this is an inevitable by-product of the imperfections of the material universe, and at other times suggests that, in the longer perspective of eternity, evil too has a place and the deeds of bad men have good consequences.

Thoughts of providence and *time often lead him to contemplate the vastness of the universe in comparison with the minuteness of a single human life, and these passages have a haunting, often a poetic quality that has impressed many readers. A typical reflection is: "Whatever befalls you was prepared for you beforehand from eternity, and the thread of causation was spinning from everlasting both your existence and this which befalls you" (10.5). This fatalism does not lead to apathy, but rather to a curious combination of resolution and melancholy. Though determined to persevere in his moral efforts, the author is often resigned to their futility: "Even if you break your heart, none the less they will do just the same" (8.4); "Who will change men's convictions?" (9.29). Marcus is also fascinated by life's transience and by the way in which all great men, even philosophers and emperors, pass on and are forgotten (e.g., 4.32). On survival after death he is agnostic; like most Stoics, he appears to have believed that the substance of the soul survived, but he wavers over the continuity of consciousness (esp. 12.5). According to some interpreters, there is a new otherworldliness in Marcus' brand of Stoicism, which is often explained by reference to a *Platonizing tendency in the school, allegedly originating with *Posidonius. It may, however, be as easily ascribed to Marcus' own temperament.

To modern eyes it is disappointing that Marcus' high principles did not lead to more radical social or political reform; he seems to see his philosophy much more as a moral framework for his own daily conduct and personal relationships. But the short book of *Meditations* has continued to provide consolation and stimulus to readers as different as Goethe and Cecil Rhodes.

BIBLIOGRAPHY: Text of *Meditations* in J. Dalfen, ed., *Marcus Aurelius ad se ipsum Libri xii*[2] (Teubner), Leipzig, 1987. Tr. and comm. in A. S. L. Farquharson, *The Meditations of Marcus Aurelius Antoninus*, Oxford, 1944. Asmis, E., *ANRW* 2, 32.3, 1989, 2228–52; Brunt, P. A., *JRS* 64, 1974, 1–20; also "Marcus Aurelius and the Christians," in C. Deroux, ed., *Studies in Latin Literature and Roman History*, vol. 1, Brussels, 1979, 483–520; Champlin, E., *Fronto and Antonine Rome*, Cambridge, MA, 1980; Pohlenz, M., *Die Stoa*,[3] Göttingen, 1964, vol. i, 341–53; Rutherford, R. B., *The Meditations of M. Aurelius: A Study*, 1989, with review by Brunt, *JRS* 80, 1990, 218–19; Theiler, W., *Kaiser Marc Aurel, Wege zu sich selbst*, Zürich, 1951.—R. B. RUTHERFORD

B

BEING. See METAPHYSICAL THOUGHT, Classical.

BION (fl. 1st half of 3rd cent. B.C.E.), of Borysthenes in the Crimaea. A travelling *sophist. The principal ancient report of his life and work is hostile and tendentious (D.L. 4.46–58). Some scholars see him as the originator of the *Cynic *diatribe and a significant influence, for example, on *Aristo of Chios and on *Epicurean *ethical writing. For others, the limitations of the evidence prohibit any overall assessment. Not in doubt is that he learned philosophy in Athens and was attracted principally by the Cynics and the Cynicizing atheist Theodorus. Surviving fragments and testimonies indicate scorn of conventions and a preoccupation with self-sufficiency. In the colorful manner remarked upon by *Eratosthenes (D.L. 4.52), Bion elaborated various strategies for rising above the vicissitudes of life and coping with poverty, vagrancy, old age, and death.

See also CYNICS and CYNICISM; DIATRIBE.

BIBLIOGRAPHY: Texts in J. F. Kindstrand, *Bion of Borysthenes*, Uppsala, 1976; O. Hense, *Teletis Reliquiae*, 1909. Hawtrey, R., *Prudentia* 9, 1977, 63ff.; Gigante, M., *Cinismo e Epicureismo*, 1992.—*MALCOLM SCHOFIELD*

BOETHIUS, Anicius Manlius Severinus (c. 480–524/6 C.E.), of Rome. Author of the *Consolation of Philosophy*, as well as numerous philosophical and theological treatises that greatly influenced the Middle Ages, Boethius transmitted philosophy to the Latin West. Orphaned at an early age, he was brought up by the illustrious Roman aristocrat Quintus Aurelius Memmius Symmachus, whose daughter Rusticiana he eventually married. Early in his career, Boethius gained a reputation as a cultivated man of learning. For many years, he also occupied a political position of trust under Theodoric the Ostrogoth, the head of the western Roman empire. In the year 510 he held the position of consul, and in 522 he and his family were singularly honored when his two sons were appointed joint consuls. Because Theodoric was an adherent of Arianism, his relations with partisans of orthodox Catholicism were of a particular concern to him. As unrest between Arians and Catholics increased, Theodoric grew increasingly anxious that the orthodox Catholic Roman aristocrats might try to overthrow his rule and seek unity with the orthodox eastern part of the empire. In this climate of anxiety and suspicion, a Roman senator named Albinus was accused of treason and condemned to death without a trial. Boethius publicly defended Albinus, with the result that his own arrest soon followed. Besides treason, the official charges against him included the implausible accusations that he practiced magic and astrology. In 524 (or 526), after a lengthy imprisonment during which he wrote his most famous work, *The Consolation of Philosophy*, Boethius was put to death.

Scholars disagree over where Boethius was educated and what his sources were. According to an older theory, Boethius studied in Athens and learned his philosophy in *Neoplatonist schools there. Another theory, associated particularly with Pierre-Paul Courcelle, maintains that Boethius studied not at Athens but at Alexandria in the school of the Greek *commentators on *Aristotle and that the head of that school, *Ammonius, son of Hermeias, was one of the main influences on Boethius. Besides the philosophical evidence for this view, there is also some historical evidence that suggests (to some scholars) that Boethius' father was prefect in Alexandria in the 480s, so that Boethius might have been in Alexandria himself. In any event, the Alexandrian schools surpassed the Athenian ones in this period. There is also a theory that Boethius studied neither in Athens nor in Alexandria, but got the material for his logical works simply from the marginalia in a copy of Aristotle's *Organon* that he owned. Although Boethius may have had and used such a volume, it is hard to imagine that the bulk of his philosophical work is nothing more than a reproduction of such marginalia, especially since the *Consolation* shows him to have had firsthand knowledge of some Greek philosophers (such as *Proclus), and his commentary on *Cicero's *Topica* also indicates that he was widely read. Whatever the final outcome of these controversies, it is clear that Boethius was heavily influenced by both Neoplatonism and *Aristotelianism.

Boethius' works include the following treatises: (i) *Consolation of Philosophy*; (ii) five theological treatises, commonly called the "*Opuscula Sacra*" (*De Trinitate, Utrum Pater et Filius, Quomodo Substantiae, De Fide*

Catholica, Contra Eutychen); (iii) *De Institutione Arithmetica*; (iv) *De Institutione Musica*; and (v) several independent treatises on *logic (*Introductio ad Syllogismos Categoricos, De Syllogismis Categoricis, De Syllogismis Hypotheticis, De Topicis Differentiis, De Divisione*). He intended to translate all the works of *Plato and Aristotle into Latin and reconcile their two philosophies, but he accomplished only a small portion of that enormous task, namely, translations of and commentaries on most of Aristotle's logical works. (For details regarding the translations of Aristotle, see L. Minio-Paluello, ed., *Aristoteles Latinus*, vols. 1, 2, 3, 5, 6, [Leiden, 1961–75].) Boethius also translated *Porphyry's *Isagôgê* and wrote commentaries on it and on Cicero's *Topica*.

There is some controversy over the dating of individual works of Boethius, but the following scheme is generally accepted. Between 500 and 511: *In Porphyrii Isagôgên editio prima; In Porphyrii Isagôgên, editio secunda; De Institutione Arithemetica; De Institutione Musica;* and *In Aristotelis Categorias*. Between 512 and 521: *In Aristotelis Perihermeneias, editio prima; In Aristotelis Perihermeneias, editio secunda; De Syllogismis Categoricis* and *Introductio ad Syllogismos Categoricos* (some scholars date Boethius' work on the categorical syllogism significantly earlier, to around 505/6); *De Syllogismis Hypotheticis; De Divisione* (though some scholars put this work in the period 505–509); *Contra Eutychen; In Ciceronis Topica*. (There may also have been commentaries on Aristotle's *Topics* and *Prior* and *Posterior Analytics* in this period.) In the last period, from 521 until his death: the remaining four *Opscula Sacra, De Differentiis Topicis*, and the *Consolation of Philosophy*. He may also have written works on astronomy and geometry and a commentary on Aristotle's *De Sophisticis Elenchis*.

Many of the ideas and positions formulated by Boethius, in areas as diverse as logic and *theology, were philosophically sophisticated and foundational for later thought. To take one example: Building on a tradition of Greek and *Christian thought, Boethius argued that God's mode of existence is not bounded by *time. Anything that exists in time exists successively; it has lost its past and does not yet have its future, so that it lives only in its present, the thin divide between past and future. God, on the other hand, has the whole of his unending life all at once, in the limitless present of eternity. Because God is eternal rather than temporal, there is no before or after in his relations with things in time, since *before* and *after* mark temporal relations. Consequently, strictly speaking, although God knows things future with respect to us, he does not have *fore*knowledge, since *fore*knowledge implies that the knower knows some things before they occur. For Boethius, then, the old puzzle concerning the compatibility of divine foreknowledge with human free will is solved by the doctrine of divine eternity; or, perhaps more accurately, on the doctrine of divine eternity the puzzle doesn't arise at all.

Boethius' influence on medieval philosophy was considerable. Until the mid–twelfth century, the medievals knew as much of Aristotle as they did know largely through his translations; his commentaries and treatises were used very widely and served to establish, among other things, a basic Latin philosophical vocabulary. In some cases—for example, in certain developments in logic—his work is the principal source for later medieval developments; and his discussion of the ontological status of Porphyrian predicables is one of the main stimuli for the long medieval controversy over universals. For the early scholastics, he was an authority second perhaps only to *Augustine among Christian philosophers. His influence can be traced throughout the medieval period, and in the Renaissance there was a resurgence of his influence in the humanist interest in *dialectic, particularly in the Boethian *Topics*.

BIBLIOGRAPHY: Texts in H. F. Stewart, E. K. Rand, and S. J. Tester, eds. and trs., *Boethius: The Theological Tractates. Consolation of Philosophy* (Loeb), Cambridge, MA, 1978. Chadwick, H., *Boethius: The Consolations of Music, Logic, Theology, and Philosophy*, Oxford, 1981; Gibson, M., ed., *Boethius: His Life, Thought, and Influence*, Oxford, 1981; Obertello, L., *Severino Boezio*, Genoa, 1974.—*ELEONORE STUMP*

BOETHUS (c. 2nd cent. B.C.E.), of Sidon (1). *Stoic philosopher, student of *Diogenes of Seleucia. We know nothing of Boethus' biographical circumstances. *Diogenes Laertius had devoted a biography to him, to judge from the so-called *Index Locupletior*.

Among the works of Boethus, the ancient sources record the following: *On Nature*, where it is asserted that the essence of the divine is the sphere of the fixed stars; *On Destiny*, which argues that everything occurs by virtue of fate; *Commentary on the "Phainomena" of Aratus*, in at least four books, concerning winds and rain and the meteorological predictions that can be drawn from them; and *On Discipline*, in at least four books. Much more interesting is a long passage in *On the Eternity of the World* by *Philo of Alexandria, who reports that Boethus and *Panaetius had abandoned the belief in the conflagration (*ekpurôsis*) and in reincarnation in favor of belief in the eternity and incorruptibility of the universe. This doctrine, together with the refusal to regard the world as a living being (*zôon*), is in obvious conflict with traditional Stoic physics. Two testimonies concerning the definition of the *soul, uncertainly attributed to the Stoic philosopher (that the soul is composed of air and fire and that, being immortal in itself, it does not await the arrival of the death of the body, but is destroyed as it departs from the body) should be read in connection with the fragments of *Porphyry's *On the Soul, Against Boethus*.

BIBLIOGRAPHY: Texts in *SVF* 3, Boethus Frs. 1–11. *DPA* 2, B47; von Arnim, H., in *RE* 3.1, 1897, 601–603.—*TIZIANO DORANDI*

BOETHUS of Sidon (2). Peripatetic philosopher. See ARISTOTELIAN-ISM, PERIPATETIC SCHOOL.

BRYSON (c. 360 B.C.E.?), of Heracleia Pontica (?). *Aristotle mentions a Bryson six times, twice as a *sophist and son of Herodoros (of Heracleia?), once as an exponent of the view that obscene language is impossible, and three times in connection with the attempt to square the circle. Aristotle does not describe how Bryson's quadrature proceeded, but implies that the argument, although "correct," was not a proof because it did not rely on any specifically geometric principles. The ancient *commentators ascribe a variety of procedures to Bryson, all involving polygons inscribed and circumscribed about a circle and the taking of some square intermediate in area between the two sets of polygons. Various attempts have been made to connect this Bryson with or disconnect him from the one or more Brysons mentioned in other sources.

BIBLIOGRAPHY: Texts in K. Döring, *Die Megariker*, Amsterdam, 1972, 62–67; 157–166 (incl. German comm.). Muller, R., *Les Mégariques*, Paris, 1985, 66–71; 174–179 (French tr. and comm.); Becker, O., *Quellen und Studien zur Geschichte der Mathematik, Astronomie und Physik*, Abteilung B, 3, 1936, 236–244.—*IAN MUELLER*

C

CALCIDIUS (fl. c. 350 C.E.). Commentator on *Plato. Waszink has shown that the correct form of his name is Calcidius, and not Chalcidius. Only one work by him is known: a translation of and commentary on Plato's *Timaeus*, both extending only to 53c. Calcidius enumerates in s. 7 of the *Commentary* a list of twenty-seven topics for discussion, of which only thirteen are preserved. He at least envisaged covering the whole *dialogue.

The identity and date of Calcidius are much disputed. His work is dedicated to a certain Osius, a friend and patron. This man has traditionally been identified with the Bishop of Corduba (c. 256–357), following the testimony of some manuscripts, but Waszink disputes this and places Calcidius—on linguistic grounds—early in the fifth century. Waszink also seeks to identify distinctively *Neoplatonic features in his doctrine and argues that the commentary is dependent on that of *Porphyry. None of this seems compelling, however. Calcidius' language certainly fits well with a later date, but is not impossible for the mid–fourth century. Nothing in his doctrines need be other than *Middle Platonic, while certain details, such as his dismissal of the introductory portion of the dialogue (17a–27b) as of purely historical interest and his use of a lambda-shaped figure to illustrate the divisions of the *soul in 35aff., seem to preclude Porphyrian influence. His most interesting points of doctrine, such as the postulation of a supreme God above Intellect in s. 176 or his doctrine of *Matter, can be accommodated to the doctrine of *Numenius (whom he quotes), and his doctrine of fate and providence closely resembles that appearing in ps.-Plutarch *On Fate*. On the whole, it seems best to regard Calcidius as essentially Middle Platonist in his inspiration. His main source may well be Numenius, but large portions of the more technical *mathematical and astronomical portions seem to be borrowed from the second century *Peripatetic Adrastus.

Calcidius' work is primarily derivative (from one or more Greek commentaries), but he is no mindless compiler. He seems himself to have been a *Christian (though he wears his religion lightly), and inserts a number of references to *Origen and other Church Fathers, to *Philo of Alexandria, and to the Scriptures, which he cannot derive from a *Platonist source.

BIBLIOGRAPHY: Text in J. H. Waszink, *Timaeus a Calcidio Translatus Commentarioque Instructus*, London/Leiden, 1962. den Boeft, J., *Calcidius on Fate: His Doctrine and Sources*, Leiden, 1970; Dillon, J., *The Middle Platonists*, London/Cornell, 1977, 401–408; Gersh, S., *Middle Platonism and Neoplatonism: The Latin Tradition*, vol. 2, Notre Dame, 1986, 421–92; van Winden, J. C. M., *Calcidius on Matter: His Doctrine and Sources*, Leiden, 1964.—*JOHN DILLON*

CALLIPHO (2nd cent. B.C.E. [?]). Callipho is known from references in *Cicero's philosophical writings, where he is repeatedly invoked, sometimes with Deinomachus, as a representative of the view that the highest *good consists of moral worth (*honestas*) combined with pleasure (*Acad. Pr.* 2.131, 137, 139; *Fin.* 2.19, 34, 5.21, 73; *TD* 5.85, 87; *Off.* 3.119). In *Academica Priora* *Carneades is said to have defended Callipho's view so assiduously that he seemed to accept it himself. It is unknown to which Hellenistic school Calliopho claimed allegiance.—*JOSEPH G. DeFILIPPO*

CARNEADES (214–129/8 B.C.E.), of Cyrene in North Africa (now in Libya). *Academic *skeptic. Carneades studied in the Academy under a certain Hegesinus and succeeded him as head of the school at some point before 155 B.C.E. In this year he was sent with two other philosophers on an embassy to Rome; while on this visit he impressed (or distressed) the Romans by arguing, on successive days, first in favor of justice and then against it. In 137 he retired from the position of head of the Academy because of ill health. He wrote nothing, but *Clitomachus, his student and eventual successor as head of the Academy, wrote a large number of books preserving his arguments, which are probably the main origin of the sizeable number of reports on Carneades' philosophical activities in *Cicero, *Sextus Empiricus, and other authors.

Carneades was the most celebrated head of the skeptical Academy after its initiator *Arcesilaus. His method, like that of Arcesilaus, was to generate sets of opposing arguments on the same subject, the result being the withdrawal of assent from either (or any) side of the opposition. Arcesilaus appears to have achieved this by arguing against whatever thesis others might propose, and it is likely that Carneades often proceeded in this way also; for example, arguments of his are recorded against the existence of the gods and against divination, and these are clearly intended to be juxtaposed with the positive arguments of nonskeptics. But sometimes Carneades would produce both sides of the opposition himself; the speeches on justice are the clearest example. The main target of Carneades' critical arguments was undoubtedly the *Stoics—especially *Chrysippus, who in the wake of Arcesilaus' attacks had elaborated and strengthened the Stoic system, and had also launched criticisms against the skeptical outlook. However, Carneades' argument against the existence of a criterion of truth, though making considerable use of Stoic concepts, is said by Sextus (M 7.159) to have been directed not just against Stoics but against all previous philosophers. Again, the *Carneadea Divisio* of which Cicero often speaks is supposedly a classification of all possible views about the *ethical end (presumably designed to induce suspension of judgment about all such views), while Carneades' subtle and interesting arguments about free will include within their scope both Stoic and *Epicurean positions. As the above remarks suggest, the subject-matter of Carneades' arguments was wide-ranging.

Carneades' successors were not in agreement about the depth of his commitment to the skeptical attitude of suspension of judgment (*epochê*). As reported by Cicero (*Acad.* 2.78), *Metrodorus of Stratonicea and *Philo of Larissa maintained that Carneades had held that the wise man might have opinions, that is, might assent to the truth of some propositions. But Clitomachus countered that Carneades had put this forward only for dialectical purposes, which is probably correct. Clitomachus appears to have been Carneades' most assiduous follower, whose interpretation of his outlook Carneades is elsewhere said to have endorsed. Clitomachus says that Carneades accomplished a Herculean task when he "rid our minds of that wild and savage monster, assent" (Cic. *Acad.* 2.108); this suggests that Carneades, besides being a strict practitioner of *epochê*, regarded the sustaining of *epochê* as of prime importance. Carneades does not seem to have advertised the merits of *epochê*, as Arcesilaus did. But this was probably due to a well-founded desire to avoid self-refutation; someone who asserts that suspension of judgment is a good thing thereby fails to suspend judgment on at least one point.

Carneades was also well known for his account of the *pithanê phantasia*, "convincing impression," which is reported most fully in Sextus (M 7.166–189) but referred to frequently elsewhere. This was a description of how one might make rational choices in the absence of any strict criterion of truth; the account is elaborate and ingenious, involving three different levels of "convincingness," yet at no point requiring one to commit oneself to the truth of any impression. It appears to be a response to the charge of *apraxia*, "inaction," leveled particularly by the Stoics—the charge that rational choice is impossible if one suspends judgment. Yet there are serious questions about its compatibility with Carneades' skeptical stance; for it may well seem itself to qualify as a philosophical doctrine to which Carneades is committed. Recent scholars have argued that it is instead meant to be taken in conjunction with some other, opposing argument, in the fashion described above—perhaps the Stoic argument for the "cognitive impression," or perhaps Carneades' own argument against any criterion of truth; or, alternatively, that he is showing the Stoics how *they* can live without a criterion of truth, consistently with their own premises, rather than claiming it as his own method. The difficulty left by both readings is that, if he does *not* offer the *pithanê phantasia* as his own doctrine, he leaves himself vulnerable to the charge of *apraxia*. However, there is perhaps a way in which he can *adopt* this doctrine without *assenting* to it. For we are told by Cicero (*Acad.* 2.104), reporting Clitomachus (who in turn is probably reproducing Carneades), that one can "approve" or "follow" impressions without committing oneself to their truth; this "approval" or "following" is sufficient to allow action, and also theoretical debate, to take place. This distinction serves as a reply to another version of the *apraxia* charge—namely, that action of any kind, rational or not, is simply impossible in the absence of assent; but it may also allow Carneades to admit that the account of the *pithanê phantasia* is *his own* position without thereby lapsing from skeptical *epochê*.

Carneades may be said to mark the climax of the skeptical Academy. With the exception of Clitomachus, as noted above, his successors seem to have abandoned the hard-line skeptical attitude. Ironically, his influence may have been greater on the Stoics than on the Academy itself, for arguably his criticisms forced the Stoics to modify some of their own uncompromising positions.

BIBLIOGRAPHY: Bett, R., *OSAP* 7, 1989, 59–94; also *The Monist* 73, 1990, 3–20; Couissin, P., in M. Burnyeat, ed., *The Skeptical Tradition*, Berkeley, 1983, 31–64; Frede, M., in *The Skeptical Tradition*, 65–94; Long, A. A., *Phronesis* 12, 1967, 59–90; Striker, G., in M. Schofield, M. Burnyeat, and J. Barnes, eds., *Doubt and Dogmatism*, Oxford, 1980, 54–83.—*RICHARD BETT*

CASSIUS the *Skeptic. Cited as a critic of the *Republic* of *Zeno of Citium, and a principal source of information about its contents (D.L. 7.32–3). He is probably to be identified with the *Pyrrhonist Cassius whom *Galen mentions as author of a book attacking inference from similar cases (*Subfiguratio Empirica* 4), and therefore no earlier than *Aenesidemus' Pyrrhonist revival of the first century B.C.E. Some scholars take Cassius to be the lately deceased doctor described by *Celsus as *ingeniosissimus saeculi nostri medicus* (*On Medicine*, Proem. 69), and so of the period of Augustus and Tiberius.

BIBLIOGRAPHY: Texts in K. Deichgräber, *Die griechische Empirikerschule*, Berlin, 1930. Schofield, M., *The Stoic Idea of the City*, Cambridge, 1991, ch. 1; Wellmann, M., *A. Cornelius Celsus*, 1913, ch. 5.—*MALCOLM SCHOFIELD*

CELSUS, Aulus Cornelius (fl. 14–37 C.E.?). Roman encyclopedist. Eight books on medicine survive from his *Artes*, which probably also comprised agriculture, *rhetoric, military science, philosophy, and jurisprudence. The section on philosophy apparently was mainly *doxographic in nature.

The extensive proemium to *De Medicina* 1–8 is of considerable philosophical interest because, in the context of outlining the history of medicine from *Homer to his own day, Celsus offers the first extant account of the controversy between the Hellenistic Empiricist school of medicine and the Rationalists (see MEDICINE, Ancient Theories of). Celsus claims that the "Rationalists" (a doxographic label of polemical convenience under which the Empiricists lumped together their methodological adversaries) posit knowledge of four things as necessary: (i) hidden causes of diseases (which entail knowledge of the constitutive principles of the body in health and in disease), (ii) evident causes (e.g., heat and cold, hunger and surfeit), (iii) natural actions (physiology: respiration, digestion, pulse), and (iv) internal parts (anatomy, "best" learned through human dissection and vivisection; see HEROPHILUS, ERASISTRATUS). However, none of the physicians explicitly introduced by Celsus as Rationalists (*Hippocrates, *Herophilus, *Erasistratus, Asclepiades of Bithynia, Plistonicus, Praxagoras) characterized his own theory in these terms; and each advocated methodological, epistemological, and medical theories that differed sharply from those of other Rationalists. It therefore is likely that Celsus' reductive, schematic characterization of "Rationalism" is drawn from a polemical Empiricist source.

The Empiricists, unlike the so-called "Rationalists," from the beginning (3rd cent. B.C.E.) gave themselves their own school label, according to Celsus; they thus represent the first ancient "school" to take its name from its guiding methodological principle. The Empiricists, he claims, accept "evident causes" as necessary but reject the Rationalists' other three "necessities" on the grounds that neither nature nor nonevident causes can be comprehended. Celsus' Empiricists argue that the medical *ars* first developed through experience and that *experientia* should continue to be its lodestar; causal knowledge in the form of physiology and pathology is of no practical use to the physician, and anatomical exploration is not only unnecessary but also misleading, because dissection induces changes in the body under investigation; furthermore, vivisection is unacceptably cruel.

Celsus offers a critique of both Rationalism and Empiricism (proem. 45–75), positioning himself as one who can steer an intermediate, moderate, non-partisan Roman course between two divergent Greek views, without blindly favoring or disfavoring either. Each, he suggests, is partly right and partly wrong. For the contradictory truths claimed by the two opposing "schools" he substitutes his characterization of medicine as an incomplete stochastic craft (*ars coniecturalis*) that relies on approximations to the truth (*proxima vero*). His opening projection of authorial evenhandedness and of Roman reasonableness masks a significantly greater explicit engagement, both sympathetic and polemical, with Rationalist theories and practices in Books 1–8 than with those of individual Empiricists. Celsus admittedly has frequent justificatory recourse to "experience" (*experimentum, experientia, usus*), but so do almost all Rationalists, too.

The medical theories and practices described by Celsus comprise regimen (Bk. 1); pathology and general therapeutics, including therapeutic regimen (Bk. 2); special therapeutics of diseases that affect the entire body (Bk. 3) and particular parts of the body (Bk. 4); pharmacology (Bks. 5–6); and surgery (Bks. 7–8). Despite his sympathetic allusions to Roman folk medicine, Celsus draws most of his information from Greek sources, for example, from Hippocratics (particularly in Books 2 and 8), Asclepiades of Bithynia (especially in Bks. 2–4), Erasistratus (3–6), and Alexandrian surgical sources (7–8). Scattered throughout these books are numerous references to anatomical, physiological, and pathological differences between the female and male bodies, to diseases never previously described in Latin, and to healing practices. Among the numerous operations described by Celsus are one for cataract and several for reversing circumcision and similar conditions. Celsus' contribution to the constitution of a scientific Latin language is significant, although he often uses Greek words, loan words, and calques and, like *Lucretius, deplores the poverty of the Latin language.

Paradoxically Celsus, the first Roman to give a systematic account of professional scientific medicine, depicts it as a product of post-Homeric decadence: Medicine was necessitated by the indolence and luxury that vitiated the bodies first of Greeks and then of Romans. In a more pristine age, the complexity of scientific medicine neither existed nor was necessary. Celsus' elegant, circumspect, and richly detailed scientific work remains an invaluable source, especially concerning Hellenistic medicine from the late fourth century B.C.E. to the founding of the Methodist school of medicine in the early first century C.E.

Texts in F. Marx, ed., *A. Cornelii Celsi quae supersunt*, Leipzig/Berlin, 1915. Sabbah, G., and P. Mudry, eds., *La médecine de Celse* (Centre Jean-Palerne, Mémoires 13), Saint-Étienne, 1994; Mudry, P., *La Préface du De medicina de Celse*, Lausanne, 1982.—*HEINRICH VON STADEN*

CHALDEAN ORACLES. The *Chaldean Oracles* are a collection of fragmentary hexameter verses attributed to Julian the Theurgist (fl. late 2nd cent. C.E.). His father, Julian the Chaldean, may also have had a hand in the collection and transmission of the *Oracles*. They reveal the clear influence of *Middle Platonist thought and were considered to be authoritative sources of revelation by later *Neoplatonists. *Porphyry, *Iamblichus, and *Proclus all wrote commentaries, now lost, on the *Oracles*. The surviving fragments are largely quotations from Neoplatonist philosophers.

The *Oracles* describe in part a system of "theurgy," a ritualistic method of communicating with the gods and procuring their activity in the material world (as opposed to "theology," speculation about the gods). Though not strictly philosophical, the theurgic aspect of the *Oracles* is buttressed by the view, derived from an amalgam of *Stoicism and *Platonism, that the various parts of the sensible world are connected via *sympatheia* to one another and to the noetic realm.

The Platonism of the *Oracles* bears similarities to the system of *Numenius, a contemporary of the younger Julian. It distinguishes first and second intellects, the former of which is also referred to as "Father," is transcendent, and is removed from concern with creation. The second, the demiurgic intellect, is a dyadic entity and has the functions of contemplating the Father's ideas and of projecting them into the material world. The material manifestation of the ideas is mediated by a third, feminine, principle, which is identified with the goddess Hecate and functions as the World Soul. Hecate may also be identified with "Power" (*Dunamis*), a principle intermediate between the two intellects, in which case it would be best to understand her as a principle whose function is to mediate generally between levels of being. The material world itself is viewed as a contaminating hindrance to the soul's communion with god. Like other Platonism-influenced religions of the time, such as *Gnosticism and *Hermeticism, the *Oracles* promise salvation to those who follow its prescriptions.

BIBLIOGRAPHY: Texts in R. Majercik, *The Chaldean Oracles: Text, Translation, and Commentary*, Leiden, 1989. Dillon, J., *The Middle Platonists*, London/Ithaca, NY, 1977.—*JOSEPH G. DeFILIPPO*

CHANGE, The Problem of. A recurring problem in Greek philosophy is a debate concerning whether change is possible and, if so, how it is and what kind of change can occur. The fact of change was at first taken for granted. Although the earliest Presocratics have nothing to say about change per se, they do assume the existence of change. The early Ionian philosophers focus on cosmogony and generate the cosmos out of some original substance or *arch*ê such as air, which is transformed into all other substances. Further developments seem to arise out of reflections on *cosmological change.

Change begins to emerge as an explicit problem with *Heraclitus, who is known to later Greek tradition for the saying that you cannot step into the same river twice (Pl. *Cra.* 402a) and who, by making the *archê* to be fire—the most unsubstantial and changeable of substances—seems to be claiming that all things are in flux. Unfortunately for the tradition, Heraclitus' "saying" is an interpretation of a passage that asserts something less than universal flux: "Upon those stepping into the same rivers flow other and other waters" (DK22B12). But even if he does not say that everything is changing all of the time, Heraclitus does in the end make change a fundamental fact without which there would be no ordered world, no cosmos: Change makes possible continuity as the flowing waters constitute the river.

The great challenge to the reality of change came from *Parmenides of Elea (founder of the *Eleatic "school"), writing possibly in reaction to Heraclitus. In the first sustained argument in Western philosophy, Parmenides argues that coming-to-be and perishing are impossible because they presuppose a change from what-is-not to what-is, and what-is-not cannot be thought or expressed. But change of place presupposes coming-to-be, and hence it must be ruled out as well. Indeed, all forms of change—coming-to-be and perishing, change of place, and qualitative change—are notions imposed on reality by mortals (DK28B8.38–41: the first implicit typology of changes). What-is must be completely changeless.

Later cosmologists generally accepted Parmenides' principle that what-is cannot come from what-is-not and accordingly ruled out coming-to-be and perishing, and with them the possibility that one substance is transformed into other substances. But, without arguing against Parmenides' criticisms of other kinds of motion, these "Pluralists" built models of change on the basis of rearrangements of a plurality of beings, each of which is changeless. For instance, *Empedocles recognized the four elements—earth, water, air, and fire—as unchanging substances that could combine in different ratios to form all other material substances such as bone and blood.

But Eleatic philosophers continued to argue against motion. *Zeno of Elea developed paradoxes associated with motion, some based on the impossibility of completing an *infinite series of stages. *Melissus argued that even if one says a new *rearrangement* comes to be, one violates the stricture against allowing what-is to come from what-is-not (DK30B7)—a criticism that strikes directly at the kind of strategy used by Empedocles.

Early atomists *Leucippus and *Democritus seemed to reject the foundations of Eleatic arguments by positing not only beings—the atoms—but also not-being—the *void—in which the atoms must move. Although the atomists developed an ingenious model, it is not clear how they avoid begging the question against their Eleatic opponents. The Eleatic challenge to motion had not been answered in a philosophical way, while theoretical attacks on motion had grown ever more damaging. It was left to *Plato and *Aristotle to use the techniques of a more sophisticated age to answer the challenge.

Plato provided an important insight into change when he suggested in the *Phaedo* that all change was from contrary to contrary (70d–71b), later adding as an afterthought that there was some subject that changed (103a–b). For Plato, however, the problem seemed not so much how to account for change as how to account for constancy and order in a world of flux. He sees reality as divided into a world of becoming populated by changeable, sensible objects and a world of being populated by changeless Forms.

Although Plato first distinguishes between alteration and locomotion in the *Theaetetus* (181c–d), his pronouncements on motion remain largely ad hoc until he discusses the highest kinds of Forms in the *Sophist*. Determining that reality must consist of both motion and rest (248–49), he includes Motion and Rest among the highest kinds, with Sameness, Difference, and Being. By blending with each other these kinds make discourse (and, presumably, the sensible world itself) possible. On this account we can see how something can be and not be in different senses, and hence we can answer the Eleatic challenge. Unfortunately, to make motion into a Form seems to preclude any internal analysis.

In the *Timaeus* Plato explores the conditions of coming-to-be in the cosmos. It is an observable fact that the elements change into one another. But if something is always changing, how can we identify it? If someone were constantly modeling shapes in gold, one could best say that the things were gold. In the original cosmos there must have been a receptacle in which random qualities appeared, which were reduced to order by the imposition of shape (*Tim.* 49–53). Here Plato comes close to a notion of *matter, but mixes his metaphors: the ground of change is like plastic matter, a womb, an apothecary's medium, a winnowing-fan, space—suggesting inconsistent properties. In the end Plato's account of change amounts to less than a coherent theory, providing not even a general description of change.

Beginning from Plato's distinctions, Aristotle goes beyond his master's analysis. His *Categories* rather unhelpfully classifies concepts expressed by action verbs as positions, states, actions, and passions (ch. 4). But is there some internal structure to changes? To treat change as a category suggests there is not. In *Physics* 1, however, Aristotle is led to analyze change as a diachronic phenomenon. Addressing the Eleatic challenge to say how what-is can come from what-is-not, Aristotle draws on the Plato's hints in the *Phaedo*: change is exchange by a subject of contrary properties. But in order to accommodate all species of change, Aristotle must broaden the scope of the analysis: In change the subject partakes in succession of *opposite* characters in the broadest sense. Not only does alteration consist of a subject being successively, for example, light and dark (having contrary qualities), but coming-to-be consists of a subject being successively, for example, not-man and man (going from a state of privation to possession). The three terms that must be present in a change, then, are a subject and two opposite predicates. A *metaphysical problem arises in this context: What is the subject that can go from being not-man to man, from being not-substance to substance? By analogy with the change of, for example, bronze into a statue, we can call the missing subject *matter* and the configuration it acquires the *form*. Viewed diachronically, matter goes from a state of privation to a state of being informed; viewed synchronically, substance is constituted of matter and form.

One feature is missing from this analysis: Since form is ontologically simple, its instantiation in matter would seem to be an all-or-nothing affair. Aristotle must introduce some new dimension to account for the gradual exemplification of form in matter in a stepwise development of the sort we observe in nature as, for example, an acorn becomes an oak tree. To meet this need he provides the theory of actuality and potentiality presupposing a continuous scale of exemplification. The acorn is potentially an oak; it becomes actually an oak as the form becomes increasingly exemplified in the matter.

Assuming that motion, not rest, requires explanation, Aristotle distinguishes between natural motion, which derives from a source in a natural body (*Phys.* 2.1), and forced motion. He later argues that every body in motion must be moved by something, and hence even natural motion presupposes an external mover. To avoid an infinite regress, we must posit a first unmoved mover for cosmic motion (*Phys.* 8), which Aristotle identifies with god (*Met.* 12). Thus physics, cosmology, and *theology are united in a transcendent final cause.

After Aristotle there was little further conceptual development in the understanding of change. Zeno's arguments against motion seem to have inspired *Diodorus Cronus to theorize that a body can *have* moved without ever *being* in motion (S.E. *M* 10.85ff.), a view that may have influenced *Epicureans, while the *Stoics were still operating with what was essentially an Aristotelian concept of change and motion (*SVF* 2.492 ff.).

BIBLIOGRAPHY: Furley, D., *Cosmic Problems*, Cambridge, 1989; Sorabji, R., *Matter, Space and Motion*, Ithaca, 1988; Waterlow, S., *Nature, Change, and Agency in Aristotle's Physics*, Oxford, 1982.—*DANIEL W. GRAHAM*

CHRISTIANITY. The Christian religion is founded upon the confessional claims that God, the creator of heaven and earth, has called humankind to inhabit the earth and to serve him; that when humanity had transgressed the divine command and fallen into sin, God entered into a covenant with Abraham, in order that the nation Israel might be a model and blessing to all of humankind; and that this covenant came to fulfillment in the life, death, and resurrection of Jesus of Nazareth, the Son of God, Messiah, and Redeemer. Christianity's doctrinal basis is to be found in the Pentateuch and in the other Old Testament writings, as well as in the written records of the life of Jesus in the Gospels of *Matthew, Mark, Luke* and *John* and the remaining books of the New Testament. The *Acts of the Apostles* recounts how, soon after Jesus' crucifixion, faith in his messianic mission spread outside the borders of Palestine, to Syria, Asia Minor, Greece, and Italy. The propagation of the Christian faith in the Hellenistic world relied heavily upon the Greek language. The church's familiarity with the Jewish tradition derived from the Greek translation of the Old Testament (the Septuagint), which originated in Alexandria in Egypt in the third to second century B.C.E.

The encounter with Hellenistic culture had far-reaching consequences for the Christian faith. Greek philosophy came to exercise an increasingly stronger influence on Christian theology as it developed. Initially, however, the church regarded its faith as radically opposed to every human doctrine or world view: The Pauline epistles posit a sharp contrast between God's salvation revealed in Jesus and "the wisdom of the world" (cf. *I Corinthians* 1.18–25; 2.6–9; *Colossians* 2.6–15).

Many interpreters have attempted to identify Hellenistic influences in the New Testament documents. The prologue to the *Gospel of John*, for example, is often said to bear the stamp of the *Stoic *logos* doctrine. And *Romans* 1.20 is often cited as teaching a natural knowledge of God. Nevertheless, careful study supports the conclusion that, apart from individual contacts in detail, the basic framework of New Testament thought is different from that of *Platonism and Stoicism (see Chadwick, p. 159). Prior to *Clement of Alexandria (c. 150–215 C.E.), Christians, except for Justin and Athenagoras, had little to do with philosophy. Even these two had virtually nothing to contribute to the *rapprochement* of Christianity with classical philosophy. The prevailing attitude among Christians was one of suspicion and antagonism (see Osborn, 1957, p. 122). That suspicion was strongly fueled by Paul's criticism of the "wisdom of the world." Clement was the first to argue that Paul was taking aim, not at philosophies that direct and encourage human beings toward a realm of transcendent, spiritual realities, but at philosophies that denied transcendence, such as *Epicurean materialism (*Miscellanies* 1.11.50.1–51.3; 6.8.67.2; cf. also Augustine *Against the Academics* 3.42). Clement argued further that one cannot do battle against that which one does not know.

The central figures in the encounter of Christianity with Greek philosophy are (i) the Apologists (2nd cent.), who strove to make the Christian faith socially and culturally acceptable (Justin Martyr, Athenagoras, Tatian); (ii) the Alexandrian School (Clement, *Origen, Athanasius); and (iii) the Cappadocians (Basil of Caesarea, his brother Gregory of Nyssa, and the latter's namesake, Gregory of Nazianzus). Of considerable influence in the Middle Ages were (iv) a body of writings under the name of *Dionysius the Areopagite. Finally (v) in Italy and Africa, Tertullian, Ambrose, bishop of Milan, and especially *Augustine, bishop of Hippo, contributed much to the encounter. Preceding all of these, however, was the Jewish theologian-philosopher *Philo of Alexandria (c. 15 B.C.E.–40 C.E.), who exercised a decisive influence on the development of Christian thought. Any account of the Christian encounter with classical thought must begin with him.

Philo is credited with being the source of the view that philosophy is the "handmaiden of Scripture." For Philo, the books of Moses were absolutely authoritative: Moses had himself been instructed by God. Moses had, however, immersed himself in philosophy while in Pharaoh's court (*On the Creation of the World* 8), and so is an exponent of the tradition of "true wisdom," of which Plato may be regarded as a later representative. Accordingly, Philo exegetes the Mosaic texts as having sublime philosophical content, even those texts where one should least suspect it. In this he is served by the methods of allegorical interpretation, a common Greek approach to the works of *Homer and *Hesiod from the sixth century B.C.E. onwards (see ALLEGORY, Classical).

The application of such spiritualizing, allegorizing exegesis of Scripture led to a dehistoricizing of the biblical texts; these texts now came to be viewed as symbolic representations of abstract philosophical themes. Thus the patriarch Abraham symbolizes the soul in search of truth, his wife Sarah represents virtue, and his slave and concubine Hagar represents "encyclic learning." Philo maintained that the texts themselves indicate the necessity or desirability of allegorical interpretation, for example, in cases where the literal text contains something "inappropriate," or in conflict with other texts. Such allegorizing paved the way for Christian writers from Origen onwards to read *Exodus* 11.2–3 and 12.35–6, passages that describe "the plundering of the Egyptians," as warrant for a positive assessment of the intellectual legacy of pagan antiquity (cf. Augustine *On Christian Doctrine* 2.60).

The Apologists of the second century endeavored to remove the reputation of criminal and antisocial conduct with which outsiders had stigmatized the Christian church. In his *Dialogue with Trypho the Jew* (c. 135), Justin Martyr presents an elaborate discussion of the differences of viewpoints between Christians and Jews.

It was Clement of Alexandria who inaugurated a tradition that sought to position Christianity positively as a rationally acceptable and intellectually responsible world view. He further introduced a distinction between "simple believers," who are unable to plumb the philosophical depths of the faith, and the *gnôstikoi*, who attain to rational understanding of the truth of the faith. He maintained that this deeper knowledge is communicated, not by the scriptural texts themselves, but by means of an ancient and still surviving secret oral tradition. Similarly, Origen and Augustine maintained that though the Scriptures constitute the sole basis for church doctrine, God nevertheless instructs the faithful through them at different levels. They, too, held that the level of faith that has arrived at rational understanding is more desirable than a faith based merely on authority. Thus theology came gradually to attain the status of "the Queen of faith."

For their part, pagan authors never acknowledged the claim made by Jewish and Christian writers to rationality or to a rational, even primitive wisdom. While Greek philosophy strongly influenced Philo and the Christian tradition, there has never been any question of influence in the reverse direction. Despite the fact that Philo is the earliest known author to have taught that the eternal Ideas are the thoughts of the divine *Logos*, that is, divine Reason—a doctrine that gained prominence in *Middle Platonism and *Neoplatonism—modern scholarship has presumed that he depended on an earlier pagan thinker unknown to us. The same holds for "negative theology," also encountered in Philo's writings; it has been argued that here Philo followed earlier thinkers within Middle Platonism, such as *Eudorus.

Celsus, a second-century Platonist, wrote a polemical tract, *True Wisdom*, in which he denounced Judaism as a perversion of Egyptian wisdom, and Christianity as a distortion of Jewish tradition. He cites numerous biblical passages and is extremely well informed about the early Christian church. Around 270, the Neoplatonist *Porphyry wrote a comprehensive work in fifteen books entitled *Against the Christians*. His teacher *Plotinus (204–269) very likely included Christians within the sweep of his grim criticism of the *Gnostics. And the Roman emperor Julian the Apostate wrote in 362/3 the three books of his *Against the Galileans*, likewise a work of Platonic inspiration.

Nevertheless, Jewish and Christian writers expressed high admiration for the products of the Greek philosophers, even if they generally avoided citing them specifically. Their appreciation was, however, selective. They scorned the materialism and hedonism of Epicureanism in abusive terms. They admired Stoicism for its lofty ethical ideals, but criticized its rejection of a transcendent reality. *Aristotelianism, they felt, failed in that it deprived the highest God of the honor due him as creator, and overvalued the "external goods." They rejected the doubt and *skepticism of the New *Academy. But for Philo and for virtually all Christian writers until the thirteenth century, Plato himself remained the exponent of the most perfect philosophy. Many of them were convinced that Plato had become acquainted with the Hebrew prophets or their writings during his sojourn in Egypt (cf. Philo *On the Eternity of the World* 3–20; Justin Martyr *Dialogue* 2.1–6; Augustine *Ag. Acad.* 2.37–43).

Augustine's conversion to Christianity, as related in *On the Blessed Life* and *Confessions*, was assisted in good measure by his recent acquaintance with Neoplatonic philosophy and Ambrose's Platonizing biblical exegesis. Had Plato lived in the fourth century C.E., he doubtlessly would have concluded—so Augustine reasoned—that his philosophical ideals were realized in the Christian church. The books of the Platonists contain many doctrines that, with only minor corrections, would be entirely acceptable to Christians. Augustine accounted for the fact that many Neoplatonist philosophers did not follow him in embracing the Christian faith by attributing that failure to their pride and conceit, their refusal to follow the example of humility given by Christ, who had laid aside his divine glory to become a man. Thus Plotinus and his students remained behind: The promised land lay within their sight, but the way of approach remained unknown to them.

This admiration for Platonic philosophy also led the way to an acceptance of Greek ontology. Although it has been claimed that Christian ontology derives entirely from original and creative reflection on God's self-revelation in *Exodus* 3.14 ("I AM [who I am]") culminating in a full-fledged "Exodus metaphysic," the evidence indicates that the Christian tradition took over the ontology of the Greeks by way of Philo. Some have claimed that the Christian/Platonic conception of God is implicitly present in the Old Testament. The suggestion, however, that a text like *Exodus* 3.14 can be utilized as basis for an ontology has generally not found favor with modern biblical scholarship.

This reliance on Greek ontology created problems for Christian thought. The Middle Platonists identified true *being with a universal, highest Intellect, that is, God, and the Platonic Ideas with the content of a lower demiurgical Intellect or Reason. But if God transcends the objects of thought, can he be known? And how can a divine thinking subject bring about the existence of concrete, material, perishable entities? Hence Jewish and Christian thinkers influenced by Middle Platonism had difficulty maintaining the doctrine of divine immutability in their accounts of the creation of the world and not compromising divine omnipotence and self-sufficiency in their discussion of a material principle. Philo "resolves" this tension by distinguishing between an absolutely transcendent and unknowable divine Intellect and the *Logos* that it brings forth, a creative power that comprehends within it all the eternal Ideas. Augustine for his part identifies the second person of the divine Trinity as the "Wisdom of God," who contains all the Ideas and who "illumines" the formless obscurity of matter into formed material objects. He takes pains to emphasize, however, that even this formless matter is a divine creation, brought forth as "almost nothing," "from nothing" (cf. *Confessions* 12).

The acceptance of a Platonic ontology had direct implications for Jewish and Christian anthropology and epistemology. Within human beings also, the distinction between a concrete, material, and perishable body and an immaterial and nonperishable soul is to be found. The vast differences of meaning between the Old Testament Hebrew *nephesh* and the Greek *psuchê* (its Septuagint translation) were completely overlooked, and the meaning of the Pauline distinction between "spirit" and "flesh" was entirely perverted. Tertullian's view of the soul's materiality is a notable exception. Augustine professes amazement at the notion that two entities of such different natures are combined within a single individual human being, a notion he finds incredible, "were it not a fact of everyday experience." After Philo (*Creation* 69), the doctrine of the "image of God" (*Genesis* 1.26–27) was understood to mean that a human being resembles God by virtue of his *logos*, the rational part of his immortal soul.

In order to come to know the divine, eternal order of being—so Christian thinkers, following their pagan Platonic predecessors, held— the soul must turn away from sensible reality. Although some influence of Plato's doctrine of Recollection can still be traced, most later Platonists, holding with Aristotle's criticism of that doctrine, preferred to speak of an "awakening" of reason or intelligence, beginning with the study of the auxiliary disciplines (*enkuklios paideia*; subsequently *artes liberales*), followed by the study of the visible cosmos, to ascend, by means of the knowledge of the order and the Ideas manifested within it, to the divine, transcendent reality of the Ideas themselves.

Contemporary assessments of the meaning of the Christian faith for the philosophical tradition are rather divergent, depending on the religious or philosophical presuppositions of the investigator. Thus the French historian E. Bréhier has claimed that throughout the entire patristic and medieval period there was no such thing as philosophy proper, given that all writers of the period were governed by the postulates of their various faiths. H. A. Wolfson, on the other hand, has argued that the Jewish writer Philo of Alexandria inaugurated a whole new philosophical tradition, one which held sway until Spinoza. In this tradition, philosophy is but a product of fallible human reason, which must be subjected to, tested against, and purified by the various foundational principles revealed by God to humankind in the Holy Scriptures. And although E. Gilson drew a sharp distinction between philosophy and theology, he nevertheless agreed that one can properly speak of a "Christian philosophy," in the sense of a philosophy that acknowledges the Christian revelation as an indispensable aid to philosophy. In such a Christian philosophy, God's glory and might find expression in a philosophy of Being and the activity of Being.

Much discussion has been devoted to the topic of the "Hellenization" of the church. A. von Harnack has represented this process as one that has enriched the Christian tradition and extended its reach. Many others, such as W. Pannenberg, following the lead of K. Barth, have lamented it as a dangerous corruption that has infected the very essence of the Christian faith. Verdicts about "Christian Platonism" have been equally diverse. C. J. De Vogel (1985) has represented the Christian faith as the fulfillment and perfection of Platonism, while H. Dörrie has argued that all Christian authors were fundamentally anti-Platonists who repudiated such Platonic dogmas as gradations within the divine, the eternity of the world, the tradition of an unchanged and eternal *Logos*, the transmigration of the soul, and the idea of the salvation of the soul through philosophy. Even granted this, however, Dörrie may still be faulted for failing to recognize the important and decisive significance of their acceptance of an essentially Platonic ontology, with its division between an intelligible and a material reality.

The dialogue between the Christian church and the Greek philosophical tradition came to a climax in the writings of Augustine and of ps.-Dionysius. In the period that followed, direct acquaintance with the sources of Greek philosophy would remain very limited until the thirteenth century. That century saw the rise of the universities, the considerable influx of texts from Byzantium, and in particular the rediscovery of the works of Aristotle. By studying and commenting on the works of Aristotle, Albert the Great and Thomas Aquinas gave new life to the dialogue. A major development in this phase of the encounter is the imposition of a territorial boundary between the realm of human (natural) reason and (supernatural) faith—related, however, in such a way that natural reason was said to be adapted to the truth, which can be fully known only by faith.

BIBLIOGRAPHY: Armstrong, A. H and R. A. Markus, *Christian Faith and Greek Philosophy*, London, 1960; Armstrong, A. H, ed., *The Cambridge History of Later Greek and Early Medieval Philosophy*, Cambridge, 1967; Bréhier, E., *Histoire de la philoso-*

phie, vol. 1, Paris, 1927, 493–4; also *Revue de métaphysique et de morale*, 1931, 133–162; Chadwick, H., "Philo and the Beginnings of Christian Thought," in Armstrong, ed., *Cambridge History*, 1967, 131–192; de Vogel, C. J., *Vigiliae Christianae* 39, 1985, 1–62; also "Antike Seinsphilosophie und Christentum im Wandel der Jahrhunderte," in *Festgabe für J. Lortz*, Baden-Baden, 1957, 527–548 (also publ. sep., Baden-Baden, 1958); Dörrie, H., *Theologische Rundschau* 36, 1971, 285–302; Gilson, E., *Being and Some Philosophers*, Toronto, 1952; also *The Spirit of Medieval Philosophy* (tr. A. H. C. Downes), New York, 1940; Harnack, A. von, *History of Dogma*, vol. 1 (tr. N. Buchanan), New York, 1961; Koch, H., *Pronoia und Paideusis; Studien über Origenes und sein Verhältnis zum Platonismus*, Berlin, 1932; Lilla, S. R. C., *Clement of Alexandria. A Study in Christian Platonism and Gnosticism*, London, 1971; Osborn, E. F., *The Beginning of Christian Philosophy*, Cambridge, 1981; also *The Philosophy of Clement of Alexandria*, Cambridge, 1957; Pannenberg, W., *Zeitschrift für Kirchengeschichte* 70, 1959, 1–45; Pelikan, J., *Christianity and Classical Culture*, New Haven, 1993; Runia, D. T., *Philo in Early Christian Literature: A Survey*, Assen, 1993; von Ivanka, E., *Plato Christianus: Übernahme und Umgestaltung des Platonismus durch die Väter*, Einsiedeln, 1964; Wolfson, H. A., *The Philosophy of the Church Fathers: Faith, Trinity, Incarnation,*[3] Cambridge, MA, 1970; also *Philo: Foundations of Religious Philosophy in Judaism, Christianity and Islam*, 2 vols., Cambridge, MA, 1947.—*ABRAHAM P. BOS*

CHRYSIPPUS (280/76–208/4 B.C.E.), of Soli in Cilicia. Third head of the *Stoic school (from 230/29). Chrysippus made most of his original contributions in *logic, providing Stoic philosophy with a firm foundation and structure. He thus played a crucial role in the school's history: "Without Chrysippus there would have been no Stoa" (D.L. 7.183). But he can also be credited with important advances in *psychology and other fields. Elaborating doctrines inherited from *Zeno of Citium and *Cleanthes, Chrysippus gave them their canonical form.

Presumably of Phoenician origin, Chrysippus moved to Athens as a young man and became a student of Cleanthes. *Diogenes Laertius portrays him as Cleanthes' star pupil, who outshone his teacher in *dialectical competence. While the latter was still alive, Chrysippus started lecturing outside the Stoic school. He also studied with *Arcesilaus and *Lacydes in the *Academy, which explains why he argued both for and against common experience and used the Academic method in dealing with magnitudes and numbers (D.L. 7.183f.). We need not assume that Chrysippus actually defected from the Stoa and was at one time an adherent of the *skeptical Academy. Diogenes attests to the recognition of systematic affinities between the Academy and Chrysippus. He represents Chrysippus' formative period as one of linear development, completed by his time with the Academics. Because of his knowledge of Academic dialectic, Chrysippus became the "cleaver of the Academic knots" (Plut. *SR* 1033e). As head of the Stoa, he devoted himself to lecturing and writing. He did not participate in politics, carefully avoiding association with any of the Hellenistic kings. Like his predecessors, he was highly regarded by the Athenian public.

Writings. Chrysippus was known for his prodigious literary output (D.L. 7.180–1). Diogenes Laertius gives a total of 705 books and appends a catalogue of titles, which has not been preserved in full (D.L. 7.189–202). Of its three main divisions (*logic, *ethics, and physics) only the logical part is very nearly complete, listing 119 titles in three hundred books. The ethics section breaks off after forty-two titles, and the physics section is lacking. But the number of books in the logical section lends credibility to the recorded total of 705 (cf. *Vita Persii*, p. 33, 1.38–9 Clausen). To the titles of the catalogue others can be added, raising their number to about 217. Particularly striking are the number and specificity of titles concerned with formal logic placed at the beginning of the catalogue. The catalogue may be taken to reflect Chrysippus' own ordering of philosophical topics.

In the first two centuries C.E., Chrysippus' treatises were still read and commented upon. Unfortunately, this did not guarantee their survival. But his status as the paragon of Stoicism made him the favorite target of polemicists like *Plutarch and *Galen, who quote several hundred Chrysippean passages as proof-texts for their criticisms. Yet the material thus preserved is not sufficient to restore any one or more treatises in whole or in part—except for a part of *On the Soul* in which Chrysippus demonstrates that the *mind resides in the heart (*SVF* 2, 879–911). A balanced reconstruction of his philosophy cannot rest on the verbatim fragments alone, but involves many indirect testimonies from a variety of sources.

Logic. In antiquity Chrysippus was considered a logician of exceptional genius. He was regarded as the Stoic who had elaborated a new, propositional logic to compete with *Aristotelian categorical syllogistic. Indeed, Stoic logic as presented by our sources is largely Chrysippean. His logic divides into two main parts, dialectic and *rhetoric. Dialectic is a complex field, involving techniques familiar from the *Platonic and Aristotelian traditions but also encompassing formal logic. To define its subject-matter, Chrysippus laid down an original theory of meaning. Meanings are technically called "sayables" (*lekta*), to be distinguished from both the corporeal entities to which they refer and from speech in its phonetic aspect. "Complete sayables" standardly consist of a subject and a predicate and come in various modes, such as questions, oaths, propositions (*axiômata*). Propositions are the subject of formal logic. They are the bearers of truth and falsity and the components of complex statements and arguments. Chrysippus laid down five "undemonstrables," that is, basic hypothetical, disjunctive, and conjunctive syllogisms, to which all other arguments can be reduced. To aid this analysis, he specified a set of at least four "ground-rules" (*themata*). Further, he explored the validity and truth-conditions of arguments. A syllogism can be treated as a conditional sentence, its two premises being the antecedent and its conclusion the consequent. If the contradictory of the consequent conflicts with the antecedent, the conditional is true (the criterion of "cohesion"). A proof is an argument with pre-evident premises and a non-evident conclusion. It formally articulates what was generally called a demonstrative "sign" (*sêmeion*). Chrysippus also considered sign-inference from the aspect of modality. One of his arguments was directed against *Diodorus Cronus' thesis that something impossible cannot follow from something possible.

Epistemology. A true proposition corresponds to the actual state of affairs in the world to which it refers. Correct evidence about existing things is conveyed to us through a cognitive presentation (*kataleptikê phantasia*). Rejecting Cleanthes' cruder explanation, Chrysippus understood the imprinting made by a presentation (according to Zeno's definition) as a qualitative change in the soul comparable with air struck by sound. He accepted the Zenonian cognitive presentation as the criterion of truth, but added sense-perception (*aisthêsis*) and preconception (*prolêpsis*). Preconceptions are general conceptions that arise naturally, though they are not innate. They are identical or congeneric with "natural" or "common notions" (*phusikai* or *koinai ennoiai*). Chrysippus claimed that the Stoic doctrines were based on common notions, such as the existence and providence of God. By means of logic, the philosopher articulates and orders these conceptions. Both coherence and correspondence as aspects of the Stoic conception of truth are relevant in this connection. The statements belonging to these presentations can thus be tested as to their truth-value. The value assigned to common notions ultimately rests on the dogma of divine providence: Even though much can, and does, go wrong in mental development, man is naturally capable of discovering truths.

Language. Chrysippus took a more nuanced view of the natural relationship of language to things than his predecessors did. While subscribing to the natural origins of language, he acknowledged its having changed in the course of time. Drawing attention to ambiguity and linguistic anomaly, he argued that between many words and their referents no one-to-one correspondence obtains. But it remains possible to reverse, through etymological derivation, the process of degeneration and uncover the true meanings and interrelations of words. The analysis of ordinary language is connected with that of common notions. Both sources furnish the raw conceptual material from which the procedure of "articulation" proceeds.

Ontology. Chrysippus regarded power to act and be acted upon as the criterion for existence or *being—a test satisfied by bodies alone. The so-called "sayables," *time, place and the *void, are incorporeal and do not share in being; they only "subsist" (*huphistasthai*) for the mind. Both corporeal and incorporeal entities are subsumed under the higher genus of the "something" (*ti*). Universals count as "quasi-somethings," lacking the specificity that marks both existing and subsisting things. They are concepts (*ennoêmata*), that is, mere figments of the mind suitable for classifying reality. In order to describe the two Stoic principles (*pneuma* and matter) and their interrelations, Chrysippus formulated the theory of four so-called genera, also called the Stoic categories: (i) substrate (or substance); (ii) qualified (further analyzed as individuating quality and common quality); (iii) disposition; and (iv) relative disposition.

*Ethical and *Political Thought.* Accepting Zeno's dictum that the goal of life consists in following nature, Chrysippus explained "nature" as pertaining to both common (i.e., cosmic) and individual nature, which are related to one another as the whole to the part. Man has to bring his nature into harmony with cosmic Nature or God. This completes a process of psycho-moral development, which starts from the first natural impulse towards self-preservation and may eventually culminate in one's choice of virtue as desirable to the highest degree. This process of "familiarization" (*oikeiôsis*) turns on one's recognition of certain things and people as belonging to oneself and a concomitant affinity with them: In accordance with his developing nature, man bestows value on things, pursuing some and avoiding others—an increasingly social and rational pattern of behavior. Like Zeno, Chrysippus regarded the external and bodily objects of our natural impulses as indifferent from a strictly moral point of view, confining "good" in its strict sense to virtue and "bad" to the passions (*pathê*). He formulated a highly sophisticated analysis of passions, explaining the various factors involved but stressing their nature as faulty value judgments. In political theory, he abandoned the classical ideal state mould, setting Zeno's vision of the city of sages and their community of property in the wider context of a *cosmic* city based on the natural law as a divine and moral principle common to gods and men alike.

Determinism. Chrysippus shares the cosmic optimism of his predecessors. We live in a providentially determined world of optimal and sensible design, devoid of caprice. In this context he explored the concept of causation. The cosmic *pneuma*, as the rational and active cause, constitutes the character of each individual thing, but also determines its environment. Thus the *pneuma* is both an internal and an external factor, the former being the "principal and perfect cause" and the latter the "auxiliary and proximate cause." In Chrysippus' analysis of a deliberate act, these two causes are represented by man's inner attitude and the external stimuli (namely, the impressions reaching his mind) respectively. Freedom resides in his mental state, that is, in his capacity to control his reactions to external stimuli. But the outcome of our actions is beyond our control, given the predetermined course of events. Thus moral evaluation and responsibility pertain to our intentions, our mental dispositions.

BIBLIOGRAPHY: Texts in *SVF* 2 and 3. Bréhier, E., *Chrysippe et l'ancien Stoïcisme*, Paris, 1951; Gould, J. B., *The Philosophy of Chrysippus*, Leiden, 1970; reviewed by A. A. Long, *CR* 23.2, 1973, 214–6; Pohlenz, M., in *Nachricht. der Akad. der Wiss. Göttingen*, phil.-hist. Kl. 1, 2.9, 1938, 173–210; Tieleman, T. L., *Galen and Chrysippus on the Soul: Argument and Refutation in the* De Placitis *Books II–III* (Philosophia Antiqua 68), Leiden, 1996—*TEUN L. TIELEMAN*

CICERO, Marcus Tullius (106–43 B.C.E.), of Arpinum and Rome. Cicero was a poet, a prodigious writer of letters, a politician, the greatest orator of his time, and the most important conveyor of Hellenistic Greek philosophy into Latin.

Cicero first encountered philosophy as a boy through lessons with *Phaedrus the *Epicurean. As a young man he heard *Philo of Larissa, at that time head of the *Academy, when he visited Rome in 87. Shortly thereafter, Diodotus the *Stoic came to live with his family, and Cicero received further training from him, especially in *dialectic. After marrying in 79, Cicero traveled east. He stayed for an extended period in Athens, at which time he heard the renegade Academic *Antiochus of Ascalon. Later in the same trip he visited Rhodes, where he studied *rhetoric with his old teacher Molon and encountered the *Platonizing Stoic *Posidonius.

Upon returning to Rome Cicero renewed his career as an advocate and politician with great success. The high point of his public career was his consulship, in 63, during which he delivered the famous *Catilinarian* speeches and played a key role in thwarting Catiline's conspiracy to seize power. He went into exile in 58 to avoid charges related to his handling of the Catilinarian conspirators. After sixteen months of exile he returned to Rome and resumed his public career. The next ten years saw the production of a trilogy on rhetorical and *political thought: *De Oratore, De Re Publica*, and *De Legibus*.

With the ascension of Julius Caesar and the fall of the Republic, Cicero withdrew from politics and began a period of impressive literary productivity. In 46 he composed *Paradoxae Stoicorum, Brutus, Orator*, and *Partitiones Oratoriae*. The next year he suffered a shattering blow when his daughter Tullia died in childbirth. Partly to console his grief, he devoted himself full-time to writing philosophy. Over the next two years he completed a series of works spanning most areas of recent philosophical debate: *Consolatio* (fragmentary), *Hortensius* (fragmentary), *Academica, De Finibus*, a translation of *Plato's *Timaeus, Tusculan Disputations, De Natura Deorum, De Divinatione, De Fato, Topica,* and *De Officiis.* After Caesar's assassination in 44, Cicero returned to politics and delivered his famous series of *Philippics* against Mark Antony. This activity led to his assassination on December 7, 43.

Cicero was hardly an original philosopher. He set himself the task of bringing Greek philosophical debates into the Latin language so that Romans could begin their own philosophical tradition. It would be going too far, however, to say that he intended only to record the views of the Greek schools in encyclopedic fashion. The works of 45–4 convey a coherent overall system, and Cicero displays modest originality (and great learning) in arranging the parts of this system, if not in the development of particular doctrines.

Epistemology and Method. In the works of 45–4, Cicero identifies himself as an adherent of the *skeptical phase of Plato's Academy that was initiated by *Arcesilaus and ended with Philo of Larissa (c. 275–80 B.C.E.). He examines the arguments for and against skepticism in *Academica,* which was published in two editions, commonly referred to as *Prior* and *Posterior,* each of which survives only in part.

Arcesilaus had revived and redirected the Academy by advancing, *contra* the Stoics, two complementary theses: (i) that there is no such thing as an impression that cannot be false (the Stoic "cognitive impression") and hence there is no certain criterion of truth and (ii) that we should suspend judgment about everything. His successor *Carneades widened the scope of (i) to include all dogmatic epistemologies, and refined (ii) by developing the idea of the "persuasive appearance" (Gk. *to pithanon,* Lat. *probabile*), which could form a reasonable basis for judgment and action without providing certainty. Carneades' successors debated whether he advanced the refinement of (ii) as his own doctrine or as a dialectical response to the Stoics. Cicero accepts the latter, more skeptical, interpretation, though he tends at times to treat the persuasive appearance dogmatically as a positive guide to life.

By the time of Cicero's main philosophical activity in 45–4 the Academy had been taken in a dogmatic direction by Antiochus of Ascalon, who accepted the possibility of the cognitive impression while simultaneously revising Stoic *ethics to make it more practical. In both these efforts he claimed to be restoring the original Academic tradition, of which he took Stoicism to be an offshoot. Cicero rejects Antiochus' dogmatizing reform of Academic *epistemology. In accord with his interpretation of Carneades, he adopts a method that requires open-minded argument on both sides of an issue and countenances the tentative acceptance of a view according to its persuasiveness and perceived verisimilitude. This stance has noticeably shaped the structure of the philosophical works of 45–4, most of which are *dialogues consisting of *pro* and *contra* disquisitions by representatives of the Hellenistic schools. When Cicero accepts a view in his own name, he tends to express himself tentatively and in terms of its persuasiveness over competing views.

*Natural Philosophy and *Theology.* In *De Natura Deorum* Cicero pits the Epicureans as defenders of mechanistic materialism and inactive gods against the Stoics as defenders of teleology and providential gods. The Academic position stands by as a *tertia via* that witholds assent from either kind of theory while recommending the nonphilosophical acceptance of Roman tradition. Interestingly, at the end of the dialogue Cicero expresses in his own voice a preference for Stoic natural theology over the Academic counterarguments. He was probably attracted to the Stoics' emphasis on providence and the overall goodness of the world, which he sees as providing a sound basis for traditional Roman moral values. He is nevertheless capable of adopting a critical attitude toward particular features of both Roman religion and Stoic theology. In *De Divinatione* he denounces belief in divination as superstition, though he recommends the continuation of divinatory practices for their civic and political benefits.

Ethics and Social Thought. For Cicero the fundamental topic in ethics is the dispute between Antiochus and the Stoics on the nature of the highest good. This debate forms the focus of *De Finibus*. The Stoics had attempted to develop a conception of the good based on man's natural impulses. They identified the primary human impulse as self-preservation, understood as the preservation of man's best part in accordance with nature. The ultimate object of this impulse they then defined as moral goodness (*honestas*) unadorned even by the so-called natural advantages (e.g., health, wealth, and life). The Stoics thus denied moral standing to all such advantages, terming them "preferred indifferents" to indicate that while the sage might choose them, they were neither good nor evil in themselves and hence could not affect one's *happiness. Antiochus criticized this conception of the good on the ground that it austerely denied the bodily part of man's nature. He revised the Stoic approach so that the good, once built up from the natural impulses, did not entirely exclude natural advantages. In *De Finibus* 5 Cicero records Antiochus' definition of the good as "life in accordance with nature," understood as including man's bodily nature and hence requiring a minimal number of the goods eschewed as indifferent by the Stoics. This view has the benefit of restoring ethical significance to the practical choices of life, though it also seems to threaten the self-sufficiency of *virtue. Cicero portrays the Antiochean spokesman trying to obviate this threat by asserting that virtue is sufficient for happiness while admitting that the natural advantages may affect the degree of happiness.

In his practical ethics Cicero accepts the compatibility of expedience and virtue. In this he follows Antiochus and the late Stoic *Panaetius *contra* the older Stoics. According to the Panaetian account outlined in *De Officiis* 1 and 2, the virtues are derived from man's natural capacities and impulses, as are individual rights such as the right to private property. Potential conflicts between the self-seeking impulses and duties imposed by virtue are supposed to be resolved by man's recognition of himself as a social being, who cannot harm his fellows without also harming himself. In an ideal political arrangement, civic law and natural law will be in accord and so too will be the interests of the individual and society. Here, as in his earlier works, *De Re Publica* and *De Legibus*, Cicero accepts as the background for his theorizing the Stoic doctrine that all men form a universal brotherhood in virtue of their common capacity for reason.

In epistemology Cicero was a fallibilist who doubted the ability of man to achieve certain knowledge, and hence he placed a high value on openness in intellectual inquiry. At the same time he was a pragmatist who saw the Stoicism of his time as providing a relatively persuasive framework for evaluating the ideals of Roman political traditions. By bringing Greek philosophy to a Latin-speaking audience he helped to secure a central role for philosophy in Roman letters. The dialogues of 45–4, especially *Academica* and *De Natura Deorum*, have at different times in the history of philosophy aroused interest, both positive and negative, in skeptical arguments. *Augustine responded to them in his influential antiskeptical treatise *Contra Academicos*. Along with the writings of *Sextus Empiricus, they were an important source for the revival of skepticism in the sixteenth century, which in turn had a great impact on the subsequent development of modern philosophy.

BIBLIOGRAPHY: Texts in J. S. Reid, ed., *Academica*, London, 1885; A. S. Pease, ed., *De Divinatione*, Urbana, 1920–23; A. Yon, ed., *De Fato*, Paris, 1950; J. N. Madvig, ed., *De Finibus Bonorum et Malorum*, Copenhagen, 1876; J. S. Reid, ed., *De Finibus Bonorum et Malorum*, Books 1 and 2, Cambridge, 1925; A. S. Pease, ed., *De Natura Deorum*, 2 vols., Cambridge, MA, 1955–58; H. A. Holden, ed., *De Officiis*, Cambridge, 1879; J. E. G. Zetzel, ed., *De Republica* (selections), Cambridge, 1995; T. W. Dougan and R. M. Henry, eds., *Tusculan Disputations*, Oxford, 1905–34. Trs. in volumes of Loeb Classical Library. Burkert, W., *Gymnasium* 72, 1965, 175–200; Glucker, J., *Antiochus and the Late Academy*, Göttingen, 1978; also "Cicero's Philosophical Affiliations," in *The Question of "Eclecticism": Studies in Later Greek Philosophy*, J. M. Dillon and A. A. Long, eds., Berkeley/Los Angeles, 1988, 34–69; Hunt, H. A. K., *The Humanism of Cicero*, Melbourne, 1954; Rawson, E., *Cicero: A Portrait*, Ithaca, NY, 1975; Süss, W., *Cicero, eine Einführung in seine Philosophischen Schriften*, Mainz, 1966.—JOSEPH G. DeFILIPPO

CLEANTHES (?331/0–230/29 B.C.E.), of Assos in the Troad (Asia Minor). Second head of the *Stoa (from 262/1). By and large he propounded the system he had inherited from his teacher *Zeno of Citium. His achievement lies mainly in the elaboration of some of its components, notably physics and *theology. His writings were soon eclipsed by those of his successor *Chrysippus and other Stoics.

The date given for Cleanthes' birth, based on *Philodemus' *Index Stoicorum* (col. 29.1–5 Dorandi), must remain uncertain in view of an alternative tradition represented by *Diogenes Laertius. Here Cleanthes is said to have died at the same age as his mentor Zeno (7.176), elsewhere specified as seventy-two on the authority of *Persaeus (7.28). This would push Cleanthes' birth forward to around 303/2 B.C.E. About the circumstances under which he came to Athens and studied there we know almost nothing. He seems to have been a loyal pupil of Zeno from the start; no other teachers or influences are recorded (apart from one late testimony mentioning the *Cynic *Crates of Thebes). There may be some truth in the suggestion found in our sources that Cleanthes, having succeeded Zeno, had considerable difficulty holding his own against attacks from philosophical opponents, notably *Arcesilaus the *Academic *skeptic. The second scholarch of the Stoa was no powerful controversialist or *dialectician. His strength lay rather in the elaboration of Stoic philosophy and its propagation through personal example. Professional rivals like the deviant Stoic *Aristo of Chios were more eloquent and attracted larger audiences (D.L. 7.182). Even during his lifetime, it fell to his pupil Chrysippus, who was proficient in dialectic, to consolidate the Stoic position and reassert the school's presence on the philosophical stage (D.L. 7.179).

Work. Cleanthes divided philosophy into six parts: dialectic and *rhetoric, *ethics and *politics, physics and theology (D.L. 7.41)—a subdivision of Zeno's tripartition into logic, ethics and physics. All six branches are represented by the extant titles of his treatises, which number fifty-seven (D.L. 7.174–75; cf. *SVF* 1, 137–9). Of Cleanthes' writings a mere handful of verbatim fragments remain, which need to be supplemented by indirect testimonies from later sources of varying date, nature and reliability. As with other early Stoics, it is often easier to attribute doctrines to the Stoa in general than specify individual contributions.

Logic. At least four treatises in Diogenes' catalogue pertain to logical subjects: *On Sophisms, On Dialectic, On Modes of Proof,* and *On Predicates.* Further, Cleanthes devoted a tract to the so-called Master Argument of *Diodorus Cronus, denying that each true statement about the past is necessary (Epictetus *Dissertationes* 2.19,1ff.). He called predicates *lekta* ("sayables"), a term he may have been the first to use in its technical Stoic sense (*SVF* 1, 488). In general, he appears to have carried Zeno's logical work further, although Stoic logic as it became known in antiquity was largely the achievement of Chrysippus.

Ethics. The large majority of the thirty-two or so titles of ethical writings concern subjects of a more practical kind. A few others, however, suggest more fundamental subject matter, notably the *On Impulse* (*Peri Hormês*, two books) and *On Appropriate Action* (*Peri tou Kathêkontos*, three books). Cleanthes' moral thought exhibits certain peculiarities reflecting his natural philosophy (inclusive of theology), while staying within the Zenonian framework. He explained "nature" in Zeno's *telos*–formula "living according to nature" as universal Nature (*SVF* 1, 555), in line with the sentiment expressed in his *Hymn to Zeus*. Equating living according to nature and living according to (moral) *virtue, he saw virtue as very much a matter of the mind's strength. This in turn is specified as the correct measure of physical tension (*tonos*) in the psychic *pneuma* ("breath"). Psychic strength thus appears as the basic virtue; for example, temperance (*sôphrosunê*) is defined as "strength in regard to acts of choice and avoidance." Cleanthes replaces practical wisdom (*phronêsis*) by self-control (*enkrateia*) in his version of the traditional quartet of primary virtues (*SVF* 1, 563). The role accorded to psychic strength—a concept largely equivalent to our idea of "will"—reflects the more general Stoic emphasis on man's responsibility for the state of his reason. Its perversion occurs when the *soul's tension relaxes, causing psychic weakness and passions. Cleanthes subscribed to Zeno's view of passions as disturbances of a wholly rational mind caused by mistaken value judgments. As to the doctrine of the different types of value and that of appropriate actions (*kathêkonta*), there were no substantial departures from Zeno either. Nor does the meager evidence for Cleanthes' political ideas point to significant modifications. Against the Cynics, Cleanthes stressed the value of the law in the context of the city-state, just as he gave the concept a prominent role to play on the cosmic level.

Natural philosophy. Of Cleanthes' physical writings, the title of his *On Zeno's Natural Philosophy* (four books) suggests the exposition of physical theories that Zeno held but did not publish in this form. His *Interpretations of Heraclitus* (four books) reflects the Stoic interest in *Heraclitus as a precursor. In general, Cleanthes followed in his master's footsteps (cf. D.L. 7.168), but he employed certain concepts in a more systematic fashion, notably the *pneuma*. Zeno had considered the soul's substance to be *pneuma* and had modeled his cosmogony on embryonic development (cf. the so-called *logos spermatikos*). Cleanthes elaborated the analogy: Just as the mind resides in the heart and is nourished from the exhalations of the blood, so the sun acts as the mind of the world, drawing its nourishment from the exhalations of the seas. Like the human soul, the sun through its rays maintains and governs the whole world down to its smallest parts, dispensing vital heat to all living creatures. In the sun the *pneuma* exists in its purest form. At the conflagration, when the world is destroyed, it absorbs the moon, stars and other heavenly bodies. The idea of tension is employed to characterize the cause of coherence and movement of the world no less than of the human frame. Cleanthes also endorsed Zeno's view on the parts and functions of the soul, taking Zeno's definition of the mental presentation (*phantasia*) somewhat crudely as an imprint involving recesses and projections in the soul, comparable to the imprint of a seal-ring in wax (*SVF* 1, 484).

Cleanthes' famous *Hymn to Zeus* (*SVF* 1, 537) reveals that Stoic theology could involve genuine religious reverence. He saw Zeus or God as the "everlasting fire," all other gods being bound to perish at the next conflagration. God is provident and cannot be held responsible for the evil men do in their folly. To explain cosmic evil, Cleanthes differentiated Providence from Fate: God does not actually want defects to occur, even though his plans make them inevitable. He tried to prove the existence of God, arguing that the ascending scale of living creatures requires there to be a perfect being (*SVF* 1, 539). In addition, he appealed to the prevalence of common religious belief, the benefits man enjoys from the earth, the awe inspired by portents, and the beauty and orderly movement of the heavenly bodies (*SVF* 1, 528). Further, he engaged in the etymological derivation of divine names and in the philosophical interpretation of myth.

BIBLIOGRAPHY: Texts in *SVF* 1, nos. 463–619; A. C. Pearson, *The Fragments of Zeno and Cleanthes*, London, 1891. Dorandi, T., *Ricerche sulla cronologia dei filosofi ellenistici*, Stuttgart, 1991, 23–28; Long, A. A., *Philosophia* 5/6, 1975/6, 133–56; Mansfeld, J., Study # 4 in *Studies in Later Greek Philosophy and Gnosticism*, London, 1989; Solmsen, F., in *Kleine Schriften*, vol. 1, Hildesheim, 1968, 436–60; Verbeke, G., *Kleanthes van Assos*, Brussels, 1949; Zuntz, G., *HSCP* 63, 1958, 289–308.—*TEUN L. TIELEMAN*

CLEMENT (Titus Flavius Clemens; c. 200 C.E.), of Alexandria, Egypt. *Christian apologist. Little is known about Clement's life. He refers to a series of teachers, blessed men whose discourses he was privileged to hear, including a Sicilian identified by Eusebius as Pantaenus, a man of *Stoic inclinations and leader of the Christian school in Alexandria in the reign of Commodus (177–192). Eusebius also says that Clement succeeded Pantaenus as head of the school and became the teacher of *Origen of Alexandria (c. 185–c. 254), who, at the age of eighteen, succeeded him, apparently after Clement left Alexandria. Eusebius asserts that Clement converted to Christianity after a thorough immersion in Greek religion, and Epiphanius says that some people make Athens Clement's birthplace. It is possible that these claims are based solely on the extensive knowledge of Greek religion (including the mysteries), literature, and philosophy that Clement shows in his writings. Clement's frequent citations and borrowings make him an important source of information on those subjects. He is also a central figure in the early Christian attempt to come to terms with Greek philosophy (see CHRISTIANITY).

Clement is the author of three major extant works, the *Exhortation to the Greeks* (*Protrepticus*), the *Educator* (*Paedagogus*), and, most important, the *Miscellanies* (*Stromata*). The *Exhortation* calls on pagans to renounce their ways and become Christians. The *Educator* is a manual of proper Christian behavior, covering everything from ear-piercing to comportment in the public baths. The Greek word *strômateis* is the plural of *strômateus*, for which LSJ gives the meaning "coverlet"; it is one of several words that were used as the title of miscellaneous collections. Clement refers to several of the books of the *Miscellanies* as "coverlets of the gnostic memoranda (*hupomnêmata*) based on the true philosophy," and in Book 1 he speaks of the work as a treasury stored up for old age as a remedy for forgetfulness. Although Clement frequently stresses the random character of his memoranda, he also makes clear that he intends to express the truth for those with the ears to hear it, but in such a way as to foil those who would misuse it. At the beginning of the *Educator* Clement implies that it and the *Exhortation* are to be followed by a work that instructs in Christian truth. Many scholars are reluctant to admit that the work referred to is the *Miscellanies* because it is so disjointed. The work is also incomplete, and many scholars think that what is printed as the last book—Book 8, a loosely organized and inconclusive compilation of mainly *Aristotelian and Stoic ideas on *"logic" and causal explanation—was not originally a part of it.

Clement's orthodoxy has also been a matter of dispute for many reasons, including his insistence that Christianity at its best is "gnostic philosophy." But there can be no question that he thinks of himself as a defender of Christianity in opposition to paganism and of the genuine Christian tradition in opposition to the extreme asceticism and libertarianism that later Christian orthodoxy labeled *Gnostic. However, because of the obscurity of the *Miscellanies*, it has to remain doubtful whether Clement had any worked-out Christian *theology. He is certain that Christian faith is necessary for salvation, but not explicit about what he calls "genuine gnostic physics" (*phusiologia*), a subject that he promises to write on after completing the *Miscellanies*, if he is able. Although Clement insists that Christianity is the only path to salvation, he thinks of philosophy as the way in which religious truth was conveyed to the Greeks, just as the Law was the way it was conveyed to the Jews. Clement also thinks that the Greeks took their philosophical ideas from the "barbarians," such as Jews, Egyptians, and Babylonians, a claim the defense of which requires heavy use of selective quotation, *allegorizing, and other dubious interpretive techniques. Clement insists that for him philosophy is not Stoic or *Platonic or *Epicurean or Aristotelian, but anything correctly spoken by any of these schools. His philosophical outlook is best classed as a very eclectic *Middle Platonism. He is most explicit in his admiration for *Plato, whom he cites frequently and refers to as noble and truth-loving; but his *ethics is importantly Stoic, and his logic and *cosmology are heavily tinged with Aristotelianism.

BIBLIOGRAPHY: Texts in O. Stählin, ed., *Clemens Alexandrinus*, Berlin, vol. 1,³ 1972; vol. 2,⁴ 1985; vol. 3,² 1970; vol. 4.1² (indices), 1980. Tr. in A. Roberts and J. Donaldson, eds., *The Ante-Nicene Fathers*, vol. 2 (repr.), Peabody, MA, 1994; G. W. Butterworth, ed., *Protrepticus* (Loeb), Cambridge, MA, 1982; J. Ferguson, *Stromata* 1–3, in *The Fathers of the Church*, vol. 85, Washington, DC, 1991. Lilla, S. R. C., *Clement of Alexandria: A Study in Christian Platonism and Gnosticism*, Oxford, 1971.—*IAN MUELLER*

CLEOMEDES (1st or 2nd cents. C.E.) is known only through a work in two books, the *Caelestia* (*Meteôra*). This work offers rare evidence of scholastic *Stoicism in the early Roman Empire and of the influence of *Posidonius on the assimilation of scientific ideas into Stoic philosophy. The surviving part of a much larger introduction to Stoicism, the *Caelestia* is a summary of the standard topics of spherical *astronomy and terrestrial geography. The account (1.7) of Posidonius' and *Eratosthenes' measurements of the size of the earth is particularly valuable, while the prefatory arguments (1.1) for the *cosmology of a finite cosmos in an *infinite *void are unique in Stoic literature. As a whole, the treatise is almost certainly a reflection of the Posidonian philosophy of science in which astronomy is classified as a subordinate *science (see Posidonius F18 Edelstein and Kidd). Cleomedes thus frequently shows how astronomers use assumptions from allied sciences, as well as from cosmology. Elsewhere, astronomical data are analysed through the Stoic *epistemological theory of the criterion, particularly in a lengthy polemic (2.1) against the *Epicurean claim that the sun is as large as it appears. The loss of the rest of the Cleomedean corpus means that these ideas are now embedded in a commonplace historical account of astronomy.

BIBLIOGRAPHY: Text in R. B. Todd, ed., *Cleomedis Caelestia* (Teubner), Leipzig, 1990. Todd, R. B., *ANRW* 2, 36.3, 1989, 1365–1378; also *Catalogus Translationum et Commentariorum* 7, 1992, 1–11; also *ANRW* 2, 37.5 (forthcoming).—*ROBERT B. TODD*

CLITOMACHUS (187/6–110/09 B.C.E.), of Carthage. *Academic *skeptic, student of *Carneades. Clitomachus was originally named Hasdrubal. According to *Diogenes Laertius (4.67), he taught philosophy in his native language before coming to Athens and meeting Carneades at the age of forty. But the chronological claim, at least, is almost certainly false; more plausibly, the *Index Academicus* says (col. 25, 2–6) that he came to Athens at the age of twenty-four and became Carneades' student four years later. In 140/139, when Carneades was still head of the Academy, Clitomachus started his own school in the Palladium; this does not seem to have been prompted, however, by any disagreement with Carneades. In 129/8, the same year as Carneades' death, Clitomachus returned to the Academy with a number of followers. But he apparently did not become head of the Academy until two years later. Carneades had retired in 137/6, and was succeeded by Carneades son of Polemarchus for six years, followed by Crates of Tarsus for a further four years (*Ind. Acad.* col. 25, 39–26,4); Clitomachus then took over and held the position until his death.

Clitomachus wrote a large number of books (more than four hundred, according to Diogenes, *ibid.*), none of which have survived. *Sextus (*M* 9.1) criticizes him for lingering excessively on points of detail, though this is primarily a methodological criticism rather than a comment on his prolixity per se. We know specifically of four books "on withholding assent" (Cic. *Acad.* 98—probably *peri epochês* in the original Greek), a work *On Philosophical Sects* (*Peri Haireseôn*, D.L. 2.92), a book addressed to his compatriots after the destruction of Carthage (Cic. *TD* 3.54), and two books dealing with difficulties surrounding Carneades' notion of the *pithanê phantasia*, "convincing impression" (Cic. *Acad.* 2.102). We have little or no indication of original thinking on Clitomachus' part; he seems to have been known, rather, for his assiduousness in preserving Carneades' arguments, and most of the testimonia relating to Carneades in *Cicero, Sextus, *Plutarch, and elsewhere probably derive ultimately from him. Cicero (*Orator* 51) indicates that Carneades himself accepted Clitomachus' renderings of his ideas. Contrary to *Philo Of Larissa and *Metrodorus of Stratonicea, he maintained that Carneades adhered strictly to the skeptical policy of suspending judgment, rather than permitting the holding of opinions; the correctness of this verdict is also suggested by Clitomachus' reported confession (Cic. *Acad.* 2.139), despite many years of association with him, that he could never understand what Carneades' own views were. If we assume that he shared the attitudes which he attributed to Carneades, Clitomachus can be considered the last rigorously skeptical member of the Academy.

BIBLIOGRAPHY: Arnim, H. von, "Kleitomachos," in *RE*. Couissin, P., in M. Burnyeat, ed., *The Skeptical Tradition*, Berkeley, 1983, 31–63; Sedley, D. N., in *The Skeptical Tradition*, 9–30.—*RICHARD BETT*

COLOTES (late 4th–early 3rd cent. B.C.E.), of Lampsacus in Asia Minor. First-generation *Epicurean philosopher and polemicist. Colotes was, and apparently remained, a member of the Epicurean school at Lampsacus. *Epicurus used to address him by the diminutive "Colotarion," and their mutual adulation was legendary. The close personal bond suggests that Colotes joined the group while Epicurus was himself still at Lampsacus, that is, in 310–307 B.C.E., before Epicurus' move to Athens. This would place Colotes' birth before 320. And since his writings engage with, among others, the New *Academics, he probably lived into the 260s or later. He apparently taught philosophy himself, numbering among his pupils one *Menedemus (of Lampsacus), later a *Cynic.

All Colotes' recorded works are polemical. Small fragments of his *Against Plato's Lysis* and the later *Against Plato's Euthydemus* survive among the Herculaneum papyri. The preserved scraps criticize *Lysis* 206–209 and *Euthydemus* 279d, perhaps treated as *"Socratic" texts, since contemporary philosophers of a Socratic bent are included in the attack. In another work, of unknown title, he inveighed against the Myth of Er from *Plato's *Republic* .

His best publicized work, however, was his *How the Tenets of Other Philosophers Make Life Itself Impossible*, which provoked *Plutarch's counterblast, *Against Colotes*. It attacked a series of philosophers allegedly committed to *skeptical positions and accused them of making life unlivable ("How shall we live, if ...?"). Starting with *Democritus, who held a special place in Epicurean critiques of skepticism, he then moved on through the remainder in apparently chronological order: *Parmenides, *Empedocles, Socrates, *Melissus, Plato, *Stilpo, and finally, unnamed, two contemporary schools, the *Cyrenaics and the New Academy of *Arcesilaus. Addressed to the Egyptian ruler Ptolemy, the tract condemned skepticism as a form of philosophical anarchy inimical to the orderliness bestowed by kingship.

It has been suggested that Colotes' critique was highly influential in later Epicureanism. However, most of his recorded criticisms are philosophically superficial, and the school never accorded him the authoritative status of his senior colleagues Epicurus, *Metrodorus of Lampsacus, *Hermarchus, and *Polyaenus.

BIBLIOGRAPHY: Texts of *Against Plato's Lysis* and *Against Plato's Euthydemus* in W. Crönert, *Kolotes und Menedemos*, Leipzig, 1905. Concolino Mancini, A., *CronErc* 6, 1976, 61–7; Einarson, B., and P. H. De Lacy, trs. and eds., *Plutarch: Against Colotes*, vol. 14 of *Plutarch's Moralia* (Loeb), Cambridge, MA, 1967; Vander Waerdt, P. A., *GRBS* 30, 1989, 225–67; Westman, R., *Plutarch gegen Kolotes*, Acta Philosophical Fennica 7, 1955.—DAVID N. SEDLEY

COMMENTARIES/COMMENTATORS. See ARISTOTELIAN COMMENTATORS.

CORNUTUS, Lucius Annaeus (c. 20–after 65 C.E.), from Proconsular Africa. Teacher of philosophy in Rome c. 50–65, who wrote on *Aristotle, *rhetoric, and poetry. Cornutus was a prominent figure who taught the poets Lucan and Persius (see *Persi Vita*). His surviving work, a *Summary* (*Epidromê*) *of the Traditions of Greek Theology*, is an extremely important compendium of *allegorical interpretations of Greek myth. Addressed to a young reader, these interpretations make extensive use of etymology. Divine names in particular, when analyzed into their component sounds, regularly provide keys to the meaning of myths. A single name may have multiple resonances: Cronus swallowing his children is time (*chronos*), into which everything that comes to be eventually disappears (6), but Cronus swallowing the stone (= the world) is "the order of the generation of the universe" (from *krainô*, "rule, accomplish," [7]). The "earlier philosophers" (35) from whom Cornutus' interpretations are derived include *Cleanthes (named once) and *Chrysippus (unnamed).

BIBLIOGRAPHY: Text in C. Lang, ed., *Cornuti theologiae graecae compendium* (Teubner), Leipzig, 1881. Nock, A. D., "Kornutus" in *RE*, Supp. vol. 5, 1931, 995–1005; Most, G. W., *ANRW* 2, 36.3, 1989, 2014–2065.—*ROBERT LAMBERTON*

CORPUS HERMETICUM. See HERMETICA.

COSMOLOGY, Classical. Classical cosmology is characterised by a variety of theories on the universe and its origins. They can be generally grouped into those that posit an "open" view of the universe, in which space is *infinite in extent, and those that posit a "closed" view, in which it is enclosed by an outer sphere of some sort. Another division, cutting across the first, differentiates theories that view the operations of the universe in purely mechanistic terms from those that understand them teleologically. Further divisions differentiate theories that view the world as being in some significant sense "alive" from those that see it as simply a composite of *matter in motion, and those that view the universe of our acquaintance as having had a beginning in *time from those that view it as eternal. All, however, agree on one thing: There has never been a beginning to, nor will there ever be a cessation from, *change* in the realm of the material. And the great majority also agree that (i) all celestial movements appear to be and are circular, (ii) the earth appears to be and is at the center of things, and (iii) the "preservation" of these *phaenomena* is an indispensable feature of any sound cosmology.

Among the Milesians, *Anaximander seems to have seen his "indefinite" or "boundless" (*to apeiron*) as being immense in extent and eternally subject to change. Whether he thought it "infinite" in the technical sense—and thus in the precise sense "open"—is very unlikely. He definitely seems to have thought, in line with ancient mythological cosmogonies, that the world of our acquaintance had a beginning in time, as did his successor *Anaximenes, whose basic substance of things, air, also seems to have been viewed as the breath-soul of a universe that is very much alive.

To what degree if any the views of these early philosophers involved conscious demythologisation of earlier, overtly religious accounts of the world and its origins is unclear. For *Thales, all things are "full of gods." For Anaximander, the *apeiron* is "divine" and "steers" all things. For Anaximenes, *air* is divine. This could be read as reductionism, but it may also have been combined with belief in the gods of popular belief. Whatever the truth of this, *Xenophanes undoubtedly attacked such gods as crude, anthropomorphic creations, affirming, according to *Aristotle, that God is in fact "identical to the one (universe)," a view apparently shared by *Heraclitus, for whom God consists of all those "opposite" things that constitute the real (DK22B67).

Many have understood *Parmenides's startling poem as an apparent doctrine of two universes, one of them (the real one) ascertainable by the *cognoscenti*, the other (the nonreal one) a mere object of opinion. But it seems more likely that he is discussing different optics on a single reality. The optic of *ascertainment* (*noein*) views the universe as a *totality* (*pan*), and as such it is one, finite, eternal, homogeneous, indivisible, immobile, a plenum (i.e., without empty spaces), and "like a well-rounded ball in mass" (i.e., spheroid). According to the optic of *opinion* it is made up of parts, subject to motion and change, and is describable in ways similar to those employed by earlier cosmologists.

Parmenides' views shocked his hearers, not least because they felt they could not fault his *logic; and much of the rest of cosmological speculation in antiquity is a conscious response to him. Even someone as friendly to his thought as *Melissus felt constrained to say that the real must in fact be infinite in extent, not finite, on the grounds that if the real were finite in extent it would have something (the *void) outside of it, which, added to the real, would constitute that seemingly forbidden thing, plurality. In other words, Parmenides is wrong in his claim that the real is finite and hence closed.

The battle lines for two major, competing cosmological systems have been drawn. While defending—against Parmenides—plurality of contents as an eternal feature of the real, *Empedocles and *Anaxagoras support Parmenides's contention that it is finite and a plenum, and in this they will be followed by *Plato, Aristotle, and many more.

They also make common cause with him on the eternal nature of the universe's constituents, but return to the commonly accepted view that the world of our acquaintance did have a beginning. They also differ from each other in their assessment of the nature of what triggers the process and its continuance, Empedocles describing it as a combination of Love and Strife (or centripetal and centrifugal force), Anaxagoras as Intelligence.

The latter concept might well be thought to have involved the introduction of a new concept, teleology, into Greek cosmology. It is certainly there by implication, but it is not clear that Anaxagoras himself had precisely teleological explanation in mind (as Plato's *Socrates was to point out with some bitterness, *Phd.* 98b), any more than Xenophanes and Heraclitus earlier, when they equated God and the real. Credit for the first clear assertion of teleological explanation in cosmology in fact goes to *Diogenes of Apollonia, for whom (as for Anaximenes earlier) air is the divine and intelligent ground of the real and is that whereby all things in nature are "disposed in the best possible way" (DK64B3). And the claim is made in the context of a return to the notion of an "open" universe, in which infinitely extended air is populated with an infinite number of "worlds."

The latter notion is as it happens a feature of the cosmological system of Diogenes's contemporaries *Democritus and *Leucippus, and he may indeed have drawn it from them. Their major claim to fame is, however, their wholly mechanistic explanation of the real without reference to teleology. The universe is one of lifeless atoms, infinite in number, eternally moving in an infinite expanse of space to produce, by haphazard, an infinity of "worlds" (we would now say galaxies), many of them not unlike our own; a universe in which "worlds" clash, are destroyed, and are constantly reborn. It is a view that constitutes the supreme challenge to those various visions of the real as finite, alive, and, under the guidance of Intelligence, moving toward and attaining rational goals.

Such visions find in Plato's *Timaeus* their most brilliant artistic and philosophical statement. Taken literally, his description involves distinctions among (i) a divine craftsman (*dêmiourgos*); (ii) empty space, which contains the "traces" of what will later constitute the four elements earth, air, fire, and water; and (iii) among other (transcendent and eternal) Forms the Form Living Creature, serving as the paradigm for that art object and living creature that will be the universe we know. At a point in time that is the beginning *of* time, the Demiurge fashions the body of the universe and also its *soul, along with the bodies and souls of the gods (conceived of as astral entities) and the rational part of human soul. The other gods then complete the construction of all other aspects of the universe and the living things within it. It is a universe that, among other things, takes account of the existence of the Ecliptic (a feature passed over in the *Republic*) and that might also have at its center a *rotating* earth, though it seems more likely that the exact countermovement to sidereal movement that Plato ascribes to the earth is formulated as an argument for its stillness rather than its motion.

The entire picture is teleological; the world is in all its structures the best that could have been constructed, given the constraints imposed by what Timaeus (following Democritus?) calls Necessity (or "Chance"), a word representing, it seems, the surd aspect of the physically real that even God cannot fully control. This remains true even if the general picture of the world's putative formation is taken in a nonliteral sense, as it was by *Xenocrates and others; on this view Plato's "productive" cause of the world is its soul, the Demiurge serving merely as a symbol for that soul or for its rational part.

Plato's discomfort with purely mechanistic explanation is also evident in other dialogues like the *Phaedrus* and *Laws*, where soul, individual and cosmic, is seen as the ultimate mover of the physical; matter as such can never of itself account for its own motion. As another teleologist, his pupil Aristotle has much sympathy for this view, but rejects both the notion of Demiurge and that of world soul in cosmological explanation (the universe of our experience is eternal and a container of living things, not itself a living thing), as well as the notion of transcendent Forms. For him the productive (or "efficient") cause of the real is rather the unmoved mover, a Mind or Intelligence that exists in a state of eternal activity untouched by potency for change in any respect.

It is a universe, modelled after that elaborated by *Eudoxus and refined by Callippus, in which the sum of movements of a particular set of contiguous and invisible spheres accounts for the perceived motion of the planet attached to the innermost one of the set, the outermost sphere of the system being that which carries the "fixed" stars. Each individual sphere depends for its movement upon the eternal motive activity of an appropriate "unmoved" substance, and these in turn depend eternally on the motive activity of the ultimate unmoved substance, that Mind that is the prime mover. The world extending from the moon to the fixed stars is perfect and changeless and is the realm of the fifth and most perfect element, *aether*; the sublunary world is the domain of change, generation, and destruction and the realm of the by now "traditional" elements earth, air, fire, and water. Like Plato's universe, Aristotle's too is single and "closed," a spheroid plenum with a spherical earth at its center, and eternally contingent for its existence and activities upon a cause other than itself.

But the notion of an "open" universe was far from dead. In the late fourth century B.C.E. *Epicurus revived the atomism of Democritus and Leucippus, adding some refinements of his own. The first of these was the view that (whatever his predecessors may have held) atoms do in fact have weight. The resulting picture for him is one of a downward "rain" of atoms, from eternity, in empty space, all of them (despite diffences in weight) moving at uniform speed and hence never colliding except on those occasions—which he does not attempt to explain—when one of them "swerves" and collides with another, setting off a train of collisions and combinations that leads to the formation of a world. The second is the strong asseveration that (whatever his predecessors may have thought) only a *finite number* of atomic shapes is needed. And the third is the contention that, while atoms are indeed physically indivisible, mathematically they are in fact further divisible, given that they have size. So refined, atomism took on new life, achieving an even wider, Latin-speaking audience with the publication, in the first century B.C.E., of *Lucretius's *De Rerum Natura*. Its main opposition, *Stoicism, would be, predictably, another *teleological* system.

The period of Greek and Greco-Roman antiquity from the third century B.C.E. onward offers largely variants on the cosmological positions discussed so far, with one significant exception. In that century *Aristarchus of Samos proposed—at least as a hypothesis—the notion that the *sun* lay at the center of things, but it was an idea that disappeared almost as soon as it was enunciated. Five centuries later *Ptolemy, building on foundations laid by Apollonius and Hipparchus, elaborated an even more impressive system of epicycles and eccentric circles than they had to explain the perceived motions of celestial bodies. But he also, significantly, continued to champion the Aristotelian distinction between an unchanging superlunary and a changing sublunary world, along with geocentricity. It was the final cosmological system propounded in classical antiquity, a system preoccupied like so many of its predecessors with preserving the particular *phaenomena* of the centrality of earth and the circular and changeless nature of the movements of celestial bodies; and it prevailed, with minor variants, till the advent of Copernicus, Galileo, and Kepler.

BIBLIOGRAPHY: Furley, D., *The Greek Cosmologists*, vol. 1, Cambridge, 1987; Neugebauer, O., *The Exact Sciences in Antiquity*,[2] Providence, 1957; Sambursky, S., *The Physical World of the Greeks*, tr. M. Dagut, London, 1956.—*T. M. ROBINSON*

CRANTOR (c. 336–276/5 B.C.E.), of Soli. Pupil of *Xenocrates and *Polemo, and the most important Old *Academic philosopher not to have been scholarch. Sources are *Diogenes Laertius 4.24–27 and *Philodemus *History of the Academy* cols. 16–18. Crantor left Soli when he was already famous. At Athens he had the reputation and opportunity to found his own school, but declined to do so, even though he numbered *Bion of Borysthenes, *Crates of Athens, *Arcesilaus, and others of note among his pupils (*ibid.* 16.30–37). He was famed partly for literary skills, which surfaced in his best-known work, *On Grief*, praised by *Cicero (*Acad.* 2.44) as well as Diogenes (D.L. 4.27). He maintained close relations with Polemo and Crates and was intimate with the young Arcesilaus. Cicero (*Acad.* 1.34) implies that he was faithful to earlier Academic traditions.

Crantor perhaps instituted the practice of commenting upon *Platonic texts. He is described by *Proclus (*In Tim.* 1.76.1–2) as the first Platonic interpreter, for although *Plutarch was able to discuss Xenocrates' interpretation of the World Soul of the *Timaeus* (Plut. *Mor.* 1012dff.), commentaries on *Plato are absent from Diogenes' list of his works (D.L. 4.11–14). Crantor's interest in interpreting the *Timaeus* was inherited by others from Soli such as Clearchus and Theodorus (Plut. *Mor.* 1022c), and by *Eudorus (*ibid.* 1020c). Surviving evidence covers three areas: (i) the status of the Atlantis story, (ii) the nontemporal cosmogony, and (iii) details of the construction of the World Soul.

(i) Proclus says that Crantor regarded the Atlantis story as *historia psilê* (*In Tim.* 1.72.1), usually interpreted as unadulterated history, yet Proclus uses the phrase in contrast to those who found profound nonhistorical meaning behind the tale. Crantor said that the story was Plato's response to those who mocked him for stealing the basic ideas of his ideal state from the Egyptians, so that he actually argued from Egyptian records that Athens had once been governed under just such a state. Crantor made reference to contemporary Egyptian priests, who knew inscriptional evidence for the story. It is unclear which points they allegedly confirmed, and Crantor's purpose was not to establish the literal truth of details.

(ii) Crantor's nontemporal interpretation of the cosmogony in the *Timaeus* is attested both by Proclus and by Plutarch. The former (*In Tim.* 1.277.8) sees Crantor as the author of the view that the world is depicted as created because of its owing its being to some external principle, that is, its derivative nature. The latter sees Crantor as viewing the psychogony as a device for expounding the variety of powers belonging to the soul (*Mor.* 1013a–b).

(iii) On his interpretation of the World Soul, Plutarch's treatise *On the Generation of the Soul* is of importance, because it mentions Crantor's work in three separate contexts: (a) the nature of the Same, Different, Divided, and Undivided (*Tim.* 35a; *Mor.* 1012d–1013f.), (b) the significance of the numbers 1, 2, 3, 4, 9, 8, 27 (*Tim.* 35b–c; *Mor.* 1027d, 1022d–28a), and (c) the number underlying the "means" (*Tim.* 35c–36b; *Mor.* 1020c–d). Crantor's approach to Same, Different, Divided, and Undivided depended on viewing Soul as a cognitive power comprehending all aspects of reality. It must grasp both intelligible (undivided) and sensible (divided) objects and appreciate both samenesses and differences within those realms and between them. Thus, on the principle that like recognizes like, the soul is composed of all four ingredients harmoniously blended (*Mor.* 1012f.–1013a). Crantor is known for having used a lambda-shaped diagram to set forth the numbers of *Tim.* 35b–c. His base figure was 384, selected to avoid fractions and often adopted later.

Crantor's *On Grief* is used extensively by Plutarch in the *Consolation to Apollonius* and by Cicero in the *Tusculan Disputations*. It was a model for later consolation literature. Evidence suggests that he drew extensively from earlier philosophy and literature, since Plutarch, whose work is full of quotations—sometimes in common with Cicero—quotes an extract that appeals to "all this ancient philosophy" (*Mor.* 104c) for the sentiment that human life is insubstantial, laborious, and unpleasant. Plutarch also quotes another extract that appeals to wise men (the Orphic/*Pythagorean tradition) who have bewailed the human lot, calling life a punishment and birth in the body a calamity (*Mor.* 115b). Crantor emphasized the naturalness, hence the rightness, of such feelings as moderate grief (*Mor.* 102c, Cic. *TD* 3.12, 3.71).

BIBLIOGRAPHY: Baltes, M., *Die Weltentstehung des platonischen Timaios nach den antiken interpreten*, vol. 1, Leiden, 1976, 82–86; Kassel, R., *Untersuchungen zur griechischen und lateinischen Konsolationsliteratur (Zetemata 18)*, Munich, 1958; Mette, H. J., *Lustrum* 26, 1984, 7–94.—HAROLD A. S. TARRANT

CRATES (late 4th cent.–c. 265 B.C.E.), of Athens. *Academic and intimate friend of *Polemo, who succeeded him in 270/69 as head of the Academy. Sources are *Diogenes Laertius 4.21–23 and *Philodemus, *History of the Academy*, cols. 15–17. His headship was brief, perhaps between two and six years (see Dorandi, p. 58). His writings included orations and books on comedy as well as philosophic works (D.L. 4.23). Diogenes emphasizes Crates' closeness to Polemo in every respect (*ibid.* 4.21), and no known doctrinal innovations occurred under his regime. He is referred to among conservative Old Academic philosophers approved by *Cicero's Varro at *Academica* 1.34, though he is not, like Polemo, a key figure in *Antiochus' history of philosophy; comparison with the preceding discussion of *Peripatetics shows that this conservatism applied to *ethics as much as to *epistemology.

BIBLIOGRAPHY: Dorandi, T., ed., *Filodemo, Storia del Filosofi: Platone e l' Academia*, Naples, 1991.—HAROLD A. S. TARRANT

CRATES (early 2nd cent. B.C.E.), of Mallos. *Stoic literary scholar. Crates worked in Pergamum, where he was presumably associated with the newly founded library. In 168 B.C.E. he served as ambassador to Rome. Lectures he delivered while recovering from a broken leg stimulated Roman interest in literary scholarship and Stoic philosophy.

Crates identified himself as a "critic" and wrote extensively on the text, diction, aesthetic evaluation, and interpretation of Greek poetry. He made significant contributions to textual criticism and the Stoic science of *grammar in conscious opposition to the analogist theories of the

Alexandrian school. By use of Stoic methods of interpretation he read *Homer, *Hesiod, and other poets as evidence of popular recognition of the truth that underlies Stoic teaching, principally in *cosmology and geography. His most notable student was *Panaetius, who may have received his first introduction to Stoicism through his early study of literature under Crates.

BIBLIOGRAPHY: Texts in H. J. Mette, *Sphairopoiia: Untersuchungen zur Kosmologie des Crates von Pergamon*, Munich, 1936; H. J. Mette, *Parateresis: Untersuchungen zur Sprachtheorie des Crates von Pergamon*, Halle, 1952. Asmis, E., *Phoenix* 46, 1991, 138–69; Lamberton, R., ed., *Homer's Ancient Readers*, Princeton, 1992, chs. 3 and 4; Pfeiffer, R., *History of Classical Scholarship from the Beginnings to the End of the Hellenistic Age*, Oxford, 1968, 234–46.—*DAVID E. HAHM*

CRATES (c. 368/365–288/285 B.C.E.), of Thebes. *Cynic philosopher and poet. Having gone to Athens as a young man, Crates became a follower of *Diogenes of Sinope and gave his wealth to the poor. He "married" *Hipparchia of Maroneia, with whom he had a son. His physical appearance (he was a hunchback and otherwise ugly) itself symbolized the Cynic rejection of conventional appearances. Of Crates' considerable poetic production, which included tragedies, the most important surviving fragments are witty and resourceful reworkings of passages from *Homer and Solon, which the ancient tradition rightly interpreted as seriocomic Cynic statements rather than mere literary parodies.

How far Crates maintained Diogenes' philosophy has from ancient times been disputed. Crates claimed to be "a citizen of Diogenes," espousing a similar cosmopolitanism; notoriously enacted Diogenes' prescriptions regarding free and public sex in his relations with Hipparchia, with whom he shared a Cynic way of life; and often expressed ethical sentiments as extreme and intolerant as Diogenes'. But he did not insist on the complete renunciation of wealth or that everybody should become a Cynic, and he conceded a certain legitimacy to existing occupations; and the deployment of his considerable charm and kindliness in proclaiming his message, comforting the afflicted and reconciling enemies, won him the titles of "door-opener" and "good spirit" and a reputation for humanity that endured throughout antiquity. Granted their obvious differences in personality and missionary approach, Crates seems himself to have followed Diogenes rigorously, while (sometimes) allowing greater latitude to others. This partial moral relativism makes him the link between "hard" and "soft" Cynicism; he is also, through *Zeno of Citium (his most famous follower), the link between Cynicism and *Stoicism.

See also DIOGENES of Sinope, HIPPARCHIA.

BIBLIOGRAPHY: For bibliography, see under CYNICS and CYNICISM.—*JOHN L. MOLES*

CRATYLUS, of Athens. Younger contemporary of *Socrates who, as a follower of the thought of *Heraclitus, significantly influenced *Plato. Nothing certain is known of the details of his life, and it is disputed among the ancient sources when exactly he came to influence Plato— whether before or after the death of Socrates. Either way, however, according to *Aristotle's account it happened at a relatively early period in Plato's development.

Cratylus' abiding claim to fame is an assertion in which, according to Aristotle, he outdoes even Heraclitus: Not only can we not step into the same river twice; we cannot step into it even once. As such it is the "ultimate" statement of the doctrine of phenomenal flux that has been attributed to Heraclitus since the beginning and is clearly based on the contention that nothing in the universe—including the knowing subject—enjoys any degree of permanence. His conclusion from this appears to have been that there is never at any moment any stable object to describe or define, so that the best policy is to remain silent and simply wave one's finger. It is a policy of what one might call "attenuated ostensive definition," in which the pointing finger calls attention to the putative existence of the putative "object," but no verbalization (of the form, "that, over there, is a cow") is allowed to mislead us into further imagining that any such object enjoys the sort of permanent features that would ever be the subject of definition in any more sophisticated sense.

In view of the above, it has surprised many people that, according to the Cratylus of Plato's *Cratylus*, he also held the view that everything has its own specific and correct name that is what it is "by nature" rather than by convention (383a). The apparent essentialism of such a view is in stark contradiction—or so it would seem—to the basic Heracliteanism attributed to him by Aristotle.

One possible solution to this problem (if it really is one) is that he held the two views sequentially and not simultaneously, at a specific time abandoning one in favor of the other. Another is that one or other of the two views has been attributed to him either falsely or misleadingly. A third possibility, attractive in view of what seems to have been his basic allegiance to the thought of Heraclitus, is that, as the result of his investigations into natural philosophy and *epistemology, he was simultaneously attracted by both views and allowed both to stand in a state of unresolved, "Heraclitean" tension—connected, and in some weak sense "one" because subsumed, like all other supposed "opposites," within that higher unity that for Heraclitus is the cosmos. A fourth possibility, consonant with the third and in some measure the second, is that his views were basically nominalist rather than essentialist, leaving him free to accept a radical doctrine of phenomenal flux while conceding the existence of enough stability amid the transience of things to ground a workable if non-Platonic theory of language and definition.

To what degree Cratylus accepted the doctrine of unity-amidst-change that is now largely accepted as having been an essential feature of Heraclitus' own thought we do not know; even on the debatable hypothesis that for some or all of his life he was a liguistic essentialist it would not follow that this particular aspect of Heraclitus' thought impressed or concerned him. Be this as it may, the doctrine of phenomenal change to be found in Plato's *Theaetetus* and *Timaeus* appears strongly to constitute "Heracliteanism" as filtered through the magnifying and perhaps selective lens of Cratylus; and to that extent his influence on the history of Greek and subsequent philosophy has turned out to be quite significant.

BIBLIOGRAPHY: Texts in DK65. Allan, D. J., *AJP* 75, 1954, 271–287; Cherniss, H., *AJP* 76, 1955, 184–186; Kirk, G. S., *AJP* 72, 1951, 225–253; Narcy, M., *Revue de Philosophie Ancienne* 5, 1988, 151–165.—*T. M. ROBINSON*

CRITIAS (c. 460—403 B.C.E.), of Athens. Sophistically inclined *littérateur*; associate of *Socrates. An Athenian aristocrat, Critias combined a career as a versatile writer and intellectual with periods of antidemocratic political activity. With the oligarchic coup of 404, he emerged as the most bloodthirsty of the Thirty Tyrants and died battling the democratic counterrevolution. Despite tactful portraits in *Plato (his nephew), he was often paired with Alcibiades as among Socrates' most corrupt "pupils."

Critias wrote recitative and dramatic poetry and "Political Constitutions" of Thessaly, Sparta, and Athens in prose and verse. Prose writings include "Aphorisms," "Conversations," and a collection of "Proemia for public speakers."

His elegant verse shows an admiration of Sparta, along with an interest in the various usages and inventions of civilization. His prose works are too little known to allow us to identify him as an original thinker, though he is said to have distinguished sensation from cognition and to have identified the soul with blood. Much attention has been drawn to a speech from the play *Sisyphus*, maintaining that religion was invented by a shrewd politician to insure that fear of the gods would make citizens obey the laws even when unobserved. This naturalistic, progressivist, and psychological account suggests *Protagoras, *Prodicus, and *Democritus, yet the *Sisyphus* is sometimes attributed to *Euripides (for the debate see Davies).

Critias is included among the *sophists by *Philostratus, but unlike most sophists he did not teach and was Athenian. He continues to hold the reputation he had among the ancients as "a layman among philosophers, a philosopher among laymen" (DK88A3).

BIBLIOGRAPHY: Texts in DK88. Davies, M., *Bulletin of the Institute of Classical Studies* 36, 1989, 16–32; Nestle, W., *Von Mythos zum Logos*,[2] Stuttgart, 1942, 400–20; Stephans, D., *Critias: Life and Literary Remains*, Cincinnati, 1939.—*ANDREW FORD*

CRITOLAUS (2nd cent. B.C.E.), of Phaselis. *Peripatetic philosopher; head of the *Lyceum. As head, Critolaus joined *Carneades and *Diogenes of Babylon on a famous embassy from Athens in 155 that first brought Greek philosophy to Rome. Little else is recorded about his life and thought, and no works or titles survive. Against the *Stoic doctrine of cosmic conflagrations, he argued that the present cosmos is eternal because it causes everything, including itself, and because it contains eternal objects and species. He also held that *soul consists of aether. In *ethics, he accused the Stoics of verbal quibbling in their analysis of the passions; and he reformulated *Aristotelian theory by defining *happiness as a "fulfillment" (*sumplêrôma*) of psychic, physical, and external goods, where virtue vastly outweighs the rest. But he broke with Peripatetic tradition to condemn *rhetoric as a pseudo-art without any methodical basis or social value.

BIBLIOGRAPHY: Texts in Wehrli 10.—*STEPHEN A. WHITE*

CYNICS and CYNICISM. The term "Cynic" ("the dog-like") has been used from the fourth century B.C.E. of *Diogenes of Sinope (c. 412/403–c. 324/321 B.C.E.), who was nicknamed "the dog" for his shamelessness, and of his followers; hence "Cynicism" as the name of the general movement. The genesis, status, significance and influence of Cynicism were controversial in antiquity and remain so. Interpretative problems arise from Cynic behavior and sayings, from the loss of nearly all Cynic writings (though this matters less in the case of Cynicism than of other philosophies), and from diverse distortions in the ancient traditions (e.g., invention of sayings and anecdotes, a general tendency of ancient biography accentuated by the flamboyant personalities and self-dramatizing tendencies of the leading Cynics, especially Diogenes; artificial integration of Cynicism into a formal philosophical succession from *Socrates to the *Stoics; bowdlerisation; polemical misrepresentation). *Diogenes Laertius, Book 6, is the most important single source for the Cynics; despite all its evidential problems, it preserves a mass of valuable information.

While there has been controversy from ancient times as to whether Diogenes or *Antisthenes, a follower of Socrates, was the true founder of Cynicism, majority opinion has always—and rightly—favored Diogenes. The claim for Antisthenes should be attributed to the general ancient desire to construct traditions based on master-pupil relationships (hence Antisthenes as Diogenes' teacher), to the specific project of tracing Stoicism back in unbroken succession to Socrates, and to Antisthenes' undoubted influence on Cynicism.

Cynicism was never a formal philosophical school but rather a way of life grounded in an extreme primitivist interpretation of the principle "live according to nature" (hence the Cynics' appeals to animals, primitive man, uncivilised barbarians, and the gods as moral standards). This principle explains all the characteristic Cynic modes of behavior and attitudes (extreme poverty and simplicity of life; rejection not only of material possessions but also of all social and political norms, of all culture, education, and intellectual speculation). As in the case of *Epicureanism, the fact that the founder's followers believed him to have discovered the truth precluded any substantial diversity or development in their thought and practice. Nevertheless, one can usefully distinguish between "hard" Cynics (rigorous exponents of the original prescription, found at all periods) and "soft" Cynics (who compromised varyingly with existing social and political institutions), between practical Cynicism (Cynicism as lived) and literary Cynicism (Cynicism as written or written about), and between Cynics (in some sense) and those merely influenced by Cynicism.

"Hard" Cynicism was best expounded by Diogenes and (to some extent) by his greatest follower, *Crates of Thebes (c. 368/365–c. 288/285 B.C.E.). From 320–220 B.C.E. "soft" Cynicism was diversely represented by Onesicritus of Aigina, whose History portrayed Alexander the Great as a Cynic philosopher-king; by the eclectics *Bion of Borysthenes, court-philosopher of Antigonus Gonatas, and Teles, school-teacher and excerptor of Cynic and other philosophers; and by Cercidas of Megalopolis, politician, lawgiver, and social reformer. Both Bion and Teles exemplify a degree of compromise between Cynics and *Cyrenaics; the elder *Aristippus became an important figure in the general "soft-Cynic" tradition. Practical Cynicism declined in the second and first centuries B.C.E. without ever dying out and revived in the early Empire. Greek cities swarmed with Cynics. Cynicism produced remarkable individuals (Demetrius, friend of Seneca; Dio of Prusa; in the second century *Demonax, Peregrinus, and *Oenomaus). The Roman authorities inevitably clashed with "hard" Cynics (qua anarchists). Later, Cynic and *Christian ascetics were sometimes confused, sometimes distinguished. (Some scholars even claim Jesus as Cynic.) Cynics are mentioned until the sixth century C.E. Continental European philosophy has shown some interest in Cynicism.

Partly in consequence of its missionary zeal, Cynicism greatly influenced Greek and Roman philosophy, rulership ideology, literature, and (later) religion. Crates' follower *Zeno of Citium founded Stoicism, a development of Cynicism with a proper theoretical grounding: Stoic *ethics are essentially Cynic ethics, Stoic cosmopolitanism a development of Cynic; Diogenes' *Republic* influenced Zeno's and *Chrysippus'. The legitimacy of Cynicism was debated within Stoicism, reactions ranging from nearly total acceptance (*Aristo of Chios) to partial acceptance (Zeno, Chrysippus), to rejection (*Panaetius), to bowdlerizing and idealizing redefinition (*Epictetus). More broadly, the very extremeness of Cynic positions on material possessions, individual ethics, and politics catalyzed the definition of other philosophies' positions: apart from the Stoics, the Epicureans, though influenced by Cynic ethics, polemicized against Cynicism. Diogenes and Crates are generally celebrated in popular philosophy. While the Cynic king is a moral concept wholly antithetical to the worldly king, Onesicritus (following Antisthenes and *Xenophon) facilitated appropriation and redefinition of that concept by rulership ideology (as later did Dio of Prusa's *Kingship Orations* addressed to the Roman emperor Trajan). Cynic ethics influenced Christian asceticism.

To maximize their audience, the Cynics (despite their avowed rejection of literature) wrote more voluminously and variously than any other ancient philosophical school: relatively formal philosophical treatises (including "*Republics*"), *dialogues, tragedies, historiography, letters, *"diatribes" (moral homilies in lecture form), various kinds of poetry and of literary parody, prose-poetry hybrids (*Menippus). The Cynic diatribe, anecdotal tradition, satiric spirit and seriocomic discourse had enormous and varied philosophical and literary influence (e.g., on the diatribes of *Seneca and *Plutarch; philosophical biography and the gospels; Roman satire; the epistles of Horace, St. Paul, and Seneca; *Lucian).

See also CRATES of Thebes, DIOGENES of Sinope, HIPPARCHIA.

BIBLIOGRAPHY: Texts in L. Paquet, *Les Cyniques grecs: Fragments et témoignages*,[2] Ottawa, 1988; *SSR* vol. 2, V B–N. Billerbeck, M., ed., *Epiktet: Vom Kynismus*, Leiden, 1978; also ed., *Die Kyniker in der modernen Forschung*, Amsterdam, 1991; Branham, R. B. and M.-O Goulet-Cazé, eds., *The Cynics: the Cynic Movement in Antiquity and its Legacy for Europe*, Berkeley, 1996; Downing, F. G., *Cynics and Christian Origins*, Edinburgh, 1992; *DPA*, vol. 2, 812–23 (on Diogenes); 496–500 (on Crates); 108–112 (on Bion); Dudley, D. R., *A History of Cynicism*, London, 1937; Goulet-Cazé, M.-O., *L'Ascèse cynique*, Paris, 1986; also Goulet-Cazé and R. Goulet, eds., *Le cynisme ancien et ses prolongements*, Paris, 1993; Höistad, R., *Cynic Hero and Cynic King*, Uppsala, 1948; Lovejoy, A. O. and G. Boas, *Primitivism and Related Ideas in Antiquity*, Baltimore, 1935; Moles, J. L., in A. Laks and M. Schofield, eds., *Justice and Generosity*, Cambridge, 1995, ch. 5; Niehues-Pröbsting, H., *Der Kynismus des Diogenes und der Begriff des Zynismus*,[2] Frankfurt, 1988; *SSR* vol. 4, Naples, 413–583.— JOHN L. MOLES

CYNOSARGES. See GYMNASIUM.

CYRENAIC PHILOSOPHY. The Cyrenaic school took its name from the native city of its members, Cyrene. Its origins are in the *Socratic circle: it was founded by *Aristippus of Cyrene (c. 435–c. 355 B.C.E.), a close associate of *Socrates. The school flourished for about a century and a half and ended in the Hellenistic period, some time between *Arcesilaus' death (242 B.C.E.) and the beginning of *Chrysippus' career in the *Stoa (232 B.C.E.).

The beginnings of the Cyrenaic school were a family affair: After Aristippus the Socratic, his daughter Arete and his grandson Aristippus the Younger successively became its leaders. In the Hellenistic era, independent sects were founded by Theodorus, Anniceris, and Hegesias, which nevertheless kept their affiliation to the orthodox branch of the school.

Although some sources maintain that the Cyrenaics dismissed the study of physics and *logic and concentrated on *ethics, others attest that they granted the usefulness of logic for philosophical argumentation and that they considered both logic and ethics parts of philosophy. They developed *epistemology as a distinct branch of inquiry, not as a part of logic.

The Cyrenaic philosophy was originally developed as an ethical doctrine with physiological and *psychological overtones. Aristippus the Socratic maintained that pleasure and pain are *pathê*, effects (undergoings, modifications, or affections) upon a subject, usually caused by contact with an external object. The term itself does not imply that what is affected is a *perceiving* subject: A stone may be affected by heat and turn hot, or a person may be exposed to heat and feel hot. Although Aristippus clearly studied the *pathê* in connection with perceivers, his doctrine in places preserves this ambiguity. While some passages yield a physicalistic conception of the *pathê*, identifying pleasure with a smooth movement and pain with a rough movement of the flesh, others report that he drew a distinction between the physical motions related to pleasure and pain and the subjective experiences of feeling pleasure or pain: These *pathê* are related to bodily motions of which the perceiver is conscious, but there may also be imperceptible motions that do not incite *pathê*. The *pathê* are short-lived, for the movements resulting in them disappear with time. The memory of past goods or the anticipation of goods to come count as pleasures, while the enjoyment of present pleasures presumably lasts only while the corresponding bodily motions are taking place. These characteristics also belong to a third category of *pathê*, probably introduced by Aristippus the Younger and identified as intermediate *pathê*. The Cyrenaics report such *pathê* by verbal or adverbial neologisms such as "being whitened" or "being affected whitely," which describe the manner in which one is affected, rather than the qualities of perceived objects.

The physiological features of the *pathê* are presupposed by the ethical doctrines of all Cyrenaic philosophers, which, contrary to what scholars commonly assume, vary considerably.

Some sources testify that Aristippus the Socratic was a hedonist positing the momentary pleasures of the present as the moral end. Others deny that he defined such pleasures as the only intrinsic *good and add that he never lectured in defence of a particular moral end. However, it seems certain that he was concerned with the moral value of pleasure and that he considered it crucial for *happiness. Contrary to other Socratics, Aristippus did not believe that the enjoyment of pleasure requires moderation: one may indulge in many and intense pleasures, provided that one can be in control of oneself. Psychological freedom in respect of pleasure is obtained by philosophical education, which provides the only means of securing the well-being of the soul. The value that Aristippus puts on such long-term activities suggests that he perceives his life as a single whole, not as a series of pleasurable incidents, and that he views particular pleasures as components of happiness, not merely as ends in themselves.

The ethics of Aristippus the Younger is marked by the definition of the moral end of each action as the particular bodily pleasure that results from it at the present moment. Each pleasure is the moral end and there can be no difference in intensity or in degree between pleasures. However, Aristippus the Younger emphasizes the importance of happiness, since he maintains that the overall goal of humans is to live pleasurably.

A subtle balance between hedonism and eudaemonism is also encountered in the ethics of Anniceris and of Hegesias. The Annicerians further clarified the concept of the moral end by arguing that pleasure and pain are necessarily related to motion and that, therefore, painlessness, which is not characterised by motion, cannot be part of the moral end. They too held that particular pleasures are the only intrinsic good. But differently from their predecessors, they attributed moral value to mental pleasures and maintained that there are circumstances in which one will act altruistically, thus indicating a concern for obtaining pleasures over an extended period of time. Hegesias was a hedonist in principle, since he too defined momentary present pleasure as the moral end. But he argued that the collection of particular pleasures constituting happiness is unattainable. This belief led him to maintain that life is a matter of indifference and that life and death are each desirable in turn. His grim ethics is moderated by the intellectualist thesis that no one errs voluntarily and by the philanthropic concern that one should not despise people but rather teach them. As to Theodorus, he introduced the concepts of joy and grief, posited joy as the supreme good, and claimed that pleasure and pain are intermediate between good and evil. His doctrine approaches the ethics of Aristippus the Socratic in that it considers wisdom and justice as goods, stresses their importance for obtaining the moral end, maintains that the wise man need not be temperate and that he is self-sufficient, and advocates cosmopolitanism. Although he does not speak openly of happiness, his doctrine clearly has eudaemonistic aspects. For since he called particular pleasures intermediates, he probably viewed them instrumentally, as means to joy. Since joy is distinct from pleasures and since its occurrence results from the exercise of wisdom, it was probably conceived as a long-term pleasurable state.

The ethical positions of the Cyrenaics are backed by an elaborate epistemological theory that claims that the nature of external objects is inapprehensible and that the only knowledge accessible to us is the awareness of our own *pathê*. In this context, the apprehension of a *pathos* probably concerns not the physical motions associated with it, but primarily the subjective experience that one has. The theses that the apprehension of the *pathê* is infallible and incorrigible and that the *pathê* themselves are private to the person who is experiencing them and are accessible to no other person emphasize the subjective character of personal experiences.

The character and analysis of subjective knowledge determines the scope of Cyrenaic *skepticism. This denies the possibility of knowing the real properties of objects, on the grounds that no epistemic link can be established between the content of one's *pathê* and the empirical qualities that they are supposed to represent. However, the Cyrenaics do not question the existence of external objects, nor do they wonder whether other people exist or whether they have *pathê*. Thus, Cyrenaic skepticism relies on the realistic presupposition that there is an external world that may be entirely misrepresented by our *pathê* and that there are people other than the perceiver inhabiting it.

BIBLIOGRAPHY: Texts in *SSR* 2. Döring, K., *Die Sokratesschüler Aristipp und die Kyrenaiker*, Stuttgart, 1988; Irwin, T., *The Monist* 74, 1991, 55–82; Laks, A., in J. Brunschwig and M. Nussbaum, eds., *Passions and Perceptions*, Cambridge, 1993, 18–49; Tsouna-McKirahan, V., *OSAP* 10, 1992, 161–192.—*VOULA TSOUNA-McKIRAHAN*

D

DAMASCIUS (c. 462–after 538 C.E.), of Damascus in Syria. Last head of the *Neoplatonic school of Athens. Damascius studied and taught *rhetoric in Alexandria and Athens, attending also the Neoplatonic schools in these two cities. He moved to philosophy under the direction of *Proclus' successors at Athens, Marinus and Isidore, revitalizing the school at Athens on becoming its head. Among his pupils was *Simplicius. On the Emperor Justinian's closure of the school in 529 (see ACADEMY), Damascius went into exile in Persia with some pupils and colleagues, but returned in 532 (his subsequent movements are unknown).

Numerous fragments of his *Life of Isidore* survive, yielding valuable information on the Neoplatonist philosophers of the fifth century C.E. Of his teaching there remain fragments from a treatise *On Number, Place and Time* (relating to *Aristotle's *Physics*), and echos of comments on Aristotle's *On the Heavens* and *Meteorology*. Some references concern his comments on *Plato's *Alcibiades I, Republic, Sophist*, and *Timaeus*; and we can still read versions of his lectures on the *Phaedo* and *Philebus*. His *Commentary on the Parmenides* and a systematic work *On [First] Principles*, covering issues relating to the Neoplatonic *metaphysical interpretation of the *Parmenides*, also survive. This teaching followed the curriculum instituted by *Iamblichus, in which the study of Aristotle leads to a cycle of Platonic dialogues read as a means for ascending to the highest philosophical knowledge.

Damascius also integrated into Platonism, as Iamblichus and Proclus had, works of ancient wisdom such as the poems attributed to Orpheus and the *Chaldaean Oracles*. In following in Proclus' steps, Damascius showed considerable critical acumen, sometimes preferring Iamblichus' views. The work *On [First] Principles* is a remarkably rigorous and sophisticated analysis of the dilemmas and limits of our conceptions of a transcendent first principle, ineffable source of all things, whereas the *Commentary on the Parmenides* begins with intelligible *being and follows the progression of lower levels of being; here Damascius applies an interpretation of the *Parmenides* different from that of Proclus. In the domain of physics, Damascius' views on *time and place are also original and interesting contributions.

BIBLIOGRAPHY: Texts in L. Westerink, ed., *The Greek Commentaries on Plato's Phaedo*, vol. 2: *Damascius*, Amsterdam, 1977; L. Westerink, ed., *Damascius, Lectures on the Philebus*, Amsterdam, 1959; C. Ruelle, ed., *Damascii successoris dubitationes ... In Platonis Parmenidem*, vol. 2, Paris, 1899; L. Westerink and J. Combès, eds., *Damascius Traité des premiers principes*, 3 vols., Paris, 1986–1991; C. Zintzen, ed., *Damascii vitae Isidorae reliquiae*, Hildesheim, 1967. *DPA* 2, 541–93.—*DOMINIC J. O'MEARA*

DAMON (active mid-5th cent. B.C.E.), of Athens. Musical and social theorist, *sophist; close associate and adviser of Pericles. He was ostracized c. 440, apparently as the intellectual *éminence grise* behind Periclean policy. He is best known from flattering references in *Plato and *Isocrates.

We know the general tendency of his thought. He made original, systematic, empirically based analyses of musical phenomena, devised a technical musicological vocabulary, and refined traditional beliefs in the effects of musical forms on character, stressing their educative role and the vulnerability of political systems to changes in musical practice. Few reliable details survive. His views on *harmoniai* probably differed from those of *Republic* 3: the "Platonized" Damon of later reports (perhaps reflecting the contents of a *dialogue *On Music* by *Heraclides of Pontus) is thoroughly suspect, as is *Philodemus' suggestion that he wrote a speech on education addressed to the Areopagus. The hypothesis that he was a *Pythagorean has virtually no foundations. Aristides Quintilianus believed he possessed Damonian descriptions of attunements, possibly those he represents elsewhere as the *harmoniai* of Plato's *Republic*; but how they were originally expressed is uncertain. Despite Damon's lasting reputation, we have only the mistiest outline of his ideas.

BIBLIOGRAPHY: Texts in DK37. Wallace, R., in R. Wallace and B. Maclachlan, eds., *Harmonia Mundi*, Rome, 1991, 30–53.—*ANDREW BARKER*

DARDANUS (c. 170–88 B.C.E.), of Athens. *Stoic philosopher, student of *Antipater of Tarsus. Dardanus was a contemporary of *Panaetius of Rhodes and of *Mnesarchus of Athens. *Diogenes Laertius wrote a biography of him, to judge from the so-called *Index Locupletior*. *Cicero (*Acad.* 2.22.69) speaks of Dardanus and Mnesarchus as *principes Stoicorum* at Athens at the time when *Antiochus of Ascalon founded the "Old *Academy," c. 100–90. Nevertheless, the hypothesis of a double scholarchate of Dardanus and Mnesarchus following the death of Panaetius has been shown to be false.

BIBLIOGRAPHY: Dorandi, T., *Ricerche sulla cronologia dei filosofi ellenistici*, Stuttgart, 1991, 29–34; *DPA* 2, D22.—*TIZIANO DORANDI*

DEMETRIUS (c. 150–c. 75 B.C.E.), of Laconia. *Epicurean exegete. A student of Protarchus of Bargilia, Demetrius probably taught first at Miletus, then moved to Athens and became a colleague of *Zeno of Sidon. His works (surviving to us in fragmentary Herculanean papyri) include *On Poetry*, *On Geometry*, *Polyaenus' Puzzles* (defending the Epicurean *mathematician), a work defending *Epicurus' view on the sun's size against *Stoic criticisms, a work on Epicurus' *theology (which includes an interesting reference to god as "dual-natured"), and a work (see bibliography) in which he discusses whether problems with various passages in Epicurus' works are to be solved by proper exegesis or by appeal to copyists' errors (which he finds by comparing his multiple copies of Epicurus' texts). *Philodemus reports his defense of "sign-inference by similarity" (*On Signs* 45-46), *Sextus his defense of the existence of proof (*M* 8.348–353) and his exegesis of Epicurus' view that *time is an "accident of accidents" (*M* 10.219).

BIBLIOGRAPHY: Puglia, E., ed., *Aporie Testuali ed Esegetiche in Epicuro* (PHerc. 1012), 1988.—*JEFFREY S. PURINTON*

DEMETRIUS (c. 355–280 B.C.E.), of Phalerum. *Peripatetic philosopher, pupil of *Theophrastus, Athenian statesman, and exile in Egypt. It is doubtful that Demetrius ever became a teaching member of the Peripatos; but as his association with Theophrastus was close, some time after the death of *Aristotle (322 B.C.E.), he used his political influence or office (beginning 317) to help Theophrastus acquire property for the school.

Demetrius was made overseer of Athens by Cassander. His governance was characterized by a property qualification for citizenship, the enactment of sumptuary legislation, and a decade of domestic peace. When Poliorcetes captured Athens (307), Demetrius went into exile, first to Thebes and then to Alexandria, where he became the adviser of Ptolemy I. He is said to have been in charge of legislation and probably influenced the founding of the Museum and the Library. He fell out of favor when Ptolemy II came to power.

Although no writing of Demetrius survives, we have *Diogenes Laertius' list of forty-five titles. *Exhortation* (to the philosophic life), *On Greatness of Soul*, *On Marriage*, and *On Old Age* addressed typical Peripatetic themes. The same is true of *On Politics*, *On Laws*, and *On the Critical Moment*. There were collections like the *Sayings of the Seven Wise*

Men and *Aesop's Fables*. A work *On (the Art of) Rhetoric* is listed; the collected *Public and Ambassadorial Speeches* were Demetrius' own political orations. *On the Iliad*, *On the Odyssey*, and *On Antiphanes* indicate interest in poetics.

Several of Demetrius' works probably offered a unique picture of the philosopher-statesman. For example, in the work *On Behalf of the Constitution* he may have explained his own legislation and governance by appealing to the Aristotelian notion of *politeia*. In *On Peace*, he may have defended his cooperation with Macedon by appealing to Aristotle, who repeatedly recognized the importance of peace over war; and in *On Fortune*, he may have followed Theophrastus, emphasizing the way fortune can determine the success or failure of sound policy. *On the Ten Years* and *A Denunciation of the Athenians* dealt with Demetrius' own experiences as an active politician.

BIBLIOGRAPHY: Texts in *FGH* 2, 1929, no. 228, 956–73, with comm., 1930, 641–53; Wehrli 4, 9–44, with comm. 45–89; P. Stork et al., in *RUSCH* vol. 10, 1998, with tr. and essays.—WILLIAM W. FORTENBAUGH

DEMOCRITUS (perhaps c. 460–350s B.C.E., though a death as early as 390s is possible), of Abdera. Atomist philosopher. *Diogenes Laertius (9.34–43) relates stories that Democritus learned *theology and *astronomy from magi left with his father by Xerxes, spent his inheritance on travel to Egypt and the east, went to Athens and heard *Socrates, met *Anaxagoras, and was an admirer of *Pythagoras. He was clearly most influenced, however, by *Leucippus, who taught the atomist philosophy at Abdera. Apparently because he developed Leucippus' philosophy in far greater detail, Democritus (nicknamed "Wisdom" because of his encyclopedic knowledge) received the title which Leucippus seems rather to deserve: "the father of atomism."

Diogenes Laertius (9.46-49) lists over sixty works attributed to Democritus: eight *"ethical," sixteen "on nature," twelve *"mathematical," eight "literary," eight "on arts" (like *medicine), and nine on "causes." *Plato allegedly wanted to burn them all, but was persuaded that copies were too widely disseminated (D.L. 40). None survive. And, of the nearly three hundred fragments of Democritus, over two hundred are ethical maxims (of uncertain authenticity); almost none address the basic atomic theory, which must be reconstructed, therefore, from *Aristotle and later *doxographers.

It is generally agreed that the Abderites conceived atomism as a reply to the *Eleatics: *Parmenides had said that Being is one and unchanging, and that Not-being does not exist; the atomists replied that Not-being exists no less than Being, that is, that both "the empty" (an *infinite *void) and "the full" (the atom, each of the infinite plurality of which is one and unchanging) exist. It is also clear that Democritus denied the reality of secondary qualities like sweetness, heat, and color: these exist in macroscopic bodies only "by convention" (our perceptions of them being nothing but subjective experiences), and atoms have only the primary qualities of shape, size, and solidity. More controversial is the thesis that Democritus also denied the reality of macroscopic bodies themselves, but the reports of Democritus' view by *Aristotle (DK68A37: one thing cannot "in truth" come to be from many atoms), *Colotes (Plut. *Against Colotes* 1110e: "compound is by convention"), and *Plutarch (*Against Colotes* 1111a: "compounds appear," but all things are really just atoms) do seem to support it.

Two reasons are given for the Abderite claim that the shapes of atoms are infinitely various: Only thus could they explain the infinitely various phenomena, and there is no reason that there should be atoms of one shape but not of another. Some sources report that the sizes of atoms were also supposed to be infinitely various, but others say that atoms are small and even (implausibly) give their smallness as a reason for their indivisibility. Other reasons given are their solidity and their partlessness. But their alleged partlessness is controversial; it is hard to imagine how Democritus could deny that one can conceive part of an atom here and part there, and, besides, some sources do speak of atoms having parts. Probably, then, atoms are theoretically divisible but physically indivisible.

Also controversial is the question of whether Democritean atoms have weight, but *Aëtius (1.12.6) and *Cicero (*Fat.* 46) flatly deny it, and it seems unlikely that Democritus anticipated *Epicurus' view that atoms tend downward in the infinite void. According to Aristotle (GC 326a9–10), Democritus said that an atom's weight is proportional to its size; and, since the size of atoms explains how they are sorted out in the vortex that produces a given cosmos (smaller atoms being driven to the periphery, larger atoms being trapped in the center), it seems likely that atomic weight was for Democritus simply atomic size considered as a cause of centripetal motion in a vortex. Note, too, Aristotle's complaints that Democritus posits no "natural" motion (*DC* 300b8–13) or origin of motion (*Phys.* 252a32): All motion is "forced," the result of collisions, and atoms now move and collide simply because they have always done so. Physical determinism is a consequence of this view of atomic motion, though some doubt Cicero's testimony (*Fat.* 23) that Democritus recognized this.

Given that the universe is infinite, there must be an infinite number of worlds at any given time. A world is formed when a set of atoms is moving in vortical fashion such that the atoms sort out like to like, with the larger and more unwieldy atoms becoming entangled at the center of the vortex to form a disklike earth resting like a lid on air below. Worlds differ; some have no sun, water, or life. In our world, life arose from the moist earth. Men developed various arts by imitating animals; weaving, for example, was learned from spiders. Different languages arose as groups of men agreed on conventional names for things. *Religion arose when images of huge, nearly indestructible, anthropomorphic beings came to men, who, unable to explain meteorological phenomena, wrongly assumed that they are caused by these beings. Whether Democritus thought that there are gods apart from these images is unclear. *Sextus (M 9.19) says he did not, but that he did think these images reveal the future and are maleficent or beneficent.

The *soul, like fire, is made up of small, spherical atoms; hence it heats the body and moves it (such atoms being especially mobile). The soul is mortal, though dead bodies still have some sensation and warmth, because not all the soul-atoms leave the body at death, and resuscitation of the dead is possible. Sensation is due to contact with the body sensed, which, in the case of vision, means that material films having the shape of the body from which they flow enter the eye. This view is attributed to Leucippus and Democritus together; a more complicated view, according to which the films first stamp an image on the air, which then enters the eye, is attributed only to Democritus. Differences in perception are explained by differences in the shapes and configurations of the atoms of the thing perceived (so that, e.g., things made of smooth atoms taste sweet) and by differences in perceivers (so that, e.g., what tastes sweet to the healthy tastes bitter to the sick).

But the fact that something tastes sweet to most people does not entail that it really is sweet. Hence, reports Aristotle (Met. 1009b11–12), "Democritus says either that nothing is true or it is unclear to us." The latter alternative would amount to skepticism, but Sextus (HP 1.213–14) insists that, whereas skeptics say they do not know whether honey is sweet or bitter, Democritus says that it is neither, presumably because, on his view, sweetness and bitterness, as macroscopic properties, do not exist. This would help explain how Democritus could say both that all perceptibles are false and that perception's reports are necessarily true: Perception reports accurately, but its objects are unreal. It would also help explain what puzzled Sextus (M 7.136): how Democritus, "although promising to support the trustworthiness of the senses, is nonetheless found condemning them." It must be admitted, however, that some of Democritus' remarks seem more radically *skeptical, for example, "in truth we know nothing about anything," a remark hard to reconcile with his claim that "in truth there exists atoms and void," his contrast of the mind's "legitimate" judgment with the senses' "bastard" judgment, and his alleged view that phenomena, concepts, and feelings are the three criteria of truth (*M* 7.135–40).

It is often said that Democritus had no systematic moral philosophy, but this impression may be due to nothing more than the loss of his ethical works and the fact that the surviving ethical fragments are mostly mere maxims. The evidence, at any rate, does suggest a consistent view of the *telos* (even if Democritus did not use that term): It is "contentment" (*euthumia*), a calm mental state disturbed by no fear, superstition, or passion. Democritus did not call this undisturbed state a pleasure, as did Epicurus later, but otherwise his views seem rather like Epicurus': Advantage is defined in terms of pleasure, contentment comes from moderation and rejection of inopportune pleasures, living virtuously frees us from fear, bodily needs are easily satisfied, and one should count one's blessings, live a simple, self-sufficient life, and not blame the gods or chance for one's misfortunes.

Though Democritus allegedly influenced *Pyrrho via the skeptical Abderites of the fourth century (from *Metrodorus of Chios to *Anaxarchus), his most important influence was on Epicurus, whose atomist school represented what seemed to later thinkers one of the two main alternative world views: "either atoms or providence," as *Marcus Aurelius puts it.

BIBLIOGRAPHY: Texts in DK68. Benakis, L., ed., *Proceedings of the First International Congress on Democritus*, 2 vols., Xanthi, Greece, 1984; Furley, D. J., *Two Studies in the Greek Atomists*, Princeton, 1967; also *The Greek Cosmologists*, vol. 1, Cambridge, 1987; also *Cosmic Problems*, Cambridge, 1989.—*JEFFREY S. PURINTON*

DEMONAX (c. 70–170 C.E.). Philosopher known from *Lucian's *Demonax* and various independently preserved *dicta*. Some of the latter could derive from (lost) written works. The *Demonax*, a paradigmatic moral biography, also has elements of indirect autobiography (Demonax evokes Lucian's self-portrait elsewhere) and of philosophical fiction in the tradition of *Xenophon's *Memorabilia* (Lucian plays Xenophon to Demonax' *Socrates, and the *Demonax* is largely anecdotal; this element does not, however, entail that everything is fictitious). Recovery of the real Demonax is therefore difficult, a difficulty compounded by Demonax' own imitation of philosophical models ("They are all admirable, but I personally revere Socrates, admire *Diogenes [of Sinope] and love *Aristippus").

Born in Cyprus of a rich and influential family, well educated, and having at various times heard the *Cynics Demetrius and Agathobulus, the *Stoic *Epictetus, and Timocrates of Heraclea, Stoic and *sophist, Demonax embraced poverty and became a philosopher. He spent most of his life in Athens, had many followers (including Lucian), eventually attained mass popularity, starved himself to death at the age of one hundred when he could no longer maintain self-sufficiency, and had a public funeral. Unusually in the ancient world, he disclaimed adherence to any particular sect while admitting personal philosophical models and sometimes accepting a Cynic affiliation. Demonax' philosophical activity consisted largely, or wholly (depending on whether or not he wrote anything), in the advocacy and practice of *virtue of a simple kind. The influence of the varied traditions of Socrates, Diogenes, Aristippus, and *Crates of Thebes (a model directly acknowledged neither by Demonax nor by Lucian) is clear, presumably partly as mediated through Epictetus' conception of the Ideal Cynic.

Demonax's advocacy of virtue consisted of advice and consolation to friends and of quips against stock Cynic targets: sophists, other philosophers, physicists, logicians, homosexuals, athletes, the superstitious, the powerful. His frankness and use of humor followed the Socratic/Cynic tradition; Lucian's insistence that he eschewed Socratic irony and Cynic abuse in favor of Attic charm is not wholly consistent with the quoted *dicta* and reflects a desire to maximize parallels with himself and minimize robuster elements. Demonax' practice of virtue imitated Diogenes' dress and simplicity of life without the ostentation and extremes of "hard" Cynicism, involved limited political participation (again contrary to "hard" Cynicism but markedly echoing Socrates' career), took a strongly philanthropic attitude to all except the incorrigibly wicked ("to err is human, to correct backslidings divine"), and alleviated strife within both family and state. This reconciling activity and the fact that he became known as a "good spirit" directly recalls Crates. Aristippus' influence emerges more generally in cheerfulness of demeanor and a certain moral relativism.

Whatever the distortions of Lucian's portrait, Demonax was clearly a philosopher of outstanding personal virtue who did much practical good.

BIBLIOGRAPHY: *DPA* 2, 718–19.—*JOHN L. MOLES*

DEXIPPUS (early 4th cent. C.E.), a follower and probably pupil of *Iamblichus. Of his teaching there remains only the earlier part of a *Commentary on Aristotle's Categories* (up to 4b23; the rest has not survived). *Porphyry and Iamblichus had included *Aristotle's *logical works in the *Neoplatonic curriculum. Dexippus follows their approach in attempting a reconciliation of Aristotle with *Platonic *metaphysics and indeed makes much use of their *commentaries on the *Categories*, contributing very little of his own, in *Simplicius' opinion. Dexippus attempts to answer *Plotinus' criticisms of Aristotle (in *Enn.* 6.1 and 3, and as reported, it seems, by Porphyry), taking account also of earlier *Stoic and *Middle Platonic criticism. This is done in the form of solutions to problems given in a dialogue between Dexippus and a pupil, Seleucus. Iamblichus' commentary on the *Categories* (lost) can be recovered in part through comparison between Dexippus and Simplicius' commentary on the *Categories*. Dexippus is also an important source for Porphyry's long commentary on the *Categories* (also lost) and for the earlier history of discussion of Aristotle's text.

BIBLIOGRAPHY: Text in J. Dillon, ed., *Dexippus On Aristotle's* Categories, London/Ithaca, 1990. Hadot, P., in R. Sorabji, ed., *Aristotle Transformed*, London/Ithaca, 1990, 125–140.—*DOMINIC J. O'MEARA*

DIALECTIC (*dialektikê*) is the art of argumentative disputation. Such an art inevitably leads to the study of arguments themselves and the development of criteria for validity; therefore, the line between dialectic and *logic is not sharp, and *dialektikê* was the usual term for logic in Hellenistic times (*logikê* first appears in the *Aristotelian commentators). Narrower conceptions of dialectic appear in *Plato and *Aristotle, and this article is mostly confined to them.

From its beginnings, dialectic was associated not only with disputation but with the specific practice of *refutation*, especially refuting others by deriving impossible or unacceptable results from premises they concede. *Zeno of Elea (mid-5th cent. B.C.E.) attacked *Parmenides' detractors in this way, for which reason Aristotle counted him as the founder of dialectic. *Socrates also refuted others from their own premises. Claiming no knowledge for himself, he insisted that he could only ask questions and never answer them; therefore, he represents his refutations as entirely the result of his interlocutors' opinions.

Plato. Plato's philosophy derived from Socrates' dialectical practice, though his understanding of dialectic changed over his long career. He regarded dialectic as the philosopher's route to wisdom (it has been said that he comes to mean by "dialectic" the correct method of philosophy, whatever that may turn out to be). A difficulty with Socratic dialectic is that it seems able only to refute and never to establish; in the *Meno*, Plato has Socrates respond to this charge with a dialectical exchange in which he extracts a geometrical proof from an uneducated slave. *Republic* books 6 and 7 presents dialectic as the crowning stage of the education of the philosopher-rulers, leading to knowledge of the Forms; as 538d–539c make evident, this dialectic is still tied to argument and refutation. (Further discussion of Plato's mature conception of dialectic would require the interpretation of his whole philosophy.)

Aristotle. Aristotle's concept of dialectic seems by contrast much humbler. He regularly contrasts dialectical argument with scientific demonstration (*apodeixis*), maintaining that dialectic cannot actually prove anything. Dialectical arguments, like demonstrations, are valid arguments; they differ from demonstrations in the premises they use. Demonstrative premises are (i) assertions, (ii) "true and primary"; dialectical premises are instead (i) questions, (ii) *endoxa* (variously rendered as "common beliefs," "reputable premises," "accepted opinions"). The *endoxa* include "what everyone thinks, or most people, or the wise (and among them, all, or the majority, or the most famous)." Since *endoxa* (however interpreted) clearly do not have to be true, dialectical arguments need not have true premises and therefore cannot establish anything. A common view is that dialectical argument is *merely plausible*, serving not actually to establish a conclusion but perhaps to render it credible to someone.

This fails to give sufficient attention to the second point: dialectical premises are questions. This has a natural explanation if we recall that dialectical arguments involve two participants: Premises must be put in the form of questions to a respondent. In fact, the Greek word translated "premise" (*protasis*) means "what is held out" (i.e., for acceptance or rejection). Those who demonstrate, by contrast, do not rely on others' opinions but take first principles as their premises. This permits a different interpretation of *endoxa*. In arguing with others, I must rely on their answers for my premises. In order to get the conclusion I want, I must be able to predict what my interlocutor will accept; a study of which premises are accepted by people in general, and by various types of person, would facilitate this. The *endoxa* may therefore be an inventory of premises acceptable (to different types of people).

Aristotle's *Topics* states as its purpose the discovery of a general dialectical *method*, for use in dialectical argument of any sort. At the foundation of this method are the *topoi* ("locations," "commonplaces"); *Theophrastus says that a *topos* is "a kind of starting point or element, by means of which we obtain starting points with respect to particular cases, definite in outline but indefinite with respect to the particulars." The examples of *topoi* in *Topics* 2–6 consist of very general principles (often reasonably characterized as logical), together with instructions for their use. The name *topos* also suggests connections with mnemonic technique (cf. *Top.* 163b28–32); the *topoi* served as a classificatory system for recalling premises when needed (timely recall is essential in a dialectical exchange). (See further Brunschwig, Stump cited below.) This same method is useful for any type of persuasive discourse, including rhetorical argument: Aristotle says (*Rh.* 1356a20–33) that *rhetoric is really part of dialectic, or a hybrid of dialectic (which provides its arguments) and a study of characters (which teaches what premises to use with which audience).

However, the *Topics* has special connections with a kind of argumentative contest practiced in Plato's *Academy, in which two disputants took on the roles of questioner and answerer respectively to debate some controversial proposition (a "problem," *problêma*), for example, "Whether the just are happier than the unjust." The answerer defended one side of this question, and the questioner undertook to derive its opposite from the answerer's responses (here again, we see refutation from a respondent's own words). Questioners could only ask yes/no questions; answerers were generally limited to assent and dissent, though they were allowed to refuse to answer badly formed and ambiguous questions. Rounds of debate were apparently judged or scored. (A number of details of the practice can be inferred from *Topics* 8.)

Aristotle also says that dialectic is useful in connection with "the philosophical sciences" (*Top.* 101a34–36). What he means is subject to more controversy, but he surely is including the procedure he calls *diaporein*, "going through the puzzles," with which he typically begins his treatment of a subject: He surveys the views of his predecessors on a subject and derives inconsistencies and difficulties from them, thus determining what difficulties his own account must solve. Since dialectic seeks to deduce consequences from the views of others, its methods are needed for a *diaporia*.

Some have suggested a loftier role for dialectic. *Topics* 101a36–b4 says that dialectic provides the "road" to the first principles on which the sciences rest and which they cannot themselves prove; *Nicomachean Ethics* 1145b2–7 implies that a criterion for adequacy in a theory is that it solve all the puzzles and leave our "common beliefs" undisturbed. Some interpreters take this as evidence that the *endoxa* have a special evidential status for Aristotle or that some version of dialectic establishes the ultimate principles of philosophy and science (Irwin's is the fullest version of such a view). Another striking text is *Metaphysics* 4, which argues that although the principle of noncontradiction, as the firmest of all principles, cannot be proved (for there is nothing more secure from which to prove it), nevertheless a kind of "refutative demonstration" can be directed at those who question it: Refutation of others is the hallmark of dialectical argument. (See Dancy on this passage.) Scholarly opinion on this issue is divided.

Eristic. Both Aristotle and Plato distinguish dialectic from *eristic*, which they characterize as verbal combat in which the object is to win at any cost. Plato's *Euthydemus* portrays (or parodies) eristic encounters; the arguments depicted are transparently bad. Aristotle defines eristic arguments as counterfeit dialectical ones that either appear to be valid without being so or have premises that appear to be acceptable to the respondent but are not. *On Sophistical Refutations* (actually the last section of the *Topics*) classifies and diagnoses such fallacies.

After Aristotle. *Cicero and other orators found the *Topics* a valuable handbook for discovering arguments, and the *topoi* play a major role in the rhetorical tradition (see *Boethius, *De Topicis Differentiis* and Stump's commentary).

BIBLIOGRAPHY: Barnes, J., *Revue internationale de philosophie* 34, 1980, 490–511; Brunschwig, J., ed. and tr., *Aristote, Topiques I-IV*, Paris, 1967; also *Wissenschaftskolleg Jahrbuch*, 1984; Dancy, R., *Sense and Contradiction*, Dordrecht, 1974; Evans, J. D. G., *Aristotle on Dialectic*, Cambridge, 1977; Irwin, T., *Aristotle's First Principles*, Oxford, 1989; Owen, G. E. L., ed., *Aristotle on Dialectic: The Topics*, Oxford, 1968; Robinson, R., *Plato's Earlier Dialectic*,[2] Oxford, 1953; Stump, E., *Boethius's De Topicis Differentiis*, Ithaca, 1978.—ROBIN SMITH

DIALECTICAL SCHOOL. A philosophical tradition closely associated with the "minor *Socratic" *Megarian (Megaric) and Eristical traditions and believed by some to have flourished c. 320–250 B.C.E. *Diogenes Laertius reports (2.106) that one *Euclides of Megara (or of Gela), who was "concerned with *Parmenidean matters," originated a tradition whose adherents "were called Megarians (*Megarikoi*), then *Eristikoi*, and later *Dialektikoi*, Dionysius of Chalcedon having first named them thus because they formulated their arguments by question and answer." Scholarly tradition, then, takes philosophers referred to as "*Megarikoi*" (e.g., Euclides and *Diodorus Cronus' contemporary, *Stilpo of Megara), those referred to as "*Eristikoi*" (e.g., Euclides' pupil and *Aristotle's opponent, *Eubulides of Miletus, and *Alexinus of Elis), and those referred to as "*Dialektikoi*" (e.g., the supposed founder of the Dialectical tradition, Clinomachus of Thurii, Diodorus Cronus, and Diodorus' pupil *Philo) as all belonging to the same tradition or school. With respect to philosophical method or style, most members of this group employed the *"dialectical" (dialogue) approach of question-and-answer and attempted to bring philosophical opponents to their conclusions by carefully constructed puzzles and indirect (*reductio*) argumentation. With respect to philosophical doctrines, many seem to have combined a Socratic interest in moral issues with some form—in some cases much attenuated—of the *Eleatic *metaphysical doctrine of the unity and changelessness of "what is."

Any further discussion of a Dialectical school must begin with the important 1977 study by David Sedley, who argues for distinct Megarian and Dialectical (and perhaps Eristical) schools. Distinguishing sharply between a "school" or *hairesis* ("normally a unified sect recognized as such by its members") and a "succession" or *diadochê* ("a neat family tree of philosophers constructed by Hellenistic biographers"), Sedley argues that the *Megarikoi* and *Dialektikoi* constituted distinct *haireseis*. He is not so certain about the *Eristikoi*, since at least one philosopher (Alexinus) is designated as both *Dialektikos* and *Eristikos* and since the uncomplimen-

tary term *"Eristikos"* ("quibbler," "argumentative logic-chopper") is unlikely to have been self-designating. Sedley concludes that the triad
Megarikoi-Eristikoi-Dialektikoi represents not a single *hairesis* but a *diadochê*
and, as such, is something of a Hellenistic fabrication. He further attempts to distinguish the philosophical concerns of the *Megarikoi* (who
were *"Cynically-inclined moral philosophers") from those of the *Dialektikoi* (who "took up the constructive study of *logic") and finds fourteen
figures bearing the latter appellation (mostly within the period 320–250
B.C.E.). The *Eristikoi*, if they existed as a "school," are said to have "built
their philosophical method around the use of logical puzzles."

While Sedley's theses are impressively developed and have been
widely accepted, his arguments are, as one would expect in light of the
dearth of evidence, not conclusive. As he points out, *"dialektikos"* designates a certain logical or argument-based approach to philosophical issues and eventually became a standard term for a logician. A number of
philosophers designated as *"Megarikos"* or *"Eristikos"* (e.g., Stilpo and
Eubulides) are characterized as masters of dialectical argument. And
both Euclides and the anonymous Megarians referred to by Aristotle
(*Met.* 9.3)—as well as the *Dialektikos* Diodorus Cronus—seem to have
been concerned to defend some form of Eleatic metaphysics, probably by
means of arguments the ancients would have termed "dialectical." In
short, it does not seem easy to distinguish Megarian and Dialectical
schools either in terms of clearly demarcated sets of philosophical doctrines or in terms of methodology. In this case, at least, the relation between "school" and "succession" remains unclear.

BIBLIOGRAPHY: Döring, K., *Die Megariker: Kommentierte Sammlung der Testimonien*
(*Studien zur antiken Philosophie*, vol. 2), Amsterdam, 1972; Ebert, T., *Dialektiker und
frühe Stoiker bei Sextus Empiricus: Untersuchungen zur Entstehung der Aussagenlogik*,
Göttingen, 1991; Sedley, D., *PCPS* n.s. 23, 1977, 74–120.—*MICHAEL J. WHITE*

DIALOGUE, Greek. *Dialogos*, derived from *dialegesthai*, "to converse."
Greek literature is characterized by dialogue from its beginning. The direct exchange of speech between two speakers is an essential feature of
the epic, a minor part of the personal lyric, and predominant in tragedy
and comedy. Philosophical dialogue, defined as philosophical questions
posed by one speaker and answers given by another, is found in Greek
dramatic literature in the comedies of Epicharmus (DK13) and in
tragedies, such as *Euripides' Antiope*, which *Plato recognized in his
Gorgias. *Aristotle regarded *Zeno of Elea as the discoverer of "*dialectic" (*Sophist* fr. 1 Ross). As a genre, the philosophical dialogue is first
represented by the authors of the *Sokratikoi logoi* (*Socratic conversations), which capture to some extent the oral nature of Socrates' inquiries. There is evidence for nine authors of such dialogues in the fourth
century B.C.E. (D.L. 2.48–125). Foremost of these were *Aeschines, Plato,

*Xenophon, and *Phaedo of Elis. Of Aeschines there are significant remains of an *Alcibiades* and *Aspasia*; of Xenophon, the conversations of *Memorabilia* 2–4, the *Symposium*, and *Oeconomicus*. Thirty-two dialogues of the Platonic corpus have Socrates as the dominant speaker, and all six of the spurious dialogues involve Socrates as the chief speaker.

The signature of Plato's Socratic dialogues is Socrates and his questions "on some philosophical or political subject, with the appropriate rendition of the character of the actors involved" (D.L. 3.48). The characters of these dialogues are almost all historical, as are some of their settings. Four of the Socratic dialogues are elaborately framed in later settings (*Phaedo, Symposium, Theaetetus, Parmenides*). Plato was responsible for the classification of dialogues as "mimetic (dramatic), narrative, and mixed" (*Rep.* 3.392c–398c), a classification later applied to his own dialogues (D.L. 3.50). Some of his later dialogues introduce characters who deliver long uninterrupted speeches (Timaeus in the *Timaeus*, Critias in the *Critias*, and the Athenian Stranger in *Laws* 5). It is clear from the dialogues that Plato regarded himself as working in a genre that most closely resembled Attic comedy and tragedy.

In one of Aristotle's dialogues, *On Poets*, there is an important discussion of the dialogue form and *mimêsis*. The dialogue is described as a form of literature "between poetry and prose" (fr. 4 Ross). The Aristotelian dialogue was regarded as a distinct development from the Platonic form. Aristotle's dialogues are contrasted with the "esoteric" writings delivered orally in his own person. They differ from the Platonic dialogue in that they have a proem written by the author in his own voice. (The *Protrepticus* is prefaced by a letter dedicatory to King Themision of Cyprus.) It is evident that the author as speaker is in control of what his characters say, and thus little care is taken with characterization (Cic. *Att.* 4.16.2 and 13.9.3–4; see DIALOGUE, Latin). Aristotle's dialogues are always reported as the expressions of Aristotle's own views (e.g., "in the *Eudemus*, Aristotle says ..."). We have the names of none of the other interlocutors, and only a hint of what was said by another speaker (*On Justice*, fr. 1 Ross). We have reports of eighteen dialogues; they are all from early in his career. Like the *Apology* and *Symposium* of Xenophon, many look back to Platonic originals, the *Eudemus* to the *Phaedo* (and the *Crito*), the *Symposium* to the *Symposium*, *Nerinthus* and the *Sophist* to the *Gorgias*, *On Justice* to the *Republic*. The most influential of his dialogues, called his "Platonic writings" by *Plutarch (*On Philosophy*, fr. 1 Ross), are the *Protrepticus* and *On Philosophy*.

The writing of dialogues continued in the *Peripatos, and *Theophrastus and *Heraclides of Pontus were important exponents of the form (particularly in Heraclides' dialogue on the woman who had stopped breathing), although both were said to lack the grace of Plato.

The Heracleidean form of the dialogue involves conversations from the past and figures like *Pythagoras and *Empedocles. In the Hellenistic age, *Epicurus wrote in dialogue form (the *Symposium*). The remarkable character of Plutarch's dialogues is obscured by the fact that they are separated in the *Moralia*. One (*On Socrates' Daimonion*) is set in Athens in 387; *On the Delayed Revenge of the Gods*, set in Delphi, involves Plutarch and his relatives, yet begins after a speech of "Epicurus." In the age of Marcus *Aurelius, we have a dialogue of *Diogenes of Oeonanda, accompanied by a prefatory letter, on *The Infinity of Worlds* (frr. 62–67 Smith). Arrian's record of the conversations of *Epictetus and *Lucian's imaginary *Demonax* (as well as many of his short philosophical dialogues) are late echoes of the first *Sokratikoi logoi*.

The occasion of a symposium is also a form that continues from Plato and Xenophon through Epicurus, and Plutarch to Athenaeus and Macrobius, and was the subject of Aristotle's dialogue, *The Symposium*.

As a form of philosophical literature, the philosophical dialogue in Greek begins by offering an alternative, actually chosen by Socrates and then exploited by Plato, to the more authoritarian forms of expression found among the Presocratics (*Heraclitus' *Logos*, *Parmenides' goddess, and *Empedocles' divine voice) as well as the long unbroken epideictic speeches of the *sophists. It also offered the possibility of combining the anonymity of the author and a staging of conflicting points of view, but without a resolution agreed on by all parties in the dispute.

BIBLIOGRAPHY: See *SSR*. Clay, D., in P. A. Vander Waerdt, ed., *The Socratic Movement*, Ithaca/London, 1994, 23–47; Hirzel, R., *Der Dialog: Ein literarhistorischer Versuch*, 2 vols., Leipzig, 1895; Jaeger, W., *Aristotle: Fundamentals of the History of his Development*,[2] R. Robinson, tr., Oxford, 1948, 24–101.—*DISKIN CLAY*

DIALOGUE, Latin. *Dialogus, disputatio* (see DIALOGUE, Greek). In Latin, the dialogue was first a literary form. The dramatic exchange of conversation characterizes a poem of Ennius, who staged a debate between life and death, and the satires of Lucilius (active around 130 B.C.E.) involve dialogue. The philosophical dialogue proper was introduced into Latin with the publication of *Cicero's *De Republica* (in 51 B.C.E.). Cicero was the major exponent of the form, and his dialogues influenced the humanist dialogues of the Renaissance in Italy.

Cicero's dialogues fall into two periods: 55–51 and 46–44. All of his dialogues are introduced by a Preface by Cicero. Unlike the dialogues of the second period, Cicero's *De Oratore* and *De Republica* are set in the past and he plays no role in them. He exhibits an awareness of a wide range of possibilities of the dialogue form: the *Platonic, the *Aristotelian, the *Heraclidean; and he knew dialogues of the *Peripatetics *Aristo of Ceos (whose *Tithonus* is recognized by his *Cato Maior*) and *Dicaearchus. Emulation of Plato is the salient feature of his *De Republica*, *De Legibus*, and even the *De Oratore* (cf. 1.28), and Platonic is the care taken to establish a significant setting. But Cicero speaks of himself as writing in the convention of Aristotle (*Aristoteleo more*) in both the *De Oratore* (of 55 B.C.E.) and in the dialogues of his second period (*Familiares*.1.9.23; *Att.* 13.19.4–5). By this he means that in his *De Oratore* he followed the method of setting out the dialectic of opposing points of view (cf. *Or.* 3.80). In the letter to Atticus he defines the Aristotelian convention as a dialogue "in which the other speakers are made subordinate to the role of the author as speaker." (This is our only explicit evidence for Aristotle as the dominating speaker in his own dialogues.)

Such a description does not fit dialogues of the first period, but it is right for the dialogues of the second period. Cicero lists most of these in the introduction to his *De Divinatione* 2: the *Hortensius* (modelled on Aristotles' *Protrepticus*), *Academica, De Finibus, Tusculan Disputations, De Natura Deorum*. His *De Legibus* is also cast in dialogue form. The memorable spectacle of *Carneades as he appeared in Rome to give both sides of the argument for and against justice (LS 68 M) had its influence on Cicero, and in the *Academica* and *De Natura Deorum* he sets out countervailing arguments concerning the gods, with an indication of his own inclination (*ND* 3., end). He also admits that his characters are not always suited to their arguments but are simply ventriloquists for a position (*Att.* 13.19.5). *Seneca's prose works always recognize an addressee, but his *Dialogi* are such only in title. *Augustine's dialogues written before his baptism in 386 C.E. bring the tradition of the philosophical dialogue to a halt, for thereafter there is only a single authority to determine the issues of inner conflict. *Boethius *Consolation of Philosophy* is a stern lecture delivered by a personified *Philosophia* to an incarcerated Boethius.

The greatest exponents of the dialogue form in Latin after Cicero were the humanists and philosophers of the quattrocento Renaissance: Bruni, Alberti, Valla, and Marsilio Ficino of the *Symposium* and Galileo of the *Siderius Nuntius* and *Dialogue concerning the Two Chief World Systems*, the last written in Italian (1632).

BIBLIOGRAPHY: Hirzel, R., *Der Dialog: Ein Literarhistorischer Versuch*, Leipzig, 1895, 1.421–565 and 2.1–64; 385–398; Lerer, S., *Boethius and Dialogue: Literary Method in the Consolation of Philosophy*, Princeton, 1985; Marsh, D., *The Quatrocento Dialogue: Classical Tradition and Humanist Innnovation*, Cambridge, MA/London, 1980.— DISKIN CLAY

DIATRIBE. A Graeco-Roman form of moralizing lecture characterized by a conversational style with abundant *rhetorical figures, anecdotes, examples, and at least some hint of *dialogue or reference to an imagined opponent. Teles, *Musonius, and *Epictetus, along with some of the speeches of Dio Chrysostom and *Maximus of Tyre, are exemplars of a genre treating standard topics compatible with *Cynic and *Stoic philosophy in a didactic setting distinct from that of the dialogue or treatise or esoteric philosophical instruction. These exemplars may be designated "primary diatribes." Further, in the tradition of mixed genres in Graeco-Roman literature from the Hellenistic Age on, literary genres such as didactic poetry, satire, epistles (*Seneca; Cynic epistles), and philosophical treatises (*Philodemus; *Plutarch) provide "secondary diatribes," by using the form with modifications (*Lucretius 3.830–1094), parodying it (Horace *Satires* 2.3), or adopting a style clearly related in themes and traits to a common form outside of the genre in use. This influential form of moralizing lecture has come to be called the diatribe, a name it may have lacked in antiquity but that, with roots in the *sophistic tradition, serves as an apt working title.

The term *diatribê* entered scholarly currency through H. Usener, whose *Epicurea* (1887) allots the title *diatribai* to the "sermones" of *Bion of Borysthenes, developer of a Cynic genre mixing seriousness and humor. Horace (*Epistles* 2.2.60) is the source for the designation *sermones*, and Usener may be correct in crediting Bion with both the development of a genre and a tendency to lighten serious topics with humor. As *Diogenes Laertius reports (4.46–57), Bion, former slave of a rhetorician, became a "many-colored sophist" (4.47) after studying with *Academics, Cynics, *Cyrenaics, and *Peripatetics and was the first to clothe philosophy in *anthina*, that is, the verbal equivalent of garb appropriate for courtesans or satyr impersonators. He was theatrical and more rhetorical than philosophical, with a taste for jokes, parody, and vulgar language. Although his position in any philosophical movement is uncertain, Bion's fragments and testimonia show a focus on *ethics and an affinity with the Cynics. His tenure at the court of Antigonus Gonatas, exercising the philosopher's right of *parrhesia* and receiving upkeep in return, belies his image as primarily a preacher to the masses. He most likely was a teacher in the tradition of the older sophists, supporting himself by lecturing to large or small groups. His legacy consisted of *apophthegmata* and *hypomnemata*, the latter probably written versions of his lectures. The titles *On Anger* and *On Slavery* survive as examples of his themes.

Diatribê used in connection with Bion appears only in Diogenes Laertius' life of *Aristippus, in a passage subject to interpretation as referring to diatribes by Bion himself or by his associates, with little evidence as to the nature of the work (or works). Must we then abandon the assumption that Bion produced anything called diatribes? In contradiction to Halbauer's (Leipzig 1911) argument that *diatribai* must refer to student lecture notes, *diatribai* appears in Diogenes Laertius' catalogues of works by Aristippus, *Zeno of Citium, and *Aristo of Chios. Earlier usage (e.g., *Plato, *Isocrates) points to a connection with speeches or lectures or the conversational teaching of *Socrates. Further, Philodemus (*Rhetorica*) uses *diatribê* in his caustic remarks about the speeches and teaching of sophists and rhetoricians, while Dionysus of Halicarnassus (15.6) refers to *politikai diatribai*. In sum, *diatribê* frequently occurs in contexts implying speaking and/or teaching, perhaps with some connotation of dwelling on one point or theme. If Bion was indeed a teaching sophist, then, it is not surprising to find *diatribê* associated with him.

The name itself is not crucial; genre, content, and style are. Even if some of Bion's works were known as diatribes, there is insufficient evidence to show whether his lectures were the generic ancestors of "primary diatribes." Nor can we prove that the *diatribai* of Zeno or Aristippus or Aristo were stylistically or generically related to Bion's. At most we can assume that Bion rhetoricized and popularized philosophy to an extent that was distasteful to some traditional philosophers but a source of inspiration to later philosophical teachers who, as their environment underwent social and political changes, could not always confine themselves to the security of an established scholarly environment. It is no coincidence that all of the writers of "primary diatribes" travelled and lectured at some point in places other than their homelands or that all of them discuss in simple style a popularized brand of Cynic and Stoic ethics that reflects the need to adapt onself to the vicissitudes of fortune.

BIBLIOGRAPHY: Kindstrand, J. F., *Bion of Borysthenes*, Uppsala, 1976; Larenti, R., *ANRW* 2, 36.3, 1989, 2105–2146; Oltramare, A., *Les origines de la diatribe romaine*, Lausanne, 1926; O'Neil, E., *Teles the Cynic Teacher*, Missoula, 1977; Stowers, S. K., *The Diatribe and Paul's Letter to the Romans*, Chico, 1981; van Geytenbeek, A. C., *Musonius Rufus and Greek Diatribe*, Assen, 1963; Wallach, B. P., *Lucretius and the Diatribe*, Leiden, 1976.—*BARBARA PRICE WALLACH*

DICAEARCHUS (fl. c. 320 B.C.E.), of Messene in Sicily. *Peripatetic philosopher; pupil of *Aristotle. Dicaearchus' interests were narrower than those of his teacher: no works on *logic, physics, and *metaphysics are reported. In *On the Soul*, which comprised the *Corinthian* and *Lesbian Dialogues*, he advanced the view that *mind and soul do not exist; there is only body configured in a certain way. In some sources, this view is interpreted as a harmony theory, but the interpretation may derive from Dicaearchus' association with *Aristoxenus, whose musical interests were well known. How Dicaearchus reconciled his view of the soul with a belief in divination through dreams and frenzy is problematic. An answer may have been given in another *dialogue, *Descent into (the Cave of) Trophonius*, in which both the luxury of the priests of Trophonius and their practice of divination were attacked.

Dicaearchus wrote on good and bad life styles. In *On the Sacrifice at Ilium*, he reported how Alexander the Great was overcome with love for a eunuch; and in *On the Destruction of Human Beings*, he presented man himself, not wild animals and natural disasters, as the greatest threat to mankind. In *On Lives*, Dicaearchus probably defended the active life over that of quiet contemplation. Whether he criticized *Theophrastus directly for championing contemplation is problematic. In any case, we need not doubt that he characterized the *Seven Sages as neither wise nor philosophic, but intelligent and capable of legislation.

Dicaearchus' *Life of Greece* was a cultural history tracing the development of human society. An initial golden age in which men lived virtuously, meeting their needs from what the earth produced spontaneously, was followed by a second period, characterized by gathering fruits and pasturing animals. The third involved the rise of agriculture, and the fourth that of civilization. Dicaearchus took notice of other cultures, and the whole work, several books long, appears to have had an evaluative slant.

Dicaearchus wrote a work entitled the *Constitution of the Spartans*. The annual reading of this work to Sparta's council of ephors suggests a picture favorable to the Spartans. He also appears to have written on the constitutions of Pellene, Corinth, and Athens. The *Tripoliticus*, perhaps identical with the *Constitution of the Spartans*, probably considered a constitution in which monarchical, aristocratic, and democratic elements were combined.

The titles *On Musical Competitions* and *On Dionysiac Competitions* may have been the whole and a part, respectively, of the same work. Dicaearchus probably discussed a range of forms, from banquet songs to dramatic productions. He provided didascalic information and took an interest in "firsts," noting innovations regarding the dithyrambic chorus and the number of tragic actors. Hypotheses of the myths of *Euripides and *Sophocles are attributed to Dicaearchus; the accuracy of the attribution, including the assignment of recently published papyrus fragments, is a matter of debate. The titles *Panathenaic* and *Olympiac* appear to refer to dialogues, which dealt with festivals and musical themes. *Homeric questions were discussed, probably within a monograph. A work *On Alcaeus* is certain. Dicaearchus's interest in proverbs is well attested.

In *Circuit of the Earth*, Dicaearchus argued that the earth has the shape of a globe. He established a main parallel of latitude running from the Straits of Gibraltar to the Himalayan mountains, made maps that were known to *Cicero, and discussed other phenomena like the cause of ebb and flood tides and the source of the Nile River. The title *Measurements of the Mountains in the Peloponnesus* appears to reflect his interest in the height of mountains; his measurements involved the use of an optical measurer.

BIBLIOGRAPHY: Texts in Wehrli 1, 13–37, with comm. 39–80; D. Mirhady et al., in *RUSCH* vol. 9, 1998, with tr. and essays.—*WILLIAM W. FORTENBAUGH*

DIOCLES of Carystus. See MEDICINE, Ancient Theories of.

DIOCLES, of Magnesia. Author of biographies of philosophers and a source for *Diogenes Laertius. Diocles' chronology is uncertain. The identification with the Diocles to whom the *Garland* of Meleager of Gadara is dedicated and the dating to the first century B.C.E. are debatable. Among his writings, two titles are attested: *Synopsis of the Philosophers* and *Lives of the Philosophers*. It is probably a case of a single work designated by different titles—a history of ancient philosophy, like that of Diogenes Laertius, without any clear distinction between biography and *doxography.

Diogenes Laertius (7.48) extracts from the *Synopsis* a detailed exposition of *Stoic *logic. It is difficult to define the precise extent of the extract. Diogenes also derived from Diocles some statements attributed to *Antisthenes (6.12–13).

Attempts to augment the number of quotations from Diocles in Diogenes Laertius are precarious. Such efforts reached their culmination in Nietzsche's unsustainable hypothesis that the work of Diogenes is nothing but a reworking of Diocles, with additions.

It cannot be proved that Diocles was the target of the *Dioclean Refutations* of *Sotion (D.L. 10.4).

BIBLIOGRAPHY: *DPA* 2, D115. Egli, U., *Das Diocles-Fragment bei Diogenes Laertius*, Konstanz, 1981.—*TIZIANO DORANDI*

DIODORUS CRONUS (late 4th and early 3rd cent. B.C.E.), a *Dialectical philosopher from the Ionian town of Iasos in Caria. According to *Diogenes Laertius (2.111), Diodorus inherited the epithet *"Kronos"* ("Old Fool") from his teacher Apollonius. Earlier scholars regularly denominated Diodorus a *Megarian; but if one distinguishes the Megarian and Dialectical schools (*haireseis*, see DIALECTICAL SCHOOL), Diodorus should be considered a Dialectician. As a dialectical philosopher in Athens, Diodorus had as pupils *Philo and the (future) *Stoic *Zeno of Citium. It appears that he eventually relocated to Alexandria, where the poet Callimachus composed a satirical epigram about him.

The meager evidence suggests that Diodorus was best known in antiquity for three philosophical contributions: his Master (or "ruling": *kurieuôn*) Argument, his account of the truth conditions of the conditional (*sunêmmenon*) form of proposition, and his arguments against the existence of motion.

According to *Epictetus (*Dissertationes* 2.19), Diodorus' Master Argument inferred (by *reductio*) from premises (i) that what is past (i.e., true in the past) is necessary and (ii) that the impossible does not follow from the possible, the conclusion (iii) that if something neither is nor ever will be the case, then it is impossible. Despite controversy concerning details of its proper formalization, the argument's basic structure seems clear. The necessity of the past postulated by premise (i) is "transferred" by premise (ii) or its logical equivalent to the future as well. Thus, the intuitive distinction between a "fixed" or *relatively* necessary past and an "indeterminate" future (characterized by *relative* possibilities, some of which fail to be actualized) cannot be maintained. The main omission from Epictetus' account is the nature of the necessary conditionals or "entailments" that the argument employs in order to tie together the past and future. The Master Argument was regarded in antiquity as having fatalistic or deterministic implications. It is, in fact, an important anticompatibilist argument that has been periodically rediscovered, for example, by Peter de Rivo in the fifteenth century and Peter van Inwagen in the twentieth.

*Sextus Empiricus (*HP* 2.110ff.) portrays Diodorus as a major figure in the Hellenistic disputes over truth or "soundness" (*hugieia*) conditions for conditional propositions. The account attributed to Diodorus of a sound conditional (one such that "it neither is nor ever was capable of beginning with a truth and ending with a falsehood") is now usually interpreted as equivalent to the omnitemporal truth of the contemporary material conditional. Why Diodorus adopted this account of the truth conditions for conditionals is not known. His account is presented by Sextus as a way of avoiding the fact that a Philonian (material) conditional can be made true simply by the independent, coincidental truth of antecedent and consequent. It is thus possible that part of his motivation was to avoid so-called paradoxes of material implication.

Diodorus argued against the existence of process (*kinêsis*) and local motion. He does not deny, however, that things are different—have different properties and are located in different locations—at different times. The result is that, although it is never true to say of something that it *is moving*, it can be true to say that it *has moved* (S.E. *M* 10.86). Diodorus evidently buttressed his denial of process by arguing that spatial extension is constituted of indivisible quanta. The *Aristotelian account of continuous and (potentially) *infinitely divisible motion, *time, and spatial extension could locate the *kinêsis* of moving in the interval of time that an object is continuously occupying less and less of its containing place and occupying more and more of a contiguous spatial area. But, Diodorus argues, it is not possible for something gradually to occupy less and less of an *indivisible* quantum and more and more of a contiguous indivisible quantum. Quantum "motion" must involve an instantaneous displacement from one quantum locus to another. The result is the elimination of Aristotelian *kinêseis* in favor of a discretely ordered sequence of static "freeze frames."

BIBLIOGRAPHY: Döring, K., *Die Megariker: Kommentierte Sammlung der Testimonien* (*Studien zur antiken Philosophie*, vol. 2), Amsterdam, 1972; Hintikka, J., *Time and Necessity: Studies in Aristotle's Theory of Modality*, Oxford, 1973, 179–213; Mates, B., *Stoic Logic*, Berkeley/Los Angeles, 1961; Schuhl, P. -M., *Le Dominateur et les Possibles*, Paris, 1960; Sedley, D., *PCPS* n.s. 23, 1977, 74–120; White, M. J., *Agency and Integrality: Philosophical Themes in the Ancient Discussions of Determinism and Responsibility*, Dordrecht, 1985.—*MICHAEL J. WHITE*

DIOGENES (2nd half of 5th cent. B.C.E.), of Apollonia, probably on Pontus Euxinos. Presocratic philosopher. We do not know Diogenes' exact dates, but his work clearly falls within the last third of the fifth century B.C.E. *Theophrastus calls him "about the youngest" of those who inquired "on nature" (DK64A5), and *Aristophanes parodied his doctrines in his comedy *Clouds*, which was performed in 423. Moreover, his views evidently built on *Anaxagoras' doctrine of the Intellect (*Nous*). Allusions to *Leucippus and *Melissus may also be detected. The reports that associate him with *Anaximenes do not mean more than that he knew the latter's work: Both took air as their first principle.

We have no precise information about Diogenes' life. He seems to have left his native Apollonia for Athens. There he apparently became famous, although his fame may have been in part negative, for he seems to have been accused of impiety (A1 and 3).

Was he a professional physician? This hypothesis is based on Diogenes' obvious interests in biological phenomena: *Aristotle's only actual quotation from him is a detailed description of the vessel system in the human body (*HA* 3.2 = DKB6). On the other hand, other Presocratic philosophers, for example, *Empedocles, display a strong interest in physiology. The very fact that Diogenes' famous description stems from his treatise *On Nature* suggests that he was a philosopher engaged in *medical matters, rather than the other way around.

Diogenes may have written other works beside *On Nature*, for *Simplicius, our main source of information about him, mentions a treatise, *Against the Natural Philosophers* (whom Diogenes interestingly called *"sophists"), a *Meteorology*, and an *On the Nature of Man*. It may be that Simplicius took for book titles what were only internal references in Diogenes' *On Nature*. On the other hand, *On Nature* seems to have been narrowly focused, for Simplicius tells us that in this work, Diogenes "proposes to demonstrate that there is much intelligence in his principle" (namely, "air"). That Diogenes wrote separate books is further suggested by the fact that Theophrastus wrote a "collection" of his views.

We have twelve fragments from Diogenes' treatise (including four isolated words or expressions). Eight of them come from Simplicius' *Commentary on Aristotle's Physics*. It is indicative of Diogenes' marginal position in the history of philosophy already in antiquity that Simplicius introduces him only to prove the negative point that he should not be associated, as Nicolaus of Damas has suggested, with the anonymous view, reported by Aristotle at *Physics* 187a12, that the principle is an "intermediate" substance. However, the quotations made to show that Diogenes' principle is in fact "air" reveal an elaborate and subtle thinker, a far cry from the reactionary eclectic he has often been taken to be (Theophrastus already called him a "confusionist," A5). What they tell us about Diogenes' principle fits nicely in the overall picture of his world that we can reconstruct on the basis of a relatively large amount of *doxographical testimonies (about thirthy-six), all ultimately derived from Theophrastus' "collection."

Diogenes' monism is not a simple revival of sixth century Milesian thought. Rather, it represents a critical reply to two major philosophical trends of his century. He rejects Empedoclean pluralism explicitly: *Change would be impossible if there were no underlying substance to the four elements (B4), an idea for which Aristotle praises him (*GC* 322b). Diogenes also dismisses Anaxagoras' problematic dualism of Intellect and *infinite stuffs, by assuming that Intelligence is immanent to a particular stuff, namely, air. Thus, his principle both is the "ruler of everything," as Anaxagoras' Intellect was (B5, cf. DK59B12), and, for all its unity, contains all the diversity that is necessary to explain "all the things that are seen to exist in this world" (B4), down to animal (as well as inanimate) species and even perhaps individuals: At any rate, B5 contains what is the first formulation of the principle of the identity of indiscernables. In some sense, air's "polytropy" (an unmistakably Odyssean attribute) is already an expression of air's "intelligence." Diogenes further demonstrated its versatility on the basis of various "signs" (*sêmeia*) taken from the entire scale of "psychic" manifestations, from magnetic attraction to rational knowledge. The standard explanation here involves a certain state of air (typically more or less humid: the drier, the better) circulating through a system of channels. It is this universal circulation that is paradigmatically illustrated by the vessel system of the human body. In his search for evidence of air's intelligence, Diogenes was led to put forward an explicitly teleological account of the kind that *Plato's *Socrates missed in Anaxagoras' treatise (Pl. *Phd.* 97c), for he appealed in this context to the beautiful organization of natural cycles (B3). The range of phenomena that he wanted to be covered by this explanation is largely a matter of speculation, although it seems unwise to trace back to him the (heavily anthropocentric) teleological arguments that we find in *Xenophon's *Memorabilia* 1.4.

Even so, it remains an historical oddity that Plato never mentions him (although Diogenes is sometimes taken to lurk behind the powerful description of earth's system of communicating channels at the end of

the *Phaedo*), and Aristotle, on the whole, so little. Aristophanes' laughter and Theophrastus' criticism have done the rest: Diogenes is, among the great presocratic thinkers, the one who has received the least attention.
BIBLIOGRAPHY: Texts in DK64. Laks, A., *Diogène d'Apollonie: La Dernière Cosmologie Présocratique* (= *Cahiers de Philologie* 9), Lille-Paris, 1983; Diller, H., in *Kleine Schriften zur Antiken Literatur*, Munich, 1971, 162–186 .—*ANDRÉ LAKS*

DIOGENES of Babylon. See DIOGENES of Seleucia.

DIOGENES LAERTIUS (c. 200 C.E.). Author of the only preserved example of an ancient "History of Philosophy." From the Renaissance until c. 1800, Diogenes Laertius was the main model for historiography of philosophy. He is known only from this work, and we know nothing about his life. His date can only be fixed by the dates of the latest personalities mentioned in his text and by the fact that he seems to have written before *Neoplatonism became influential (c. 250 C.E.). His work, dedicated to a woman interested in *Platonism (bk. 3, 47), seems to have been titled *Compendium of the Lives and Opinions of Philosophers*.

Diogenes' work belongs to a type of literature that was called *Successions*. In works of this sort, the biographies of philosophers seem to have been arranged in series, with teacher followed by student within each major philosophical school—hence the title.

Diogenes' preserved text is divided into ten books, as follows: (1) Introduction and various wise men. *(2)–(7): The Ionian tradition:* (2) The Ionian physicists, *Socrates, and the minor *Socratic schools down to the early third century B.C.E.; (3) *Plato; (4) the *Academy down to *Clitomachus (late 2nd cent. B.C.E.); (5) *Aristotle and the *Peripatetics down to *Lyco (late 3rd cent. B.C.E.); (6) *Antisthenes and the *Cynics down to the end of the third century B.C.E.; (7) *Zeno of Citium and the *Stoics down to at least *Chrysippus (late 3rd cent. B.C.E.), and in the missing end of the book perhaps even down to the first century C.E. *(8)–(10): The Italian Tradition:* (8) *Pythagoras and his early successors, *Empedocles; (9) *Heraclitus, the *Eleatics, *Leucippus and *Democritus, *Protagoras and *Diogenes of Apollonia, *Pyrrho; (10) *Epicurus.

Though Diogenes only offers *Lives* of of the founders of *Pyrrhonism and *Epicureanism, he mentions other members of these schools—in the case of the *Skeptics, even down to the second century C.E., the *terminus post quem* for his work.

Diogenes' book is basically a compilation of excerpts from a large number of sources: In the biographical sections he often tells us which sources he is using, while the philosophical sections in general appear without any indication of their origin and seem unlikely to have come from Diogenes' biographical sources.

The quality and structure of Diogenes' book is very uneven: some *Lives* are nothing but anecdotes and aphorisms, while others are mainly *doxographical. Some *Lives* have long and detailed sections on philosophy (so Zeno of Citium in 7), others have short and inadequate sections (e.g., Aristotle in 5.28–34). Diogenes does not show any signs of having read the works of the philosophers whose lives he describes and whose doctrines he reports, yet in Book 10 he has preserved four long original writings by Epicurus that constitute the most important evidence for Epicurus' philosophy from before the period of *Cicero. On the other hand, his many and often randomly selected sources allow us to get an impression of the Hellenistic tradition of philosophical biography. In many of the *Lives* he quotes letters that must be pseudepigraphical writings of the Hellenistic or early Roman period, but because he seems to have had a predilection for old documents, he has preserved the testaments of four Peripatetics (Aristotle, *Theophrastus, *Strato, and Lyco) and a number of catalogues of the books written by philosophers.

Most of Diogenes' biographies include various items like birth, parents, name, appearance, relationship to other philosophers, travels, life style, and circumstances of death. There is, however, no particular order in which these items are presented. The dominant element in all the biographies is Diogenes' use of anecdotes. This interest leads him sometimes to refer to the same anecdote in more than one *Life*. In any case, these anecdotes reveal how the later tradition viewed the main characteristics of a particular philosopher. This use of anecdote should come as no surprise. It was very difficult to find documentary evidence concerning a deceased person unless that person was a famous public figure or had left written works from which it was possible to extract biographical information. Thus most of the dates Diogenes offers derive from *Apollodorus' poem *Chronica* and not from documentary evidence. Often literary works were exploited without regard for the fact that it is anything but likely that the content of a fictional work applies to its author. Diogenes' factual information must always be viewed with some skepticism, and there are many obvious mistakes. The *Lives* may have been written with less artistic skill than, for example, *Plutarch's or Suetonius' biographies, but they are not unlike other ancient *Lives* of philosophers.

Diogenes devotes considerable space to presentations of the doctrines of the major philosophical schools: The *Life* of Plato (3.48–109) is a general introduction to the study of the *Corpus Platonicum*. As an account of Plato's philosophy it may be inadequate, but it nevertheless resembles other Platonic writings of the second century C.E. The section on Aristotelian philosophy (5.28–34) is far less satisfying, but all three of its parts seem to go back to the Hellenistic period. The section 7.38–160 is the most comprehensive account of Stoic philosophy we have from antiquity, and the section on *logic is especially important. The survey of the Skeptic tropes (9.79–105) is shorter than in *Sextus Empiricus but otherwise comparable. Epicurus' letters and his forty "Principal Doctrines" in Book 10 are invaluable because no other sources preserve so much authentic material. When he places these aphorisms at the end of his work, Diogenes admits that he considers them a culmination of philosophical wisdom.

For the Presocratic philosophers Diogenes has used a "doxographical" source similar to other accounts in *Hippolytus and several other authors in late antiquity; ultimately, it derives from Aristotle and Theophrastus (see DOXOGRAPHY). In the case of Pythagoras, Diogenes presents an excerpt from Aristotle and an excerpt from Alexander Polyhistor (1st. cent. B.C.E.), thus providing us with a much earlier (Hellenistic) expression of Pythagoreanism than we find in other sources of the second century C.E. or later.

Diogenes' philosophical sections vary as much in quality and comprehensiveness as his biographical chapters. Obviously, he is no philosopher, but he has preserved much of philosophical significance. He seems to have had no influence in antiquity, but since Walter Burley's *On the Life and Manners of the Philosophers* (early fourteenth cent.), the Latin translation of the *Lives* by Ambrosius Traversarius (1432), and the *editio princeps* of the Greek text in 1533, Diogenes Laertius has been the most important single source for the lives and often for the doctrines of the major ancient philosophers.

BIBLIOGRAPHY: Text and translation in R. D. Hicks, ed. and tr., *Diogenes Laertius: Lives of Eminent Philosophers*, 2 vols. (Loeb), London, 1925; Long, H. S., *Diogenis Laertii Vitae Philosophorum*, Oxford, 1964 (a new Teubner ed. of the Greek text is in preparation). Giannantoni, G., ed., *Diogene Laerzio: Storico del pensiero antico*, Naples, 1986; essays in *ANRW* 2, 36.5–6, 1992, 3556–4307; Mejer, J., *Diogenes Laertius and His Hellenistic Background*, Wiesbaden, 1978.—*JØRGEN MEJER*

DIOGENES (probably 2nd cent. C.E.), of Oenoanda in Lycia. *Epicurean philosopher. Nothing is known of his life, except from his monumental inscription. In this he describes himself as standing at "the sunset of life" and suffering from stomach problems assuaged by a diet of curds.

Diogenes' complex philosophical inscription, cut on the wall of a stoa in his native city, constitutes the last chapter of the history of Epicureanism in antiquity. The first inscribed blocks were discovered in 1884. Displayed on three registers of a wall (c. 100 meters long) is a series of philosophical writings and personal documents. The central register holds Diogenes' introduction to the inscription as a whole. Here he presents himself as offering on his stoa "remedies" for the moral sufferings of mankind. In the Physics Treatise that follows, Diogenes defends Epicurean physics against the "*Socratics," attacks Presocratic theories of

*matter, offers a theory of dreams, an account of the origins of civiliza-
tion, *astronomy, and *theology. On the bottom course he displays his
*Ethical Treatise. After an anti-Stoic polemic, he discusses passions and
actions; asserts the primacy of the *soul, while denying it can exist apart
from the body; attacks metempsychosis; returns to dreams; and offers his
vision of a golden age. On the top course runs his Old Age Treatise. The
wall also displayed a *dialogue on innumberable worlds, Diogenes' maxims, epistolary, testament, and some letters of *Epicurus.

Diogenes preserves texts of Epicurus not known from other sources,
and Epicurus' ethical maxims underwrite Diogenes' Ethical Treatise. But
his conception of his evangelical stoa, his writings, and style are very
much his own. He favors dialogue and polemic. He is our best source for
the social history of Epicureanism in the second century C.E.

BIBLIOGRAPHY: Texts in A. Casanova, *I Frammenti di Diogene d'Enoanda*, Florence,
1984; M. F. Smith, *Diogenes of Oenoanda: The Epicurean Inscription*, Naples, 1992.
Clay, D., *ANRW* 2, 36.4, 1990, 2446–2559.—*DISKIN CLAY*

DIOGENES (date unknown), of Ptolemais. *Stoic philosopher, known
only through a single reference to him by *Diogenes Laertius (7.41), who
claims that he places *ethics first among the three Stoic parts of philosophical discourse (ethics, physics, and *logic).—*IAKOVOS VASILIOU*

DIOGENES (c. 228–140 B.C.E.), of Seleucia on the Tigris in Babylon. Fifth
scholarch of the *Stoa, student of *Chrysippus and *Zeno of Tarsus,
teacher of *Antipater of Tarsus, *Apollodorus of Seleucia, *Panaetius of
Rhodes and the philologist *Apollodorus of Athens. Diogenes' fame
spread to Italy through his participation, along with *Critolaus and
*Carneades, in the historic Athenian embassy of philosophers to Rome
(156/5 B.C.E.). A defender of Chrysippean orthodoxy, Diogenes was responsible for several new formulations of Stoic doctrines. A focus of
scholarly debate is now whether Diogenes initiated some of the changes
to the doctrine of the early Stoa that are characteristic of *Posidonius and
Panaetius and that seek an accommodation with *Platonic and *Aristotelian doctrines.

Diogenes divided philosophy into physics, *ethics, and *logic, following *Zeno of Citium and Chrysippus (D.L. 7.39). In the first of these,
according to fragments of his *On Music* in *Philodemus, he may have anticipated Panaetius or Posidonius in dividing the soul into different
parts; he also adopted from *Speusippus a division of perception into
congenital and "scientific" kinds. *Galen (*On the Doctrines of Hippocrates
and Plato* 2.128.32–132.16 DeLacy) quotes Diogenes' defense, in *On the
Governing Part of the Soul*, of Chrysippus' location of the governing part
in the heart: for the meaningful voice arises from the chest. Diogenes also
continued Chrysippus' line on the gods: He defended his master's *alle-

gorical interpretation of the gods in his treatise *On Athena* (Philod. *On Piety* col. 8 Henrichs; Cic. *ND* 1.41); in *On Mantic* (Cic. *On Divination* 1.6, 84, 2.90) he defended Chrysippus' position that it follows from the divine providence that the gods must give signs of the future to men; he also intervened on behalf of Zeno's argument that, since it is right to honor the gods, they must therefore exist (S.E. *M* 9.133–136).

Diogenes' political thought added to the early Stoic account of the sage who follows "common reason" in the community of wise men and gods an account of the sage's place in more typical human settings. According to quotations in Philodemus, in his *On Rhetoric* Diogenes equated *rhetoric with *politics and attributed both to the sage alone; in ordinary human societies, he claimed further, "cities," and their "magistrates" were only loosely so called. It is not clear whether he also anticipated Panaetius by attempting to give practical moral guidance to those still "making progress." *Cicero (*Leg.* 3.13f.) praises Diogenes' contributions to political philosophy and the role of magistrates, probably in reference to his *Laws* (Athenaeus 526c–d). Diogenes also wrote a treatise *On Noble Birth* (Athenaeus 168e). In the ethical sphere, he gave reformulated definitions of the good ("what is perfect by nature": *SVF* 3, 40), the goal ("rationality in the selection and rejection of the things according to nature": *SVF* 3, 44ff.), and justice ("disposition which distributes to everyone what he deserves": *SVF* 3, 47). A debate between Diogenes and Antipater, probably constructed by *Hecato, is portrayed by Cicero (*Off.* 3.49b–57). Here Diogenes is made to argue that the wise man must tell a buyer facts that would lower the market value of his goods only insofar as civil law requires such disclosure, although he may not "conceal" such facts if asked. Finally, the *sophistic and *Peripatetic idea that music could be used to train the passions of the young was adapted by Diogenes in his *On Music* with reference to the Stoic theory of natural affinity (*oikeiôsis*).

Under the logical part of philosophy we have a report from Diogenes' *Art On Voice* (D.L. 7.55–58) detailed enough to show that *grammatical science was based on Stoic handbooks of this type. This book, together with his *Dialectical Art* (D.L. 7.71), provided definitions for the key concepts of Stoic logic and rhetoric.

BIBLIOGRAPHY: Texts in *SVF* 3, 210–243; source texts in A. Henrichs, *CronErc* 4, 1974, 5–32; D. Delattre, *CronErc* 19, 1989, 49–143; R. Janko, *CronErc* 22, 1992, 123–130; A. J. Neubecker, ed., *Philodemus, Über die Musik IV. Buch*, Naples, 1988; new ed. expected by D. Delattre; S. Sudhaus, ed., *Philodemus Volumina Rhetorica*, Leipzig, vol. 1, 1892, vol. 2, 1896; J. Hammerstaedt, *CronErc* 22, 1992, 9–117; new ed. expected by D. L. Blank, D. Obbink, and J. Hammerstaedt. Diogenes Laertius 7.55–58, 71 (= *FDS* 476, 536, 914); Cicero, *Off.* 3.50–57, 91–92. Brunschwig, J., in J. Brunschwig, *Papers in Hellenistic Philosophy*, Cambridge, 1994, 170–189; Dyck, A. R., *A Commentary on Cicero, De Officiis*, Ann Arbor, 1996, *ad* 3.49b–57; Obbink, D., and P. A. Vander Waerdt, *GRBS* 32, 1991, 355–396; Pohlenz, M., *Die Stoa*,[2] Göttingen, 1959, 180–190; Schäfer, M., *Philologus* 91, 1936, 174–196; Schenkeveld, D. M., *Mnemosyne*, ser. 4.43, 1990, 68–108.—*D. L. BLANK*

DIOGENES (c. 412/403–c. 324/321 B.C.E.), of Sinope on the Black Sea. Nicknamed "the dog." Founder of *Cynicism ("doggishness"). The general distortions in the ancient traditions about Cynicism multiply in the case of Diogenes, himself a flamboyant self-dramatist, who provoked extremes of admiration, hostility, and imaginative invention, leading to the creation of a rich and varied Diogenes-legend. All accounts, ancient and modern, are, therefore, necessarily controversial, but the ancient traditions show certain constants, and *Diogenes Laertius (6.70–3) arguably preserves Diogenes' essential thought.

Many elements of Diogenes' biography remain disputed: In principle, a skeptical and minimalist reconstruction must be correct. Accused with his father, moneyer at Sinope, of "defacing the currency" (a phrase that was to yield a potent metaphor), Diogenes was exiled some time after 362 B.C.E. and spent the rest of his life in Athens and Corinth. (His capture by pirates, consultation of Delphi, and discipleship of *Socrates' follower *Antisthenes are fictitious; his meeting with Alexander the Great may be historical.)

Diogenes had many followers, including *Crates of Thebes and the Alexander-historian Onesicritus (the notion of Cynic "pupils" is problematic, since (i) in Cynicism individuals had to attain philosophical salvation by their own efforts; (ii) a Cynic philosopher had no teaching in the usual sense of the term to impart; and (iii) he could not possibly accept payment for his moral exhortations). Notwithstanding ancient and modern doubts, it is certain that Diogenes expounded his views in a *Politeia* (*Republic*—reconstructible from D.L. 6.72 and *Philodemus' *On the Stoics*) and several tragedies.

Over the years Diogenes evolved a distinctive and original way of life from diverse, mainly Greek, elements: the belief (espoused by certain types of holy men and wise men) that wisdom was a matter of action rather than thought; the principle (advanced by various *sophists, fifth-century primitivists, and Antisthenes) of living in accordance with nature rather than law/convention; the tradition, perhaps sharpened by contemporary disillusionment with the *polis*, of promulgating ideal societies or constitutions; a tradition of "shamelessness" (reflected by the symbol of the dog in literature and by the supposed customs of certain foreign peoples); Socratic rejection of all elements of philosophy except practical *ethics; Socrates' pursuit of philosophy in the *agora* rather than in a school; an anti-intellectual tradition; the tradition (variously represented by Odysseus, Heracles, the Spartans, and to some extent by

Socrates) of physical toughness as a requirement of *virtue; the image of the suffering hero and the wanderer (Odysseus, Heracles, various tragic figures); the tradition of mendicancy (represented both in literature and in life); the life of asceticism and poverty (as represented by various wise men and holy men and laborers); the tradition of the wise or holy man who promises *happiness or salvation to converts; and various humorous traditions (the jester's practical and verbal humor; Old *Comedy's outspokenness and crudity; Socrates' seriocomic wit).

Diogenes pursued a life as close as possible to the "natural" life of primitive man, of animals, and of the gods. This entailed the minimum of material possessions (coarse cloak, staff for physical support and protection, purse for food) and of sustenance (obtained by living off the land, begging, and stealing), performance in public of all natural functions, training in physical endurance, and a wandering existence in harmony with natural conditions. Freedom, self-sufficiency, happiness, and virtue supposedly followed. It also entailed not merely indifference to civilized life but complete rejection of it and of all forms of education and culture as being not simply irrelevant but inimical to the ideal life. Hence Diogenes' attacks on convention, marriage, family, politics, the city, all social, sexual, and racial distinctions, worldly reputation, wealth, power and authority, literature, music, and all forms of intellectual speculation. Such attacks are imposed by the Cynic's duty metaphorically to "deface the currency." Hence the modern implications of the word "cynic" are misleading. Indeed, humane attitudes came easily to Diogenes (e.g., his advocacy of sexual freedom and equality stemmed naturally from rejection of the family).

Although proclaiming self-sufficiency, Diogenes tried to convert others by his own outrageous behavior (which went beyond the requirements of the natural life), by direct exhortation employing all the resources of his formidable wit and *rhetorical skills, and by various written works. Such writings, which compromise the ideal of the practical demonstration of philosophical truth and the formal rejection of literature, did not imply real debate with conventional philosophers. Diogenes sparred verbally with *Plato but dismissed his philosophy as absurd; his *Politeia*, while a serious statement of Cynic positions, parodied "serious" philosophers' pretensions.

Diogenes' missionary activity entailed what his aggressiveness sometimes obscured: recognition of the common humanity of Cynics and non-Cynics. "Philanthropy" (concern for one's fellow human beings) is integral to Cynicism and essential to Diogenes' celebrated concept of "cosmopolitanism" (the belief that the universe is the ultimate unity, of which the natural and animal worlds, human beings, and the gods are all intrinsic parts, with the Cynic representing the human condition at its best—at once human, animal, and divine).

Ancient and modern reactions to Diogenes range from appreciation of his wit to admiration (often tinged with exasperation) for his integrity, denial of his philosophical significance, revulsion at his shamelessness, dislike of the threat he posed to conventional social and political values, and misguided attempts to make him respectable. Yet, whatever the detailed distortions in the *Stoic history of philosophy, it was right to locate Diogenes firmly within the great tradition, as even Plato half-conceded when he dubbed him a "mad Socrates" (D.L. 6.54).

See also CYNICS and CYNICISM, CRATES of Thebes, HIPPAR-CHIA.

BIBLIOGRAPHY: For bibliography, see under CYNICS and CYNICISM.—*JOHN L. MOLES*

DIOGENES (2nd or 1st cent. B.C.E.), of Tarsus. *Epicurean philosopher. Diogenes travelled widely delivering lectures (collected in at least twenty books), largely on *ethics but also covering physics. He also wrote an *Epitome of Epicurus' Doctrines*, which discussed sex and marriage; and he discussed literary problems and improvised poetry "in a tragic style." His works, scant references to which survive, were standard authorities and are cited alongside *Epicurus on basic issues: Kinetic and static pleasures alike involve both body and soul; virtue is good only because of pleasure, not intrinsically; and virtue does not eliminate pain. His literary interests, while arguably heretical, reflect the favorable estimate of literature advanced by *Zeno of Sidon and *Demetrius of Laconia, then put into practice by *Philodemus and *Lucretius; with them, Diogenes probably deserves credit for helping broaden the appeal of Epicureanism and enhance its popularity in the Roman world.

BIBLIOGRAPHY: Texts listed in *RE* 5, 776–7.—*STEPHEN A. WHITE*

DIONYSIUS (c. 330–c. 250 B.C.E.), of Heraclea on the Pontus. Son of Theophantus and pupil, successively, of his fellow-citizen *Heraclides, *Alexinus of Elis, *Menedemus of Eretria, and *Zeno of Citium. These associations imply that Dionysius must have been born around 330 at the latest; he lived to be eighty years old. He remained an adherent of *Stoicism for much of his life, but after being struck by a painful disease found that he could no longer maintain the doctrine that pain is no evil and adopted a hedonistic philosophy, of the *Cyrenaic rather than the *Epicurean variety, if the stories told about his later life are to be believed; but probably these should be taken with a pinch of salt. He was afterwards known as *ho metathemenos*, the Renegade.

*Diogenes Laertius (7.167) has preserved the titles of nine of his works, seven on *ethics and two on historical subjects. He adds that he was also interested in literature and wrote poetry. Only one extract from his philosophical writings has been preserved, by *Cicero (*TD* 3.18); there he maintains a conventional Stoic position, that the wise man will feel no anger.

BIBLIOGRAPHY: Texts in *SVF* 1, 422–34. Dorandi, T., ed., *Filodemo, Storia dei filosofi: La stoà da Zenone a Panezio*, Leiden, 1994, 17f.; von Arnim, H., in *RE* 5.973; Pohlenz, M., *Die Stoa*,[2] vol. 1, 27, Göttingen, 1959.—H. B. GOTTSCHALK

DIONYSIUS the Areopagite. See (PSEUDO-) DIONYSIUS the Areopagite.

DIONYSODORUS. See EUTHYDEMUS.

DISSOI LOGOI, the title given by modern scholars to a short anonymous piece of *sophistic writing, preserved in the manuscripts of *Sextus Empiricus and first printed in 1570 by Stephanus under the title *Dialexeis*. The title *Dissoi Logoi*, which is now preferred by scholars, is taken from the formula used in the first paragraph of the work and repeated at the beginning of each of the next three chapters, namely, "two-fold arguments are expressed in Greece by those who concern themselves with philosophy, concerning what is good and what is bad, ... what is beautiful and what is ugly, ... what is just and unjust, ... what is true and what is false." The dialect is a form of literary Doric, which has led to conjectures that the author may have been a *Pythagorean and that the work may have been written in Sicily or southern Italy. There is, however, no positive evidence to support these speculations, and the manuscript tradition is quite definite in attributing the work to "an anonymous author."

Discussions as to the date of composition are based on the following statement in 1.8–10: "and in the case of war (and I shall speak first of the most recent events) the victory which the Spartans won over the Athenians and their allies was good for the Spartans but bad for the Athenians and their allies." The same argument is then applied to the Persian wars and the Trojan war, the war between the Thebans and the Argives, the Lapiths and Centaurs, and the gods and giants. The first-mentioned war seems clearly to be the Peloponnesian war that ended in 404 B.C.E. As all the other wars were previous to it, the statement that the Peloponnesian war was the most recent would be technically true right down to the present day. But it remains the more natural interpretation to suppose that the statement was made in a period of some twenty years after the end of the war, and fairly certainly before the battle of Chaeronia in 338 B.C.E. when Macedonia under King Philip secured a dominant position in the Greek world as a whole. This conclusion, challenged by some scholars, will provide a date of 400–380 B.C.E. for the composition of the work. The anonymous author will then be the earliest surviving writer to offer a general analysis of the sophistic movement.

The pattern of argument is established in the first chapter and is followed consistently throughout the remainder of the treatise. "Some say that the good is one thing and the bad is another thing while others say that each is the same and that the same is good for some but bad for others and that for the same person it is on one occasion good and on another occasion bad." Such a formulation is potentially ambiguous, and in fact it has been translated and understood in different ways by some modern scholars. To say that the good and the bad are the same might mean that the meaning of the two terms is to be taken as identical, or it might mean that any one thing is (or may be) both good and bad (either simultaneously or at different times and in different relationships). But the examples given, both in the first chapter and throughout the treatise, seem to establish beyond reasonable doubt that it is the second interpretation that is in fact correct. In other words, the meanings of "good" and "bad" are always different—it is the things to which the terms are applied that can sometimes be good and sometimes bad, or both good and bad at the same time because what is good for one person may itself at the same time be bad for another person.

This amounts to a doctrine of relativism. In the first six chapters or sections of the *Dissoi Logoi* it is argued that this relativism should be understood as applying first to the terms "good" and "bad," then to "beautiful" and "ugly" (*kalon* and *aischron*, which mean, respectively, what is noble and so to be admired, and what is shameful and so to be rejected), then to "just" and "unjust," to "true" and "false" in the case of propositions, and to the teachability of wisdom and virtue.

Parallels to this kind of relativism are clearly expressed in doctrines expounded by a number of different sophists, especially *Protagoras, *Hippias, and *Gorgias, which has led some scholars actually to assign the authorship of the treatise to one or another of these sophists. But in fact the older sophists were all in one way or another giving expression to doctrines of moral relativism (see Kerferd, ch. 9). It is much safer to regard the *Dissoi Logoi* as exemplifying the relativism of the sophistic movement as a whole than as having reference exclusively to one or two individual sophists.

After the discussion of the six different applications of relativism the treatise concludes with three further sections by way of appendages. In these it is argued that election by lot is a bad method of election for democracies, that the art of the *dialectician (who is a person skilled in argument) is the same as the art of the statesman, and that the art of memory is invaluable both for intellectual wisdom and the conduct of life.

BIBLIOGRAPHY: Text in DK90. Tr. in R. K. Sprague, *The Older Sophists*, Columbia, SC, 1972, and M. Gagarin and P. Woodruff, eds., *Early Greek Political Thought from Homer to the Sophists*, Cambridge, 1995. Kerferd, G. B., *The Sophistic Movement*, Cambridge, 1981; Robinson, T. M., *Contrasting Arguments: An Edition of the* Dissoi Logoi, New York, 1979; Untersteiner, M., *Sofisti testimonianze e frammenti*, Fasc. 3, Florence, 1954, 149–191.—*G. B. KERFERD*

DOXOGRAPHY is a nineteenth-century term, made famous by Hermann Diels' *Doxography Graeci* (Berlin 1879), in which he collected a number of texts that report the views of Greek philosophers from *Thales to mid–first century B.C.E. In the preface to this collection Diels discussed the characteristics of these texts, which exhibit so many similarities that they can with some justification be considered as belonging to a particular tradition. Diels' establishment of this "doxographical tradition" has dominated the discussion of the sources for early Greek philosophy for more than a century. It is important to note that the term "doxography" is modern, based on the title of a number of ancient books called *Peri ton doxon...* (= *On the opinions of...*); other titles use the terms *dogmata* and *areskonta* (= Lat. *placita*).

The two texts that constitute the main specimens of doxography are, first, pseudo-Plutarch's *Placita Philosophorum*, also copied out by Eusebius in his *Praeparatio Evangelica*, books 14–15, and translated into Arabic c. 900 C.E., and second, the very similar anonymous excerpts in *Stobaeus' *Anthology* (*Eclogae* 1.10–46 and 4.36–37; 50a 30 Hense). The texts of these two sources were printed in parallel columns by Diels (*DG* 273–444). They consist of entries or questions on philosophical and other matters, arranged in five books dealing with (i) *cosmology and (*meta)-physics, (ii) the heavenly bodies, (iii) meteorology, (iv) *psychology and perception, and (v) human physiology and embryonics. Under each entry is listed the views of a number of philosophers, from the Presocratics to the first century B.C.E. (and even in a few cases later), views that purport to give answers to topics like "On the *void," "On *time," "How did the world originate?" "What is the nature of the heavenly bodies?" "Are sense impressions true?" "How does conception take place?" The selection of philosophers is far from systematic, and their views are presented as simple statements of fact, without any context or arguments. For example, in ps.-Plutarch (1.21) under the heading "Time" we are told that according to the *Pythagoreans time is the movement of the sphere of the surrounding; according to *Plato time is a mobile image of eternity or an interval in the movement of the universe; while according to *Eratosthenes it is the journey of the sun. What matters, obviously, is the variety of opinions, not the thinking or argumentation of individual philosophers as such.

Both ps.-Plutarch's and Stobaeus' accounts must have been based on the same source, who according to Diels was someone called *Aëtius, an otherwise unknown writer of a doxographical work to be dated c. 100 C.E. (see AËTIUS). This work in its turn seems to be based on similar works from the first century B.C.E. and even the earlier Hellenistic period, since the earliest trace of it is found in *Chrysippus in the third century B.C.E. One or more of these works were extremely popular in the Roman period, and we can recognize their influence in, for example, *Cicero, Varro, Athenagoras, Soranus, and the *Historia Philosopha*, falsely attributed to *Galen.

A different kind of doxography is found in (primarily) the church fathers *Hippolytus and Theodoretus, *Diogenes Laertius, and ps.-Plutarch's *Stromateis* (= *Patchwork, Miscellanies*). These doxographies differ from the first kind in that they present the views of each philosopher in a separate chapter, but they are similar to it in that they report on the same five areas (see above), in the same order and often with the same wording. While some of these doxographical reports contain important information, others demonstrate that the knowledge about earlier Greek philosophy in late antiquity can be confused and misleading. It is important to notice that both kinds of doxography basically abstain from criticizing or discussing the views presented, as is also clear from some remarks quoted by St. *Augustine in his preface to *De Haeresibus*: "A certain Celsus [otherwise unknown] has presented the views of all philosophers who founded philosophical schools down to his own period ... in six rather large volumes. He did not refute any of them, he just explained what they thought, with such brevity that both style and content gave room, not for praising and criticizing, nor for confirming or defending, but only for explaining and presenting their ideas. For Celsus mentioned more than one hundred philosophers, not all of whom even founded their own schools, since he was of the opinion that he ought not to neglect those philosophers who followed their teachers without dissent."

Quotations from *Theophrastus in the work of the Aristotelian *commentator *Simplicius in the sixth century C.E. demonstrate that the sections on the Greek philosophers from Thales to Plato in the doxographical sources must ultimately go back to Theophrastus, who both in independent treatises (on *Democritus, *Anaxagoras, etc.) and in his philosophical works discussed his predecessors. It is not certain that all this information is derived from his *Peri Phusikôn Doxôn* (= *Physical Opinions*, as the likely meaning is), though this has often been assumed, since Theophrastus, like *Aristotle, used to discuss the historical development of ideas as a preliminary step to his own philosophy. It is not known who changed the Aristotelian-Theophrastean way of discussing predecessors according to the affiliation of their views into the less problem-oriented system we find in the so-called doxographers. It is important to notice that although each doxographer seems to have changed and added to the account of his immediate predecessor, the fact that several sources attribute the same view to a particular philosopher does not by itself increase the likelihood that it reflects the original ideas of that philosopher. All it means is that this was a standard item within the doxographical tradition.

Though "doxography" in a strict sense originally applied only to those sources that seem to derive from Theophrastus, it later came to be used to include any ancient source that reports the views of earlier philosophers. It has been suggested by M. Giusta that, corresponding to the doxographies on physics and metaphysics, there must have been another doxographical tradition dealing with *ethics. There seems, however, to be general agreement that the existence of such a parallel tradition cannot be established. The similarity between various texts (e.g., some of Cicero's and *Seneca's), though impressive, can be explained as a result of a common way of dealing with these questions.

There is another type of philosophical historiography that may be called doxographical, namely, a series of works called *Peri Haireseôn* (= *On the Sects*), written in the second and first centuries B.C.E. These works are all lost and only known from references and quotations, particularly in Diogenes Laertius. Only one substantial excerpt, by *Arius Didymus and preserved by Stobaeus (*Eclogae* 2.7, 37–152 Hense), can possibly be attributed to works of this type. It appears that these works dealt only with the Postsocratic schools of philosophy and hence primarily with ethics and also that they offered systematic accounts of the philosophical doctrines, so that the views of each school on a particular philosophical topic were presented in separate sections.

In late antiquity, in the church fathers, for example, there can be little doubt that doxographical works of one type or another were the sources consulted by most students of philosophy. Only few of the original works by Presocratic and Hellenistic philosophers were available outside Alexandria and other centers of scholarship. Hence the study of doxography and of the transmission of philosophical texts in antiquity is important for a proper evaluation of the significance of late testimonies and of their interpretations vis-à-vis the original statements by earlier philosophers.

BIBLIOGRAPHY: Giusta, M., *I dossografi di etica*, vols. 1 and 2, Torino, 1964–68; Mansfeld, J., *ANRW* 2, 36.4, 1990, 3056–3239; also in *RUSCH*, vol. 5, 1992, 63–111; Mejer, J., *Diogenes Laertius and His Hellenistic Background*, Wiesbaden, 1978, 75–89; *RUSCH*, vol. 1, 1983; Stokes, M. C., *One and Many in Presocratic Thought*, Washington, DC, 1971, 66–85.—*JØRGEN MEJER*

E

ELEATIC SCHOOL. Name given to *Parmenides and the philosophers (*Zeno of Elea and *Melissus of Samos) who adopted his views. *Plato's *Sophist* 242d3–6 mentions an "Eleatic group" that goes back to *Xenophanes or even earlier. The connection of Xenophanes with the Eleatic school is tenuous: The link is sometimes made on the basis of Xenophanes' account of a single unchanging god, but this is dubious. There may not have been an Eleatic "school" at all in the normal sense. Whereas Plato tells us in the *Parmenides* that Zeno was a student of Parmenides, it is doubtful that Melissus studied with Parmenides (as opposed to merely studying his work). The sophist *Gorgias is also linked to the Eleatic school through his work "On that which Is Not."

The Eleatic philosophers shared the conviction that what is must be perfect, unchanging, whole, complete, and a unity. Parmenides provided arguments for the impossibility of what is not and deduced these characteristics from an analysis of the nature of *being. According to Plato, Zeno defended Parmenides against his detractors by arguing that the assumption of plurality entailed contradictions. Moreover, in his paradoxes, Zeno argued against the possibility of motion. Melissus expanded on Parmenides' claims, arguing explicitly that Being is one and that void is impossible. In addition, Parmenides had argued that what is is limited, held in the fetters of a mighty bond, while Melissus argued that Being is unlimited.

Parmenides' views were highly influential on later Presocratic thought; and while there are Eleatic influences on Plato's thought, Plato and *Aristotle presented arguments against the Eleatic positions on unity, being, *change, and motion.

BIBLIOGRAPHY: For bibliographical information, see the entries on PARMENIDES, ZENO of Elea, and MELISSUS.—*PATRICIA CURD*

EMPEDOCLES (c. 492–432 B.C.E.), of Acragas (modern Agrigento) in Sicily. Presocratic philosopher. We know that Empedocles' family had been prominent for at least two generations, since his grandfather had the resources to enter a horse race at the Olympian games. Like his father Meton, Empedocles was politically active and is said to have aided his city's transition from tyranny to democracy in 472. But most of the information about his life is mere legend. Much of the anecdotal material was probably inspired by his own poetry; for example, the stories of his *Pythagorean connections, his role as a doctor, miracle-worker, and magician, and even some of the many legends about his death.

His intellectual context is easier to establish. His thought was affected by Pythagoreanism and by the mystery religions which flourished in Italy and Sicily. It is also obvious that *Parmenides' poem had the most profound influence on his thought and work.

Empedocles' poetry survives only in quotations by later writers; in fact, more directly quoted material of his work survives than of any other pre-Platonic philosopher. Yet there is considerable uncertainty about the form which the work took. Long-standing tradition (based on *Diogenes Laertius) holds that there were two separate works of philosophical poetry, one *On Nature* and one entitled *Purifications*; the same source mentions a short poem on *medicine, an *Expedition of Xerxes*, and a hymn to Apollo (both said to have been burned by his sister), and some epigrams and tragedies of dubious authenticity. Most scholars pay little attention to any alleged works except the *On Nature* and *Purifications*; though a medical poem may have been the basis for his reputation as a doctor, we cannot identify any fragments that could not just as easily have come from a poem on natural philosophy. The main controversy is whether there were originally two distinct poems, one on nature and one on religious purifications. The report in Diogenes Laertius (8.77) is the best evidence for there having been two separate works, yet even he only reports a total length for the two works together. No other source claims that the works were distinct, though some authors cite from *Purifications* and some from *On Nature*. It has proven difficult to assign our surviving fragments with confidence to two separate works. Hence some scholars prefer to regard the two poems mentioned by Diogenes as alternative descriptions of one long poem that would be the source of all the surviving fragments. Certainty is impossible.

Like the other pluralists, Empedocles faced the challenge of explaining the natural world despite Parmenides' apparent demonstration that *change and plurality were impossible. He postulated the existence of

four "roots" or elemental forms of *matter (earth, air, fire, water), none of
which changed in quality or quantity. These were the *"beings" that met
the strict standard set by Parmenidean reasoning. They were unborn,
undying, and permanently self-identical. Yet there were four beings,
whereas Parmenides claimed that only *one* thing existed. Either Empedocles took advantage of the apparent fact that Parmenides did not argue
formally for uniqueness (at least not in the fragments that we possess), or
he regarded the postulate of plurality as justified by the explanatory
work it could do: Without some plurality, no explanation of the world of
appearance was possible—as even Parmenides conceded in the second
half of his poem. Similarly, the possibility of motion must have been assumed by Empedocles, though he offered an explanation in the form of
two other entities (usually regarded as corporeal), Love and Strife, which
acted as motive powers for the four roots. *Aristotle and his *commentators often complained that the causal power exercised by Love and Strife
was nonteleological and that "chance" was given too much work to do in
the system.

Once the four roots, Love, and Strife have been postulated, Empedocles explains virtually everything else by reference to them. The action of
Love and Strife causes mixture and blending of the roots, and the resul-
tant compounds are the things we see: Earth, sky, plants, animals, even
our own selves are mixtures of the roots. Any mixture will eventually
become unmixed and perish. Hence any compound is by its very nature
mortal; only simples are immortal (which is probably why the roots,
Love, and Strife were all referred to by divine names). This theory seems
to commit Empedocles to a kind of two-level ontology, with immortal
pure entities having full being, and mixtures possessing a lesser degree
of reality.

Empedocles also held that change, which his theory defended
against Parmenidean stasis, occurred in a cycle. There is a kind of perfection in the complete and seamless mixture of all the roots that Love creates when she unites them harmoniously in the shape of a sphere. But
Strife is an equally potent force, and its prerogatives were equally important: Complete separation of each root from the others must also occur.
Hence he held that the history of the cosmos consisted of an endless cycle
of alternation (governed by "oaths" that guarantee balance) between the
complete dominance of Love and the unfettered sway of Strife. In the
condition of complete Love, the total mixture does not admit of differentiation; and under total Strife there is no mixture and so no compound
entities at all. Any differentiated cosmos, such as the one we observe,
must occur at some intermediate stage or stages in the alternation between these two extreme conditions, when both Love and Strife act on
the roots. There is considerable controversy over the symmetry of this

cycle: Are differentiated worlds created in both stages (increasing Love and increasing Strife) or in only one (increasing Love)? The ancient sources are ambiguous, and scholars divided.

Either in a separate poem or in the work on nature, Empedocles developed a theory of transmigration. But the migratory entity was not labelled "soul," as it was later by *Plato and perhaps also by early Pythagoreans. What survived bodily death was called a *"daimôn"* or divinity, and it could be reincarnated in virtually any living thing: Empedocles himself said that he had been male and female, a bush, a bird, a beast, and a fish; certain species of animal and plant were privileged, and it seems that moral and intellectual excellence would be rewarded by a movement up the scale of reincarnation. Eventually a *daimôn* could attain the status of a true god. What is not clear, though, is whether these migratory *daimones* were immortal in the same way that the roots were or whether they perished (like other "long-lived *daimones*") when Love or Strife held sway.

Within the framework of his *metaphysics and cyclical *cosmology, Empedocles undertook to give a more or less materialistic explanation of a very wide range of phenomena: the heavenly bodies and their motions; the origin of animal species; the structure of matter, both animate and inanimate; sense perception and thought (the subject of a long discussion in *Theophrastus' *De Sensu*); and processes such as breathing and reproduction. In all cases the central explanatory device was a theory of matter that relied on the mixture of the four roots. Mixture, like sense perception, was explained in terms of "pores" or passages in the structure of matter. It is not clear how this theory can be reconciled with Empedocles' emphatic Parmenidean denial of the existence of *void, nor is it clear whether the fundamental structure of matter is particulate. More important than these obscurities, though, are several conceptual breakthroughs that would bear considerable fruit in later philosophy and science: the use of numerical ratios in the explanation of different kinds of matter and tissues (bone is two parts water, four parts fire, two parts earth, while blood is an equal blend of all four roots), the idea that sense perception occurred when material effluences from the surfaces of physical objects entered the sense organs through pores in the body, and the essential similarity of thought and perception.

But perhaps the most important legacy of Empedocles to later Greek philosophy and *science was the most basic part of his theory: the idea that there were four and only four basic kinds of matter, with every other physical entity to be explained as some mixture or combination of these simples. A theory that began as a brilliant attempt to reconcile Parmenidean reasoning with the evidence of the senses became a cornerstone of qualitative physics that survived until the dawn of modern science.

BIBLIOGRAPHY: Texts in DK31. Bollack, J., *Empédocle*, Paris,1965–69; Inwood, B., *The Poem of Empedocles*, Toronto, 1992; Mourelatos, A. P. D., *PBACAP* 2, 127–194; O'Brien, D., *Empedocles' Cosmic Cycle*, Cambridge, 1969; Osborne, C., *CQ* 37, 1987, 24–50; Solmsen, F., *Phronesis* 10, 1965, 109–48; Wright, M. R., *Empedocles: The Extant Fragments*, New Haven/London, 1981; Zunzt, G., *Persephone*, Oxford, 1971.— *BRAD INWOOD*

EPICTETUS (c. 50–130 C.E.), from Hierapolis, in Phrygia. *Stoic philosopher, student of *Musonius Rufus. Born into slavery, Epictetus served for a time as slave to Nero's freedman Epaphroditus in Rome. Later, he moved to Nicopolis across the Adriatic sea, where he set up a philosophical school for young men. Like *Socrates, the philosopher he admired most, Epictetus did not compose any writings. His teachings were written down by a student, the historian Arrian. They consist of *Diatribes* (in four books), a collection of lectures and conversations, and *Handbook (Encheiridion)*, a compendium of his teachings.

Epictetus was thoroughly familiar with all branches of Stoic philosophy, but focussed his own concern on practical *ethics. The cornerstone of his ethics is a distinction between what is in our power and what is not in our power. The only thing in our power is our own mental disposition. The rest—our bodies, our family, our fortune, in short, all circumstances external to the inner self—is outside our power. How we fare in these externals makes no difference to our *happiness. We should, therefore, give our full attention to what is in our power. This consists basically in the use of our "impressions" (*phantasiai*), that is, in our choice (*prohairesis*). Impressions come, in the first place, to our senses from outside. From sensory impressions, we acquire impressions belonging to our *mind, called "ruling principle" (*hêgemonikon*). A person has the power of assent or dissent to impressions, or may simply suspend judgment. How a person judges an impression depends on his or her mind. A person acquires a morally good disposition by learning how to judge impressions correctly. Using a typically vivid image, Epictetus demands that our judgments must be firm, not like wax melting in the sun (*Diatribes* 3.16.9). Persons who follow every impression are madmen (1.28.33). Those who discriminate among them on the basis of a good moral disposition are happy.

The most prominent concept in Epictetus' writings is freedom. This surely has something to do with his own slavery. But it is also firmly grounded in Stoic doctrine and, in particular, Epictetus' demand for the correct use of impressions. Our response to impressions makes us free, whatever our external circumstances. A slave can be free, as can any person oppressed by society or fate. Like all Stoics, Epictetus believed that whatever happens to us is fated, even our own decisions. Yet this does not mean that we are not in charge of making our decisions. Epictetus is committed to a compatibilist position on free will. Because our decisions depend on our own mental state, we have the freedom to make them and are responsible for them. The good person lives entirely as he wishes; he is completely unhindered. A beloved son or daughter may die; he may be sent into exile or cast into chains—none of this matters. The real slaves are the powerful friends of Caesar who fear for their lives; a senator enjoys the "sleekest" slavery (4.1.40). The only safe fellow-traveler is God, not Caesar (4.1.98).

Along with *Seneca, Epictetus made prominent in Stoicism the notion of "inner god." Both are influenced by Alcibiades' description of Socrates' inner sanctuary, his soul, in *Plato's *Symposium*. While adhering to the Stoic doctrine of an immanent cosmic deity, Epictetus internalizes God and *religion by identifying the mind within us as a deity. We must have allegiance to this deity more than to Caesar (1.14.17). Epictetus urges us to look inward, not outside ourselves, for our happiness; this is where we truly find God. Orthodox Stoicism demands an adjustment of one's personal rational capacity to the reason that governs the universe. Epictetus does not abandon this doctrine, but shifts attention away from an integration of the individual within the world to the inner perfection of oneself. He asks us to admire not the world, but rather the human soul, as God's artifact.

This internalization shows itself in a reevaluation of Stoic *virtues. Epictetus has little to say about the four cardinal Stoic virtues: prudence, justice, temperance, and courage. Instead, he gives an altogether new emphasis to two virtues of his own choosing: sense of shame or respect (*aidôs*) and faith (*pistis*). These qualities are inner-directed; they define a new kind of religion, the devotion to one's own inner god. The good person has, above all, respect for himself and faith in himself.

In a sense, then, Epictetus thus recommends a withdrawal from the world. But despite a certain disdain for the world, he is sure of the ability to overcome it; he is not depressed by it. He speaks of life as a festival (1.12.21, 4.1.108): We participate cheerfully in a round of affairs, then take our departure without complaining. Similarly, he compares life to a comfortable inn (2.23.36). We stay for a while, then move on. His internalization of virtue is confident and spirited.

Epictetus is drawn strongly to *Cynicism. Like *Zeno of Citium, the founder of Stoicism, he values the Cynics' exclusive concern with virtue. But he views Cynicism quite differently from Zeno. For Epictetus, the Cynic philospher has a special role as messenger from God (3.22.23). He is delegated by God to show humans where they have gone wrong and to turn them to virtue. Because of his immersion in the world, the Cynic must be free of personal distractions, such as a wife and children. By contrast, the Stoic wise person makes friends with other wise persons and participates in the world without trying to reform it. Without explicitly rejecting the Stoic ideal of the wise person, Epictetus opts for the Cynic. We can detect Epictetus' own preference in his choice of a model. He is a practical philosopher who strives above all to teach others to be virtuous.

More forcefully than any other philosopher in antiquity, Epictetus seeks to impel his listeners into an effort to improve themselves. He emulates Socrates in this goal, but uses methods of his own. In his commentary on Epictetus' *Handbook*, *Simplicius observes that Epictetus' teachings are so effective that "whoever is not wholly dead is prodded by them" and that "whoever is not moved by these discourses could be straightened out only by the courts in Hades." Epictetus urges his students, one by one, to look closely at their weaknesses as a preliminary to improving their character. His teaching is not gentle. He compares the philosopher's school to a hospital: One comes out in pain, not with a feeling of pleasure (3.23.30). Moral improvement, like medical treatment, is painful. Epictetus is clearly a psychiatrist, and his method is to inflict pain. This, he believes, is the first step in the process of healing. Epictetus has no sympathy with those who would deceive themselves, who run way from a recognition of their faults, who feel sorry for themselves, who want a little sympathy from their teacher. He berates a sick student for wanting to go back home to recuperate (3.5). He will not coddle his students. He is a hard taskmaster, accused of being an "uncaring old man" (2.17.38). Standing in lieu of a parent, he cares enough to lecture them on physical as well as moral cleanliness. More than anything, Epictetus wants to teach the young men in his school to lead self-respecting lives when they go back out into the world.

BIBLIOGRAPHY: Texts in W. A. Oldfather, ed. and tr., *Epictetus*, 2 vols. (Loeb), London/Cambridge, MA, 1925. Bonhöffer, A., *Epictet und die Stoa*, Stuttgart, 1890, repr. 1968; also *Die Ethik des Stoikers Epictet*, Stuttgart 1894, repr. 1968; Hershbell, J., *ANRW* 2, 36.3, 1989; Hijmans, B. L., *Askesis: Notes on Epictetus' Educational System*, Assen, 1959.—ELIZABETH ASMIS

EPICUREANISM. A philosophical tradition based upon the teachings of *Epicurus and his early followers. Along with *Stoicism and *Skepticism, it was one of the three major Hellenistic moral philosophies. Most of the writings of Epicurus are completely lost or survive only in fragments; and the majority of our Epicurean texts come to us not from Hellenistic Athens, but from the era of the Roman Republic and Empire. In addition to the sympathetic account of *Diogenes Laertius, our main sources include: *Diogenes of Oenoanda, *Lucretius, *Philodemus, and the (often hostile) treatments by non-Epicureans such as *Cicero, *Plutarch, *Seneca, and *Sextus Empiricus. Because so few of our sources are con-

temporary with Epicurus or his first disciples, the early history of Epicureanism is difficult to reconstruct. The problem is compounded by the
fact that most of our later sources are heavily influenced by a hostile
tradition that portrayed the Epicureans as intemperate, licentious, and
anti-intellectual, a misrepresentation that lingers in our modern term
"epicurean." Although Epicurus had many adherents throughout the
Mediterranean world and although the Garden (the original headquarters of Epicureanism) remained active for several hundred years, Epicureanism seems never to have enjoyed complete respectability in Greek
or Roman society.

Relationship to Other Philosophical Systems. Although Epicurus himself
apparently claimed to be self-taught, the ancient tradition recognized in
Epicureanism the influence of the atomists *Democritus and *Leucippus,
as well as the importance of *Anaxagoras, *Archelaus, and *Pyrrho.
Modern scholarship adds various others to this list, including *Aristotle,
*Diodorus Cronus, *Eudoxus, *Plato, and *Theophrastus. The *doxogra-
phers cited by Diogenes Laertius (Book 10) assert that Epicurus heard
personally the lectures of the Democritean *Nausiphanes, the *Platonists
Pamphilus and *Xenocrates, and the *Peripatetic Praxiphanes. Diogenes
Laertius also reports that hostile sources claimed that Epicurus was influenced by *Aristippus; but Epicurean hedonism, with its emphasis
upon the simple pleasures of a quiet life, was in fact quite distinct from
the hedonism of the *Cyrenaics.

Epicureanism shared with the other Hellenistic schools the conception of philosophy as a cure for human suffering. As a system that emphasized the *happiness of the individual and the integration of theory
and practice, the Garden had much in common with the Stoa in particular. Despite this similarity, the Roman sources consistently portray the
Epicureans as the rivals of the Stoics, and modern scholarship has often
assumed that the two systems developed in opposition to each other
from the very beginning. Fundamental issues such as the Garden's denial
of divine providence, its withdrawal from public life, and its rejection of
conventional Greek education certainly distinguished it from the Stoa.
The traditional opposition between Stoics and Epicureans cannot be
traced back to Epicurus' lifetime, however: Although *Zeno of Citium
and Epicurus were contemporaries, we have no evidence for hostilities
between them, and Epicurus cannot have confronted the views of
*Chrysippus, who was still a child when Epicurus died. Thus it may be
significant that Plutarch (*Mor.* 1086e–f and 1108b) does not include any
Stoics in his list of philosophers criticized by the early Epicurean
*Colotes. Some extant sources suggest that early Epicureanism defined
itself mainly in opposition to the *Academy, the Presocratics, and early
Skepticism; and it is possible that animosity between Stoics and Epicure-

ans did not crystallize until the era of Cicero, when Epicureanism came to be viewed (by Epicureans as well as by outsiders) as the antithesis of Roman Stoicism.

The First Epicureans. According to Diogenes Laertius, Epicurus had already attracted students in Mytilene and Lampsacus before founding the Garden at Athens (c. 307 B.C.E.); and several of these early disciples (including Colotes, Leontius, *Metrodorus [of Lampsacus], Pythocles, and *Hermarchus) seem to have formed the center of Epicurus' original circle in Athens. Lacking early texts, we cannot know how closely Epicurus' teachings in the East approximated his mature philosophy, but it is generally thought that the system was essentially complete before Epicurus' return to Athens. Some scholars, however, assign a more formative role to the Garden's proximity to the other Athenian schools.

The nature of our sources makes it difficult to know exactly how to characterize the Garden as first established by Epicurus. Modern scholarship depicts the Garden variously as a philosophical school, a center for the production of Epicurean books, an alternative community, a radical social experiment, or a combination of these categories. The *Life* and the will of Epicurus (as reported by Diogenes Laertius) portray the Garden both as a shared dwelling place and as the site of philosophical discussions, although the will also suggests that some members lived in a separate house. Modern treatments of Epicureanism have often asserted that a rigid hierarchical social order was maintained in Epicurus' Garden, a view based primarily upon an idiosyncratic reading (first formulated by DeWitt, 1936) of Philodemus' *On Frankness*. It now seems likely that Philodemus' discussion (and that of his source *Zeno of Sidon) pertains to later philosophical groups and that Philodemus' various titles for teachers do not reflect a strict ranking system. It is even possible that the early Epicurean system of education was egalitarian in practice as well as in theory and that the Garden was open to persons normally excluded from the other schools.

Ancient authorities cite slaves (especially a man named Mys) and women (e.g., Leontion, Erotion, Hedeia, Nikidion, and Themista) who were associated with the first generation of the Garden, but the various biases of the sources make them problematic. Diogenes Laertius, when defending Epicurus against detractors (10.9–10), praises Epicurus' gentleness towards servants and asserts that Mys and other slaves joined him in philosophical study. In contrast, the stereotype of the irresponsible and immoral Epicurean is prominent in writers such as Plutarch, who portrays the women not as students of philosophy but as instruments of pleasure on a par with the allegedly abundant Epicurean wines and foods. Cicero, while recording ridicule of the Garden for its inclusion of women, provides us with evidence that Leontion was indeed a disciple who authored a treatise against Theophrastus (*ND* 1.93). It has been suggested recently that the (possibly erotic-sounding) names of Epicurean women were invented by a hostile outsider, but epigraphic sources prove that the names themselves are authentic Greek names. Several first-generation Epicurean women, including Hedeia, Nikidion, and Mammarion, also appear in the texts of the later Epicurean Philodemus, who had a serious interest in Epicurean biography. Few slaves or women are associated with subsequent generations of the Garden, however; and it may be significant that Philodemus names four original authorities for Epicureanism (Epicurus, Hermarchus, Metrodorus, and *Polyaenus), to whom he refers to collectively as *hoi andres* ("the men").

Also present in the Garden during these early years was Timocrates, the brother of Metrodorus and a disgruntled Epicurean. Diogenes Laertius recounts that this Timocrates wrote an exposé that detailed the alleged corruption of the Garden. Sedley (1976) has argued that Timocrates thus inaugurated the anti-Epicurean tradition that pervades the works of Cicero, Plutarch, and others.

At the death of Epicurus, the directorship of the Garden passed on to Hermarchus, and then to *Polystratus.

The Later History of Epicureanism. Modern scholarship has often portrayed Epicureanism as an extremely conservative system that tolerated no innovation or development. This view is not completely groundless: Among later Epicureans there was a tendency to regard certain early writings as canonical scripture, and Philodemus (1st cent. B.C.E.) warned his contemporaries that rejection of these texts was akin to parricide. Followers were encouraged to memorize the *Kuriai Doxai*; and generations of Epicureans idealized Epicurus and preserved his cult through the celebration of his birthday, the wearing of rings, and the erection of statues. Recent scholarship, however, has begun to view the history of Epicureanism as more complex than the traditional approach has supposed. Philodemus' concern to authenticate certain Epicurean texts (while condemning others) may itself be an indication of doctrinal shifts. New fragments of Diogenes of Oenoanda demonstrate that even the *Kuriai Doxai* were subject to change: His inscribed set of doctrines matches precisely with neither the Vatican Sayings nor the *Doxai* as preserved by Diogenes Laertius. The papyrus fragments of Epicurus, as well as the titles of non-extant Epicurean books, also demonstrate that the three epistles of Epicurus recorded by Diogenes Laertius are not representative of the range and sophistication of Epicurus' work as a whole. The scarcity of early Epicurean texts will always make the development of Epicureanism difficult to trace, but the longevity of the school and the diversity of its adherents assured the Garden a varied history.

After the death of Epicurus, followers appear not only in Greece but also in Syria, Egypt, and Asia Minor. Little is known about Epicurean circles of the late third and second centuries B.C.E., but papyri from Herculaneum, such as a fragmentary biography of the second-century Syrian Epicurean Philonides, have begun to fill some gaps. An important adherent in Greece at the end of the second century B.C.E. was *Demetrius of Laconia, who specialized in the exegesis of early Epicurean texts. Among the better-known Epicureans who were born further from Athens, Diogenes Laertius mentions in particular *Diogenes of Tarsus, the two Ptolemaei of Alexandria, and Zeno of Sidon. Zeno, who was head of the Garden during the early first century B.C.E., was especially significant because he developed Epicurean responses to current philosophical debates. Most noteworthy were his critique of Stoic *logic, his response to the Academic *Carneades (214–129 B.C.E.), and his innovative analysis of Epicurean scientific method. Beginning with the work of Asclepiades of Prusa during the first century B.C.E., Epicureanism also began to influence the Greek *medical tradition.

Epicureanism was at first slow to gain adherents in Italy, but according to Plutarch (*Life of Pyrrhus* 20.6; cf. Valerius Maximus 4.3.6), news of the Garden had reached (and shocked) Rome as early as Epicurus' lifetime. Cicero, who suggests that Epicureanism was the first Greek philosophy to be expounded in Latin, claims that early Epicurean texts in Latin found many readers among the uneducated but that they were of poor quality (*TD* 4.3.7). The Epicurean popularizers Amafinius (late 2nd or early 1st cent.), and Catius (d. 45 B.C.E.), for example, were especially inadequate as translators of key terms (Cic. *Ad Familiares* 15.19.2). By the late Republic, however, the Garden was rapidly gaining followers among the Roman elite. Two students of Zeno of Sidon seem to have been the most influential scholars of Epicureanism in Italy around this time. These were Siro, whose circle of students in Campania may have included the young poet Vergil, and Philodemus of Gadara, whose numerous Epicurean works have survived in papyrus fragments from Herculaneum. *Phaedrus, who succeeded Zeno as director of the Garden, also had some Roman students of note, including Cicero's friend Atticus.

The fragmentary texts of Philodemus contain a wealth of information about Epicureanism as practiced among the Greek-speaking inhabitants Italy in the first century B.C.E. Philodemus is especially critical of Stoic *political theory; and like his contemporary Cicero, he tends to describe Epicureanism and Stoicism as polar opposites. Epicureanism at this era was not monolithic, however. Philodemus writes of energetic disputes over Epicurean doctrine between his own circles in Campania and Epicureans in Rhodes, Cos, and elsewhere. His response to such controversies was to appeal to the authority of Athens (including his own teacher

Zeno) and to exhort dissident Epicureans to return to the original texts of Epicurus, Hermarchus, Metrodorus, and Polyaenus. Philodemus also differs from his Roman contemporary Lucretius. His elaborate descriptions of the gods, for example, contrast sharply with Lucretius' reticence and may represent Philodemus' (or Zeno's) own response to recent accusations that the Epicureans were atheists. Also very unlike Lucretius is the sympathetic attitude toward grieving expressed in Philodemus' *On Death*.

While Philodemus is clearly immersed in contemporary discourse, the poet Lucretius displays no obvious connections with Epicurean circles in Rome, Campania, or elsewhere. Although the *De Rerum Natura* is our most important Epicurean source in Latin, it is difficult to prove that Lucretius used anything but original texts of Epicurus as his source for Epicurean doctrine; and scholars disagree as to whether Lucretius' exposition of Epicureanism ought to be regarded as strictly orthodox or specifically Roman. Some of Lucretius' presentations of Epicureanism seem to be engaged with the contemporary debate between the Stoa and the Garden, but even this is a controversial issue because Lucretius never mentions the Stoa by name. The recent discovery of fragments of *De Rerum Natura* in Herculaneum, however, suggests at the very least that Lucretius was read by Epicureans like Philodemus.

The late Republic is sometimes described as the only era in which numbers of Epicureans abandoned Epicurus' dictum *lathe biôsas* ("live unknown") and became politically active. Those Epicureans who took political action were not aligned with one particular party or class, however. While Cassius the tyrannicide was an Epicurean, there were also many Epicureans among the friends and supporters of Caesar.

Open adherence to Epicureanism seems to have declined in Rome during the last quarter of the first century B.C.E. as the values promoted by Augustus became increasingly associated with Stoicism. Some scholars detect sympathy for Epicureanism in the works of Vergil, Horace, and Ovid, and some would describe the patron Maecenas as an Epicurean, but no major Epicurean texts from this era survive. Evidence for the first century C.E. is also inconclusive, much of it coming from Jewish and *Christian critiques. *Philo of Alexandria's attacks on the Epicurean concepts of corporeal gods, indivisible atoms, and a universe governed by chance, for example, suggest an active Epicurean community in Alexandria; and Paul's epistles and other New Testament texts may provide evidence for an Epicurean presence in Athens, Colossae, Corinth, Philippi, and Thessalonica. Seneca's broad knowledge of Epicurus also suggests a continued presence of Epicureans in Rome.

The second century C.E. saw a great revival of Epicureanism, especially in Greek-speaking communities in Greece and Asia Minor. Some of the evidence is indirect: *Galen's eight (non-extant) works against the Epicureans suggest an ongoing debate; and Plutarch's attacks upon Epicureanism indicate that he considered the Garden a serious threat to Graeco-Roman society. Many scholars consider Trajan's wife Plotina to have been a disciple of Epicurus, and a bilingual inscription from 121 C.E. records her successful petition to Hadrian on behalf of the Athenian Epicureans, who had requested the right to choose their head from among non-Roman citizens. Further imperial recognition came from Marcus *Aurelius, who endowed chairs for the Academy, *Lyceum, Stoa, and Garden. Our most important source for the shape of Epicureanism in second-century C.E. Asia Minor is the inscription of Diogenes of Oenoanda, who offers Epicurean wisdom to "all Greeks and barbarians." From Diogenes we know that Epicureanism still had adherents, not only in his province of Lycia but also in Rhodes, Lindos, Chalcis, and Thebes. Important testimony to the vitality of Epicurean communities elsewhere in the Roman Empire is also found in *Lucian's *Alexander the False Prophet*, a work that describes the efforts of Epicureans to expose an especially popular oracle monger. While this text is not a rich source for doctrinal details, it reveals much about the social and cultural location of Epicureanism—and its adversaries—in the second century.

Discussions of Epicureanism in a variety of later writers, including Claudian, *Porphyry, and Christian apologists such as *Clement of Alexandria, Lactantius, *Origen, and Tertullian, attest to the survival of Epicureanism into the next three centuries.

For Epicurean doctrines, see EPICURUS, LUCRETIUS and other Epicurean figures.

BIBLIOGRAPHY: Articles in *CronErc*; Association Guillaume Budé, *Actes du VIIIe Congrès*, Paris, 1968 (contains over thirty articles on the history of Epicureanism); Bollack, J., and A. Laks, eds., *Etudes sur l' épicurisme antique*, Lille, 1976; Carratelli, G. P., ed., *SUZÊTÊSIS: Studi sull' Epicurismo Greco e Romano offerti a Marcello Gigante*, 2 vols., Naples, 1983; Castner, C., *Prosopography of Roman Epicureans: from the Second Century B.C. to the Second Century A.D.*, Frankfurt am Main, 1988; DeWitt, N., *CP* 31, 1936, 205–11; *GRBS* 30.2, 1989 (Proceedings of conference, "Tradition and Innovation in Epicureanism," Duke University, April, 1989); Ferguson, J., *ANRW* 2, 36.4, 2257–2327; Long, A. A., *Hellenistic Philosophy: Stoics, Epicureans, Sceptics,*[2] Berkeley, 1986; Nussbaum, M., *The Therapy of Desire: Theory and Practice in Hellenistic Ethics*, Princeton, 1994; Sedley, D. N., in J. Barnes and M. T. Griffen, eds., *Philosophia Togata*, Oxford, 1989, 97–119; also "Epicurus and his Professional Rivals," in J. Bollack and A. Laks, eds., 119–159.—*PAMELA GORDON*

EPICURUS (341–270 B.C.E.), of Samos. Founder of *Epicureanism. Epicurus set up a philosophical school c. 307 B.C.E. in Athens, in a garden; hence the name "Garden" (*Kêpos*) for Epicureanism. He was joined in his school by numerous friends, including *Hermarchus, *Metrodorus (of

Lampsacus), and *Polyaenus, who were known, along with Epicurus, as the founding fathers of Epicureanism. Epicurus wrote many books, of which only a tiny part is preserved. We have three complete *Letters*: the *Letter to Herodotus*, a summary of his physics; the *Letter to Pythocles*, a summary of his meteorology and *astronomy; and the *Letter to Menoeceus*, a summary of his *ethics. In addition, there are two collection of aphorisms: the "Authoritative Opinions" (*Kuriai Doxai*), which set forth in easily memorized form the fundamental doctrines of Epicureanism, and the Vatican Sayings. Fragments of his large work *On Nature* have been preserved on papyri found at Herculaneum (near Naples). There are other fragments and a large number of reports by ancient authors. A major, though controversial, source for Epicurus' teachings is *Lucretius' poem *On the Nature of Things*.

Epicurus' philosophical aim was to teach others how to be happy. He believed that in order to attain *happiness, people must be freed of their anxieties, primarily the fear of the gods and death, and must learn how to limit their desires. Consequently, they must learn physics. For only physics will teach them that the gods do not rule this world or interfere in any way in their lives, and it will tell them that the *soul is destroyed at death. The gods do not rule either a person's life, for they are wholly detached from this world, or an afterlife, for there is none. It is up to each person to fashion his or her life to be as happy as possible. The goal of life is pleasure, and the highest pleasure is the absence of both physical and mental pain. In order to have the maximum of pleasure, a person must learn how to keep desires within natural limits. By calculating the amount of pleasure and pain involved in each action, a person can choose a course of life that is predominantly pleasant.

Epicurus intended his philosophy to be accessible to all persons, male and female, educated or not. His school notoriously included women (see EPICUREANISM). He addressed his teachings to the humble no less than the socially prominent, to ignorant "villagers" (as *Cicero puts it) no less than accomplished intellectuals. The range of his writings reflects this concern. There are maxims to be memorized by those who want a short course in philosophy, and there are technical writings for more advanced students, ranging from summaries to highly detailed expositions. Just as anyone, no matter how underprivileged, could be happy, so anyone, no matter how uneducated, could learn to be happy. The only real type of education is Epicurean philosophy, which is available to everyone; indeed, traditional education is a hindrance.

Epistemology and Physics. Epicurus divided philosophy into two main parts, physics and ethics. Under physics he included epistemology, which he called "canonic." This is preliminary to the investigation of nature. "Canonic" is derived from the *kanon*, "rule," by which knowledge is measured. Epicurus proposed an empiricist epistemology. He held that sensory phenomena serve as "signs" of what cannot be observed. All hypotheses must be checked against sensory data, and the sensory data must be pure of any interpretation. Epicurus believed that such pure sensory information exists in the form of perceptions that have not been joined by belief. Whenever we see, hear, and so on, we receive an impression from outside that is "true," for it corresponds to an external state of affairs. To this impact from outside, we add an opinion "from within ourselves"; and this opinion may be true or false (*Letter to Herodotus* 50–51). It is true when confirmed by a present perception, false when it is not confirmed in this way. The technical term for sensory confirmation is "witnessing" (*epimarturêsis*); for nonconfirmation, "no witnessing" (*ouk epimarturêsis*). For example, we may receive an impression of a round tower, then add the opinion that the tower in the distance is round. This opinion turns out to be false; for when we come up close, we see the tower as square. Both impressions are "true," but the opinion that there is a round tower in the distance is falsified by the subsequent impression of a square tower. The subsequent opinion that the tower is square is confirmed by perception.

It is a matter of considerable doubt and controversy, from antiquity to the present, how such necessarily "true" sensory impressions can serve as confirmation of beliefs and so as the foundation of knowledge. According to Epicurus' physical theory, every sensory impression corresponds to a configuration of *atoms that makes an impact on the sensory organ. But this configuration need not correspond to a particular external source. Granted that we can distinguish between an impression and an opinion (and this is itself dubious), it is not clear how this distinction allows us to get a cognitive grip on the external world. Epicurus and his followers themselves struggled with this problem. They insisted that their physical theory confirms their initial methodological assumptions. The reason, it seems, is that the theory shows not only that every sensory impression corresponds to an atomic configuration but also that external objects present themselves by atomic streams that can preserve a continuity with the object, so as to correspond exactly to the external object.

Physical inquiry begins with a distinction between what is observed and what cannot be observed. In addition to the observational evidence, it is necessary to have concepts in order to formulate a question or hypothesis. If these concepts are already contaminated by untested presuppositions, then the inquiry is bound to fail. Epicurus thought that the initial concepts of investigation are constructed out of sensory impressions in such a way that they are wholly confirmed by these impressions. He called these concepts "preconceptions" (*prolêpseis*). They must be accepted as true; for although they are judgments, they are firmly based on sensory evidence. A theory about what cannot be observed is shown to be false by "counterevidence" (*antimarturêsis*); it is confirmed by there being "no counterevidence" (*ouk antimarturêsis*). The method of "counterevidence" consists in deducing an observational consequence from the contradictory of the hypothesis. If this consequence is observed not to be true, the initial hypothesis is confirmed. For example, take the hypothesis that there is *void. If there were no void, Epicurus argued, then bodies would not be able to move. But they are observed to move, hence there is void. It is a vexed problem of Epicurean epistemology how the absence of counterevidence can confirm a hypothesis. Epicurus' followers *Zeno of Sidon and his associates thought they had an answer: They held that all physical theories are inferences showing the similarity of what is not observed to what is observed.

Equipped with both sensory observation and concepts, the investigator aims to discover the unobservable nature of things. Epicurus constructed a series of deductions as the foundation of his physics (*Letter to Herodotus* 38–44). The first principle is that nothing comes to be from nonbeing, the second that nothing is destroyed into nonbeing. Epicurus is usually thought to have taken over these principles from *Parmenides. But, as Lucretius shows in detail, he seems to have proved these principles by "counterevidence," by reducing the contradictory of each hypothesis to an observational consequence that is in conflict with what is observed. Thus the opinon that nothing comes to be from nonbeing is confirmed by the observed regularity of natural processes.

After concluding that the universe is always the same in respect to what exists, Epicurus argues that it consists of bodies and void, and nothing else. He argues in turn that bodies are either complexes of atoms, or atoms themselves. Atoms are unchanging, unsplittable bodies that come in countless shapes and sizes. The universe is *infinite, as are the atoms and the void. Atoms move very fast through the void, colliding and getting entangled with each other to form complexes. The largest type of complex is a world system. Since there is no reason why, in an infinite expanse of atoms and void, there should be a limit to the number of world systems, there are infinitely many worlds. Everything that happens in the universe is caused by the movements of atoms in the void.

Epicurus' physics is strongly indebted to his atomist predecessors *Democritus and *Leucippus, but there are some striking departures. One of the most interesting is the atomic swerve. Epicurus held that the weight of the atoms causes them to fall downward in straight lines. At indeterminate times and places, however, the atoms swerve by a minimal distance (Lucretius 2.243–45). This deviation allows the atoms to collide and consequently get entangled with each other. It also accounts for free will. One puzzle of Epicureanism is how a random movement can result in free will.

The division of the universe into atoms and void implies that there is no special soul stuff or other divine stuff. Each living creature has a soul that consists of fine atoms dispersed throughout the body. These atoms are scattered upon death. Humans have an especially fine concentration of atoms in the chest, which constitutes the *mind. Perception and thought consist of interactions between ourselves and the outside world. We perceive secondary qualities, such as colors, flavors, and sound, when atoms from outside collide with the sensory organ. The external objects themselves are composed of atoms that have only shape, size, and weight. There are gods, but they are fine complexes of atoms in the spaces between worlds. Though immortal, they are themselves products of atoms. They do not act in any way upon the world or intervene at all in human lives. The atoms are sufficient to account for the order in the world.

Ethics. All animals seek to have pleasure and avoid pain. This aim is obvious, Epicurus held, from birth; and it is the highest goal in life. What distinguishes humans from other animals is that we have the ability to calculate how to obtain the greatest amount of pleasure. Reason, along with the rest of human virtue, is a means to the attainment of pleasure. Since there can be no greater pleasure than the absence of pain (called "catastematic" pleasure), it does not matter how much sensual pleasure (classified as "kinetic" pleasure) a person has. Mental pleasure, more-over, far outweighs bodily pleasure. By focussing our minds on pleasant thoughts, we can avoid feeling both bodily and mental pain. Even a person undergoing the worst tortures can be happy.

Although Epicurus' hedonism was widely condemned in antiquity as a philosophy fit for pigs, some ancients also praised it for being admirably pure. Epicurus did not preach austerity, but accepted it as compatible with happiness. He drew a distinction among three kinds of desires: natural and necessary, natural and unnecessary, and unnatural and unnecessary. The first type is exemplified by the desire for food, drink, and other necessities of life; and it is easy to satisfy. The satisfaction of the second type of desire is unnecessary for pleasure but is nonetheless welcome, because it varies our experience of pleasure. Examples are the desire for good wine, or music, or the company of friends. The third type of desire must be avoided, for its satisfaction brings more pain than pleasure. Examples are the desire for wealth, power, limitless sex, or relentless study. There is a natural limit to pleasure, which any human being can and must learn in order to be happy.

Epicurus proposed a kind of recipe for happiness, called *tetrapharmakon* or "fourfold remedy." It consists of keeping in mind the first four "authoritative" opinions. The first is that the gods do not punish or reward; the second is the famous saying, "Death is nothing to us"; the third is that the highest pleasure is the elimination of pain; the fourth is that prolonged pain is tolerable, while acute pain is short. If we adhere to these principles, Epicurus held, nothing prevents us from living a life like that of the gods.

BIBLIOGRAPHY: Texts in Arrighetti, G., ed., *Epicuro Opere*,[2] Turin, 1973; Bailey, C., ed., *Epicurus: The Extant Remains*, Oxford, 1926; A. A. Long and D. N. Sedley, eds., *The Hellenistic Philosophers*, 2 vols., Cambridge, 1987; Usener, H., ed., *Epicurea*, Leipzig, 1887. Asmis, E., *Epicurus' Scientific Method*, Ithaca, 1984; Everson, S., in Everson, ed., *Epistemology*, Cambridge, 1990, 161–83; Mitsis, P., *Epicurus' Ethical Theory*, Ithaca, 1988; Rist, J. M., *Epicurus: An Introduction*, Cambridge, 1972; Sedley, D., in *Syzetesis*, vol. 1, Naples, 1983, 11–51; Striker, G., *AGP* 59, 1977, 125–42; Taylor, C. C. W., in M. Schofield et al., eds., *Doubt and Dogmatism*, Oxford, 1980, 105–24.—*ELIZABETH ASMIS*

EPISTEMOLOGY. See KNOWLEDGE, Classical Theories of.

ERASISTRATUS (c. 315–240 B.C.E.?), of Iulis on Ceos. Physician. Erasistratus may have practised both at the Seleucid court in Antioch-on-Orontes (Syria) and in Alexandria; personal connections with the *Peripatos are attested but controversial. Several hundred fragments and testimonia survive. Within *medicine, Erasistratus distinguishes between its scientific (*epistêmonika*) parts (aetiology, physiology) and stochastic parts (therapeutics, semiotics).

Erasistratus is the only ancient *scientist other than *Herophilus to whom ancient sources attribute systematic scientific dissection of human cadavers. *Celsus claims that Erasistratus also vivisected convicted criminals. Four general features of Erasistratus' method are noteworthy: (i) He takes a functional approach to his anatomical discoveries (e.g., he both offers the first reasonably accurate description of the heart valves and demonstrates that their function is to ensure the irreversibility of the flow through the valves). (ii) He often verifies hypotheses by means of experimentation. (iii) He adopts an overarching teleological perspective but sets limits to teleological explanation. (iv) Individual bodily processes are explained mechanistically, notably by the principle that *matter naturally moves by "following toward what is being emptied," that is, if matter is removed from any contained space, other matter will rush in to take its place, since a natural massed *void is impossible. Erasistratus uses this major mechanistic principle (later called *horror vacui*) to unite all physiological functions in a single, comprehensive model, within which *pneuma* is central. The left ventricle of the heart pumps vital (*zôtikon*) *pneuma* into the arteries with each contraction (*sustolê*), the nerves distribute psychic (*psuchikon*) *pneuma* from the brain, and the veins distribute blood from the liver. All organic structures consist of "triple-braided strands" (*triplokiai*) of arteries, veins, and nerves.

Internal causes of diseases are mostly instances of different types of bodily matter, which normally are separated, somehow not remaining separated. Such pathological movements of matter often are also explained in terms of the *horror vacui* principle. Like Herophilus, Erasistratus believes that there are no diseases peculiar to women. He recommends preventive regimen and mild, noninvasive measures that will ensure the return, to its natural place, of matter that has strayed.

Erasistratus' influence on subsequent Greek medicine was considerable; even his most vociferous critic, *Galen, took over central features of his anatomical and physio-pathological theories.

BIBLIOGRAPHY: Texts in I. Garofalo, ed., *Erasistrati fragmenta*, Pisa, 1988. Harris, C. R. S., *The Heart and the Vascular System in Ancient Greek Medicine*, Oxford, 1973, ch. 4.—*HEINRICH VON STADEN*

ERATOSTHENES (c. 276–194 B.C.E.), of Cyrene in North Africa. An eclectic scholar and *scientist whose principal efforts were devoted to geography, but who also published works of philosophy, literary criticism, *mathematics, and history and composed narrative poetry to boot. All these works have been lost except for a few valuable fragments. Eratosthenes headed the Alexandrian Library for about half a century, taking over that post from Apollonius of Rhodes around 247 and holding it until his death. The verdict on his philosophic career has been passed, though no doubt too harshly, by *Strabo: "His work entitled *On the Good* shows ... that he walked a middle course between wanting to be a philosopher and not having the rigor to discipline himself for this way of life and therefore advancing only as far as *seeming* philosophical" (*Geography* 1.2.2). Strabo also reports that Eratosthenes was a pupil of *Zeno of Citium at Athens, but his instructor in *Stoicism was actually *Aristo of Chios, one of Zeno's students; the *skeptic *Arcesilaus, who headed the *Academy in its middle period, was another of his early teachers. Later, Eratosthenes received instruction from Lysanias and Callimachus at Alexandria and thereafter inclined to the humanistic philology of these men rather than to any doctrinaire *ethical teaching.

In geography Eratosthenes is best known for his accurate measure of the circumference of the earth, by a mathematical procedure described by Tozer and Bunbury (see bibliography). His *Geographica* in three books presented an overall system of global geography incorporating the recent eastern explorations of Alexander the Great. Eratosthenes was roundly attacked by Strabo for not treating *Homer's *Odyssey* as part of the geographic record (see STRABO), but here he seems more nearly in line with modern approaches than were his Stoic adversaries. He retorted thus to the rigidly historical criticism prevalent among his peers: "You can find the route Odysseus wandered when you find the cobbler who sewed the bag of the winds" (referring to the episode of the Aeolian winds in *Odyssey* Book 10). In mathematics Eratosthenes is credited with the "sieve" for finding prime numbers that still bears his name. As a historian he produced a list of victors in the Olympic games going back five hundred years, an important step in the standardization of ancient chronology. Not much is known about the treatise *On the Good* mentioned by Strabo, but in general Eratosthenes' philosophic works seem to have been largely compilations or surveys of ethical thought rather than original contributions.

BIBLIOGRAPHY: Texts in G. Bernhardy, ed., *Eratosthenica*, Berlin, 1822; Bunbury, E. H., *A History of Ancient Geography*, vol. 1, London, 1879, ch. 16; Pfeiffer, R., *History of Classical Scholarship: From the Beginnings to the End of the Hellenistic Age*, Oxford, 1968, 163–170; Thalamas, A., *La Géographie d'Eratosthène*, Versailles, 1921; Tozer, H. F., *History of Ancient Geography*, New York, 1965, 158–168.—*JAMES ROMM*

ERETRIAN SCHOOL. See MENEDEMUS of Eretria.

ERISTIC. See DIALECTIC.

ETHICAL THOUGHT, Classical. "Ethics" was first defined as a separate category of philosophy by *Aristotle and remains one in some later theories, notably the *Stoic. But ethical thinking is an important strand in ancient philosophy from the Presocratics to *Neoplatonism. For Aristotle, "ethics" means "things related to character (*êthos*)," and the nature and formation of a good character is a central concern of Classical ethical thought. But the defining question of ancient ethical thought is, rather, "How should one live?" or, more precisely, "How should a human being shape his or her life?" The question of the best goal or end (*telos*) for shaping one's life is a recurrent one, typically framed as a question about the nature of human "happiness" or "flourishing" (*eudaimonia*) or the human "good" (*agathon*). It is characteristic of Classical thought that the answer to this question is not seen as provided by divine law or individual autonomy but by shared rational debate or *dialectic. Although the answers offered were sometimes presented as consistent with "nature" (*phusis*) or the "natural order" (*kosmos*), it was recognized that there was room for argument about what was "natural." An image that sums up much that is typical of ancient ethical thinking is that of human beings as participants in three interconnected types of dialogue: interactive social dialogue, reflective debate, and the "dialogue" between the parts of the personality (or *"soul," *psuchê*) that constitutes psychological life and the formation of character.

The Greek Poets. The characteristic form of Classical ethical philosophy is partly prefigured in *Homeric epic (c. 8th cent. B.C.E.) and Attic *tragedy (5th cent. B.C.E.), poetic genres that had a special status in Greek education and artistic life from the fifth century B.C.E. onward. These genres present, in narrative and dramatic form, debate about ethical issues (e.g., about what legitimates revenge or friendship bonds, or about the best life a human being can lead) that arise out of crises in interpersonal and communal life. Questions about human emotions (what motivates anger or passionate lust and how far can these be controlled?) also form part of this debate. Although these questions are often couched in terms of "honor" and "shame," some recent scholarship suggests that Greek poetic thinking envisages the "internalization" of these values in a way that anticipates Greek philosophical ideas about virtuous motivation. In Greek poetry the gods do not represent the source of ethical norms for human life, as does the Biblical God; instead, the ethical status of divine actions and attitudes constitutes one of the issues raised.

The Presocratic Philosophers. The Presocratics (7th–5th cent. B.C.E.) treat ethics (and *psychology) only as part of their project of studying nature or reality as a whole. Thus, they explore in their own way the question of the linkage between the natural order, human personality, and social norms, that is a characteristic theme of Classical thought. Examples of the linkage between nature and social norms include *Anaximander's (c. 610–540 B.C.E.) analysis of the natural order in terms of retribution and injustice and *Empedocles' (c. 493–c. 433 B.C.E.) analysis of this in terms of alternating patterns of Love and Strife. The *logos* ("reason") of *Heraclitus (fl. c. 500–480 B.C.E.) represents (i) the central principle of nature, (ii) (ideal) law (*nomos*), and (iii) human thought or rationality. *Pythagoras (6th cent. B.C.E.) saw number theory as the basis for (i) an analysis of the elements of the universe; (ii) organized forms of communal life; (iii) an understanding of the nature of the *psuchê,* and of the management of diet and desire. An implication of this type of thinking, also found in *Platonic and *Stoic thought, is that the more "rational" you become in your character and life, the more you become capable of understanding the rationality of the natural order. Presocratic thinking includes explicit ethical criticism of traditional and poetic ways of conceiving the gods (e.g., *Xenophanes, 6th cent. B.C.E.), or a redefinition of the "divine" and of its role in the origin and workings of the universe (e.g., *Anaxagoras, c. 500–c. 428 B.C.E.). The provocative, sometimes oracular, style typically adopted by Presocratic philosophers seems designed to stimulate disagreement and debate with other thinkers and with conventional opinion.

*The *Sophists and *Socrates.* In the second half of the fifth century B.C.E., Athens became a focus of Greek intellectual life and the context for debates that have far-reaching implications for subsequent ancient ethical thought. The most prominent is that about the relationship between nature (*phusis*) and law or convention (*nomos*), whose importance is reflected in, for example, *Aristophanes' *Clouds* (423 B.C.E.), a satire of contemporary intellectual life. Positions adopted include the claim that human nature and desire is inevitably in conflict with law (*Antiphon; "Callicles" in *Plato's *Gorgias*); and that laws are a mode of "social contract" to prevent the mutually destructive conflict that would otherwise naturally occur (Guthrie, chs. 4–5). However, there is, perhaps, a more important contrast, between the characteristic ethical approaches of the sophists and Socrates, which is expressed vividly (though in a highly partisan and fictionalized form) in Plato's early *dialogues. The sophists were itinerant professional teachers, who usually taught the art of public persuasion or *rhetoric. In identifying the basis of ethical norms, they tend to locate this in social institutions or practices. The position ascribed to *Protagoras (c. 485–415 B.C.E.) in Plato's *Protagoras* (320–8) is that justice and the other virtues are promoted, in any given society, by public and private persuasion and are a necessary precondition of human communities and hence of human survival. This may be taken as a "communitarian" account of the basis of ethics, which Protagoras himself may have combined with ethical relativism.

Socrates (469–399 B.C.E.) is presented by our sources (especially Plato, also Aristotle and to a lesser extent *Xenophon) as practising a distinctive method of systematic questioning, conducted with one person at one time and aiming at producing a logically consistent set of beliefs. Typical questions are: what is virtue (or a given virtue), how is it acquired, and how does it affect action? Socrates claims not to know the answers to these questions, but his procedure implies a distinct approach to ethics. By contrast with the communitarian position of Protagoras, Socrates' method implies that dialectical analysis is a necessary preliminary for acquiring the virtues; simply acquiring beliefs from the discourse of one's community is not enough. Ideas that seem to have recurred in Socratic *dialogues are the so-called paradoxes: that virtue is one, that virtue is knowledge, and that nobody does wrong willingly. Although these ideas are never put forward as definite doctrines by Socrates (who claims always to seek a type of knowledge he does not possess), the implied position is that virtue depends on dialectical understanding and that, once acquired, virtue determines action and feeling in a way that rules out weakness of will or wrongdoing. The opposition and interplay between communitarian and dialectical accounts of the nature and transmission of virtue remains fundamental in ancient ethical enquiry.

Plato. Whereas Socrates wrote nothing, Plato (c. 429–347 B.C.E.) practised philosophy (in part at least) through the medium of written dialogues, combined in his later life with dialectical teaching in the philosophical "'school" or research center that he founded, the *Academy.
Plato's early dialogues take the form of representing the Socratic method
of dialectic. Since Plato was a creative philosopher and even the early dialogues are more or less fully fictionalized, it is impossible to draw a precise distinction between the early philosophy of Plato and the work of
Socrates. In the middle period, Plato's dialogues are often seen as exploring implications of Socrates' method and arguments that were not developed explicitly by Socrates. The ideas pursued include these: that the
psuchê (conceived as the locus of life, knowledge, and the direction of action) is immortal (e.g., *Phaedo*); that love or desire (*erôs*) is essentially a
mode of self-immortalization, and that the highest kind of love is that for
*knowledge of objective truth (*Symposium*, *Phaedrus*). A recurrent idea is
that the deepest knowledge (indeed, the only understanding that can
properly count as *knowledge*, in the full sense) is dialectically based
knowledge of objective, fundamental truths. This is usually known as
Plato's theory of Forms; the Forms are characterized as what is "essentially" just, or "the Just itself." In the middle period, the central concern
is with Forms of ethical norms, such as "good," *agathon* (*Republic*), and
"fine" or "beautiful," *kalon* (*Symposium*).

The *Republic* can be seen as combining the Socratic approach with a
type of communitarian one. The program of ethical education proposed
for the guardians in the ideal state implies that ethical virtue depends
both on the development of right beliefs in the right kind of community
and on the conversion of these into knowledge of objective truth by dialectic, which in turn provides the basis for shaping communal beliefs.
This two-stage program of education also shapes the three functions of
the *psuchê* (reason, spirit, appetite) so as to render them progressively
more harmonized with ethical truth. This interrelated political and psychic ideal forms part of a defence of the claim that complete virtue
(understood as "justice," *dikaiosunê*), constitutes happiness (*eudaimonia*).
Plato's last work, the *Laws*, also combines a communitarian approach to
the development of virtue (focussing on the development of right beliefs,
feelings, and desires by public persuasion and social institutions) with
the assumption that there are objective ethical standards. In another late
work, the *Timaeus*, Plato, like the Presocratic philosophers, connects the
rationality of the universe with that of human beings as psychological
(and psychophysical) wholes. In the *Philebus*, in a move that is characteristic of several late Platonic works, Plato reexamines the ideas of his own
middle-period dialogues and offers a new account of the relationship

between knowledge and pleasure, combined with an outline of a new *metaphysical framework.

Aristotle. Plato's pupil Aristotle (384–322 B.C.E.) is the first Greek thinker to demarcate ethics as a distinct branch of philosophy, one closely linked with *politics; his way of conceiving ethical enquiry is widely followed in later ancient thought. Although the ethical treatises (principally, *Eudemian Ethics* and *Nicomachean Ethics*) seem not to have been available in the Hellenistic period, the school that Aristotle founded, the *Lyceum or *Peripatos, perpetuated his approach. The central ethical question for Aristotle is, How should a human being shape his or her life as a whole? What should be taken as the goal (*telos*) of life, or the human good (*agathon*), which is assumed to be identical with happiness (*eudaimonia*)? Aristotle's answer, like Plato's in the *Republic*, is that it is virtue (*aretê*). More precisely, it is psychological activity or life "according to virtue" (*NE* 1.7). For Aristotle, this does not mean, however, that "external" goods such as health, wealth, social position, and the state of one's family are without significance in determining happiness (*NE* 1.8, 10–11). Aristotle subdivides virtue into that of character (*êthos*) and intellect (*dianoia*), though these are partly interdependent and virtue in the fullest sense involves both types. Ethical virtue is defined by the fact that the virtuous person does virtuous acts "for the sake of the fine" (*kalon*) or "for its own sake," and does so in a way that hits the "mean" (*meson*) between defective extremes of action and feeling. The virtuous person acts in this way because of a combination of a correct pattern of motivation (*hexis*, disposition) and correct practical reasoning (*phronêsis*). Failure to develop ethical virtue results in a character and life that is marked either by defectiveness/vice (*kakia*) or by the "weakness of will" (*akrasia*) of those who are not fully virtuous in their sensual desires.

Aristotle's ethical approach, like that of Plato's, can be seen as combining communitarian and dialectical strands. He stresses that ethical reflection needs to be based on the (prereflective) shaping of character; he seems to think that this can occur in conventional societies (not just the ideal state in which Plato places this process). The ethical virtues he discusses, including tact, magnificence, and magnanimity (*megalopsuchia*), are based on conventional Greek ethical thought. However, Aristotle sees the role of ethical philosophy as revisionary and directive and not just as the codification of conventional beliefs. On friendship, as well as redefining the conventional ideal (which can be seen as that of either altruism or shared life and mutual benefit), he presents this ideal, unconventionally, as a means of virtuous self-love and of extending one's own (virtuous) existence (*NE* 9.4,8,9). In *NE* 10.7–8, though not in *EE*, he presents contemplative rather than ethical/practical virtue as the highest possible human (or rather "divine") activity. Scholars disagree sharply about the significance of this last move. Some hold that it is inconsistent with the emphasis on ethical virtue (as the main or equal constituent of human happiness) elsewhere in the ethical works. Others argue that it is consistent with the preference for contemplative wisdom (*sophia*) over practical wisdom (*phronêsis*) in *NE* 6.7,13, as well as with Aristotle's metaphysical account of what "god" means (*Met.* 12.9).

Hellenistic Philosophy. In the Hellenistic Age (323–31 B.C.E.) and under the Roman Empire (31 B.C.E. onward), ethical debate centers on the positions of the various philosophical schools (Academy, Lyceum, *Epicurean, Stoic) and on modifications and combinations of these. A recurrent idea throughout the Hellenistic and Roman periods is that philosophy is a mode of "therapy," aiming to cure false beliefs and the resulting misguided emotions and desires. Much of our evidence of Hellenistic ethics derives from later sources, some of whom (including *Cicero, *Plutarch, and *Galen) are hostile to some of the theories for which they constitute important sources.

Epicurus. Epicurus (341–271 B.C.E.), unlike Plato, Aristotle, and the Stoics, identifies the goal of life not with virtue but with pleasure. In this respect, as in some others, he draws on the thinking of *Democritus (b. 460–57 B.C.E.), who presented "cheerfulness" or "peace of mind" (*euthumia*) as the goal. However, Epicurus conceives this goal in a form that brings it closer to those other theories than one might expect. Pleasure is defined negatively as absence of physical pain (*aponia*) and absence of disturbance of mind (*ataraxia*). As in most other ancient theories, the stress is on framing a certain kind of *life*, not on maximizing episodes of pleasure. (The *Cyrenaics, by contrast, who are also hedonists, adopt the latter approach.) A key part of Epicurus' method is to distinguish between types of desire (natural, necessary, and nonnecessary) and of pleasures ("static" and "kinetic") in order to promote the kind of life that is as free as possible from physical pain. A further part is the critique of goals (such as political power or wealth) and fears (such as fear of death and punishment in the afterlife) that disrupt peace of mind. An understanding of the true nature of the universe, as Epicurus conceives this to be, is a crucial part of this program. This enables one to recognize that the gods play no part in the direction of the universe (or in human affairs) and that death is simply the decomposition of a certain arrangement of *atoms.

Epicurus has a complex, and seemingly contradictory, view on the role of virtue, especially justice, and friendship in the pursuit of pleasure. Virtue is presented as purely instrumental to the overall goal of pleasure and not as an inherent good; but it is also seen as "inseparable" from the pleasant life (LS 21B[6]). Analogously, friendship is valued as a means of mutual help (and as an important component of a pleasurable life); but the friendship valued is one in which we love friends as we love ourselves (LS 22E–I, O). Justice is presented not as an objective norm but simply as "a guarantee of utility with a view to not harming another and not being harmed" (LS 22A). But the ideal Epicurean society is imagined to be one in which "everything will be full of justice and mutual friendship" (LS 22S). Although this set of ideas raises difficult issues, a key underlying thought is that it is the kind of virtues—including justice and friendship—informed by *Epicurean* objectives that are valued in an unqualified way.

Stoicism. Whereas Epicureanism remained a relatively uniform system, Stoicism evolved under the successive heads of the school, while retaining a central core. In ethics, the essential claim is that virtue is not just the overall goal of life but the only good, and that the other so-called good things (e.g., health, wealth, social status) are, by comparison, "matters of indifference" (*adiaphora*). However, it is acknowledged that these are, at least, "preferable"; and selection between "matters of indifference" is seen as a way of making progress towards the state of full virtue (or "wisdom") in which one's character and life is wholly shaped by the recognition that virtue is the only good. The Stoics stress that it is natural for human beings, as rational animals, to develop in this way (this development forms part of *oikeiôsis*, "appropriation" or "familiarization"). Another part of this process is that whereby human beings develop the motivation to benefit other human beings as such, through the extension outward of virtuous affection for children, friends, and fellow citizens. The Stoics believe that the universe is a rationally, providentially ordered whole; a further function of human rationality is to understand the ordered and providential character of the universe.

On the relationship between the Stoic and the conventional conceptions of what "virtue" means, different Stoics adopt different positions. *Zeno of Citium (334–262 B.C.E.) apparently drew a sharp contrast between the ideal community (that of the wise) and conventional societies guided by false beliefs. (He may have been influenced by the *Cynics, who defined true ethical values as those of "nature" by contrast with "convention.") Later Stoics, especially *Panaetius (c. 185–c. 110 B.C.E.), emphasize, rather, that human beings can make progress towards full virtue by performing the "appropriate acts" (*kathêkonta*) linked with their social roles in conventional societies.

In ethical psychology, the Stoics argue that the human capacity for rationality pervades all aspects of action, feeling, and desire. Adult human action is analyzed as an impulse (*hormê*) that is the outcome of "assent" to a rational (verbalizable) impression. *Chrysippus (c. 280–c. 206 B.C.E.), the most important Stoic thinker, emphasized that human psychology was, in this respect, strongly unified. The emotions (*pathê*) of nonwise people reflected (or rather *were*) beliefs; and the agitated, "sick" character of these emotions reflected the falsehood of their understanding of what was really "good," a sickness for which Stoic philosophy offered the only real therapy.

Skepticism. The founder of skepticism was believed to be *Pyrrho (c. 360–c. 270 B.C.E.). From the mid-third to the first century B.C.E. this position was adopted by the Platonic Academy, whose adherents saw themselves as perpetuating the Socratic conception of dialectic as ongoing search. It was restated by *Sextus Empiricus (2nd cent. C.E.). Skeptics deny the possibility of knowledge, as distinct from (undogmatic) belief or "appearance." They claim that the recognition that knowledge is unavailable leads to "suspension of judgment" and yields peace of mind (*ataraxia*). It does so partly by preventing the inner torment that results from trying to reconcile the (inevitable) contradictions that arise on any topic with a dogmatic claim to knowledge. It produces moderate feeling (*metriopatheia*), because the skeptic does not claim to *know* that anything is bad and so does not have the intense emotional reactions that result from this supposed knowledge.

Roman Philosophy. Roman thinkers transmit or modify Greek (especially Hellenistic) theories rather than evolving new ones. *Lucretius incorporates Epicurean ethics into his poetic restatement of the Epicurean conception of the universe (*De Rerum Natura*). He emphasizes that the Epicurean view of the virtues differs from the conventional Greco-Roman one, and offers (in Bk. 5) a developmental account of the origin of justice in conventional societies. Cicero is a major source for all Hellenistic philosophy, including ethics. He adopts a nondoctrinaire philosophical position (a version of Academic skepticism) but favors the Stoic ethical approach, which he sees as more compatible with Roman moral attitudes. In *De Finibus* he analyses the positions of the schools on the central question of the "ends" or goals of life; in *Tusculan Disputations* he examines their strategies for curing passions and distress. In *De Officiis* he draws on Panaetius' thinking on "appropriate acts" to combine Stoic practical ethics and Roman ideals. *Seneca writes essays and letters (and, arguably, tragedies too) to promote Stoic ethical ideas, especially regarding the "therapy" of the passions. The cure of the passions and practical advice is a prominent theme in Greek ethical philosophy of the period, including the Stoic teachings of *Epictetus (c. 55–c. 135 C.E.) and the essays of the eclectic thinker Plutarch (c. 50–c. 120 C.E.).

Neoplatonism. A feature of later antiquity is the close study of the texts of Plato and Aristotle and the philosophical development of their ideas. The *Enneads* of *Plotinus (205–270 C.E.) synthesize Platonic and Aristotelian thought; in particular, they represent an intensified form of Platonic middle-period idealism. Plotinus defines three fundamental forms of reality (in ascending order of *being and value): *psuchê* (understood as nonmaterial), intellect, and the one (or good). He argues that human beings are naturally inclined to aspire toward the highest possible state of being, that is, toward psychic being rather than bodily, intellectual rather than sensual or emotional, and, ultimately, a state of union with the one or good.

*Augustine (354–430 C.E.) describes in the *Confessions* the philosophical and spiritual journey by which he returned to the *Christianity in which he was brought up. He was drawn first to *Manicheanism, which saw the universe as a struggle between two fundamental principles, good and evil, and then to Neoplatonism, which saw the universe rather as a combination of the real (nonmaterial) elements and matter, which, though not sharing in fundamental being, was not bad in itself. Neoplatonic thinking about the relationship among the three fundamental realities helped him to frame an account of the three persons of the Trinity. Finally, he moved to a theorized Christianity, in which evil is explained by the fact that, although God created the universe, human beings are free to reject God's love, and human sin is redeemed by God's grace, as expressed in the incarnation. Although Augustine's spiritual journey draws on Greco-Roman philosophy, his final position on the ethical status of the human and the divine is substantively different from anything in Classical thought.

BIBLIOGRAPHY: General: Annas, J., *The Morality of Happiness*, Oxford, 1993; Gill, C., *Personality in Greek Epic, Tragedy, and Philosophy: The Self in Dialogue*, Oxford, 1996; Guthrie, W. K. C., *A History of Greek Philosophy*, vol. 3, Cambridge, 1969; Irwin, T., *Classical Thought*, Oxford, 1989; Nussbaum, M. C., *The Fragility of Goodness: Luck and Ethics in Greek Tragedy and Philosophy*, Cambridge, 1986; Prior, W. J., *Virtue and Knowledge: An Introduction to Greek Ethics*, London, 1991; Williams, B., *Shame and Necessity*, Berkeley, 1993. On particular topics: Annas, J., *An Introduction to Plato's Republic*, Oxford, 1981; Irwin, T., *Plato's Ethics*, Oxford, 1995; Kenny, A., *Aristotle on the Perfect Life*, Oxford, 1992; Kraut, R., *Aristotle on the Human Good*, Princeton, 1989; LS; Nussbaum, M. C., *The Therapy of Desire: Theory and Practice in Hellenistic Ethics*, Princeton, 1994; Rorty, A. O., ed., *Essays on Aristotle's Ethics*, Berkeley, 1980; Schofield, M., and G. Striker, eds., *The Norms of Nature: Studies in Hellenistic Ethics*, Cambridge, 1986; Vlastos, G., *Socrates: Ironist and Moral Philosopher*, Cambridge, 1991; also *Socratic Studies*, M. Burnyeat, ed., Cambridge, 1994—
CHRISTOPHER GILL

EUBULIDES. See MEGARIAN SCHOOL.

EUCLID (c. 300 B.C.E.), of Alexandria (?), Egypt. Putative author of a series of *mathematical texts, of which the most famous is the *Elements*. Nothing is known with certainty about Euclid, including when and where he lived. The date and place given here are conventional, but not improbable. The differences among the works that have come down under Euclid's name make it very difficult to suppose that they should be ascribed to one person. Discussion will be limited to works thought to be authentic that have come down to us in Greek under Euclid's name: the *Elements*, the *Sectio Canonis*, the *Phenomena*, the *Optics*, and the *Data*.

The *Sectio Canonis* uses arithmetic propositions and a vague physical theory of pitch and musical concordance set out in a prose introduction to justify deductively (i) the specific correlations between musical intervals and numerical ratios associated with the *Pythagoreans; (ii) certain impossibility results, such as the nonexistence of a semitone; and (iii) the construction of a certain tuning or system. At least some of the mathematical argument of the *Sectio* was known to *Archytas.

The *Phenomena* has a prose prologue offering empirical reasons for a standard Greek geometrical picture of the cosmos in which the sphere of the fixed stars rotates uniformly about a fixed axis. In the body of the treatise Euclid gives geometric arguments concerning the risings, settings, and locations of fixed stars. From an *astronomical point of view, the treatise is very elementary. Its main significance is perhaps as an illustration of the importance the Greeks attached to deductive rigor.

The *Optics* has sometimes been interpreted as a treatise on perspective. In it Euclid gives a deductive account of the appearance of objects to an eye on the assumption that there are straight rays emanating from the eye and that, for example, the apparent height of an object varies directly with the size of the angle made by rays connecting the eye with the top and bottom of the object.

The fundamental notion of the *Data* is the concept of being given. The work begins with a series of definitions explicating this notion. For example, the first says that areas, lines, and angles are given in magnitude if it is possible to "furnish" (*porisasthai*) things equal to them. It is seems reasonably clear that the point of the treatise is to show which geometrical properties can be determined when others are, so that the treatise is an attempt to provide a heuristic for searching for proofs. But the formal presentation seems an impediment to the goal.

In outward appearance the *Elements* is a unified mathematical treatise in thirteen books built up deductively from first principles called definitions, postulates, and common notions. But examination shows that it is some kind of compilation of a variety of materials unified more by style than by content. In the first book Euclid proves the fundamental facts about plane rectilinear figures. The subject of Book 2 is what has been called geometric algebra, a fundamental Greek geometric technique for proving equalities among rectilinear figures and constructing rectilinear figures equal to given areas. Book 3 introduces the circle as a subject, and Book 4 treats the inscription of rectlinear figures in circles and closely related topics. In Books 1–4 Euclid makes no use of the theory of proportionality, which he introduces in Book 5. Since in Book 6 Euclid uses proportions to prove equivalents of propositions proved in Books 1–4 without proportions, it seems clear that Euclid designed the *Elements* to show the possibilities of avoiding proportions in parts of plane geometry.

Book 5 is generally thought to be based on original work by *Eudoxus. It is a logical tour de force in which fundamental laws of proportionality are proved on the basis of definitions strikingly similar to Richard Dedekind's definition of real numbers as "cuts" in the system of rational numbers. Euclid calls the objects involved in proportions magnitudes. The topic of Books 7–9 is arithmetic. Euclid gives a new definition of proportionality for numbers and proves for them some of the same laws that he proved for magnitudes in Book 5. In Book 10 Euclid brings together the two conceptions of proportionality in a way that has been interpreted as a clear sign of the disunity of the *Elements*. The major topic of the book is a partial classification of "irrational" straight lines, lines that have no common measure with a given straight line, and the squares on which have no common measure with the square on the given straight line. This very difficult book is thought to be based on work done by *Theaetetus. Book 11 establishes fundamental results in solid geometry, making full use of proportionality. From a foundational point of view it is much less satisfactory than Books 1–4. Like Book 5, Book 12 is a logical tour de force and thought to be based on work by Eudoxus. In it results are proved using what is called the method of exhaustion, a forerunner of the modern notion of integration. In the final book Euclid constructs the five regular solids, employed by *Plato in the *Timaeus*, and circumscribes spheres around them. This book is thought to be based on work by Theaetetus.

In later antiquity and in modern times, Euclid's *Elements* was the embodiment of mathematics for many philosophers. For us this is no longer true, but it is certainly the work that gives us our best chance of understanding the mathematical background not only of later philosophers but also of Plato and *Aristotle and perhaps also of earlier philosophers. Euclid's other works did not achieve anything like the prestige of the *Elements*, but they too are undoubtedly good indices of the sort of formal mathematical work being done in the fourth century B.C.E.

BIBLIOGRAPHY: Texts in J. L. Heiberg and H. Menge, eds., *Euclidis Opera Omnia*, 9 vols. (Teubner), Leipzig, 1883–1916. Heath, T. L., *The Thirteen Books of Euclid's Elements*,[2] 3 vols., Cambridge, 1926; Mueller, I., *Philosophy of Mathematics and Deductive Structure in Euclid's Elements*, Cambridge, MA, 1981.—*IAN MUELLER*

EUCLIDES (c. 450–380 B.C.E.), of Megara (or of Gela). An associate of *Socrates who founded a "school" at Megara (see MEGARIAN SCHOOL). Aulus Gellius (7.10) carries an anecdote that has him alive just before the Peloponnesian war, when Megarians were banned from Athens (*Thucydides [1.139] speaks of a commercial ban; *Plutarch, *Pericles* 30 speaks of one that squares with Gellius' anecdote, but this evidence is widely discounted). The ban, real or fictitious, would have dated from 433/432. *Plato's *Theaetetus* opens with Euclides' narration to his associate Terpsion (about whom we have no other information) of his recent encounter with the dying *Theaetetus; Theaetetus' death is currently put in 369.

*Diogenes Laertius (2.108) ascribes six *dialogues to him; they were apparently referred to by *Panaetius as *"Socratic," although he was in doubt either about their authenticity or about their historicity (D.L. 2.64). Of these dialogues, apparently not so much as a line has survived.

According to Gellius' anecdote, Euclides entered the city disguised as a woman every night to converse with Socrates. In the beginning of Plato's *Theaetetus* he is made to speak of frequent visits to Socrates in the course of which he wrote down and corrected the rest of the dialogue. He and Terpsion are among those listed in Plato's *Phaedo* as present at Socrates' death. Afterwards, it is reported, Plato, among other unnamed followers of Socrates, "fearing the savagery of the tyrants" (D.L. 3.6, 2.106, citing Hermodorus, a student of Plato's—"the tyrants" would have to refer to the radical democrats who condemned Socrates), went to Megara to stay with Euclides.

"He used to pursue the study of *Parmenides' writings" (D.L. 2.106), and his main reported view would have to derive at least as much from Parmenides as from Socrates: "He asserted that the *good (was) one, called by many names: sometimes wisdom, sometimes god, sometimes mind, etc.; while he would reject things opposed to the good, saying that they are not" (D.L. 2.106). Similarly *Cicero (*Acad. Pr.* 2.42.129) puts him in the *Eleatic succession: "*Xenophanes ..., Parmenides, and *Zeno (of Elea) ..., afterwards Euclides, student of Socrates, a Megarian," and says of all in the succession, "they used to say that that alone was good that was one and alike and always the same." And *Aristocles, as quoted by Eusebius (*PE* 14.17), ascribes to "the circle of *Stilpo and the *Megarians" the view that "that which is is one and the other is not, and neither is anything generated or destroyed or moved in any way." These passages can be read either distributively (Euclides would be making something's being good and its being one somehow equivalent and pronouncing of each thing that it is one and good) or collectively (he would be saying that some single thing is the good). If he was also denying reality to anything but the good, the distributive reading has him making existence go together with unity and goodness and the collective reading makes him an extreme monist. The latter fits with his interest in Parmenides, and this picture lends plausibility to the idea that Aristocles would have included Euclides among "Stilpo and the Megarians."

Nothing in the surviving texts indicates any reasoning that might have led Euclides or any other Megarian to their conclusion. It is natural to suppose that, if Socrates had anything to do with it, it is connected with his insistence in Plato's *Protagoras* on the unity of *virtue; in 7.161 Diogenes refers the claim that the virtues are one, called by many names, to the Megarians. And it can hardly be coincidence that the claim that the One and the Good are the same is ascribed to Plato (Ar. *Met.* 1.6, 988a7–17; cf. 14.4, 1091b13–14). But both of these claims are ones for which the arguments are far from clear, and the thesis ascribed to Euclides goes very far beyond either of them.

(Scholars such as Schleiermacher and Zeller used to ascribe to Euclides and the Megarians a theory of Forms very like Plato's; this theory was supposed to have been the object of the Eleatic Stranger's attack on "the friends of the Forms" in Plato's *Sophist* 246b–c, 248a. There was, in fact, no evidence to support this, and it was decisively rebutted by Gillespie.)

If Euclides was an extreme monist, there is a very good chance that such arguments as he had in favor of this position were *reductiones ad absurdum*, as are those of Parmenides and Zeno of Elea. It may be this that stands behind Diogenes' saying (2.107) that "he would object to proofs not for their premises but for their conclusion." But Euclides and other Megarians had a reputation for contentiousness (see the verses of *Timon quoted by Diogenes, 2.107), so perhaps the citation of Euclides' propensity for attacking conclusions rather than premises is merely supposed to be an indication of his shallowness.

Diogenes (2.107) also tells us that Euclides "would reject argument by analogy, saying that it was fashioned either from similars or from dissimilars, and if from similars, it ought to be concerned with the things themselves rather than things similar to them, and if from dissimilars, the comparison is irrelevant." This foggy argument appears to put Euclides at quite a remove from Socrates, who seems to have been fond of analogy.

*Melissus had already pointed out that *skepticism with regard to the senses is a consequence of radical monism; and if Euclides adopted such a monism, he must have realized it, too, but there is nothing to show that he did, save *Seneca's blanket condemnation in *Epistulae Morales* 83.44,45 of "the *Pyrrhonists, Megarians, Eretrians, and *Academics" (along with *Protagoras and others) as having "introduced a new sort of knowledge: to know nothing" and having "destroyed the hope of knowing anything."

BIBLIOGRAPHY: Gillespie, C. M., *AGP* 24, 1911, 218–241. See also under MEGAR-
IAN SCHOOL.—*R. M. DANCY*

EUDAIMONIA (HAPPINESS, FLOURISHING). See ETHICAL
THOUGHT, Classical.

EUDEMUS (2nd half of 4th cent. B.C.E.), of Rhodes. A student of *Aristotle, often mentioned in conjunction with *Theophrastus. In a charming
story in Aulus Gellius (13.5), when Aristotle was dying, he chose Theophrastus over Eudemus as his successor in the *Lyceum. Eudemus apparently returned to Rhodes on Aristotle's death and founded his own
school; *Simplicius (*In Phys.* 923.9–15) mentions an exchange of letters
between him and Theophrastus on a textual question in Aristotle's
Physics. Simplicius also (924.13) mentions a biography of Eudemus by
one Damas, of whom nothing else is known.

There are ascribed to Eudemus in various places (see Wehrli) two
books of *Analytics*, a *Categories*, *On Expression* (*Peri Lexeôs*), *On the Angle*,
Physics, and histories of geometry, arithmetic, and *astronomy. Simplicius refers to Eudemus as "the most genuine of Aristotle's comrades" (*In
Phys.* 411.15–16) and says that he "follows Aristotle in all things" (133.
22). Though not entirely true, this appears not far off.

In *logic, Eudemus and Theophrastus (who are always mentioned together in this connection) made various modifications to Aristotle's syllogistic; *Alexander, in his commentary on the *Prior Analytics*, cites the
following (Alexander is echoed by the other *commentators on most of
these points): (i) Theophrastus and Eudemus devised a direct proof of
the convertibility of universal negative propositions (Alexander 31.4–10;
contrast Ar. *APri.* 1.2, 25a14–17). (ii) They adopted the *peiorem* rule in
modal logic: "that the conclusion is always assimilated to the lesser and
weaker of the premises" (Alexander 124.13-14; by contrast Aristotle allowed certain combinations of necessary and assertoric premises to yield
necessary conclusions, as in *APri.* 1.9). (iii) They defended the convertibility of universal negative problematic propositions (Alexander 220.9–
16, against Ar. *APri.* 1.17, 36b35–37a31). (iv) They also did extensive
work on hypothetical syllogisms (Alexander 389.31-390.3; Philoponus, *In
APri.* 242.18–19, speaks of "treatises of many lines" on the subject).

Eudemus is said to have claimed in *On Expression* (Alexander *In
APri.* 16.15–17, scholium in *APri.* ed. Brandis [in *Aristotelis Opera* 4]
146a24–27) that "is" in "Socrates is" is a predicate term; he may thus
have been the first to have contradicted Kant's claim that existence is not
a predicate. Alexander's notice of this is phrased in a way that makes it
appear to contradict Aristotle (at least under Alexander's interpretation
of Aristotle: 15.14–22).

All we know of *On the Angle* is that Eudemus argued in it that the angle is in the category of quality on the ground that straightness is a quality, fractures are qualities, and an angle is a fractured straightness (Proclus *In Eucl.* 125.6–13).

The most substantial remains of Eudemus' work are from the *Physics*; this seems to have been a paraphrase of or commentary on Aristotle's *Physics*. Simplicius, in the introduction to his commentary on *Physics* 7, says (*In Phys.* 1036.13–15): "Eudemus, having followed the main points in the entire treatise up to this point, passes by this book as superfluous, and proceeds to what is in the last book."

Eudemus' historical works were of very great importance; much of what we know about the early history of *mathematics, including astronomy, is traceable to Eudemus. *Proclus three times quotes him by name for historical points (*In Eucl.* 299.3, 333.6, 352.14), and Proclus' report of the history of geometry before *Euclid (64.16-68.6) seems to be taken from Eudemus. Simplicius quotes long extracts from Eudemus describing *Hippocrates of Chios' quadrature of the lune (*In Phys.* 60.22-68.32). Eutocius quotes him for *Archytas' solution to the problem of the duplication of the cube (commentary on Archimedes *On the Sphere and the Cylinder* 2, in *Archimedis Opera Omnia* ed. Heiber/Stamatis 3.84.12–88.2). The extracts preserved from Eudemus' histories of arithmetic and astronomy (see Wehrli, frs. 143–149) are less extensive, but illustrate his importance for the transmission of what knowledge we have.

Seven passages in *Aelian's *On the Nature of Animals* (collected in Wehrli, frs. 126–132) name a Eudemus as the source for wild stories about animals, but, although *Apuleius (*Apologia* 36) credits Eudemus along with Aristotle, Theophrastus, and *Lyco with books on the generation of animals, these passages seem unlikely to have come from our Eudemus.

The treatise entitled *Eudemian Ethics* in the corpus Aristotelicum was taken in the 19th century to be Eudemus'; it is now thought to be Aristotle's (see Rowe, 9–14).

BIBLIOGRAPHY: Texts in Wehrli 8. Rowe, C. J., *The Eudemian and Nicomachean Ethics: A Study in the Development of Aristotle's Thought*, PCPS Supp. no. 3, 1971.— R. M. DANCY

EUDORUS (fl. c. 25 B.C.E.), of Alexandria. *Platonist philosopher. Of Eudorus' life we know nothing, except that he precedes *Arius Didymus, who used his work, and that he disputed with the *Peripatetic Aristo as to the source of the Nile. His works are all lost, but included *An Analytical Account of Philosophy* (*Diairesis tou kata Philosophian Logou*), a summary of the *ethical section of which is preserved in *Stobaeus; and commentaries on *Plato's *Timaeus* (used by *Plutarch),*Aristotle's *Categories* (a

hostile analysis), and possibly also his *Metaphysics*. Influenced by *Neo-pythagoreanism, Eudorus seems to have turned the very *Stoicized Platonism of *Antiochus of Ascalon in a more transcendental direction.
BIBLIOGRAPHY: Dillon, J. M., *The Middle Platonists*, London/Ithaca, 1977, 114–35; Moraux, P., *Der Aristotelismus in der Antike*, vol. 2, Berlin, 1984, 509–27.—*JOHN DILLON*

EUDOXUS, of Cnidus. *Mathematician, *astronomer, geographer, and philosopher associated with *Plato's *Academy and subsequently head of his own school in Cnidus. None of his writings has survived. The accounts of his life conflict (see Merlan): he may have been born as early as 408 or as late as 390 B.C.E. *Diogenes Laertius (8.86–87) tells us that he studied geometry with *Archytas (perhaps it is for this reason that Diogenes lists him among the *Pythagoreans) and *medicine with Philistion of Sicily and that he traveled to Athens, to Egypt, to Cyzicus, and back to Athens, by which time he had a number of followers. It is possible he was left as interim head of the Academy in 367 when Plato went to Sicily; in that year *Aristotle arrived at the Academy (see the *Vita Marciana* and *Vita Latina* of Aristotle). Diogenes again tells us that he lectured, apparently in Cnidus, on the gods, the universe, and astronomy (8.89) and that he died at the age of fifty-two (8.91).

A scholion to *Euclid, *Elements* 5, reports that "some say that the book is a discovery of Eudoxus, the teacher of Plato." Discounting the confusion over who taught whom, this squares with what *Eudemus (cited in Proclus *In Euclid*. 67 and 68) tells us about Eudoxus. In *Elements* 5 Euclid develops a general theory of proportion applicable to geometrical and numerical magnitudes alike, and Aristotle speaks of the discovery of this generalized theory as recent (*APo*. 1.5, 74a17–25). Its most important virtue is its ability to handle proportions among nonnumerical magnitudes: the number-system of the period countenanced no fractions, much less irrational numbers, and only by means of such a theory as Eudoxus' could the ratio between, for example, the side of a square and its diagonal be brought within mathematical purview. Eudoxus is frequently hailed as a precursor of Dedekind (see Stein). Among his other mathematical discoveries were the proof that the volume of a cone is a third that of a cylinder with the same base and height and likewise for the volume of a pyramid relative to that of a prism (Archimedes *Ad Eratosthinem Prooemium*, Heiberg/Stamatis 2, 430.1–9) and further results that, like these, are to be found in Euclid *Elements* 12.

The application of geometry to astronomy provided Eudoxus' most influential achievement. Eudemus and/or Sosigenes (cited in Simplicius *In DC* 488.18–24) tells us that Eudoxus was the first to respond successfully to Plato's challenge to provide a set of uniform and orderly motions that would "save" the apparent but quite irregular motions of the planets, sun, and moon. He did this by associating each planet with a point on the surface of a sphere that rotated on an axis fixed within another sphere that, in turn, rotated on another axis, up to four spheres per planet, and three each for the sun and moon. This system was taken up by Aristotle in *Metaphysics* 12: in chapter 8 he describes some of the problems with and modifications to the scheme that led to its revision by himself and Callippus (see also Simplicius *In DC* 492.31–497.8).

This system was soon superseded by the *Ptolemaic system, but it retained its influence, mostly because Aristotelian views about *matter could provide a physics for it, whereas none was provided for Ptolemaic physics. It is to Eudoxian spheres that Copernicus' title *On the Revolutions of the Heavenly Spheres* refers (see Kuhn, 59). Eudoxus also wrote at least two books describing his observations of the fixed stars, *Mirror* and *Phaenomena*.

The fragments of Eudoxus' work *Circuit of the Earth* (for which see Lasserre 96ff.) show that his interests were not merely geographical: Eudoxus included a great amount of ethnographical detail as well.

In *Metaphysics* 13.5, 1079b18–23 Aristotle remarks that Plato's Forms do not explain other things by being present in them, "for then they might perhaps be thought to be causes in the way that white is, by being mixed into the white thing; but this account, which first *Anaxagoras and later Eudoxus, in the course of discussing difficulties, used to state, as did certain others, is very easily overthrown"; he then alludes to numerous absurdities entailed by the theory. *Alexander of Aphrodisias, commenting on the doublet of this passage in 1.9, 991a14–19, lists some purported absurdities, and he speaks of himself as relying on Aristotle's lost *On Ideas*. The theory Eudoxus seems to be espousing has the "form" white causing things to be white by acting as a pigment mixed into those things, and it appears to have excited at least some discussion in the Academy: Apart from the objections Alexander lists, some of which in any case may go back to Aristotle, Plato in *Sophist* 247a–c raises objections that would apply to a theory of this kind (see Dancy).

Aristotle says (*NE* 10.2, 1172b9–10) that "Eudoxus thought pleasure to be the good because he saw all (things), both rational and irrational, aiming at it." Aristotle downplays this argument from the universal pursuit of pleasure for hedonism by going on to comment (1172b15–18) that Eudoxus' arguments were credited not so much for their intrinsic merit as because of Eudoxus' own excellence and moderation. But the argument from universal pursuit appears at the beginning of Plato's *Philebus* (11a–b), strongly suggesting that Eudoxus may be one of Plato's targets in that dialogue, and it also plays a positive role in Aristotle's own account, for example, at 7.13, 1153b25–32. It may suitably claim parentage for the argument employed by *Epicureans and *Stoics alike nowadays referred to as the "Cradle Argument."

BIBLIOGRAPHY: Texts and comm. in F. Lasserre, *Die Fragmente des Eudoxos von Knidos*, Berlin, 1966. Dancy, R. M., *Two Studies in the Early Academy*, Albany, 1991, 3–59 and 121–146; Gosling, J. C. B., and C. C. W. Taylor, *The Greeks on Pleasure*, Oxford, 1982, 255–283; Kuhn, T., *The Copernican Revolution: Planetary Astronomy in the Development of Western Thought*, Cambridge, MA/London, 1957; Merlan, P., *Studies in Epicurus and Aristotle*, app., *Klassisch-Philologische Studien* 22, Wiesbaden, 1960, 98–104; Stein, H., *Synthese* 84, 1990, 163–211, partially repr. in W. Demopoulos, ed., *Frege's Philosophy of Mathematics*, Cambridge, MA /London, 1995, 334–357.—*R. M. DANCY*

EUDROMUS (c. 2nd cent. B.C.E.). *Stoic philosopher. Eudromus wrote a book on *ethics and, in agreement with *Chrysippus, hierarchically ordered the three areas of Stoic philosophical discourse, giving first place to *logic, followed by physics and ethics. He called each of these "species" (*eidê*) (D.L. 7.39–41).—*IAKOVOS VASILIOU*

EUNAPIUS (c. 346–after 414 C.E.), of Sardis. *Sophist, historian, and biographer. After an early *Neoplatonic education in Sardis, Eunapius went to Athens at the age of fifteen to study with the *Christian sophist Prohairesias. He returned, perhaps in less than a year, when his Christian mentor was banned from teaching by the non-Christian emperor Julian. In Sardis he continued to study philosophy while embarking on a lifelong career of teaching *rhetoric. He is also said to have acquired an extensive knowledge of *medicine.

Eunapius' major work was a *History*, of the period from 270 to 404 C.E. In keeping with the fashion of the times, it wedded biography and historical narrative. A committed pagan, Eunapius took pains to praise the defenders of paganism and to blame many of the problems of the period on Christianity and Christian emperors. His *Lives of the Philosophers and Sophists*, written between 396 and c. 399 C.E., consists of a series of biographies of (i) Neoplatonic philosophers from *Plotinus to Eunapius' teacher, Chrysanthius, (ii) leading sophists of the day, and (iii) five physicians with rhetorical training ("hiatrosophists"). The work illustrates Eunapius' admiration for Greek culture in general and his personal commitment to the particular religious and theurgic brand of Neoplatonism espoused by *Iamblichus. The *Lives*, which survives intact, is an important source of knowledge of the school of Athens and the pagan reaction to the rise of Christianity in the fourth century C.E.

BIBLIOGRAPHY: Texts in J. Giangrande, ed., *Eunapii Vitae sophistarum*, Rome, 1956; W. C. Wright, ed., *Philostratus and Eunapius: The Lives of the Sophists* (Loeb), London/New York 1921; R. C. Blockley, *The Fragmentary Classicising Historians of the Later Roman Empire*, 2 vols., Liverpool, 1981–83 (fragments of the *History*).

Penella, R. J., *Greek Philosophers and Sophists in the Fourth Century A.D.: Studies in Eunapius of Sardis*, Leeds, 1990.—*DAVID E. HAHM*

EURIPIDES. See POETS, TRAGIC.

EUTHYDEMUS (5th cent. B.C.E.), of Chios. An *eristic *sophist who evidently worked with his older brother Dionysodorus. They joined the colony at Thurii (founded in 443) but left under a cloud and taught oratory for a fee. The pair is known to us mainly through *Plato's dialogue *Euthydemus*, but *Aristotle mentions Euthydemus, and *Sextus Empiricus lists the pair among those who reject the criterion of truth. According to Sextus their view is relativistic (*M* 7.64), but Plato treats Euthydemus' view as a distinct alternative to *Protagoras' relativism. Euthydemus, on his view, held that everyone always has every property at the same time (*Cra.* 386d). Hawtry and many other scholars have held that the targets of the *Euthydemus* are fourth-century figures and not the brothers from Chios. The argument Plato has them give for the impossibility of contradiction (*Euthyd.* 285d7–286b6) is that of *Antisthenes (Ar. *Met.* 1024b32).

They used a playful style of argument apparently designed to defeat any opponent on any subject, but leading to absurd conclusions. Their favorite argument scheme turns on what Aristotle calls fallacies of accident; virtually all of their arguments depend on overlooking precise qualifications. For example, if your dog has puppies, then, because he is your dog and a father, he is your father (*Euthyd.* 298e). Plato seems to think they delivered such arguments merely to stun, and Sextus takes the pair simply as denying the possibility of knowledge. We must, however, remain open to the possibility that the purpose of their arguments was to teach the importance of careful speaking. This would help to explain their high reputations as teachers of forensic oratory (*Euthyd.* 272a).

BIBLIOGRAPHY: Hawtrey, R. S. W., *A Commentary on Plato's Euyhdemus*, Philadelphia, 1981; Kerferd, G. B., *The Sophistic Movement*, Cambridge, 1981; Sprague, R. K., *The Older Sophists*, Columbia, SC, 1972, 294–301.—*PAUL WOODRUFF*

EXCELLENCE, VIRTUE (ARETÊ). See ETHICAL THOUGHT, Classical.

G

GALEN (129–c. 210 to 215 C.E.). Born in Pergagmum in Greek Asia Minor, Galen studied philosophy under reputable *Platonists, *Stoics, and *Aristotelians before turning to *medical studies with equal dedication and catholicity. In tune with the eclectic philosophical tenor of the times, he was inclined to stress the harmony to be found in the philosophical and *scientific tradition; but he did not do so blindly, being prepared to take issue even with his two great masters, whose essential agreement he stressed in the characteristic *On the Doctrines of Hippocrates and Plato*.

Galen settled in Rome at the age of forty, where he became first the acquaintance and then the personal physician of the philosopher-emperor Marcus *Aurelius and his family. He also wrote voluminously, on philosophy and linguistics as well as medicine, much of the latter *oeuvre* surviving (the monumental edition of C. G. Kühn, Leipzig, 1821–33), some of it in Arabic and other languages (Hebrew and Armenian, as well as in medieval Latin translation).

Much of his philosophical work is lost; however, enough survives, in particular treatises and in the form of comments scattered throughout his medical writings, to allow an assessment of his achievement. The division between philosophy and medicine was not, in the ancient world, a firm one. Much of the content of the disputes between the various contending medical sects of the time (see MEDICINE, Ancient Theories of) was philosophical in content, concerned with the nature and accessibility of *knowledge, the relation of reason to therapy, and the structure of explanation.

The key to Galen's medical philosophy is his Hippocratism. He sought to restore to center stage the figure and reputation of the semilegendary Coan physician (see HIPPOCRATES); about a quarter of his surviving writing consists in detailed commentary on Hippocratic texts. But he was no slavish acolyte; he thought Hippocrates had pioneered the correct method in medicine, without having discovered all of medical truth. But, Galen thinks, if prosecuted honestly and diligently, the Hippocratic method will eventually yield the whole of medical science. His conception of medical science is Aristotelian. Medicine is in principle completable, and the complete science will take the form of an apodeictic exposition of its axiomatic structure, in which theorems are derived from prior axioms, including definitions (expressing, for example, the real nature of a particular disease) and *metaphysical principles such as "nothing occurs without a cause." Any imprecisions in medical science result, Galen thinks, not from the nature of the subject-matter itself, but rather from the difficulty of making accurate enough determinations of the crucial physical quantities involved (such as temperature and pulse rate).

Galen thus agrees with the Rationalist doctors who held that proper therapy required an understanding of the underlying physical realities of the body. He adopted a version of Hippocratic humoral theory, in which the fundamental constituents of the human system were blood, phlegm, and yellow and black bile, each of which was associated with a pair of the fundamental qualities of hot, cold, wet, and dry. Disease is defined as "impairment of some natural function"; and diseases occur from excess or deficiency of any of these qualities, either singly or in combination; in addition there are four types of organic disease, and a general category he calls "breakdown of cohesion," which may occur either to the organic or to the uniform parts of the body.

The qualities are theoretical entities, identified in particular substances by their causal powers rather than by their phenomenal appearances. Thus chilled white wine is, for Galen, hot and dry in temperament, since its effect is to heat and desiccate. Yet Galen's medicine also owes something to the Empiricists (see MEDICINE), since he too thinks that actual experience and observation are essential to the construction of medical science. Medicine, even theoretical medicine, cannot be practiced within the confines of one's study. Testing is required to confirm the results of theoretical speculation and to adjudicate between the conflicting theoretical pronouncements of the various Rationalist schools, and experience is needed to suggest the direction in which those speculations might profitably be pursued. Galen happily allows that Empiricists may, with certain limitations, become good doctors, although their rejection of any theoretical substructure to their empirical generalizing makes it harder for them, he thinks, to extend their understanding into new domains. Thus Galen succeeded in unifying the Empiricist and Rationalist approaches and effectively thereby put an end to the history of sectarian strife between the schools.

Galen is passionately committed to the view that medicine involves continuous research, and here he goes beyond Empiricism. He wrote several large texts on anatomy (the usefulness of which Empiricists denied), in which he describes the performance of sophisticated experiments on live animals (one which uncovered the function of the recurrent laryngeal nerve), as well detailed and precise observations in dissection, all of which he thought absolutely fundamental to a proper understanding of anatomy without which no knowledge of the body's functions could be won. In order to treat disease, the impairment of those functions, we need to know what they are and how they operate (treatment for Galen is, as it was for the Hippocratics, allopathic: excess of heat requires cooling; if something impairs a function, the impediment must be removed).

Anatomical study also offers concrete proof of the providentiality of nature. Galen is strongly committed to teleological explanation in nature. For Galen, as for *Aristotle, nature does nothing in vain. Unlike Aristotle, however, Galen attributes this purposeful arrangement to a divine Artisan on the model of *Plato's *Timaeus*: and his teleology is more all-embracing and thoroughgoing than that of his predecessors. In his great treatise *On the Function of the Parts* he takes Aristotle and others (such as the third century B.C.E. Alexandrian doctor *Erasistratus) to task for failing fully to appreciate the extent of nature's design and for daring to assert that some organic parts have no function at all. They only say this, he thinks, because they have failed to investigate the matter with sufficient acuity. Indeed, teleology is for Galen a methodological principle: the existence of an organ is a challenge to determine its purpose and hence its contribution to the functioning of the body as a whole.

Galen also inherits from Aristotle the fundamental framework of the four causes (although he has little time for the formal cause, and equally has nothing much to say about the Platonic Ideas), to which he adds the *Middle Platonic category of the instrumental cause. He also makes room for the Stoic-influenced divisions within the catgeory of efficient causation, which had arisen in the medical schools in order to develop a scheme of explanation sophisticated enough to do the necessary analytical work in medical theory. Thus Galen differentiates between antecedent causes, the initial, external events that trigger pathogenic processes (as excessive exposure to sunlight can cause fever); the internal preceding causes, which are the dispositional structures of particular individuals' bodies in virtue of which they are susceptible to certain types of harmful influence; and the containing causes of the disease itself, the patient's morbid dispositions thus actualized, actually causing impediment to some function. This classification allows Galen to rebut the argument of Erasistratus that antecedent causes are not causes at all, since they are not invariably followed by their supposed effects (see MEDICINE): given that different patients have different internal structures there is no reason why, for example, if excessive heat is a cause of fever in some cases, it should be in all.

Galen was equally catholic in his *logical tastes, adopting both Aristotelian and Stoic types of syllogism (although not uncritically: he rejects the third Stoic indemonstrable, on the grounds that its conclusions may be purely contingent, and hence tell us nothing genuine about the structure of the world). But he saw, with greater clarity than any other ancient logician, the limitations of both systems; unlike his contemporary *Alexander of Aphrodisias he was perfectly well aware that innumerably many inferences (effectively those whose premises involve multiple generality) cannot be modelled by *Peripatetic syllogistic; and he essayed his own, albeit somewhat naive, analysis of such "relational" arguments.

Galen's *epistemology was fundamentally Aristotelian. The sense-organs are "natural criteria," and nature does nothing in vain. Hence animals are naturally constituted to take on form, and no inductive problem of the sort that usually plagues empiricist accounts of concept-formation need arise. And by going to work on these naturally arising conceptions we may, by dint of hard work, come to an understanding of the real, definitional principles of things upon which all genuine scientific knowledge is based.

Galen's moral *psychology (which is mostly to be found in *On the Doctrines of Hippocrates and Plato*) is Platonic in inspiration. He accepts tripartition of the soul, although he argues for it on the basis of physiological considerations, establishing by experiments in neural anatomy that the brain really is, *contra* the Stoics and Aristotelians, the body's control center. He attacks the unified psychology of orthodox Stoicism on the grounds that it cannot adequately account for the phenomena of psychic conflict; and while the Stoics recommended the complete eradication of the emotions, Galen, again following a Platonic lead, argues rather that they should be domesticated from their original savage state and put to useful work, supplying the psychological drive required to become a better person.

Galen is a great believer in moral self-improvement, and he prescribes a course of self-psychotherapy for those who wish to improve themselves. Disagreeing with the Stoics that emotions are simply false judgments writ large (if they were, Galen argues, no one would, as people do, continue to experience emotional affect after recognizing that what initially gave rise to it was a false assessment), Galen nonetheless holds that we may, by an extensive course of spiritual exercises, learn to emphasize the good and rational within us while at the same time causing that part of our psyche that is responsible for emotional overreaction to atrophy. We become calm by practicing calmness. Thus, although the emotions are not purely cognitive, we may still, if we work with a will and are helped by our friends, undertake cognitive steps to tame them. At the same time, Galen believed (and wrote a treatise to the effect) that our mental states are consequent upon our physical temperament; and although Galen expresses caution in regard to the substance of the soul, he finds it difficult to see how something with such obvious corporeal effects could itself fail to be material; moreover, he inclines towards determinism (he thinks punishment is justified not because the criminal in any strong sense deserves it, but simply because criminal natures demand that sort of treatment). The cognitive components of the autotherapy must themselves ultimately be given an explanation in terms of physical conditions.

For Galen, *ethics cannot be divorced from scientific practice: One who is to be a good doctor must possess the requisite virtues of character (primarily honesty and diligence) in addition to having a suitable endowment of natural ability. Galen wrote a short treatise entitled *The Best Doctor Must be a Philosopher*, and he meant it absolutely literally. Not only must the good doctor understand physics in order to understand physiology; he must be steeped in logic, both in order to refute plausible *sophistry (which Galen considers to be the degenerate order of the day in the medicine of his time) and to build a valid superstructure upon the foundational principles of the science. And none of this can be done without the drive and commitment to the truth of the good man. Thus, for Galen philosophy and medicine are unified by more than merely methodological ties.

BIBLIOGRAPHY: Texts in C. G. Kühn, ed., *Galeni Opera Omnia*, Leipzig, 1821–33; J. Marquardt, I. v. Müller, G. Helmreich, eds., *Galeni Pergameni Opera Minora*, 3 vols., Leipzig, 1884–93; G. Helmreich, ed., *Galenus: De Usu Partium*, 2 vols., Leipzig, 1907–9; P. H. De Lacy, ed., *Galeni de Placitis Hippocratis et Platonis*, 3 vols., *Corpus Medicorum Graecorum* V, 4,1,2, Berlin, 1978–83. Frede, M., in Frede, *Essays in Ancient Philosophy*, Oxford/Minnesota, 1987, 279–300; Hankinson, R. J., *Galen on the Therapeutic Method, Books I and II*, Oxford, 1991; also *ANRW* 2, 36.5, 1992, 3505–3522; also in J. Brunschwig and M. C. Nussbaum, eds., *Passions and Perceptions: Studies in Hellenistic Philosophy of Mind*, Cambridge, 1993, 184–222.—R. J. HANKINSON

GEMINUS (1st cent. B.C.E.) was a Greek author, probably from Rhodes. He wrote works on physical theory, *mathematics, and the allied *sciences of *astronomy and optics. In his only surviving treatise, the *Isagôgê eis ta Phainomena* ("Introduction to the Phenomena [sc. of astronomy]") he dealt with the standard topics of spherical astronomy; he described the signs of the zodiac and the constellations and surveyed basic lunar theory. He contributed nothing to planetary theory, but his account of calendaric computation and the appended calendar (perhaps derived from an earlier source) have occasioned interest among chronologists. Geminus is often called a *Stoic, and Stoicism may form the background to his rejection of astrology. He also wrote an epitome of *Posidonius' *Meteôrologica*, the surviving fragment of which (= Posidonius F18 Edelstein and Kidd) deals with the subordinate relation of astronomy to physical theory. This philosophy of science does not, however, influence the *Isagôgê* as it does *Cleomedes' *Caelestia*, nor in general can Geminus be seen as an obvious follower of Posidonius. In the fifteenth century an excerpt from the *Isagôgê* became known as the *Sphaera* of *Proclus and had a wide currency as a textbook in the Renaissance.

BIBLIOGRAPHY: Text in G. Aujac, ed., *Géminos: Introduction aux Pheonomenes*, Paris, 1975. Todd, R. B., *Revue d'Histoire des Textes* 23, 1993, 57–71; also *Catalogus Translationum et Commentariorum* 8 (forthcoming).—*ROBERT B. TODD*

GNOSTICISM. Gnosticism, or Gnosis, is the term given to a cluster of theosophical systems arising around the beginning of the Christian era and flourishing particularly in the second and third centuries C.E. These systems are characterized by a strongly dualistic worldview, a negative attitude to the physical world, and a belief in salvation for a small elite through ascetic practices (or alternatively, but less characteristically, libertinism) and the acquisition of hidden "knowledge" (*gnôsis*). The systems had little formal structure, but were dependent rather on the personalities of a number of charismatic individuals who usually composed sacred books, either in their own names or in those of mythical or historical figures. Some of these books (though, unfortunately, none of the main works of the chief figures) have been rediscovered in Nag Hammadi in Egypt since 1945. Before that our information was almost entirely derived from hostile sources, usually orthodox *Christian writers— particularly Irenaeus of Lyons (c. 130–200), *Hippolytus of Rome (c. 175– 235), and Epiphanius of Salamis (c. 315–403).

The origins of the Gnostic movement are obscure and much disputed. The main problem is whether a distinctively pre-Christian Gnosis can be discerned or whether all that we know as Gnosticism arises from unorthodox Christian reactions to the Old and New Testaments. There seems now to be a consensus that the roots of Gnosticism are to be seen, if not in Iranian dualism—as was the view of such scholars as Wilhelm Bousset and Richard Reitzenstein—then at least in the milieu of unorthodox Judaism, the Judaism of intertestamental apocalyptic and wisdom literature, which goes back at least to the second century B.C.E. (e.g., *Book of Daniel*)—as is the view of such scholars as Gilles Quispel and Kurt

Rudolph. Followers of such movements believed that the world was soon to end, being now in the grip of evil demons, and that only a small elite, those to whom the apocalypses have been revealed, could be redeemed by this hidden knowledge. The sectaries of Qumran, authors of the Dead Sea Scrolls, may be seen as part of this milieu. Certain personalities of the Old Testament, such as Adam, Seth, Cain, Shem and Noah, are picked out as spiritual ancestors (cf., e.g., *The Apocalypse of Adam* or *The Three Steles of Seth*). Such figures as Enoch, Baruch, and Ezra are presented as paradigms of the elect who can reach true knowledge of God. God himself, now raised to an almost unbridgeable transcendence, is given intermediaries such as the Son of Man or Wisdom (Sophia), through whom he may communicate with the world. All that is needed for fully developed Gnosticism is the idea that the world is the creation of, and the domain of, a positively evil, or at least ignorant and perverse, deity. That is a legacy to Gnosticism from the strong dualism of Iranian religion.

While unorthodox Judaism may be seen as the seedbed of Gnosticism, we must also recognize that Greek philosophical ideas, particularly those of *Platonism and *Pythagoreanism, play an important part in its development, at least in its second-century form. It can be viewed as part of the "underworld" of later Platonism, other manifestations of which are the *Hermetic corpus and the *Chaldaean Oracles*. The god of this world, though owing much to the Yahweh of the Old Testament, nevertheless acquires the title of Demiurge, borrowed from *Plato's *Timaeus*. The ideal world, or *Plêrôma*, likewise is a concept borrowed from the intelligible world of Forms presented in that dialogue. It is not for nothing that heresiologists like Hippolytus accuse the Gnostics of deriving their ideas from one Greek philosophical school or another, despite the fanciful nature of the connections that they discern.

The earliest Gnostic leader identified by the orthodox tradition was Simon of Samaria, a contemporary of the Apostles. Simon is presented in the *Acts of the Apostles* (8.9–25) as a mere venal charlatan, trying to jump on the bandwagon of Christianity. He is better seen, however, as an independent teacher arising from a dualistic Samaritan tradition and presenting an early form of the later "Barbelognostic" system represented in the *Nag Hammadi* corpus by the *Exegesis on the Soul*. According to this system, the Supreme God projects a female principle, his Thought (*Ennoia*) which by its fall brings the world into being and itself into servitude, a state from which it must be rescued by a savior figure. Followers of Simon in the latter part of the first century are Menander and Satornilos, the latter of whom, probably the author of the "Great Proclamation" (*Megalê Apophasis*), introduces the notion of two distinct types of man—one wicked, the other good—and of Christ as a Gnostic redeemer, coming to save only the good.

Gnosticism reaches its climax, however, in the second half of the second century, spreading out from Syria-Palestine in the direction of Alexandria and of Rome. Three teachers of particular importance in this period are Basilides, Marcion, and Valentinus, all of whom originated in, or spent time in, Alexandria and who subsequently gravitated to Rome. The majority of all Gnostic literature known to us, including the Nag Hammadi corpus, dates from this period, as do the sects best known both from the heresiologists and from original writings, the Ophites, Naassenes, Cainites, Sethians, Valentinians, and Peratae. By the end of the fourth century, after the triumph of orthodox Christianity, most Gnostic sects were eliminated, and their writings destroyed, except for the *Manichaeans and their offshoot the Mandaeans, the latter of whom survive in Iraq to the present day.

All the developed Gnostic systems share concepts with Greek philosophy, particularly Platonism, and it is not always clear, in relation to later Platonism, in which direction the influence goes. Besides the Demiurge and the intelligible cosmos, Basilides' concept of a primal god that is "nonexistent" and Valentinus' idea of the "preexistent forefather" seem to owe something to an interpretation of the famous description of the Good in Plato (*Rep.* 6, 509) as "beyond *being," while such concepts as *Ennoia* and *Sophia* seem to be mythological personifications of the Platonic-Pythagorean Indefinite Dyad. On the other hand, the motif of the "fall" of *Sophia,* which creates the physical cosmos, seems to contribute something to *Plotinus' doctrine of the creative "fall" of the *soul (much though Plotinus objects to the world-negating attitude of the Gnostics, cf. *Enn.* 2, 9). The influence of a Gnostic worldview on Middle Platonists such as *Plutarch, Atticus, or *Numenius is more pervasive than on Plotinus, though, as has been said above, influences are plainly working in both directions.

BIBLIOGRAPHY: Grant, R. M., *Gnosticism and Early Christianity,* New York, 1966; Layton, B., ed., *The Rediscovery of Gnosticism,* 2 vols., Leiden, 1980–81; Pagels, E., *The Gnostic Gospels,* New York, 1975; Quispel, G., *Gnostic Studies,* Leiden, 1974–75; Rudolph, K., *Gnosis: The Nature and History of Gnosticism,* tr. R. M. Wilson, San Francisco, 1984.—*JOHN DILLON*

GOOD, The. See ETHICAL THOUGHT, Classical.

GORGIAS (c. 485–early 4th cent. B.C.E.), of Leontini in Sicily. Rhetorician and teacher of *rhetoric. Gorgias lived to a very advanced age, certainly after the death of *Socrates in 399 B.C.E. He was a disciple of the Sicilian philosopher *Empedocles, and made a famous visit to Athens in 427 as a leader of an embassy from his native city. He travelled extensively in the Greek world as a teacher of rhetoric, for which he received considerable sums of money in payment. He also taught pupils at Athens and was well known for public speeches delivered there as displays of his rhetorical skills and technique. Summaries and actual parts of at least six of these speeches survive to the present day, namely, a *Funeral Oration*, an *Olympic Oration*, a *Pythian Oration*, an *Encomium to the Eleans*, an *Encomium to Helen*, and an *Apology of Palamedes*.

His claims to have been a philosopher rest upon his teachings, first in physics and *psychology and second in *epistemology and ontology. In *Meno* 76c–e *Plato is quite explicit in ascribing to Gorgias a developed doctrine of perception based on Empedocles' doctrine of effluences from external objects passing through pores in the perceiving subject. For perception to take place, the effluent shapes must fit exactly into pores and so be neither too large nor too small. A unifying feature in Gorgias' thought would seem to have been his doctrine of the *logos*, a term that may be translated to both "speech" and "language" as well as "argument expressed in words." A simple enough extension from the last of these three translations leads to the meaning, "the structure of things themselves." In his treatment of rhetoric Gorgias seems to have analyzed the importance of the use of *logos* for persuasion, in particular its use "at the right time" in relation to any given situation. Particularly intriguing was his use of the term *dikaia apatê* ("justified deception") as the basis of a theory of tragedy and of literature in general.

By far the most important of Gorgias' treatments of *logos* is found in his treatise entitled *On That Which Is Not, or On Nature*. This, regrettably, does not survive in any complete form, but is available to us in two separate summaries, one by *Sextus Empiricus and the other in the treatise probably wrongly attributed to *Aristotle under the title *On Melissus, Xenophanes and Gorgias*. It is clear the Gorgias' argument was presented in three stages: (i) nothing is; (ii) even if it is, it cannot be known to human beings; (iii) even if it is and is knowable, it cannot be indicated and made meaningful to another person. It is beyond question that Gorgias' treatise was highly technical in character. But its interpretation is difficult. Essentially, there have been three distinguishable approaches in modern times. For long it was dismissed simply as a parody or joke against all previous philosophers, or at best as a purely rhetorical exercise in arguments in support of a wholly paradoxical conclusion. On this view there is simply no basis for any meaningful philosophy. Nothing whatever exists, and even if it did exist, it could neither be known or given meaningful expression. Hence all attempts at philosophizing are vain and ridiculous. A second line of interpretation applied to Gorgias' treatise saw it less as a joke than a full-scale and carefully orchestrated attack on the philosophic doctrines of the *Eleatics and to a large extent those of all the physical philosophers before Gorgias. On this view the verb "to be" in Gorgias' treatise does not mean "to exist," and the argument is directed against *Parmenides' contention that only *Being exists. For Gorgias neither Being nor Not-Being exists, and the result is a position of complete philosophic Nihilism. Parmenides had destroyed the manifold world of appearances but retained the unitary world of true Being. Gorgias cleared the slate completely to leave us simply with: nothing. A third and more positive approach to Gorgias' treatise is based on a new and perhaps better understanding of the use of the verb "to be" in Greek philosophy both before and after the *sophists. On this view the primary and possibly exclusive use of the verb "to be" is to function as a copula between a subject and a predicate—in other words, to make predicative statements of the form "X is Y." What Gorgias may really have been concerned with was the relationship among words, thoughts, and things. This may be expressed in modern terms as the problem of meaning and reference. Protagoras had argued that all perceptions are true and so are of the things that are, as they are. Gorgias was maintaining that the *logos* of a thing must be understood in three ways, as: (i) the principle or nature or constituent of things themselves, (ii) what we understand that to be, and finally (iii) the verbal descriptions that we give for our own use and for our attempts to communicate with others. We are fundamentally mistaken if we attempt to understand uses (ii) and (iii) as applying in sense (i). In the first part of his treatise Gorgias denies being in the predicative sense to phenomena. In the second and third parts he argues that even if we concede this kind of being to phenomena, we must still separate being from thinking and the words in which thinking is expressed.

BIBLIOGRAPHY: Texts in DK82 and in Buchheim, T., *Gorgias von Leontinoi, Reden, Fragmente und Testimonien, grischisch-deutsch,* Hamburg, 1989. Tr. in R. K. Sprague, *The Older Sophists,* Columbia, SC, 1972, and M. Gagarin and P. Woodruff, eds., *Early Greek Political Thought from Homer to the Sophists,* Cambridge, 1995. Dodds, E. R., *Plato: Gorgias,* Oxford, 1959; Kerferd, G. B., *Phronesis 1,* 1955/6, 3–25; Newiger, H. J., *Untersuchungen zu Gorgias' Schrift Über das Nichtseiende,* Berlin, 1973.—G. B. KERFERD

GRAMMAR (*grammatikê [technê]*), the study of reading and writing or, in a more specialized form, philology and the study of literature. In the fifth century B.C.E. philosophers and *sophists began inventing grammatical terminology for discussions of the moral content of poetry. *Protagoras distinguished three genders of nouns, "masculine, feminine, thing" (Ar. *Soph. El.* 173b19ff.) and four types of discourse, "prayer, question, answer, order" (D.L. 9.54) and censured two errors in the first line of *Homer's *Iliad*: *mênis* ("wrath") is a masculine concept in a feminine word, and the imperative *aeide* ("sing") addressing a goddess should be in "prayer" form. *Plato attests his predecessors' concerns with literary criticism (Protagoras in *Prt.* 339bff.), parasynonyms (*Prodicus in *Prt.* 339eff.), and the origin of names and their relation to the things they name (*Cratylus*). Plato himself explained the possibility of false statement by analyzing sentences into name (*onoma*) and verb (*rhêma*), such that a sentence always involved combining a name with a verb (*Soph.* 261dff.). *Aristotle's work with true and false sentences kept the analysis into name and verb as the significant parts of a sentence (or "parts of speech," *Int.* 16a3 ff.), other words being seen in relation to these. The demands of describing artistic composition led Aristotle to more detailed analyses of diction (*lexis*) in his *Poetics* (19–22) and *Rhetoric* (Bk. 3). In this he was followed by *Theophrastus, who first listed the "virtues of diction": purity or Hellenism, clarity, appropriateness, ornament (FHS&G fr. 684).

Although the above involve observations that will be of use to grammar, they were not made in the context of a project corresponding to our grammar, an explanation of rules for speaking and writing correctly in everyday situations. The first such project was probably a part of *Stoic *logic, which was divided into *rhetoric, treating "speaking well," and *dialectic, "correct conversation" (D.L. 7.42). Stoic dialectic in turn was divided into the study of intelligible "things signified" or *lekta* ("sayables"), types of sentences and their parts, and corporeal "voice" (*phônê*), sound elements, their combinations, and significant expressions. In order to avoid false assents, it was important for the Stoics to understand the structure and relations of things signified, which was ultimately the structure of the *logos or reason that governed the universe, but also to grasp the relation between the signifieds and the signifying voice, so that they could express the signifieds and interpret expressions correctly. Thus, Stoic dialectic always involved both the signifieds and the expressions: Parts of speech were distinguished according to their type of signification, and these types were reflected in morphological distinctions; the combination of expressions was seen as being governed by the combinatorial properties of what they signified, the syntax of *lekta*.

On the level of the expressions, what Aristotle and Theophrastus had given as a theory of artistic diction was divided by the Stoics between rhetoric and the study of voice included under dialectic: rhetoric dealt with artistic expression and the "higher" virtues of style—clarity, appropriateness, ornament, and brevity—while dialectic treated purity or correctness, called "Hellenism." The summary of the Stoic theory of voice in *Diogenes Laertius 7.55–59, mostly drawn from *Diogenes of Babylon, begins with phonology, the study of *lexis* or voice qua nonsignificant, then moves to *logos* or significant speech and its parts—name, common noun/adjective, verb, conjunction, article, followed by the virtues and vices of speech. Diogenes treated the study of voice as a *technê* ("art," "discipline"), implying that it contained rules compiled according to certain canons of investigation, presumably including those discussed by grammarians: Correct forms could be discovered by analogy, common usage, etymology, and historical research in books. The other canons would ultimately be rejected by *Epicureans and *Skeptics, who championed usage alone.

*Crates of Mallos, a first- or second-generation pupil of Diogenes, developed at Pergamum a comprehensive art of literary criticism (*kritikê*). In the formulation of his pupil Tauriscus, criticism was divided into "logical, empirical, and historical" parts (S.E. *M* 1.248), the first corresponding more or less to Diogenes' treatment of voice. Meanwhile, Crates' Alexandrian rivals, including Aristophanes of Byzantium and Aristarchus, had been collecting masses of linguistic observations and rules for their philological work on classical texts. The first Alexandrian treatise on grammar was written by Crates' contemporary Dionysius the Thracian, a pupil of Aristarchus. While Dionysius' *Art of Grammar* defines "grammar" as the whole study of literature ("grammar is an expertise for the most part of what is said in poets and prose-writers," 1.1), it begins with phonology and the parts of speech, the topics treated by Diogenes of Babylon and by Tauriscus' logical part of criticism.

The treatise preserved under Dionysius' name does not cover the remaining parts of literary study and may be a later compilation, but we have substantial information about the *On Grammar* of Dionysius' pupil Asclepiades of Myrlea. Asclepiades (S.E. *M* 1.252) divided grammar into three parts, "technical, historical, and grammatical" (about poets and prose-writers). Asclepiades' technical part corresponds closely to the contents of Diogenes' *On Voice*: elements, syllables, *lexis*, parts of *logos*, orthography, Hellenism (analogy and etymology, the vices of barbarism and solecism). The Roman type of grammatical treatise, inspired by Crates but continued under the influence of Alexandrians, is concerned more exclusively with the topics of this "technical" part (hence "technical grammar"); its three parts deal with phonology, parts of speech, and virtues and vices of speech. It is no accident that technical grammar in Alexandria began with a contemporary of Crates and that its Roman variant includes stray topics from Stoic dialectic (definition, species, genus). These facts, among others, betray the origin of technical grammar in the Stoic theory of diction. Apollonius Dyscolus in the second century C.E. was the first grammarian to write a treatise on syntax, a subject derived from the Stoic syntax of *lekta*.

BIBLIOGRAPHY: Blank, D. L., *Ancient Philosophy and Grammar*, Chico, CA, 1982; Fehling, D., *Rh. Mus.* 108, 1965, 212–379; Frede, M., in Frede, *Essays in Ancient Philosophy*, Oxford/Minneapolis, 1987, 301–337; 338–359; Pinborg, J., in *Current*

Trends in Linguistics, vol. 13, *Historiography of Linguistics*, The Hague, 1975, 69–126; Sluiter, I., *Ancient Grammar in Context*, Amsterdam, 1990.—*D. L. BLANK*

GYMNASIUM. Along with the theater and the temple, the gymnasium developed into a building type and an institution that distinctively characterized the Greek *polis* as a collective mode of living. A gymnasium brought identity, shared purpose, and prestige to a political community. During the Hellenistic period the gymnasium became an emblem of the ongoing process of "Hellenization" and constituted a particularly notable benefaction for wealthy individuals or rulers to provide for a city. A gymnasium was the single most important instrument of the aggressive expansion of Greek culture (*paideia*) into the larger "Hellenistic" world of new cities and kingdoms being administered by the successors of Alexander the Great.

The gymnasium originated as a public space that served as a place of exercise and as a civic center. Such nonmonumental gymnasia were established in certain sanctuary properties during the archaic period. Sparta and city-states inspired by Spartan institutions appear not to have established public gymnasia on this model, but the early development of gymnasia was by no means confined to Athens. Associated with the evolution of the *polis* form of society in numerous Greek-speaking areas, the gymnasium provided public facilities for exercising because of the community's need to defend itself with a physically fit citizen army and because of the increasingly intense competition for prestige in the form of victories at the Panhellenic Olympic Games (founded 776 B.C.E.; reorganized 6th cent. B.C.E.) and at such intra-city contests as the Panathenaic Games in Athens (founded 566 B.C.E.).

During the sixth century B.C.E., gymnasia spaces were laid out more formally and became more extensively developed as sites for individual exercise and recreation, for athletic practice and competition, and for military drills associated with hoplite warfare. Most notably at Athens, but also in other Greek city-states, the gymnasia nurtured the practice of *paiderastia*, a mode of socialization by which an older male developed an erotic relationship with a younger male and took on the role of mentor.

There were three major gymnasia at Athens: the *Academy, the *Lyceum, and the Cynosarges, all of them located in spacious sacred precincts outside the city wall and named after the cult-figures associated with the sanctuaries into which the practice of physical exercising was introduced In the course of the fifth century B.C.E. at Athens, additional facilities were developed to promote the multiple civic purposes served in the gymnasia, and—probably as part of the Periclean building program—architecturally significant monumental gymnasium buildings were constructed in all three areas. The Cynosarges became the gymnasium frequented by half-Athenians such as Themistocles, while the Academy and Lyceum were used by citizens.

Gymnasia evolved into centers of intellectual education and philosophical exchange. In the second half of the fifth century B.C.E. itinerant teachers of wisdom, known as *sophists, regularly visited the gymnasia when they traveled to Athens. There a sophist could rely on finding a ready supply of potential clients for his teaching—individuals and groups of men open to learning while they were exercising their bodies at their "leisure" (scholê). Athens made no provision for formal education of citizens beyond the private elementary teaching that took place between a slave teacher and a small boy. When boys became adolescents, education was left to the informal arrangements and vicissitudes of paiderastia. Because of the demands of Athenian democratic society, requiring direct participation of male citizens in the assembly and in the courts, the teaching of the sophists—with its emphasis on rhetorical presentation as well as on intellectual arguments and issues—found a very responsive market in Athens. The Athenian *Socrates, who opposed the teaching of the sophists and their tendency to professionalize and commercialize the educational process, also frequented the Athenian gymnasia—to confront the sophists and to promote his own vision of "philosophical" learning, as opposed to "sophistic" teaching, among the citizenry gathered there.

Gymnasia became more enduringly identified with higher education and philosophical teaching in the fourth century B.C.E. After the death of Socrates (399 B.C.E.)—and largely thanks to his immediate followers (Sokratikoi; see SOCRATIC CIRCLE)—the institutionalization of higher education further evolved into more permanent schools in Athens and other Greek city-states. Unlike the temporary, entrepreneurial "schools" founded by the first generation of traveling sophists, fourth-century schools were confined to a particular location and often made provision for continuation over generations after a school-leader (scholarchos) left or died. Legally speaking, the "founding" and operation of a philosophical school remained informal, not involving charter or regulation by the city-state; the ongoing groups of philosophers did not constitute religious cults but were rather purely secular associations dedicated to the pursuit of higher learning. A favorite location for such an institutional initiative was a public gymnasium.

The first philosopher to establish an ongoing group of this kind at Athens appears to have been *Antisthenes, a *Socratic who taught at the Cynosarges gymnasium in the 390's B.C.E., before the Athenian rhetorical teacher *Isocrates established a rival school in his own home. Although there may have been only a spiritual connection between Antisthenes's school in the Cynosarges and the later *Cynic movement in Athens, Antisthenes provided a model that the practice of school-founding in the fourth century B.C.E. would follow and elaborate.

When *Plato returned to Athens in 387 B.C.E., having been away on various travels for most of the decade following his teacher's death, he associated himself with another gymnasium, the Academy, where he established an ongoing group of philosophers, buying a nearby small estate in which to reside and extend the facilities of his community beyond what was available in the Academy. These two properties, Plato's private estate and the public Academy sanctuary with its gymnasium facilities, formed the basis of the school which Plato at his death handed over to his successor, his nephew *Speusippus. Through a succession of scholarchs the Academy continued over time as a haven for professional philosophers and as a collective group promoting a kind of philosophical education in an ongoing community. "Philosophy" was defined as a way of life with an institutional form, not just as a noetic activity. Although *"Platonism" continued to be studied and practiced in some form throughout antiquity, there is no evidence that the Academy at Athens survived as a center for philosophical education after Sulla's disastrous siege of the city in 86 B.C.E. Only mythology supports the common view that Plato's Academy had a continuous existence at Athens until the emperor Justinian "closed the philosophical schools" in 529 C.E.

*Aristotle, a non-Athenian from Stagira (Macedonia) and a former student at the Academy, established himself and his followers in the Lyceum gymnasium at Athens in 336 B.C.E. After Plato's death in 347, Aristotle and colleagues from the Academy left Athens and formed a philosophical association in Asia Minor, first in the Troad and later in Mytilene (on Lesbos). From there Aristotle was called to the Macedonian court to tutor the young Alexander.

Supported by Macedon, Aristotle carried on an elaborate empirical research program as the foundation for his philosophical writing and teaching. Eventually, after thirteen years away, he returned to Athens to found a school of his own there. He chose not to associate himself and his followers with the Academy, which was continuing under Speussipus's successor, *Xenocrates of Chalchedon, perhaps because Aristotle judged his philosophical program no longer compatible with the textual and *dialectical orientation of the Academy. The Lyceum included the first systematic collection of books and research materials, which became the model for the great Library at Alexandria through the agency of the *Peripatetic philosopher *Demetrius of Phalerum. The community of Peripatetic philosophers consisted largely of non-Athenians who could not own land or exercise other privileges of citizenship. Nevertheless because philosophical schools were regarded as a benefit—a source of intellectual prestige, economic value, and civic pride—even largely foreign groups were officially encouraged to practice philosophy and allowed to use public facilities such as the Lyceum. Despite some political backlashes because of the Lyceum's Macedonian political connections, the school continued to function until it was severely damaged during Sulla's siege of Athens in 86 B.C.E.

Even after they were occupied by philosophical communities, the gymnasia continued to serve their other civic purposes—as cult centers and as places for exercise, athletic practice, and military drills—and were supervised by a publicly elected official, the gymnasiarch. During the Hellenistic period, when Athens was no longer a military power and largely an educational center, the institution of the Athenian *ephêbeia* (compulsory military service for eighteen-year-old males) continued to make use of the gymnasia and began to incorporate lectures of philosophers into their training regimen. When Romans came into more intimate contact with Greek culture (c. 150 B.C.E.), elites began to travel to Athens to enter the ephebeia or participate in the philosophical schools. *Cicero, who had studied in Athens, noted that a discus might fly by as a group was engrossed in philosophical study at an Athenian gymnasium. After Sulla's widespread destruction, however, Athens declined as an educational center and was not restored to a prominent place for philosophical teaching and learning until Hadrian invested Roman funds to renew the city (2nd cent. C.E.).

The two major philosophical schools founded at Athens during the Hellenistic period, the *Stoa and the Garden, did not use gymnasium property or facilities. *Zeno of Citium (on Cyprus) associated himself with the Stoa Poikilê in the Agora, while *Epicurus, an Athenian citizen, set up his more inwardly looking school in his private home.

Two additional public gymnasia were built at Athens toward the end of the third century B.C.E., the Diogeneion and the Ptolemaion (probably the benefaction of Ptolemy III Philopater); both were located inside the city-walls and became centers for the *ephêbeia* and for philosophical education. The Ptolemaion was the site of the first public library at Athens.

See also ACADEMY, LYCEUM, PERIPATETIC SCHOOL.

BIBLIOGRAPHY: Delorme, J., *Gymnasion: Étude sur les monuments consacrés à l'éducation en Grèce*, Paris, 1960; Forbes, C. A., *CP* 40, 1945, 32–42; Habicht, C., *Hellenistic Athens and Her Philosophers*, Princeton, 1988; Jaeger, W., *Paideia*, vols. 1–3, tr. G. Highet, New York, 1945; Kyle, D. G., *Athletics in Ancient Athens*, (*Mnemosyne* suppl. 25), 1987; Marrou, H., *A History of Education in Antiquity*, tr. G. Lamb, New York, 1956; Miller, S. G., *Arete: Greek Sports from Ancient Sources*, Berkeley, 1991; Travlos, J., *Pictorial Dictionary of Ancient Athens*, London, 1971; Wycherley, R. E., *The Stones of Athens*, Princeton, 1978.—*JOHN PATRICK LYNCH*

H

HAPPINESS (*EUDAIMONIA*). See ETHICAL THOUGHT, Classical.

HECATAEUS (c. 350–290 B.C.E.), of Abdera. Man of letters with philosophical interests. Hecataeus wrote *On the Poetry of Homer and Hesiod*; *On the Hyperboreans*, a work utopian-philosophical in nature; *On the Philosophy of the Egyptians*; and a work midway between history and fantasy, used by Diodorus Siculus in the first book of his *Library of History*. A long passage on the origin of the universe and of civilization reveals the clear influence of *Democritus' ideas. The attribution to Hecataeus of a work *On the Jews* is erroneous.

BIBLIOGRAPHY: Texts in DK73; *FGH* 264. Spoerri, W., "Hekataios," in *Reallexikon für Antike und Christentum* 14, 1988, 275–310.—*TIZIANO DORANDI*

HECATO (2nd to 1st cent. B.C.E.), of Rhodes. *Stoic philosopher, student of *Panaetius. Hecato may have accompanied Panaetius to Rome and was in contact with the Scipionic Circle, as the dedication of his work, *On Duties* (to Q. Aelius Tubero), indicates. Other works include *On the End*; *On Goods*; *On Virtues*; *On Passions*; *On Gratitude*; *On Paradoxes*; and *Adages*. He concerned himself chiefly with *ethics. *Cicero made use of *On Duties* in the third book of his work of the same name, while the treatise *On Gratitude* was probably the source of *Seneca's *De Beneficiis*.

Hecato provided a schoolish formulation of Panaetius' philosophical ideas. On some points, however, he took different positions or went further. He defined all the cardinal *virtues as "theoretical," that is, based on knowledge, and to these he opposed those that are "non-theoretical," for example, health, beauty, strength of spirit, and courage. In contrast to Panaetius he emphasized the importance of case-by-case analysis and defended the concept of personal utility as against that of duty toward one's own kind. He maintained that between benefactor and beneficiary there exists a reciprocal relationship of affection based on feelings and not on personal advantage.

BIBLIOGRAPHY: Gomoll, H., *Der stoische Philosoph Hekaton*, Bonn, 1933; Pohlenz, M., *Die Stoa*, Göttingen, vol. 1, 240f.; vol. 2, 123f.—*TIZIANO DORANDI*

HEGESIAS. See CYRENAIC PHILOSOPHY.

HERACLIDES (?380s–c. 310 B.C.E.), of Heracleia Pontica. Student of *Plato and contemporary of *Aristotle. Heraclides probably entered Plato's *Academy in the 360s and remained there until the death of *Speusippus in 339. Having failed in his bid to succeed Speusippus, he retired to his home town on the Black Sea coast of Turkey. He may have been influenced by Speusippus and Aristotle as well as Plato. The surviving fragments of his works also show the influence of earlier philosophers, probably mediated through the Academy.

Like Aristotle and other students of Plato, Heraclides transcribed Plato's lecture *On the Good*. He wrote independent works on a large variety of subjects, including *"dialectics," *ethics, *political philosophy, and *religion, as well as literary and historical topics. He is best known today for two of his *scientific theories. First, he partly anticipated Tycho Brahe in his account of planetary movements: He postulated an *infinite universe in which the earth rotates on its axis from west to east in one synodic day, while the sun revolves around the earth from west to east in a year, presumably in the plane of the ecliptic. Mercury and Venus, the inner planets, revolve around the sun on epicycles; we do not know his views on the outer planets. Second, he held that matter is composed of two kinds of particle separated by microvoids. There are "corpuscles" (*ongkoi*), which are compounded of "fragments" (*thrausmata*). Corpuscles may be broken down into fragments, but fragments cannot be broken down any further. Corpuscles have at least some of the sensible qualities of midsized objects but fragments do not.

Both theories show the influence of Plato's *Timaeus*. In that work, at 38d, Plato describes but does not explain the movements of Mercury and Venus, and many readers have seen a reference to an axial rotation of the earth at 40b–c. Moreover, at 54dff. Plato describes the four elements as each consisting of minimal particles shaped like one of the regular solids, which in their turn can be resolved into two kinds of triangle. But whereas Plato has two-dimensional triangles as the ultimate constituents of matter, Heraclides substitutes three-dimensional "fragments"; whereas Plato views the elementary particles as geometrical constructs, Heraclides holds that they are aggregates of matter. Nevertheless, his doctrine of two stages of aggregation stands in contrast with other contemporary *atomistic theories and was clearly inspired by Plato.

Heraclides' account of the *soul is related to Plato's in much the same way. Like Plato, he affirmed the soul's immortality and the idea of reincarnation; unlike Plato, he claimed that it is material, being constituted of "light," the finest kind of matter. Between incarnations, souls not corrupt enough to be confined in hell congregate in one part of the heavens, where they make up the Milky Way. Apparently this "Heavenly Hades" was situated immediately below the sphere of the sun.

These doctrines were contained in a revelation supposedly vouchsafed by Pluto and Persephone to a certain Empedotimus, and with them we have crossed the boundary between Heraclides' scientific views and his ethical and religious *dialogues. Here his outlook was puritanical. The lust for pleasure, he believed, corrupts individuals and societies alike, with dire results; for the gods observe human behavior and ensure that crimes are punished. In the dialogue *On Pleasure* he seems to have made some attempt to analyze the *psychology of pleasure and even of the "politics of envy," but on the whole his teaching was rather trite. The popularity of these writings rested on their style and presentation. His speakers were famous historical figures or wise men, including *Pythagoras, *Empedocles, Abaris (a notorious Scythian *Shaman*), and perhaps Zoroaster; and his dialogues contained uplifting sermons, historical or quasi-historical anecdotes, and miracles and revelations such as the one mentioned above. One described a banquet Empedocles gave to celebrate his resurrection of a woman who had lain in a coma for thirty days while her soul had temporarily left her body, and ended with his apotheosis. It included a description of the woman's condition and how Empedocles cured her, as well as Pythagoras' famous parable defining the philosophic life; probably both were narrated during the banquet. Against this fantastic background Heraclides preached the dualism of soul and body and the ideal of the contemplative life adopted by Plato's Academy.

Heraclides left no school. *Cicero admired his style and sometimes emulated his dialogues, but only the physician Asclepiades of Bithynia (active in Rome c. 100 B.C.E.) took his ideas seriously. Although generally following the views of *Epicurus, he adopted Heraclides' two-level corpuscular theory, presumably because he found it useful for explaining physiological processes.

BIBLIOGRAPHY: Texts in Wehrli 8. Gottschalk, H. B., *Heraclides of Pontus*, Oxford, 1980.—*H. B. GOTTSCHALK*

HERACLIDES (fl. 85–65 B.C.E.?), of Tarentum. Physician of the Empiricist school (see MEDICINE, Ancient Theories of). About ninety fragments and testimonia concerning several treatises survive, including *On* *the Empiricist School* and works on regimen, therapeutics, pharmacology, and *Hippocratic exegesis.

A pupil of Mantias (*Herophilus' famous follower), Heraclides turned against the Herophileans, becoming a theoretically nuanced Empiricist who exercised a significant moderating influence on Empiricist doctrine. Although he viewed experience (*empeiria*) as the foundation of *medicine, he parted ways with earlier anti-aetiological Empiricists by freely deploying causal explanation. Physiology, which some Empiricists rejected, arguing that nature cannot be known (see CELSUS), is explicitly accommodated in Heraclides' theories (e.g., he developed his own theory of the pulse in extensive polemics against Herophilus' theory). It is a measure of Heraclides' influence that he is the Empiricist cited most often by later authors (e.g., *Celsus, *Galen).

BIBLIOGRAPHY: Texts in K. Deichgräber, *Die griechische Empirikerschule*[2], Berlin/ Zurich, 1965.—*HEINRICH VON STADEN*

HERACLITUS (allegorist). See ALLEGORY, Classical; HOMER.

HERACLITUS (late 6th–5th cent. B.C.E.), of Ephesus. Presocratic philosopher distinguished by the power of his vision of unity amid change and the paradoxicality and occasional opaqueness of his expression. Of his life almost nothing is known for certain, except that he lived in Ephesus. Though very likely of aristocratic background, he seems nonetheless to have deliberately distanced himself from involvement in the political scene.

It is a matter of dispute whether he wrote a treatise and, if so, whether it was entitled *On Nature*. The apophthegmatic, not to say hierophantic material that has survived in fragmentary form may reflect a prose style of that order or a particular speaking style, or both; fragment 1 (DK22B1) looks a lot like the opening words of a book, others seem more like a collection of his *dicta* on various topics.

In possibly deliberate answer to *Xenophanes' pessimism about the attainment of *knowledge (DK21B34), Heraclitus claims that knowledge is possible and that it constitutes one single thing: "the one wise thing is to know the plan (*gnômê*) which steers all things through all things" (B41). This appears to refer to the overall divine plan for the operation of the real, and he admits that ascertainment of it is beset with pitfalls, such as relying on what poets tell us (B104), accepting uncritically what the senses tell us (B46, 107), or looking for obvious rather than hidden connections among things (B54). On the other hand, success is possible if one focusses on the real constitution (*phusis*) of things, something achieved by paying attention to their "common" or universal aspect (B2). Important, too, are precise observation, especially with the sense of sight (B101a), experience (B55), and open-mindedness to possibilities (B18).

The "plan" of things is also described as that everlasting "statement" or "account" (*logos) that holds forever, even if "people prove forever un-comprehending of it, both before they have heard it and when once they have heard it" (B1). The utterer of this account is in some straightforward sense presumably Heraclitus himself, but more important it is the source of even his utterance, an entity that he calls variously "that which alone is wise" (B32) and that "which is unwilling and willing to be called by the name Zeus" (*ibid.*). Descriptively the account is that everlastingly true statement that describes a reality everlastingly stable and everlastingly subject to change; prescriptively it is that divine law (*nomos*) that under-pins all human law (B114).

The essence of the account is that "all things are one" (B50), despite surface change and diversity. This is expressed paradoxically in a num-ber of the fragments as though apparent "opposites" in nature (day/night, winter/summer, satiety/famine) are in some apparently pantheis-tic sense one and the same (B67), but his meaning appears to be that many apparent opposites show "connectedness" (and in that weaker sense show unity) in various subtle and little-noticed ways. Such con-nectedness/unity could be that of inseparability (night/day, B67) or of perspective ("a road up or down [an incline] is one and the same [road]" B60), or of varying effect ("sea[-water] is very pure and very foul water—for fish drinkable and life-sustaining, for people undrinkable and lethal," B61).

This one, unified and interconnected world seems to be Heraclitus's "God" (B67), whose "plan" and activity constitute its law and operations (B114). Its unity and inner-connectedness are famously compared to the "back-turning" (possibly "back-stretching") connectedness of the string(s) and frame of a bow or lyre (B51). It is everlasting; it is not made by any "god or man"; and it is "an ever-living fire, being kindled in mea-sures and being put out in measures" (B30). "Fire" here seems to be both a metaphor and something more than a metaphor, symbolizing in a par-ticularly vivid way the fact of unity-amid-change and at the same time articulating what for Heraclitus is the most basic and significant element in the real.

This fire presents itself, either diachronically or synchronically or both (B30, 31), as earth and water as well as fire (air is not mentioned); and Heraclitus may just possibly have believed (as the *Stoics said he did) in periodic "conflagrations," when all things for a time become sim-ply fire again, before a new process of elemental transformation begins. Whatever the case, the essential point to be stressed is the unity amid the change rather than the change itself; violent as change in the world may be (a notion famously expressed in the phrase "War is father of all and king of all," B53), and so universally pervasive as to call into question the substantiality of anything whatever ("We step and do not step into the same rivers; we are and are not," B49a), from a God's-eye-view all is part of the plan that produces, through change, that higher unity that is the cosmos itself (B41).

At the human level, Heraclitus believes in *soul (*psychê*) as both our life-principle and the principle of our moral and rational activities. It seems to range in makeup from fiery dryness (constituting pure rationality and goodness) to the very opposite state, extreme wateriness (manifested, he suggests, with particular clarity in the phenomenon of drunkenness, where the soul in question is nearing the point of destruction by liquefaction). This very materialist view is, however, difficult to reconcile with his apparent belief in an afterlife, immortality, and—for a few—possible divinization (B21, 27, 53, 62, 63); perhaps he felt attracted to both notions for different reasons and chose in the end to leave them in the state of balanced tension that characterizes the components of the rest of his cosmos.

*Politically, he seems to have had a strong confidence in the protective powers of a city's law (B114). From the rest of this fragment and from his attacks on his native Ephesians (B121), one can infer that for him good law is in some real sense a reflection of divine law (though what this amounts to in detail is not spelled out) and that such good law is by similar parallelism not infrequently imposed by a single strong ruler. One can fairly assume, despite the lack of detail in his remarks, that his own preferred political system was as aristocratic as his cosmos and his own likely provenance and that he had little sympathy for the rising phenomenon of democracy. As for his views on poets, politicians, other philosophers, and "ordinary" people in general, these are characterized by a general acidity and contempt.

In terms of the history of Presocratic philosophy, Heraclitus is, despite the power of his prose and philosophical imagination, a marginal figure, who seems to have been significantly less influential than his near contemporary *Parmenides. A heavily overstressed version of his views on change did however—via *Cratylus—very much influence *Plato, and in more recent times Hegel and Marx have quarried the fragments for the putative origins of their own dialectical theory.

BIBLIOGRAPHY: Texts in DK22; Kahn, C. H., *The Art and Thought of Heraclitus*, Cambridge, 1979; Marcovich, M., *Heraclitus. The Greek Text with a Short Commentary*, Merida, 1967; Robinson, T. M., *Heraclitus: Fragments, A Text and Translation with a Commentary*, Toronto, 1987. Gigon, O., *Untersuchungen zu Heraklit*, Leipzig, 1935; Kirk, G. S., *Heraclitus. The Cosmic Fragments*, Cambridge, 1954; Reinhardt, K., *Parmenides und die Geschichte der griechischen Philosophie*, Bonn, 1916.—T. M. ROBINSON

HERILLUS (3rd cent. B.C.E.), of Carthage (or Chalchedon, if a variant manuscript reading is correct). *Stoic philosopher, student of *Zeno of Citium. *Diogenes Laertius (7.165–166) says he wrote a few powerful works in reply to Zeno and lists the following lost books: *On Training, On the Passions, On Belief, The Lawgiver, The Midwife, The Challenger, The Teacher, The Reviser, The Examiner, Hermes, Medea, Dialogues,* and *Ethical Themes.* Diogenes Laertius and *Cicero outline his doctrines as follows: (i) the chief end (*telos*) is knowledge (*epistêmê*); (ii) the chief end is distinct from the subordinate end (*hupotelis*)—the nonwise aim at the subordinate end, while only the wise aim at the chief end; (iii) all things between *virtue and vice are indifferent. Interpretations of his philosophy vary. Some have interpreted the knowledge he set up as the end as theoretical knowledge, but most have taken it as knowledge in a *Socratic, *ethical sense, as Diogenes Laertius (7.165) seems to indicate ("knowledge, that is, to live always directing everything towards living with knowledge and not being misled by ignorance. And he said that knowledge is a habit in the reception of images which cannot be upset by argument"). His distinction (ii) between end and subordinate end is unclear. He seems to have originated the term *hupotelis* ("subordinate end"), and it has been variously interpreted as equivalent to Zeno's "things preferred" (*proêgmena*), to objects of a creature's first impulse, or to things that "appear good" to a creature. His teaching that (iii) everything except virtue and vice is indifferent resembles the view of *Aristo of Chios. Later writers viewed him as a heterodox Stoic. *Cleanthes wrote a work *Against Herillus,* and Cicero reports (*Fin.* 2.43) that no one after *Chrysippus bothered to refute him. Cicero (*Or.* 3.62) says there was a philosophical school named after him.

BIBLIOGRAPHY: Texts in *SVF* 1, 409–421. Hirzel, R., *Untersuchungen zu Ciceros Philosophischen Schriften,* vol. 2, Leipzig, 1882, 45–58; Ioppolo, A. M., *Phronesis* 30, 1985, 58–78; von Arnim, H., "Herillos" in *RE.—WALTER G. ENGLERT*

HERMARCHUS (perhaps 330s–250s B.C.E.), of Mytilene on the island of Lesbos. *Epicurean philosopher and cofounder of the Epicurean school, who on *Epicurus' death (271) succeeded him in the headship for an unknown period. Originally trained in *rhetoric, he probably met Epicurus at Mytilene when the latter founded his first school there c. 311. Later he moved to the school's Athenian headquarters, the Garden, founded in 307. Epicurus, *Metrodorus of Lampsacus, Hermarchus, and *Polyaenus were, as co-founders, accorded authority status by later Epicureans, who referred to them collectively as "the men."

Hermarchus' works, much admired and quoted, were listed as: *Epistolary Writings (Epistolika), Against Empedocles* in 22 books, *On the Sciences,*

Against Plato, and *Against Aristotle.* Most surviving citations come from the first two.

Against Empedocles dealt with religious and moral issues raised by *Empedocles. As well as defending Epicurus' anthropomorphic *theology (frs. 32–3 Longo Auricchio), Hermarchus developed a detailed theory of the origins of laws on killing (fr. 34 = Porphyry *On Abstinence* 1.7–12). The differential laws on voluntary homicide, involuntary homicide, and animal slaughter were devised to enforce on the unreflective masses the code of conduct that thinking people already approved on grounds of social utility. Homicide disrupts society, but animal killing is justified by considerations of human safety and nourishment and by animals' inability to form contractual relations of justice with us.

Epicurus, although an admirer, considered Hermarchus intellectually somewhat intransigent. Hermarchus was nevertheless among the school's most powerful thinkers and exerted an important influence on later Epicureanism.

BIBLIOGRAPHY: Texts in F. Longo Auricchio, *Ermarco, frammenti,* Naples, 1987. Alberti, A., in A. Laks and M. Schofield, eds., *Justice and Generosity,* Cambridge, 1995, 161–90. Vander Waerdt, P. A., *TAPA* 118, 1988, 87–106.—*DAVID N. SEDLEY*

HERMETICA. Egyptian religious and philosophical texts. The texts are called "Hermetica," because many are ascribed to "Hermes Trismegistus" (= Thoth). They include, of philosophical and *theological interest, seventeen treatises in Greek in the *Corpus Hermeticum* (*CH*), the Latin *Asclepius*, forty texts and fragments in *Stobaeus' *Anthologia,* three texts in Coptic found at Nag Hammadi, a text in Armenian, and a few other fragments. There are also some "technical" Hermetic treatises on astrology, *medicine, alchemy, magic, and theurgy.

Some of the "technical" Hermetica may be dated to the third century B.C.E., if not earlier, but the philosophical Hermetica are usually dated to the second century C.E. *Plutarch, in *On Isis and Osiris* (c. 120 C.E.), seems unaware of a collection of Hermetic texts, while *Clement of Alexandria (*Miscellanies,* 200–210 C.E.) notes treatises ascribed to Hermes Trismegistus. Some Hermetica were surely written after 210 C.E., and some may have been written considerably earlier. Those who wish to trace the origins of Greek philosophy to Egypt may claim that the origins of the Hermetica lie before the time of *Pythagoras, so that Greek philosophers could have learned from the Egyptian tradition.

The Hermetica present themselves as native Egyptian, even if most were written in Greek. They appear to have been produced by a religious community with roots in the Egyptian temple tradition and branches in Egyptian gnosticism. The *Corpus Hermeticum* seems to be a Byzantine collection; Stobaeus, around 500, did not to know the *CH* as such, but Michael Psellus, in the eleventh century, did.

The Hermetica always have a primarily *religious goal; the role of philosophy in achieving that goal is clear: "Without philosophy it is impossible to be perfectly pious. He who learns of what nature things are, and how they are ordered, and by whom, and to what end, will be thankful for all things to the Creator" (Stobaeus 2B.2–3; Fowden, 101). Human beings have a double nature: part is like the divine, part is material. Gaining knowledge of God, of humanity, of the universe—the step-by-step understanding of Reality—is a divinization of the divine part; knowing what God knows makes a person one with God (*Ascl.* 7).

The material world is "the receptacle of all the sensible forms or qualities of bodies, none of which can be invigorated without God. For God is everything; everything comes from him; everything depends on his will" (*Ascl.* 34). Fate, Necessity, and Order are expressions of the divine plan, revealed visibly in the everlasting rotation of the universe. The sun is a delegated craftsman of God, binding "heaven to earth, sending essence below and raising *matter above" (*CH* 16.5). The sun, "like a good driver, steadies the chariot of the cosmos and fastens the reins to itself to prevent the cosmos going out of control. And the reins are these: life and *soul and spirit and immortality and becoming." The sun is also in charge of *daimones*, who are the instruments of "fate" in human affairs. The image of the sun as source of illumination leads to consideration of an analogous source of intellectual and spiritual illumination. "If anyone has a ray of the sun shining on the rational part of his soul the effect of the *daimones* is nullified" (*CH* 16.16).

The emphasis on an inner source of knowledge made the Hermetica attractive to some *Gnostic and *Christian philosophers in late antiquity; the attitude of other philosophers of the period to the Hermetica was ambiguous. Tertullian (mid-3rd cent.) cited a theoretical Hermetic text; *Porphyry (*Life of Plotinus* 16) recounts the hostility of the great Egyptian philosopher to gnostic and magical uses of philosophy, doubtless including Hermetism (cf. Fowden, 203), although he clearly had assimilated their message. More sophisticated, more philosophically rigorous, than the Hermetic tradition, *Plotinus was still an Egyptian. Porphyry was more sympathetic to Hermetism; according to *Iamblichus he had read Hermetic texts, though he did not cite them explicitly. Iamblichus (c. 300 C.E.), especially in *De Mysteriis*, used these texts, along with others, to construct his own syncretic version of *Neoplatonism. Lactantius, at about the same time, enthusiastically used Hermetica to support Christian ideas. *Augustine (in *City of God*, 410-426 C.E.) was frankly antagonistic to the Hermetic texts; consequently they became, in the West, something of an "underground" literature. In Byzantium, Michael Psellus was impressed by the similarities of expression between the Hermetica and the Bible (Copenhaver, xl-xli). In the Renaissance, Hermes Trismegistus was seen as one of the great springs of ancient wisdom, and of course the Hermetica continue to be an honored source for mystical and esoteric philosophical traditions.

For the historian of Classical philosophy the significance of the Hermetica lies primarily in their witness to the indigenous philosophical tradition of Greco-Roman Egypt. These texts comprise one of the most important sources for the history of a truly "African" philosophy. At the same time we recognize that these texts have inspired the religious imaginations of many devout philosophers from antiquity to the present.

BIBLIOGRAPHY: English tr. of *Corpus Hermeticum* and *Asclepius* in B. P. Copenhaver, *Hermetica*, Cambridge, 1992. Ambrose, E. A., *The Hermetica: An Annotated Bibliography*, St. Louis, 1992; Festugière, A. -J., *La révélation d'Hermès Trismégiste*, Paris, 1944–1954; Fowden, G., *The Egyptian Hermes*, Cambridge, 1986; Mahé, J. -P., *Hermès en Haute-Egypte*, Quebec, 1978–1982.—*ANTHONY PREUS*

HERODOTUS (c. 484–c. 425 B.C.E.), of Halicarnassus. Historian. Exiled from Halicarnassus, Herodotus travelled widely (e.g., to Egypt, Tyre, the Black Sea) with longer stays at Samos and Athens. He joined the Panhellenic colony of Thurii in south Italy (founded in 444/3) and wrote the *Histories* during c. 450–425 (the last securely dateable events mentioned in his work belong to the first years of the Peloponnesian War). His chief subject is the rise of the Persian empire (to 5.27), followed by the Persian Wars (499–479 B.C.E.). The division of the *Histories* into nine books is of Alexandrian origin.

Philosophy was indispensable for the birth of historiography; it fostered the rejection of mythopoeic explanations and the formulation of criteria for truth and influenced views of the physical and natural worlds, including man. Among philosophers and *sophists Herodotus names only two (while mentioning most of those reckoned among the *"Seven Sages"): *Thales (1.74: the prediction of the solar eclipse of 28 May 585; cf. 1.75, 170) and *Pythagoras (4.05). He alludes to various ideas of others without naming them: for example, *Anaximander (the *gnômê*, 2.109; map of the world, 5.49), *Xenophanes (fossils, 2.11–12), *Anaxagoras (Nile flooding from melting snow, 2.22).

More often it is difficult to identify specific sources, although a general influence is clear. He views the physical world as one of balancing polarities. In geography, for example, the Nile is balanced by the Danube (2.31–34), Egypt by Scythia (cf. 4.36), and the edges of the world, where the rarest and most valuable things are found together with extremes of climate, by Greece, which enjoys a blend of the extremes (3.106) at the center. In the natural world, the small number of offspring of noxious creatures is balanced by the prolific reproduction of their victims (3.108, attributed to the *pronoia* of the deity). In the moral world *tisis* or retribution, usually at human hands though occasionally the divine, follows upon wrongdoing (2.120). Those great in size, prosperity, or power will suffer reversal, both individuals and states (1.5; 7.10), again sometimes because of divine envy (1.32; 3.40; 7.10). Even mere hubristic thoughts might bring retaliation (1.34). Herodotus' view of causation is most often couched in terms of guilt or blame for wrongdoing (*aitiê*, proem 1.5). Most often he prefers human to *theological explanations (the whole of 7.133–137 is instructive). He is strongly influenced by the "tragic" paradigm of *koros-hubris-apatê-atê*. *Nomos* is the hallmark of culture worldwide (3.38); for example, of religious practices (2.3–4) and national character (7.101–104). Here he is probably influenced by *Protagoras, whom he may have known at Thurii.

His criteria for truth owe much to philosophy, as does his reliance on personal inquiry (*historiê*) and his privileging of sight over hearing (1.8; 2.99, 147). Poets and legends are viewed with distrust as prone to falsehood, sometimes deliberate (2.116, *Homer), and as using unverifiable data (2.21, 23 on the Ocean). The *spatium historicum* (which begins roughly 700–650 B.C.E.) is demarcated from the *spatium mythicum* (2.142–146); the phrase "the first of whom I/we know" (1.5, 12–13; 3.122) is frequently used to signal the demarcation. Rationalization (2.52–57), analogy (2.31–34), and probability are common methods of seeking truth, as is cross-checking (2.44).

Herodotus shares many interests with the sophists on topics such as *nomos*, forms of government (3.80–82, the debate on democracy, oligarchy, and monarchy), language, and invention as proof of cultural advance. With the *medical writers he shares an interest in climate, sicknesses, and anthropology (e.g., 3.12 on the thickness of Persian and Egyptian skulls; 1.71, 7.102 and 9.122 on "hard" and "soft" cultures).
BIBLIOGRAPHY: Irwin, T. H., *Classical Thought*, Oxford, 1989, 26–28; Lloyd, G. E. R., *Polarity and Analogy*, Cambridge, 1966, 431–435; also *Magic, Reason and Experience*, Cambridge, 1979, 29–32; Nestle, W., *Vom Mythos zum Logos*,[2] Stuttgart, 1942, 503–14.—*T. J. LUCE*

HEROPHILUS (c. 330–260 B.C.E.?), of Chalcedon. Alexandrian physician. Almost three hundred testimonia and fragments of his works survive. He wrote on anatomy, the pulse, semiotics, mental disorders, the classification of dreams, midwifery, regimen, therapeutics, ophthalmology, pharmacology, and the interpretation of *Hippocratic texts. Making use of analogical reasoning, he developed detailed theories despite his emphasis on the provisionality of theory. His dictum "first the phenomena" and his causal hypotheticalism may have prompted some of his followers to turn to the Empiricist school (see MEDICINE, Ancient Theories of; HERACLIDES of Tarentum).

One of only two ancient *scientists (see ERASISTRATUS) to perform systematic scientific dissections of human cadavers (and possibly vivisections of condemned criminals), Herophilus made numerous influential anatomical discoveries. These include the nerves, the distinction between sensory and "voluntary" (i.e., motor) nerves, the distinctions among four coats of the eye, various fine cerebral and vascular structures, and, using the analogy of the male parts, the ovaries, which he called the female "twins" (*didumoi*, "twins" being a traditional term for the male testicles).

Herophilus locates the command center (*hêgemonikon*) of the body in the fourth cerebral ventricle. From the brain, sensory and "voluntary" nerves proceed like offshoots, permitting transmissions to and from parts of the body, apparently by means of *pneuma* that flows through the nerves. This *pneuma* is ultimately derived from the air through respiration, which is attributed to a natural tendency of the lungs to dilate and contract through a four-part cycle. Herophilus' *On Pulses* became the foundation of most ancient pulse theories. A "power" or "faculty" (*dunamis*) flowing from the heart through the coats of the arteries causes the regular dilation (*diastolê*) and contraction (*sustolê*) of the arteries, which thus "pull" a mixture of *pneuma* and blood from the heart and distribute it throughout the body. The veins, by contrast, distribute only blood.

Herophilus tried to demystify the uterus by claiming that it is constituted of the same elements and governed by the same faculties as the rest of the body. "Affections" such as conception, parturition, and lactation are, of course, unique to women, but there are no diseases peculiar to women. He also discussed menstruation, the causes of difficult childbirth, and whether a fetus is a living being; and he developed an instrument for use in abortions.

*Galen, Vesalius, and other later anatomists recognized that Herophilus' anatomical discoveries and anatomical accuracy represent a pioneering achievement.

BIBLIOGRAPHY: Texts in H. von Staden, *Herophilus: The Art of Medicine in Early Alexandria*, Cambridge, 1989.—*HEINRICH VON STADEN*

HESIOD (trad. date: late 8th cent. B.C.E.). With *Homer, Orpheus, and Musaeus, one of the mythic hexameter poets at the beginning of the Greek literary tradition. Since the bulk of the poetry in question emerges out of preliterate oral traditions in which the speaker or *persona* serving as the mouthpiece must be assumed to have evolved along with the other traditional material, no claims of an autobiographical nature should be taken at face value. The Hesiodic *persona* is specific to only two surviving archaic poems, the *Theogony* (where the speaker identifies himself as Hesiod [22], and describes his initiation into poetry on Mt. Helicon), and the *Works and Days*, a didactic poem whose speaker is a rustic poet who addresses to his brother Perses (a mute *persona*) a great deal of advice about the necessity of hard work and the techniques of farming (and incidentally seafaring), along with advice of a more general nature, much of it proverbial, culminating in a list of lucky and unlucky days for various undertakings. The manuscript tradition also preserves a poem on the *Shield of Heracles* attributed to Hesiod, and numerous other works survive only in fragments. The issue of the authenticity or spuriousness of individual lines, passages, and whole poems attributed to Hesiod has been a troublesome one since antiquity.

As the only archaic Greek theogony preserved intact, Hesiod's account of the generations of the gods and his rudimentary cosmogony provide an important point of reference for prephilosophical Greek *theology and *cosmology. He provides the background against which we must assess not only Homeric ideas on these subjects (where both similarities and differences are highly significant) but also those of *Pherecydes of Syros and the Orphics. At the same time, we have no reason to take the Hesiodic account as authoritative. It was one among several competing archaic poetic accounts of the gods and the cosmos.

In its overall development, Hesiod's *Theogony* starts from the "gaping" (*chaos*) that separates Earth and Tartarus, presented as the first entity to exist, and then populates those realms (along with Heaven and the Seas) with deities. Each successive generation is patriarchal. The first dominant deities, Uranus and then Cronus, are monsters who obliterate their offspring. Zeus' triumph, first over Cronus, liberating his siblings, and then over the other Titans, forms the basis for a new distribution of honors that establishes the rights and privileges of the Olympian deities who now govern the order of the universe. The succession myth and other motifs have Near Eastern precedents.

The most Hesiodic of myths—narrated in somewhat different form in each of the two central poems—is that of Prometheus, the fire-bringer and trickster, to whom is attributed the invention of the partition of sacrificial victims. Zeus' response to being cheated in this distribution was to deprive man of fire. Prometheus stole it back for mankind, and the creation of woman (Pandora) was Zeus' revenge for the theft of fire. A grim misogyny pervades both poems. This account of the dynamics of the relations of the gods and mankind, along with the myth of the ages of mankind developed in the *Works and Days* (106–201), constitutes the core of the anthropological speculation to be found in archaic Greek poetry.

The *Works and Days* weaves together with invective and advice a series of *ethical claims of considerable importance. The insistent association here of Zeus with justice (*dikê*) marks the distance between the generally amoral Homeric deities and Hesiod' s vision of a universe in which the gods and their power are a guarantee that right will prevail over criminality, or at the very least, that criminality will bring divine retribution.

BIBLIOGRAPHY: Texts in Solmsen, F., et al., eds., *Hesiodi Theogonia, Opera et Dies, Scutum, Fragmenta Selecta*, Oxford, (OCT), 3rd ed., 1990; Texts, comm. and biblio. in M. L West, *Theogony*, Oxford, 1966; also *Works and Days*, Oxford, 1978. Lamberton, R., *Hesiod*, New Haven, 1988.—*ROBERT LAMBERTON*

HIEROCLES (fl. c. 120 C.E.), of unknown provenance. *Stoic philosopher. The sole evidence for his life stems from Aulus Gellius (*Noctes Atticae* 9.5.8), who calls him *Stoicus, vir sanctus et gravis* ("a Stoic, a revered and serious man"), and says that he was frequently cited by the *Platonist Calvenus Taurus for his opposition to *Epicurean hedonism. Some dozen excerpts of his work on practical *ethics are included in *Stobaeus' anthology. In 1901 a papyrus was discovered in Egypt containing the opening columns of a work by Hierocles entitled *Ethikê Stoicheiôsis* ("Elements of Ethics"). Linguistic parallels prove that this is the same man as Stobaeus' Hierocles. The papyrus represents a significant addition to what was previously known about the way Stoics sought the foundation for ethics in an animal's instinctual desire for self-preservation (*oikeiôsis*).

As was already clear from *Cicero *De Finibus* 3.16, the Stoics argued that this desire could not exist unless animals "perceived themselves." But this primary step in their argument is neither emphasized nor justified in Cicero's summary. Hierocles dwells upon it at great length. First, he adduces evidence to show that animals do perceive themselves; next, he seeks to prove that they perceive themselves continuously; finally, he argues that they perceive themselves as soon as they are born. Having demonstrated that self-perception is prior to the perception of anything else, he concludes that animals must be well-disposed to their own self-image. This instinctual disposition, he then argues, entails animals' desire for self-preservation since any other attitude would be inconsistent with the way they perceive themselves.

The papyrus is too defective to show how Hierocles made the transition from animal behavior in general to the goal of human beings. However, we can conjecture that he explained it by refinements in the way human beings perceive themselves as they mature. He is our unique evidence for a terminological distinction among four kinds of *oikeiôsis*. Over and above the initial *oikeiôsis* to oneself, he refers to *oikeiôseis* to blood relations, external possessions, and things useful for preserving one's constitution.

The excerpts of Hierocles in Stobaeus deal with *kathêkonta*, the Stoic term for actions proper to human nature. They include advice on how one should behave towards parents and other relatives and also the reverence appropriate to gods and fatherland. The content of Hierocles' material on family life has some affinity to the work of *Musonius Rufus, but the style of the two Stoics differs. Musonius' work, like that of *Epictetus, is the record of oral delivery. Hierocles expounds his teaching with a good many literary flourishes.

The point of greatest interest in the Stobaeus material is Hierocles' model of the mind as the center of a series of concentric circles (6.671); the first of these contains the body, and the remainder, as their radius increases, contain one's family relationships, neighbors, fellow citizens, and the like, concluding with the whole human race. Hierocles proposes that a person should contract the circles towards the center, with the aim of reducing the distance between oneself and one's fellow human beings. He also recommends giving more distant relatives the names of those who are closer (calling cousins, siblings, etc.).

Hierocles' way of treating his subjects has more in common with the great Stoic philosophers of the past than with the moralizing typical of other Roman Stoics. Given our pathetically little evidence for the first-hand writings of professional Stoics, the Hierocles papyrus is an extremely valuable find.

BIBLIOGRAPHY: Texts in Stobaeus, *Eclogae*, C. Wachsmuth and O. Hense, eds., 1884–1912: 1.63, 64; 2.181; 3.660, 730, 731; 4.502, 503, 603, 640, 660, 671, 696; *Ethikê Stoicheiôsis*, G. Bastianini and A. A. Long, eds., *Corpus dei Papiri Filosofici Greci e Latini* (*CPF*) I, vol. 1**, Florence, 1992, 268–451, with supp. comm. in *Studi su codici e papiri filosofici*, Florence, 1992, 221–49. Brunschwig, J., in G. Striker and M. Schofield, eds., *The Norms of Nature: Studies in Hellenistic Ethics*, Cambridge/Paris, 1986, 113–45; Inwood, B., *OSAP* 2, 1984, 151–84; Long, A. A., *Stoic Studies*, Cambridge, 1996, 250–263; Pembroke, S. G., in A. A. Long, ed., *Problems in Stoicism*, London, 1971, 114–49.—*A. A. LONG*

HIEROCLES (5th cent. C.E.), of Alexandria. *Neoplatonist philosopher, student of *Plutarch of Athens (d. 431/2) at Athens. Hierocles taught in Alexandria and possibly temporarily in Byzantium (Constantinople), where he was persecuted for his pagan opinions and condemned to exile. We possess a commentary of his on the *Carmen Aureum*, a work for beginning students of philosophy, as well as brief fragments (reported by Photius) of his treatise in seven books, *On Providence*.

Contrary to longstanding opinion (see Kobusch and Aujoulat in bibliography) in the wake of K. Praechter's theories, Hierocles' system of philosophy—his doctrines of the creation of the world, the demiurge, *matter, providence, and the destiny of *souls—does not depart from the Neoplatonism of his day. He did not perpetuate the theses of *Middle Platonism, particularly those of the pagan *Origen, nor was he contaminated by *Christianity. On the contrary, recent studies have been able to prove that Hierocles was influenced—via his teacher Plutarch—by the Neoplatonist *Iamblichus and that his philosophy, not only from a historical but also from a systematic point of view, occupied a middle ground between that of Iamblichus and that of *Proclus. Similarly, the historical attention that Hierocles throws on the development of the *Platonic school supports the inference that he is an adherent of a typical, even late Neoplatonic philosophical system. The contents of Books 4 and 5 of *On Providence*, with their systematic incorporation of the *Chaldean Oracles*, of theurgy, and of the *Orphica*, presuppose a degree of development of Neoplatonist doctrine that was attained only between Iamblichus and Proclus—a time that coincides exactly with that of Hierocles. The brilliance of his style and the ease with which he could develop his ideas in front of his audience were widely admired by his contemporaries.

BIBLIOGRAPHY: Texts in F. W. Köhler, ed., *In Carmen Aureum* (Teubner), Stuttgart, 1983; fragments of *On Providence* in Photius, *Bibliotheca*, cods. 214 and 251, ed. R. Henry, Paris, 1962 and 1974. Aujoulat, N., *Le néoplatonisme alexandrin: Hiéroclès d' Alexandrie*, Leiden, 1986; Hadot, I., *Le problème du néoplatonisme alexandrin: Hiéroclès et Simplicius*, Paris, 1978; also *Revue des Études Grecques* 103, 1990, 241–262 (review of Aujoulat); also *Revue des Études Grecques* 103, 1990 (final response to Aujoulat); Kobusch, T., *Studien zur Philosophie des Hierokles von Alexandrien*, Munich, 1976; Praechter, K., "Hierokles," in *RE* 8, 2, 1913.—*ILSETRAUT HADOT*

HIERONYMUS (mid-3rd cent. B.C.E.), of Rhodes. *Peripatetic philosopher. Hieronymus was disliked by *Lyco and critical of *Arcesilaus. His writings, which were admired for style, survive only in fragments. Almost all involve *ethical themes, such as anger, eros, education, and inebriation; many recount anecdotes about poets and earlier philosophers; a few discuss *rhetorical style. Hieronymus was accused of apostasy for equating happiness with "absence of disturbance (*aochlêsia*)," but he probably sought to update *Aristotelian theory. Like *Epicurus, he made equanimity the criterion for *happiness, but he avoided hedonism by denying that pleasure is intrinsically good; and while endorsing the *Stoic thesis that *virtue is necessary for avoiding disturbance, he followed *Aristotle in denying that it is sufficient for happiness. He probably also helped develop the Peripatetic theory of "moderate passions" from Aristotle's doctrine of the mean.

BIBLIOGRAPHY: Texts in Wehrli 10. Arrighetti, G., *Studi classici e orientali* 3,1954, 111–28.—*STEPHEN A. WHITE*

HIPPARCHIA, of Maroneia. *Cynic female philosopher. According to the ancient tradition, Hipparchia was the daughter of wealthy parents and the sister of Metrocles, one of the followers of *Crates of Thebes. She became enamored of Crates and wished to marry him. Her parents naturally objected to this challenge to the concept of the arranged marriage, especially as Crates was ugly and (by now) a pauper, and Crates himself tried in public to dissuade her. Finally he stripped naked in order to demonstrate all that the Cynic life involved, and when she persisted in her desire the two lay down in the *agora* and consummated their union, much to the embarrassment of *Zeno of Citium, Crates' closest follower, who threw a cloak over them. Thereafter Hipparchia shared a full Cynic life with Crates. They had one son. Hipparchia is credited with the ready wit and rhetorical resourcefulness characteristic of the Cynics.

Though embellished in detail (the intervention of Zeno, for example, symbolizes a point of difference between Cynicism and *Stoicism: Orthodox Stoicism moved away from the Cynic doctrine of "shamelessness"), the story of the union of Crates and Hipparchia, or "dog marriage," as it became known, is basically historical. Their union perfectly exemplified the sexual teachings of Crates' master, *Diogenes of Sinope: Sex, as a natural function, should be performed in public and "the man who persuades should go with (= 'have intercourse with') the woman who persuades" (D.L. 6.72). More generally, the episode illustrates the extreme radicalism of "hard" Cynicism's assault upon convention, its insistence upon the union of teaching and practice, and its commitment (arguably unparalleled elsewhere in ancient philosophy and thought) to the complete equality of the sexes.

See also CRATES of Thebes, DIOGENES of Sinope.

BIBLIOGRAPHY: Rist, J. M., *Stoic Philosophy*, Cambridge, 1969, ch. 4. For further bibliography, see under CYNICS and CYNICISM.—*JOHN L. MOLES*

HIPPIAS (5th cent. B.C.E.), of Elis. *Sophist and younger contemporary of *Protagoras. Hippias was still alive at the time of *Socrates' trial in 399 B.C.E. He travelled widely in the Greek world as a professional sophist, though visiting Athens somewhat rarely. He claimed mastery over the whole sphere of human knowledge and also the majority of human skills. It was said that he appeared at Olympia wearing clothes and shoes together with a ring, scraper, and oil flask all completely of his own making. He left a very large number of writings in both prose and verse, dealing with historical, *mathematical, artistic, and *grammatical questions as well as tragedies, epics, and dithyrambs, none of which has survived. Of considerable importance was a work entitled *Synagôgê*, from which we have what seems to be the introductory paragraph. This suggests that the work as a whole was a collection of passages from the earlier writers, both Greek and non-Greek, and that it was the first historical *doxography that included extracts from the Presocratics. Unfortunately none of this has survived in its original form; it may be the source of quotations found in later authors. Attempts by scholars to reconstruct what may have been Hippias' own philosophical doctrines, by attributing to him works that actually survive, such as the *Dissoi Logoi*, the *Anonymus Iamblichi* and the Proem to *Theophrastus' *Characters*, should probably be dismissed as lacking in foundation. We have two works in the Platonic corpus, the *Hippias Major* and the *Hippias Minor*, which are really only concerned with ridiculing Hippias in his confrontations with Socrates and give us very little actual information about Hippias himself.

He is, however, depicted by *Plato in the *Protagoras* as present together with a number of other sophists at the house of Callias in Athens about 433 B.C.E. when these others are seen to be asking Hippias a series of *astronomical questions on nature and the heavenly bodies while he was seated in his chair and was distinguishing and explaining in turn the subjects of their questions (Pl. *Prt.* 315c). Much later than Plato we find *Proclus attributing to Hippias a solution of the problem of trisecting an angle and of squaring the circle by the invention of the curve, later known as "the quadratrix," a name that may well be a translation of Hippias' own term, the *tetragônizousa* (DK86B21). Later in the *Protagoras*, in an attempt to resolve an argument between Socrates and the other sophists present, Hippias is represented as having said (337cff.) that he regarded all those present as kinsmen, relatives, and fellow-citizens by nature, but not by law. For by nature like is akin to like, whereas law acts as a tyrant among human beings and compels them to do or submit to many things contrary to nature. On the basis that like is by nature akin to like, he further argued that men should draw the logical consequence from this. Unfortunately it is not made clear what Hippias supposed this consequence to be, which has led scholars to a variety of conjectures. He may have been advocating the unity of mankind as a whole, as would be the case if he were recognizing as friends and kinsmen the men of all cities and nations. But he may have been confining his remarks to Greeks only and so simply be advocating Panhellenism, or possibly he was arguing only for the unity of wise men, whether Greek or barbarian.

BIBLIOGRAPHY: Texts in DK86. Tr. in R. K. Sprague, *The Older Sophists*, Columbia, SC, 1972, and M. Gagarin and P. Woodruff, eds., *Early Greek Political Thought from Homer to the Sophists*, Cambridge, 1995. Woodruff, P., *Plato: Hippias Major*, Indianapolis, 1982.—G. B. KERFERD

HIPPO (2nd half of 5th cent. B.C.E.). Presocratic philosopher. Hippo (called Hipponax in some testimonies), a minor natural philosopher, was a younger contemporary of *Anaxagoras and *Empedocles. His doctrines were parodied by Cratinus (c. 420 B.C.E.) in his comedy, *The Omniscients*. He is often referred to as Hippo "the atheist." Whether he deserved this epithet more than Anaxagoras or *Diogenes of Apollonia (both of whom were accused of impiety) is difficult to decide. His *cosmological and physiological interests are typical for early writers "on nature." He seems to have been a monist and to have taken "moisture" as the principle from which everything else derives (according to some testimonies, including *Aristotle, he spoke of "water" or even "the cold," but this is probably inaccurate). *Hippolytus, however, says that Hippo operated with two principles, water and fire. This may have been true only of the cosmogony. Life-related phenomena such as *soul, sensation, semen, and embryology—in which Hippo was apparently mostly interested—were certainly explained by reference to the virtues of fluids. It is also significant that the only quotation we happen to have argues that all drinkable water come from the (salty) sea, although this of course is only an answer to a standard cosmological question. On the whole, Hippo appears to have been to *Thales, with whom his name remains associated after Aristotle (*Met.* 984a7), what Diogenes of Apollonia was to *Anaximenes. His relationship to *Pythagoreanism, although suggested by some sources, is tenuous.

For us, Hippo's doctrines remain extremely shadowy. If we trust Aristotle, this may not be a great loss, for he considered Hippo's thought to be simplistic (*loc. cit.*), and called his doctrine of the soul "trivial" (*DA* 405b2). But we cannot be certain about this. "Trivial" is a term Aristotle also applies to *Melissus, and *Theophrastus calls Diogenes of Apollonia's theory of cognition "naive," neither of which is entirely fair. In any case, Hippo's physiological doctrines seem to have had some influence on *medical literature, for Censorinus and the *Anonymus Londinensis* report his views in some detail.

BIBLIOGRAPHY: Texts in DK38.—*ANDRÉ LAKS*

HIPPOCRATES of Chios. See MATHEMATICS, Earlier Greek.

HIPPOCRATES (c. 460–370 B.C.E.?), of Cos, and the **HIPPOCRATIC CORPUS**. The historically elusive Greek physician Hippocrates was already renowned by the time of *Plato and *Aristotle. However, none of the pre-Alexandrian characterizations of Hippocrates is entirely compatible with any of the more than sixty extant treatises attributed to Hippocrates in antiquity (the "Hippocratic Corpus"). Furthermore, not even the Hippocratic treatises believed to have been written as early as the fifth century B.C.E. (e.g., *Airs Waters Places*, *Sacred Disease*, *Prognosis*, *Prorrhetic* 2, *Epidemics* 1, 3, *Art*, *Ancient Medicine*, *Nature of Humans*, *Regimen in Acute Diseases*, and *Winds*) can be ascribed with certainty to the historical Hippocrates. The doctrinal, methodological, stylistic, and lexical heterogeneity displayed within the Hippocratic Corpus suggests that its texts were written in more than one location by a variety of authors (mostly 430–340 B.C.E.) drawing on divergent traditions and that these texts were gradually assembled under the name "Hippocrates." The assimilation of texts to the Corpus continued in the Hellenistic Age and in the Roman

Empire: *Heart, Nutriment, Law, Precepts, Decorum,* and *Physician,* for example, seem to be postclassical works.

Method, Epistemology, Causation. Some Hippocratic works advocate or display close "clinical" observation, using all the senses (e.g., *Prorrhetic 1, Prognostic, In the Surgery, Diseases 2, Epidemics,* the description of an epileptic seizure in *Sacred Disease*). Others add that only reason can complete the interpretation of sensory signs (*Prognostic*). Furthermore, some texts display a keen interest in generalizable models of physical causation, whereas others do not. The secularization of causation—explicitly substituting "natural," physical causes for divine causes—is a key move in the early Hippocratic strategy of scientific authority, for example in explanations of the Scythians' impotence (*Airs Waters Places*) or of epilepsy (*Sacred Disease,* which also offers the first sustained criticism of magic). According to *Art* and *Airs Waters Places,* every disease has a natural cause that invariably produces the same result under the same conditions; *Regimen in Acute Diseases* recognizes that a similar effect can be brought about by different causes; *Nature of Humans* distinguishes between *general* diseases caused by miasmic air (which affects numerous people in similar ways) and *particular* diseases caused by individual regimen. The distinction between cause and coincidence also is deployed in some Hippocratic works (e.g., *Regimen*).

A different, more cautious view of causal generalization is advanced in *Ancient Medicine,* whose author criticizes new theorists who put forward reductive causal "hypotheses" (the hot, cold, dry, and wet) to explain diseases. In one of the earliest attested uses of the word *philosophia* (as a representative of which he introduces *Empedocles), this author fences off *medicine from "philosophy," castigating those "physicians and *sophists" who claim that it is impossible to attain medical knowledge without first "knowing" what a human being is; the latter investigation, he argues, belongs to *philosophia* and is irrelevant for medical practice, whose proven method is to start from past observations about the effects of regimen. By contrast, *Nature of Humans* and *Regimen* begin by offering a general theory of a human being, and several Hippocratic works (e.g., *Fleshes, Regimen 1, Sevens*) even suggest that *cosmology is essential to understanding the human medical microcosm.

Pathology. Hippocratics often interpret diseases as an imbalance in the natural state of the body (see ALCMAEON), brought about by internal or external factors or both. Some present the environment, including seasons and winds, as a central determinant (e.g., *Airs Waters Places, Epidemics, Aphorisms, Humors,* sections of *Diseases of Women*). *Nature of Humans* at times emphasizes interactions between environment, regimen, and humors, whereas relations between diet and exercise tend to dominate in *Regimen,* which sees fire (hot and dry, providing motion to the body) and water (cold and wet, providing nourishment) as the constituents of living beings.

The theory of bodily "humors" or liquids, whose excess or deficiency can cause imbalance and hence disease, appears in divergent versions in the Corpus. *Diseases* 1 and *Affections*, for example, usually (see below) attribute diseases to the dominance of two humors, phlegm and bile. By contrast, after criticizing medical and philosophical monists (including the *Eleatic *Melissus), *Nature of Humans* argues that four humors—phlegm, yellow bile, black bile, blood—are the constituents of the body. Further four-humor theories include phlegm–bile–blood–water (*Generation/Nature of the Child, Diseases* 4) and phlegm–bile–black bile–water (*Remedies, Affections* 36). Many Hippocratic treatises, however, do not make systematic use of humoral theory. The epideictic work *Winds*, for example, argues that air within the body is the principal cause of illness.

Deontology. The famous *Oath* does not reflect all the divergent Hippocratic deontological perspectives. Responsibility to one's *technê*, understood as a result-oriented professional expertise and a practice consistent with that expertise, often is depicted as the physician's prime motivation. This also entails responsibility for the reputation of one's *technê*. The concern with reputation, perhaps along with the relative insecurity of the physician within the social and economic order, is a reason both for the defensive posture of some texts (e.g. *Art, Law*) and for the significant role ascribed to accurate prognosis (e.g., *Prognostic, Prorrhetic* 1–2, *Coan Prenotions, Airs Waters Places, Internal Affections, Diseases* 1–2, *Regimen in Acute Diseases: Appendix, Crises*, the surgical treatises). The frequent prognosis of incurability and death, the polemics against charlatans, and the deontological emphasis on the avoidance of ostentation and theatricality likewise seem to be motivated in part by a concern with "shame" and reputation. The fact that some Hippocratic physicians were itinerant (cf. *Epidemics, Airs Waters Places, Prorrhetic* 1) might have intensified such concerns. Sensitivity toward the patient, and the physician's affective and sexual self-control are further recurrent themes (*Physician, Decorum, Precepts, Oath, Testament*).

A pluralism of traditions also becomes visible in Hippocratic theories of reproduction and embryology, in gynecology, and in therapeutics. Many of these often contradictory traditions became culturally obligatory points of departure for all subsequent European medicine, at least until the early modern era.

BIBLIOGRAPHY: Texts in É. Littré, ed. and tr., *Oeuvres complètes d'Hippocrate*, 10 vols., Paris, 1839–1861. Jouanna, J., *Hippocrate*, Paris, 1992.—HEINRICH VON STADEN

HIPPOLYTUS (d. c. 235 C.E.), of Rome, reputed author of the *Refutation of All Heresies*, a major source for the history of Greek philosophy. The work survives in two parts. The manuscripts of Book 1, which was first printed in 1701, ascribe it to *Origen of Alexandria; it is almost entirely a *doxographical survey of Greek philosophy from the sixth to the fourth century B.C.E. An anonymous manuscript of the bulk of Book 4 and the remaining Books 5–10 was discovered in a monastery in the nineteenth century; it was published together with Book 1 as a work of Origen in 1851. The contested but widely accepted identification of the author of the *Refutation* is based on a complex chain of arguments. Autobiographical material in Book 9 shows that the author was engaged in bitter controversy with Pope Callistus (reigned 217–222), whom the author survived. The attachment of the name "Hippolytus" to the *Refutation* rests on a variety of overlapping lists of works, sometimes with ascriptions to an approximate contemporary of Callistus named Hippolytus. The next step in the determination of the author of the *Refutation* is his identification with a Saint Hippolytus thought to have been martyred with Pope Pontianus shortly after 235. Eusebius says that Hippolytus the author was a bishop "somewhere," and it seems most plausible to accept the claim of some sources that he was Bishop of Rome. But since the name "Hippolytus" does not occur on any of the standard lists of papal successions, it is generally assumed that his election was contested and, indeed, that he was the first known antipope and the only antipope who is also a saint.

Hippolytus appears to have been the last Roman *Christian author to write in Greek until the eighth century. Although he became virtually unknown as an author in the West, many of his works were preserved in the East in their original language or in translation. In addition there is a substantial number of fragments that have not yet been pulled together in a systematic way. Needless to say, controversy surrounds the works and fragments. Much of Hippolytus' writing was exegetical, but he did influential work on biblical chronology and on the determination of the date of Easter.

The *Refutation* is not a fully coherent work, but Hippolytus' basic idea is to "refute" various heresies by showing that they are "identical" with one or another pagan theory. The identifications are usually far-fetched and, not surprisingly, show no sense of the relevance for interpretation of historical or literary context. Moreover, it is quite clear that at least on some occasions Hippolytus simply copied from other sources. Much of the *Refutation* is of more interest to students of heresy than to students of philosophy. Nevertheless, Hippolytus is of considerable value as a source for the way in which various philosophers (particularly *Aristotle, *Plato, and the *Pythagoreans) were understood in the early part of the common era, for certain doxographical information (particularly about *Anaximander and *Anaximenes) and for the fragments of *Empedocles and *Heraclitus.

BIBLIOGRAPHY: Text of *Refutation* in M. Marcovich, ed., *Hippolytus, Refutatio Omnium Haeresium*, Berlin/New York, 1986; Works in M. Geerard, *Clavis Patrum Graecorum*, vol. 1, Brepols, 256–278. Tr. of *Refutation* in A. Roberts and J. Donaldson, eds., *The Ante-Nicene Fathers*, vol. 5 (repr.), Peabody, MA, 1994. von Dölinger, J. J. I., *Hippolytus and Callistus*, tr. A. Plummer, Edinburgh, 1876; Mansfeld, J., *Heresiography in Context*, Leiden/New York/Cologne, 1992; Mueller, I., *ANRW* 2, 36.6, 1992, 4309–4374.—*IAN MUELLER*

HOMER (8th cent. B.C.E.?), probably from Ionia. Epic poet, credited with composing the *Iliad* and *Odyssey*; other poems were also attributed to him in antiquity. Nothing is known about his life; the biographical information in ancient *Vitae Homeri* may preserve conventions developed within a "rhapsodic" performance tradition active up to the fourth century B.C.E. (see *Plato's *Ion*). Because variations flourished in this originally oral-poetic art form, the text of the Homeric poems was not firmly established until the Hellenistic period; thus Plato and *Aristotle's citations differ in a number of readings from the later canonical versions. As the earliest, longest, and richest Greek poems to survive, Homer's work exerted enormous influence not only on most later literature but on thought and behavior throughout Greco-Roman antiquity. The *ethical, *theological, and *cosmological perspectives offered by him were givens for the philosophical tradition. Even if reviled, the authoritative epics could never be ignored.

The historian *Herodotus (2.53) claimed that Homer and *Hesiod first taught the Greeks about the gods' names and activities. This view of Homeric theology as personal mythologizing marks the earlier criticism of epic's anthropomorphic gods by the poet-philosopher *Xenophanes of Colophon (6th cent. B.C.E.), who said "Homer and Hesiod attributed to the gods shameful things and reproaches—stealing, committing adultery and deceiving one another" (DK21B11). That Xenophanes performed his own philosophical poetry in the manner of a rhapsode may explain this antagonism to the older poet. At the same time, the monotheistic tendency of Xenophanes' thought recalls the Homeric depiction of Zeus authorizing all cosmic action with a nod of his head (B23–26). Innovation in Greek thought would always face similar obstacles in breaking free of the Homeric world-view.

Another Ionian philosopher, *Heraclitus of Ephesus (c. 500 B.C.E.) said that "Homer was worthy to be thrown out of the games and beaten" (DK22B42). Since Heraclitus scorned most of his predecessors, there may not be a rationale for the rejection. Apparently, he characterized Homer as an astronomer (scholia at *Iliad* 18.251), perhaps in a context that included B53—"war as father of all makes some gods, some men, some slaves, some free"—which has been thought to imply criticism of Homer's line (*Iliad* 18.107), "would that strife (*eris*) might perish from the earth." A similar distaste for defects in Homeric theology underlies the story that *Pythagoras saw Homer and Hesiod being punished in Hades (Hieronymus of Rhodes 42, Wehrli 10).

A more sustained attack on Homer's gods comes from a different direction in Books 2 and 3 of Plato's *Republic*. Socrates is made to show how the epics are inappropriate for teaching the guardians of the ideal state: Homer depicts the gods as angry, lustful, and deceptive and heroes as overpowered by their emotions (377d–391e); furthermore, his art-form involves dangerous *mimêsis* of speeches in which unacceptable sentiments are voiced. Here it must be remembered that Plato associates Homeric art with the extravagant dramatic performances of the rhapsodes. The critique of Homer in *Republic* 10 dwells again on epic's mimetic quality: Not only is the poet imitative, but Homer failed to impart knowledge to his own contemporaries and thus can be of little service to the state.

In other *dialogues, Plato's Socrates, while effusive in praise of Homeric verse, makes it clear that the poet, lacking *dialectic, is no philosopher. In the *Protagoras* we can see the sort of appeals to Homeric authority that Plato is countering: Socrates' nemesis the *sophists associated themselves with Homer, claiming him and other early poets as crypto-sophists (316c–e). Thus it appears that Plato's ultimate rejection of Homer reflects his contemporary social context.

Counterpointing the rationalizing and demythologizing traditions were equally early claims that Homer represented the height of wisdom. From Plato's indirect critique, we glimpse two major strategies for saving Homeric authority: *allegorical interpretation and appeal to the poet's encyclopedic practical knowledge.

When Socrates at *Republic* 378d rejects Homeric stories of divine strife even if these are "composed with hidden meanings" (*en huponoiais*), he refers to the former technique, practiced widely in his time (e.g. Xenophon *Symp* 3.6 on Stesimbrotus of Thasos). The earliest specific interpretation of Homer attested, by Theagenes of Rhegium (c. 525 B.C.E.), uses allegory to explain the battle of gods in the *Iliad* as the clash of the elements fire and water (DK8.2 = scholion B at *Iliad* 20.67). Such an interpretation may have been meant to defend the poet from the criticism of Xenophanes. Later, *Metrodorus of Lampsacus (DK61A3–4) said the gods and heroes of Homer were fictions representing the sun (Achilles), earth (Helen), liver (Demeter), and so on. The allegorical method was explicitly levelled against Plato's arguments rejecting Homer by the

Homeric Allegories of *Heraclitus (1st cent. C.E.). On the other hand, we owe to the *Neoplatonist *Porphyry (232–c. 305 C.E.), a disciple of *Plotinus, the elaborate allegories that read the Homeric poems as stories of the Platonic *soul's journey through the material world. His *Essay on the Cave of the Nymphs* is a tour de force interpretation of *Od.* 13.102–12 as a message about abandoning the sensual. More extravagant still is the allegorical exegesis of Homer by *Proclus (c. 410–85 C.E.).

Allegorical readers assumed that Homer knew, but concealed in myth, metaphysical truths that later philosophers discovered. By contrast, those who appealed to Homeric wisdom in practical matters read Homeric speeches and descriptions as if these were overt instructions about behavior and professional skills (cf. Pl. *Ion*; *Rep.* 598e). In addition to *Protagoras, the sophist *Hippias of Elis seems to have discoursed this way (*Hp. Mi.* 363), using the Homeric Nestor as a preceptor in his (lost) *Trojan Discourse*. Similar use of Homer for ethical argument may underlie the remark of *Anaxagoras that the poetry was concerned with *virtue and justice (DK59A1) and was also likely featured in the essays on Homer by *Antisthenes (446–366 B.C.E.), by some accounts the father of *Cynicism. In winnowing ethical truths from Homer, Antisthenes is said to have anticipated *Zeno of Citium, whose five books on Homeric problems sought to clear Homer of self-contradictions, without, it seems, the use of allegory (see *SVF*1.274).

Regardless of their philosophical relationship to his thought, philosophers persisted in imitating, quoting, and analyzing Homer's verse. *Empedocles and *Parmenides chose to compose in evocative Homeric style. Plato quotes from Homer 112 times, and his own prose is full of Homeric touches (see ps.-Longinus *De Sublimitate* 13). His narratological analysis of *Iliad* Bk.1 (*Rep.* 393–394) anticipates Aristotle's deep appreciation for Homeric art in the *Rhetoric* and *Poetics*. In turn, *Peripatetic work, starting from Aristotle's own *Homeric Problems* (Rose, frs. 142–79), guided the textual criticism of the Alexandrian scholars Zenodotus, Aristophanes of Byzantium, and Aristarchus, who determined the present shape of the poems.

BIBLIOGRAPHY: Buffière, F., *Les mythes d'Homere et la pensée grecque*, Paris, 1956; Havelock, E., *Preface to Plato*, Cambridge, MA, 1963; Lamberton, R., *Homer the Theologian*, Berkeley, 1986; also Lamberton and J. Keaney, eds., *Homer's Ancient Readers*, Princeton, 1992; Richardson, N., *PCPS* 201, 1975, 665–81; Tate, J., *CQ* 23, 1929, 142–54 and *CQ* 24,1930, 1–10.—*RICHARD P. MARTIN*

HYPATIA (d. 415 C.E.), of Alexandria. Pagan *mathematician, *astronomer and philosopher, daughter of the mathematician *Theon and teacher of Synesius of Cyrene, *Neoplatonist and *Christian bishop. Hypatia, a virtuous virgin, taught publicly both in Athens and Alexandria and attracted numerous students. Friend of the Christian prefect of

Egypt Orestes, she became an object of hostility to Cyril, patriarch of Alexandria (later Saint Cyril), and was horribly murdered by a Christian mob. Cyril's hostility probably stemmed more from concern for personal power and political rivalry with Orestes than from *theological or ideological considerations.

Hypatia revised the third book of Theon's *Commentary on the Almagest* (the great textbook on astronomy of *Ptolemy of Alexandria); lost works include editions of the mathematicians Diophantus of Alexandria and Apollonius of Perge and an edition of Ptolemy's *Handy Tables*. All these were basic text editions, perhaps with some elementary explanatory additions. Claims for Hypatia's philosophical significance and originality find little support in the ancient tradition and seem incompatible with these written works. Hypatia is important, rather, as an inspirational and influential teacher and as a pagan cultural icon and martyr.

BIBLIOGRAPHY: Text of *Commentary on the Almagest* in A. Rome, ed., *Studi e Testi* 106, Rome, 1943. Beretta, G., *Ipazia d'Alessandria*, Rome, 1993; Cameron, A., and J. Long, *Barbarians and Politics at the Court of Arcadius*, Berkeley, 1993; Dzielska, M., *Hypatia of Alexandria*, tr. F. Lyra, Cambridge, MA, 1995.—*JOHN L. MOLES*

IAMBLICHUS (c. 245–325 C.E.), of Chalcis in Coele Syria. *Neoplatonist philosopher, who studied with Anatolius (possibly the Anatolius who was teacher of *Aristotelian philosophy in Alexandria) and probably with *Porphyry, founder of an influential school in Syria at Apamea or at Daphne near Antioch. Little of his extensive work survives: the first four volumes of a nine (or ten) volume compendium of *Pythagorean philosophy incorporating excerpts taken from *Plato, from *Aristotle and from *(Neo-)Pythagorean sources (*On the Pythagorean Life*; *Protrepticus*, believed to include matter from Aristotle's lost *Protrepticus*; *On General Mathematical Science*; *On Nicomachus' Introduction to Arithmetic*); and the "Reply of Abammon to Porphyry's *Letter to Anebo*," known by its Renaissance title as *On Mysteries*. Otherwise, we have access only to fragments surviving from some of Iamblichus' lost works: *On the Soul*, *On the Gods*, *On Statues*, an extensive exposition of *Chaldaean *theology, Iamblichus' letters, and, most important of all, *commentaries (which were fundamental texts in later Greek Neoplatonism) or interpretations concerning Aristotle's *Categories*, *Prior Analytics*, *De Interpretatione* and *On the Heavens*, Plato's *Timaeus*, the *Phaedrus*, *Parmenides*, and other Platonic *dialogues.

Iamblichus' pupils, including *Dexippus, Theodore of Asine, Sopater, and Aidesius, themselves founded schools and contributed to the evolution of the Neoplatonist school at Athens whose members credited Iamblichus with determining the direction taken by later Neoplatonic philosophy. His innovations include a standard school curriculum composed of texts of Aristotle and of two cycles of selected dialogues of Plato; an exegetical system for reading Plato, each dialogue considered as having a particular finality relating to the stages of the ascent of the *soul to the Good; the exploitation of *mathematical ideas in *ethics, physics, and *metaphysics ("theology"); the diversification of the Neoplatonic system of reality including possibly the introduction of "henads" subordinate to the ultimate principle; the systematic integration into *Platonism of the "theologies" of the ancients (Egyptians, Persians, Chaldaeans, Orphics, Pythagoreans), their demonology and rites, in particular Chaldaean theurgy. Previously dismissed by modern scholars as having betrayed the tradition of "Greek rationalism," Iamblichus is currently the object of reevaluation.

BIBLIOGRAPHY: Texts: Pythagorean compendium volumes edited separately by H. Pistelli, N. Festa, and L. Deubner (Teubner), Leipzig, 1888 onwards; F. Romano, *Giamblico Il Numero e il divino* (text and Italian tr.), Milan, 1995; English tr. of *Pythagorean Life* by G. Clark, Liverpool, 1989, by J. Dillon and J. Hershbell, Atlanta, 1992; French tr. of *Protrepticus* by E. des Places, Paris, 1986; *On Mysteries*, text and French tr. by E. des Places, Paris, 1966; comm. on Aristotle, fragments in B. Larsen, *Jamblique de Chalcis*, Aarhus, 1972; comm. on Plato, fragments with English tr. in J. Dillon, *Iamblichi Chalcidensis in Platonis dialogos ... fragmenta*, Leiden, 1973. Blumenthal, H., and G. Clark, eds., *The Divine Iamblichus*, Bristol, 1993; Dillon, J., ANRW 2, 36.2, 1987, 862–909; O'Meara, D., *Pythagoras Revived*, Oxford, 1989.—DOMINIC J. O'MEARA

INFINITE, The. Greek adjective *apeiros* (from which the neuter substantive *apeiron*), "unbounded," "endless," "indefinite," "infinite"; formed from *peirar* or *peras*, "limit," with alpha-privative. *Homer applies the related adjectives *apeirôn* to a crowd and to sleep (*Odyssey* 6.286) and *apeiresios* to land, people and ransom (*Iliad* 1.13).

*Anaximander was, according to *Simplicius (DK12A9), the first to treat the *apeiron* as a principle or origin (*archê*) of existing things. In view of the paucity of texts, it is difficult to decide whether "indefinite" or "unbounded" is his intended sense of the term. It appears that the *apeiron* surrounds the cosmos as a physical domain; it may thus extend limitlessly outward and at the same time not be internally differentiated according to opposites.

The *Pythagoreans headed their list of opposites, according to *Aristotle (*Met.* 1.5, 986a22–b2), with the contrast between limit (*peras*) and unlimited (*apeiron*), corresponding to that between odd and even numbers respectively. Limit was associated also with masculine and good, unlimited with feminine and bad, among other properties. The *metaphysics of this arrangement is obscure.

*Parmenides' radical conception of *being entailed that anything of which it may be predicated that "it is not" has no existence; hence the denial of *void and of becoming of every kind, since "becoming" would imply that a thing "was not" at an earlier time. The cosmos is conceived as an unchanging finite sphere "limited on every side" (DK28B8.42–44); beyond its perimeter is nothing, and infinite spatial extension is thus eliminated. *Zeno of Elea argued (e.g., in the conundrum concerning Achilles and the tortoise [DK29A26]) that if space is infinitely divisible, then any motion must involve an infinite number of prior moves, which is impossible in a finite *time. Alternatively, as in the paradox of the arrow (A27), at any individual instant no motion is possible, and hence motion is impossible in the sum of the moments. The implication, it appears, is that being is indivisible and unchangeable, as argued by Parmenides. Zeno does not seem to have addressed the issue of infinite extension. *Melissus, however, accepted the infinite extension of the void surrounding the Parmenidean cosmos; he may have seen spatial unboundedness as parallel to the temporal eternity of the universe (DK30B3). *Empedocles too described the universe as infinite (*apeirôn* [DK31B28]).

*Anaxagoras explained *change or transformation as the emergence in a substance of previously obscured elements that become dominant. He supposed, accordingly, that there is a portion of all elements in every bit of a thing, with no lower limit at which the elements may be isolated in pure form (e.g., DK59B6,11,12). This notion entails infinite divisibility and, correspondingly, infinite multiplicity or quantity. Anaxagoras appears to have believed in multiple worlds (B4), and may have held that the universe is boundless.

The *atomists *Leucippus and *Democritus proclaimed the spatial infinity of the universe (comprising both solid *matter and void on their view) and accordingly the numerical infinity of its constituent particles (DK68A37). However, they denied the infinite divisibility of matter (DK67A13; 68A48b), perhaps in response to Zeno's arguments, and held that particles of matter were irreducible because of either their hardness or their smallness. The details of Democritean minimalism remain obscure; in particular, it is uncertain whether Democritus' atoms are merely physically indivisible, in which case they would not counter Zeno's puzzles, or are indivisible in an absolute or *mathematical sense.

*Plato, in the *Timaeus* (53c–54b), posited tiny triangles as the consituent elements of the physical world; these would appear to be indivisible, an interpretation perhaps confirmed by *Aristotle's assertion in *Metaphysics* 1.9 (992a23) that Plato believed in indivisible lines. Since he knew that lines could be incommensurable, it is possible that Plato restricted indivisibility to physical entities and allowed for the infinite divisibility of mathematical or ideal magnitudes. Plato rejected the infinite extension of the universe. In the *Timaeus* he maintained that time began with the creation of the universe (38b); hence, the past does not extend infinitely.

Aristotle too denied the possibility of infinite spatial extension and accordingly concluded that the physical universe is finite (*Phys.* 1.9). Since Aristotle denied the existence of void whether inside or outside this world, an infinite universe must take the form of an infinite sensible body, but it is part of the definition of body that it is bounded by a surface. Further, an infinite body is inconsistent with the Aristotelian doctrine of natural place (*Phys.* 3.5). Thus spatial magnitudes cannot be infinite, whether actually or potentially. Time is infinite because the elements of which it is comprised (e.g., days) do not actually persist (see below, penultimate paragraph). In *Physics* 5–6, Aristotle denied the possibility of indivisible magnitudes. Aristotle argued that if motion is continuous, then an object in traversing any interval will necessarily occupy at some instant the midpoint of that interval (*Phys.* 6.1). This difficulty can be eluded only if time too is composed of indivisible instants and if objects are imagined as moving by quantum leaps: one minimum of space in a minimum of time. Aristotle further argued that a minimal entity must be partless and hence can have no edges; accordingly, minima can be in contact only as wholes to wholes (*ibid.*). Thus, minima cannot be imagined as coalescing to form a finite entity. Any spatial magnitude, such as a line, is divisible, no matter how small it is, and in this sense all intervals are infinitely divisible. They are so, however, only potentially, since actually it is impossible to divide a line an infinite number of times. With the doctrine of potential divisibility, Aristotle sought to neutralize the paradoxes proposed by Zeno (*Phys.* 6.2, 9).

It is uncertain whether or not Aristotle's arguments were directed against the atomists, but they evidently had a considerable influence on *Epicurus' reappropriation of Democritean physics. Epicurus seems to have accepted Aristotle's contention that spatial minima entail the quantization of time and motion (fr. 278 Usener—this doctrine may have been propounded by *Diodorus Cronus as well). According to Simplicius, Epicurus held that over minimal intervals an atom may be said, not to move, but to have moved (*ibid.*). Epicurus further adopted the view that minima cannot be free-standing but, like points in lines, necessarily exist only in aggregates. Consequently, Epicurus distinguished between the atom, which was physically unsplittable as a consequence of its material solidity, and the minimum or theoretically indivisible quantity (*Letter to Herodotus* 58–59). Because the minimum, however small, is finite, it can, unlike a point, serve as a unit of measure of magnitudes. Epicurus agreed with Democritus, as against Plato and Aristotle, that the universe extends infinitely, and consequently the number of atoms and of local worlds is held to be infinite (*Letter to Herodotus* 45). The number of kinds of atoms, however, is described as incomprehensible but not strictly infinite (there is, accordingly, an infinite number of atoms of any particular kind). What status incomprehensibly large magnitudes had in Epicurean theory, and what their relationship might be to the size of minima, remain unclear. The idea of quasi-infinite magnitudes was apparently raised previously by *Xenocrates, the third head of the Platonic *Academy.

The *Stoics agreed with Aristotle that there exists only one world and that it is finite (*SVF* 2.531–535). They differed, however, in acknowledging the existence of void outside this world, and held that this void is infinite in extension (*SVF* 2.503). Like Aristotle, the Stoics rejected the idea of indivisibles and maintained that both bodies and mathematical entities are divisible to infinity (*SVF* 2.482). Whether the complete fusion of bodies, as in the case of wine and water, involves infinite divisibility is unclear. In answer to Democritus' puzzle (DK68B155) about whether the surfaces produced by slicing a cone parallel to the base are equal (in which case the cone will be a cylinder) or unequal (in which case it will be step-like), *Chrysippus maintained, according to *Plutarch, that the surfaces will be "neither equal nor unequal" (*SVF* 2.489). It is possible that this and other formulations of the kind addressed the properties of limits, which the Stoics apparently considered to be incorporeal. Time too, according to the Stoics, is both infinite in extension and infinitely divisible (*SVF* 2.509).

The *Christian philosopher *Philoponus exploited Aristotle's arguments concerning the impossibility of traversing an infinite number of stages to refute Aristotle's assumption that time has no beginning. If that were the case, Philoponus contends, then the universe must have gone through an infinite number of years. In addition, each new year will increase the sum of the infinite, which is absurd (*De Aeternitate Mundi* 9–17 Rabe). The Aristotelian response, as Simplicius notes (*In Phys.* 506 Diels), is that past years exist only potentially; hence, the sum of years is not actually increased.

The mathematicians generally thought in terms of geometrical entities and hence did not construct their theorems to cover infinite magnitudes. They did, however, conceive of limiting cases. For example, *Eudoxus, a contemporary of Plato, appears to have treated the circle as a limit of the polygons inscribed within it (cf. Euclid *Elements* 12.2); subdivision of the polygonal segments is thus assumed to be in principle unlimited or inexhaustible. In their strict demonstrations, the mathematicians employed formulas of the form, "for every x there exists a y," in order to deal with indefinitely large or small quantities. In his treatise, *The Method*, *Archimedes used indivisibles as a heuristic device in mathematical proofs, but what his debt to atomistic theories may have been remains moot.

BIBLIOGRAPHY: Kretzmann, N., ed., *Infinity and Continuity in Ancient and Mediaeval Thought*, Ithaca, 1982; Mondolfo, R., *L'infinito nel pensiero dell'antichità classica*, Florence, 1956; Sorabji, R., *Time, Creation and the Continuum*, London, 1983.—*DAVID KONSTAN*

ISOCRATES (437–338 B.C.E.), of Athens. Educator, student of *Gorgias and possibly *Socrates. After a brief career writing speeches for others to deliver in the law courts, Isocrates opened an enormously successful and influential school in Athens c. 392 that was its first permanent school of higher learning. Among his students were the philosopher *Speusippus, the historian Theopompus, and politicians Timotheus, Isaeus, and Hypereides. Isocrates' writings functioned both as models for his students to emulate and as popular essays aimed at influencing current events. All of his educational writings have survived except for portions of *Against the Sophists*. A lost *Art of Rhetoric* falsely attributed to him was probably a collection of his writings rather than a separate treatise. Nine letters and a small sample of speeches from his days as a speechwriter are extant as well. Isocrates is also well known for his refinement of prose composition using long and involved periodic sentences.

Though history would enshrine him as a great teacher of rhetoric, Isocrates described his teaching as "philosophy" and eschewed the word *rhêtorikê* throughout his writings. He described philosophical education as the cultivation of the *psuchê* (*"mind" or "soul") and as *logôn paideia, "education in discourse." In particular, Isocrates believed the purpose of higher education was to prepare students for civic leadership. "Love of wisdom" is responsible for establishing civic institutions and for educating morally responsible leaders. For Isocrates, moral and intellectual development are closely linked. He may have been the first to offer the analogy that philosophy trains the *psuchê* as gymnastics trains the body. Refusing to separate thought from expression, he believed that training his students to think and speak nobly encouraged them to *be* noble.

Isocrates believed that proper philosophical education must prepare students to contribute to the common weal through thoughtful words and deeds. He claimed that teachers of philosophy agree that the well-educated person must be able to deliberate about matters of public importance and provide wise counsel to the *polis*. Education not directed toward such ends should not be called "philosophy." Isocrates claimed, "I do not think we should give the name 'philosophy' to a study that has no immediate benefit for speaking or action; instead I call it mental exercise and preparation for philosophy" (*Antidosis* 266). Because Isocrates believed that certainty and *knowledge (*epistêmê*) are not possible on matters of social importance, he called "philosophers" only those who pursued *phronêsis*, or "practical wisdom."

The primary vehicle through which Isocrates believed students could learn *phronêsis* was through the composition of discourse concerned with important *ethical and *political themes. He disparaged forensic oratory as unimportant and self-serving. Epideictic speeches should be crafted with an eye toward the ethical lessons that can be drawn from the subject at hand. Isocrates' chief preference was for deliberative discourse concerned with the important issues of the day. Familiarity with such material, in modern terminology, conditions or socializes students to handle their own affairs in a noble way, "so that speaking and thinking well will bring together the love of wisdom and love of honor to those well-disposed toward discourse" (*Antidosis* 277).

The vast majority of Isocrates' essays are explicitly moral and political. Many of his compositions addressed actual, not hypothetical, audiences and were intended to move them toward specific actions. Isocrates urged young leaders such as Nicocles, Demonicus, and Alexander the Great to study philosophy and live just lives. Following the ill-conceived "Social War," he tried to persuade his fellow Athenians to reverse the policy of aggression. After the Thebans destroyed Plataea, Isocrates encouraged Athenians to help their long-time ally to rebuild. An opponent of long standing of the anti-Macedonian war party, he hailed the peace between Philip and Athens in 346 B.C.E. His several discourses on behalf of Panhellenic unity, in which he urged the Greek city-states to cease warring against each other, became famous in his own time and their theme remains his best-known theme. Though he was not as influential a politician as Demosthenes, Isocrates did influence Greek politics and shape public opinion far more than did many other philosophers and orators of his own time.

Historians often pit Isocrates against *Plato in a battle of rhetoric versus philosophy. An account more faithful to Isocrates' texts would view the clash as one between two competing visions of higher education in general and between two approaches to philosophy in particular.

Many of Isocrates philosophical beliefs are consistent with aspects of Deweyan pragmatism: Respect for informed opinion should replace the quest for certainty; pedagogy should be moral and aimed at civic participation; and practical is preferable to speculative philosophy.

BIBLIOGRAPHY: Texts and translations in G. Norlin and L. van Hook, eds. and trs., *Isocrates* (Loeb), Cambridge, MA, 1928–1945. Jaeger, W., *Paideia: The Ideals of Greek Culture*, vol. 3, Oxford, 1943; Mathieu, G., *Les Idées Politiques d'Isocrate*, Paris, 1925; Schiappa, E., in S. Mailloux, ed., *Rhetoric, Sophistry, Pragmatism*, Cambridge, 1994.—*EDWARD SCHIAPPA*

K

KNOWLEDGE, Classical Theories of. According to *Plato's *Phaedo*
*Socrates' predecessors had asked whether "it was blood we think with,
or air, or fire, or ... whether the brain provided our senses of hearing,
sight, and smell, which give rise to memory and opinion, and ultimately,
when memory and opinion have acquired stability, to knowledge" (96a–
b). Since accounts along these lines had been proposed by *Empedocles,
*Anaximenes, *Heraclitus, and (probably) *Alcmaeon, these inquiries can
be dated to the beginning of the fifth century B.C.E. But it was already a
commonplace of early Greek poetry that mortals "think such things as
they meet with" and, as a consequence, know hardly anything at all (cf.
Iliad 2.484–87; *Odyssey* 18.130–37, Archilochus fr. 70, Semonides fr. 1).
This "poetic pessimism" evolved into a (moderate) form of philosophical
*skepticism when *Xenophanes—and later *Democritus—argued that
our inability to observe the realities firsthand precluded our knowing
anything for certain about them (DK21B34; DK68B6–10, 117).

Xenophanes did, however, attempt to explain various natural phenomena by reference to familiar substances and forces (cf. DK21B27–33).
His assertion that "by seeking they discover (a) better" (B18.2) can be
read as a statement in support of the novel form of "inquiry" (*historiê*)
conducted by the philosopher-scientists of Miletus. Although the evidence for a scientific *Pythagoreanism dates from a later period, it is possible that the inquiry Heraclitus attributed to *Pythagoras (in DK22B129)
involved the study of numbers in connection with natural phenomena.
Heraclitus appears to distance himself from the Ionian scientific tradition
when he claims to have "inquired of himself" (B101) and (in B40) includes several Ionian inquirers among those who prove that "much

learning does not teach *nous* ("wisdom" or "understanding")." His insistence that things apparently opposed to one another are actually in agreement (B8, 51, 59–62) and that men of experience still lack knowledge (B1, 17, 34, 45, 72) appear to have been designed to provoke his audience into reflecting on nature's hidden principles of unity. At about the same time, *Parmenides composed an elaborate poetic account of an *elenchos* or critical examination of the possible ways of thinking and speaking about "what is." He concluded that all testimony of human "eye, ear, and tongue [i.e., speech]" must be repudiated (DK28B7) since reasoned argument proves that "what is" must be an eternal, motionless, fully realized, and indivisible whole (B8). In similar poetic language Empedocles promised knowledge of the "four roots of all things" (DK31B6) to all those who would listen to his divinely inspired words (B131) and pursue "pure meditation" (B110). In short, in addition to pursuing the physiological inquiries Plato mentioned, a number of presocratic thinkers claimed a special wisdom for themselves and inaugurated a tradition of inquiry through observation, reflection, and the use of reasoned argument.

*The *Sophists, Socrates, and Plato.* Toward the end of the fifth century B.C.E. sophistic teachings such as *Protagoras' view of man as "the measure of all things" (DK80B1) and *Gorgias' Parmenidean-style critique of the possibility of knowledge (DK83B3) raised a potent challenge to intellectual inquiry and brought the topics of truth, knowledge, and the reliability of the senses, into the foreground of philosophical discussion.

The Socrates of Plato's early *dialogues also disavowed knowledge, at least with respect to moral matters. These disavowals have frequently been discounted as dramatic hyperbole or the usual Socratic irony (or, more recently, as a "complex irony" involving two senses of "know"), but they may be read with complete consistency as a sincere disavowal of *wisdom* or *expert knowledge* concerning "the most important things"— the defining qualities of moral excellence. Although Socrates evidently believed that mortals could never discover nature's basic principles (cf. *Phd.* 96c; Xen. *Mem.* 1.1.18–20), he appears to have devised his distinctive question-and-answer form of *elenchos* in the hope of acquiring wisdom concerning *virtue or, failing that, at least to remove the single greatest impediment to a successful search, the false conceit that one already knew.

In the *Meno* Plato opposed the relativism of the sophists by arguing that everything called by the same name (including virtue) must possess a single common characteristic. He also rejected the sophistic paradox of inquiry by arguing that in a sense we can learn what we already know. If (as many would have assumed) our *souls exist before the present life, we must already have knowledge within us which (as demonstrated through Socrates session with Meno's slave) can be "recollected" or re-covered "from within." Recollection (or Anamnesis) is identified as a process of "reasoning out the cause" (*aitias logismôi*, 98a), and the result-ing rational account is what distinguishes knowledge from mere true opinion. The moral of Plato's discussion appears to be that inquiry, teaching, and learning are possible if (by employing Socratic rather than sophistic techniques) we activate our powers of reasoning in order to re-discover the object of our search. Here, as in the *Republic*, Plato's view is shaped in important ways by the choice of geometry as a paradigm case of knowledge.

In the *Phaedo* and *Republic* Plato explores the conditions essential to all knowledge and meaningful discourse. At the heart of his account is a distinction between Forms (roughly speaking, idealized versions of the essential natures Socrates had investigated) and appearances. The former possess the stability, reality, and truth required for discourse and knowl-edge while the latter have a determinate and knowable nature only to the extent they "imitate" or "participate in" one of these eternal, immutable, and perfect prototypes. While the contrast of the one (knowable) reality and the many (opinable) appearances reveals Plato's debt to Parmenides, the frequent use of ratios or progressions (as in the simile of the divided line) reflects Plato's fervent Pythagoreanism. Through the famous similes of sun, line, and cave of the central books of the *Republic* Plato sets out an account of the absolute perfection and invariability of the objects in the intelligible realm as well as the completely *a priori* character of the exam-ination of hypotheses (or *"dialectic") through which we come to know them. Yet even knowledge of Forms is subordinated to the more pro-found grasp of "the Good"—described only in outline as an understand-ing of how all things are ordered together in the best way (*Rep.* 6, 505; 7, 531; cf. *Phd.* 99c, *Tim.* 28a–d).

In a number of late-period works Plato raises questions related to knowledge but (except for the *Timaeus*, whose place in the order of dia-logues remains a matter of debate) the theory of Forms plays no explicit role in any of his discussions. The *Theaetetus*, for example, revisits the question of whether sense perception is knowledge; but rather than simply noting that no Form (or Idea) is ever encountered in sense experi-ence, Socrates argues at great length that sense perception reaches nei-ther existence nor truth, both hallmarks of knowledge. On occasion, however, the *Theaetetus, Sophist, Statesman,* and *Philebus* allude to a supreme science that is said to involve mastery of an entire network of relationships among various abstract ideas (or "kinds"). Here, as on some occasons in the *Republic*, the focus of Plato's interest is not knowl-edge in general, but the supreme philosophical science that can provide us with the most penetrating and comprehensive understanding of reality.

Aristotle. Aristotle sought to fashion philosophical accounts that could accommodate the views of his predecessors as well as many current popular opinions. As a result, a variety of ideas about knowledge find a home in his epistemology. In the *Metaphysics* he endorses the commonsense opinion that the senses furnish us with much knowledge (980a25–26). Sense perception is also said to yield "experience" (*empeiria*) when repeated perception enables us to detect recurring sequences of events (980a15–16; cf. the view expressed in the latter half of the *Phaedo* passage quoted above). As both Socrates and Plato had held, artists and master-craftsmen possess a special knowledge in so far as they understand the general principles of their art—a knowledge of "the why" as well as "the that" (980a24–30). We are said also to possess an intuitive form of knowledge (*nous*) of the first principles of a science (*APo.* 2.19) and, in a practical context, of the right thing to do in specific circumstances (*NE* 6, 1143b11–14). There is also the knowledge that comes into being when our minds take on the intelligible form or "the what-it-is-to-be" of the object (*DA* 3.4, 429b5ff.) and the special complex form of knowledge identified at *Posterior Analytics* 1.2 as *epistêmê apodeiktikê* or "demonstrative knowledge."

The basic principle of Aristotle's account of demonstrative knowledge harkens back to Plato's *Meno*: "We think we know each thing … strictly speaking, whenever we think we know the reason or cause (*aitia*) which accounts for it, that it is the cause, and that this could not be otherwise" (71b9–12). In addition, the premises of a syllogism productive of demonstrative knowledge must be true, relate to facts more basic than those stated in the conclusion, and be accepted by us with a greater degree of conviction than any statement derived from them (71a–72a).

In the celebrated concluding chapter of the *Posterior Analytics* Aristotle argues that the first principles of a body of scientific knowledge must be known through induction (*epagôgê*) "since that is how sense perception implants the universal," and by "intuition" (*nous*), since where there can be no further explanation there can be no *epistêmê* either. On Aristotle's view, then, Democritus, *Anaxagoras, and the other early inquirers into nature were in a sense correct: We have no option but to begin from the things "more knowable" to us (the things we meet with in sense experience) and move toward things less immediately evident to us but "more knowable in themselves" (the first principles). But in a different sense Plato was also right: All knowledge—in the sense of demonstrative knowledge—requires prior knowledge of general truths. To know a thing scientifically, we must reflect on truths we have learned from experience in order to find both the premises and conclusions we must have in order to construct our demonstrations (*APri*. 1.30, 46a).

Aristotle's claim that we can possess *nous* of first principles has often been viewed with suspicion (certainly the abrupt and eleventh-hour manner in which it makes its appearance in his account does not inspire confidence). But Aristotle was not the first to characterize knowledge of basic truths and concepts as a matter of *nous* or *noêsis* (cf. Heraclitus DK 22B40 quoted above; Pl. *Prm.* 132a). In addition, forms of the verb *noeô* had appeared earlier in the *Posterior Analytics* in connection with a process through which sense perception discloses the connections between things (cf. 71b32, 77b31, 80b12). Moreover, *nous* is characterized here in 2.19 not as a *dunamis* (or *faculty*) through whose operation we discover first principles, but rather as the *hexis* or *state* we achieve when we know them. Thus the plausibility of Aristotle's account rests mainly on whether (as claimed at 100a3–b5) our knowledge of universal principles can be adequately accounted for by reference to the capacity we possess to form general concepts through the repeated perception of particulars. But Aristotle does not help matters when he characterizes first principles as "immediately convincing in themselves" (*Top.* 1.1, 100b18) or (as above) as "more convincing than anything derived from them," thus suggesting that we might ascertain their truth independently of sense experience.

Despite the "inclusivist" spirit that shaped it, Aristotle's account of knowledge featured a number of novel ideas. For the *logical structure required for demonstrative science, he drew on his invention of the categorical syllogism. In what he characterized as his major advance over earlier thinkers (cf. *PA* 1.1, 642a), he grounded the objectivity and necessity of scientific definition and knowledge in the fixed combination of attributes that was the "what-it-is-to-be" of each kind of thing. He held also that his idea of "essential explanation" advanced the understanding of the "reason why" well beyond any point reached by previous thinkers (*Met.* 1.7, 987bff.). In place of the theory of Forms, which he considered both otiose and saddled with insuperable logical difficulties (cf. *Met.* 1.9), he attributed our knowledge of universal concepts to the soul's capacity to abstract attributes from sensible spatial magnitudes (*DA* 3.8). The separate productive or "active intellect" (430a) that helps us to acquire such knowledge represented a novel adaptation of Anaxagoras' idea of an "unmixed" cosmic *nous*.

The Legacy of Platonic and Aristotelian Accounts of Knowledge. The ancient Greek skeptics rightly saw themselves as heirs to an intellectual tradition that went back to Xenophanes, Parmenides, Democritus, and Socrates (cf. Cic., *Acad.* 1.43 ff.; D.L. 9.66; Timon frs. 59, 60, 818–820). Although Aristotle consistently rejected skepticism with regard to knowledge, in many ways Greek skepticism represents a consolidation and extension of views that appear in his writings. His discussion of the relativity of appearances in *Metaphysics* 4.5 and 4.6 foreshadows many of the skeptical "tropes" of *Aenesidemus (cf. S.E. *HP* 1). In 4.4 Aristotle anticipates (and rejects) the later skeptical argument based on an infinite regress of justification, and in 4.5 he anticipates the common later objection that the skeptic cannot live according to his teachings (cf. the *Epicurean defense of sense experience on the basis of the demands of daily life in *Lucretius 4.469).

On some accounts Plato's skepticism concerning the senses impeded the development of modern (empirical) science. But on occasion important scientific breakthroughs have resulted from just the intellectual "brainstorming" Plato advocated, and for all its "other worldly outlook" the theory of Forms did allow for *some* knowledge of the everyday world (cf. *Rep.* 7, 520c). Nevertheless, Plato's strong preference for the knowledge that lay "within" made his philosophy congenial to many early Jewish and *Christian thinkers. A mystical strain entered into the *Neoplatonic tradition when *Plotinus taught that all forms of reality emanated from an ultimate "One" that lay beyond all knowledge and being (a view inspired—though hardly implied—by the comparison of the Good and the Sun at *Republic* 6, 505–9 and the arguments for the utter simplicity of a "One" at *Parmenides* 137–42). One important legacy of this doctrine, presented by *ps.-Dionysius the Areopagite and at a later date by Nicholas of Cusa, was that God can be known only through a *via negativa*, that is, only in terms of what God is not.

Philosophers who have defended generally rationalist accounts of knowledge accept the thesis proposed by Plato (and earlier by Parmenides) that only through the exercise of our rational faculties can we ascertain the truth about reality. The influence of Plato's rationalist epistemology is especially marked in the accounts of knowledge given by St. *Augustine, by Ficino and other members of the fifteenth-century Florentine Academy, and by the Cambridge Platonists of seventeenth century England. In his "pre-critical" *Inaugural Dissertation*, Kant also defended a view along Platonic lines when he held that sense perception gives us knowledge of things as they appear while reason gives us knowledge of things-in-themselves.

Several important developments in contemporary epistemology can be linked with Plato's *Theaetetus*. The philosophy of logical atomism developed earlier in this century by Russell and Wittgenstein bears a striking resemblance to the "dream theory of knowledge" presented at 201–202 (cf. Wittgenstein's *Philosophical Investigations*, Secs. 48ff.). Theaetetus' definition of knowledge as "true belief with an account" (201d) is identified in many contemporary discussions as the prototype of the "justified true belief" analysis of "S knows that *p*." The "regress of reasons" problem raised at 209–10 also remains a live issue in epistemology, especially in connection with foundationalist views of knowledge.

The enormous influence of Aristotle's ideas on Western philosophical and scientific thought dates mainly from the twelfth century, when the Greek texts studied and introduced into Western Europe by Arabic scholars began to be made available in Latin translations.

Virtually every major feature of Aristotle's epistemology was incorporated within Aquinas' account of knowledge. Aquinas held, for example, that in cognition the mind becomes assimilated to and isomorphic with its object; that human beings acquire knowledge through sense perception as well as through a rational grasp (or *intellectus*) of self-evident and necessarily true first principles; and that *scientia* is knowledge of the truth of propositions established by means of demonstrative syllogisms. He also rejected the idea of independently existing universals in favor of the view that we acquire knowledge of universals by means of an active intellect that enables us to abstract universals from sensible particulars.

A large portion of medieval discussion of the origins and nature of knowledge assumed the *De Anima* account of our knowledge of concepts in terms of the mind's reception of the intelligible form of an object through a process of abstraction from sense perception, as well as the *Posterior Analytics* view of demonstrative knowledge as the arrangement of concepts acquired from sense experience within a larger syllogistic structure. The form of medieval *Aristotelianism known as scholasticism relied more on abstract (often abstruse) argument and on the authority of the words of Aristotle himself than on any lessons that might be learned from experience. But there was also an important empirical strain in the later Aristotelian tradition reflecting Aristotle's own interest in the study of nature (e.g., William Harvey, whose *De Motu Cordis* marks the emergence of modern physiology, was a product of the Aristotelian school at Padua). Although Aristotle's scientific views were a frequent target of criticism for Renaissance philosophers and scientists, new scientific theories were commonly presented and defended within the framework provided by Aristotle's conception of demonstrative knowledge.

Aristotle's view of scientific explanation as syllogistic demonstration by means of the middle term has long since given way to more plausible accounts of the character of scientific theorizing. The development in this century of formal logical systems of vastly greater scope and flexibility has also reduced his doctrine of the syllogism to mainly historical interest. But we owe to Aristotle our basic conception of the sciences as organized bodies of knowledge differentiated by their special domains of inquiry and explanatory principles. Aristotle's accounts of moral knowledge and training are also still relevant to issues in contemporary moral philosophy and psychology.

BIBLIOGRAPHY: Barnes, J., M. Schofield, and R. Sorabji, eds., *Articles on Aristotle 1: Science*, London, 1975; Everson, S., ed., *Companions to Ancient Thought 1: Epistemology*, Cambridge, 1990; Irwin, T., *Aristotle's First Principles*, Oxford, 1988; Lear, J., *Aristotle: The Desire to Understand*, Cambridge, 1988; Lesher, J., *OSAP* 12, 1994, 1–34; Reeve, C., *Socrates in the Apology*, Indianapolis/Cambridge, 1989; White, N., *Plato on Knowledge and Reality*, Indianapolis, 1976.—*J. H. LESHER*

L

LACYDES (3rd cent. B.C.E., d. 206/5), of Cyrene. *Academic *skeptic. Lacydes succeeded *Arcesilaus as scholarch of the Academy in 241/40 B.C.E. Ancient testimony betrays some confusion about how long he retained this position, however. This seems to be because Lacydes entrusted his responsibilities to his fellow Academics, Telecles and Evander, during his lifetime, perhaps because of poor health. In any case, Academic tradition holds that the succession passed through Evander to Hegesinus, who was in turn succeeded by *Carneades.

The oldest and most informative testimonies make no mention of any books by Lacydes, but a much later report of questionable reliability speaks of works on philosophy and nature. No information bearing directly on Lacydes' philosophical views and activities has come down to us. The bulk of the testimony we have consists of a comic anecdote, which is not without philosophical interest, however. In the story, Lacydes is first led to embrace the skeptical philosophy of Arcesilaus and avow the incomprehensibility of all things by his slaves, who secretly pilfer household stores that he believes secure. Then, tricked by easily detected tampering with the seals on the storeroom's doors into maintaining that he knows them to have been altered, Lacydes is confronted by the slaves with his own skeptical position. In the end, he is driven to acknowledge that philosophy is one thing, life another. The anecdote thus belongs to the ancient genre of stories intended to illustrate the incompatibility between the skeptic's philosophical views and his actions. If, as has been suggested, it goes back to a contemporary comedy or satire, it shows that the Academy was already identified in the public's eye with skepticism in Lacydes' time.

In view of the apparent modesty of Lacydes' achievements, it is surprising to find him credited with founding the New Academy, an honor that is usually reserved for Arcesilaus, who is almost certainly responsible for all that is distinctive and original about the Academy's philosophy in this period. Scholars have speculated that he was viewed as the founder of a school because views that had belonged to Arcesilaus became the views of the Academy under his leadership.

BIBLIOGRAPHY: Texts in H. J. Mette, *Lustrum* 27, 1985, 39–148, 39–51. Capelle, W., "Lakydes," in *RE* 1.12, cols. 530–34; Goedeckemeyer, A., *Die Geschichte des griechischen Skeptizismus*, Leipzig, 1905, 46ff.—*JAMES ALLEN*

LEUCIPPUS (fl. c. 435 B.C.E.), of Miletus (or Elea or Abdera). *Atomist philosopher. The teacher (or at least elder colleague) of *Democritus at Abdera, Leucippus seems to deserve the title "the father of atomism" more than Democritus, though their respective contributions to the Abderite philosophy cannot be determined with certainty. Having allegedly studied *Eleatic philosophy, he broke with the Eleatics in teaching that not-being (i.e., an *infinite *void) exists no less than *being, that being is not a unity, but an infinite plurality of indivisible bodies, and that these "atoms" are eternally moving and colliding in the void. This permitted him to explain how perceptible things can come into being (by the aggregation of atoms) and can undergo qualitative alteration (by the rearrangement of atoms) while yet conceding to the Eleatics that what *really* exists can do neither. It also permitted him to explain the existence of an infinite number of transitory worlds, each arising, without any maker, when atoms form a vortex that sorts them like to like. All this was presumably explained in *The Great World-order*, attributed to Leucippus by *Theophrastus (though to Democritus by others). He also wrote *On *Mind*, whence comes his only surviving fragment (DK67B2): "Nothing comes into being at random, but everything for a reason and by necessity." Democritus was more prolific, and fuller on certain matters (most notably, *ethics, about which Leucippus seems to have said little or nothing), but otherwise seems to have followed Leucippus, breaking with him only on minor points (e.g., in denying that the sun is farther away than the stars).

See also DEMOCRITUS and bibliography there.

BIBLIOGRAPHY: Texts in DK67. Bailey, C., *The Greek Atomists and Epicurus*, Oxford, 1928.—*JEFFREY S. PURINTON*

LOGIC is the theoretical study of logical consequence. One statement is said to be a consequence of a group of others if it is impossible for that statement to be false and all the statements in that group true. An argument is said to be *valid* if its conclusion is a consequence of its premises. A statement, or proposition, is (approximately) a sentence capable of being true or false; thus, a theory of logical consequence requires a theory of statements and an account of what makes them *true* and *false*. Logic studies validity by determining what *forms* of argument are valid (and so valid in virtue of their form); a logical theory therefore rests on a theory of the logical forms of statements and arguments. Other concepts important to logical theory are *proof* or *demonstration* (an argument that establishes or explains some truth), *modal* concepts (possibility, impossibility, necessity), and *definition*. From *Aristotle forward, Greek logical theorists addressed all these topics with considerable sophistication.

Early history. As good a candidate as any for the title "earliest logical inquirer" is *Zeno of Elea (mid-5th cent.), who attacked *Parmenides' detractors by deducing contradictions from their own premises; Aristotle counted him as the founder of *dialectic, probably for this reason. *Socrates' practice of refutation has much the same structure, despite its different purpose. Aristotle credits Socrates with two innovations: *inductive arguments* (inferring a generalization from a series of its instances) and *universal definitions*. The latter may mean just that he argued about definitions, but it may also mean that he developed logical procedures for testing them. Many sophists developed paradoxical or ingenious arguments (see, e.g., *DISSOI LOGOI*). However, there is little indication of logical theorizing.

Plato. Though Plato offers no real logical theory, his *dialogues contain many discussions of very general principles that might be called logical; his argumentative practice is highly sophisticated, and he often discusses the validity or invalidity of an argument itself (see, e.g., the appearance of a form of the principle of noncontradiction in *Republic* 4 and such passages as *Euthyphro* 10–11). He introduces or borrows (e.g., from *mathematics) some technical terminology, such as "quality" (*poiotês*), "noun" (*onoma*), "verb" (*rhêma*), "hypothesis." A theory of truth for predications is sketched in *Sophist* 262–263; some have seen the nucleus of Aristotle's syllogistic in *Phaedo* 103–105. Definition was a particular concern of Plato's, and a method of Division for discovering definitions appears in *Sophist* (independent evidence confirms the importance of defining to the *Academy).

Aristotle. It was Plato's student Aristotle who first produced a true logical theory. At its basis is a theory of the bearers of truth, which are *declarative expressions* (*logoi apophantikoi*) or simply *propositions* (*protaseis*). A single proposition consists of a *predicate* that is either affirmed or denied of a *subject*, for example, "Socrates is seated" affirms "is seated" of the subject Socrates. He distinguishes such individual predications from *universal* ones having general terms as their subjects, for example, "Humans are animals." Universal predications may be *universal* (*katholou, kata pantos*), *particular*, or *indefinite* (Aristotle sometimes treats the last as in effect particular). *On Interpretation* discusses relations among such "categorical" (the term is not Aristotle's) propositions: "Every A is B" and "Some A is not B" are contradictories (exactly one of them must be true); likewise "No A is B" and "Some A is B."

Aristotle's *Prior Analytics* contains the first theory of validity. He defines a *deduction* or *syllogism* as "an argument in which, some things being supposed, something different from the things supposed follows of necessity because of their being so" (24b18–20; cf. *Top.* 100a20–22). This comes close to a general definition of validity (though it requires that an argument have more than one premise and that the conclusion be different from every premise). Aristotle begins by considering combinations of two categorical premises sharing one term, classifying the combinations into three *figures* according as the shared term (the *middle*) is subject of one and predicate of the other (*first figure*), predicate of both (*second figure*), or subject of both (*third figure*). For each combination, he either shows a conclusion will follow for any premises of that form or shows, by ingenious counterexamples, that no form of conclusion always follows.

To show that conclusions follow, he uses a procedure of *reducing* (*anagein*) one argument to another. This consists of constructing a series of steps from the premises in question to a premise pair already known to yield a conclusion, which is thereby shown to follow from the original pair. At each step, Aristotle relies on *conversion* (developed in *APri.* 1.2): The *converse* of a categorical proposition is what results when its subject and predicate are interchanged, and Aristotle shows (*APri.* 1.2) that "No A is B" and "Some A is B" entail their respective converses "No B is A" and "Some B is A," while "Every A is B" entails its partial converse "Some B is A." The four valid forms of the first figure are taken as "perfect" or "complete" deductions not in need of proof; other concludent premise pairs give "incomplete" or "potential" deductions that are "completed" by the reduction process. In his exposition of this theory (called the "syllogistic" by later writers), Aristotle borrows the device of using letters from Greek mathematics so as to give fully general proofs.

The syllogistic is a remarkable achievement itself, but Aristotle carries it still further. In *APri.* 1.7, he shows that a simpler system is possible that dispenses with two of the four first-figure forms by reducing them to the others; this is a striking anticipation of modern metalogical investigations. It has also been argued (Smiley) that he undertook to prove the completeness of his system (in the modern metalogical sense) in *APri.* 1.23. The latter part of *APri.* 1 is largely concerned with showing that every valid argument whatever can be shown to be valid using only the methods of the syllogistic (this often requires developing ways to transform other arguments into appropriate categorical form).

In *APri.* 1.8–22, Aristotle adds a theory of propositions qualified with "necessarily," "possibly," and the like. The resulting *modal syllogistic* (not Aristotle's term) is far less satisfactory: Some modern interpreters have attempted to make sense of his results, but a larger number try to explain what they take to be his errors or confusions. Many scholars think this is a later addition to the *Prior Analytics*, perhaps never brought to perfection.

The *Prior Analytics* claims that the syllogistic is the general theory of validity for all kinds of argument; in other treatises, Aristotle explores the special properties of those varieties. The *Posterior Analytics* examines *demonstration* (*apodeixis*) or scientific proof: A demonstration is an argument that produces or constitutes scientific knowledge (the details belong to *epistemology, not logic).

In the *Topics*, Aristotle presents a method for *dialectical* argument, that is, disputation (see DIALECTIC). Despite his frequent declarations that there is only one correct account of validity, applicable to scientific as well as dialectical arguments, scholars have often noted that the *Topics* seems to know nothing of the syllogistic; it has frequently been concluded that this treatise was written before the syllogistic was developed and rests on some earlier logical theory. (Such developmental claims should be regarded with caution, however.) *On Sophistical Refutations,* which is really the last section of the *Topics*), discusses fallacies, that is, arguments that appear to be valid but are not or that have misleading premises, diagnosing the sources of their deceptive character. Finally, the *Rhetoric* says that the *rhetorical art is composed of a grafting together of dialectic and a theory of character-types (*Rhet.* 2.23 contains much material from the *Topics* in condensed form).

The *commentators grouped *On Interpretation,* the *Analytics, Topics,* and *On Sophistical Refutations* together as Aristotle's logical works under the title *Organon* ("instrument"). The first treatise of the *Organon* was the *Categories,* which says little about inference but does discuss and elaborate some of the classificatory apparatus used in the *Topics* (some think the correct title of the treatise should be *Introductory Material for the Topics*). Its most celebrated doctrine, the theory of *categories* (also found in *Top.* 1.9), is better discussed under Aristotle's *metaphysics. See ARISTOTLE.

*Megarian, *Dialectical Schools.* An independent line of investigation into argumentation descended from *Euclides of Megara (c. 435–c. 365 B.C.E.), a *Socratic who may also have been influenced by Parmenides. His pupil *Eubulides is credited with discovering a number of logical puzzles, some of which remain troublesome today (the Liar, the Sorites). His student Apollonius taught *Diodorus Cronus (d. c. 284), a gifted and influential logician. Within Diodorus' circle (the "dialectical," i.e., logical, school), there was intense interest in *conditional* propositions (of the form "If A, B"). They were agreed that a "sound" (*hugies*) conditional is one in which the consequent follows from the antecedent, but they differed about the definiton of "follows from." Diodorus said that a conditional "If A, B" is sound if it neither was nor is possible for A to be true and B false; his student *Philo said that "If A, B" is sound if it is not the case that A is true and B false. Diodorus' logical concerns were partly motivated by arguments for determinism. His own "Master Argument" first sought to establish that three propositions are mutually inconsistent: (i) all past truths are necessary; (ii) the impossible does not follow from the possible; (iii) something is possible which neither is nor will be true. Diodorus himself accepted (i) and (ii) and rejected (iii), leading to a definition of the possible as that which either is or will be true; since it follows that whatever will not be true is impossible, this comes very close to determinism.

Aristotle responds to what is probably an ancestor of the "Master" in *De Interpretatione* 9: If every proposition must at any time be either true or false and if every past truth is necessary, then a past utterance of a proposition about the future must now be either necessarily true or necessarily false; therefore, nothing is possible but what happens. To avoid this conclusion, which he rejects, Aristotle imposes some constraint on the principle of Bivalence (every proposition is either true or false) for future propositions; scholars differ widely about just what that is, however, and about the nature of his response.

Stoic Logic. *Zeno of Citium (334–262 B.C.E.), the founder of the Stoic school, learned logic from Diodorus; *Chrysippus (c. 280–c. 206), the "second founder" of Stoicism, became the most celebrated logician of the Hellenistic period. Unfortunately, no Stoic logical treatise has survived, and we must rely on fragmentary reports from often hostile sources (*Sextus Empiricus, the Aristotelian commentators). Even with these handicaps, Stoic logic clearly shows itself as a highly sophisticated system.

The bearer of truth of falsehood was the *proposition* (*axiôma*), which the Stoics distinguished from speech, a sentence, or a thought: A proposition is a "sayable" (*lekton*), defined as that which barbarians who hear a (Greek) sentence fail to grasp. Propositions are divided into *simple* and *nonsimple*: the nonsimple are composed of one or more propositions joined by a *connective* (*sundesmos*). Different connectives produce different types of non-simple propositions: "and" produces conjunction (*sumpeplegmenon*), "or" (*êtoi*) a *disjunction* (*diezeugmenon*), "if" a conditional. The status of negations is not fully clear: formed with "not" (the Stoics preferred *ouchi*, which can negate any sentence as a prefix) they would appear to be non-simple, and the Stoic indemonstrables (see below) treat negation on a par with conjunction and disjunction, though the sources never count them among the types of non-simple proposition. Conjunction and disjunction are truth-functional, corresponding to modern conjunction and exclusive disjunction. Conditionals were generally not treated truth-functionally; Chrysippus defined a sound conditional as one the antecedent of which "conflicts" (is inconsistent) with the denial of its consequent.

An argument is a system of premises (*lêmmata*) and a conclusion (*epiphora*). It is *concludent* (*perantikos, sunaktikos*) if the conditional having the conjunction of its premises as antecedent and its conclusion as consequent is sound (thus, there is a close link between the definition of soundness for conditionals and the account of validity). The Stoics held that the validity of any valid argument could be demonstrated by reducing it to five *indemonstrable* argument forms using four "basic rules" (*themata*). Our information about these is very fragmentary; the five indemonstrables are known, but only one of the four basic rules is preserved (though plausible guesses have been made about the others), and we have a scrap or two illustrating a reduction. It does appear that they developed something approaching a modern natural-deduction system for propositional logic.

Little is known about Stoic views on predication. The Stoics criticized Aristotle's syllogistic as resting on a wrong construal of categorical sentences: They held that "every human is mortal" should be analyzed as "If something is human, it is mortal" (a close parallel to the analysis of modern logic).

The renaissance of the *Peripatetic school after *Andronicus and the declining interest in Stoic logic even among the Stoics gave Aristotle's logic a new prominence but led to (or intensified) a controversy between Stoic and Peripatetic logic that sometimes appears based on misunderstanding: To modern interpreters, Stoic propositional logic and Peripatetic logic are complementary rather than rival theories. In fact, later Greek and Latin handbooks of logic draw on both traditions, treating Aristotelian figured arguments as one variety ("categorical") of syllogism, Stoic-style propositional arguments as another ("hypothetical"); see, for example, *Galen's *Introduction to Logic* (*Eisagôgê Dialektikê*). The interest in metalogic so prominent in Aristotle and the early Stoics disappears; logic becomes merely an adjunct to the study of rhetoric and philosophy.

BIBLIOGRAPHY: Ackrill, J., *Aristotle's Categories and De Interpretatione*, Oxford, 1961; Barnes, J., *Aristotle's Posterior Analytics*,[2] Oxford, 1994; Brunschwig, J., ed., *Les Stoiciens et leur logique*, Paris, 1978; Corcoran, J., *AGP* 1973; Döring, K., *Die Megariker*, Amsterdam, 1972; Frede, M., *Die Stoische Logik*, Göttingen, 1974; Gould, J., *The Philosophy of Chrysippus*, Leiden, 1970; Hintikka, J., *Time and Neces-*

sity, Oxford, 1973; LS §§ 31–38; Lukasiewicz, J., *Aristotle's Syllogistic from the Standpoint of Modern Formal Logic*,[2] Oxford, 1957; Kneale, W. and M., *The Development of Logic*, Oxford, 1978; McCall, S., *Aristotle's Modal Syllogisms*, Amsterdam, 1963; Mates, B., *Stoic Logic*, Berkeley, 1961; Mueller, I., in J. M. Rist, ed., *The Stoics*, Berkeley, 1978, 1–26; Patzig, G., *Aristotle's Theory of the Syllogism*, Dordrecht, 1968; Schuhl, P.-M., *Le dominateur et les possibles*, Paris, 1961; Smiley, T., *AP* 14, 1994, 25–38; Smith, R., *Aristotle's Prior Analytics*, Indianapolis, 1989.—ROBIN SMITH

LOGOS. The term *logos* covers a very broad field of meaning. Generally it means "word," "speech," and the contents of speech, "argument," or "account." More specific denotations include "calculation," "measure," or "proportion." In philosophical contexts it usually denotes "reason" or "rational principle." The term plays a predominant part in Greek thought, from *Heraclitus to the Church Fathers.

Heraclitus quite deliberately plays on the various meanings of *logos*. He may use it to refer to his own account or to the universal law (DK22 B1), which is "common" to all, although men do not understand it (B2; 50), and which is manifest as fixed proportions (B83), as the constant relation between opposites (e.g., B88; 111; 64; 32), or as unity behind plurality. It is a universal law as well as a creative principle that makes the world a *kosmos*, and in this sense it seems to be interchangeable with "God" (B67). It is, however, also coexistent with the physical constituent of the world, fire (B31). In fact, Heraclitus did not distinguish between the concrete and the abstract, and the "concrete" meaning is apparent in the idea that man literally inhales the divine *logos* when awake (B26; A16).

In Heraclitus *logos* comes near to meaning "rational thought" or "argument," and in general the concept is often contrasted with *mythos*, a type of narrative that does not call for argument. During the early development of *rhetoric the *sophists analyzed *logoi*, here understood as "arguments," as part of their general preoccupation with the effects of language. The preoccupation tended to lead to relativism ("making the weaker cause the stronger"), against which *Plato reacted with such vehemence.

Plato and *Aristotle do not use *logos* as a technical term in any strict sense, but their use nevertheless has significant philosophical implications. The Platonic *dialogues all but personify *logos* as the argument leading the interlocutors wherever it will (*Tht.* 191a; *Prt.* 333c). A true *logos*, however, has to be an organic whole (*Phdr.* 264c), adapted to its audience; but true *logos* and true philosophy coincide, being reflections of the true structure of reality.

More theoretically Plato analyzes *logos* as argument or language. In the *Phaedo* (99dff.) *logoi* are regarded as better images of reality than are physical objects, because universals (ideas) are reflected in *logoi*. The

Cratylus is dedicated to the character and status of language on the basis of the sophistic question whether language exists by nature or by convention. Its conclusion seems to be that language should be regarded both as a closed system of signs and as a reflection of a prelinguistic content, transcending language proper. Further, for Plato *logos* is a necessary but not a sufficient condition for knowledge. *Socrates' interlocutors have to "render an account" (*logon didonai*) of their alleged insight (*La.* 187e; *Phd.* 95d), and in the *Meno* knowledge is stated to be true belief accompanied by an account (*logismos*). This does not mean, however, that *logos* by itself justifies true belief (98a; cf. *Tht.* 201cff.). The idea of *logos* as a condition for knowledge is elaborated in the *Seventh Letter* (342aff.).

In Aristotle, too, *logos* may signify language, argument, or, simply, reason. It may mean "definition" or "formula," but in a broader sense than the more technical *horismos*. Often Aristotle distinguishes between priority in definition (*logos*), in knowledge, or in time (*Met.* 1028a32ff.) or between a conceptual or theoretical point of view (*logikôs*) and one which refers to observable facts (1029b13ff.; 1072a22, *Phys.* 204b4). Thus form is conceptually "separate" (*logôi chôriston*), while in the physical world it coexists with matter (*Met.* 1042a29). Following Plato (*Soph.* 261cff.) Aristotle analyzes *logos* ("sentence") as a complex unity of meaningful parts (*Int.* 16b26ff.).

For the *Stoics, the concept of *logos* is of cardinal importance. *Logos* is the principle that governs the world, making it a rational unity, and sets the moral law for men. Man participates in *logos*, but human *logos* is imperfect, whereas the divine *logos* is a universal principle, immanent in nature as a whole. Hence, the concept is operative on two levels—the divine and the human—and this tension the Stoics traced back to Heraclitus, whom they in several respects considered their spiritual ancestor.

Stoic *epistemology is based on a representative theory of perception. A cognitive presentation (*phantasia katalêptikê*) is accepted by assent (*sunkatathesis*, D.L. 7.45ff.; S.E. *M* 3.397ff.), and the further activity of reason or *logos* consists in the formation and application of concepts. Along with *phantasiai katalêptikai*, right reason or coherence, *orthos logos* (D.L. 7.54) is mentioned as a criterion of truth. Human reason reflects divine reason; and insofar as man is able to understand nature as one coherent system, he has made the world his own "possession" (*oikeiôsis*, Cic. *Acad.* 2.38).

The linguistic expression of human reason is a statement (*logos*). According to Stoic semantics (D.L. 7.62) the meaning of the linguistic sign, the "sayable," is incorporeal, already subsisting in the corporeal presentation (S.E. *M* 8.70). *Logos* is an articulated meaningful utterance. A *logos* is uttered, what is meant (*to lekton*) is said (D.L. 7.57ff.). *Logic in the strict sense deals with the formal relation between *lekta*. In the last resort, however, pure formal logic is considered a rational tool for attaining knowledge of the world.

Physics is concerned with the divine *logos*, the universal law, structuring the world. According to *Chrysippus everything, however minute, happens in accordance with nature (*phusis*) and with its reason (*logos*). Though nature is one corporeal substance, one can nevertheless distinguish conceptually between two aspects: an active creative principle and a passive one, *matter (*SVF* 1, 84). *Logos* as a creative principle may be regarded from several points of view. If the physical aspect is emphasized, *logos* acts as fire (cf. Heraclitus) or as breath (*pneuma*) pervading the whole world (*SVF* 2, 1027; 473). If emphasis is laid on *logos* as governing principle, it may be called God, providence, or fate.

The world is limited in *time as well as in space. It passes through a finite course of events, predetermined by *logos* or God. In the beginning God laid down certain "seminal principles" (*logoi spermatikoi*), determining the subsequent series of events. Free will seems to be included in this causal nexus (Alexander *On Fate* 181.13ff.).

Stoic ethics implies that the moral good for man is to live in accordance with nature. The *logos* of nature is identified with the moral law, laid down by God. As a fully developed moral being, man will give his assent (*sunkatathesis*) to universal law, and he will make the world his own "possession" (*oikeiôsis*). Reason and *virtue imply each other, and at the final stage man (the "wise") has identified himself with *logos* and virtue (D.L. 7.85ff.; Cic. *Fin.* 3.16ff.).

The first century B.C.E. is marked by an eclectic fusion of *Platonic and Stoic ideas, operative into succeeding centuries. This is apparent already in *Philo of Alexandria, who welded together the Greek and Jewish traditions. According to the book of *Genesis*, interpreted *allegorically, God created the intelligible as well as the physical world, and he created man by means of the eternal *logos* (Philo *On the Creation of the World* 29; 69). *Logos* may be regarded as transcendent, coequal with God, or as a mediator between God and the world (*ibid.*, 20; 31; *On God's Immutability* 31).

The assimilation of Stoic elements to a Platonic philosophy of transcendence characterizes *Gnosticism (*Corpus Hermeticum* 1.8ff.) and *Neoplatonism. In *Plotinus the creative "power" by means of which nature or *soul—emanated from *nous*—gives structure and form to matter (*Enn.* 3.8,2 ff.; 2,16) is called *logos*. *Logos* is not a separate *hypostasis*, but in a late treatise (11ff.) it acts, so to speak, on behalf of providence, bestowing upon each man his lot and adapting everything in the world to its order.

The *Christian tradition begins with the *Gospel according to St. John*, which may have been influenced by Gnosticism. In the prologue (*John*

1.1ff.) *logos* is identified with Christ, but is also preexistent in God. In early Christian thought this idea is often brought into confrontation with the pagan tradition (see CHRISTIANITY). The doctrines of creation in *time and the incarnation were at issue, but very often the Gospel was subjected to an *interpretatio Platonica*, as in the case of Justin Martyr and *Clement of Alexandria. To Clement the incarnation was almost synonymous with God's immanence in the world (*Miscellanies* 5.1ff.; 1.17). The same attitude to the incarnation can be found in *Origen of Alexandria. In his polemics against Platonism he frequently refers to St. John's Gospel (*Against Celsus* 7. 42ff.), but he actually draws heavily on the *Middle Platonic concept of God. In Gregory of Nyssa this is adapted to a systematic Trinitarian theology (*Oratio Catechetica* 3 [*Patriologiae Graeca* 45.17]).

In a well-known passage (*Confessions* 7.9) *Augustine likewise makes use of St. John's Gospel, but for him the incarnation is to be understood literally. Christ is really the Son of God, and he is really the Word of God. In human beings the "word" (*verbum = logos*) is a vestige of the divine one, but differs radically. Mental language is a precondition for understanding the spoken word (cf. *Teacher* 9.26), and the "inner word" (*verbum mentis*) appears as the final stage in Augustine's analysis of human consciousness and self-consciousness (e.g., *Trinity* 9.11,16). To him *verbum mentis* primarily refers to man's understanding of his own self, whereas in scholastic thought the primary meaning is simply "concept."

BIBLIOGRAPHY: Armstrong, A. H., ed., *The Cambridge History of Later Greek and Early Medieval Philosophy*, Cambridge, 1967, 137–92 (Chadwick on Philo); 195–268 (Armstrong on Plotinus); Boeder, H., *Archiv für Begriffsgeschichte*, 1958, 82–112; Christensen, J., *An Essay on the Unity of Stoic Philosophy*, Copenhagen, 1962; Derbolav, J., *Platons Sprachphilosophie in Kratylos und in den späteren Schriften*, Darmstadt, 1976; Guthrie, W. K. C., *A History of Greek Philosophy*, vol. 1, Cambridge, 1962, 419–34 (on Heraclitus); vol. 3, 1969, 176–225 (on the Sophists); LS.—
KARSTEN FRIIS JOHANSEN

LUCIAN (c. 120–180 C.E.), of Samosata, in ancient Syria. Lucian was one of the most original and engaging figures of postclassical Greek culture. Although long associated with philosophy, he was not a philosopher but a *sophist, satirist and parodist who, following *Plato, the *Cynics (e.g., *Menippus), and the Old *Comic poets (e.g., *Aristophanes), took philosophers and their discourse as one of his principal subjects. He produced a large, diverse, and singular corpus, comparable in size to that of Plato. Formally the *dialogue (in both Platonic and Cynic—or Menippean—forms) dominates (thirty-six of seventy-three prose works), but there are also memorable satiric narratives, satiric *diatribes, and many lectures or critical essays in his highly variegated *oeuvre*. Lucian was taken up as a model of the witty, erudite cultural critic by the Humanists of the Renaissance and is historically significant for transmitting Cynic and *Skeptic traditions to Europe. David Hume is said to have read Lucian's comic *Dialogues of the Gods* on his deathbed.

Lucian's work is philosophically significant in at least three senses. First, he is important as a source of ostensibly "eye-witness" accounts of contemporary philosophical and religious figures like *Demonax of Cyprus, whom Lucian claimed as a teacher, or the notorious Cynic Peregrinus of Parium and the "false-prophet" Alexander of Abonoteichus, both extremely influential figures in their day and, as such, mercilessly anatomized by Lucian in satiric narratives in which *Democritus and *Epicurus provide the philosophical armature. Second, he provides a general commentary on and evaluation of the reception of classical philosophical traditions in the polyglot cultural landscape of the Roman empire. He is suspicious of the inflated value of tradition(s) in a classicizing culture. Accordingly, two works satirize the experience of "conversion" to classical philosophical traditions. Similarly, the hilarious *Philosophers for Sale!*, in which the founding fathers of Greek philosophy are auctioned off as slaves, uses parody and caricature to satirize *all* the idols of the philosophers' tribe, sparing none. The philosophical import of texts in these first two categories is more or less overt and explicit. Third, Lucian is noted for the philosophical implications of his practice as a seriocomic (*spoudogeloios*) writer of dialogue, satire, and parody, which are generally Cynical or Skeptical in tendency.

While Lucian's parodic treatment of philosophers and their discourse make him indispensable reading for any student of the history of philosophy, the value of good parody resists summary by its very form, as does a literary repertoire of over 170 characters. Lucian's own philosophical stance is consequently elusive and is never stated directly. If we consider his oeuvre as a whole, however, there are clear patterns of aversion and affinity. Lucian is attracted to the *Epicureans for their rational hedonism and critique of religious ideology; to the Cynics for their courageous practice of *parrhêsia* ("free speech")—the moral basis of satire—and their unflinchingly satiric perspective on the *ancien régime*; to the *Pyrrhonean Skeptics for their "suspension of judgment" on such questions as the value of philosophy as an activity or an institution. It makes sense, therefore, that Lucian has been of most interest to satirists (e.g., Rabelais, Jonson, Swift, Voltaire), skeptics (e.g., Hume), and highly literary thinkers of skeptical tendency (e.g., Montaigne, Diderot, Nietzsche) who do not fit easily into the history of philosophy. From Erasmus to Macaulay Lucian was regarded as "the last great master of Attic eloquence and Attic wit." In an age as awash in parody, cynicism, and religious entrepreneurs as it is alienated from its own traditions, he is finding new audiences.

BIBLIOGRAPHY: Texts and trs. in A. M. Harmon, K. Kilburn, and M. D. Macleod, eds. and trs., *Lucian: Works* (Loeb), Cambridge, MA, 1913–1917, vols. 1–8; and H. W. and F. G. Fowler, *Lucian: Works*, Oxford, 1905, vols. 1–4. Branham, R. B., *Unruly Eloquence: Lucian and the Comedy of Traditions*, Cambridge, MA, 1989; Duncan, D., *Ben Jonson and the Lucianic Tradition*, Cambridge, 1979; Jones, C. P., *Culture and Society in Lucian*, Cambridge, MA, 1986; Relihan, J. C., *Ancient Menippean Satire*, Baltimore, 1992; Robinson, C., *Lucian and His Influence in Europe*, Chapel Hill, 1979; Sloterdijk, P., *Critique of Cynical Reason*, tr. M. Eldred, London, 1988.—R. BRACHT BRANHAM

LUCRETIUS (90s–50s B.C.E.). Titus Lucretius Carus, Roman poet and *Epicurean, author of the philosophical poem *De Rerum Natura* (*On the Nature of Things*), one of the great works of Latin literature and our principal ancient source for *Epicurus' *atomic theory.

Little is known about Lucretius' life. St. Jerome, making additions to Eusebius' *Chronicle* under the year 94 B.C.E., wrote "Titus Lucretius the poet is born. After being driven mad when he drank a love potion, he wrote a number of books in between periods of insanity. *Cicero later edited them. He killed himself by his own hand during his forty-fourth year of life." Jerome's account of the dates of Lucretius' birth and death are problematic, and scholars are generally content to give approximate dates in the 90s and 50s B.C.E. The other details of Jerome's report are generally viewed with suspicion. Some have taken the stories of the love potion, insanity, and suicide as possible and partially corroborated by passages from the poem, but most dismiss the stories as anti-Epicurean polemic. Jerome's statement that Cicero "edited" the *De Rerum Natura* is also controversial. Cicero refers to Lucretius once, in a letter of 54 B.C.E.: "The poems (*poemata*) of Lucretius are as you describe, full of flashes of genius, but also great artistic craft"), but there is no agreement about what, if anything, Cicero had to do with the final editing of the poem. The *De Rerum Natura* itself provides little information about Lucretius. The poem is addressed to Memmius, probably to be identified with Gaius Memmius, Roman noble and patron of the poet Catullus, which indicates Lucretius was known in upper-class Roman society. It is likely he was from Rome, but other suggestions have been made. The poem also reveals that Lucretius was well educated in both Greek and Latin literature. We know nothing of the intellectual circles he moved in, but he is praised by Virgil at *Georgics* 2.490–492: "Happy he who was able to understand the causes of things and has cast beneath his feet all fears, relentless fate, and the shrieks of hungry hell." He is mentioned by Ovid, Statius, and others. Fragments of his poem have recently been identified among the charred papyrus rolls from the Epicurean library buried at Herculaneum during the eruption of Vesuvius in 79 C.E.

Sources and Style. De Rerum Natura is a poem composed of approximately 7,400 lines of Latin dactylic hexameter divided into six books. It is classified as didactic epic, designed to instruct and written in a high poetic style. Lucretius was influenced by many ancient writers, including *Hesiod, *Euripides, Aratus, *Thucydides, Ennius, and Cicero, but above all by Epicurus and *Empedocles. From Epicurus Lucretius received his philosophical inspiration and doctrines, and Lucretius worked closely from Epicurus' writings, most of which are now lost to us. Of particular importance was Epicurus' major work, the *Peri Phuseôs* (*On Nature*) in thirty-seven books. Lucretius' title *De Rerum Natura* is a Latin translation of Epicurus' Greek title *Peri Phuseôs*, and many details of Lucretius' exposition probably derive from Epicurus' great work. Empedocles, the Greek author of a philosophical poem also titled *On Nature*, was Lucretius' chief poetic inspiration. Epicurus had taken a dim view of writing poetry (D.L. 10.120). Empedocles provided a model of how a philosophical poem could be written. Lucretius praises Empedocles as an inspired poet (1.705–741), and Lucretius' opening of Book 1, with its invocation of Venus and mention of her opposite Mars, owes much to Empedocles' principles of Love and Strife. The *De Rerum Natura* is written in a clear, powerful style characterized by vivid imagery, alliteration, repetition, archaisms, and the occasional invention of striking new words. Lucretius presents himself as a poet embarking on a bold new venture that will assure him fame and bring *happiness and philosophical salvation to his readers.

Content. The six books of the poem fall into three groups of two: (i) Books 1 and 2 treat the nature of the atom; (ii) Books 3 and 4 the nature of the *soul; and (iii) Books 5 and 6 the nature of the world. Book 1 opens with an invocation to Venus as mother of the Roman race, generating force of nature, and personification of Epicurean pleasure and includes an address to Memmius, an attack on *religion, the setting out of philosophical principles, the existence of *void and atoms, a critique of earlier philosophers (*Heraclitus, Empedocles, *Anaxagoras), and the *infinite nature of *matter, space, and the universe. Book 2 begins with praise for Epicurean philosophy, is devoted to the motions, shapes, and characteristics of atoms, and explains the birth and death of worlds including our own. Book 3 praises Epicurus' accomplishments and sets out the nature of the soul in atomic terms, arguing that the soul is mortal and concluding with a *diatribe against the fear of death. Lucretius begins Book 4 by describing his poetic mission and then explains some *psychological matters: the nature of atomic images, their role in perception and thinking, and the processes of digestion, movement, sleeping, and dreaming. He ends with a spirited diatribe against the passion of love. Book 5 praises Epicurus as the savior of mankind, discusses the birth and growth of our world, argues against divine agency, treats the heavenly bodies, and discusses the origin and growth of life and human society on earth. Book 6, too, begins with praise for Epicurus and discusses meteorological and geological topics, including thunder and lightning, clouds and rain, earthquakes, volcanoes, magnets, and plagues. Book 6 ends with an account of the great plague at Athens based on that of the historian *Thucydides.

As this summary of contents reveals, the poem deals primarily with Epicurean physical theory. Lucretius does not provide an explicit account of Epicurean *ethical theory in the poem, but his chief purpose is ethical. He hopes to dispel the fears people have of the gods and death by providing a clear and persuasive account of how the world works in atomic terms. The poem is unfinished, although scholars disagree to what extent. Some suggest that Lucretius intended to add to the poem, fulfilling his promise at 5.155 to write more about the gods, clearing up the many repetitions found throughout the work, and perhaps ending the poem on a different note than with the account of the plague at Athens. Others have argued that the poem is substantially finished and that the repetitions and ending serve intended philosophical purposes. The *De Rerum Natura* survived the Middle Ages in only two manuscripts, but it has been very popular and influential since the Renaissance.

BIBLIOGRAPHY: Texts in C. Bailey, *Lucretius: De Rerum Natura Libri Sex*, 3 vols., Oxford, 1947; C. Giussani, *T. Lucreti Cari De Rerum Natura Libri Sex*, 4 vols., Torino, 1896–1898. Boyancé, P., *Lucrèce et l'épicurisme*, Paris, 1963; Clay, D., *Lucretius and Epicurus*, Ithaca/London, 1983; Dalzell, A., *Classical World* 66, 1972–73, 385–427; 67, 1973–74, 65–112 (bibliography); Dudley, D. R., ed., *Lucretius*, London, 1965; Gale, M., *Myth and Poetry in Lucretius*, Cambridge, 1994; Kenney, E. J., *Lucretius, Greece and Rome: New Surveys in the Classics* 11, Oxford, 1977; Segal, C., *Lucretius on Death and Anxiety*, Princeton, 1990; West, D. A., *The Imagery and Poetry of Lucretius*, Edinburgh, 1969.—*WALTER G. ENGLERT*

LYCEUM, The. The Lyceum was a large sanctuary dedicated to Apollo Lykeios ("Wolf-god") and located just outside the eastern section of the Themistoclean defence wall of Athens. The sanctuary was fitted out with public facilities for exercising, including a monumental gymnasium building provided in the time of Pericles. The site became a center for philosophical, as well as gymnastic, activity in the fifth century B.C.E. Itinerant *sophists gathered followings there, and *Socrates frequented the Lyceum to oppose their teaching and to promote his own view of philosophy. A century later, in 335 B.C.E., *Aristotle and his followers made use of the sanctuary as the site for their school, which became known as the Lyceum or the *Peripatos (after the walkway within the gymnasium complex).

Through a succession of scholars the Lyceum continued to be the site of an ongoing philosophical school until Sulla's destructive siege of Athens in 86 B.C.E., which caused major damage to both the *Academy and the Lyceum. During the Hellenistic period, after the death of Aristotle's successor *Theophrastus, the Lyceum declined in importance as a philosophical school and showed less institutional vitality than the Academy and its newer rivals, the *Stoa and the Garden. Much of the kind of philosophical work which Aristotle and Theophrastus initiated in the Lyceum at Athens went on in the new intellectual center of Alexandria, which was better funded to carry on empirical research. Invasions of Athens during the third century B.C.E. and the removal of the library of Aristotle and Theophrastus to Skepsis in the Troad may have contributed to the Lyceum's decline and to its inability to compete with the Museum and Library at Alexandria.

See also GYMNASIUM, PERIPATETIC SCHOOL, ACADEMY.

BIBLIOGRAPHY: Brink, K. O., "Peripatos," in *RE* suppl. 7, cols. 899–949; Lynch, J. P., *Aristotle's School: A Study of a Greek Educational Institution*, Berkeley, 1972; Ostwald, M., and J. P. Lynch, in D. M. Lewis, J. Boardman, S. Hornblower, and M. Ostwald, eds., *The Cambridge Ancient History*, vol. 6, *The Fourth Century*,[2] Cambridge, 1994, ch. 12a, 592–633.—*JOHN PATRICK LYNCH*

LYCO (c. 300–c. 225 B.C.E.), from the Troad. Head of the *Lyceum after *Strato, whose will designated him successor. Wealthy and worldly, Lyco was a popular teacher, attracted major benefactions, and directed the school for forty-four years. *Aristo of Ceos, a favorite student, probably succeeded him. Lyco was also noted for athletic prowess, lavish feasts, and political service to Athens. His bombastic style elicited the nickname "Glyco" ("Sugar"). His forte was moral education, not theory or research, and the Lyceum waned philosophically under his direction. Anecdotes and anthologies exhibit his flair for stylish moralizing, but no book titles are recorded; and, apart from his will, only a lurid tableau of drunkards and two fragments on *ethical theory survive. He characterized happiness as "true joy"; despite the semblance of hedonism, he probably meant to defend *Aristotelian doctrine in *Stoic terms, since "joy" is a Stoic technical term for the rational satisfaction caused by genuine good and experienced only by the *virtuous.

BIBLIOGRAPHY: Texts in Wehrli 6.—*STEPHEN A. WHITE*

M

MANICHAEANISM, historically, is the religion founded by the Parthian theosophist Mani (216–276 C.E.), once thought merely to have superadded a *Gnostic-*Christian mythology of his own to the native dualism characteristic of Iranian religion. Discovery of new texts in the present century has made the picture much more complex, and Lieu's 1992 survey does much to bring the general reader abreast of these. Mani was not interested in the philosophical implications of his "Manichaean" dualism (which was more absolute than most Gnostic or Zoroastrian versions; thus the adjective has become a sobriquet for good-evil dualism in general) but in the elaboration of his fantastic mythology of the war of darkness and light and the battles of various heavenly and demonic beings. By these struggles the seeds of light, which he called the "suffering Jesus" (Latin *Jesus patibilis*), came to be entrapped in living entities, men, animals, and plants, in this demonically created cosmos and must be released to their heavenly origin by the efforts of believers. At the end of this struggle the two kingdoms will be forever separate. A class of Elect observed the full rigorous austerities, including complete abstinence from sex, necessitated by the religion's hatred and suspicion of the material world, helped by ordinary believers (Hearers) under milder discipline who prepared their vegetarian food (its digestion by an Elect released the seeds of light in the food to the kingdom of light they came from); and they served as energetic apostles of the doctrine to East and West. Their success was so great that their sects persisted in India and China through the Middle Ages, though they were as energetically disliked and persecuted by Hindus, Buddhists, and Taoists as by the Christians and Moslems of the West. In the Roman Empire they had great initial successes against Christianity in the fourth century. Their pointed criticisms of the Old Testament (which they despised even more than the Gnostics as an immoral production of the god of this world) and the evil of this world, and their rigorous austerities, which outbid those of the orthodox, made them very effective. Indeed, their main place in Western philosophical history is due to the hostility of St. *Augustine, who spent nine years as a Hearer before becoming disillusioned and being converted to orthodoxy. Typical arguments against them are set out in *Confessions* 3–5. He remained an implacable opponent of the sect throughout his orthodox life. On the other hand his own doctrines, particularly his Old Testament criticism and his dark emphasis on original sin and predestination, show that the influence of their austere and hopeless view of this world never entirely left him.

Orthodox persecution, both in Eastern and Western Christianity, and the equal hostility aroused by the sect in the Moslems effectively marginalized Manichaeanism properly so-called by the early Middle Ages. But "Manichaean"—because of St. Augustine's powerful influence—was the common term of opprobrium for every strictly dualist or even more mildly Gnostic heresy that arose in the Middle Ages. In the East, the most important were the Paulicians in Bulgaria and the Bogomils, whose influence was felt throughout the Byzantine world and in Russia, and in the West the Cathars and Albigenses of France, wiped out with horrific persecutions lasting from 1208 to 1330. The persistence of Manichaean dualism in the Christian world had as its most striking result in orthodox thought a strict limitation of obsession with the evil of this world, the encouragement of what affirmation theologians thought possible of its goodness as God's work, and the finding by theologians from Augustine onwards of antidualist solutions to the problem of evil.

BIBLIOGRAPHY: Brown, P., *Augustine of Hippo*, Berkeley/Los Angeles, 1967, chs. 4–5; Lieu, S. N. C., *Manichaeanism*,[2] Tübingen, 1992; Runciman, S., *The Medieval Manichee*, Cambridge, 1948.—*DAVID ARMSTRONG*

MANILIUS, Marcus (1st cent. C.E.), of Italy. Latin didactic poet, author of the *Astronomica*, the oldest surviving complete work on astrology. Apart from his poem in five books, nothing is known about his life: Books 1 and 2, extolling the greatness of Augustus Caesar, were written while that emperor still lived; Book 4 describes Libra as the sign of the reigning emperor Tiberius. The poem was in progress when Augustus died in 14 C.E. No later events are mentioned.

The *Astronomica* is a poetic treatment of *astronomy and astrology. Book 1 treats the origin and nature of the universe (a created universe composed of the four elements) with a catalogue of stars and planets, finishing with a poetically impressive passage on the dire influence of comets. Book 2, after a preface on Manilius' predecessors in didactic poetry and on the doctrines of *Stoicism, lists the influences of the zodiacal signs and the twelve Houses. Book 3 lists astrologically significant points on the zodiac and the influences that govern the length of life. Book 4 describes the influence of each zodiacal degree, finishing with an astrological geography. Book 5 lists the extrazodiacal constellations—an excuse for poetic development of the themes suggested by each sign. The poem concludes with a description of the six stellar magnitudes, comparing the stars of differing magnitudes with the ranks of human society, a typically Stoic microcosm/macrocosm comparison.

Manilius works in the tradition of didactic poetry, including Aratus' *Phaenomena* (Stoic) and *Lucretius' *De Rerum Natura* (*Epicurean), against whom Manilius writes. Astrology was congenial to Stoicism: The world is a living organism, each part in sympathy with the other; human *souls are akin to the stars (2.115: "who can know Heaven except by the gift of Heaven?") and the most noble will return to their celestial home; Nature is arrayed in ranks like the senators, knights, and plebs of Roman society (5.733ff.); God's beneficence is revealed in the heavens as well as in moral law. Each of these doctrines occurs in Manilius. He refutes Lucretius' Epicurean teaching, most strikingly in anthropology: Lucretius postulates an evolutionary progress from cavemen to contemporary society. Manilius in contrast emphasizes that from the beginning the gods inspired wisdom and knowledge, particularly the science of the heavens.

Manilius' poem is a tour de force, especially his attempt to versify numbers, degree-coordinates, and geometrical figures. His astrological doctrines had little influence on later writers, but his poetry (particulary Book 2) has been admired and quoted since his rediscovery in the Renaissance.

BIBLIOGRAPHY: Text in A. E. Houseman, *M. Manilii Astronomicon,*[2] Cambridge, 1937. Text and tr. in G. P. Goold, *Manilius Astronomica* (Loeb), Cambridge, MA, 1977.—*MARK T. RILEY*

MARCUS AURELIUS. See AURELIUS, Antoninus Marcus.

MATHEMATICS, Earlier Greek. Our word "mathematics" is derived from the Greek word *mathêmatikos* (educated, learned), the adjectival derivative of the noun *mathêma* (subject of study), itself derived from the root of the verb *manthanein* (learn). Throughout antiquity these words retained a general sense. However, at some point the noun and adjective also acquired a more specific sense. Traditionally this more specific sense was associated with the *Pythagoreans. For contemporary readers the *locus classicus* for understanding the specific sense is the passage in *Republic* 7 in which *Socrates describes the five disciplines (*mathêmata*)—arithmetic, plane geometry, solid geometry, astronomy, and harmonics—

which potential philosopher-kings were to learn before turning to *dialectic and the ascent to the Good. In later, more scholastic discussions plane and solid geometry are combined as geometry, producing what is frequently referred to as the quadrivium: arithmetic, geometry, astronomy, and music.

Greek mathematics begins and develops along with philosophy in the sixth and fifth centuries B.C.E. The first names in the history of Greek mathematics are *Thales and *Pythagoras. In the later fifth century we begin to find people whose role in the histories of mathematics dwarfs their negligible or nonexistent role in histories of philosophy, notably Meton and Euctemon of Athens and Hippocrates and *Oenopides of Chios. This trend continues in the fourth century, when the central figures for the history of mathematics are the Pythagorean *Archytas, *Theaetetus, and *Eudoxus. The earliest extant mathematical texts date from the later fourth and third centuries.

It is generally agreed that the characteristic achievements of Greek mathematics are the development of rigorous deductive proof and the geometrical representation of the cosmos for astronomical and geographical purposes. But it is frequently supposed that other cultures provided the Greeks with data and general truths on the basis of which they developed their own theories. Less than a century ago it was standardly assumed that more or less the only sources for Greek mathematical ideas were Egyptian, but beginning in the earlier part of this century scholars have moved away from claims of Egyptian influence toward claims for the Babylonians. The discovery and translation of Babylonian clay tablets made clear that the Babylonians had reached a much higher level in mathematics than the Egyptians. The richness of this material provided a way of "explaining" what would otherwise be a Greek mathematical miracle: If Pythagoras enunciated the "Pythagorean" theorem, he got his knowledge of it from the Babylonians; if Thales predicted a solar eclipse, he did so on the basis of Babylonian records. Needless to say, such claims raise serious questions about the chronology of Babylonian accomplishments; and there are serious issues of transmission. The point of view adopted here is that there is no convincing evidence of Babylonian influence on Greek mathematics before the Hellenistic period.

Most scholars would admit the viability, if not the correctness, of this point of view in the case of astronomy. But many scholars are impressed by the fact of Babylonian knowledge of the Pythagorean theorem centuries before its alleged discoverer lived; and they seem to be even more struck by the parallels between Babylonian "algebra" and a technique fundamental to Greek geometry frequently called geometric algebra, which can be illustrated by a proposition proved by *Euclid as *Elements* 6.29:

To a given straight line [AB] to apply a parallelogram [AB'C'D] equal to a given rectilineal figure [b] and exceeding by a parallelogrammic figure [CBB'C'] similar to a given one [EFGH].

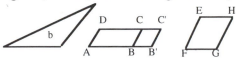

Scholars who were unaware of Babylonian "algebra" already realized that if AB and b were taken as known quantities a and b, and EFGH was taken to be a square, then BB' could be taken as the solution of the equation "$x^2+ax=b$." Many of them also assumed that 6.29 and related propositions were simply generalizations of translations of algebraic problems and propositions into a geometric notation; for them Greek geometry, a largely qualitative science, was a disguised algebra, a science of calculation and measurement. The decipherment of Babylonian problem texts provided concrete historical evidence of a calculational predecessor from which Greek geometric translation could take place. The motivation for the adoption of such an apparently cumbersome representation was provided by the Greek demand for logical rigor and perhaps by the discovery of incommensurability and the realization that not all quantities could be represented by integers and ratios between integers. It is important to see that the algebraic interpretation of Greek mathematics is an interpretation and that the hypothesis of Babylonian influence is a conjecture that can only be supported by the historical priority of the Babylonians and the (partial) intertranslatability of Babylonian and Greek mathematical materials. There doubtless always was a body of Greek calculational and metrical techniques, knowledge of which has been largely lost to us while the more abstract, theoretical mathematics so highly prized by Greek intellectuals was preserved. But the main body of Greek mathematical materials is geometric and descriptive, not metrical and calculational, and the evidence does not warrant taking those materials to be translations of a mathematics of another kind.

It would be possible to argue on the basis of testimony from later antiquity that most of the mathematics known to Euclid was known to Thales and to Pythagoras or the early Pythagoreans. But the reliability of most of that testimony has been questioned, and it cannot be said that any substantial consensus has been reached on the character and content of Greek mathematics in the early period. What follows is a concise interpretive summary of the evidence for each of the four mathematical sciences.

Geometry and the Idea of Proof. Thales is credited with the proof or discovery of quite elementary geometrical theorems. It is difficult to see why he would have even formulated some of them unless he was working with a reasonably rigorous notion of proof. Pythagoras or early Pythagoreans are credited with establishing a range of specific geometric propositions and some general accomplishments, including the construction of the five regular solids used by *Plato in the *Timaeus* and treated in Book 13 of the *Elements*, the study of irrational quantities, and geometric algebra. The first of these is now generally thought to be the work of Theaetetus in the fourth century; the discovery of incommensurability, a necessary preliminary to the notion of irrationality, is now usually placed in the last quarter of the fifth century, the age of Hippocrates of Chios, the first person to whom one can assign the use of geometric algebra with any confidence. The main evidence for Hippocrates as geometer is *Simplicius's long account (ultimately derived from *Eudemus) of his quadratures of lunules, moon-shaped figures contained by two circle circumferences. Hippocrates is also said to have been the first person to write elements of geometry, and he is associated with the method of analysis or reduction of the problem of proving a proposition to the problem of proving another. His contemporary and fellow citizen Oenopides is reported to have been concerned with two very elementary geometric constructions, again suggesting an interest in foundational matters.

Simplicius's account of Hippocrates' quadratures raises a number of questions, three of which illustrate major problems of interpreting late fifth-century mathematics.

(i) Simplicius says that Hippocrates proved the equivalent of proposition 12.2 of Euclid's *Elements*: "Circles are to one another as the squares on their diameters." Euclid provides a rigorous proof of this result, using what is called the method of exhaustion, a method of indefinitely close approximation generally thought to have been worked out by Eudoxus in the fourth century. It seems unlikely that Hippocrates could have proved 12.2 in a rigorous fashion, but it is not clear whether he simply assumed it or offered some less than rigorous proof for it.

(ii) Clearly the formulation of 12.2 rests on some notion of proportionality. Simplicius's presentation suggests that Hippocrates treated proportionality in terms of the notion of part and that his conception of proportionality was adequate for at most commensurable magnitudes. In Book 7 of the *Elements* Euclid defines proportionality for numbers in a way that could easily be extended to commensurable magnitudes. In Book 5 he gives a characterization of proportionality for what he calls magnitudes. This definition, which applies to both commensurables and incommensurables, is generally thought to be due to Eudoxus, as is the original of Book 5, in which various laws of proportionality are proved in what is perhaps the finest Greek achievement in the domain of abstract *logical deduction. Clearly the (apparently unanswerable) question of how Hippocrates dealt with proportionality is connected with the question of the time of the discovery of incommensurability and its effect on Greek mathematicians and with the general question of the rigor of late fifth-century Greek mathematics.

(iii) The question of rigor is also raised by remarks of Aristotle suggesting that Hippocrates argued fallaciously from his essentially sound quadratures of lunules to the possibility of squaring the circle. Whatever one thinks Hippocrates may have done, there can be no question that in the late fifth century thinkers of various kinds concerned themselves not only with the quadrature of the circle but also with the construction of a cube twice the size of a given one and the trisection of an arbitrary angle. The existence of these concerns suggests that more elementary problems had been solved by this time, although we have no way to tell what constituted a satisfactory solution.

It seems clear that the fundamentals of deductive method had been worked out by the end of the fifth century. For us, Greek deductive method is codified at the end of the fourth century, but there is good reason to think that a substantial amount of work was done during that century, in which at least two books of elements were written. When we try to move back before the later fifth century we are confronted with insoluble problems. There seem to be three broad interpretive choices: to suppose that Greek geometry had already taken on a deductive form in the sixth century; to suppose that it underwent a slow development based on internal mathematical and logical considerations; to suppose some external influence. Recent proponents of the last view have focussed on the hyperrational deductivism of *Parmenides, but their arguments seem more speculative than do arguments based on the questionable ancient testimonies concerning Thales and Pythagoras. The more humdrum second alternative may be our best interpretive option.

Astronomy. The situation with geometrical astronomy is much the same. The full geometrical model of the cosmos with spherical earth at the center of spherical heaven is ascribed to both Thales and Pythagoras. But the wide variations in the *cosmological speculations of the presocratic philosophers—including Thales himself—make it seem unlikely that the idea of a spherical earth in the middle of a spherical heaven found much use in the sixth and fifth centuries. There is strong evidence for the existence of the model only in the fourth century. Plato clearly relies on it in the *Timaeus*, and Eudoxus used it in developing the first geometric account of planetary motion. Aristotle makes the model a standard part of cosmological speculation.

The earliest Greek solar-lunar cycle, a correlation of lunar months with solar years, is ascribed to a very shadowy sixth-century figure, Cleostratus of Tenedos. The next ascriptions relate to the later fifth cen-

tury. The pivotal early cycle, for much of later Greek astronomy, standardly called the Metonic cycle, is due to Meton and Euctemon. There is
no clear evidence that anyone attempted to use the numbers from these
cycles in connection with geometrical astronomy until the time of Hipparchus. However, there is good evidence that Meton and Euctemon
tried to determine the occurrence of solstices observationally. Although
there are attestations of such observations as early as *Anaximander, it
seems likely that, in this case too, Greek mathematics begins to take off in
the late fifth century.

Harmonics. The beginnings of harmonics should probably be attributed to the early Pythagoreans. There is no satisfactory evidence for
an alternative account. Although the traditional story of Pythagoras's
discovery of the numerical expression of the fundamental musical concords—octave as 2:1, fifth as 3:2, and fourth as 4:3—contradicts the laws
of nature, it seems clear that these relationships were formulated as
truths by the early fifth century and represented geometrically by the
tetraktys in which the four numbers expressing the concords are seen to
sum to 10, the Pythagorean perfect number:

It also seems likely that early Pythagoreans represented the three ratios
in their lowest common numbers as 12:6, 9:6, and 8:6, and called 9 (= $\frac{12+6}{2}$)
the arithmetic mean of 12 and 6, and 8 (= $\frac{2\cdot12\cdot6}{12+6}$) their subcontrary (later
harmonic) mean. In contexts in which means are discussed the third ba-
sic mean is the geometric, the geometric mean between x and y being the
z such that x is to z as z is to y. Additions to the number of means are
credited to the Pythagorean Hippasus (early 5th cent.), Archytas, and
Eudoxus. Theaetetus developed a classification of certain "irrational"
straight lines based on the three means, a classification that is embodied
in another form in Book 10 of Euclid's *Elements*. On the basis of the form
of this book and remarks in Aristotle some scholars have credited
Theaetetus with developing the first adequate theory of proportionality
for commensurable and incommensurable quantities.

Euclid's *Sectio Canonis* uses unsatisfactory arguments to deduce the
correlations between the fundamental concords and the corresponding
ratios. The mathematically more significant part of the *Sectio* involves
certain impossibility proofs, for example, the proof that there is no such
thing as a semitone. Euclid takes for granted that any interval corresponds to a numerical ratio and that the addition and subtraction of intervals are represented by what we would call the multiplication and
division of corresponding fractions. Since the tone is the difference be-

tween a fifth and a fourth, it is represented by the ratio of 9 to 8 ($\frac{9}{8}$ being equal to $\frac{3}{2} \div \frac{4}{3}$). Euclid proves generally that the tone is not divisible into any number of equal intervals. For if it were divisible into n equal intervals one would have numbers m, m_1, m_2, ... , m_n such that 9 is to 8 as m is to m_n and m is to m_1 as m_1 is to m_2 as ... as m_{n-1} is to m_n. But the impossibility of such numbers is proved in Book 8 of the *Elements*. Euclid's reasoning—and thus deductive harmonics—can be traced back to Archytas, who (assuming genuineness of relevant fragments) is our earliest source for the doctrine of the three means and for the idea of the quadrivium and also the author of an elaborate stereometric construction of a cube twice the size of a given one. It would seem that he must have known a considerable amount of the arithmetic and geometry of Euclid's *Elements*. There is also confused evidence that *Philolaus worked with the basic ideas of mathematical harmonics, but we are left with surmise for the period prior to Philolaus.

Arithmetic. The *tetraktys* is an example of what is called a figurate number, the representation of a number as a geometrical figure. It represents 10 as a triangular number. In *Nicomachus's *Introduction to Arithmetic* and other later Pythagorean/ Platonic works we find a full-fledged development of a theory of figurate numbers in which numbers of a given shape are generated by a uniform procedure starting from 1. For example, the triangular numbers are 1, 1+2, 1+2+3, 1+2+3+4, and so on, and the squares are 1, 1+3, 1+3+5, 1+3+5+7, and so on.

There is no real trace of figurate numbers in the *Elements*, although some of Euclid's vocabulary, such as "square," may derive from them, and there is no other compelling early evidence for the use of figurate numbers. Nevertheless, the ideas in play here are usually assumed to be early Pythagorean. In the *Elements* Euclid presents arithmetic deductively, treating numbers as straight lines and addition and multiplication of numbers as concatenation of lines, so that, if the straight line AB represents the number n, 3·n is represented by any straight line 3 times as long as AB. It seems plausible to assume that Archytas already developed arithmetic deductively, but attempts to assign a deductive arithmetic to any earlier time in any specific way remain speculative.

In summary it can be said that we have direct knowledge of Greek mathematics only in the Hellenistic era and later, but the most significant interaction between Greek philosophy and mathematics appears to have occurred in the preceding period. We are able to reconstruct with varying degrees of probability some of the mathematical accomplishments of fourth-century mathematicians, notably Archytas, Theaetetus, and Eudoxus. We can also see with reasonable certainty that fundamental mathematical ideas had emerged in the later fifth century, but as we move back in time evidence becomes sparser and more controversial. However, it seems clear that the achievements of the later fifth century presuppose earlier developments. And it seems likely that these developments were internal to Greek mathematics and go back to Thales and Pythagoras in the sixth century.

BIBLIOGRAPHY: Barker A., ed., *Greek Musical Writings*, vol. 2, Cambridge, 1989; Becker, O., *Das mathematische Denken der Antike*, Göttingen, 1957; Burkert, W., *Lore and Science in Ancient Pythagoreanism*, tr. E. L. Minar, Jr., Cambridge, MA, 1972; Dicks, D. R., *Early Greek Astronomy to Aristotle*, Ithaca, 1970; Heath, T., *A History of Greek Mathematics*, 2 vols., Oxford, 1921; Neugebauer, O., *The Exact Sciences in Antiquity*,[2] Providence, 1957; van der Waerden, B. L., *Science Awakening*, tr. A. Dresden, New York, 1963.—*IAN MUELLER*

MATTER, Classical Theories of. *Aristotle probably coined the word *hulê* as a technical term for matter, the stuff that composes physical objects. He also initiated the systematic study of matter, though earlier Greek philosophy, in its search for the basic principle or principles at work in the cosmos, has much to contribute to the history of matter-theory.

The first book of Aristotle's *Physics* introduces the technical notion of matter to deal with the problem of *change. The problem, which Aristotle inherited from *Parmenides, is this: How can something come to be that was not there before? If it was not there before, it has come to be from nothing, and that is impossible. If it was there before, no coming-to-be has occurred. How, then, can anything come to be? Aristotle proposed that change involves both the replacement of something and a continuant that survives the replacement. So the emergent object is not entirely new: Something was there all along, which comes to be characterized in a new way. In nonsubstantial change (changes of quality, quantity, and place), the continuant is a physical object, which changes in its properties or location. In substantial generation, a physical object is the product of change, so something else must serve as the continuant. To account for this case, Aristotle posited matter. A new substance comes to be when matter that lacked a certain form acquires it.

Aristotle often characterizes matter as "that from which a product is generated, which is present in the product." Matter is what preexists a change, constitutes the generated product, and is left behind when the product is destroyed. Once the concept of matter is so defined, earlier Greek philosophy offers many theories of matter, though not characterized as such by their authors. In *Metaphysics* 1 Aristotle says that, of his four causes (material, formal, final, efficient), most of his predecessors recognized only the material cause. They mainly disagreed about the number and sort of materials. *Thales was the first to hold this sort of theory, and he regarded water as the single original stuff. *Anaximander, *Anaximenes, and *Heraclitus were also material monists.

Once Parmenides had challenged the possibility of change, later Presocratics proposed theories of matter that aimed to preserve change from his objections. *Empedocles with his theory of four "roots" (earth, water, air, and fire), *Anaxagoras with his theory of universal mixture, and *Democritus with his theory of *atoms and *void were among the pluralists. Though their alternatives differed, they shared a common theme. The basic materials are ungenerated and imperishable, and other things are produced through their combination or separation. The charge leveled against these proposals by *Plato and Aristotle was that they failed to give an adequate account of how materials become organized in ways that are complex and beneficial. The pluralists were content to credit complex structure to the chance interactions of the basic materials. Although modern-day science finds resonances in the scientific theories of the early pluralists, Plato and Aristotle thought that material explanations were inadequate to account for all the phenomena. They believed that complex organization required natural goals and so preferred teleological explanations to purely mechanical ones.

Perhaps Plato would have denied that he had a concept of matter in the sense under discussion. Even so, the *Timaeus* offers a mathematical account of the construction of bodies out of simpler materials. According to Timaeus, the divine Demiurge constructs the bodies of earth, water, air, and fire out of two sorts of triangles. Looking to the eternal Forms as models, he then constructs complex bodies out of these four bodies. Aristotle identified Platonic matter, not with the triangles, but with another entity discussed in the *Timaeus*, the receptacle. The receptacle was introduced as a medium for becoming, and Timaeus calls it space. Aristotle claims that Plato identified matter and space and treated the receptacle as what "participates" in Forms. The receptacle, though it has no character in its own right, takes on perceptible qualities. As a subject for properties, the receptacle resembles Aristotelian matter.

Aristotle's interpretation of Plato indicates that he attributes to matter a second role. In addition to serving as a continuant in change, Aristotelian matter is also a subject for predication. If we analyze an object, form makes the object the sort of thing that it is, whereas matter makes it the individual that it is. In some contexts at least, he treats form as responsible for an object's "suchness" and matter as responsible for its "thisness," its numerical distinctness from other things.

Since antiquity scholars have thought that Aristotle believed in prime matter, an ultimate stuff that is actually nothing but potentially everything, and that this doctrine was grounded both in his theory of change and in his theory of predication. This view of Aristotle's position is now controversial. He uses the expression *prôtê hulê* ("prime matter"), but not for an ultimate uncharacterized stuff. Some scholars have argued that he explains elemental transformation without appeal to a simpler stuff. On this view earth, water, air, and fire are his ultimate matter and are distinguished from each other by pairs of contraries (the hot, the cold, the wet, and the dry) and by their natural linear motions toward or away from the center of the cosmos. A fifth element, aether, which is imperishable, composes the superlunary sphere and has a natural circular motion.

In the Hellenistic period the *Epicureans revived atomism. Like the early atomists, the Epicureans believed that the division of matter will uncover solid, indivisible bodies, *infinite in number, which move through infinite empty space. In the course of their motion atoms collide and sometimes combine into compounds. Whereas the early atomists believed that atoms move randomly through the void, the Epicureans thought that atoms move downward through the void at equal speeds. Given this view, they needed to explain why collisions between atoms occur. They proposed that occasionally atoms swerve slightly from their course. Quite possibly they introduced uncaused atomic swerves because they thought that indeterminism at the atomic level would help to account for freedom of the will.

The rival *Stoic school advocated both materialism and determinism. Like Aristotle and unlike the atomists, they believed that matter is continuous. They posited two principles, one active (God) and one passive (indeterminate matter). Although there is some dispute even in the ancient testimony, they probably regarded the principles of corporeal bodies as themselves corporeal. The Stoics believed that God is the *logos and designing fire, an idea earlier espoused by Heraclitus. Their view about God and matter may also derive from reflection on the Demiurge as craftsman and the receptacle as recipient of qualities in Plato's *Timaeus*, and on the criterion of *being mentioned in Plato's *Sophist*—being as a power to act or to be acted upon. But unlike Plato, the Stoics were thoroughgoing materialists. Since the Stoic God is an all-pervading immanent causal principle, any object and the world as a whole can be analyzed as a composite of God and matter. Bodies are unified and differentiated by their innate *pneuma*, a blend of fire and air, which varies in degrees of tension.

The contrast between corpuscular and continuum theories of matter and between structural and functional theories, first formulated and debated on the ancient stage, has dominated the ongoing history of matter-theory.

See also CHANGE, Classical Theories of.

BIBLIOGRAPHY: Furley, D. J., *The Greek Cosmologists*, vol. 1: *The Formation of the Atomic Theory and Its Earliest Critics*, Cambridge, 1987; and also *Two Studies in the Greek Atomists*, Princeton, 1967; Gill, M. L., *Aristotle on Substance*, Princeton, 1989; McMullin, E., ed., *The Concept of Matter in Greek and Medieval Philosophy*, Notre Dame, 1963; Sorabji, R., *Matter, Space, and Motion: Theories in Antiquity and Their Sequel*, London, 1988; Toulmin, S., and J. Goodfield, *The Architecture of Matter*, London, 1962.—MARY LOUISE GILL

MAXIMUS (2nd half of the 2nd cent. C.E.), of Tyre. Orator of the Second *Sophistic who for a time lived in Rome under Commodus (180–192 C.E.). He is probably not identical with Claudius Maximus, the teacher of the later emperor Marcus *Aurelius in 152 C.E. Forty-one declamations (*Dialexeis*), popular lectures on common ethical and religious topics, are extant. Regarding artistic form as more important than logical content, he would often attack and defend the same thesis in his declamations, which included discussions of *Homer, *Socrates, *Plato, *Diogenes of Sinope, and *Epicurus. Though a self-professed *Platonist, he incorporated some *Stoic doctrines. He was not an original thinker; nevertheless, his argumentation is typical of the popular philosophy of his time.

BIBLIOGRAPHY: Texts in M. B. Trapp, *Maximus Tyrius: Dissertationes*, Stuttgart/ Leipzig, 1994; G. L. Koniaris, *Maximus Tyrius: Philosophumena—Dialexeis*, Berlin/New York, 1995. Szarmach, M., *Maximos von Tyros: Eine literarische Monographie*, Torun, 1985 (with bibliography); Trapp, M. B., *Studies in Maximus of Tyre. A Second Century Philosopher and his Nachleben, A.D. 200–1850*, Diss. Oxford, 1986.—JÜRGEN HAMMERSTAEDT

MEDICINE, Ancient Theories of. With the partial exception of *On Ancient Medicine* (and to an extent the *Epidemics*), the treatises of the *Hippocratic Corpus tend to hypothesize more or less elaborate theoretical schemes (of humors, and so on) in order to account for the functioning and disfunctioning of the human body; and in general they embody the faith, to be found elsewhere in Greek theoretical science, that the world in all its phenomenal diversity can be given a satisfying account in terms of some small stock of fundamental entities.

This faith begins to come under fire in the post-Classical period. Diocles of Carystus (fl. c. 350 B.C.E.) held that explanation is not in all cases possible: Some things simply have to be accepted as inexplicable, while explanation in terms of fundamental principles is in some cases neither appropriate nor possible. Some issues are too controversial to allow such an approach, and experience is generally a better guide to medical practice. "Explanations" are often no more than rhetorical devices to enable the theorist to make a favorable impression.

Diocles' empirical approach is echoed in the fragments of the third century B.C.E. Alexandrian physician *Herophilus. Herophilus discovered the differentiation between motor and sensory nerves and postulated, on the basis of widespread experiment on live subjects (perhaps including humans), the existence of four vital capacities. Yet he too was wary of grand theory, saying that the phenomena should be accorded fundamental importance. *Galen indeed reports that he accepted causes "only hypothetically," saying that they were by nature undiscoverable. Moreover, Galen ascribes to him a a set of structurally similar dilemmatic skeptical arguments designed to show that there can be no causes (e.g., causes must either (i) precede, (ii) succeed, or (iii) be contemporary with their effects, but none of (i)–(iii) is possible).

Herophilus's contemporary *Erasistratus argued that the alleged antecedent causes of diseases (the external influences that trigger diseases: overheating, excessive labor, refrigeration, etc.) were not really causes at all, since they were not in all cases succeeded by their supposed consequences (not everyone exposed to excessive sunlight develops a fever). Causes should be invariably correlated with their effects, and thus only the immediate causes of events are genuinely their causes (see further GALEN). He opposed the postulation of specific organic "faculties" (attraction for urine by the bladder, for example), arguing that physiological fluid dynamics relied only on the abhorrence of a vacuum. This principle he considered also responsible for the transfusion of blood from the veins (where it belonged) to the arteries (which should, he thought, properly contain only *pneuma*, the vital modification of air) across the capillaries, which he discovered (although not, of course, their function). This transfusion was brought about by excess of blood, itself brought about by immoderate ingestion of nutriment.

Serapion, one of Herophilus's pupils, established the school of medical Empiricism, building on his Herophilean inheritance. The Empiricists avoided theoretical speculation, basing their therapies on observations of pathologically significant sets of signs and symptoms and past successes in treating them. Empirical medicine consisted in building up a vast accumulation of Humean data of constant (or regular: the Empiricists did not require their concatenations to be invariable) conjunctions of empirical phenomena, on the basis of not only personal observation but also the reports of others, whose reliability was itself to be determined by empirical testing. Possible therapies might be suggested by past experience or, in cases where none was relevant, simply by inspiration or luck. Medicine grows by a long process of trial and error.

Later Empiricists invoked a process called "transition to the similar," whereby if particular cases were similar in some ways to previously recorded instances, then similar remedies might be essayed with some expectation of success. But transition was never regarded as a method of discovery; rather, it suggests possible interventions that must then be tested empirically; and some hard-line Empiricists rejected it altogether as smacking too much of reason and theory.

The Empiricists claimed that the hidden facts (if any) in virtue of which their remedies worked were forever inaccessible. The Rationalists (as their theoretical opponents came compendiously to be known) disagree about the fundamental facts, disagreements that are undecidable since there is no agreed criterion for their resolution. Moreover, knowledge of these theoretical arcana is unnecessary for successful therapy, while the Rationalists' theoretical terms merely redesignate the evident phenomena that they claim to explain. The Empiricists allow inference from evident signs to equally evident consequences, while rejecting the Rationalist claim to be able to deduce hidden causes from the observable phenomena.

But the Rationalists fought back. Asclepiades of Bithynia (fl. c. 125 B.C.E.) charged the Empiricists with inconsistency: They claim to be purely empirical and to make no unwarranted rational assumptions, yet their practice relies on their ability to classify syndromes as being similar to one another. But every case is, in some respect, *sui generis*, while different types of syndrome share irrelevant features. The Empiricist owe us an account of how to determine *relevant* similarities, but to do that requires theoretical assumptions. Even if they can evade that problem, they derive their theorems on the basis of experience of many similar cases— but how many times is many? If one is not enough, why should two be? And if two are not, why three? They are vulnerable to a soritical argument.

The Empiricists, in the person of Menodotus, their greatest practitioner of the second century C.E., reply—as recorded in Galen's treatise *On Medical Experience*—that they need no *theory* of relevance: After a while certain things strike them as being significantly similar, and that is simply part of the appearances themselves. Whether they actually are significantly similar is another matter; but empirical testing will, in the long run, distinguish useful from useless correlations. Again, they require no logical rebuttal of the sorites: After a certain time, a theorem will seem to be established. How much time will vary from case to case, being a matter of psychology rather than logic.

The picture is further complicated by the arrival in the first century C.E. of medical Methodism. Medicine, for the Methodists, was easy: There are two basic pathological conditions or "communalities," constriction and relaxation. These communalities are evident to anyone with a little training, and the proper (allopathic) treatment (styptics for relaxation, laxatives for constriction) is equally obvious. The Methodists discountenanced Empiricist evident sign-inference, employing an argument isomorphic to Erasistratus's against antecedent causes: The same phenomenal sign should invariably be succeeded by the states they indicate, but this is not the case: Empiricist semiotics is chimerical.

The differences between the schools involve their attitudes to explanation. Galen considers the case of a man bitten by a rabid dog: The Rationalist will talk of how his internal constitution has been upset by the particular power of the rabid bite; the Empiricist (who will admit antecedent causes into his syndromes, as signs of future events) will also hold the dog's particular condition therapeutically relevant, on the basis of past experience. The Methodist, however, will take no notice of the dog and simply treat the bite as an ordinary wound. Thus the schools differ not merely in their general approaches to therapy but fundamentally in their attitudes to what can and cannot be known and to what is or is not required knowledge for the successful doctor (see further GALEN).
BIBLIOGRAPHY: Frede, M., *Galen: Three Treatises on the Nature of Science*, Indianapolis, 1985; also *Essays in Ancient Philosophy*, chs. 12–15, Oxford/Minneapolis, 1985; Hankinson, R. J., *Phronesis* 32, 1987, 329–48; also in D. Furley, ed., *Routledge History of Philosophy*, vol 2: *Aristotle to Augustine*, London, 1997.—R. J. HANKINSON

MEGARIAN SCHOOL. *Euclides founded a "school" in the town of Megara, just across the isthmus from Athens, c. 400 B.C.E. It was apparently short-lived, and its history is somewhat confusing. *Diogenes Laertius (2.106) says of Euclides that "those after him were called Megarians, then *eristics, and later *dialecticians, because of their setting out their arguments in question and answer." But in 2.113 he quotes "Philippus the Megarian" to the effect that *Stilpo of Megara "drew away" several of the dialecticians to the school of Megara, and elsewhere reports various attacks on "the dialecticians" (7.163, 10.8, 10.24), and he and other ancient authors use "dialectician" as a label for *Diodorus Cronus and for *Philo the Dialectician. Thus it looks as if the label "dialecticians" in 2.106 may refer to a separate school or sect. But it does not seem likely that anyone called himself an "eristic"; this label was probably attached to certain of the Megarians because of their argumentative tendencies (see also DIALECTICAL SCHOOL).

Eubulides and Paradoxes. Even Euclides was branded an "eristic," but such labels must have come into their own in connection with Euclides' student, Eubulides, with whom a number of *sophistic paradoxes are associated: "the liar, the undetected man, Electra, the veiled man, sorites, horned one, and baldheaded man" (D.L. 2.108). These are spelled out in various places.

The "liar": "If you state that you are lying, and state the truth, you are lying" (Cic., *Acad.* 2.95).

The "undetected" and the "veiled" are presumably of the same form; the latter, it appears from *Lucian (*Vitarum Auctio* 22, where it also appears that the "Electra" is just another variant), runs: If you know your own father, and don't know the veiled person before you, but that person is your father, you both know and don't know the same person.

The "sorites" (Nemesius *De Natura Hominis* 44; see also Cic. *Acad.* 2.49; D.L. 7.82): If you take one grain of sand from a heap (*soros*), what is left is still a heap; so no matter how many grains you take one by one, the result is always a heap. The baldheaded man seems to be a variant on this.

The "horned one": "If you haven't lost something, you have it; you haven't lost horns; therefore you have horns" (D.L. 7.187).

These arguments are spelled out not in connection with Eubulides and the Megarians, but in connection with *skepticism: If they had any serious purpose among the Megarians, it may have been that of casting doubt on knowledge obtained through the senses or on discourse about matters of sense, since it appears that the Megarians were extreme monists who denied the reality of *change (see EUCLIDES and STILPO). The papyrus fragment of *Epicurus' *On Nature* 28 appears to be attempting to engage some of these arguments, and that by itself may lend them a little more weight.

Eubulides engaged in some sort of a dispute with *Aristotle; it may have turned on some of these arguments (Aristotle takes up something like the liar in *Soph. El.* 24 and 25), or on the notion of possibility (see below); unfortunately, all we hear about the dispute is *ad hominem* argument of the worst possible sort (D.L. 2.109; Aristocles, cited in Eus. *PE* 15.2,5, etc.).

Other Megarians. Diogenes (2.112) tells us that among those who came after Euclides were Clinomachus of Thurii, Ichthyas son of Metallus, and Stilpo of Megara. The first of these "was the first to write about propositions, predications, and so on," according to Diogenes; the terminology is suspiciously *Stoic. It is he who apparently gave rise to the "dialectical" school or sect (*Suda* s.v. "Socrates"). Ichthyas had a dialogue written against him by *Diogenes of Sinope (the *Cynic) (D.L. 2.112). Stilpo, the most famous of the Megarians, was either a student of Euclides or of one Thrasymachus of Corinth, an associate of Ichthyas (D.L. 2.113; Thrasymachus is also mentioned in Athenaeus 9.509c, and apparently nowhere else).

Eubulides numbered among his students the orator Demosthenes (D.L. 2.108 and elsewhere), *Alexinus of Elis, "a most contentious man, because of which he was called Elenxinus" (2.109: the pun is on the Greek for "refutation," *elenchos*), who is supposed to have argued with *Zeno of Citium, and Apollonius Cronus, the teacher of Diodorus Cronus (2.110), who taught Philo as well as his own daughters (D.L. 7.16, Clement *Miscellanies* 4, 19.121.5), and, apparently, Zeno as well (D.L. 725). All this is chronologically a bit hectic, but possible. However, the claim that Stilpo taught Bryson (who may have been his son) and that *Pyrrho of Elis studied with Bryson seems out of the question.

About the views of these people we have almost nothing. Aristotle attacks "the Megarians" in *Metaphysics* 9.3 for their denial of the distinction between actuality and potentiality; since his conception of motion involves that distinction, and potentiality always points to the possibility of change (see *Phys.* 3.1–3, *Met.* 9.1–2), if the Megarians were static monists, they would have denied that there was any such distinction.

BIBLIOGRAPHY: Texts in K. Döring, *Die Megariker: Kommentierte Sammlung der Testimonien*, Amsterdam, 1972; see also *SSR.—R. M. DANCY*

MELISSUS (5th cent. B.C.E.), of Samos. Little is known of Melissus' life. An *Eleatic philosopher and an admiral who defeated the Athenian fleet under Pericles in 441 B.C.E., he apparently wrote a single book. *Diogenes Laertius says that Melissus was the pupil of *Parmenides, but although Melissus studied and was influenced by the work of Parmenides, it is doubtful that he was his student. It is difficult to fix the chronology, but Melissus probably criticized *Anaxagoras and *Empedocles. Some of his arguments may attack *Leucippus, although the relation of Melissus to the development of Presocratic *atomism is controversial. All of the surviving fragments of Melissus are preserved in *Simplicius' *commentaries on *Aristotle's *Physics* and *De Caelo*. There is also an account of Melissus in the pseudo-Aristotelian treatise *De Melisso Xenophane Gorgia* (*MXG*).

Melissus' arguments are an exploration of what must be the case if something is. It is an open question whether he began by assuming that something is (the view of *MXG*) or argued that there must be something rather than nothing (suggested by Simplicius *in Phys.* 103.18). The extant fragments argue that what is is ungenerated and always was and always will be just what it is. Having no beginning and no end, it is thus unlimited in *time. From this Melissus further concludes that what is must be unlimited in magnitude. This last step is dubious; Melissus was castigated by Aristotle for his faulty reasoning (*Soph. El.* 168b), and it is likely that this is the argument Aristotle had in mind. The inference to unlimited magnitude is difficult to understand; Simplicius, who reports the argument, says that Melissus did not mean by "magnitude" extension in space, but rather the greatness or the perfection of its being (*in Phys.* 109.32–34). This links Melissus' argument with Parmenides' comparison of the perfection and completeness of what is with the bulk of a well-rounded sphere (DK28B43–45).

From the fact that *being is unlimited, Melissus deduces that it is one: "for if it were two, they would not be unlimited, but would have limits against each other" (B6). Here Melissus explicitly argues for the numerical monism of being, and this is an advance on Parmenides, who had said that being is one and continuous (28B8.6) but gives no argument for its numerical unity. In B7 Melissus further explores the nature of the one unlimited being. It is, he says, "eternal, unlimited, one and all alike." It neither loses anything nor becomes larger, nor can it be rearranged; it suffers neither pain nor anguish. All of these characteristics are denied to what is because of its unity: Any such change would destroy the unity of being. (The denial of pain and anguish is mysterious; both Empedocles and *Diogenes of Apollonia have been suggested as targets of the argument, but no completely satisfactory interpretation of it has yet appeared.) The denial of rearrangement is important, for it seems to undermine a possible response to Parmenides. The pluralists (Anaxagoras and Empedocles) and the atomists (Leucippus and *Democritus) argued against Parmenides that what is real does not come to be or pass away, but what seems to be generation and corruption is simply a rearrangement of beings, each of which satisfies Parmenides' requirements for what is. Melissus denies the cogency of this response. Moreover, Melissus argues that none of what is can be empty (since what is empty is nothing), thus denying the possibility of a *void, differences in density and rarity, and motion: if there is no void, what is cannot move.

In DK30B8 Melissus rejects arguments for plurality based on sense experience. "If there were a many," he says, "they would have to be as I say the One is." Yet the many of sense experience change in many ways, and are thus unlike the One; plurality is thus impossible. It has been argued that Melissus' assertion here influenced the development of ancient atomism, for each atom is like a One—although Melissus has already rejected both the void and the possibility of rearrangement of what is, two fundamental tenets of atomism. Finally, in B9, Melissus argues that the unity of being entails that what is cannot have body. This argument sits uneasily with the claim that being is unlimited in magnitude, although plausible interpretations of the two claims have been offered (see Furley and Curd).

*Plato and Aristotle treated Melissus lightly: Plato mentions him only twice, and Aristotle dismissed Melissus' arguments. Both Plato and Aristotle link Melissus with Parmenides, seeing him merely as an apologist for Parmenidean thought, thus underestimating his originality. Melissus was the first of the Eleatics explicitly to call what is "the One," and he also presents specific arguments against void and the rearrangement of what is. Thus, it is possible that it is his version of Eleaticism that was attributed to Parmenides by Plato (in the *Parmenides*) and by Aristotle.

BIBLIOGRAPHY: Texts in DK30. Booth, N. B., *AJP* 79, 1958, 61–65; Curd, P. K., *AP* 13, 1993, 1–22; Furley, D., in K. J. Boudouris, ed., *Ionian Philosophy*, Athens, 1989,

114–122; Reale, G., *Melisso: Testimonianze e Frammenti*, Florence, 1970; Solmsen, F., in Solmsen, *Kleine Schriften*, vol. 3, Hildesheim, 137–149.—*PATRICIA CURD*

MENEDEMUS (c. 340–c. 265 B.C.E.), of Eretria. *"Socratic" philosopher, who founded the short-lived Eretrian school. Menedemus left no writings, and very little is recorded about his ideas; his impact derived mainly from personal probity and a talent for disputation, not original insights. In his youth he was drawn to philosophy by *Stilpo; he later studied at the school founded by *Phaedo in Elis and also visited Athens. By 300 he returned to Eretria, where his frugal lifestyle, stern rectitude, and bluntness won respect and attracted students. Very active politically, he held high office and served his city repeatedly in diplomatic negotiations. But opponents drove him to retire late in life to the Macedonian court of Antigonus Gonatas, where he eventually ended his life by fasting. In his thought, as in his conduct, Menedemus was endebted to Stilpo and other *Megarians. Anecdotes report him discussing logical puzzles with *Alexinus and criticizing *Persaeus the *Stoic. He explored problems in predication, negation, and conditionals; and, adapting Socratic views about *virtue, he claimed that *knowledge is the only *good, though called by many names. *Timon of Phlius compared him to *Arcesilaus.

BIBLIOGRAPHY: Texts in *SSR*. Knoepfler, D., *La vie de Ménédème d'Érétrie de Diogène Laërce*, Basel, 1991.—*STEPHEN A. WHITE*

MENEDEMUS (3rd cent. B.C.E.), of Lampsacus on the Hellespont. *Cynic philosopher, follower first of *Colotes, pupil of *Epicurus, then of the Cynic Echechles, who was a follower of Cleomenes and Theombrotus, who were followers of Metrocles, brother of *Hipparchia. The description in *Diogenes Laertius (6.102) of Menedemus' extravagant and theatrical dress and behavior confuses him with *Menippus. This Menedemus (not *Menedemus of Eretria) and Colotes attacked each other in writing concerning the value of poetry, poverty, and self-sufficiency, in a dispute partially reconstructible from Herculanean papyri. Nothing else is known about Menedemus, but he is an important illustration of the facts that for a time Cynicism did have something of a tradition based on master-follower relationships, that Cynics sometimes engaged in more or less formal debate with other philosophers, and that *Epicureans were always hostile to Cynics (a hostility here presumably exacerbated by personal bitterness).

BIBLIOGRAPHY: Gigante, M., in M.-O. Goulet-Cazé and R. Goulet, eds., *Le cynisme ancien et ses prolongements*, Paris, 1993, 198–203; *SSR* 4, 581–83.—*JOHN L. MOLES*

MENELAUS (fl. 100 C.E.), of Alexandria. Geometer and *astronomer. Menelaus' principal work, the *Sphaerica*, a treatise in three books on spherical geometry, is lost in Greek but is extant in Arabic translation and in Latin and Hebrew translations based on the Arabic. Other works, now lost, include the *Elements of Geometry*, *On Weights*, and a book *On Triangles*. There are references to Menelaus' study of a "paradoxical curve" (otherwise unspecified) and to a treatise, *On Chords*. *Proclus mentions Menelaus' alternative proof of *Euclid's prop. 25 in Book 1 of the *Elements*.

Menelaus' *Sphaerica* recasts and extends the field of spherical geometry, as inaugurated by Euclid, Autolycus, *Theodosius, and Hipparchus. He avoids *reductio ad absurdum*, even where that reasoning is adopted in parallel passages of the others. Book 3 is of greatest interest: Starting with its first proposition—a key result on the ratios associated with pairs of segments intercepted in a configuration of four intersecting arcs of great circles (the "Menelaus" theorem)—Menelaus develops a sequence of identities that provide the geometric basis for the solution of spherical triangles. In the treatment of this material in *Ptolemy's *Syntaxis* (1.13), the first of Menelaus' theorems becomes (unacknowledged) the basis for all the computations of spherical triangles.

Ptolemy's more concise account ought entirely to have supplanted Menelaus' *Sphaerica*. In fact, however, the latter continued to be expounded by later teachers and retained its interest among Arabic astronomers and the medieval scholastics.

BIBLIOGRAPHY: Björnbo, A. A., *Studien über Menelaos' Sphärik*, in *Abhandlungen zur Geschichte der mathematischen Wissenschaften* 14, 1902, 1–154; Krause, M., *Die Sphärik des Menelaos aus Alexandrien in der Verbesserung von Abû Nasr Mansûr b. 'Alî b. 'Irâq*, in *Abh. Gesell. Wissen. zu Göttingen*, 3rd ser., vol. 17, 1936; Heath, T. L., *A History of Greek Mathematics*, vol. 2, Oxford, 1921, 260–273; Pedersen, O., *A Survey of the Almagest*, Odense, 1974, 69–78.—*WILBUR R. KNORR*

MENIPPUS (1st half of 3rd cent. B.C.E.), of Gadara in Syria. *Cynic philosopher or Cynic-influenced writer. According to ancient traditions Menippus was a Phoenician slave of a Pontic master (whence his association with Sinope, birthplace of *Diogenes) who obtained freedom either by begging or by usury, became a Theban citizen and a follower of *Crates of Thebes, acquired a large fortune, lost it, and hanged himself. The association with Crates is plausible; the rest should be dismissed as fabrication stemming variously from contamination with the biographies (or pseudo-biographies) of Diogenes and *Bion of Borysthenes, malicious invention and false inference from Menippus' own writings.

*Diogenes Laertius (6.101) attests thirteen books, of which he lists six titles: *Necromancy*; *Wills*; *Letters Artfully composed in the Character of the Gods*; *Against the Physicists, Mathematicians and Grammarians*; *The Birth of Epicurus*; *The Twentieth Days Worshipped by them* (sc. the *Epicureans, who met on the twentieth day of the month in commemoration of *Epicurus and his pupil *Metrodorus of Lampsacus). Other attested titles are *Symposium*, *Sale of Diogenes* (an important item in the development of the Diogenes-legend), and *Arcesilaus*. None of these works survives, but some are variously and controversially reconstructible, partly from direct evidence, partly because Menippus had an enormous (albeit in detail highly controversial) literary influence upon (among others) Meleager of Gadara, Varro's *Menippean Satires* (especially), the *Satires* of Lucilius and Horace, *Seneca's *Apocolocyntosis*, Petronius' *Satyricon*, *Lucian (especially), and *Apuleius. The *Necromancy* (itself modeled on *Odyssey* 11) was particularly influential.

Scholars both ancient and modern debate whether Menippus' work was seriocomic (exploiting the recognised technique of investing serious moralizing in comic guise) or merely comic/entertaining (the same debate occurs even within the interpretation of satire as a literary genre). In favor of the former is one ancient tradition, which appeals to the association with Crates, aspects of Menippus' biography (or pseudo-biography), the *Sale of Diogenes*, and the attacks on useless knowledge (as Cynics regarded physical philosophy, etc.), on bogus religiosity, and on philosophers such as *Arcesilaus the *Academic, the Epicureans, and the *Stoics, whose doctrine of cosmic conflagration was mocked in the *Symposium*. The latter interpretation emphasizes the other ancient tradition, emphasizing Menippus' sheer literary inventiveness, which exceeded that of Diogenes and Crates and included the mixture of prose and verse, his extravagant and theatrical self-presentation (D.L. 6.102—wrongly attributed to Menedemus), and the example of his literary descendant Lucian, whose moral seriousness is at least problematic.

The difficulty of deciding between the two views is compounded by the fact that even serious Cynics (as Diogenes and Crates should be classed) exploited humor, exaggeration, and theatrical self-presentation as means of propagating their philosophical message and that even serious Cynic teaching is itself largely devoted to attacks on the many things to be rejected rather than to positive advocacy of the one true way of life (which is simple and easily attainable). Nevertheless, it seems clear that Menippus did align himself with the tradition of Diogenes and Crates, and the apparent seriousness of the *Sale of Diogenes* is not easily deconstructed. Menippus should therefore be regarded as a Cynic philosopher who increased the proportion of the comic and greatly extended the range of Cynic literary exposition, thereby producing rich material for development by subsequent non-Cynics, but did not himself abandon the serious.

BIBLIOGRAPHY: Helm, R., *Lucian und Menipp*, Leipzig, 1906; Relihan, J. C., *Ancient Menippean Satire*, Baltimore/London, 1993, esp. ch. 3.—*JOHN L. MOLES*

METAPHYSICAL THOUGHT, Classical. "Metaphysics" (*ta meta ta phusika*) names a discipline practiced, from the 2nd cent. C.E. on, by the *Peripatetic and *Platonic schools, and also names two "classic" early Peripatetic texts, a long treatise by *Aristotle and a short one by *Theophrastus. The phrase *ta meta ta phusika* is first attested, as a title for both treatises, in Nicolaus of Damascus (1st cent. C.E.), but is probably earlier as a title for Aristotle's work. While the title comes from the arrangement of this treatise after Aristotle's physical works, this arrangement is determined by the perceived logical order of the subjects of Aristotle's different treatises and the recommended order for instruction; there is no basis for the modern legend that the title originates in a library catalogue. (The systematic arrangement of Aristotle's works is often credited to *Andronicus of Rhodes [1st cent. B.C.E.], but the texts had clearly been given some systematic and pedagogical order before Andronicus' edition; it is controversial how far Aristotle himself intended this order.) The phrase "*ta meta ta phusika*" is intended as equivalent to Aristotle's "wisdom," "first philosophy," and "*theologikê.*" Its advantage over these other names is that it is more specific. Thus the *Stoics use "*theologikê*" to name the discipline that studies gods or divine things; but since these gods are themselves natural bodies, *theologikê* is a part of physics, although it may be the final, crowning part of physics, and although *Cleanthes distinguished it from physics in a stricter sense (D.L. 7.41). The title "*ta meta ta phusika,*" for a discipline occupying the same place as Stoic *theologikê*, makes it clear that the divine objects to be studied (unlike the divine objects studied in Aristotle's *De Caelo*) are beyond the physical world.

Although Aristotle uses "wisdom" and "first philosophy" for the same discipline, these names are not interchangeable and are used in different contexts. "Wisdom" (discussed mostly in *ethical contexts) designates a certain intellectual virtue, namely, whatever knowledge is most desirable for its own sake and not for any practical consequences. "First philosophy" specifies the object of this knowledge and contrasts it with other disciplines: If there were only physical substances, then "physics would be the first science" (*Met.* 1026a27–9), but if (as Aristotle thinks) there are eternal unchanging substances separate from *matter, then first philosophy can be *contrasted* with physics as the science of the best and most divine kind of substance. Aristotle thinks that none of the existing sciences will do as first philosophy. In the early *Topics* (105b19–29) Aristotle recognizes the tripartition of *"logic," "physics," and "ethics" elsewhere credited to his *Academic contemporary *Xenocrates, in which all *theoretical* philosophy (knowledge pursued only for its own sake) would fall under physics. But now Aristotle seeks a further theoretical discipline. One candidate would be Platonic *dialectic, which, beyond examining hypotheses by question and answer, also classifies and defines and so seeks to grasp the eternal Forms of the definienda. Aristotle admires the practice of dialectic and the ideal of a universal presuppositionless science, but rejects *Plato's exaggerated claims for dialectic. Aristotle contrasts dialectic (which aims at defending or refuting, before a general audience, the claim *that* S is P) with the specialized causal investigations (seeking the real reason *why* S is P), which alone can produce scientific knowledge. The knowledge (and the scientific definitions) of the forms of natural things can be grasped only by physics, not by dialectic; and the forms reached in this way are not separate eternal substances but depend for their existence on matter. If separate eternal substances do exist, then they can be known (if at all) only by another causal inquiry, which, unlike physics, would lead us from manifest sensible effects to a cause separate from sensible things.

Both Aristotelian and post-Aristotelian metaphysics continue the discussions of Presocratic physicists "on first principles" [*peri archôn*], while insisting that the truly *first* principles are beyond physics—the very last Greek metaphysical work, by *Damascius, is again called "*Peri Archôn*." But the metaphysician cannot simply ask, "What are the principles?"—that is, "What is *prior* to everything else that exists?" Since these principles are known only as causes of more manifest effects, we must ask *what effects* the sought-for principles cause, and (since there are several ways of answering a "why" question) *in what ways* they are causes. The answers to these questions determine what a philosopher takes the scope of metaphysics as a science to be. The clarification of these "preliminary" questions may occupy much of his work. Notoriously, Aristotle's *Metaphysics* spends only a short time actually discussing nonphysical substances (and much of this discussion is critical rather than positive); Theophrastus' *Metaphysics* consists entirely of preliminary *aporiai* without explicit solutions.

Aristotle asserts that metaphysics "considers being as being, and its *per se* attributes" (*Met.* 1003a21–22)—attributes such as unity and plurality, said of all beings. The context shows that he is asking what "the principles and the highest causes" are causes *of*, and is answering that they are causes of being as being—causes, to the things that are, of the fact that they are (a26–32). The argument apparently rests on the principle (cited by *Proclus in *Elements of Theology* 56–60, 70–72) that the highest causes are causes of the most universal effects. (Aristotle argues that all beings are connected enough to have a common cause.) This does not settle the scope of metaphysics, since "is" (and "one" and "many") have different senses and since there are different kinds of causes explaining why something is.

In *Metaphysics* 6 Aristotle gives four senses in which something can be said to be: a true statement *is*, and a false statement *is not*; X *is* Y whenever the same thing happens to be both X and Y, as the carpenter *is* musical; X *is* what it is its nature to be, as this horse *is* a horse and this white thing *is* white; X *is* when it is actually what it is potentially, as the fluteplayer *is* fluteplaying. Aristotle dismisses the first two ("being as truth" and "being *per accidens*") and investigates "being in the sense of the categories" (and its most important case, being as *ousia* or substance), and "being as actuality," to see whether the sought-for principles will be found as causes of being in one of these senses.

The causes of being in these different senses will be causes in different ways. The cause of *ousia* to X is the *ousia of* X, that is, the answer to "what is X?" The investigation of causes of being in this sense rejoins the Presocratic search for principles as the *natures* of manifest things ("What is man?" "Fire!"—cf. *"Hippocrates" On the Nature of Man* 1). The question "what is X?" can be answered in two ways, either by giving the *subject* [*hupokeimenon*] of X, that is, a Y such that Y *is* X, or by giving the *essence* [*ti ên einai*] of X, that is, a Y such that X *is* Y, or so that for X to be is for it to be Y. The *ousia* of X in the first way is its material cause ("flesh and bone"); the *ousia* of X in the second way is its formal cause, expressed by a genus-differentia definition ("wingless biped animal"—*eidos* means both "form" and "species"). Aristotle argues that the principles sought by metaphysics are not causes in either of these ways: He is especially concerned to answer Plato's claim that the *ousiai*-as-forms of manifest things are separate eternal substances. In *Metaphysics* 7–8 and *Physics* 2, Aristotle argues that, although the *ousia* or nature of a physical thing is more properly its form than its matter, this form is an immanent or inseparable form, and it is physics that properly studies both the form and the matter.

Aristotle asserts that the principles sought by metaphysics are causes of being as actuality—causes, to what is potentially X, of its actually being X. A cause of being in this sense is an *efficient* cause. Efficient causes, unlike formal causes, are temporally prior to their effects; some efficient causal chain might lead up from a physical effect to an eternal nonphysical first cause. Typically the efficient cause of a natural individual is a previous individual of the same species: Aristotle thinks these causal chains lead to infinite series without a first cause; but he argues that the cycles of sublunar generation require the eternally constant rotations of the heavens for their continuance and that these rotations require an eternally unchanging substance as their efficient cause. The principles so reached are not *potential* efficient causes, like "housebuilder," but *actual* causes, like "housebuilder housebuilding." Aristotle argues in *Metaphysics* 9 and 12 that actuality is "prior" (in several senses) to potentiality and thus that the principles (being prior to everything else) must be entirely actual causes: If the efficient principles were, like *Anaxagoras' *nous* before the creation of the ordered world, merely potential causes, nothing else could actualize them. The first principle must be, not only eternal, but purely and eternally actual. Aristotle takes over from Plato's *Timaeus* and *Philebus* the Anaxagorean thesis that the first efficient cause is *nous* (Reason), but he rejects his predecessors' descriptions of its causality—notably any description implying that *nous* is itself affected in acting on other things—as inadequate to an eternally fully actual *nous*. Aristotle concludes that *nous* moves the heaven only by causing the heaven to know and desire it; *nous* is an efficient cause only by being a final cause. He therefore agrees with Plato that the first principle is a separate Good-itself; he thinks he has shown, better than Plato, how it is a cause *qua* good (and not merely *qua* One and cause of unity). But Aristotle draws only a very thin causal connection between the first principle and ordinary objects, entirely mediated by the heavenly rotations; many philosophers might find this disappointing as an explanation of the phenomena as consequences of the Good.

The Stoics continue the discussion *peri archôn*, but firmly under the rubric of physics: the *ousia* of things is the passive matter out of which they were formed, but the "cause" of things (their efficient cause, but also, as the "quality" through which things have their characteristic predicates, comparable to an Aristotelian formal cause) is the portion of God or the world soul in them and actively forming them; but both these *archai* are bodies, interpenetrating to form the physical world. The revival of metaphysics as a discipline begins with a rebellion against these Stoic corporeal *archai*. The Platonists of the first centuries C.E. reclaim Plato as a dogmatic philosopher (against the *skeptical Academy), then as an anticorporealist (against Stoicizing interpretations). To establish the *archai* as incorporeal and to understand what these *archai* might be like, they ally themselves with the *Peripatos, and call on the neglected Aristotelian discipline of metaphysics. Thus *Alcinous' *Introduction to the Doctrines of Plato* (2nd cent. C.E.) replaces the usual division of philosophy into logic, physics, and ethics, with a division into *dialektikê, theôrêtikê*, and *praktikê*, dividing theoretical philosophy (following Aristotle) into physics, *mathematics, and *theologikê*. As a specimen of *theologikê*, we have Alcinous' account of the principles. God (the demiurge of the *Timaeus*) is eternally actual *nous*; he is superior to the world-soul, a merely potential *nous* dependent on God for illumination; the Ideas, objects of God's thought and his models for creation, are simply God's acts of thought and do not exist outside him. Matter too (the receptacle of the *Timaeus*) is incorporeal, as are the qualities and active powers existing within matter and acting upon it. Now the Stoics, too, recognize a divine *nous* that forms the world according to a preexisting plan, using active qualities (such as heat) to shape a preexisting passive matter into the desired order. But the Stoics identify these principles either with the active body (God as the totality of the *pneuma* pervading matter) or with the passive body (matter itself). The Platonists' task is to show that these principles are incorporeal and to distinguish the different incorporeal principles, some superior and separate from bodies, others derivative and inseparable from bodies. Different Platonists distinguish more or fewer incorporeals, but Alcinous is typical of his time in identifying the first principle with *nous* and making this superior to *souls, which are in turn superior to the incorporeal but inseparable qualities or active powers, which in turn act upon matter to produce bodies (later Platonists tend to distinguish more and more levels of being).

The Platonists, like the Peripatetics, require a metaphysical discipline to prove the existence of incorporeal principles, to show how these should be conceived (and to give criteria for distinguishing different levels of incorporeals), and to show how they are causes. Metaphysics, like other disciplines, was sought in "classic" texts. Peripatetics and Platonists alike turn back to Aristotle's *Metaphysics*, first as a source for particular distinctions and arguments, then as a systematic basis for instruction.

The great reviver of Aristotle's *Metaphysics* was the Peripatetic *Alexander of Aphrodisias (c. 200 C.E.), but the Platonists share in this return to the text: *Porphyry says that "Aristotle's treatise *Metaphysics* is condensed ... in *Plotinus' writings" (*Life of Plotinus* 14). Porphyry is thinking, for example, of Plotinus' argument against the Stoics, in *On Nous, Ideas, and Being*, that *nous* exists separate from (and prior to) souls and is identical with the intelligible objects it contemplates (namely, the Ideas). Although souls *can* perceive intelligible objects, they are not essentially *actually* knowing but require an efficient cause to make them actually know. Plotinus, following Aristotle's argument for the priority of actuality, argues that this efficient cause must be an actually knowing *nous* and (barring an infinite regress) a *nous* that is *essentially* actually knowing. Plotinus' main aim is to show, against Stoics and against Platonists who do not distinguish enough levels of incorporeals, that *nous* is something prior to soul and thus that the first principle (be it *nous* or something prior to *nous*) must be prior to soul. Thus Plotinus appropriately calls on Aristotle, who shares his concern to argue against too "low" a conception of the first principle. Plotinus concludes, with Aristotle, that an essentially actual *nous* cannot know objects *external* to itself (otherwise its knowing would depend on things outside it and would not be essential); here the adoption of Aristotle's argument is more paradoxical, since Aristotle intended to argue against Platonic Ideas as objects of the demiurge's contemplation. For Plotinus, the argument shows merely that the Ideas are not external to *nous* but are different components or aspects of *nous*; against Aristotle, *nous'* self-knowledge must have this internal complexity, because it is the source of complex intellectual knowledge in souls, and each of the many forms present in souls must preexist in a higher way in *nous*.

While Plotinus' use of Aristotle is still sporadic, later Platonists, especially Proclus and his followers in the fifth and sixth centuries C.E., use Aristotle systematically and teach and write *commentaries on his treatises, although they may disagree with him on specific issues. The Platonists are interested in using Aristotle, and especially the techniques of Aristotelian metaphysics, in order to extract a teachable scientific doctrine from Plato's suggestive but imprecise descriptions of his principles. The Platonists share Aristotle's concern to avoid inappropriately "low" descriptions, especially those that attribute to intelligibles the peculiar characteristics of the sensibles. Aristotle was especially useful against Stoics or Stoicizing Platonists; and Aristotle's characterizations of intelligible realities (notably, as pure actuality) give criteria for when a description is inappropriate. Embarrassingly, Aristotle's criticisms of unworthy descriptions of the divine are often directed against Plato. The Platonists do not want Plato to have maintained such doctrines (e.g., that intelligible Forms resemble the sensibles and are members of the same species, that the demiurge acts after a period of inactivity, that thinking is a circular motion of an extended soul); and they use Aristotle's arguments, together with a principle of charity, to argue that Plato cannot have intended these doctrines, and that he intends terms taken from sensible things to be understood *allegorically. So fifth- and sixth-century Platonists say either that Aristotle's criticisms of Plato are misunderstandings or that Aristotle did not even *intend* to criticize Plato, but only disciples who took Platonic metaphors literally.

Nonetheless, late ancient Platonists were not simply Aristotelians: They defend crucial Platonic theses, including the immortality of the soul, the plurality of Forms in *nous*, and divine providence over the whole sensible world. The last two theses are connected: *nous* cannot exercise providence unless it contains a representation of the sensible world and of the different species within it. The Platonists' metaphysics differs from Aristotle's in defending thicker causal connections between the sensible world and the first principles. In the teaching systematized by Proclus, and shared by all fifth and sixth century philosophers, beings at each level of the hierarchy are causes of the next lower level in each of three ways, as efficient, final, and formal (or "paradigmatic") causes. This echoes Aristotle's doctrine of the coincidence of the efficient, final, and formal causes of a natural thing; but whereas Aristotle thinks that most upward causal chains (apart from the special cases of the heavens, and perhaps rational souls) lead only to immanent forms, Proclus thinks that they lead at each step to a higher ontological level, and thus to separate substances, and ultimately to the Good. Proclus defends separate paradigm-forms, and a Being-itself and a One-itself (the latter identified with the Good), by strictly causal arguments. Proclus implicitly concedes to Aristotle that the consideration from dialectic, that being and unity are the most universal predicates, is insufficient to show that Being and Unity are first principles; but he maintains, against Aristotle, that causal argument will reveal a wider range of separate principles than Aristotle recognizes (including Being and Unity) and a broader connection between these principles and material things.

Much of the work of Proclus and his school is exegetical: In metaphysics, commentaries were produced not only on Aristotle's *Metaphysics* (a lost commentary by Simplicius, besides *Syrianus' hostile commentary on books 3, 4, 13, and 14, and Asclepius' student notes), but also on Plato's *Parmenides* (by Proclus and Damascius), and on the Platonic texts collected for commentary in Proclus' *Platonic Theology*. But there is also a radically *anti-exegetical* metaphysical work, Proclus' *Elements of Theology* (and, under Proclus' influence, Damascius' *Peri Archôn*). These *Elements* are intended to recall *Euclid's *Elements of Geometry*, which Proclus also commented on. Like Euclid, Proclus appeals neither to authority nor to sense-experience, but tries to prove each claim, relying only on what he has said earlier in the same work. But, holding metaphysics to be an unhypothetical science, Proclus avoids calling on postulates proper to his subject: Everything is to be deduced "from scratch" (presumably Proclus appeals to common notions, without listing them explicitly). Nonetheless, the doctrine Proclus claims to deduce is recognizably the fifth-century scheme, based ultimately on Platonic and Aristotelian texts; Proclus even introduces such terms as "soul" and "*nous*," implicitly defining them in proving the existence of entities deserving these names. The *Elements* elaborates the logical substructure for Proclus' commentaries. A commentator's first task is to decide what each word in the text refers to. This often involves deciding where it belongs in the hierarchy of being: for example, if one authority says "every soul is immortal" while another says "only *nous* is immortal," these can both be right only if "soul" means exclusively *rational* souls, and if "*nous*" designates rational souls as well as reason-itself. To make these decisions, the commentator must know what levels of being are available and what predicates may be legitimately applied at each of these levels. The *Elements* collects the rules for deciding these questions, allowing Proclus (in the *Platonic Theology*) to discover in the Platonic texts a complete ontological system. The *Elements* divides beings by their degrees of unity or multiplicity, and of change

and changelessness, and investigates their causal relations. A first principle can be proved, with the *Parmenides*, as a source of unity or, with Aristotle, as a source of motion: Bodies are moved nonmovers, receiving their
motion immediately from natures or immanent forms, which are moved
movers, and ultimately from souls, which are self-moved movers, and
from *nous*, which is an unmoved mover; each term in the chain has a different relation to spatial and temporal divisibility. Proclus' method is
dogmatic and his resulting theology baroque, where Aristotle's method
was aporetic, his results largely negative, and his positive theology
spare; but Proclus is the first philosopher to systematically take up Aristotle's challenge to investigate being and its *per se* attributes, to sort out
their different kinds and their different kinds of causes, and to examine
which causal paths lead up to principles separate from matter and to the
Good as the first principle of all.
BIBLIOGRAPHY: For bibliography, see under major figures, schools and movements
discussed.—*STEPHEN P. MENN*

METRODORUS (early 4th cent. B.C.E.), of Chios. Variously described as
a follower of *Democritus, of the Democritean Nessas of Chios, and of
Metrodorus of Abdera. Two fragments of *On Nature*, Metrodorus' only
known philosophical work, survive. It began, "None of us knows anything, not even whether or not we know, nor do we know what not
knowing and knowing are, nor whether or not anything at all exists"
(DK70B1). Yet, like Democritus, he did not let this *skepticism prevent
him from presenting a positive philosophy: The universe is *infinite, it
consists of *atoms and *void, and there are an infinite number of worlds.
*Doxographers mention his views on various meteorological phenom-
ena. His chief importance, however, is as a link in the succession of
skeptical Democriteans, which leads through his follower Diogenes of
Smyrna to *Anaxarchus, *Pyrrho the skeptic, and *Epicurus' teacher
*Nausiphanes; and the main challenge is to reconcile the reports of his
radical skepticism with his endorsement of atomism and his other surviving fragment: "All things which one conceives exist" (B2).
BIBLIOGRAPHY: Texts in DK70.—*JEFFREY S. PURINTON*

METRODORUS (331–278 B.C.E.), of Lampsacus. *Epicurean philosopher, and a cofounder of the school, which revered his memory with a
monthly feast. His association with *Epicurus dated from the latter's
foundation of a circle at Lampsacus in 311. Metrodorus accompanied
him to Athens when he moved his school's headquarters there in 307,
but did not live to succeed him as scholarch. Metrodorus' sister and two
brothers joined the school, although one brother, Timocrates, later defected to become its leading detractor. Metrodorus formed a union with

the Epicurean ex-courtesan Leontion: their two children included a son named Epicurus.

Epicurus' *On Nature* 28 (296 B.C.E.) is addressed to Metrodorus, whose early views on the character of language as purely conventional are critically recalled. Metrodorus himself wrote voluminously. More than twenty titles are known, including *On the Gods*, *On the Senses*, *On Poetry*, *Against the Doctors*, *Against the Dialecticians*, *Against Those who Say that the Study of Physics Produces Good Orators*, and further polemical works against named targets; also a number of letters and *ethical treatises, from which most of his testimonia derive, including his influential *How our Own Responsibility for Happiness is Greater than that of Circumstances*. These works, along with those of Epicurus, *Hermarchus, and *Polyaenus, later formed the authoritative canon of Epicurean scriptures.

His felicitous turns of phrase led to various of his *ethical dicta becoming virtual Epicurean clichés, including those that survive as *Gnomologium Vaticanum* 10, 14, 30–1, 47, and the famous 51 on sexual continence, addressed to the youthful prodigy Pythocles. Some of Metrodorus' phraseology recurs in Epicurus' own writings, reflecting their close philosophical symbiosis.

BIBLIOGRAPHY: Texts in A. Körte, ed., *Metrodori Epicurei Fragmenta* (*Neue Jahrbücher* supp. 17, 1890), 529–97. Erler, M., in H. Flashar, ed., *Die Philosophie der Antike 4: Die Hellenistische Philosophie*, Basel, 1994, 216–22.—*DAVID N. SEDLEY*

METRODORUS (late 2nd cent. B.C.E.), of Stratonicea. *Academic philosopher, student of *Carneades. According to *Diogenes Laertius (10.9), he was an *Epicurean before studying with Carneades. He claimed to be one of Carneades' closest adherents (*Index Academicorum Philosophorum Herculanensis* 26; Cic. *Or.* 1. 45 and *Acad.* 2. 16). No writings of his are known. He is best remembered for his interpretation of Carneades' view that the wise man may "perceive nothing but still hold opinions" (Cic. *Acad.* 2. 78). In opposition to *Clitomachus, who said that Carneades maintained the view for dialectical purposes and did not accept it himself (and thus that Carneades advocated a strong form of *epochê*, or suspension of belief), Metrodorus maintained that it was Carneades' own view (and therefore that Carneades held a weak form of *epochê*). *Cicero endorsed Clitomachus' view against Metrodorus, as have most recent scholars, but Metrodorus found an ally in *Philo of Larissa, who was influenced by Metrodorus' interpretation of Carneades. *Augustine (*Against the Academicians* 3.41) credits Metrodorus with saying that members of the Academy had adopted the *skeptical position that nothing could be known not because they endorsed the position themselves, but merely as a defense against the *Stoics.

BIBLIOGRAPHY: Brochard, V., *Les Sceptiques Grecs*,[2] Paris, 1932, 187–188; Sedley, D., in *The Skeptical Tradition*, M. Burnyeat, ed., Berkeley, 1983, 9–29; Striker, G., in M.

Schofield, M. Burnyeat, and J. Barnes, eds., *Doubt and Dogmatism*, Oxford, 1980, 54–83; Zeller, E., *Die Philosophie der Greichen in ihrer geschichtlichen Entwicklung³*, vol. 3.1, 1880, 523–525.—*WALTER G. ENGLERT*

MIDDLE PLATONISM. See PLATONISM.

MIND, Classical Theories of. *Anaxagoras (500–428 B.C.E.) was the first philosopher to make mind (*nous*) an important explanatory principle. As the universal principle that set the other elements into motion, *nous* was itself a material element. Treating mind and more generally soul as a natural phenomenon was not peculiar to Anaxagoras but was characteristic of Classical philosophers.

Presocratics. While not oblivious to the connotations of mind in our sense, the early philosophers emphasized the shared constitution of soul and body. For *Anaximenes (fl. 526 B.C.E.), the soul like everything else consists of air; for *Heraclitus (fl. 500), of fire. From drunkenness to disease, according to Heraclitus, states of the body that cloud judgment are due to the presence of internal dampness that threatens the soul with destruction. The *atomists, *Leucippus (fl. 440–35 B.C.E.) and *Democritus (fl. 420), appealed to the atomic structure of objects of all sorts to explain their properties. Because the soul, the seat of cognition, extends throughout the body, making it alive, the soul must, they argue, consist in atoms that are extremely fine, highly mobile, and spherical. The soul is held together by the body; when the body disintegrates with death, the soul does so as well.

Today these early materialist theories seem overly simplistic and yet the conception of psychological explanation underlying them is promising. The study of mind is naturalized; the principles used in psychological explanation are the same as those used in any other physical theory. The building-blocks are in place for a unified theory of all of nature, including human beings.

A more complex picture of the soul emerges in the writings of philosophers with religious as well as naturalistic concerns. The soul, the *Pythagoreans believe, migrates from one body when it dies, to another body. The soul thus conceived is an autonomous individual whose identity is not dependent upon its belonging to any particular body. Another proponent of transmigration, *Empedocles (fl. 450 B.C.E.) posits a soul consisting of a mixture of the basic constituents of the universe, namely, fire, air, water, and earth and the forces of attraction and repulsion. There is little evidence that the Presocratic philosophers recognized the inherent tension between naturalized psychology and more dualistic thinking.

Plato. In Plato's *Meno*, the story of transmigration is used to introduce the doctrine that learning is recollection (81a–86b), and this thesis in turn serves as a premise in an argument for the soul's immortality in the

Phaedo (73a–76e). Unlike his philosophical precedessors, Plato recognizes that if the person is in some sense his or her soul and the soul survives the death of the body, there must be an ontological difference between soul and body, mind and *matter. In the *Phaedo*, Plato defends the immateriality and simplicity of the soul in contrast to the body. If the soul is wholly unlike the body, Plato reasons, the soul must be indestructible since the body is subject to decay and death. If the presence of a soul in a body is required for life, then the soul must be essentially, not just accidentally, alive. Plato's clarity about the requirements of psychological dualism is unparalleled in the Classical period, and later his analysis serves as the basis for the dualistic theories of the *Neoplatonists.

The human soul for Plato, as for his contemporaries, is both the animating principle of the body and the seat of consciousness. In various situations from those calling for courage or moderation to those calling for mental self-discipline, the soul's different roles may be, and often are, in conflict. For this reason, Plato posits a tripartite soul in the *Republic*, consisting of appetites, emotions, and reason. Psychic conflict is made intelligible by appeal to a conception of the soul such that the soul is closely connected to the body at the level of appetite and relatively separate from the body at the level of reason. In the *Timaeus*, a "probable story" is told about physical reality that includes a detailed treatment of the soul's relation to the body. The appetites are situated in the lower portion of the body; the emotions in the chest, and reason in the head. The soul is in motion essentially and autonomously, and it is the source of motion and change in the body. In these works, Plato attempts to give a detailed, naturalistic explanation of psychic function that is consistent with his dualism.

Aristotle. Aristotle is the first to articulate the parameters of psychology as a discipline. In *De Anima* 1, he argues that an alternative to Presocratic materialism and Pythagorean and Platonic dualism is needed. A human being is not merely a body nor a composite of two substances, a mind and a body. The soul is the form or actuality of the body. A human being is the realization of a particular form (the rational soul) in a particular body. The rational soul contains potentially the animal, perceptive soul (the constellation of perceptual capacities including the individual senses and the capacity to feel pleasure and pain) which in turn contains potentially the vegetative, nutritive soul (the constellation of the functions characteristic of all life forms, namely, digestion, reproduction, elimination, respiration).

The nature of soul, Aristotle believes, can only be understood through the detailed examination of actual life forms. Aristotle carefully constructs an analytic account of human cognitive functions in the *De Anima, De Sensu, De Insomniis,* and *De Memoria.* This results in a fully developed theory of the perceptual functions, including the five senses, the common sense, the capacity for apperceptual awareness, and imagination. These capacities are realized in specific bodily organs. Rationality is the capacity to use the particulars presented sensorially in perception and imagination to apprehend universals. Perception is the realization of a sensible form, a ratio (*logos*) of sensible qualities, in a percipient; thought is the realization of an intelligible form in a rational being.

Just as color is the immediate cause of seeing, the object of thought is the immediate cause of the activity of thinking but unlike color, how the intelligible object, typically a universal, occasions the thought is less clear. In *De Anima* 3.5, Aristotle hypothesizes that there is a kind of mind (*nous*) that is active in a way that is analogous to the way light enables a percipient to see color. It is unlikely that by positing active mind Aristotle intended to abandon psychophysical hylomorphism in favor of dualism; the concept of active mind, however, was so interpreted by later philosophers.

Aristotle's definition of the soul enables him to conceive the human being as a single substance while giving the vital and cognitive functions of the soul their due. Of the ancient accounts, Aristotle's is the psychological theory with the most explanatory power. Hellenistic theories of mind can be seen as attempts to develop pre-Aristotelian psychology in a way that meets Aristotle's objectives without appealing to the difficult notion of enmattered form.

Hellenistic Philosophy. Materialism is the dominant conception of mind in the Hellenistic period (323–31 B.C.E.). The *Epicureans and the *Stoics claim that what is real is material and minds are real and hence material. Sophisticated and detailed accounts of cognitive activity that emphasize physical causes and causal processes are also characteristic of the period. Even the Hellenistic *skeptics, who do not construct accounts of the mind of their own, presuppose mind-body materialism when arguing against other philosophers.

Epicureanism. Like the Presocratic atomists, *Epicurus explains psychological phenomena by appealing to the atomic structure of the soul. Instead of positing a single type of psychic atom, Epicurus posits at least three and probably four types, namely, fire-like, air-like, and wind-like atoms and a fourth nameless type that is responsible for cognition. Fiery atoms explain the heat of the body, windy ones its motion, airy ones its capacity for rest. The preponderance of one type of atom over another explains differences of character. Stags have a windy soul and lions a fiery one, as do people who are quick to anger. The Epicurean soul is centered in the heart and extends throughout the body. Physical causes have psychological effects (e.g., bodily injury causes the experience of pain), and psychological causes have bodily consequences. Such interactions are relatively easy to explain because both soul and body consist of atoms. Another crucial advantage of materialism is, according to Epicurus, the elimination of the fear of death. Sentience depends upon the coherence of the psychic atoms; at death both psychic and bodily atoms are dispersed, and simultaneously the conditions for the experience of pleasure and pain are destroyed.

Perception is the reception by a bodily organ of a stream of atoms from an external object (*Letter to Herodotus* 47–53). The direct result of physical causal processes, perceptions are always true. Illusory appearances are not false perceptions, Epicurus argues, because the sense is accurately reporting the pattern of the atoms received; for instance, traveling a great distance, the edges are worn off the pattern produced by a square tower, and thus the perception of a round tower is true. Immediate perceptions through the senses and the intellect are the basis of preconceptions, general ideas, and beliefs about what is not directly observable.

Stoicism. According to the Stoics, all of reality is material and interconnected; *pneuma* (breath) permeates inert matter, giving it the character it has throughout the cosmos. *Pneuma* is expressed as soul in the cosmos, which is a single living being, and in individual living things. The soul that permeates a human body is the source of life, sentience, and reason in that body. The ruling principle (*hêgemonikon*) has its seat in the heart and extends throughout the body; among its centralized functions are presentation, assent, impulse, and reason, and it has seven peripheral parts, namely, the five senses, seed, and utterance.

The Stoics developed a detailed account of cognition to support the claim that one type of presentation, the apprehensive presentation (*katalêptikê phantasia*) cannot be mistaken because it "is stamped and impressed exactly in accordance with what is" (D.L. 7.46; cf. S.E., M 7.228–241). A rational being has presentations, which are implicitly propositional, for "thought, which has the power of utterance, expresses in language what it experiences through presentation" (D.L. 7.49). Presentations serve as the basis for preconceptions and common notions, which in turn support a variety of mental operations yielding complex thoughts and generalizations.

Rather than parcel out the functions of the mind to distinct faculties with different bodily centers, the early Stoics argue for the physiological and psychological unity of cognitive and affective activity. Ancient criticisms notwithstanding, the Stoic conception of a single center for all cognitive and affective functions marks a significant advance beyond earlier theories. Plato divided the soul into three parts, and Aristotle rejected partition in favor of different functions exercised through distinct faculties. The conception of a fully integrated psychic system was not found before the Hellenistic Stoics, and regrettably at least one later Stoic, *Posidonius, seems to have reverted to the Platonic picture and distinguished between the passions and reason.

Later Developments. The third and fourth centuries C.E. saw the resurgence of dualism in *Neoplatonism and the modification of psychophysicalism in *Peripatetic philosophy. Later Greek *Aristotelianism reached its zenith in the writings of *Alexander of Aphrodisias (c. 200 C.E.). Alexander's *De Anima* follows Aristotle's *De Anima* in structure and content. Familiar with Stoic psychology and skeptical criticisms, Alexander strengthens Aristotle's arguments, and he incorporates certain Stoic elements into the Aristotelian framework. Alexander also develops Aristotle's notion of an active mind in a way that underscores its independence from the body.

According to the Neoplatonist philosopher *Plotinus (204–270 C.E.), the soul is superior to and largely independent of the body. Embracing Plato's myths about the prior existence and afterlife of the soul, Plotinus posits an eternal soul that takes on a particular human body. The human soul is the seat of consciousness. The vital functions that Aristotle assigns to the nutritive soul Plotinus attributes to the cosmic soul. The human soul has the capacity to direct its attention either to the higher realm of the intelligibles or to the lower realm of the sensible and corporeal. The emphasis on psychic perspective generates a notion of self as defined by mental activity, and Plotinus describes his own mystical experience as waking up outside his body (*Enn.* 4.8.1). The relation between the individual soul and its body is said to resemble that of light to illuminated air. Like light, the soul is present as a whole throughout the body and yet it remains irreducibly distinct from the body. Nevertheless, the account of perception given by Plotinus borrows heavily from Aristotle's, and he seems to allow material bodies to affect the soul indirectly by causing the sense organ to take on a form that is accessible to the soul.

The restoration of Platonic dualism in Neoplatonic philosophy of mind held great appeal for the early and Medieval *Christian philosophers. *Augustine (354–430 C.E.) adopted and refined the Neoplatonic picture to make it consistent with Christian dogma. Like Plotinus, Augustine posits a transcendent Intellect that is the seat of the intelligible Forms, which he identifies with the mind of God. The human soul, a rational substance, is distinct from the body and survives the death of the body. The individual embodied soul should, as Plotinus and Plato recommend, attempt to separate itself from the corporeal realm as far as possible by focussing its attention on the intelligibles and not on its body or other bodies. The soul has three powers, memory, understanding, and will. The soul is superior to the body, and thus it cannot be affected by the body. Faced by the challenge of explaining perception, Augustine postulates that the soul creates a form that corresponds to the form of the changes in the percipient organ caused by the impact of the external object on the organ. Perception is the soul's grasp of the form as it exists in the soul; thus, even in perception the soul is essentially active and the body passive.

The study of mind was initiated by the earliest Greek philosophers, and it continued to be a central preoccupation of philosophers throughout the classical period. Their goal was to describe the makeup and functioning of the soul in the body. Materialist, dualist, and hylomorphic theories of mind vied for dominance. Even more striking than classical contributions to the debate about the relation between mind and body are their analyses of cognition, which from Aristotle to Augustine are remarkably detailed and sophisticated.

BIBLIOGRAPHY: Annas, J., *Hellenistic Philosophy of Mind*, Berkeley, 1992; Beare, J., *Greek Theories of Elementary Cognition from Alcmaeon to Aristotle*, Oxford, 1906; Bremmer, J., *The Early Greek Concept of the Soul*, Princeton, 1983; Emilsson, E., *Plotinus on Sense-Perception: A Philosophical Study*, Cambridge, 1988; Modrak, D. K. W., *Aristotle: The Power of Perception*, Chicago, 1987; Nussbaum, M., and A. Rorty, eds., *Essays on Aristotle's De Anima*, Oxford, 1992.—DEBORAH K. W. MODRAK

MINOR SOCRATICS. See SOCRATIC CIRCLE.

MNESARCHUS (c. 170–88 B.C.E.), of Athens. *Stoic philosopher, student of *Diogenes of Seleucia and *Antipater of Tarsus. Mnesarchus was a contemporary of *Panaetius of Rhodes and of *Dardanus of Athens. *Cicero (*Acad.* 2.22.69) speaks of Dardanus and Mnesarchus as *principes Stoicorum* at Athens at the time when *Antiochus of Ascalon founded the "Old Academy," c. 100–90 B.C.E. It has been shown, however, that the hypothesis of a double scholarchate of Dardanus and Mnesarchus after the death of Panaetius is false. Of his philosophical thought we know very little. In *psychology, he, like Panaetius, denied that language (*to phônêtikon*) and the procreative faculty (*to spermatikon*) were independent parts of the *soul, and he reinscribed them, along with sensory perception, in the sphere of the *aisthêtikon* as opposed to the *logikon*. He employed a distinction between *kata to idiôs poion* and *kat' ousian poion* and located in *pneuma* the *prôtê ousia* (primary substance) of the universe. He intervened in the debate over *rhetoric, maintaining that only the sage possesses the *aretê* of true oratory.

BIBLIOGRAPHY: Dorandi, T., *Ricerche sulla cronologia dei filosofi ellenistici*, Stuttgart, 1991, 29–34; von Fritz, K. V., "Mnesarchus," in *RE* 15.2, 2272–2274.—TIZIANO DORANDI

MONIMUS (4th cent. B.C.E.), of Syracuse. *Cynic philosopher, student of *Diogenes of Sinope and *Crates of Thebes. According to *Diogenes Laertius 6.82–83, Monimus was the slave of a Corinthian banker who knew Xeniades, the master of Diogenes of Sinope. Wishing to follow Diogenes, Monimus pretended to be mad until his master released him from service. Diogenes Laertius reports that he wrote some "playful pieces which concealed serious intent," as well as *On Impulses* (two books) and a *Protrepticus*. Fragments of his writings reveal that he was a Cynic with *skeptical views. His most famous saying occurs in two slightly different versions: "Everything as we conceive it is delusion" (Menander fragment, preserved in D.L. 6.83; cf. Marcus Aurelius *Meditations* 2.15), and "all things are delusion" (S.E. *Against the Logicians* 2.5), which *Sextus glosses as "the opinion that things which do not exist do exist." Sextus lists him among the philosophers who did away with the criterion of truth (*ibid.* 1.48) and reports that he and *Anaxarchus compared all that exists to scene paintings, saying that they are like things encountered in dreams and fits of madness (*ibid.* 1.87–88). Two further sayings of his are preserved, "Wealth is the vomiting of Fortune" (Stobaeus 4.31C.89), and "It is better to be blind than uneducated, for while the one falls into a ditch (*bothron*), the other falls into disaster (*barathron*)" (Stobaeus 2.31.88).

BIBLIOGRAPHY: von Fritz, K., *RE* "Monimus."—*WALTER G. ENGLERT*

MUSONIUS RUFUS (c. 30–100 C.E.), of Volsinii (modern Bolsena) in Etruria. *Stoic philosopher. Though an *eques*, not a senator, he became a leader of the "philosophical opposition" to the emperor Nero. He accompanied Rubellius Plautus into exile (62 C.E.) and advised him to meet death bravely. When back in Rome he was himself exiled, on suspicion of involvement with the Pisonian conspiracy, to the desolate island of Gyaros. Recalled by Galba, he unsuccessfully preached peace to the Vespasianic armies closing in on Vitellius and successfully prosecuted Egnatius Celer, false accuser of the Stoic Barea Soranus. Exempted from the initial philosophical purge of 71, he was exiled later in Vespasian's reign and publicly protested against the gladiatorial contests held in the theatre of Dionysus in Athens. He was recalled by Titus, a personal friend. In Rome, Gyaros, Greece itself, and the East, Musonius, unusually for a Roman, taught philosophy and did so largely, perhaps exclusively, in Greek. His many pupils included both Greeks and Romans and important philosophers of the next generation (notably *Epictetus and Dio Chrysostom). He died before 101 C.E.

Musonius may have written philosophical letters (though those extant are spurious), but his teaching survives in twenty-one *"diatribes" (single-theme moral lectures), evidently recorded by pupils, and various *dicta* and anecdotes. The diatribes are as follows: (i) *That there is no Need to use Many Proofs for One Problem*; (ii) *That Man is Born with an Inclination towards Virtue*; (iii) *That Women too should Study Philosophy*; (iv) *Whether*

Daughters should Receive the Same Education as Sons; (v) *Whether Theory or Practice is more Effective*; (vi) *On Training (askêsis)*; (vii) *That One should Despise Hardships*; (viii) *That Kings also should Study Philosophy*; (ix) *That Exile is not an Evil*; (x) *Whether the Philosopher will Prosecute Anyone for Personal Injury*; (xi) *What Means of Livelihood is Apppropriate for a Philosopher?*; (xii) *On Sex*; (xiii) *What is the Purpose of Marriage?*; (xiv) *Whether Marriage is an Obstacle to the Pursuit of Philosophy*; (xv) *Whether Every Child that is Born should be Raised*; (xvi) *Whether One should Obey One's Parents in All Things*; (xvii) *What is the Best Viaticum for Old Age?*; (xviii) *On Food*; (xix) *On Clothing and Shelter*; (xx) *On Furnishings*; (xxi) *On Hair-cutting*.

The general picture is clear. Consistently with his choice of diatribe-format, Musonius rejects technical philosophy and mere intellectualism [(i)] and concerns himself with practical moralizing on central questions: the acquisition and practice of virtue, the moral role of hardship, family and gender relationships, sex, ways and styles of life, old age, material possessions. In its acceptance of the practical attainability of virtue his stance is positive and optimistic and also, by contemporary standards, notably humane (a lofty conception of marriage, near-acceptance of sexual equality, rejection of litigiousness, of exploitation of slaves, and of exposure of children). Consistently with his own career, there is some concern with politics in the narrow sense (how to bear exile, the need for kings to be philosophers). The philosophical position is formally Stoic (e.g., the exploitation of the doctrine of moral indifferents), but it is that brand of Stoicism that not only rejects formal philosophy in favor of practical moralizing but also comes close to embracing *Cynic positions and primitivism (the emphasis on moral and physical training, on the positive role of hardship, on extreme simplicity of life, elevation of manual labor, appeal to *Diogenes of Sinope and *Crates of Thebes as exemplars). This Cynic strain is, however, tempered by acceptance of, even enthusiasm for, conventional social and political institutions (marriage, the family, kingship).

While Musonius was not a great thinker, he was the very type of the philosopher *engagé* and the consistent integrity of his example and of his teaching inspired many, won him a reputation as the Roman *Socrates and strongly influenced Epictetus and Dio Chrysostom.

BIBLIOGRAPHY: Texts in O. Hense, ed., *Musonii Reliquiae*, Leipzig, 1905. Charlesworth, M. P., *Five Men*, Cambridge, MA, 1936, 33–62; Goulet-Cazé, M.-O., *L'Ascèse Cynique*, Paris, 1986, 185–88; 213–18; Lutz, C. E., YCS 10, 1947, 3–147; van Geytenbeek, A. C., *Musonius Rufus and Greek Diatribe*, Assen, 1963.—*JOHN L. MOLES*

N

NAUSIPHANES (late 4th cent. B.C.E.), of Teos. *Democritean philosopher, teacher of *Epicurus. In his youth, Nausiphanes admired the character of the *skeptic *Pyrrho (D. L. 9.64), while maintaining his own doctrines. His claim (according to *Seneca) that nothing visible is more true than not smacks of Democritean skepticism (cf. *Metrodorus of Chios). He wrote the *Tripod* (*logic, *ethics, and physics?), on which Epicurus reportedly drew for his *Canon* or *epistemology; he may have transmitted to Epicurus the principles of Democritean physics. In ethics, Nausiphanes substituted the term *akataplêxia* ("undauntability") for Democritus' *athambiê*, "fearlessness"; cf. Epicurus' *ataraxia* or "imperturbability." If the biographical tradition may be trusted, Epicurus denied the influence of Nausiphanes, insulting him as "illiterate" and a "whore"; see also Epicurus' *Letter to the Philosophers of Mytiline* and *Philodemus, *To the Friends of the School* fr. 116 (ed. A. Angeli [Naples 1988]). Nausiphanes' interests included *mathematics and music. His views on *rhetoric are discussed critically in Book 6 (renumbered 5 by T. Dorandi, *ZPE* 1990, 85) of Philodemus' *On Rhetoric*, a crucial source. Nausiphanes held, contrary to Epicurus, that the physical philosopher should engage in politics; he will excel as an orator because he knows the innate goal (*telos*) of human nature (to seek pleasure and avoid pain), and he can present his ideas clearly.

BIBLIOGRAPHY: Texts in DK72. Longo Auricchio, F., and A. Tepedino Guerra, in F. Romano, ed., *Democrito e l'atomismo antico*, Catania, 1980, 467–77.—*DAVID KONSTAN*

NEMESIUS (c. 400 C.E.), bishop of Emesa in Syria, known only as the author of *On the Nature of Man.*, a rich compendium of ancient *psychological views from the Presocratics to the *Neoplatonists. In the first part of the book (1–2), Nemesius characterizes the human being as existing on the boundary between the intelligible, divine world and the sensible world and as capable of ascent to the intelligible or descent to the carnal; he argues that the *soul is an immortal, incorporeal substance. In the last part (28–42), he argues against fatalism and insists on human freedom and divine providence. The middle part (6–27) is marked by a strong interest in the physiological.

BIBLIOGRAPHY: Text in M. Morani, ed., *Nemesii Emeseni De Natura Hominis* (Teubner), Leipzig, 1987. W. Telfer, ed. and tr., *Cyril of Jerusalem and Nemesius of Emesa*, London, 1955.—*IAN MUELLER*

NEOPLATONISM. See PLATONISM.

NEOPYTHAGOREANISM. See PYTHAGOREANISM.

NICOMACHUS (1st, or 1st half of 2nd cent. C.E.), of Gerasa (probably in Syria). *Neopythagorean *mathematician and philosopher. Nicomachus' date is determined by his reference to *Thrasyllus (d. 36 C.E.) and a testimonium that *Apuleius (b. 123 C.E.) translated his *Introduction to Arithmetic*. Extant are the *Introduction to Arithmetic* and the *Manual of Harmonics*. Extensive extracts of the *Theology of Arithmetic* appear in the *Theology of Arithmetic* now attributed to a source using *Iamblichus and in an epitome by Photius (*Bibliotheca*, cod. 187, 142–6). *Porphyry's *Life of Pythagoras* contains extracts of his *Life of Pythagoras*. Nicomachus mentions an *Introduction to Geometry* and an intent to write an *Introduction to Harmonics*. This may be the treatise *On Music*, cited by Eutocius, commenting on *Archimedes, and the *Great Book on Music* known in the Arab tradition.

Nicomachus projects *Pythagorean reverence for numbers onto a *Platonic division between a world of *being (pure numbers) and a world of becoming. The eternal beings are matterless and ever similar to themselves and only *become* accidentally in as much as they belong to items of the world of becoming; these bodily items are then called homonymous *beings* derivatively from their participation in the eternal entities. The eternal entities are ordered from the Unit (*monas*), which is congruent with God. By doubling itself, the Unit or the Same forms the Pair (*duas*) or Other, from which the other numbers derive. The categories and everything else then derive from number.

Containing little original mathematics, the *Introduction to Arithmetic* presents no formal proofs. Its purpose is rather to provide systematic (if sometimes artificial) classifications and generations of numbers from basic classifications and the unit, so as to provide understanding of number *in general.* For one cannot know every number individually. Nicomachus has four treatments of numbers: absolute quantity (e.g., odd/even), relative quantity (e.g., equal, multiple), number as shape, and ten kinds of proportion.

The *Introduction* was a preparation for the *Theology*, perhaps as reasoning is for *dialectic in *Plato's divided line. The *Theology*, its first book on the unit through tetrad and its second on the pentad through decad, concerns these basic numbers *individually*. Each number is characterized mathematically and assigned to divinities and various qualities, for example, God to the unit, justice to the pentad, the whole and the cosmos to the decad. Some see in *Introduction* 1.6 a distinction between Scientific Numbers (as used in ordinary arithmetic and involving the combining of units) and Form Numbers, with the *Introduction* concerning one and the *Theology* the other. This might be Nicomachus' view, but given the respective subjects of the treatises the passage does not require this.

BIBLIOGRAPHY: Text of *Introduction to Arithmetic* in R. Hoche, ed., *Introductionis Arithmeticae Libri II*, Leipzig, 1866; tr. by M. D'Ooge, *Introduction to Arithmetic* (includes studies by F. Robbins and L. Karpinski), New York, 1926. Text of *Manual of Harmonics* in C. Janus, ed., *Musici Scriptores Graeci*, Leipzig, 1895; tr. and study by F. Levin, *The Harmonics of Nicomachus and the Pythagorean Tradition*, University Park, Pa., 1975. Fragments from *Theology of Arithmetic* in V. de Falco, ed., *Ps.-Iamblichus. Theologoumena Arithmeticae*, Leipzig, 1922; tr. by R. Waterfield, *The Theology of Arithmetic Attributed to Iamblichus*, Grand Rapids, 1988. Dillon, J., *The Middle Platonists*, Ithaca, 1977; O'Meara, D. J., *Pythagoras Revived*, Oxford, 1989.—HENRY MENDELL

NUMENIUS (2nd cent. C.E.), of Apamea in Syria. Influential *Platonist philosopher (also referred to as a *Pythagorean). Of some of Numenius' works (*On the Secret Doctrines of Plato, On the Indestructibility of Soul, The Hoopoe, On Numbers, On Place*) very little is known, whereas substantial fragments from two of his other works survive: a *metaphysical dialogue *On the Good*, and an informative history of *Plato's *Academy (*On the Divergence of the Academics from Plato*) designed to show how much the Academy had corrupted Plato's teaching. He claimed this teaching was Pythagorean, relating it to the ancient wisdom of the Brahmans, Magi, Egyptians, and Jews whose scriptures he interpreted allegorically. He shared ideas with *Gnosticism and with the *Chaldaean Oracles. In his metaphysics he argues for intelligible being as that on which material reality depends, intelligible *being depending on a first god, the Good, which is difficult to grasp, but which inspires a second god to imitate it, turning to matter and organizing it as the world. *Matter is evil, as is life in the body for our soul. Numenius had considerable influence on *Plotinus (who was accused of plagiarizing him), on *Amelius, on *Porphyry and on later *Neoplatonists, in particular Theodore of Asine.

BIBLIOGRAPHY: Texts in E. des Places, *Numénius Fragments*, Paris, 1973. Dillon, J., *The Middle Platonists*, London/Ithaca, 1977, 361–79; Frede, M., "Numenius," *ANRW* 2, 36.2, 1987, 1034–75.—*DOMINIC J. O'MEARA*

O

OENOMAUS (probably 2nd cent C.E.; possibly 1st half of the 3rd cent. C.E.), of Gadara, near the Sea of Galilee. *Cynic philosopher, perhaps identical with the Abnimus mentioned in the Talmud as a friend of the famous Rabbi Meir (2nd cent. C.E.). His work, *The Swindlers Unmasked*, written against divination, survives in fragments. In *The Dog's Own Voice* he probably defended his ideas about Cynicism. He also wrote *On Diogenes, Crates and the other Cynics, The Philosophy according to Homer*, and, like *Diogenes of Sinope, a *Republic* and *Tragedies*. An *Epigram* is dubious.

Oenomaus revived the literary Cynicism of Diogenes, *Crates of Thebes and *Menippus. With his biting wit and subtle parodies he treated religious and social questions and Cynicism itself, directing his commentary at a learned readership. The extant fragments of his writings ridicule popular beliefs in oracles and refute *Stoic and *Middle Platonic attempts to combine fate and free will. He even employed Stoic *epistemology against the Stoics themselves. He probably criticized contemporary Cynics for imitating their famous predecessors, and, significantly, he did not quote those earlier Cynics as examples to follow.

There are affinities between the writing of Oenomaus and *Lucian, and the latter's use of Menippean literary features may be due to Oenomaus' influence. *Christian writers appreciated his arguments against oracles and superstition: Eusebius copied nearly forty pages of them. In his attacks against Oenomaus and his followers, Julian the Apostate treated him as the major exponent of the new Cynicism.

BIBLIOGRAPHY: Fragments of *The Swindlers Unmasked* in J. Hammerstaedt, *Die Orakelkritik des Kynikers Oenomaus*, Frankfurt am Main, 1988. Hammerstaedt, J., *ANRW* 2, 36. 4, 1990, 2834–2865 (with bibliography); also in M.-O. Goulet-Cazé and R. Goulet, eds., *Le Cynisme ancien et ses prolongements*, Paris, 1993, 399–418; Luz, M., *Journal for the Study of Judaism* 23, 1992, 42–60.—*JÜRGEN HAMMER-STAEDT*

OENOPIDES (5th cent. B.C.E.), of Chios. Unknown except for surviving reports by diverse authors from *Plato to *Proclus concerning matters in *astronomy, geometry, meteorology, and *cosmology. The casual reference to Oenopides in Plato's *Amatores* (123a–b) may well have occasioned the tradition purportedly going back to *Eudemus that Oenopides discovered the obliquity of the zodiacal belt (or circle, as some have it). By the third century C.E., as the practice of converting *mathematical and *logical relations into historical accounts became established, Oenopides was credited with discovering a calendrical cycle in which each year has 365 and 22/59 days. Later authors identify this 59-year cycle as his Great Year in which the seven planets return to their initial relative positions. Proclus attributes to Oenopides views about the distinction of theorems and problems in geometry, as well as interest in the application of areas (that is, in the problem of constructing a figure equal to a given figure in area, at given point on a given line).

See also MATHEMATICS, Earlier Greek.

BIBLIOGRAPHY: Testimonia in DK41.—*ALAN C. BOWEN*

"OLD OLIGARCH" (wrote probably between 446 and 424 B.C.E.), of Athens. The anonymous author of a treatise on the government of Athens, which survived under false attribution to *Xenophon as the *Constitution of the Athenians*. It is dated by most modern scholars by an event it mentions (446 B.C.E.) and a prominent one it omits (424 B.C.E.); in any case it clearly belongs to the political discussion that took place at the time of the Peloponnesian War. The "Old Oligarch" appears to have been a disgruntled exile from Athens, and his treatise invites comparison with debates on constitutions at *Herodotus 3.80–82 and *Euripides' *Suppliants*, lines 399–456.

Although opposed to democracy, the "Old Oligarch" defends the Athenian system against the most common criticisms leveled against it. He concedes that democracy subverts good law, but admits that it works well in the interests of the common people, and that the Athenian system effectively preserves itself. The author also observes how Athens' control over its empire is built on its support for democracies in the subject cities.

BIBLIOGRAPHY: Text and tr. in G. W. Bowersock, ed., *Xenophon*, vol. 7 (Loeb), Cambridge, MA, 1984. Tr. in R. K. Sprague, *The Older Sophists*, Columbia, SC, 1972, and M. Gagarin and P. Woodruff, eds., *Early Greek Political Thought from Homer to the Sophists*, Cambridge, 1995. W. K. C. Guthrie, *The Sophists*, Cambridge, 1971.—*PAUL WOODRUFF*

OLYMPIODORUS (before 510–after 565 C.E.), of Alexandria (?). Alexandrian *Platonist and pupil of *Ammonius. Among attested commentaries, we have those on the *Categories* and *Meteororologica* of *Aristotle, and three on *Plato. For other works see Westerink, 21ff. Of chief interest are his Platonic commentaries, to which are related the anonymous *Prolegomena to Plato's Philosophy* and the extensive scholia on the *Gorgias*. Extant commentaries concern *Alcibiades I*, *Gorgias*, and *Phaedo* (the last a small fragment only), the first three *dialogues of the post-*Iamblichan Platonist curriculum; they provide evidence for the student's first encounter with Plato in an Alexandrian school now usually specializing in Aristotle.

Westerink (23) rightly mentions the "extreme pliability" of his doctrine, which seems designed to cause minimum offense to *Christian students without sacrificing Platonist principles. This particularly applies to theology and to interpretation of pagan divinities encountered in Plato's works. Little trace of *Plotinus or of the elaborate *metaphysics of *Proclus or *Damascius is found. Important to the interpretation of the Platonic commentaries are (i) a multilevel theory of *virtues, accounting for their different treatment in different dialogues; (ii) an *allegorical treatment of myth similar to that of Proclus; (iii) and a division of *rhetoric into a flattering kind, a philosophic kind, and an intermediate kind represented by great Athenian statesmen.

BIBLIOGRAPHY: Tarrant, H., *Byzantinische Forschungen* 22, 1996, 179–190; Westerink, L. G., *The Greek Commentaries on Plato's Phaedo*, vol. 1, *Olympiodorus*, Amsterdam, 1976.—*HAROLD A. S. TARRANT*

ORIGEN (3rd cent. C.E.). Pagan *Platonist philosopher, who, with *Plotinus, studied philosophy under *Ammonius Saccas in Alexandria (Egypt) in the 230s and himself taught Longinus, *Porphyry's teacher in Athens before Porphyry joined Plotinus in Rome. Origen also visited Longinus in Athens and Plotinus in Rome. The arguments against identifying this Origen with his *Christian homonym, *Origen of Alexandria, are strong; only two (lost) works are ascribed to the (pagan) Origen: *On Demons* (used by Porphyry and concerning, it appears, different types of demons) and *That the King Alone is Creator*, an ambiguous title that could refer either to the (human) king as poet, or to the first principle or god (the "king" of *Plato's *Second Letter* 312e) as being the demiurge of the world. Origen is reported by *Proclus as having (like *Numenius) thought of the first principle as intellect and as absolute *being, denying existence to a principle transcending being and corresponding (in the *Neoplatonic view) to the One of the first hypothesis of Plato's *Parmenides* (137cff.).

BIBLIOGRAPHY: Schwyzer, H., in G. Boss and G. Seel, eds., *Proclus et son influence*, Zurich, 1987, 45–59. Weber, K., *Origenes der Neuplatoniker*, Munich, 1962.— DOMINIC J. O'MEARA

ORIGEN (c. 185–254/5 C.E.), of Alexandria. *Christian philosopher and exegete. Origen was born in Alexandria of a Christian father, Leonides, who perished in a persecution organized by Septimius Severus in 202. Well educated by his father, Origen became a teacher and, at the age of seventeen, at the request of the bishop, Demetrius, took over the head-ship of the catechetical school. To increase his effectiveness in relation to the Alexandrian intelligentsia, many of whom were influenced both by philosophy and by forms of *Gnosticism, he attended the lectures of the *Platonist *Ammonius Saccas (later also frequented by *Plotinus), and in the next two decades forged for himself a remarkable philosophical position, based on selected passages of Scripture (mostly *allegorically interpreted), but much influenced by contemporary Platonism.

This emerges most notably in his systematic work *On First Principles* (*De Principiis*), produced before his departure from Alexandria to Caesarea in 231, and in his commentary on St. John's Gospel (in thirty-two books, of which just ten survive). The move to Caesarea was caused by a quarrel with Bishop Demetrius, who became increasingly disturbed by Origen's doctrinal positions, and objected to his being ordained by the Bishop of Caesarea on a previous visit there.

Despite his concern for orthodoxy, Origen adopted some doctrines offensive to the church establishment. He saw the cosmos, and all creatures, as developing from the *Logos* of God, and being ultimately subsumed back into the *Logos*. This involved asserting the reincarnation of the individual soul and the denial of eternal punishment to anyone (even the Devil would ultimately be saved, he was alleged to have asserted).

Origen went on to open a school in Caesarea, and to compose many other works, including commentaries on most of scripture, most notably on *the Gospel According to St. Matthew* and on the *Song of Songs*, and an important apologetic work, the *Contra Celsum*, a refutation of an attack on Christianity by a Platonist polemicist of the previous century.

Origen died in 254 or 255, following imprisonment and torture during the persecution of Decius in 250–1. His influence on the Christian tradition of biblical exegesis, despite the condemnation of his doctrines, was very great, especially in the Eastern church (though both *Augustine and Ambrose in the West learned much from him). The majority of his work has perished, and of what survives, much (including most of the *De Principiis*) is available only in the tactfully laundered Latin versions of his Roman admirer Rufinus, so that a full appreciation of his philosophical position is denied to us.

BIBLIOGRAPHY: Tr. of *De Principiis* by G. W. Butterworth, London, 1936; of *Contra Celsum* by H. Chadwick, Cambridge, 1953. For biographical details, see Eus., *HE* Bk. 6. Chadwick, H., *Christianity and the Classical Tradition*, Oxford, 1966; Daniélou, J., *Origen*, tr. W. Mitchell, New York, 1955; De Faye, E., *Origène, sa vie, son oeuvre, sa pensée*, 3 vols., Paris, 1923–1928; Trigg, J. W., *Origen*, Atlanta, 1983.— *JOHN DILLON*

P

PANAETIUS (c. 185–109 B.C.E.), of Rhodes. *Stoic philosopher and head of the Stoic school from 129 until 109 B.C.E. Student of *Diogenes of Babylon and *Antipater of Tarsus. From 144 on, Panaetius came frequently to Rome, where he became a member of the Scipionic circle, a group of prominent Romans associated with Scipio Africanus the Younger and much interested in Greek culture. Panaetius' writings are known only through reports by later authors. He is often regarded as the founder of the "Middle Stoa" (a modern coinage), which is distinguished from the early Stoa by its receptiveness to the influence of *Plato and *Aristotle.

Panaetius continued the trend, begun by his teachers, of focussing on practical *ethics. His ethics is the first major reform of Stoic ethics. He was the first in a series of Stoics to adapt Stoic ethics to the concerns of the Roman ruling class. While adhering to the system of moral development proposed by his Stoic predecessors, Panaetius shifted attention away from the attainments of the wise to the duties of the leaders of society. His ethical teachings have been preserved primarily by *Cicero, who used them as a basis for his own adaption of Stoic ethics in his *On Duties*.

Panaetius refined the Stoic account of duties by adding many insights of his own. His fundamental innovation is a distinction among four personae (*prosôpa*), roles in life (Cic. *Off.* 1.107–121). The first two personae constitute the nature of a human being. A person has, first, a generic nature as a member of the human race, and, second, an individual nature, consisting of personal physical and mental attributes. Third, a person has a role determined by circumstances; examples are political

power, wealth, noble birth, and their opposites. The fourth role is determined by one's own choices. These include choice of career, such as philosophy, law, or *rhetoric, and choice of the *virtue in which one wishes
to excel.

While observing the demands of our universal human nature,
Panaetius insists, we must follow our individual nature. There is no
point in fighting our own nature and attempting the impossible. Just as
an actor chooses roles that suit his particular talents, so a person must act
in conformity with his own natural endowments. Panaetius' reformula-
tion of the goal of life as "living in accordance with the starting-points
given to us by nature" (fr. 96 van Straaten) takes account of both kinds of
nature. By recognizing individual constraints, Panaetius adapted Stoic
ethics to the needs of every human being. Even though he addressed his
advice primarily to a political elite and focussed on leadership qualities,
his emphasis on individual traits and fortunes broadened the field of
Stoic ethics from the primarily intellectualist concerns of the early Stoa to
the recognition of diverse practical talents. Panaetius is the founder of a
theory of individual personality. Whereas all Stoics proposed a single
goal in life that is the same for all humans—the *happiness that attends
perfect rationality, Panaetius emphasized that there are different approaches to this goal, depending on a person's natural predisposition,
circumstances, and choices. Just as archers aim for a single target by aiming at different lines on the target, Panaetius argued, so humans aim for
the single goal of happiness by aiming at different virtues (fr. 109 van
Straaten).

Panaetius reinterpreted the four cardinal Stoic virtues of prudence,
justice, temperance, and courage. By recasting courage as "greatminded-
ness," Aristotle's paramount ethical virtue, he demoted military valor
and gave priority to the courage displayed in civic life (Cic. *Off.* 1.61–
192). Mere fighting prowess, he maintained, is something humans share
with beasts. Panaetius assigned new importance to the cooperative
virtues by substituting sociability for justice and by making justice and
liberality the two main subdivisions of sociability (*Off.* 1.20). Temperance
underlies all the virtues while forming a category of its own (*Off.* 1.93–
151). Panaetius redefined it as the "fitting" or "decorum" (*prepon*) and assigned a large place to the social graces.

Panaetius also introduced some important changes into Stoic psychology. Instead of positing a single, unitary *mind whose sole function is
the exercise of reason, Panaetius proposed two kinds of mental motion,
reason and impulse. Impulses are separate from reason and must obey it
(frs. 87–89 van Straaten). This dualism is indebted to Plato's separation of
spirit and desire from reason in his tripartite soul. While separating the

emotions from reason, Panaetius agreed with the rest of the Stoics that pleasure is an irrational impulse that must be shunned.

BIBLIOGRAPHY: Texts in M. van Straaten, *Panétius*, Amsterdam, 1946. Tr. in M. T. Griffin and E. M. Atkins, *Cicero: On Duties*, Cambridge, 1991. De Lacy, P., *Illinois Classical Studies* 1977, v. 2, 163–72; Dyck, A., *Mus. Helv.* 38, 1981, 153–61; Gill, C., *OSAP* 6, 1988, 169–99; Pohlenz, M., *Antikes Führertum, Cicero De officiis und das Lebensideal des Panaitios*, Leipzig, 1934.—*ELIZABETH ASMIS*

PANTHOIDES (fl. c. 299–265 B.C.E.). *Logician belonging to the *Dialectical School. Teacher of a *Peripatetic named *Lyco (D.L. 5.68), Panthoides worked exclusively on logic (S.E. *M* 7.13). He wrote a work entitled *On Ambiguities (Peri Amphiboliôn)*, to which *Chrysippus wrote a response (D.L. 7.193).

The most substantive information about Panthoides' philosophical views comes in connection with *Diodorus' "Master Argument" (Epictetus *Discourses*, 2.19, 1–5; see DIODORUS CRONUS; LOGIC). The following three propositions conflict: (i) every truth about the past is necessary, (ii) something impossible does not follow from something possible, and (iii) there is something possible which neither is nor will be true. Diodorus uses the first two propositions to conclude that, contrary to (iii), nothing which neither is nor will be true is possible. *Epictetus claims that the circles of Panthoides, as well as *Cleanthes, however, retain (ii) and (iii) by denying (i).

BIBLIOGRAPHY: See bibliography under DIALECTICAL SCHOOL; DIODORUS CRONUS.—*IAKOVOS VASILIOU*

PARMENIDES (late 6th to mid 5th cent. B.C.E.), of Elea or Hyele (the Roman and modern Velia), in southern Italy. The central figure of the *Eleatic School, the most influential of the Presocratic philosophers, and the first among them who may reasonably be called a *metaphysician. Testimony in *Diogenes Laertius 9.21–23 places Parmenides' *floruit* (40th year) at 500 B.C.E. By contrast, *Plato's *dialogue *Parmenides*, the dramatic date of which is 451–449, involves an encounter in Athens (also alluded to at *Tht.* 183e and *Soph.* 217c) of the "very young" *Socrates with Parmenides at age "sixty-five at most." Though Plato's testimony was already impugned in antiquity (Athenaeus 11.505f.), the much earlier date attested in Diogenes is even less credible; for it appears to draw on a transparently artificial scheme of the succession of prominent historical personages employed by the chronologist *Apollodorus of Athens (2nd cent. B.C.E.). There is some suggestive evidence (ancient testimony, archaeological findings at Velia, thematic indications) that Parmenides was by profession a physician.

In their traditional use, the terms "School of Elea" or "Eleatic School" refer not just to Parmenides and *Zeno of Elea but also to *Xenophanes of

Colophon (who spent the major part of his life in southern Italy and Sicily) supposedly as founder of the school, and to *Melissus of Samos, viewed as an an Ionian acolyte. Apart from shared themes that may be noted through comparative study of these four philosophers and beyond the obvious likelihood of some association between the two persons whose native city was Elea, the "Eleatic school" has no historical reality. The grouping appears to have been prompted by such tendentious or playful remarks of Plato's as "the Melissuses and Parmenideses" (*Tht.* 180d) and "the Eleatic nation, starting from Xenophanes and even earlier..." (*Soph.* 242c). See also ELEATIC SCHOOL.

*Metaphysics and *Cosmology.* What has been preserved of Parmenides' work is about twenty fragments (quotations in later authors) of a didactic poem in dactylic hexameter—close to 150 lines in all. Ancient sources also provide us with "testimonia" concerning Parmenides' doctrines and his life—a body of some two hundred passages.

The narrative prologue of Parmenides' poem describes a mysterious journey that culminates in an encounter with a goddess, who announces that she will deliver a revelation concerning not only "Truth" but also "*Doxai*," the misguided "Opinions of Mortals." In the "Truth" part of her discourse, the goddess points out two routes (*hodoi*) that are open to thinking or knowing: "it is, and it cannot not be"; and "it is not, and it rightly is not" (DK28B2.3 and 2.5). The second of these routes she rejects as "one from which no tidings ever come." She also rejects a third route (cf. B6 and B7), one that would combine the first two. Her proscription of the second and third routes also implies rejection of the entities referred to by the expressions "what-is-not" and "nothing." Dwelling on the consequences of strict adherence to the first route, she develops (B8.1–38) distinct proofs that *to eon* ("what-is," or "the real," or *"Being")* must bear the following attributes: "unborn and deathless"; "altogether one, cohesive" or "indivisible"; "immobile"; and "fully actualized" or "perfect" (*tetelesmenon*). Except for referring to it as "what-is," the goddess offers no positive specification of the subject of her deductions; but she also makes it obvious that the ephemeral, multiform, and variable objects of ordinary experience could not possibly qualify (B8.39–41). To convey the absolute integrity, coherence, and perfection of what-is, the goddess introduces the simile (*enalinkion*) of a well-made sphere: "well-rounded from all sides"; "thrusting out equally from the center in every way"; "same with itself from all sides"; "lying uniformly within limits" (B8.42–49).

The goddess emphatically warns at the outset (B1.30) that the part on "*Doxai*" offers "no genuine trust"; and she later prefaces its exposition with a notice that it comprises a "deceptive order of words" (B8.50–52). Given such express disparagement, it is not surprising that the contents of *"Doxai"*—which was, nonetheless, the longer of the two parts of Parmenides' poem—are poorly represented in the preserved fragments. By drawing also on testimonia, we can perhaps get a glimpse of salient concepts and themes. *"Doxai"* expounded a dualistic cosmology and cosmogony. It presented the cosmos as resulting from the mixing of thing-like characters or powers (*morphai, dunameis*) in accordance with this scheme of contrariety: (on the positive side), fire, bright, mild, light in texture and weight, sprightly; (on the negative side) night, thickly textured, heavy, sluggish (B8.55–60).

Remarkably, *"Doxai"* also included reference to four major cosmological and *astronomical discoveries of the time. Whether these discoveries were made by Parmenides or are simply reported by him, they are more securely attested in this context than they are in other attributions (to earlier or later alleged discoverers). Parmenides knows that the moon derives its light from the sun; he knows that the morning star and the evening star are the same object (and thus also that the object is a planet); and he is credited with introducing the standard division of the earth into five zones (arctic, antarctic, two temperate, and torrid), which implies belief in the sphericity of the earth. Moreover, even if the *sphaira* in "Truth" is only a simile, several details in *"Doxai"* suggest that he also envisaged spherical shape and concentric structure for the entire cosmos.

Two Strains in Parmenides' Argument. Some harrowing ambiguities in the text of "Truth" make it difficult to interpret securely the logical structure of key passages and to surmise Parmenides' philosophical motives. In one very telling passage, however, we have clear hints of a double rationale: "What birth would you seek of it? Having grown how, and from where? Nor will I permit you to say, 'from what-is-not'; for it is neither sayable nor thinkable [*or* 'knowable'] that it is not. Besides, what requirement could have impelled it, starting from nothing, to come into being later rather than sooner?" (B8.6–10). The two assertoric sentences in the middle offer some sort of semantic or *epistemological principle: One cannot speak or conceive of what-is-not. The rhetorical questions at the two ends of the quoted passage are expressions of a rationalist demand for intelligibility in explanation: first a simple appeal to considerations of causal intelligibility ("What birth ...?"); then, at the end, appeal to what later came to be known as the Principle of Sufficient Reason ("Why ... later and not sooner?"). Taken together, the two rhetorical questions support one of the axioms of classical rationalist metaphysics, best known in its medieval Scholastic version, *ex nihilo nihil fit*, "nothing can come into being out of nothing."

Monism. Plato gives this epitome of Parmenides' philosophy: "All things are (*or* all is) one." This formula, which is conspicuously absent in the fragments of "Truth," provided the model for interpretations of Parmenides from Plato onward. *Aristotle adopts Plato's formula and embellishes it in a syllogism (cf. *Met.* 1.5, 986b18 ff.): What would exist next to (besides) what-is would be what-is-not; but what-is-not is nothing; so, necessarily, what-is is one (unitary). The syllogism is then repeated, with slight variations and amplification, in accounts of Parmenides by *Peripatetic authors and by the *Neoplatonic *commentators.

This Platonic-Aristotelian image of Parmenides has been challenged primarily because of the almost studied avoidance in the preserved fragments of what would be the ultimate inference: that what-is must be a single, all-encompassing, and undifferentiated One. That inference was indeed drawn by Melissus, whose argument parallels in many other respects that of Parmenides. And it is in the fragments of Melissus that "the One" appears as the subject of the deductions and that infinity (*apeiron*) plays the role of crucial attribute in the argument (there could not be two or more infinites). The inference to "all is one" may have also been drawn by Zeno, whose paradoxes of motion and plurality are plausibly read—in agreement with Plato's testimony—as the negative corollary to Parmenidean monism, namely, that the familiar world of plurality and *change is fundamentally incoherent.

If Parmenides is not a monist in quite the sense conveyed by Plato's formula, he may still be a monist in another sense. It has been suggested that he argues for "predicational monism," the thesis that no more than a single predicate, the same in all instances, may be applied to anything that properly qualifies as "what-is." Farthest removed from the Platonic reading is yet another alternative: that he allowed for both a plurality of subjects and a plurality of predicate types, provided that each what-is, taken in itself, is absolutely simple and indivisible—a universe of metaphysical and logical monads.

Other Questions in the Interpretation of "Truth." The verb forms *esti*, "is," and *einai*, "to be," appear without a subject in the goddess's presentation of the two "routes." Did Parmenides, nonetheless, envisage a subject (say, "the All," or "Reality," or even "the subject of discourse") in the expectation that his hearers or readers would silently supply it? Or is the absence of subject part of a strategy to allow the identity of the subject to emerge through the deduction of the relevant attributes?

What precisely is the syntax and sense of the verb *einai*, "to be," in its thematically crucial uses (the ones in the statement of the routes and in the articulation of the deductions)? Does the verb have the force of existence ("it exists," "to exist," "existent"), or does it have veridical force ("it is the case," "it is so," etc.)? Or does the verb function as bare copula, lacking both an explicit subject and an explicit predicate complement?

What is it that Parmenides found so objectionable about the second route and about what-is-not? Is he assuming a referential conception of meaning? That is, does he suppose that reference either to nonexistent entities or to non-actual states-of-affairs is impossible? Or is he worried that reports that merely tell us what a given subject "is not" will never yield any knowledge of the subject? Or is his intuition one of the causal inefficacy, and thus metaphysical irrelevance, of what-is-not? Or does he simply want to uphold a model of "robust reality," according to which no tinge of negativity is present in a reality that is fundamental or ultimate?

At B8.5 (cf. B8.19–20) Parmenides states that "what-is never was, nor will it be, for it is now." Do these lines propound a nontemporal conception of reality? Or do they state a doctrine of sempiternity (what-is exists at absolutely all times, in a sempiternal "now")? Or do they suggest that what-is has the nature of an instantaneous event?

These and related issues continue to be vigorously debated in the scholarly literature. They have important repercussions on any philosophical appraisal of Parmenides' thought.

Issues in the Interpretation of "Doxai." Scholarly discussion has focused on B8.54, in which the goddess diagnoses the fatal mistake mortals commit as they adopt a dualistic cosmology, and on B1.31–32, which are the goddess's programmatic lines concerning the two parts of the poem. Depending on different resolutions of the ambiguities in these two crucial texts, readers have found support for strikingly different interpretations of the *"Doxai"*: (i) as a phenomenology, a doctrine of how appearances are bound to present themselves to mortal sensibility; (ii) as the best possible articulation of the world grasped by the senses; (iii) as mere polemic against the earliest cosmologies; or (iv) as an instructive specimen of a false metaphysics, a case study in human delusion.

Unresolved issues aside, a significant linguistic pattern in the *"Doxai"* is clearly discernible: The goddess uses language that is pointedly reminiscent of language used with reference to what-is in "Truth"; and she also uses language that is pointedly in contrast to her account of what-is. The *"Doxai"* may thus serve not only as a dialectical foil to "Truth"; it may also provide us with a semantic commentary on "Truth." For example, when the goddess states in "Truth" that "all of it is full of what-is," the applicable sense of "full" is not the literal one in which physical bodies "are full of" or "are filled by" the reified contraries of the *"Doxai."*

Self-referential Inconsistency in Parmenides' Argument. Against his monistic version of Parmenides, Plato advances a devastating ad hominem objection: Parmenides himself speaks of naming what-is, and does so with alacrity; he concedes, therefore, at least one other reality, that of language, of the name (*Soph.* 244d). Even if we do not accept Plato's version of Parmenides, we may nonetheless fault the goddess for self-referential inconsistency on grounds similar to Plato's or on other grounds. Does she not avail herself freely of the "is not" route as she rules out inadmissible attributes of what-is? Moreover, it is highly problematic for the goddess to proclaim that "nothing outside [*or* 'other than'] what-is exists or will exist" (B8.36–37). For what of the realm of "*Doxai*"? Whether it represents a scheme of appearances or the record of mere delusion, some principle or factor other than what-is must be acknowledged.

Parmenides' Influence. One does not need answers to such ad hominem objections nor does one need a definitive interpretation of the poem in order to appreciate the enormous impact Parmenides' thought had on later philosophy. Of the two strains distinguished above, the semantic-epistemological strain was largely ignored by the other natural philosophers of the fifth century B.C.E. But in the *sophistic movement, issues and paradoxes that involve reference to what-is-not and to "nothing" are prominent—and the connection with Parmenides is unmistakable. These issues are of central importance also for some of the minor *Socratics in the fourth century: *Antisthenes' doctrine that it is impossible to propound the contradictory of a given proposition is a dialectical descendant of Parmenides' proscription of what-is-not; and the *Megarians' *logic of sheer actuality can be traced back to Parmenides' deduction of the fourth attribute of what-is, "fully actualized."

The semantic-epistemological strain also mediates the connection of Parmenides to Plato. In the middle dialogues Plato virtually echoes Parmenides: "that which *absolutely-is* is knowable absolutely; that which *altogether-is-not* is altogether unknowable" (*Rep.* 5.477a). The realm of absolute Being turns out to be the realm of intelligible Forms. At least in those contexts in which the Forms are characterized as logically simple (*monoeides*), each of the Forms taken separately satisfies all four requirements for what-is posited in Parmenides' "Truth." Moreover, the realm of Platonic *doxa*, the realm of "equivocal" entities which *in-some-ways-are but in-some-ways-are-not*, is prefigured in the "*Doxai*"—even if Parmenides did not at all envisage, as Plato did, a metaphysics of degrees of reality. Eventually Plato sought a more inclusive theory. In the *Sophist*, now in carefully phrased opposition to Parmenides, he develops a metaphysics that secures semantic and cognitive legitimacy even for what-is-not.

The rationalist strain, with its characteristic adherence to the twin principles, "No generation from, and no perishing into, nothing," is evident in the connection to Melissus, and also in the connection with the natural philosophers of the middle and late fifth century B.C.E. (*Anaxagoras, *Empedocles, *Philolaus, the *atomists *Leucippus and *Democritus, *Diogenes of Apollonia). Melissus bases the entirety of his deduction of the attributes of what-is on the twin rationalist principles.

The post-Parmenidean natural philosophers, for all their wide differences as to what should count as fundamental reality, are in agreement that the reality at issue is unborn, imperishable, and immune to any sort of internal change.

Especially striking is the influence—again via the rationalist strain—on Aristotle. The fundamental thought-structures in Aristotle's metaphysics—substance vs. the other categories, qualitative alteration, the contrast between potentiality and actuality, the distinction between *matter and form—have been very aptly interpreted as components in Aristotle's highly sophisticated answer to Parmenides. Change, Aristotle argues (e.g., in *Phys.* 1.8–9), is conceptually articulated and modulated in such a way that we are never faced with an unintelligible transition from nothing to what-is, the sort of transition Parmenides had inveighed against at B8.6–10; an underlying substrate persists across all types of change; and potentialities are specifically adapted to the corresponding actualities. In further observance of Parmenidean strictures, Aristotle insists that substantial forms neither come into being nor perish and that actuality is logically and metaphysically prior to potentiality (the principle that "man begets man"). Most remarkably, Aristotle's unmoved mover (which is absolutely simple in its nature as sheer actuality) is perhaps the only concept that meets unequivocally all of Parmenides' requirements for what-is in all of ancient philosophy.

BIBLIOGRAPHY: Texts in DK28. Aubenque, P., ed., *Études sur Parménide*, 2 vols., Tome I, *Le Poème de Parménide: Texte, traduction, essai critique* (by Denis O'Brien with Jean Frère); *Tome II, Problèmes d'interprétation*, Paris, 1987; Barnes, J., *AGP* 61, 1979, 1–21; also Barnes, *The Presocratic Philosophers*, 2 vols., London, 1979 (in one vol., rev., 1982); Coxon, A. H., *The Fragments of Parmenides, Phronesis* supp. vol. 3, Assen/Maastrich, 1986; Curd, P. K., *Phronesis* 36, 1991, 241–264; Furth, M., *JHP* 6, 1968, 111–132; repr. in A. P. D. Mourelatos, ed., *The Presocratics*, Princeton, 1993, 241–270; Gallop, D., *Parmenides of Elea, Fragments: A Text, with an Introduction. Phoenix* supp. vol. 18 (= *Phoenix* Presocratics, vol. 1), Toronto, 1984; Kahn, C. H., *Rev. Met.* 22, 1969, 700–724; Mourelatos, A. P. D., *The Route of Parmenides: A Study of Word, Image, and Argument in the Fragments*, New Haven, 1970; Owen, G. E. L., *CQ.* n.s. 10, 1960, 84–102; repr. in R. E. Allen and D. J. Furley, eds., *Studies in Presocratic Philosophy*, vol. 2, *Eleatics and Pluralists*, London, 1975, 48–81.—
ALEXANDER P. D. MOURELATOS

PERIPATETIC SCHOOL. By the "Peripatetic School" may be understood both the institution founded (at least in a loose sense) by *Aristotle in Athens that ceased to exist in 86 B.C.E. and the wider group of people known as "Peripatetics" who followed Aristotle's thought and developed it through many centuries and in many parts of the world—in such a way that even when they produced views of their own they shared some fundamental assumptions with him. Since there were Peripatetic schools outside Athens from an early date and since Peripatetic teaching continued in Athens and elsewhere after the end of the *Lyceum, a clean division cannot be made.

The school was started by Aristotle at the Lyceum in Athens in 335 B.C.E. alongside the already existing *Academy founded by *Plato. It became a society devoted to study and education that passed from one generation to another by the will of the head. The establishment included a library and probably a museum. Aristotle set out to produce, in a series of lectures, and by written records, a kind of encyclopedia of all human knowledge, from *logic to poetics, including natural *science and *ethics, largely preserved in his "esoteric" writings. Several of his followers also engaged in this work: *Eudemus wrote histories of *mathematics and *theology, Meno wrote a history of *medicine, and *Theophrastus covered botany. In addition, the constitutions of many Greek and some non-Greek states were gathered in a collection. After Aristotle's departure from Athens in 323 as persona non grata because of his Macedonian connections, and his death a year later, his colleagues apparently put his papers in order so that records of his work have survived to this day with great fidelity to their originals. After a period of obscurity, in which Aristotle was known for his lighter "exoteric" works, later Peripatetics took the esoteric as a starting point for their own studies but were not subservient to them.

Aristotle was much influenced by his teacher and colleague Plato, but criticized him and extended his interests beyond him. He laid the foundations of predicate logic with the categorical syllogism. He introduced certain concepts into thought: the categories, including substance, quantity, quality, and relation; the four "causes"; form and *matter; and potentiality and actuality. These were applied to the processes of the natural world and beyond: In any individual thing one could distinguish between the form that made it the kind of thing it was, a chair or an oak tree, and the matter of which it was made, which would remain with a different form when the thing came to die or be destroyed. Matter and form could also be seen as causal agents, along with that which brought them together, the maker of the object or the father of the offspring, and the purpose for which this was done. The idea of purpose informed his outlook, not only in biology but also in ethics, *politics, and theology. He treated the *soul as the form of the body, in animals and even in plants as well as in humans, but allowed for an intellect in the human soul that in some form might survive death. He also produced an influential account of God as the first mover, beyond the universe but influencing it, as well as works on *rhetoric and the theory of drama. His accounts of *virtue as a mean and of a tragedy as catharsis acquired wide circulation.

These ideas are well known, but some aspects of his thought have been given less attention, in particular his physiological ideas. These stimulated later work in practical experimentation, particularly by *Strato and later Hero. The theory of spirit or *pneuma* seemed to provide a vehicle for the soul and appears frequently in later thought. His theories of space, *time, and motion aroused considerable controversy.

Theophrastus continued Aristotle's project (i) in original works, like his two botanical works, his *Characters*, comic sketches that influenced later European literature, and his little *Metaphysics*, a critical study of *metaphysical problems that covered a wide field beyond the views of Aristotle himself and may have been written while Aristotle was still alive; (ii) in a collection of the opinions of earlier thinkers on many subjects that became the foundation of later *doxography; and (iii) in what amounted to commentaries on Aristotle's esoteric writings, of which a large part of his *On the Soul* survives, and portions of others. He and Eudemus found flaws in Aristotle's modal logic and developed the areas of hypothetical syllogisms and prosleptic syllogisms. Whether he influenced the development of propositional logic by the *Stoics is disputed. He may also have introduced the notion of the criterion of truth and went beyond Aristotle in setting out an empiricist theory of *knowledge. He argued that there is a natural affinity between all human beings, and beyond that between them and animals, because of their common ancestry or their sharing in common features like blood and flesh. He argued against meat eating and animal sacrifice and said that the wise man should not marry because of the consequences. But here as elsewhere we cannot be certain that these arguments represent his final thought.

Strato was particularly interested in the scientific side of Aristotle's thought; he is known for his theory of microvoids, which explained compressibility and has an influence on Hero's practical developments. He also worked on the theories of space, time, and motion and explained the workings of the universe without reference to God. On *psychology he argued that the soul was unitary and noted the part played by thought in perception.

Other early members of the Peripatos were *Dicaearchus, who denied the existence of the soul and said that life depended on the arrangement of elements in the body. He also believed in prophecy in dreams, however, and considered a practical life the most valuable. He also wrote on the development of mankind and on politics. *Aristoxenus is known for his work on music, but also for a theory of the soul as "harmony." Clearchus may have argued that there is evidence that the soul can leave the body and return to it and may have taken Greek philosophy to India. *Demetrius of Phalerum was an orator and statesman. Phaenias was noted for works on logic, botany, and history. The underrated Eudemus of Rhodes worked with Theophrastus on modal logic and set up a flourishing school in Rhodes. He is said to have treated hypothetical syllogisms more widely than Theophrastus, though still not extensively. In his *On Speech* he discussed questions and terms, and his work on physics continued Aristotle's and Theophrastus' treatments of time, place and movement. *Heraclides of Pontus is called a Peripatetic by *Diogenes Laertius, but he was also attached to the Academy, and his views are eccentric.

Non-philosophers who were classed as Peripatetics included Menander the comic playwright and Satyrus, who wrote chatty biographies, including one of Euripides which has partially survived. *Erasistratus the physician is said to have been a pupil of Theophrastus and to have used Strato's teachings, and *Aristarchus the astronomer was a pupil of Strato.

A number of works received into what is known as the Aristotelian Corpus are unlikely to be by Aristotle himself, and many of them probably spring from the early Peripatetic school, although for many there are still scholars who argue that they are by Aristotle. These include the *Magna Moralia* and the *De Mundo*; works on colors and on sounds, and sets of problems on many subjects including mechanics have been attributed to Theophrastus, Strato, or one of their associates. The account of Peripatetic ethics by *Arius Didymus given by *Stobaeus names few names and summarizes developments after Theophrastus.

The history of the school in Athens after *Lyco, Strato's successor who died about 225 B.C.E., is obscure, and—unlike the Stoics, the *Epicureans, and the Academic *Skeptics—has attracted little attention. But there is evidence that its members continued to work on some of the themes of Aristotle and made some important innovations. We are dependent for our information mainly on the interests of those who reported on it, like *Cicero, though a few actual fragments of works survive in papyrus form. *Critolaus, a pupil of Lyco's successor *Aristo of Ceos, represented Athens—along with *Diogenes of Seleucia and *Carneades from the Academy—at the famous meeting in Rome in 156 B.C.E. when the Romans were first made aware of Greek philosophy. This implies that the Peripatos was still prominent, and it was numbered among the four main schools of the time, that of *Epicurus being the one unrepresented at Rome. Aristo himself is dismissed as unimportant by Cicero, and there is much uncertainty about whether he or the Stoic *Aristo of Chios wrote the works listed by Diogenes Laertius. *Philodemus, however, has preserved some passages from his writings on character, including a treatment of arrogance. Yet another Aristo, from Cos, attacked rhetoric. Critolaus' pupil, Diodorus of Tyre, was concerned with the nature of the soul and emotions.

We can still distinguish certain broad themes in Peripatetic thought. In psychology the evidence is scanty and may be misleading. If we accept it, views ranged from the complete materialism and denial of a separate soul to belief in a soul that could be separated from the body. But inconsistencies in the accounts suggest that we should be cautious. In physics the correct way to define time, space, and motion was debated at length, and in ethics problems like the nature of *happiness were discussed. The themes of biography, styles of living, and proverbs and riddles also recur.

During this early period Aristotle was best known outside the school for his exoteric works, written in an attractive style for a wider public. But in the first century B.C.E. *Andronicus of Rhodes edited and published Aristotle's esoteric works and arranged them in order. He also wrote *commentaries on the *Physics, Ethics,* and *Categories.* His successor, Boethus of Sidon—to be distinguished from the Stoic *Boethus of Sidon—wrote at length on the theory of categories and on the soul and had subtle views on time. Aristo of Alexandria also wrote on the categories, a subject so popular that the Stoic *Athenodorus, the Platonist *Eudorus, and a *Neopythagorean also joined in. Commentaries on many of Aristotle's works were written for several centuries to come, many incorporating elements of *Neoplatonism remote from Aristotle. These commentaries have survived in large numbers. *Alexander of Aphrodisias is the greatest and most reliable. The original works of Aristotle and some of his successors passed into Arabic culture, and Averroes wrote commentaries that, translated into Latin, vastly influenced Western thought in the Middle Ages. Averroes was himself regarded as a Peripatetic at the time.

Thus the Peripatetic school's influence extended to Alexandria—where Strato was tutor to Ptolemy Philadelphus—to Rome, to the Arab world, and ultimately to medieval western Europe, where Aristotle was treated as the source of all knowledge, though people differed about how his works should be interpreted. Through Thomas Aquinas in particular he came to have a tremendous influence on *Christian theology. Parts of Theophrastus' teaching on the human soul were also much studied. Earlier, as long as the small city state existed, the political influence of the Peripatos was considerable: from Aristotle's connections with Hermias of Atarneus and Philip and Alexander of Macedon, to Athenion, called a Peripatetic, but also the "tyrant" who gave Athens a new constitution in the first century B.C.E. In a final irony, he brought about the destruction of the Lyceum by the Romans.

BIBLIOGRAPHY: Texts and notes in Wehrli. Moraux, P., *Der Aristotelismus bei den Griechen,* vol. 1, Berlin, 1973; De Vogel, C. J., *Greek Philosophy: A Collection of Texts with Notes and Explanations,* vol. 2, Leiden, 1953, 230–67.—*PAMELA M. HUBY*

PERSAEUS (c. 307/6–c. 243 B.C.E.), of Citium in Cyprus. Persaeus was brought up by *Zeno of Citium and lived in his house; hence the story that he was Zeno's slave. He was sent by Zeno in his stead along with Philonides to Antigonus Gonatas in response to persistent invitations to join him. There he stayed "having chosen the court, not the philosophical, life" (*Index Stoicorum* col. 13), and was eventually entrusted with the defence of the Macedonian garrison of Acrocorinth (c. 244). When the Macedonians were driven from it by Aratus of Sicyon, Persaeus sustained such wounds that he took his own life (*ibid.* col. 15). The story that this catastrophe converted him from adherence to Zeno's paradox that only the wise man can be a general sounds *ben trovato* (Plut. *Life of Aratus* 23).

The catalogue of his writings (D.L. 7.36) suggests that his philosophical preoccupations were predominantly *ethical and *political. Most notable is a treatise *Against Plato's Laws* in seven books. From his *Spartan Constitution* there survives information on the Spartan communal meals, and his *Notes on/Dialogues at Symposia* (reproducing material from *Stilpo and Zeno) provide evidence that he discussed standard questions about, e.g., appropriate topics of conversation and the acceptability of drunkenness on such occasions. His *On Gods* is said to have endorsed *Prodicus' view that men worship as divinities primarily the things that feed and sustain them, and then those who have discovered arts pertaining to these, like Demeter and Dionysus. Although he was Zeno's favorite pupil, there is no sign that he contributed to *Stoic theory.

BIBLIOGRAPHY: Texts in *S V F* 1, 435–62. Deichgraber, K., *R E* 19, 926–31.— *MALCOLM SCHOFIELD*

PHAEDO (5th and 4th cents. B.C.E.). The facts of Phaedo's life are uncertain. While *Plato named after him the *dialogue dedicated to the last hours of *Socrates, neither *Xenophon nor *Aristotle ever mentions Phaedo. According to some late sources, Phaedo was a native of Elis, coming from a noble family, who on the fall of his city was taken captive and was brought as a slave to Athens. There he frequented the circle of Socrates, who eventually induced Alcibiades or Crito or Cebes to ransom him. From then onwards, Phaedo became one of the most intimate disciples of Socrates and, after his death, moved back to Elis, where he founded the Elian school. It may be, however, that the dramatic events of Phaedo's life are a biographical invention similar to other stories of conversion to philosophy attributed to several *Socratics.

Phaedo's writings belong to the genre of Socratic discourses. According to *Diogenes Laertius (2.105), his dialogues *Zopyrus* and *Simon* are certainly authentic, whereas the dialogues *Nicias, Medius* (or *Medeius*), *Antimachus* or *The Elders*, and *The Cobblers's Tales* (or, perhaps, *Scythian*

Tales) are considered spurious. The *Suda* omits this last work and adds to the list three more dialogues, *Alcibiades, Simmias,* and *Critolaus*.

The *Zopyrus* owes its title to a professional physiognomist of the Periclean age. It may have contained a discussion of physiognomic principles concerning the relation between physical appearance and character, stressing the power of philosophical education and habituation to transform entirely one's natural disposition.

Simon was probably named after Simon the cobbler, a historical personage and a friend of Socrates. As a literary figure, Simon was a creation of Phaedo and, perhaps, of *Antisthenes. The dialogue may have been used as a source for the Twelfth and Thirteenth Socratic Letters, but its content is uncertain. It may have discussed various conceptions of *virtue and its relation to pleasure and perhaps defended the view that certain pleasures deriving from good actions and from a virtuous disposition are compatible with virtue—an intermediate position between *Aristippus' hedonism denounced in the Twelfth Letter and an extreme asceticism. This position is close to the views of Antisthenes and fits well with Simon's praise of Antisthenes in the Letters.

A theme connecting *Simon* to the *Zopyrus* and exploited by all the Socratics is the predominant importance of philosophy over the privileges of birth and mundane education. In the Thirteenth Letter, Simon is presented as another Socrates, attracting the noblest and most gifted among the youth despite his humble origins and profession.

BIBLIOGRAPHY: Gigon, O., *Mus. Helv.* 3, 1946, 1–21; Rossetti, L., *Studi Urbinati* 47, 1973, 364–81; von Fritz, K., *Philologus* 90, 1935, 240–244; von Willamowitz-Moellendorf, U., *Hermes* 14, 1879, 187–193.—*VOULA TSOUNA-McKIRAHAN*

PHAEDRUS (5th cent. B.C.E.) came from the Attic deme of Myrrhinus. He appears in several *Platonic *dialogues, but otherwise is almost unknown. The date of his birth is uncertain. On the one hand, in Plato's *Phaedrus* *Socrates occasionally calls him "dear boy" and "young man," which expressions, if taken literally, suggest that Phaedrus was very young at the dramatic date of the dialogue and that his birth may be fixed around 425 B.C.E. On the other hand, several passages in the *Phaedrus* suggest that the dramatic date of the dialogue coincides with Phaedrus' mature years. Besides, in the *Protagoras*, whose dramatic date is 432 B.C.E., he is presented as older than Agathon, born in 447; in the *Symposium*, whose scene is situated in 416, he appears close to middle age; and Phaedo is said to have spoken of him in the *Simon* as a close contemporary of Alcibiades. This evidence places his date of birth around 450 B.C.E.

Little is known of Phaedrus' life, aside from the fact that he was reasonably well off, but that at some point he lost his fortune, not through his own fault or malice, and subsequently married a relative. His death is placed either in the 390s or in 401 B.C.E.

No writings of his survive or are reported. Although he was a friend of Socrates, he probably was not a philosopher. In the *Protagoras* he appears as a student of *Hippias, and in the *Phaedrus* he is prepared to speak about *rhetoric, a chief subject of instruction of the *sophists, and he is acquainted with many important figures of the intellectual life of the fifth century B.C.E. Thus Phaedrus probably had a good general education that allowed him to follow, to a certain extent, a philosophical argument.—*VOULA TSOUNA-McKIRAHAN*

PHAEDRUS (c. 138–70 B.C.E.), of Athens. *Epicurean philosopher. Nothing of Phaedrus' philosophical writings survives. We know of only one title, *On the Gods*, which *Cicero requested from Atticus (*Att.* 13.39.2). Phaedrus' main influence seems to have depended on his character. He was head of the Epicurean community in Athens from the death of *Zeno of Sidon until Patron succeeded to the headship at the death of Phaedrus in 70. Phaedrus moved between Athens and Rome, where Cicero followed his lectures in 88, the year Cicero became acquainted with *Philo of Larissa (*Brutus* 306). From his appeal to Memmius to abandon his plans for building on the site of the dilapidated buildings of *Epicurus' Garden, it is clear that the example of Philo had come to diminish his high opinion of Phaedrus (*Ad Familiares* 13.1, 51 B.C.E.).

Cicero and Athenian inscriptions are our only sources for his activities as a member and director of the Epicurean school. They reveal not a hint of his philosophical attitudes. Cicero praises him for his nobility, sense of duty, and companionship (*Philippics* 5.13, *Ad Familiares* 13.1). Phaedrus was from an important Athenian family, attested in honorary decrees of the second and first centuries B.C.E. His Roman pupils in Athens honored him with statues placed on the acropolis (Atticus in *Inscriptiones Graecae* 2^2 3897/3896 and Lucius and Appius Saufeius in *IG* 2^2 3899) and in the Eleusinion. Unimpressive as a philosopher, he was evidently crucial in the maintenance of the school in Athens and its representation in Rome.

BIBLIOGRAPHY: Erler, M., in H. Flashar, ed., *Grundriss der Geschichte der Philosophie: Die Philosophie der Antike*, vol. 4, Basel, 1994, 273–275; Raubitschek, A. E., *Hesperia* 16, 1949, 96–103.—*DISKIN CLAY*

PHERECYDES (6th cent. B.C.E.), of the Cycladic island of Syros. Early writer of Ionic prose, sage, *theologian, proto-*cosmologist. His *floruit* may tentatively be placed in the 540s, but the biographical tradition is an unhelpful collection of tales of wonder-working and prophecy, closely bound up with the traditions of *Pythagorean biography. Many later

Pythagoreans recognized Pherecydes as *Pythagoras' teacher, but this tradition should not be confused with historical fact.

Pherecydes is credited with the invention of prose (frs. 2, 9–12 Schibli), and *Diogenes Laertius preserves the opening sentence of what in his time passed for Pherecydes' book: "Zas and Chronos always were, and Chthonie; Chthonie received the name Ge since Zas gives her Earth as her gift of honor" (fr. 14). Diogenes also reports (on the authority of Theopompus) that Pherecydes was "the first to write about nature and the gods" (fr. 1) and it is possible that a title (probably *On Nature* and/or *On the Gods*) lurks in that description. *Aristotle placed Pherecydes in a group of "theologians" whom he described as "mixed, by virtue of not putting everything mythically" and who "make the first generating entity the best" (*Met.* 14.4, 1091b = fr. 81). This description suggests a thinker intermediate between the poetic "theologians" (*Homer and *Hesiod) and the beginnings of a cosmogonic speculation that might properly be called philosophical. Pherecydes' revision of the succession myth would seem to have eliminated the Hesiodic transfers of power from more primitive generative deities to those who preside over the improved order of the world as we know it. This picture of a transitional thinker, using the deities inherited from the poetic cosmologies and a largely (though no longer entirely) mythic discourse to elaborate a more refined and reflective cosmology, is consistent with the available evidence. Pherecydes is only very rarely (and belatedly) called a philosopher. He clearly stood, along with the other "sages," on the cusp between the old, poetic traditions of wisdom and the beginnings of what the Greeks called philosophy.

BIBLIOGRAPHY: Text and tr. in DK7 and H. S. Schibli, *Pherekydes of Syros*, Oxford, 1990. KRS, 51-70; West, M. L., *Early Greek Philosophy and the Orient*, Oxford, 1971, 1–75.—*ROBERT LAMBERTON*

PHILO (c. 20 B.C.E.–45 C.E.), of Alexandria. Jewish philosopher and exegete of Scripture. Philo was a member of one of the richest and most prominent Jewish families in Alexandria and plainly received an excellent, but entirely Hellenized, education. In later life he seems to have "rediscovered his roots," and thereafter devoted himself to reinterpreting the Jewish intellectual heritage, and in particular the Pentateuch, the "books of Moses," in terms of Greek philosophy—more particularly *Platonism. His rationale for doing so was that *Plato was a follower of *Pythagoras, who in turn had learned all that was valuable in his doctrines from disciples of Moses. Philo thus saw himself as reclaiming the philosophical heritage of Moses from the Greeks, and to achieve this he used as an interpretative key the method of *allegorical exegesis primarily developed by the *Stoic commentators on *Homer of the School of Pergamum, such as *Crates of Mallos.

Armed with this tool, he embarked upon a vast project of exegesis. First, he produced a sequence beginning with the essay *On the Creation of the World* and continuing with lives of the Patriarchs—seen as "living laws"—including a life of Moses (which seems modelled on the existing life-myth of Pythagoras). He followed this by a series of works on the Ten Commandments and the particular laws that fall under each of these. This sequence ends with the treatise *On Rewards and Punishments*. Next, we find an even more heroic project, a virtual line-by-line exegesis of *Genesis*, beginning with the the the books of *Allegories of the Laws* and continuing, with sundry gaps, to the treatise *On the Change of Names*, which is an exegesis of *Genesis* 17.1–22. To this sequence he appended three books *On Dreams*, of which the latter two are extant, dealing with the dreams of Jacob (*Dreams* 1) and those of Joseph, Pharaoh, and the chief baker and butler (*Dreams* 2). Finally there is a third sequence—surviving as a whole only in Armenian—which covers *Genesis* and *Exodus* in the form of *Problems and Solutions*.

In what order these three great sequences were composed is not clear, but the first one seems to show both more complete Hellenic influence and a less developed system of allegory than the other two, while the *Problems and Solutions* certainly appear less elaborate than the line-by-line commentary. There are also a number of essays unconnected with these sequences, such as those *On the Eternity of the World* and *On Providence*, and an account of the Embassy to Gaius on behalf of the Jewish community of Alexandria on which Philo served in 39 C.E. (the only certain date we have for his life).

To speak of Philo's philosophical position is perhaps somewhat rash, since it is not universally agreed that he has a coherent one, but it can best be seen as a form of *Middle Platonism, which adopts many *Stoic formulations (though firmly rejecting Stoic materialism and their doctrine of an immanent divinity) and is also much influenced by *Neopythagorean transcendentalism and number mysticism. It corresponds most nearly, in fact, to what we know of the philosophical position of his older contemporary *Eudorus of Alexandria. Philo has a more pronounced *Logos-doctrine than any known Platonist before *Plotinus, and one can discern also a distinctive streak of Jewish piety and a great personal reverence for God and for monotheism, unusual for a Greek philosopher. This piety also leads on occasion to a downgrading of the ability of the human intellect (unaided by God's grace) to comprehend truth, which comes out curiously, at times, as *skepticism. Indeed, Philo is able to make use at one point (*On Drunkenness* 162–205), of *Aenesidemus' ten tropes against dogmatism—a most unexpected development.

Other distinctive doctrines are those of the "powers" (*dunameis*) of God, the creative and the administrative, which Philo terms Goodness and Sovereignty and which, with God himself, he sometimes views as a triad (cf. *On Abraham* 120ff.), and that of God's Wisdom (*sophia*), an entity for which there is some warrant in earlier Jewish thought but which also fills the role of the Platonist/Neopythagorean Indefinite Dyad. Sometimes we find the *Logos* portrayed as the offspring of God and Sophia (*On Flight and Finding* 109; *On Husbandry* 51), and producing in turn the two chief Powers (*On the Cherubim* 27ff.)

In the area of *ethics, Philo combines Stoic, Platonist, and *Peripatetic influences in interesting ways. For instance, though he is normally an advocate of the extirpation of the passions (*apatheia*), as opposed to their mere control (*metriopatheia*), he is prepared to recognize the latter as a state proper to the *prokopton*, the man still progressing in virtue (symbolized by the figure of Aaron, as opposed to Moses, the perfected sage, *Allegories* 3.132). In *psychology, Philo basically observes a bipartite division of the *soul into rational and irrational parts, but he sees no contradiction in making use also, when the exegetical situation calls for it, of the tripartite division of the *Republic* and elsewhere and even of the Stoic division into the "ruling element" and seven physical faculties (e.g., *Creation* 117, where he is in the process of extolling the number seven, and a group of seven dependent on a monad is what he needs).

In *logic, similarly, we find Philo operating with a mixture of Peripatetic and Stoic logical terminology and presenting a number of interesting developments. As regards the categories, we find him, like Pseudo-Archytas and Eudorus, presenting the order "Substance—Quality—Quantity" (*On the Decalogue* 30f.) and speaking of the categories as being "in nature," making explicit an uncertainty left by *Aristotle as to whether they were categories of speech or reality. He is also, however, prepared to utilise the Stoic categories, as when he identifies the manna in the desert with the Stoic supreme category *ti*, "something," at *Allegories* 3.175.

Even if one does not accept Philo's philosophical position as a coherent one, the vast corpus of his works remains a most useful source for the history of Greek philosophy, and in particular for later Platonism and Stoicism.

BIBLIOGRAPHY: Texts in Cohn and Wendland, *Philonis Alexandrini Opera quae Supersunt*, 7 vols., Berlin, 1896–1915; also Loeb ed. by F. H. Colson and G. H. Whitaker, with two supp. vols. by R. Marcus, of texts preserved only in Armenian. Bréhier, E., *Les idées philosophiques et religieuses de Philon d'Alexandrie*, Paris, 1950; Dillon, J., *The Middle Platonists*, London/Cornell, 1977, ch. 3; Runia, D., *Philo of Alexandria and the Timaeus of Plato*, Leiden, 1986; Wolfson, H. A., *Philo: Foundations of Religious Philosophy in Judaism, Christianity and Islam*,[3] 2 vols., Cambridge, MA, 1962.—*JOHN DILLON*

PHILO (158–84 B.C.E.), of Larissa in Thessaly. *Academic philosopher and head of the school from 110/109 B.C.E. until its breakup in 88. After studying with Callicles the Carneadean in Thessaly, Philo came to Athens at the age of twenty-four, where he studied with *Clitomachus for fourteen years as well as with other philosophers, including a *Stoic (Philod. *Hist. Acad.* col. 33). When the position of philosophers at Athens became untenable because of the pro-Mithridatic faction, he left for Rome, where he wrote the two *Roman Books*. These adopted a radical position capable of being viewed as involving both false historical claims and an untenable *epistemological position (Cic. *Acad.* 2.11, 18). Before Philo died, he had influenced *Cicero considerably.

Philo belonged to the same tradition as *Carneades and Clitomachus, though it would be inaccurate to refer to him as a *skeptic. While he maintained the battle against the Stoic theory of knowledge, and in particular against the *katalêptikê phantasia*, the school had long been engaging in genuine teaching. *Arius Didymus (in Stobaeus *Selections* 2.39. 20ff., Wachsmuth) preserves what purports to be Philo's division of moral philosophy—in fact a theory of moral education much influenced by *Plato's *Sophist* (230b–e). Protreptic encourages the taking of the cure, while contrary advice is refuted. False doctrines are driven out, and healthy ones are substituted. Thereafter *happiness is promoted, both in personal *ethics and in *politics. Doctrinal handbooks are needed for those without time for a fuller moral education.

From this division it is clear that both elenctic and didactic processes are to be employed, which helps explain Philo's belief that there was but one Academy, not (as *Antiochus thought) an "Old" and a "New" Academy disagreeing over the possibility of knowledge. The final break with Antiochus came after Philo had written his allegedly radical *Roman Books*, to which Antiochus replied with his *Sosus*. The supposed "skepticism" of the Carneadean school had with Philo become little more than an ideal of continued investigation, unhampered either by unwarranted conviction or by the uncritical acceptance of the doctrines of an authoritative figure.

*Sextus (*HP* 1.235) says that Philo made things comprehensible in their own nature, but not in such a way as to satisfy the Stoic criterion. One should compare Cicero *Acad.* 2.33, where the Stoic criterion, which demands that something be seen as true in such a way that it could not be false, is said to be all that moderate Academics resist. *Numenius (fr. 28 des Places) implies that the evident clarity (*enargeia*) and agreement (*homologia*) of things influenced his return towards a more confident epistemology; compare Cicero *Academica* 2.34, where those same moderate Academics admit that things can be evident, that is, true and securely impressed upon the mind.

The texts referred to above may be supplemented by the account of the Academy of the time given by *Aenesidemus in the first book of his *Pyrrhonian Logoi*, a summary of which is preserved by Photius.

BIBLIOGRAPHY: Hankinson, R. J., *The Skeptics*, London/New York, 1995; Glucker, J., *Antiochus and the Late Academy* (= *Hypomnemata* 56), Göttingen, 1978; Mette, H., *Lustrum* 28–29, 1986/87, 9–63; Tarrant, H., *Scepticism or Platonism?* (*Cambridge Classical Studies*), Cambridge, 1985.—HAROLD A. S. TARRANT

PHILO the Dialectician (late 4th and early 3rd cent. B.C.E.). Pupil of the *Dialectical philosopher *Diodorus Cronus. Philo is particularly associated with two *logical issues. One pertains to the Hellenistic disputes concerning truth or "soundness" (*hugieia*) conditions for the conditional (*sunêmmenon*) form of proposition: according to *Sextus Empiricus (*HP* 2.110, *M* 8.113), Philo held that a sound conditional is one "that does not begin with a truth and end with a falsehood." This account has been interpreted as equivalent to the modern account of the "material conditional." However, Hellenistic accounts often did not clearly distinguish between the truth/soundness of a conditional proposition and the entailment of consequent by antecedent. Thus, the examples given by Sextus for true conditionals with false antecedents are ones in which the antecedent is understood to entail the consequent.

The other doctrine attributed to Philo pertains to the alethic modalities: According to *Boethius and others, Philo held that possibility (of a proposition's being true or of a state of affairs' being actualized) consists exclusively in "internal" capacity for being actualized. Thus, the impossible is what cannot, "according to its proper nature," be true; the necessary is what cannot admit of falsity, and the nonnecessary is what can admit of falsity. It seem clear that Philo's account represents an attempt to allow unactualized possibilities and, as such, involves repudiation of the sort of fatalism inherent in Diodorus Cronus' equation of the possible with what either is or will be the case. In judging of possibility, Philo apparently wished to prescind from "external" factors that might causally influence the actualization of a state of affairs: thus, it is possible that a piece of wood be burned even though (i) it never will be burned and (ii) external circumstances, for example, its location at the bottom of the ocean, prevent its being burned.

BIBLIOGRAPHY: Kneale, W., and Kneale, M., *The Development of Logic*, Oxford, 1962; Mates, B., *Stoic Logic*, Berkeley/Los Angeles, 1961; Sedley, D., *PCPS* n.s. 23, 1977, 74–120.—MICHAEL J. WHITE

PHILODEMUS (c. 110–40 B.C.E.), of Gadara in Syria. *Epicurean philosopher and poet. After studying with *Zeno of Sidon, head of the Epicurean school in Athens, Philodemus settled in Rome, where he taught Epicureanism to prominent Romans, notably Piso, father-in-law of Caesar. His philosophical writings are strongly indebted to Zeno. They come to us from the so-called Villa of the Pisones at Herculaneum. Charred and buried in the eruption of Vesuvius in 79 C.E., the texts were excavated in the mid-eighteenth century. The better-preserved papyri throw a unique light on the philosophical controversies in which the Epicureans were involved in the time of Zeno and Philodemus. Against attacks by *Academics, *Stoics, and others, the Epicureans defended *Epicurus' doctrines, often by reformulating them in detail, while insisting that they were faithful to Epicurus.

Philodemus was interested especially in *ethics, along with literary and musical theory. His writings range from rather technical reports of philosophical debates, especially those in which his teacher Zeno had a leading part, to highly personal essays addressed to the ordinary reader. The reports usually contain summaries of the opponents' arguments, together with detailed replies by the Epicureans. Philodemus' own philosophical contribution consists primarily in adapting Epicurean ethics to the concerns of his Roman audience. He is particularly effective in engaging the reader with gentle, yet passionate appeals to learn Epicurean tranquillity. While proclaiming himself a follower of Epicurus, he reformulates Epicurean doctrine by heeding both the objections of other philosophers and the anxieties of the ordinary person.

Among Philodemus' better-preserved ethical writings are *On Household Management*, showing how a philosopher should support himself; *On Frankness*, on the psychotherapy of verbal admonitions; *On Anger*, on keeping anger within natural limits; and *On Death*, on conquering the fear of death. Philodemus defends Epicurean theology in *On the Gods*. He attacks traditional religion and defends Epicurean piety in *On Piety*. His *Rhetoric*, *On Poems*, and *On Music* are valuable sources of information about Hellenistic developments in these fields. In *On Poems*, Philodemus criticizes Hellenistic literary theorists in detail and presents his own view of poetry as a union of form and content. Among his few *epistemological writings, *On Signs* is one of the most interesting documents in the history of *scientific method. It may be regarded as the first systematic defence of induction. Philodemus argues that the Epicurean method of using sensory phenomena as signs of what cannot be observed is the only valid method of scientific investigation.

BIBLIOGRAPHY: Texts in F. Sbordone, ed., *Ricerche sui Papiri Ercolanesi*, Naples, 1969–83, vol. 2, *On Poems* A, B, C, ed. Sbordone; vol. 3, *Rhetorica* 1, 2, ed. F. Longo Auricchio; vol. 4, *On Poems* D and E, ed. M. Nardelli. Also in M. Gigante, dir., *La Scuola di Epicuro*, Naples, 1978–, *On Signs*, eds. P. De Lacy and E. De Lacy; *On Anger*, ed. G. Indelli; *On Poems* 5, ed. M. Mangoni. See also *CronErc*. Dorandi, T., *ANRW* 2, 36.4, 1990, 2328–2368; Asmis, E., *ANRW* 2, 36.4, 1990, 2369–2406.—
ELIZABETH ASMIS

PHILOLAUS (c. 470–385 B.C.E.), of Croton (or Tarentum) in southern Italy. Presocratic philosopher in the *Pythagorean tradition. *Plato (*Phd.* 61d) implies that he was still alive in 399 and that Simmias and Cebes had heard him speak in Thebes, but there is little other reliable evidence about his life. He is the first Pythagorean to have written a book. It was still available to *Aristotle's pupil Meno in the late fourth century, but only fragments have been preserved. Moreover, several of the Pythagorean pseudepigrapha were forged in Philolaus' name, and fragments derived from and testimonia based on these books have also been preserved. A consensus has emerged that some ten of the twenty-six surviving fragments are from Philolaus' genuine book (DK44B1–6, 6a, 7, 13, 17). The book followed a typical Presocratic structure: An assertion of basic principles is followed by a cosmogony leading up to *astronomical, *psychological, and *medical theories.

Philolaus argues that the cosmos and everything in it was put together out of two types of elements, limiters and unlimiteds. It is most likely that by unlimiteds Philolaus means elements that are not in themselves defined by any quantity or structure. These would include the "stuffs" such as air, water, hot, and cold, commonly chosen as elements by earlier Presocratics, but Philolaus is the first to create an abstract category that includes all such elements under the title "unlimiteds." However, Philolaus is critical of previous Presocratics for relying solely on this type of element and argues that another type, limiters, is necessary. Limiters are elements that define quantities and structures. Presocratic philosophers had used structural ideas prominently in their systems, but Philolaus is original in identifying them as a distinct class of entities. Thus, in Philolaus' astronomical system the central fire is a combination of the "unlimited" fire and the "limiter" center. Moreover, limiters and the unlimited are bound by *harmonia.* Philolaus presents the diatonic scale as an example. It is composed of the unlimited continuum of sound limited by a set of notes. However, these notes are inserted not at random, but in a pleasing order (*harmonia*) that is governed by whole-number ratios (1:2 = octave, 3:4 = fourth, 2:3 = fifth).

Thus, with the introduction of harmonia, number makes its entrance into Philolaus' system. He does not say that things are made up of numbers (Aristotle's interpretation of the Pythagoreans), but rather asserts that it is through numbers that things are known. In response to *Parmenides' call for a completely determinate object of *knowledge, Philolaus suggests that we know something when we can specify the numbers that define the harmonia according to which its limiters and unlimiteds are put together. Philolaus also employed a method of inquiry in which the first step is to define a set of starting points (*archai*), which are the minimum set of elements necessary to explain a given phenomenon. In the study of reality in the most general sense, it is the limiters, unlimiteds, and harmonia themselves that are the *archai*. In a narrower field such as the pathology of the human body, the set of *archai* that Philolaus uses to explain the phenomena become more specific: bile, blood, and phlegm as unlimiteds and heating and cooling as the limiting mechanism.

Philolaus drew a parallel between the birth of the cosmos and the birth of a human being. The cosmos starts from a fire that breathes in the unlimiteds breath, *time, and *void just as the human embryo is originally hot before drawing in cooling breath. Philolaus' astronomical system is famous as the first to make the earth a planet. However, it does not orbit around the sun; along with the sun, moon, five planets, the fixed stars, and a mysterious counter-earth (introduced to make the orbiting bodies total the perfect number ten), it circles the central fire.

Philolaus anticipates aspects of Platonic and Aristotelian psychology. As in Plato, different psychic faculties are tied to specific parts of the body. The soul is not tripartite, however. Four *archai* are identified as necessary to explain human beings. The genitals are identified as the seat of generation and are regarded as common to all living things. The navel is called the seat of "rooting" and is the *archê* peculiar to plants, while the heart is the locus of life and sensation and characteristic of animals. Intellect is located in the head and is the *archê* unique to humanity.

Controversy over the authenticity of the fragments has obscured Philolaus' important place in the Presocratic tradition until recently. Some have wanted to see Philolaus as a number mystic trying to express the wisdom of his master Pythagoras in terms of Presocratic philosophy. Others regard him as a serious theorist on nature but as heavily dependent on Pythagoras for his basic principles. Given the state of our knowledge, it is impossible to be certain about what debt if any Philolaus owed to Pythagoras. However, recent scholarship has shown him to be an original thinker who was responding to central problems in the tradition of Presocratic writing on nature, medicine, and astronomy. While Philolaus followed the way of life of a Pythagorean, his book may owe more to *Anaxagoras and Parmenides than to Pythagoras. It was an important influence on Plato's *Philebus* and the basis of Aristotle's account of Pythagoreanism, although the fragments also reveal that Aristotle's account is distorted in important ways.

BIBLIOGRAPHY: Texts in DK44. Burkert, W., *Lore and Science in Ancient Pythagoreanism*, tr. by E. Minar, Cambridge, MA, 1972; Huffman, C. A., *Philolaus of Croton: Pythagorean and Presocratic*, Cambridge, 1993; Kahn, C., in A. P. D. Mourelatos, ed., *The Pre-socratics*, New York, 1974.— CARL A. HUFFMAN

PHILOPONUS, John (c. 490–570 C.E.), also John the Grammarian, of Alexandria. *Christian *commentator on *Aristotle, student of *Ammonius, son of Hermeias. The name "John" implies that Philoponus was a Christian from birth, while "Philoponus" ("lover of work") is a nickname. About his life little other than his rivalry with the commentator *Simplicius is known. In late life Philoponus turned to Christian theological controversies; in 680/681 C.E. his views were (posthumously) declared anathema. Partly as a result, his philosophical and scientific views had little direct influence until his rediscovery in the Renaissance, when he inspired Galileo, among others.

While much of his corpus is lost, the major surviving texts can be divided into (i) commentaries on Aristotle (e.g., *Categories*, *Prior* and *Posterior Analytics*, *Meteorologica* 1, *Generation and Corruption*, *De Anima*, and the *Physics*—the commentary on the *Metaphysics* is spurious); (ii) writings on the creation and destruction of the world (e.g., *De Aeternitate Mundi contra Proclum*, *Contra Aristotelem*, and *De Opificio Mundi*); and (iii) theological treatises (e.g., *The Arbiter*, *Apologies*, and *Against the Fourth Council* on monophysitism; e.g., *On the Trinity* and *Against Themistius* on tritheism; and, e.g., *On the Resurrection* on the theory that the resurrected shall be without earthly bodies). There are also extant works on *grammar, *astronomy (the earliest treatise on the astrolabe), and *mathematics. The *medical manuscripts are unlikely to be authentic.

While Philoponus rejected many *Aristotelian physical tenets, his opposition was nonetheless inspired by Aristotelian philosophical principles. He argued, for example, that the world must both have been created and come to destruction, because an *infinite universe would entail a more than finite existence and, as Aristotle argued, no actual infinity can exist. Similarly, in the field of dynamics, Philoponus argued that (*contra* Aristotle) motion in a vacuum would not have infinite velocity; instead, all motion has finite velocity and a vacuum would only eliminate resistance. He also rejected Aristotle's account of projectile motion; instead of a external force moving the object, Philoponus claimed that the agent transferred an internal force ("impetus") to the object in motion. Impetus theory had the further consequence that there was no need for a fifth element to explain circular (heavenly) motion—God had merely impressed a circular motion in the mundane matter of the (now perishable) heavens.

At a more abstract level, Philoponus attacked the Aristotelian account of space/place (*topos*) and the categories. He returned to the view (rejected by Aristotle) that the space of an object was the extension it occupied (this also entailed that an extension, i.e., space, could be a *void). Space *qua* three-dimensional extension was clearly distinguished from its occupying body and became the ultimate substrate. Thus Philoponus (disturbing the Aristotelian categorial hierarchy) places extension in the category of substance, not quantity.

Philoponus' theology too was motivated by Aristotelian philosophical principles: there could be only one nature in Christ, since there was only one *hupostasis*. Each member of the Trinity was an independent *hupostasis*; consequently, there exist three Gods and three substances. Finally, the resurrected (immortal) *soul requires a new immortal body, not merely the (traditional) resurrected earthly body.

Because of his heterodox views, Philoponus' influence was felt first upon Islamic science and philosophy, through which he became known to the West in the thirteenth century. Only in the Renaissance were significant Latin translations available.

BIBLIOGRAPHY: Texts in *CAG* 13–17; Rabe, H., ed., *De Aeternitate Mundi contra Proclum*, Leipzig, 1899. Sorabji, R., ed., *Ancient Commentators on Aristotle*, London/Ithaca, 1987–; also Sorabji, ed., *Philoponus and the Rejection of Aristotelian Science*, London, 1987.—*LAWRENCE P. SCHRENK*

PHILOSTRATUS, Flavius (c. 170–245 C.E.), of Lemnos. Philostratus studied under some of the famous *sophists of the late second century C.E., became a member of the literary circle of Empress Julia Domna (d. 218 C.E.), and was active both as an official and as a teacher in Athens. He is known for two major works: *The Life of Apollonius of Tyana* (or, more accurately, *In Honor of Apollonius of Tyana*), commissioned by the Empress and thus begun before her death; and *The Lives of the Sophists*, completed before 238 C.E. The biography of Apollonius of Tyana (1st cent. C.E.) is an attempt to defend this "holy man" against charges that he was nothing more than a magician. Apollonius is presented as a philosopher of *Neopythagorean garb who travels all over the world and meets Indian sages, Egyptian priests, Greek philosophers, and even the Roman emperor. Like any other sophist, he knows at every encounter what to say and to say it eloquently; in addition, he sometimes demonstrates his superhuman powers. Philostratus has clearly combined elements from the Greek novel, the exotic travel accounts that were popular in the early Roman empire, and hagiographic literature. Recent scholarship, however, has stressed that Philostratus also had access to genuine source material, and many of the features attributed to Apollonius can be paralleled from descriptions of historical figures. While the work has little philosophical significance, it gives a lively impression of the social setting of intellectual activities in the Roman empire during the first and second centuries C.E.

The *Lives of the Sophists* is a sweeping history of so-called sophists, from *Gorgias in the fifth century B.C.E. to the culmination of the *"Second Sophistic" at the end of the second century C.E. (the term was coined by Philostratus himself and covers all sophists from the fourth century B.C.E. onward—see also SOPHISTS). His two longest biographies are of

Polemo and Herodes Atticus, both of whom belong to the generation preceding Philostratus. The main emphasis is on the oratorical performances of the sophists, and Philostratus gives many examples of their style. Gossip, anecdotes, and dramatic events fill up the major parts of the biographies.

BIBLIOGRAPHY: Texts in C. L. Kayser, ed., *Corpus Philostrateum*, Zürich 1853; Leipzig, 1871, repr. 1964. Texts and trs. in A. R. Benner, and F. H. Forbes, eds., *The Letters of Alciphron, Aelian and Philostratus* (Loeb), London, 1949; F. C. Conybeare, ed. and tr., *Life of Apollonius of Tyanna* (Loeb), London, 1912; W. C. Wright, ed. and tr., *Lives of the Sophists* (Loeb), London, 1922. Anderson, G., *Philostratus: Biography and Belles Lettres in the Third Century A.D.*, London, 1986; Bowersock, G. W., *Greek Sophists in the Roman Empire*, Oxford, 1969; also Bowersock, ed., *Approaches to the Second Sophistic: Papers presented to the 105th Annual Meeting of the American Philological Association*, University Park, PA, 1974.—*JØRGEN MEJER*

PLATO (427–347 B.C.E.). Athenian philosopher. Plato's family was deeply involved in the city's politics. Two members of the Thirty, a group of antidemocratic leaders who briefly took control of Athens in 404, were his relatives: *Critias, his mother's cousin, and Charmides, her brother. Like a number of other young people of his time, he attached himself to *Socrates and was present at his trial (*Ap.* 38b), although he did not witness his death in prison (*Phd.* 59b). The influence of Socrates is most clearly evident in his early works. In addition, we are told by *Aristotle (*Met.* 987a32) that in his youth he became familiar with *Cratylus and thereby with the doctrines of *Heraclitus; the impact of these and other thinkers, such as *Parmenides and the followers of *Pythagoras, is apparent in his middle and later writings. Despite his intellectual bent, Plato contemplated a political career, as we are told in the *Seventh Letter* (324b–c); but the trial and death of Socrates convinced him that he should abstain from direct involvement in political life (325b–326b).

Ancient sources indicate that after the death of Socrates in 399 he left Athens and visited Megara, Cyrene (in North Africa), Italy, Sicily, and Egypt (D.L. 2.106, 3.66; Cic. *Rep.* 1.10.16; *Fin.* 5.29.87; *Acad.* 1.10.16). These travels increased the range of ideas that were to influence his philosophical development. Cyrene was the home of *Theodorus, a *mathematician who appears as the teacher of *Theaetetus in the *dialogue of that name. In Italy he visited *Philolaus, *Archytas, and Timaeus, all followers of Pythagoras. Philolaus had offered money to help Socrates escape from prison (*Cri.* 45b), and two of his students, Simmias and Cebes, are major characters in the *Phaedo*. Archytas, whose friendship with Plato is alluded to in the *Seventh Letter* (338c–339d), was both a mathematician and a political leader—a combination of talents that may have encouraged Plato in his writing of the *Republic*. Megara was the home of *Euclides, a follower of Socrates (*Phd.* 59c) and the founder of a school of *logicians (see MEGARIAN SCHOOL.).

These travels came to an end in 387, when Plato returned to Athens and established the *Academy, a society devoted to the investigation of philosophical problems and the training of future political leaders and a rival to the school of *Isocrates. Among its best-known members were Aristotle, *Speusippus, and *Xenocrates; although *Eudoxus, a mathematician and *astronomer, may not have been a member (this is a matter of scholarly dispute), he and Plato were certainly in contact with each other.

In 367, after the death of Dionysius, the tyrant of Syracuse, and the succession of his son, also named Dionysius, Plato was induced to return to Sicily to undertake the education of the city's new ruler. Dion, the brother-in-law of the elder Dionysius, was a devoted friend of Plato's and was instrumental in persuading him to take on this task. But the pedagogical experiment was a disaster, and Plato returned to Athens in 365. Four years later, he was again prevailed upon by Dion and Dionysius to return, but once more the project ended in utter failure. In 353, Dion was killed in an expedition he led against Dionysius. This series of events is the subject of several of Plato's *Letters*, including the Seventh. Plato's epitaph for Dion, preserved by *Diogenes Laertius (3.30), testifies to the depth of their friendship. We know of no further disruptions in Plato's philosophical career after his return from Sicily in 361. Upon his death in 347, Speusippus became the head of the Academy; he was in turn succeeded by Xenocrates.

The authenticity of the following works, listed alphabetically within chronological groups, is widely accepted:

Early works: *Apology, Charmides, Crito, Euthydemus, Euthyphro, Gorgias, Hippias Minor, Hippias Major, Ion, Laches, Lysis, Menexenus, Protagoras.*

Middle works: *Cratylus, Meno, Parmenides, Phaedo, Phaedrus, Republic, Symposium, Theaetetus.*

Late works: *Critias, Laws, Philebus, Politicus, Timaeus, Sophist.*

The division of Plato's works into these three periods is also generally accepted, and for the most part there is agreement about which works belong to which periods. But there are some disputed cases: The *Euthydemus* and the *Timaeus* are thought by some to be middle dialogues, and the *Cratylus* has been taken to be early. Some scholars have tried to establish a more precise ordering of the dialogues; and although these efforts are in some cases disputed, in others a consensus has emerged about a dialogue's position within its chronological group. For example, the *Gorgias* is widely thought to be among the latest of the early works. If the *Euthydemus* and the *Cratylus* belong to the early group, they are

among that period's later works; if they are middle dialogues, they belong to the earlier part of that period. The *Meno* is certainly among the
first of the middle dialogues, and it is soon followed by the *Phaedo*. The
Republic is widely thought to postdate the *Phaedo*, and the *Parmenides* and
Theaetetus are generally considered to be among the latest within the
middle period. The *Phaedrus* and *Symposium* are more difficult to locate
among the middle works, although most assume that the *Phaedrus* is the
later of the two and that it probably postdates the *Republic*. As for the late
works, cross-references suggest that the *Sophist* precedes the *Politicus*
(*Soph.* 217a, *Pol.* 257a, 258b) and that the *Timaeus* precedes the *Critias*
(*Tim.* 27a). A conjecture based largely on stylometric studies is that they
were written in the following order: *Timaeus, Critias, Sophist, Politicus,
Philebus, Laws*. But there is considerable disagreement about the quality
of the evidence for such fine-grained chronological claims. Ancient
sources testify that the *Laws* was Plato's last work, although its length
makes it likely that its composition occupied many years, and Plato
could have been writing other dialogues during this period as well. We
will return to chronological issues below (see *Chronology*).

Other extant works were attributed to Plato in antiquity, but their
authenticity has come into doubt in the modern period: *Alcibiades I,
Alcibiades II, Cleitophon, Epinomis, Hipparchus, Minos, Rivals* (alternatively
called *Lovers*), and *Theages*. The *Epinomis* is thought by some scholars to
be the work of Philip of Opus; but if it is Plato's, it certainly belongs to
his late period. The other works just mentioned have strong affinities to
the dialogues of Plato's early period and are thought by some contemporary scholars to be genuine. A brief work called *Definitions* is included
among the medieval manuscripts of Platonic writings, but it is universally agreed to be spurious. Ancient sources attribute to Plato a group of
thirteen *Letters*, but their authenticity is a controversial matter, and it is
highly doubtful that all are genuine. One of them, the Seventh, contains
several pages of philosophical exposition, but it declares that Plato's
deepest thoughts have never been committed to writing. If genuine, this
is a work of considerable importance; many scholars agree that even if it
is spurious, it provides useful information about Plato's pedagogical
failures in Sicily, mentioned above.

Methodological Issues: How Should the Dialogues be Read? Plato is an
enigmatic writer. He never allows himself to be one of the interlocutors
of his dialogues; rather, the principal figure is usually Socrates. (There
are, however, important exceptions among some middle and later works:
the conversation of the *Parmenides* is dominated by Parmenides; that of
the *Sophist* and *Politicus*, by an Eleatic stranger; and Socrates is entirely
absent from the *Laws*). For whatever reason, Plato has chosen not to
speak directly to us, and therefore questions arise about how we should

gather the meaning of his works. For example: Should we assume that Plato himself endorses the conclusions about which his speakers are agreed? When they disagree (as they do in several of the early works), does Plato take the side of the principal character? Since Socrates is often the main interlocutor and his speech is laced with irony, might he not intend the opposite of what he says? When the progress of a dialogue seems to overlook an obvious alternative or when an argument seems conspicuously weak, might Plato be prompting his readers to discover for themselves the neglected alternative or the fallaciousness of the argument? We must also reckon with the fact that in the *Phaedrus* (274b–278b) Plato has Socrates express serious reservations about the value of written compositions. And in the *Seventh Letter* (341b–344e), he says that he has never committed his deepest thoughts to writing.

Impressed by these difficulties, we might decide either that there is no such thing as Plato's philosophy and that his writings are mere occasions for intellectual exploration and play, or that the main philosophical point of each dialogue is hidden, the apparent conclusions serving merely as a mask for esoteric doctrines. There is a grain of truth in each of these approaches: Most students of Plato's works agree that in certain passages he is exploring possibilities without deciding between them and that at times he intends the reader to draw a conclusion that he does not spell out. Nonetheless, it is generally accepted that Plato does have a philosophy, one that is for the most part overtly defended by the principal speakers of the dialogues. Reading him in this way does not prevent us from recognizing the absence of rigidity in his thinking. At every stage of his development, he shows his awareness of gaps and difficulties in the positions he was taking; and his thinking evolved as he tackled these problems. So, although the dialogues must be read with special sensitivity to contextual clues, because of the indirect way Plato presents his ideas, we can often be reasonably certain that he accepts the positions and arguments propounded by his main speakers.

There are some notable exceptions to this general rule: for example, we may legitimately wonder whether Plato accepts the hedonism for which Socrates seems to argue in the *Protagoras* (351a–354d), or the theory of divine inspiration proposed at the end of the *Meno* (99c–100c), or either of the two theories of names propounded in the *Cratylus*. Even so, the more important point is that the principal doctrines of the dialogues express Plato's own philosophy: There is a realm of eternal and changeless objects called "Ideas" or "Forms"; these are the most real entities and the basic objects of *knowledge; the Form of the Good is the highest object of understanding; the observable world is a deficient reflection of the Forms; the *soul, or at least the reasoning part of it, does not die, but is separated from the body when the latter perishes; and the *virtues of the

soul—wisdom, courage, temperance, and justice—are incomparably better for us than any other sorts of good. As we shall see, Plato may have
modified or even abandoned some of his principal tenets; but even if he
did, the point remains that the dialogues are his vehicles for the presentation and defense of his own philosophical outlook.

Plato's attitude towards writing as expressed in the *Phaedrus* does
not undermine this approach; on the contrary, that dialogue affirms the
value of writing as a reminder of thoughts arrived at in conversation
(276d). The main point Plato wishes to make in the *Phaedrus* about the
written word is that wisdom cannot be acquired simply by reading, that
instead one must work out one's position through spoken dialogue with
others. But he would hardly have bothered writing the dialogues had he
not believed that, after one has gone through the *dialectical process of
philosophical discovery, there is some value in leaving a record of the
conclusions at which one arrived and the path one took to reach them.
Here we have at least part of the explanation for Plato's use of the dialogue form in his writing: The use of interlocutors is a reminder that
conversation, not declamation, is the proper way to arrive at philosophical truth. This is why he continues to use the dialogue form even when
there is no genuine opposition of views and the use of several speakers
seems rather mechanical. What we have in these cases (e.g., in the
Timaeus and the *Laws*) is in effect a treatise, but Plato still casts his
thought in the form of a dialogue because this represents the primacy of
conversation and the derivative value of writing. In other works, such as
the *Gorgias* and the *Phaedo*, where there is a genuine clash of views, the
dialogue form has obvious advantages: It is a natural vehicle that allows
Plato to expose the weakness of initially attractive positions and to show
how his own favored views can best be defended against criticism. We
need not, therefore, regard the fact that Plato does not speak to us directly in his own voice as an indication that as a rule he intends to sub-
vert or distance himself from the conclusions of his principal speakers.

What has been said here gives no key to the solution of specific problems about why Plato writes the dialogues as he does. For example: Why
in the *Crito* does he give to the personified laws of Athens the role of presenting Socrates' reasons for remaining in prison (50a–53e)? Why do so
many of the early dialogues end in disagreement or perplexity? Why is
the order of speeches in the *Symposium* disrupted from its original plan
because Aristophanes develops the hiccups (185c)? Why in this dialogue
is the presentation of the theory of Forms assigned to a priestess, Diotima
(201d–212b)? Why does Plato choose to end this work with the speech of
Alcibiades (212c–222c)? What is the significance of the fact that the *Phaedrus* is set in the countryside rather than the agora or some interlocutor's
home (227a–230e)? Why does Socrates play a minor role in certain dia-

logues and none at all in the *Laws*? Why is the *Theaetetus* interrupted by a digression in which Socrates defends the unworldliness of philosophers (171d–177c)?

The multiplicity of these questions calls attention to the point that, even after we agree that Plato intends his writings to be a vehicle for the expression of his philosophy, difficult problems remain about how to extract his thoughts from his words. Scholars differ not only in their solutions to the questions just raised but also in their estimate of the urgency of these questions for the understanding of Plato. Some would say, for example, that we cannot know why the *Phaedrus* has a pastoral setting, for there are simply too many possible explanations, but that fortunately nothing of importance hangs on this question. Similarly, it might be said that the demotion of Socrates as a speaker in the *Parmenides, Sophist,* and *Politicus* can be explained in many different ways, that we are in no position to choose among alternatives hypotheses, and that in any case the content of what is being said can be understood without determining why it is Parmenides rather than Socrates who says it. But other scholars are convinced that the dramatic interaction among characters and the setting of dialogues provide crucial clues to their interpretation. There seems to be no systematic way to resolve these differences. One must simply proceed case by case, using one's judgment to assess whether Plato is planting a clue that is crucial to the understanding of his philosophy or whether he is instead supplying, for dramatic or historical reasons, details whose philosophical significance should not be exaggerated.

These are not the only problems of interpretation that Plato's readers must confront. For in addition to his writings, we have reports, from Aristotle and others, that ascribe to him mysterious doctrines that seem, at least on the surface, to have little or no relation to the content of the dialogues. Some hold that Plato's most profound thoughts were communicated orally and not in writing, and that Aristotle is revealing these mysteries to us. We will return to this issue below (see *Other Later Developments*).

The Chronology of the Dialogues and Plato's Departure from Socrates. Plato's writings, as we have seen, are divided into three groups—early, middle, and late—although in a few cases there is disagreement about where a particular dialogue belongs. What is the basis for this division?

To begin with, we know that the life and philosophy of Socrates profoundly influenced Plato. There can be no other explanation of the fact that he made Socrates the principal interlocutor of so many of his dialogues and that he wrote an eloquent defense of him in the *Apology*. It is plausible to suppose that this work was written at an early point in his career, when the trial of Socrates was still fresh in his memory and the impact of his defense would be greatest. Furthermore, there is a group of dialogues that are also thought to be early because of a number of shared features: They are vivid and brief portraits of Socrates' method of examining himself and others; they focus principally on *ethical questions; they are largely exploratory in character; and although they do not reach positive results acceptable to all parties, they often strongly convey the suggestion that virtue is a form of knowledge. Now, Aristotle tells us that Socrates characteristically asked questions but did not answer them (*Soph. El.* 183b7–8); that he was not interested in the natural world but focussed exclusively on ethical matters (*Met.* 1.6, 987b1–2); and that he identified virtue with knowledge (*NE* 1147b17–19). Since the impact of Socrates was presumably greatest during the earliest part of Plato's philosophical career, it is plausible to assume that the dialogues in which the features mentioned by Aristotle are most fully on display are those that Plato wrote first. He was during this period pursuing the mutually supporting goals of preserving the memory of Socrates, vindicating his way of life, and giving his teacher's philosophical views their best defense.

Having agreed that the "Socratic dialogues," as they are sometimes called, are earlier than the rest, we should also notice some philosophical differences between them and Plato's later works. Socrates says in the *Apology* that he does not know whether death is a long sleep or whether we continue to live in the underworld (40c–d); by contrast, in the *Phaedo*, Plato offers a series of proofs for the eternal existence of the soul (to be supplemented by further proofs in the *Republic* and *Phaedrus*). Similarly, the early dialogues fail to find definitions of the virtues upon which all interlocutors can agree; in the *Republic*, however, we find definitions of courage, temperance, wisdom, and justice—and these definitions are backed by an elaborate moral and *political theory. The Socrates of the early dialogues equates virtue with knowledge and never countenances the possibility that nonrational aspects of human motivation are capable of overwhelming reason; by contrast, in the *Republic*, the nonrational parts of the soul are divided off from the rational, and their power to overturn reason is affirmed. Accordingly, the *Republic* does not equate virtue merely with knowledge; rather, the virtues of temperance, courage, and justice are understood to involve the right relationship between the rational and nonrational parts of the soul. Whereas the *Apology* portrays Socrates as an innocent victim of unfounded prejudice, Plato tells us in the *Republic* (539a–b) that young people should not be exposed to moral controversy until they have had a rigorous mathematical training. Evidently, having achieved some distance from his teacher, Plato comes to see some merit in the charge that Socrates corrupted the young. It would be absurd to suppose that the *Republic*, with its elaborate political and moral theory, successfully defended definitions, and fear of the harm that can be done by moral inquiry, was written in Plato's early period and that such Socratic dialogues as the *Charmides*, *Laches*, and *Euthyphro* were written after it. Accordingly, works that bear strong philosophical similarities to the *Republic* cannot be placed among the early dialogues.

The middle works exhibit a far wider scope than do the early dialogues, which are devoted principally to the defense of the ethical outlook Plato had inherited from Socrates. Although *metaphysical and *epistemological assumptions are made in this early period, there is no interest in exploring them for their own sake; they are in the background and are put in service of the moral life. But then, as Plato moves into his middle period, there is a broadening of interests, a greater ambitiousness in the projects he undertakes, and a shift in philosophical orientation. In the *Cratylus*, for example, he discusses at length two different theories of how names acquire their meaning—a topic that seems at best remotely connected to the concerns of the Socratic dialogues. In the *Meno*, he becomes more self-conscious about methodological and epistemological issues, and he seeks illumination in the method of hypothesis employed by mathematicians and the doctrine of reincarnation accepted by the Pythagoreans. Ancient sources attest to Plato's association with some of the leading mathematicians of his time, and we can see from the *Republic* how important he took mathematical studies to be for the development of philosophical skills and insights. During this period, when Plato was writing the *Phaedo*, *Republic*, *Symposium*, and *Phaedrus*, there is a burst of confident and highly programmatic theorizing. The nature and eternality of the soul are revealed; grand theories of human motivation are sketched; an ideal city is described; the nature of the virtues is discovered. At the center of the project lie the Forms, the nonsensible and unchanging objects that are the primary objects of human knowledge and aspiration.

It would be a mistake, nonetheless, to think that Plato had made a complete about-face after he composed the early dialogues. Had he decided that his teacher was completely misguided in his philosophy, he would hardly have allowed him to continue to play the role of chief interlocutor and expounder of Platonic theories. Socrates revealed to Plato the fruitfulness of the search for definitions and the power that dialogue has, when properly conducted, to transform one's life by rooting out false belief and discovering new truths. And one of the guiding ideas of the early dialogues—that there is more need of expertise in moral matters than in any other area—is the seed that grows into the ideal of the philosophical ruler in the *Republic*. Plato's relationship to the ideal of his youth and to the youthful ideas of the early dialogues is complex, and cannot be accurately portrayed as one of continuous development or to-tal reversal.

Thus far, we have seen why the *Republic* and other closely related di-alogues cannot be early works. But why not consider it and its kin to be late dialogues rather than products of his middle period? In fact, why should we distinguish between a middle and a late period at all? Why not divide the dialogues into two groups (the early and the rest) rather than three (early, middle, late)?

To begin with, there is strong evidence that the *Republic* was written before the *Laws*. For example, the former announces with considerable fanfare that, ideally, wives and property should be held in common (451c–471c); the latter quietly endorses this as an ideal but proposes a second-best arrangement that preserves traditional institutions (739c-e). These and other passages strongly suggest that the *Republic* is the earlier work, which is how Aristotle regarded them (Ar. *Pol.* 1264b26–7). In fact, as was mentioned earlier, it was thought in antiquity that the *Laws* was Plato's last work; whether this is correct or not, it is reasonably and widely assumed that it was in any case among his last compositions. This is a significant point, because since the nineteenth-century scholars have undertaken a series of increasingly complex and sophisticated studies of Plato's style, and their tests have converged upon the result that there is a group of dialogues that bear much more stylistic similarity to the *Laws* than do dialogues outside the group; these are the works listed above as late: *Critias, Philebus, Politicus, Timaeus, Sophist* (arranged alphabetically). Most scholars would agree that the philosophical content of these works also indicates that they were written after such middle works as the *Phaedo*, the *Symposium*, and the *Republic*. Doubts have been raised about the *Timaeus*, however, because to some its philosophical orientation seems akin to that of the middle rather than the late dialogues. We will return to this issue at the end of the next section.

The Theory of Forms. It is widely agreed that at least during his middle period the Forms were at the center of Plato's philosophy. But what are these objects? Why does Plato believe they exist? Answers to these ques-tions must begin with a certain assumption made by Socrates in the *Meno* and several of the early dialogues. In the *Euthyphro* (6d–e), he says that piety is a single thing that is present in every pious action and that it has a single "idea" or "form" (the Greek word here is *idea*). Similar assump-tions are made in the *Laches* about courage, in the *Charmides* about tem-perance, and in the *Meno* about virtue. What is this single thing that is here called an *idea*? In the early works, Socrates never raises that ques-tion. Instead, he focusses all of his attention on the defects of the answers given by his interlocutors to his definitional questions. He merely asserts that piety is a single thing in order to reject attempts to define it in terms of a conjunction of unrelated characteristics or examples. Similarly, in the *Meno*, he insists that virtue cannot be one sort of thing in men, another in women, one sort of thing in children, another in adults; there must be some single *eidos* that all of their virtues have, something that makes them all virtues (72c). Socrates is making a debatable point; although he calls our attention to it, he never allows his interlocutors to propose objections to it. He is, to use Aristotle's terminology (*Met.* 987b2–3), positing the existence of universals, but he does not so much argue for as presuppose their existence and advances no theory about their nature.

In the *Phaedo*, however, Plato for the first time focusses his attention on the nature of the entities presupposed by the Socratic search for definitions, and he is eager to show his readers what a momentous step it is to recognize the existence of these objects. He gives an argument to show that equality itself must be distinguished from the equal objects that we observe by means of the senses. The argument is that, because we have knowledge of equality, we recognize equal sticks to have an imperfection that equality itself escapes. What is this imperfection? Equal sticks, he says, appear equal to one but not to another (74b). What this means is a matter of scholarly controversy: Is he saying that a given stick appears equal to a second stick and unequal to a third? Or is his claim that a given stick can be taken by one person to be equal, and by another to be unequal? Is he alluding to the existence of perceptual errors, or is he speaking of a case in which the conflicting appearances of equality and inequality are veridical? Even if we read the passage to be referring to the experiences of two different observers, we can make good sense of Plato's argument by taking him to be talking about veridical experiences: a given stick *is* both equal (to a second stick) and unequal (to a third), and so it is *rightly* seen by one person as equal and another as unequal. By contrast, equality itself is evidently not something that is also unequal. Since the Form of equality is that by virtue of which anything is equal, it is rightly called equal; it has its equality perfectly because there is no basis for saying that it is also unequal. It should be noticed that Plato's argument in the *Phaedo* does not allege that sensible objects are only approximately and never exactly equal in length, nor does it claim that we never observe that they are equal. Scholars have sometimes assumed that this was Plato's meaning, but such an interpretation is now widely rejected. (After all, wouldn't Plato admit that those two cows over there are exactly equal in number—not approximately equal—to these two cows over here?) What the argument does assume is that we have knowledge of equality, for it attempts to explain how we acquire such knowledge. Of course, Plato cannot mean by this that all human beings, however uneducated, actually know geometry; for the knowledge the soul had prior to embodiment is lost at birth and must be regained through careful study. So when he says in this passage that "we" have knowledge of equality and tries to explain how such knowledge is possible, he is referring to people who have mathematical sophistication. His claim is that the sort of expertise that is possible in geometry and all other genuine branches of knowledge can be acquired only if there are nonsensible and unchanging objects that serve as the objects of scientific study. We cannot explain the possession of knowledge or the possibility of acquiring it by appealing to our perception of equal sensible objects, because those objects have an imperfection that makes them inadequate as the basic epistemic objects. Equal sticks are as much an example of equality as inequality, since each member of the pair is also unequal to other sticks; but the Form is precisely what equality is and can never be characterized as unequal. This is why someone who knows what equality is must have acquired this knowledge by looking to the Form and not merely to objects whose equality is detected by the senses.

This argument in the *Phaedo* should be connected with the many places in the dialogues where Plato contrasts the permanence and changelessness of the Forms with the constant flux of the sensible world (*Phd.* 78d–79a, *Cra.* 439c–e, *Symp.* 211a–b, *Rep.* 479a–d, *Tim.* 49c–d, 51e–52a). When reading such passages, it is important to realize that Plato construes *change more broadly than we commonly do: he uses the Greek term *genesis* (coming into being, becoming, changing) to characterize not only the possession of different characteristics at *different* times but also the possession of opposite qualities at the *same* time. If, for example, someone is tall (in relation to a second person) and short (in relation to a third), he is someone who "changes" (*gignetai*), in the sense that he can be characterized in opposite ways (*Tht.* 152d–e). The argument of the *Phaedo* can therefore be expressed by saying that because equal sticks change (from being equal to being unequal), we must have acquired our knowledge of equality from something else, namely, the sort of equality that does not change. This way of putting Plato's point is adopted by Aristotle when he says that Plato posited the existence of Forms because he took sensible objects to be in constant flux and argued that definitions must therefore apply to things beyond the sensible world (*Met.* 1.6, 987b4–7).

Plato clearly believes that what he says about equality and the contrast between equality itself and the many sensible equals applies in other cases as well—for example, to beauty, goodness, justice, and piety. We must posit such objects, he says (*Phd.* 75d), whenever we raise questions and give answers, using the phrase "what is itself ..." (i.e., what is itself equal, beautiful, etc.). He is clearly referring back to the Socratic questions raised in the early dialogues and is claiming that to ask, as Socrates did, "What is X?" is to inquire about a Form. He characterizes all such objects in a way that he had never done in the earlier dialogues: they are unchanging, everlasting, imperceptible, and knowable solely by means of reasoning (78d–79d); and he claims, building on the argument of the *Meno*, that the soul once knew them when it was disembodied but lost that knowledge when it entered the body it presently occupies. At the end of the *Phaedo* (103dff.), he seems to be assuming that there are Forms of hot, cold, snow, fire, two, three, odd, even, sickness, fever, soul. In the *Republic*, he countenances such other geometrical Forms as the diagonal and the square (510d–e) and Forms of craft products, such as a Form of bed and one of table (596b); in the *Timaeus* (51c–52d) and *Parmenides* (130c), there are Forms of fire, earth, and other physical elements; in the *Parmenides* (130c) and *Philebus* (15a) there is the Form of human being. In the *Parmenides*, Socrates balks at the existence of Forms of hair, mud, and dirt, but he is immediately rebuked by Parmenides, who says that this reluctance is the product of Socrates' youthfulness (130c–e).

These passages raise an obvious difficulty: How are we to generalize from what Plato says about equality in the *Phaedo* to construct an argument that purports to prove the existence of Forms in all of these other cases as well? The argument in the *Phaedo* rests on the point that sensible objects are related to each other in contrary ways: The same sticks are both equal and unequal. But if the argument depends essentially on that feature of sensible objects, then it cannot in any obvious way be applied to man, fire, bed, and so on. Nothing is both a bed and the opposite of bed, since beds have no opposite. A common response to this problem is to suppose that Plato develops one or more additional arguments, beyond the one he uses in the *Phaedo*. But what additional argument does he offer?

Some students of Plato propose that he gives what is called a "one over many" argument: Roughly formulated, it holds that whenever a number of different things have some one thing, F, in common, there must be some further object—the Form of F—that makes them all F. Aristotle attributes such an argument to the Platonists (*Met.* 1.9, 990b13), and obviously it would generate Forms of man, fire, bed, mud, and so on. Furthermore, we do seem to find something like this approach in Plato; in the *Euthyphro*, for example, he assumes that there is a Form of piety because there must be some single thing that the many different things that are pious have in common (5c–d). He puts the idea more generally in the *Republic* when he justifies the assumption that there is a Form of bed: "We are in the habit of positing some single Form for each multitude to which we attach the same name" (596a).

There is a problem, however: In the *Politicus*, Plato says that there is *not* a Form for every name. He notes that there is no single *genos* (kind, species) of *barbaroi* (non-Greeks), even though there is a single name, *bar-*

baros; and if we made up a name to designate all numbers other than ten thousand, that would not designate a *genos* either. It is reasonable to assume that when Plato is talking about *genê* here (plural of *genos*), he is referring to Forms and is saying that there is no guarantee that every word in our language or in a language we make up corresponds to a Form. There are Forms corresponding to names only when those names designate objects that have real unity and are not a merely arbitrary conglomerate. What Plato seems to be presupposing is that an inquiry into the question, "What is a barbarian?" would not produce genuine knowledge, because there is no genuine science that involves the positing of barbarians as a real species of objects. If he wishes to uphold the claim he makes in the *Republic* that there is a Form "for each multitude to which we attach the same name," then he must assign a special meaning to "name" and deny that "barbarian" is really a name. And if there is a one-over-many argument that is independent of the argument in the *Phaedo* for a Form of equality, then that argument must be formulated in such a way that it generates Forms only for genuine unities and not for any arbitrary collection of objects. Plato never bothers to spell out such an argument, but perhaps this is because he wants his readers to fill in these details for themselves.

A different possibility is that he generates Forms of circle, bed, fire, and so on by generalizing from the argument he gives in the *Phaedo*, rather than by relying on another argument that is entirely independent of it. On this reading, when he says in the *Republic* that we are to posit "some single Form for each multitude to which we attach the same name," he is not giving an argument that is unrelated to the one he presented in the *Phaedo*. Rather, he is assuming that just as equal sticks have one kind of imperfection that requires us to find an object of knowledge outside the sensible world, so other types of observable objects have other imperfections that again require the positing of Forms. He cannot claim that artifacts have the same sort of imperfection as equal sticks, since it is not the case that whatever is a bed is also not a bed. But beds are subject to change over time, and eventually perish; furthermore, they have many features that have nothing to do with the fact that they are beds. Plato may be assuming that these are imperfections that make observable beds ineligible as the principal objects of the craftsman's knowledge. According to this way of thinking, the craft of bed-making would not be a genuine craft if it chose some particular wooden bed as the object of its study or even if it chose a group of well-designed beds. For such objects are filled with features that are irrelevant to their being beds and eventually they will deteriorate and go out of existence. Accordingly, the status of bed-making as a craft cannot depend on the close observation of those particular beds. Instead, if it is a genuine branch of knowledge, it must look to something other than observable beds—and the object to which it looks is what Plato calls the Form of bed. Similarly, he would say, to achieve a proper understanding of the natural world, we must not take these many perceivable examples of fire and earth to form the basic objects of our study. Just as a geometer must realize that he is not studying these particular lines in his diagram, but is proving theorems about the nature of triangles, numbers, and equality, so students of the cosmos or the human body should recognize that their ultimate concern is with the Forms of fire, air, and health. This does not mean that they are to pay no attention whatsoever to the observable world; rather, the study of objects that can be sensed is to be pursued to the extent that it serves a higher epistemic goal, the understanding of the Forms.

We have been discussing the Forms of Plato's middle dialogues without using the word "universal," for Plato himself does not have any term that corresponds to this. It is Aristotle who invented the word *katholou*, which is rendered by our "universal." But even though this is Aristotle's word and not Plato's, it is reasonable to ask whether the Forms count as universals as Aristotle conceived of them. And it might at first seem that Aristotle himself must give a negative answer to this question. For he vehemently denies that there are such things as Plato's ideas (*Met.* 1.9, 990a34–991b9), and yet he is convinced that the sorts of entities he calls universals do exist. If he says that universals exist but that Forms do not, must he not be viewing the Forms as a different kind of entity, and not as universals at all?

Before answering this question, we should realize that as Aristotle reads Plato, Forms are by their nature the sorts of objects whose existence is independent of the sensible world. The Form of human being, for example, does not owe its reality to the existence of individual human beings, and there would be such a Form even if there were no observable objects at all. And Aristotle rejects the existence of Forms precisely because they have this feature. He thinks that if there were no particular human beings, there would be no universal predicated of human beings. Whether he is right about this or not, he has in any case identified an important difference between his theory and Plato's, for Plato does take at least some of the Forms to exist independently of sensible objects. The *Timaeus* describes the creation of the cosmos as the work of a divine craftsman who looks to the eternal Forms as patterns, which presupposes that the Forms of fire and earth exist independently of observable fire and earth. (It should be noticed, however, that this creation story does not commit Plato to believing in the independent existence of Forms of artifacts.)

This enables us to see how Plato's Forms qualify as universals in Aristotle's sense, even though Aristotle believes that universals exist but Forms do not. A universal, according to Aristotle, is "of such a nature as to be predicated of many things" (*Int.* 17a39–40). A Form, however, has a further feature beyond the one described in this definition: It is not only predicated of many things (there is one Form of fire, but there can be many fires that share in it), but it is also capable of existing separately from those many objects. Aristotle thinks there are no such things as Forms because he holds that whatever is predicable of many objects—and he assumes that Forms have this feature—must depend for its existence on the objects of which it is predicated, a dependency that Plato takes Forms to lack. This does not commit Aristotle to denying that Plato's Forms are universals: They meet his definition of universals, but they fail to exist because they have a further feature—ontological independence—that universals cannot have.

Some scholars have argued, however, that taking Forms to be universals is a mistake—that they are really extraordinary particulars rather than universals. According to this reading, the Form of circle is a perfectly circular object, and the Form of human being is a particular human being—one who is a perfect human being. It is widely agreed that Plato's theory, so understood, is absurd. For can we take seriously the suggestion that there is a certain individual human being who is incorporeal, unobservable, and eternal? Plato's theory is much more palatable if it holds that the Form of human being is the universal or property that all humans have in common, and is not itself one more human being, differing from others by being a perfect exemplar of the species.

The question whether Forms are universals or perfect particulars is often raised in scholarly discussions of a notorious argument in the *Parmenides* (131e–132b). It is one of four arguments that are posed as difficulties for the theory of Forms, and it holds that the theory is threatened with an infinite regress. The argument begins by noting that a Form is posited whenever a number of things share a certain feature; for example, if many things are large, then there is one and the same Idea of large, in virtue of which we apprehend that the large things are large. But now consider this second group of things: both the many large things and the large itself. There must be another Idea of large, in virtue of which the members of that second group are large. And so on: Instead of there being one Form of large, there are infinitely many. (This is often called the "Third Man Argument" because discussions of it in antiquity were expressed in terms of the Form of man rather than the Form of large. The first man is an ordinary sensible man, the second is the Form, and the third is the additional Form arrived at by means of the regress argument.) No explicit reply is made to this objection in the *Parmenides* or any other dialogue. Instead, Parmenides tells Socrates (135b–d) that he should not give up his belief in the Forms and that he should engage in further study, which is provided to him in the second half of the dialogue.

It is widely recognized that the inference to a second Form of large presupposes two assumptions that are not made explicit in the text. The first is that the Form of F is itself F; the second holds that if something is F then it is not F in virtue of itself. If the Form of large is not itself large, or if it is large in virtue of itself, then there is no need to posit a second Form of large. Although scholars are generally agreed that assumptions like these two are needed, they differ markedly in their views about how Plato himself regarded the regress argument. One interpretation, advocated by Vlastos in an article that created extraordinary interest in the Third Man Argument (1954), is that Plato failed to recognize the tacit assumptions on which the argument rests, and wrote this part of the *Parmenides* as an admission of "honest perplexity": He saw that there was a deep problem in his theory, but did not know how to solve it. Others (e.g., Strang, 1963) hold that Plato did recognize the assumptions at work in the argument, realized that his metaphysics absurdly conceived of the Form of large as a particular large object, and radically revised his theory in the later dialogues. Another opinion, defended by Cherniss (1957), is that Plato took the Third Man Argument to rest on a confusion and therefore saw no need to make radical revisions in his theory. In fact, according to Cherniss (1957), Plato had already suggested a solution to the problem in Book 10 of the *Republic* (597c–d), where he argues that there could not be more than one Form of bed, since if, *per impossibile*, there were, those two "Forms" would share in another, and that other would be *the* Form. According to this line of thinking, although Plato does say the Form of equality is equal (*Phd.* 74b–d), that beauty is beautiful (*Phd.* 100c) and that justice is just (*Prt.* 330c), he has a way of construing such sentences that avoids any commitment to the notion that the Forms are particulars rather than properties. So read, his theory does not conceive of the Form of large as a large object or the Form of human being as a particular human.

No consensus has been reached about which of these approaches is best supported by Plato's writings. The issue cannot easily be resolved by attention to the late dialogues, because although it is generally agreed that in these works Plato continues to affirm the existence of Forms (although now they are often called "kinds"), it is uncertain whether these objects are thought of in precisely the way they were in the middle works. To many, the lateness of the *Timaeus* provides strong confirmation that Plato's thinking about the Forms did not change in significant ways. That is why Owen sought to show the defectiveness of stylometric studies that draw the conclusion that the *Timaeus* is a late dialogue and therefore postdates the *Parmenides* (1953). Owen's arguments have not been widely accepted, but the issue is far from settled, because many scholars hold that the evidence of stylometric studies is not strong enough to require us to accept implausible conclusions about Plato's philosophical development.

Ethics and Politics. It is clear from Plato's writings that he is deeply disturbed by the moral climate of his time. The opinions of the masses are molded by the meretricious and unreflective works of the poets; some of the *sophists—Callicles in the *Gorgias*, *Thrasymachus in the *Republic*—have abandoned moral standards altogether, although others (*Protagoras) teach a form of conventionalism; *religious practices do not promote true piety but instead undermine the virtues (*Rep.* 364b–365a). The standard by which most people make decisions is pleasure (*Prt.* 353c–354e), and for this reason Plato regards it as an urgent philosophical task to understand what pleasure is and to reject its credentials as an independent criterion for deciding what is good and bad. This task occupies him throughout his career; pleasure is examined in the *Gorgias*, the *Republic*, the *Laws*, and most thoroughly in the *Philebus*.

Plato's most wide-ranging treatment of moral and political issues and his fullest integration of these themes with his metaphysics and epistemology are found in the *Republic*. Here he gives an elaborate argument for the conclusion that being a just person is a great good. The argument begins in Book 1, but this part of the *Republic* ends in the manner of many early dialogues, and Socrates expresses dissatisfaction with his results. This has led some to regard Book 1 as an early dialogue; but others hold that it is too closely connected with later features of the *Republic* to have been written in ignorance of what would follow. In any case, Plato makes it clear that justice and the other virtues are not the only goods worth having; they are desirable both for their own sake and for the sake of the extrinsic rewards that they normally bring. In the main body of the *Republic*, however, he sets aside these extrinsic rewards, because he thinks it important to show that even when they are excluded—in fact, even when they are replaced by their opposites—it is still the case that for one's own good one should be a just person. (It should be noticed, incidentally, that whereas Socrates had claimed, at *Apology* 41d, that a good person cannot be made worse off, Plato holds that it is better to combine justice with other goods than to be just and lack those goods.)

The great difficulty in understanding the *Republic* is to see whether and how its different components hang together as an argument for the goodness of justice. Plato evidently believes that he has achieved important results by the end of Book 4, for here he gives definitions of the cardinal virtues (something that had eluded Socrates in the early dialogues), and he affirms that justice can now be seen to be related to the soul as health is to the body: Both health and justice involve a certain balancing of elements, and just as life would not be worth living if one's body has been ruined, so it would be all the more unbearable if one's soul has been destroyed by injustice (444c–445b). It is evident that Plato's emphasis is not primarily on the performance of just acts, but on the development and maintenance of an inner harmony. Just acts are no doubt a necessary condition of achieving this condition, but they are not sufficient; Plato says nothing to suggest that if one acts justly solely as a means to extrinsic rewards and the avoidance of punishment, then one has moved closer to being a just person or that one benefits in any way from one's actions.

But it would be a mistake to think that Plato has completed his defense of justice at this point in Book 4 or that what follows is the beginning of an entirely new argument for the goodness of justice. Rather, he makes it clear that there is a single argument for this conclusion that stretches from Book 2 to Book 9 at 580c. (The two arguments that follow this, which affirm that the just person experiences pleasures that are greater in reality and quantity, are mere supplements; when Plato gives them, he has already fulfilled the promise he made in Book 2 to show how beneficial justice is.) Book 4 should therefore be regarded as a sketch of an argument that Plato completes in the remainder of the work. We are told in this middle book that the soul has three parts and that justice involves the proper working of these parts in relation to each other: Reason must rule, spirit must be its ally, and appetite must obey. But he has at this point told us little about what it is for reason to rule, for he has not yet described the philosopher, the paradigm of reason's dominance. It emerges, as we read beyond Book 4, that Plato does not equate the rule of reason merely with rational planning and control over one's impulses. If that were all there is to justice, then a cool-headed scoundrel might have a just soul. Rather, Plato makes it clear that the fully just person is someone whose reason is engaged in the study of the Forms, because these are the highest objects with which reason can deal. And he argues that those who study the Forms will undergo a transformation in their values: They will see the sensible world and its rewards as a realm inferior to the world of intelligible objects. The Forms exhibit the highest order that any objects can attain, and by contemplating them the philosopher's soul comes to share in that order. This is why it is best to have a just soul and to lead a just life: It is a life spent in devotion to and imitation of the best objects there are. And we can see why Plato assumes that a just person will refrain from the sorts of activities that are ordinarily considered unjust. Philosophers, because of their love of the Forms, become lovers of proper order in the sensible world as well. They wish to imitate the harmony of the Forms, and so in their relations with others they are loathe to do anything that violates the proper order among people. Furthermore, the normal incentives of human injustice—lust, avarice, hunger for power, aggressiveness—are absent in those who have been transformed by their love of Forms. Even though Plato in this way maintains a link between perfect justice as a state of the soul and just behavior as ordinarily understood, it should be recognized how far he has moved from the ordinary conception of what just persons are like. To be fully just, one must have studied arithmetic, geometry, *astronomy, harmonics, and dialectic. Two virtues that are ordinarily kept distinct—theoretical and practical wisdom—are joined by Plato; he thinks that neither one can be fully possessed unless it is combined with the other.

It is often thought that Plato's attempt to defend this radical claim involves him in a serious internal difficulty. The activity that the philosophers love most of all is the study of Forms; since it is directed at the best objects, it is the best activity for them to undertake. At the same time, he insists that justice requires them to interrupt this activity in order to help rule the city. He appeals to a notion of reciprocity in order to defend the justice of this requirement: Having received benefits from the city, they must make a fair return (519c–520e). Yet his argument seems to involve a difficulty: It would be unjust for a philosopher to refuse to help rule the city; yet would it not be advantageous to refuse, since avoiding this responsibility would allow more time for the best activity, the contemplation of the Forms? Plato's attempt to show that justice is always advantageous seems to contain a counterexample to that claim. Scholars have tried to provide answers to this objection, but thus far no consensus has been achieved about how serious a difficulty this is for Plato and whether he has the resources to avoid it.

Plato's politics in the *Republic* are deeply antidemocratic: He associates freedom with the license to do as one pleases and rejects the idea that all citizens should have an equal say in political matters. It should be noticed, however, that he does not try to justify political institutions merely by assessing the effect that they have on the philosophical elite. He explicitly rejects the idea that institutions should be arranged to benefit only a few leading citizens: Just as a statue's parts must be combined with a view to the whole work, so the various components of a city must accept whatever institutions will best promote the well-being of the whole polity (419a–421b). Here Plato is proposing that the common good, not just the good of philosophers, must be sought in political matters. Yet it is not easy to see how this part of his moral philosophy can be integrated with the rest. The central difficulty is that if justice consists in the harmonious rule of reason and if this psychological condition requires a study of the Forms, then only philosophers can be just. But if nonphilosophers cannot develop the virtues, then how can they lead good lives? And if they cannot lead good lives, how are they benefitted by the institutions of the ideal city? Perhaps Plato's idea is that non-philosophers can develop something akin to true virtue if they are properly educated, but this line of thought is left undeveloped in the *Republic*.

Far more attention is paid to the training of nonphilosophers in the *Laws*. Here Plato has a more accommodating attitude towards democratic values: some combination of monarchic and democratic elements must be achieved in every successful political system; it is possible not only to have too much freedom and equality but also to have too little (693d–701e). Does this mean that Plato now thinks that even if the philosophical regime described in the *Republic* were possible, it would not be worthwhile to aim at it? He does not reject his earlier ideal so directly. For even though in the *Laws* he designs a city in which nonphilosophers are fully involved in political decision making, land is privately owned, and the family remains the medium in which future generations are produced, he takes himself to be constructing a second-best regime, and he still holds that it would be best if women, children, and property are held in common (739a–c). His project, apparently, is to describe the best system that can be achieved when philosophers play a smaller role and the divisiveness that comes with private ownership is tolerated but kept within bounds. Private life is heavily regulated, poetry is censored, true religion is taught and enforced by penal sanctions, women are trained for public life and have military and civic responsibilities, all of which indicates that some of the leading ideas of the *Republic* are still at work. But instead of relying on expertly trained rulers, the city constructed in the *Laws* relies on the rule of law, elaborate systems of voting, and careful public scrutiny of elected leaders. If there is any role at all for philosophers to play, it involves their study of the unity of virtue and their participation in the "nocturnal council" that is briefly described at the end of the work (961aff).

Other Late Developments. A large part of Plato's philosophy—and, some would claim, its most impressive part—has not yet been mentioned. In the *Phaedrus*, the second half of the *Parmenides*, the *Theaetetus*, and the late works, he develops new philosophical methods and investigates problems that had been neglected or treated too briefly in earlier works. In many of these dialogues, there is a strong interest in taxonomy as a method of investigation: Love in the *Phaedrus* and pleasure in the *Philebus* are studied in part through an examination of their varieties. This method of "collection and division," as Plato calls it, involves recognizing unities in disparate phenomena and dividing unities into their proper subdivisions. Someone who has real understanding of music, for example, must not only see sound as forming a unitary field of study but must also know how it is to be divided into a definite number of elements. More generally, it is not enough to recognize that there is one kind uniting a plurality of phenomena: One must possess a classificatory scheme that determines the exact number of subgenera that fall under that kind.

The late dialogues not only introduce new methods but also tackle problems that had long been on Plato's agenda but received too little attention in his earlier works. The theory of Forms, as we have seen, is based on the thesis that the basic objects of knowledge must be something unperceivable, because the familiar objects of the senses have imperfections that prevent them from playing a primary epistemic role. In the *Theaetetus* he further develops his case for the epistemological insufficiency of the senses by arguing against the thesis that perception by itself constitutes knowledge. That thesis is connected to the Protagorean doctrine that everything that appears to us is true, which is in turn supported by the Heraclitean thesis that sense organs and objects of perception are fluctuating in a way that creates unique appearances at every moment. Plato does not explicitly tie his refutation of these connected claims to his doctrine that Forms are the fundamental objects of knowledge, but presumably he assumes that he has made this epistemological corollary of his metaphysics more acceptable by showing that the senses cannot by themselves give us understanding.

The *Theaetetus* also shows Plato struggling with a problem for his own epistemology: He had always assumed that knowledge involves the ability to give a *logos* (an account) of the object of knowledge (*Meno* 98a, *Phd.* 76b, *Rep.* 534b) but had never said what is involved in giving a *logos*. In the *Theaetetus*, he finally faces this problem. Several alternative definitions of *logos* are proposed, but each is found unsatisfactory. Are we to take these results at face value, or is Plato prompting us to reach certain conclusions on our own? Just as the Socratic dialogues leave us with the question whether we should take his professions of ignorance at face value, so Plato in the *Theaetetus* leads us to wonder whether there is more up his sleeve than he admits. It is probably no accident that in this dialogue Socrates does not propound views of his own, as he does in other middle dialogues, but occupies a role similar to the one he had played in the early dialogues; but precisely what Plato means to accomplish by this reprise is unclear.

There is a further problem tackled in the *Theaetetus* that has been on Plato's mind for some time, having made its first appearance at *Euthydemus* 283e–284c: how are false judgments and statements possible? A false statement is one that says what is not, but how can there be such a thing as what is not? The strictures raised by Parmenides against all talk of not-being (and therefore all talk of perishing, coming into being, and any other sort of change) had cast a cloud over the legitimacy of studying the natural world; and although such students of nature as *Anaxagoras, *Empedocles, and the *atomists had tried to accommodate themselves to the logic of Parmenides, no philosopher before Plato had taken on the project of refuting him. The *Theaetetus* devotes considerable attention to the problem, but finds no way to resolve it. In this case, however, we can be reasonably certain that Plato's confession of failure is sincere, for he returns to the problem again in the *Sophist* and proposes an elaborate solution—one that had presumably eluded him in the earlier work. His strategy for showing the legitimacy of talk about not-being involves demonstrating that once we understand what is involved in *being* and perceive its complex relationships with other kinds—such as motion, rest, sameness, and difference—then the acceptability of talk about not-being can also be established.

Plato's philosophy of the natural world is most fully presented in the *Timaeus*: it tells the story of the creation of *time, the world soul, and material bodies by a divine craftsman who looked to the Forms and transformed moving bodies that were once too disorderly even to be named into a beautiful and measured cosmos. The outlook of the *Timaeus*, which emphasizes the ungrudging goodness of a creator who designed a world of great harmony and beauty, is sometimes thought to be at odds with the more pessimistic perspective of the *Phaedo*; in that earlier dialogue, the material world is portrayed as a locus of punishment and the senses are described as impediments to full understanding, which can be fully achieved only after the soul is liberated from the body by the latter's death. There is no logical contradiction in holding that the whole sensible cosmos is both beautiful and ugly— beautiful in comparison with the small, disorderly chunks of reality around us; ugly in comparison with unheard harmonies—but it would be difficult to look at the world from both of these perspectives at the same time. In any case, Plato's conception of nature as the result of divine craftsmanship was rejected by Aristotle, who held that the presence of purpose does not presuppose the existence of a rational designer, but it was embraced by the *Stoics.

What is unique to Plato's *cosmology is the idea that all *matter is developed from regular solid figures, which are in turn constructed from two types of triangles; just as *Democritus and later *Lucretius sought to explain macroscopic properties by appealing to the shapes of atoms, so Plato goes into considerable detail about how natural phenomena result from varying combinations of the basic triangles. A further innovation of Plato's cosmology is his postulation of a third kind of entity: In addition to the Forms and the observable and always changing objects that have the same names as the Forms, there is *chôra* (space), an eternal and imperceptible object that serves as the receptacle in which all change occurs

(52b). What seems to motivate Plato's postulation of this third entity is his belief that the objects of perception are constantly shifting and therefore dependent entities: There must be something that serves as an anchor for their transformation, something in which the change takes place. This is the receptacle of all becoming (50b). The receptacle thus plays a double role, since it is both the substratum of all transformations and the spatial element in which all change occurs.

The most mysterious and controversial component of Plato's late metaphysics comes to us not from the dialogues themselves but from reports of later writers who attribute to him doctrines that seem to have no basis at all in his writings. According to these accounts, Plato did not think that the Forms were the most fundamental entities in terms of which all else should be explained, for the Forms themselves could in some sense be derived from two other sorts of objects, which he called "the one" and "the indefinite dyad" (which is sometimes also spoken of as "the great and the small"). Aristotle attributes to Plato the view that the one is the cause of the essence of the Forms, whereas the great and the small provide the matter upon which the one operates, as form operates on matter (*Met.* 1.6, 987b18–988a17). He also associates Plato with the view that Forms are numbers (*Met.* 1.9, 991b9–10). What is his basis for attributing these strange doctrines to Plato?

A plausible response is that they were proposed by Plato in conversations or lectures, but not expressed in writing. Surely a philosopher as devoted as was Plato to the value of dialogue and as mindful of the dangers of writing would have held some views that he did not commit to print. And we have excellent evidence that Plato proposed some doctrines that are not found in the dialogues, because at one point Aristotle makes a distinction between what Plato says about place in the *Timaeus* and what he says in his "so-called unwritten opinions" (*Phys.* 4.2, 209b14–15). We are also told by Aristotle's student, *Aristoxenus, that Plato delivered a lecture on the good that disappointed his audience because it dealt with mathematics rather than generally recognized human goods.

The fact that Plato orally proposed ideas not found in the dialogues does not mean that Aristotle or anyone else in antiquity must be taken as a reliable interpreter of the content of those verbal opinions. And since Aristotle's reports about Plato's generation of Forms from the one and the great and the small are not accompanied by the statement that *these* opinions of Plato's were expressed orally but never in written form, it is possible that Aristotle is describing in strange terms a doctrine that he perceives (or thinks he perceives) in Plato's written dialogues. Aristotle's credentials as a fair and accurate reporter of Platonic doctrine are open to question; and some scholars, notably Cherniss (1945), have argued that his reports regarding the one and the indefinite dyad are misreadings and were never intended as reports of oral doctrine. But many other scholars, most prominently Krämer (1990), believe that Plato orally proposed a bold and elaborate metaphysical scheme that went beyond anything he expressed in the dialogues and that Aristotle's reports about the one and the indefinite dyad are based on these oral opinions.

However, even among those who agree that in conversations or lectures Plato proposed a metaphysics that he chose not to put in the dialogues, there is strong disagreement about the weight that should be attached to the reports we have of these oral opinions. Some scholars, led by Krämer, take the unwritten doctrines to be the underlying basis of everything Plato wrote; they explain the fact that he did not write them down by appealing to his distrust of the written word. Other scholars, following Vlastos (1963), take the fact that he did not commit these late metaphysical speculations to writing as an indication that these were tentative ideas in which he lacked confidence. But even if Plato was as fully confident in his unwritten doctrines as he was in the philosophy he expressed in the dialogues—and we have no way of knowing this— the obscurity of the oral doctrines and the paucity of our information about them are serious obstacles to allowing them to play a controlling part in our interpretation of his writings.

Plato Today. Plato's influence waned after the fourth century B.C.E., and for several hundred years the Hellenistic schools—Stoics, *Epicureans, and *Skeptics—were the dominant intellectual forces of the ancient world. But the first century B.C.E. witnessed a revival of *Platonism; resuscitated and transformed, his philosophy flourished in late antiquity and exerted a powerful influence on medieval and Renaissance thought. It is easy to see the affinities between Platonism and *Christianity that made his philosophy ripe for adaptation by religious thinkers: In both systems of thought, the objects of sense have a lesser degree of reality and are mere images that point the way to a divine realm. The similarities are even more pronounced when one considers the thesis of later Platonism that all reality is an emanation from a single divine being that is equated with unity and goodness and lies outside time.

The religiosity of Plato was regarded as the most important component of his philosophy until the present century. What is remarkable is that he continues to be read, studied, and taught even in a largely secular intellectual environment. Historical journals overflow with studies of the dialogues, new translations emerge almost every year, graduate seminars on Plato are commonplace, undergraduate majors are required to read his works, and some of the dialogues are the staples of introductory courses. Plato's continuing presence in academic life seems paradoxical, when one considers how unfashionable so many of his ideas have become: It is now widely assumed that perception is at least one form of knowledge and perhaps the only kind there is; that bodies—not souls and universals—are the basic realities; that death is not to be longed for, but to be regarded as a great evil, because it is the end of consciousness; that justice is not primarily a matter of internal harmony but of political institutions whose proper role is restricted to the regulation of external behavior. In all of these respects, we live in a deeply anti-Platonic age. How then can we explain the fact that Platonic studies still thrive, both in the classroom and on the printed page?

Perhaps part of the answer is that every age needs its enemies. There are some writers we love to hate, because they dramatically express doctrines that strike us not only as false but as offensive and dangerous. For some, Plato is just such an enemy. Where can we find a more bitter attack on democratic values than in the *Gorgias* and in the *Republic,* and when has there been an event more embarrassing to democracy than the one portrayed in the *Apology*? Where else can we find a more infuriating advocate of censorship? It is part of our self-image that we listen to those who oppose our values, and perhaps for this reason Plato has become an indispensable part of our democratic culture. Furthermore, his gifts as a stylist are evident even in translation; when these literary qualities are combined with the power of his doctrines to provoke an emotional response, his continuing fascination is understandable.

But this cannot be the whole story. Modern intellectual life contains many warring factions, and Plato's dialogues contain many worlds; some of these worlds provide hospitable homes for contemporary forms of Platonism. In the philosophy of mathematics, some of the most influential theoreticians consider themselves to be Platonists and hold that mathematical truths are descriptions of an imperceivable and timeless realm of objects. In metaphysics, the existence of universals remains a live option. In epistemology, Plato's conception of knowledge as superior to mere belief, because it involves a rational account, still has many defenders; so too does his attack on the relativism of Protagoras. The relationship between morality and self-interest remains an unresolved issue of great importance, and it is difficult to find a more sustained examination of this topic, in antiquity or in any other period, than in the *Republic.* Although readers of earlier centuries often reacted to Plato's discussions of love and sexuality in the *Symposium* and *Phaedrus* with embarrassment, these works are now regarded as among his most brilliant creations precisely because of their profound approach to subjects about which philosophers have generally said too little. Plato has in this way contributed to a broader conception of the province of moral philosophy. Furthermore, those who take logic and the study of language to be central features of philosophy have found such works as the *Parmenides* and the *Sophist* to be among his most acute and penetrating compositions; in fact, in Britain and the United States, the study of Plato underwent a great revival in this century when scholars working under the influence of a linguistically oriented philosophy turned their attention to the subtle arguments of these dialogues. The question whether Plato modified his theory of Forms in light of self-criticism has been pursued with great vigor and insight by scholars for whom the nature of universals and the rational basis for articulating the world into types are live issues. The conclusion we must draw, then, is that Plato is not only a deeply religious philosopher and an enemy of modern thought but is also a source of inspiration and ideas in a secular age. Perhaps the most extraordinary facet of his philosophy is that it combines these opposing features.

BIBLIOGRAPHY: Texts in J. Burnet, ed., *Platonis Opera* (Oxford Classical Texts), 5 vols., Oxford, 1900–1907. Translation in J. M. Cooper and D. S. Hutchinson, eds., *The Complete Works of Plato*, Indianapolis and Cambridge, MA, 1997. Allen, R. E., ed., *Studies in Plato's Metaphysics*, London, 1965; Annas, J., *An Introduction to Plato's Republic*, Oxford, 1981; Brandwood, L., *The Chronology of Plato's Dialogues*, Cambridge, 1990; Burnyeat, M., *The Theaetetus of Plato*, Indianapolis, 1990; Cherniss, H. F., *Aristotle's Criticism of Plato and the Academy*, Baltimore, 1944; also *The Riddle of the Early Academy*, Berkeley, 1945; also "The Relation of the *Timaeus* to Plato's Dialogues," *AJP* 78, 1957, 225–66 and repr. in Allen, ed., *Studies*, 339–278; Fine, G., *On Ideas: Aristotle's Criticism of Plato's Theory of Forms*, Oxford, 1993; Grote, G., *Plato and the Other Companions of Sokrates*,[2] 3 vols., London, 1867; Guthrie, W. K. C., *A History of Greek Philosophy*, vols. 4 and 5, Cambridge, 1975, 1978; Irwin, T. H., *Plato's Ethics*, Oxford, 1995; Krämer, H. J., *Plato and the Foundations of Metaphysics*, Albany, 1990; Kraut, R., ed., *The Cambridge Companion to Plato*, Cambridge, 1992; Moravcsik, J. M., *Plato and Platonism*, Cambridge, MA, 1992; Meinwald, C. C., *Plato's Parmenides*, New York, 1991; Morrow, G. R., *Plato's Cretan City: A Historical Interpretation of the Laws*, Princeton, 1960; Nussbaum, M. C., *The Fragility of Goodness: Luck and Ethics in Greek Tragedy and Philosophy*, Cambridge, 1986; Owen, G. E. L., "The Place of the *Timaeus* in Plato's Dialogues," *CQ* 3, 1953, 79–95 and repr. in Allen, ed., *Studies*, 313–338; also repr. in M. C. Nussbaum, ed., *Logic, Science, and Dialectic: Collected Papers in Greek Philosophy*, Ithaca, NY, 1986; Patterson, R. *Image and Reality in Plato's Metaphysics*, Indianapolis, 1985; Penner, T., *The Ascent from Nominalism: Some Existence Arguments in Plato's Middle Dialogues*, Dordrecht, 1987; Reeve, C. D. C., *Philosopher-Kings: The Argument of Plato's Republic*, Princeton, 1988; Ross, W. D., *Plato's Theory of Ideas*,[2] Oxford, 1953; Ryle, G., "Plato's *Parmenides*," *Mind* 48, 1939, 129-51, 302-25 and repr. in Allen, ed., *Studies*, 97–147; Sayre, K. M., *Plato's Late Ontology: A Riddle Resolved*, Princeton, 1983; Strang, C., "Plato and the Third Man," *PAS*, supp. vol. 37, 1963, 146–64 and repr. in Vlastos, ed., *Collection*, vol. 1, 184–200; Vlastos, G., "The Third Man Argument in Plato's *Parmenides*," *PR* 63, 1954, 319–49 and repr. in Allen, ed., *Studies*, 231–263; also review of *Arete bei Platon und Aristoteles* by H. J. Krämer, *Gnomon* 41, 1963, 641–55 and repr. in Vlastos, *Platonic Studies*,[2] 370–398; also ed., *Plato: A Collection of Critical Essays*, vols. 1

and 2, Garden City, NY, 1970; also *Platonic Studies,*[2] Princeton, 1981; White, N. P., *Plato on Knowledge and Reality,* Indianapolis, 1976.—*RICHARD KRAUT*

PLATONISM. As a coherent and structured philosophical system, Platonism should be regarded as beginning, not with *Plato himself, but among his immediate successors in the Old *Academy, and in particular with the third head of the Academy, *Xenocrates. The second head, Plato's nephew *Speusippus (scholarch 347–339 B.C.E.), held idiosyncratic views that found their way into the main stream of Platonism only much later. In particular, he postulated (probably for logical rather than for mystical reasons) a first principle superior to *Being as well as Goodness, a concept that surfaces again only in *Neopythagorean circles from the early Principate on, this time with overtones of negative *theology.

Plato himself, though he undoubtedly held strong views on most subjects, was careful to keep his philosophy aporetic and open-ended. However, he may be said to have bequeathed to his successors certain guiding principles by which Platonism was ever afterwards characterized, among which may be particularly mentioned (i) a strong contrast between an immaterial realm of perfect, unchanging Forms (the realm of Being), graspable only by intellection, and the sense-perceptible, physical world of ever-changing phenomena (the realm of Becoming); (ii) a belief that the human *soul is immortal and the most essential aspect of ourselves, which our whole purpose in life should be to purify, and that soul in general is the motive force in the world; and (iii) a strong contrast between *knowledge in the strict sense (*epistêmê*), which relates to the realm of Forms and true being and involves being able to give a reasoned account (*logos*) of what one knows, and "opinion" (*doxa*), which relates to the phenomena of the physical world.

We may divide Platonism in the ancient world into four main periods, which will be surveyed in turn.

The Old Academy (347–267 B.C.E.). Plato's followers continued to develop his ideas freely after his death. After the formal secession of *Aristotle in 335 to found his own school, however, a process of codification of doctrine seems to have begun under Xenocrates (scholarch 339–314), partly in reaction to Aristotle's unremitting criticisms. It seems to have been Xenocrates who was responsible for the official edition of Plato's works, and it may have been under his scholarchate that such a document as the *Seventh Letter* was produced, but firm evidence is lacking. At all events, a system of Platonist doctrine emerges in this period, with the following characteristics:

(i) A first principle that is termed a monad but is a self-thinking Intellect, rather like Aristotle's, the contents of whose mind are probably the Forms (cf. Xenocrates frs. 15,16 Heinze) and from whose interaction with

an indefinite dyad the whole cosmos, in its various levels, is derived
(*Theophrastus, at *Met.* 6a23ff., particularly commends Xenocrates for his
comprehensiveness in this respect).

(ii) The definition of soul as "self-motive number," a formulation that
caused some confusion in later times but that seeks to combine the two
chief aspects of the soul's nature as set out in the *Phaedrus* and the
Timaeus (in Xenocrates' interpretation), its role as the initiator of all motion, and its construction on the basis of all the harmonic ratios, which is
the basis of its ability to cognize every level of the universe.

(iii) An *ethical system based on the recognition of "the primary natural instincts" (*ta prôta kata phusin*, frs. 78–9) as the basis for an ethical
theory. At least with his successor *Polemo (scholarch 314–267 B.C.E.),
this seems to have resulted in a view that the end of life (the *telos*) was
"life according to nature," but this did not, as with the *Stoics later, involve the dismissal of physical or external goods or the doctrine that the
passions should be extirpated rather than moderated. In fact, Old
Academic ethics seem to have been easily reconcilable with Aristotelian
principles, with the result that the doctrines of the *Nicomachean Ethics*
could be adopted effortlessly by later Platonists, such as *Plutarch or
*Alcinous.

(iv) A formalization of the Platonic *logical processes of collection
and division, as introduced in the *Phaedrus* and demonstrated in the
Sophist and *Politicus* (the Aristotelian system of categories or of syllogistic
does not seem to have been adopted into Platonism before the Middle
Platonic period).

(v) A formal division of the subject-matter of philosophy into the
three topics of physics, ethics, and logic (in that order, Xenocrates fr. 1),
such as was later adopted by the Stoics.

We have a list of fully seventy-six works by Xenocrates (all now lost),
which cover between them all aspects of philosophy and may be seen as
laying the basis for the later Platonist system. We may also note, in the
case of both Xenocrates and of Speusippus before him, a tendency to
adopt *Pythagoras retrospectively as an ancestor of Platonic doctrine, a
move that was to have considerable influence in later times. Other distinguished members of the Old Academy include Philip of Opus, probable editor of *The Laws* and author of the *Epinomis*; *Heraclides of Pontus
(who defected to Aristotle's school); and *Crantor of Soli.

The New Academy (267–80 B.C.E.). With Polemo's successor *Arcesilaus (scholarch, 267–241), the Platonist tradition takes a remarkable turn,
though one that could, and did, reasonably appeal for authority to the
*Socratic, aporetic aspect of Plato's teaching. What precisely set this off is
not certain, but it is probably a reaction to the dogmatic tendencies of
contemporary Stoicism. Certainly the main thrust of Arcesilaus' philo-

sophical activity was polemical, his chief targets being the Stoic theory of knowledge, specifically the doctrines of *enargeia* ("perspicuity") and *sunkatathesis* ("assent"). He asserted that the sort of certainty that the Stoics claimed was not attainable and that the only rational attitude to physical phenomena was to withhold assent (*epochê*). Like Socrates, he published nothing but was enormously influential nonetheless, stimulating *Chrysippus to many refinements on *Zeno of Citium's teaching. A good source for his teaching, as for that of the later Academic scholarch *Carneades, is Cicero's *Academica*. Arcesilaus' position, as we learn from *Acad.* 1.45, was not that nothing can be known. Even that assertion would be too dogmatic. We cannot even be certain whether anything can be known or not. He certainly claimed that his position was true to the spirit of Plato (*ibid.* 46), a claim tenable if he concentrated on the earlier, aporetic *dialogues and such a later one as the *Theaetetus*, which indeed seems to have been of importance for the *skeptical Academy.

Arcesilaus' immediate successors seem to have contributed nothing, but fourth in succession to him arose a philosopher of major importance, Carneades (scholarch c. 160–129). He revived Arcesilaus' acute criticisms of Stoic *epistemology, but also, in response to criticisms of Chrysippus and others, seems to have devised a system of three levels of "probability" (*pithanotês*), by observance of which one would be enabled to make practical decisions without assenting to the perspicuity of impressions. What status Carneades himself accorded this system we cannot be sure, since he, like Arcesilaus, wrote nothing, and his views are relayed to us by his pupil *Clitomachus, who himself maintained that he could never be sure what his master actually believed.

The New Academy's position was effectively undermined by its last scholarch, *Philo of Larissa, who went so far as to deny that Platonists claimed that things were nonapprehensible, but only that the Stoic criterion of certainty was unworkable. His precise position is not easy to recover, but it left the way open for his dissident successor *Antiochus to reassert the dogmatic tradition of Platonism, augmented with a liberal dose of Stoicism.

Middle Platonism (80 B.C.E.–c. 250 C.E.). This is the generally accepted term for the Platonism of the period extending from the returning of the Platonic Academy to dogmatism from various degrees of skepticism, by Antiochus of Ascalon (c. 130–69 B.C.E.) in about 80 B.C.E. to the distinctive developments in doctrine made by *Plotinus in the years following 244 C.E., when he set up his school in Rome. Antiochus claimed to be returning the Academy to its Platonic roots, but in reality he introduced into it a considerable degree of Stoic doctrine, to the extent that it is not clear that he believed in immaterial reality at all. Certainly he operated with a Stoic-style system of an active and passive principle within the universe, taking the demiurge of the *Timaeus* as representing the Stoic *Logos*. He also adopted the Stoic formulation of the purpose of human life as "living in concordance with Nature."

However, he certainly inaugurated a trend, developed after his death in a much more transcendentalist mode by Platonists in Alexandria in particular (such as *Eudorus [fl. c. 25 B.C.E.]), which built up a comprehensive body of doctrine, incorporating not only much Stoicism, but also many *Peripatetic formulations (such as the view of God as a mind thinking itself, the doctrine of the "mean" in ethics, and the whole of Aristotelian logic) and a considerable injection of Pythagoreanism, including a strong tendency to number mysticism and a reassertion of the immaterial nature of reality. Eudorus, for instance, postulated a system involving a One superior to a pair of Monad and Dyad, and reformulated the *telos*, or purpose of life, as the more Platonic one (cf. *Tht.* 176a–b) of "assimilation to God."

These developments must not, however, be seen as betokening mere "eclecticism." Antiochus had a definite view of the history of philosophy, according to which both Aristotle and Zeno of Citium were in various ways followers of Plato, who were merely developing lines of thought implicit in the dialogues, while later Platonists such as Eudorus saw Pythagoras as a major influence on Plato. What we see, in fact, is a living philosophical tradition, grounded in the Platonic dialogues (and in the so-called unwritten doctrines), but adopting and adapting doctrines and formulations of later schools found to be compatible with Plato.

Within this broad consensus (Platonism in this period was not a rigid school, nor does there seem to have been a physical Academy in Athens that could dispense dogma), there were possibilities of veering towards either Stoicism or Peripateticism, particularly in the sphere of ethics. Atticus (fl. c. 170 C.E.) is an example of the former tendency, Plutarch (c. 45–125 C.E.) of the latter, while *Numenius of Apamea (fl. c. 150 C.E.) is a prominent representative of the Pythagoreanizing wing.

Distinctive doctrines of the period are, in *metaphysics, the view of God as a self-absorbed Intellect, whose thoughts are the Platonic Forms (if this was not already accepted in the Old Academy), this divine intellect being also a perfect unity (the Pythagorean Monad), for which a source was found in the Good of the *Republic*; a secondary divinity, either a demiurgic figure, derived from the *Timaeus*, or a version of the Stoic *Logos*; and a World Soul, also derived from the *Timaeus*, but owing something also to the Pythagorean Indefinite Dyad.

In ethics, we find Aristotle's *Nicomachean Ethics* very widely accepted as a basic source of doctrine (e.g., by Plutarch and by Alcinous in his *Didascalicus*), though some (such as Atticus) championed Stoic *apatheia* (extirpation of the passions) over Aristotelian *metriopatheia* (moderation of the passions); and in logic, Aristotelian syllogistic, as amplified by Theophrastus, reigns more or less supreme, though there are traces of an interest in both Old Academic division and the basic argument-forms of Stoic logic.

Within Middle Platonism, a special place must be accorded to the Neopythagorean tradition. Some of its members, such as Moderatus of Gades (late 1st cent. C.E.), actually took quite a hostile view of Platonism, alleging that it had plundered all its best ideas from Pythagoras without proper acknowledgement, but generally, as in the case of *Nicomachus of Gerasa (fl. c. 125 C.E.), and Numenius of Apamea (fl. c. 150), they fit comfortably into the Platonist spectrum of doctrine. A large body of Pythagorean pseudepigrapha also grew up, from the late Hellenistic period on, which sought to reclaim most of Stoicism and Peripateticism, as well as Platonism, for Pythagoras or other Pythagoreans. Notable Platonizing documents include "Timaeus Locrus" On the Soul of the Universe, and On Nature (the "original" of Plato's Timaeus), and Ocellus Lucanus On the Nature of the Universe.

An interesting subject of controversy arising in this period is how far the New Academy is to be accepted as part of the Platonist tradition. Antiochus plainly dismissed it as an aberration, but later Platonists such as Plutarch chose to embrace the aporetic polemic of the New Academics as an integral part of the Platonic tradition (while others, such as Numenius, persisted in rejecting them), and a curious notion grew up, possibly going back to Philo of Larissa himself, that such men as Arcesilaus and Carneades had dogmatized in private, reserving their skeptical stance for public polemic with the Stoics (cf. S.E. HP 1.234).

While the Middle Platonic period can boast no clearly great philosophers, it is important as the formative era of later Platonist scholasticism, which was both to dominate late antiquity and to dispute the field with *Aristotelianism during the Middle Ages and the Renaissance.

Neoplatonism. "Neoplatonism" is the commonly accepted modern term for that period of Platonism following on the new impetus provided by the philosophical speculations of Plotinus (204–269 C.E.). It extends, as a minimum, to the "closing" of the Platonic School in Athens by Justinian in 529, but maximally through Byzantium, with such figures as Michael Psellus (1018–1078) and Gemistus Pletho (c. 1360–1452), the Renaissance (Ficino, Pico and the Florentine Academy) and the early modern period (the Cambridge Platonists, Thomas Taylor), to the advent of the "scientific" study of the works of Plato with Schleiermacher (1768–1834) at the beginning of the nineteenth century.

Neoplatonism proper may be divided into three main periods: (i) that of Plotinus and his immediate followers, *Porphyry (234–c. 305) and *Amelius (3rd cent. C.E.); (ii) the "Syrian" School of *Iamblichus and his followers (4th cent.); and (iii) the "Athenian" School begun by *Plutarch of Athens, and including *Syrianus, *Proclus, and their successors, down to *Damascius (5th–6th cents.).

(i) Plotinus and his School. Plotinus' innovations in Platonism (developed in his essays, the *Enneads*, collected and edited by his pupil Porphyry after his death) are mainly two: (a) above the traditional supreme principle of earlier Platonism (and Aristotelianism), a self-thinking intellect, which was also regarded as true being, he postulated a principle superior to intellect and being, totally unitary and simple ("the One"); (b) he saw reality as a series of levels (One, Intellect, Soul), each higher one outflowing or radiating into the next lower, while still remaining unaffected in itself, and the lower ones fixing themselves in being by somehow "reflecting back" upon their priors. This eternal process gives the universe its existence and character. Intellect operates in a state of nontemporal simultaneity, holding within itself the "Forms" of all things. Soul, in turn, generates *Time and receives the Forms into itself as "reason principles" (*logoi*). Our physical, three-dimensional world is the result of the lower aspect of soul ("nature") projecting itself upon a kind of negative field of force, which Plotinus calls *"matter." Matter has no positive existence, but is simply the receptacle for the unfolding of soul in its lowest aspect, which projects the Forms in three-dimensional space. Plotinus often speaks of matter as "evil" (e.g., *Enn.* 1.8), and of the soul as suffering a "fall" (e.g., 5.1.1), but in fact he sees the whole cosmic process as an inevitable result of the super-abundant productivity of the One and thus "the best of all possible worlds."

Plotinus was himself a mystic, but he arrived at his philosophical conclusions by perfectly logical means, and he had not much use for either traditional religion or any of the more recent superstitions. His immediate pupils, Amelius (c. 225–290) and Porphyry (232–c. 310), while somewhat more hospitable to these, remained largely true to his philosophy (though Amelius had a weakness for triadic elaborations in metaphysics). Porphyry was to have wide influence, both in the Latin West (through such men as Marius Victorinus, *Augustine, and *Boethius), and in the Greek East (and even, through translations, on medieval Islam), as the founder of the Neoplatonic tradition of *commentary on both Plato and Aristotle, but it is mainly as an expounder of Plotinus' philosophy that he is known. He added little that is distinctive, though that little is currently becoming better appreciated. Indeed, his doctrine of the One, which equates it with the highest element, or "Father," of the noetic triad may well have influenced the development of *Christian trinitarian doctrine.

(ii) Iamblichus and the Syrian School. Iamblichus (c. 245–325), descendant of an old Syrian noble family, was a pupil of Porphyry's but dissented from him on various important issues. He set up his own school in Apamea in Syria and attracted many pupils. One chief point of dissent was the role of Theurgy (really just magic, with philosophical underpinnings, but not unlike Christian sacramental theology). Iamblichus claimed, as against Porphyry, that philosophical reasoning alone could not attain the highest degree of enlightenment without the aid of theurgic rites, and his view on this was followed by all later Platonists. He also produced a metaphysical scheme far more elaborate than that of Plotinus, by a scholastic filling in, normally with systems of triads, of gaps in the "chain of being" left by Plotinus' more fluid and dynamic approach to philosophy. For example, he postulated two first principles, one completely transcendent and ineffable, the other the source of all creation, thus "resolving" a tension in Plotinus' metaphysics.

Iamblichus also took a distinctive line on the question of the nature of the soul, rejecting Plotinus' doctrine that the highest element of the human soul remained "above," in uninterrupted contact with the noetic world, and indeed that the soul is not affected in its essence by stimuli from the physical world. For Iamblichus, the human soul is a thoroughly mixed entity, preserving no direct contact with the noetic realm and experiencing both permanence and change in its essence; and this view was adopted by his successors, against the more optimistic stance of Plotinus.

Iamblichus was also concerned to fit as many of the traditional gods as possible into his system, which attracted the attention later of the Emperor Julian (331–363), who based himself on Iamblichus when attempting to set up an Hellenic religion to rival Christianity, a project which, however, died with him.

(iii) The Athenian School. The precise links between the pupils of Iamblichus and Plutarch of Athens (d. 432), founder of the Athenian School, remain obscure, but the Athenians always retained a great respect for the Syrian. Plutarch himself is a dim figure, but Syrianus (c. 370–437), though little of his writings survives, can be seen from constant references to him by his pupil Proclus (412–485) to be a major figure and the source of most of Proclus' metaphysical elaborations.

The Athenians essentially developed and systematized further the doctrines of Iamblichus, creating new levels of divinity (e.g., intelligible-intellectual gods, and "henads," or unitary archetypes of Forms, in the realm of the One—though they rejected Iamblichus' two Ones). This process reached its culmination in the thought of the last head of the Athenian Academy, Damascius (c. 456–540).

The drive to systematize reality, and to objectivize concepts, exhibited most dramatically in Proclus' *Elements of Theology* but also (though with much acute critical analysis) in Damascius' *De Principiis*, is a lasting legacy of the later Neoplatonists and had a significant influence on the thought, among others, of Johannes Scotus Eriugena, Nicolaus of Cusa, and Hegel, and on the whole German idealist tradition.

BIBLIOGRAPHY: Armstrong, A. H., ed., *The Cambridge History of Later Greek and Early Mediaeval Philosophy*, Cambridge, 1967; Cherniss, H., *The Riddle of the Early Academy*, Berkeley/Los Angeles, 1945; Dillon, J., *The Middle Platonists*, London/Ithaca, 1977; Gersh, S., *Middle Platonism and Neoplatonism: The Latin Tradition*, Notre Dame, 1986; Long, A. A., *Hellenistic Philosophy*,[2] London/Los Angeles/ Berkeley, 1986; Merlan, P., *From Platonism to Neoplatonism*, The Hague, 1953; Wallis, R. T., *Neoplatonism*, London/Ithaca, 1972.—*JOHN DILLON*

PLOTINUS (204/5–270 C.E.), perhaps of Lycopolis in Egypt. *Neoplatonist philosopher.

Life. Plotinus studied *Platonism with *Ammonius Saccas in Alexandria in Egypt in 232–242, joining then Gordian III's expedition against the Persians in which the emperor was murdered (244). He escaped to Antioch, moving on to Rome, where he was received in the household of the patrician Gemina. There he founded an unofficial school in which he taught, assisted by a group of close pupils, *Amelius at first (246) and then later (263) *Porphyry. The classes were attended by men and women of diverse cultural backgrounds, high-ranking politicians, doctors, and men of letters. Our principal biographical source, Porphyry's *Life of Plotinus*, gives a detailed portrait of the life of the school. Discussions might begin with a text of *Plato as discussed by an earlier (2nd cent. C.E.) Platonist commentator such as *Numenius or Atticus. *Aristotelian *commentators, among them Adrastus and *Alexander of Aphrodisias, were also read. Plotinus would give free rein to the discussion and was slow to intervene. Discussion could also turn on the resolution of a philosophical problem, such as the relation between *soul and body, as raised presumably by a passage in Plato. Plotinus began to compose treatises in connection with these discussions in 254, increasing the scope of his writing with Porphyry's arrival in 263. (Porphyry provides a chronology of the treatises in *Life* chs. 4–6.) Some texts were inspired by a polemic that opposed Plotinus and his assistants to *Gnostics, whose doctrines began to pose a serious threat in the school to what Plotinus considered to be the correct interpretation of ancient truths expressed in Plato. Plotinus attempted (unsuccessfully) to use his friendly relations with the emperor Gallienus (253-68) and his wife to found a "Platonopolis"; what this project involved is unclear (a scheme to organize a city inspired by Plato's *Republic* or *Laws*? A more modest plan for a sort of philosopher's monastery?). Porphyry claims that Plotinus, even if of a contemplative disposition, assumed practical responsibilities successfully. Porphyry left for Sicily in 268 for health reasons. Plotinus himself fell ill (his illness is not clearly identified) and retired to the country house of a former pupil near Minturno (Campania) where he died attended by another pupil, the doctor Eustochius. Various readings of the report of his last words are possible: "I try [or: 'Try'] to lead the god in us [or: 'you'] up to the divine in the universe" (*Life* 2.26–7).

Works. Plotinus' works circulated, if restrictedly, already in his lifetime. Amelius compiled a hundred volumes of notes based on Plotinus' lectures and a (lost) edition of Plotinus may have been prepared by Eustochius. However, in his *Life of Plotinus* Porphyry asserts his claim to be Plotinus' authorized editor, even if he did not publish his edition (the *Enneads*), prefaced by the *Life*, until some thirty years after Plotinus' death. It is this edition that has prevailed. Porphyry took great liberties in organizing the edition. He divided up some of Plotinus' treatises so as to increase their number to fifty-four, the product of the perfect number six and the number of totality, nine. Thus, for example, 6.4 and 6.5 originally formed one treatise. Porphyry then distributed the texts in six sets (1–6) of nine treatises each ("nines," *enneades*), the sets representing successive stages in the ascent of the soul (of the reader) from moral questions (sets 1, 2) and the material world (set 3) to soul (4), Intellect (5), and the One (6). Plotinus' treatises (cited therefore according to set number and number in the set, e.g., 3.9) were not, however, written in view of this arrangement, to which their content does not correspond very well. And in one case, it seems, the distribution meant the dispersal of four parts of one treatise in different places in the edition (3.8; 5.8; 5.5; 2.9). Porphyry did not, however, intervene much, it seems, in correcting Plotinus' very free and personal Greek. Porphyry also gave titles to the treatises or used those already current in the school. The division into chapters was made by Marsilio Ficino in his magnificent Latin translation of 1492. The first printed edition of the Greek text was published in 1580, the first edition based on modern critical principles by P. Henry and H.-R. Schwyzer in 1951–73.

Preliminaries to Reading the Enneads. (i) Plotinus' treatises show the influence of *Aristotelian aporetics in the sense that they often cover a series of questions or difficulties (e.g., 3.6.1; 4.3.1; 1.8.1) that Plotinus sets out to resolve in critical discussion of earlier, current or possible approaches to the matter (see 3.7.1 for a statement of method). The interpretation of relevant passages in Plato plays a central role. In reading a Plotinian treatise, one therefore needs to be aware of its *dialectical context and character, and the history of the problems under discussion, in particular the options taken by Plotinus' immediate Platonic and Aristotelian predecessors (about which we are unfortunately not always well informed). Plotinus also includes *Stoic positions in his analysis, as he does (but to a lesser extent) Presocratic, *Epicurean and *Skeptic views. Thus critical reaction to much of Greek philosophy of the classical, Hellenistic, and imperial periods constitutes the background to Plotinus' reading of Plato. If historically anachronistic, this scope permits of an approach to Plato that is perhaps more philosophically rich and interesting than what is possible in some modern, somewhat academic and puritan versions of Plato. Certainly there are few who can come as near as Plotinus does to Plato's imaginative brilliance and intellectual depth.

(ii) In seeking to resolve problems and criticize inadequate positions, Plotinus' ultimate object is to facilitate, through knowledge, the reader's access to the Good: developing understanding from a situation of confusion, error, or ignorance means a transformation of the self that seeks to know (see below, *Human Soul*). Thus Plotinus' writing is marked by a strong protreptic, moral purpose (for an example, see 6.9), which is characteristic indeed of much of Greek philosophical writing. We may feel at times that the underlying goal somewhat precipitates or overdetermines the critical discussion. Plotinus is aware of his purpose and brings out the moral significance, to those inquiring into a question, of the inquiry itself (e.g., 4.3.1).

(iii) Part of the difficulty in reading Plotinus derives from our ignorance of the immediate dialectical context of the treatises, an ignorance that results in seeing the treatises as unintelligible or "mystic," an ignorance somewhat diminished by modern research on Plotinus' immediate Platonic predecessors. However, Plotinus remains a difficult author and some scholars have resorted to interpretative categories (e.g., the "subjective" versus the "objective" viewpoint in Plotinus, the "psychological" versus the "ontological") in order to sort out puzzling features. It may be that an analysis of these features from within Plotinus' own framework might put in question the necessity and usefulness of such categories.

(iv) In view of the importance of the matter for Plato and Aristotle, the modern reader cannot but raise the question of intellectual development in Plotinus' case, given the unique opportunity provided by Porphyry's chronological listing of the treatises (*Life*, chs. 4–6). Earlier attempts to trace such a development, involving arbitrary declarations of texts as inauthentic, have not been accepted. In general it seems advisable to interpret the treatises as a fairly cohesive if nonsystematic work. We should note also that the treatises were written only in the last quarter of Plotinus' life and that some evolution in Plotinus' style (at first somewhat scholastic, his writing becomes freer and more nuanced) also occurs. It is not, however, impossible that some doctrinal evolution might be demonstrated. In any case, it is preferable to read the treatises in chronological order, reading the divided texts as continuous, seeing how points are raised and taken up again later, rather than in Porphyry's artificial enneadic ordering. Sometimes references to Plotinus include the number, given in brackets, of a treatise in the chronological order (e.g., 3.8.[30]).

First Principles. At the beginning of his *Physics* and *Metaphysics*, Aristotle surveys his predecessors' views on the number and kinds of first principles (*archai*) required to account for the physical world. Inspired by Plato's *Timaeus*, Plotinus' Platonic predecessors listed as first principles the transcendent Forms, *matter, and a divine intellect or demiurge. In Aristotle's case, immanent form and matter may be cited, as well as the unmoved mover, a transcendent self-thinking intellect (*Nous*). For the Stoics, God, as an immanent creative force, and passive matter were first principles. Plotinus lists three such principles: Soul, Intellect (*Nous*), and the One (he does not include matter, perhaps because of its essentially negative, nonproductive function; see below, *Matter and Evil*) and argues that this is Plato's list and is superior to others (5.1.8–9). (In 2.9.1 he argues against the Gnostics for economy in the number of principles, an economy not observed by his Neoplatonist successors.) His reasoning is essentially this: (i) Plotinus shares with Stoicism the idea of a rational force unifying, organizing, and vivifying bodies, a force he identifies with the world soul of the *Timaeus* and whose specific functions he defines in terms of the hierarchy of vital functions of Aristotle's *De Anima*. As the unifying principle sustaining bodies, soul cannot itself be body (5.1.2; see the anti-Stoic arguments in 4.7.2ff.), but is prior to body as the cause prior to the effect of which it is constitutive. (ii) Soul organizes bodies according to rational principles, an art, which is not, Plotinus argues, proper to soul: Soul has the potentiality to think these principles and as such is not the actuality of thought that such a potentiality presupposes. (The Aristotelian principle of the priority and independence of specific actualities in relation to corresponding potentialities plays an important part in Plotinus' notion of causality and is combined here with the idea of an agent or active intellect in Aristotle's *De Anima* 3.4–5.) The presupposed actuality of thought corresponds to Aristotle's divine intellect (*Nous*), but is Platonic in the sense that the objects of its thought are soul's models, the transcendent Forms (5.1.3–4). If some Platonists had already adopted Aristotle's *Nous* as first principle, not all agreed that the Forms were internal to its thinking. Plotinus argues, however, that if this thinking is to be absolutely primary and true, there can be no externality separating the subject and object of thought: *Nous* and the Forms must be one (5.5.1–2). (iii) Against Aristotelians and Aristotelianizing Platonists, however, Plotinus claims that *Nous* cannot be ultimate: As the multiplicity of Forms and the duality of subject and object constitutive of all thought, *Nous* is causally dependent in that all multiplicity presupposes as prior to it the principle constitutive of its unity (5.1.4–5). Prior then to

Nous is the ultimate first principle that, as prior to all multiplicity, can be called the "One" (i.e., the non-multiple).

Problems Concerning the One. Plotinus' "One" has predecessors: the *Neopythagorean reduction of things to a number series flowing out from a "one"; Aristotle's reports on Plato's first principles (*Met.* 1.6); and, in Plotinus' opinion, the Form of the Good of Plato's *Republic* and the "one" of the *Parmenides* (137cff.). However, Plotinus both articulates the grounds for postulating the One and is fully aware of the dilemmas that arise thereby. As what is prior to thought in its highest form (*Nous*) and the Forms that are primary *being, the One is "beyond" thought and being (see *Republic* 509c; however, Plato's Good is a Form, which is not the case for Plotinus' One). The One cannot therefore be thought and still less spoken. We speak "as if" we could speak of the One; but in speaking of it, calling it "the One" or "the Good," we refer in fact to the multiplicity and deficiency of the things we know as they presuppose something radically different (6.9.3; 5.3.14). *Enneads* 6.8 is a fine study of the problem posed by the inadequacy of language, in connection with the predication of freedom of the One.

Derivation. (i) Plotinus' list of first principles differs from those common among his Platonist predecessors in that the latter see their principles as equally primary factors contributing to the organization of the world, whereas Plotinus' list is a reductive series: the world presupposes in its constitution soul, which presupposes *Nous*, which in turn presupposes the One. Thus everything has whatever type of existence it has, mediately or immediately, from the One. Plotinus is therefore confronted with an acute form of the classic Greek problem of how the many comes from the one (5.1.6). One image he uses here is that of an outflowing from a source, emanation, but this is merely an image, limited by its material connotations, not an explanation.

(ii) The derivation of things follows the reverse order of their reduction to one ultimate principle. Thus the first problem concerns the constitution of *Nous* from the One. Given the difficulties involved here (above, *Problems Concerning the One*), Plotinus nevertheless suggests (a) that natural (biological) and immaterial realities, in attaining the perfection of their nature, become productive and that it is implausible that the One, the most perfect of all (in its causal priority and integrity of existence), should be nonproductive; and (b) that each reality consists in an internal act that is its life and gives rise externally to a secondary act that is its image (e.g., the sun and sunlight), the One thus having a secondary act, an intellective potentiality (which Plotinus identifies with the "indefinite dyad" Aristotle attributes to Plato) that in some relation of orientation to the One becomes the articulated expression or image of the One (5.4.1–2;

5.1.6–7). Plotinus' account is, however, fraught with interpretative and philosophical difficulties.

(iii) The constitution of soul is explained along the same lines; it is the manifestation or image or articulation at a greater degree of multiplicity of *Nous*, just as *Nous* is the determinate expression or image of the One (5.2.1). Here also the mechanism of an orientation upwards (*epistrophê*) of a potentiality allows for the constitution of this potentiality as an expression of its cause while freeing this cause from implication in action on its effect. This is the causal relation linking Aristotle's unmoved mover to its world, a relation already used by earlier Platonists (see *Alcinous *Handbook*, chs. 10, 14).

(iv) The physical world is constituted similarly, according to 3.8: it results as an expression or by-product of contemplation by soul of higher realities. Plotinus is anxious here to exclude the use of artisanal (demiurgic) procedures and mechanisms such as had been ridiculed by critics of Plato's *Timaeus*. Plotinus' approach entails that soul produce outside itself a sort of indeterminacy or potentiality, matter, that becomes the world in relation to soul. There are, however, great difficulties here: How could soul, expression of the Good, produce matter, which is absolute evil (1.8; see below, *Matter and Evil*)? Some scholars doubt that soul produces matter, and the *Enneads* are not entirely explicit on this point (but see 3.4.1). How can matter, which is absolutely impassible, become articulated in relation to soul? Plotinus speaks in 3.8 of soul producing lower levels of itself, in particular its lowest level, *phusis* (nature), and of soul going down to organize what is below it.

Intelligible and Sensible Reality. Aristotelian criticism takes as decisive Plato's apparent inability to explain how sensible particulars participate in the Forms, how Forms are present in these particulars. In Plotinus soul acts as the mediator of intelligible principles in the sensible world. However, the presence of soul in body remains to be explained: How can soul, which Plotinus defines, in contrast to body, as nonquantitative and nonlocalized, be "in" body? In handling this issue in 6.4–5, Plotinus indicates that the larger question of the relation between sensible and intelligible reality is at stake. Insisting on the need to avoid the category mistake of thinking of soul *as if* it were a body and *then* asking how soul could be present in body, Plotinus elaborates a description of the kind of unified whole that is intelligible reality, which distinguishes it from the spatially dispersed multiplicity of the sensible world. Intelligibles constitute among themselves relations of one/many, whole/parts of a kind different from relations obtaining between bodies: All intelligibles are in each other, while each intelligible remains distinct. This means that *Nous* and soul are multiplicities in unity ("all souls are one"), present in whole or in part depending on the receptivity of particular bodies. Participation is then a function of bodily receptivity, leaving unaffected the unity and integrity of the intelligible order. Thus soul is present both as one, throughout the separate parts of the body, and as many powers, in function of the different capacities of the different parts of the body. The need to keep soul unaffected by the body leads Plotinus to subtle analyses of perception and other soul/body relations seen from this perspective (3.6.1–5; 4.3). Body is also temporal, living the fragmented image of nontemporal integral ("eternal") intelligible life that soul produces in constituting the world (3.7). Thus the world has no beginning in *time (another point on which Aristotle criticized Plato), but is made with time by soul, which is itself the extratemporal expression of *Nous* and of the One.

Matter and Evil. Matter is a kind of impassible background against which the world of sensible objects appears through the agency of soul. It is not then Aristotelian matter (potentiality determined), but corresponds more to the "receptacle" of the *Timaeus* through which pass images of the Forms while remaining unaffected (2.4–5; 3.6.7–19). As nonform, nonmeasure, absolute indeterminacy, matter fits our notion of evil defined as opposed to the Good (1.8). Matter is then evil per se and the principle of secondary evils: natural evils (e.g., sickness) arising in bodies in which form fails to dominate matter and moral evils (vice) when souls turn away from the Good and become engrossed in material (false) goods. Anticipated by Numenius, Plotinus' position here is ably criticized by *Proclus in his *De Malorum Subsistentia.* How could matter be both the product of the Good (through soul) and absolute evil? If matter is the principle of moral evil, what of moral responsibility? How can soul be affected by what is inferior to it? There are earlier references in Plotinus to some moral failing as the source of evil for souls (5.1 [10].1): How does this relate to the view expressed in 1.8 [51], a late treatise? At any rate Plotinus does not share Gnostic notions of the world as the work of a demiurge who acted through ignorance and moral perversion. Nor does he accept the Epicurean view of the world as a result of irrational movements. If capable of vice, soul comes to the world primarily in order to express the Good in organizing it (4.8). Against the darkness of matter, the world is light, beauty, a rational order produced by soul inspired by *Nous*, a living whole expressed by the (Stoic) concepts of providence and cosmic sympathy (3.2–3).

Beauty. The experience of beauty is as significant for Plotinus as it is for Plato. His first (and probably most read) treatise, 1.6, criticizes the Stoic account of beauty as symmetry (with good color) as not covering noncomposite beauty. Plotinus argues that form, all form, is what makes a physical object beautiful, a position more reminiscent of Aristotle than of Plato, who refers to a *particular* Form of beauty. However, like Plato, Plotinus emphasizes the experience in the soul of recognition in the object of the presence of Form, the reminiscence in soul of its kinship with the Forms, of its intelligible origin. Moral and intellectual beauty also relate to Form: The beautiful soul is one that is most itself, nearest to intelligible Form. Thus primary beauty (and the source of all other beauty) is Form, that is, *Nous* (see also 5.8). Plotinus allows (5.8.1) that artists need not simply imitate visible things but may have insight into the transcendent principles, the Forms that produce these things—a seminal suggestion for Renaissance theories of artistic creativity. What of the relation between Beauty and the Good, between the *Phaedrus* and the *Republic*? Left undecided in 1.6, this issue is discussed in 5.5.12 and 6.7.22 and 32. If beauty is intelligible Form and if the Good (the One) is "beyond" Form, then beauty is subordinate to the Good. Or rather one might say that it is the "light," "grace," or "life" of the Good shining in intelligible beauty that moves us, that we desire. The love of beauty is part of a wider love of the Good, a love that is infinite, since its object is beyond finitude (6.7.32).

The Human Soul and the Path to the Good. (i) Following Plato, Plotinus identifies our soul, particularly its higher aspects, as our true self (1.1). As particular souls we are present to particular bodies, just as world-soul is present to the universe as a unified whole. All souls are one, if also discrete entities. This means that we are always *metaphysically linked to intelligible reality, whatever our moral state, a part of us remains "above" (a novel claim rejected by Plotinus' Neoplatonist successors), just as all intelligible reality is potentially present to us at all times. However, we focus our selves at particular levels in existence, in different activities: Thus our selves are mobile; we are what we do (3.4). If our roots in intelligible reality ground our freedom (which Plotinus associates with knowledge, 6.8.1–5), allowing us to transcend the determined life of the universe (providence), we can degrade ourselves by living inferior lives, forgetful of what we originally are (*Nous* as our "fatherland"), identifying ourselves with and loving things inferior to us.

(ii) If *ethics concerns the true human good and the means to attain it, Plotinus' treatises are largely ethical in purpose, seeking to bring our souls to self-awakening, self-discovery, self-knowledge, which becomes knowledge of intelligible reality, a life according to *Nous*, which is how Plotinus defines the good life, *eudaimonia* (1.4). For this purpose, moral dispositions are required, the "civic" virtues of Plato's *Republic* 4, which condition lower desires related to the body, and the purificatory virtues of the *Phaedo*, which liberate us from concern with material objects (1.2). The arguments of philosophy are also necessary, since their aim is knowledge, whose highest form is the self-knowledge of *Nous*. This self-knowledge is nondiscursive in the sense that no externality or process of thought separates the subject from the object of thinking. In our present condition we think in relation to objects external to us and by virtue of processes of *logic. However, Plotinus accepts Skeptic arguments that under such conditions knowledge cannot be assured (5.5.1). Ratiocinative knowledge of externals must then become, through philosophy, the nonmediated unity of subject and object of thought, which alone can claim to be true knowledge and self-knowledge (see also 5.3.1–6). This is the life of *Nous* that Plotinus describes himself as having attained in 4.8.1. (The Aristotelian tradition also knows of this [momentary] sharing by the philosopher in the life of divine intellect.) At this point philosophy, as ratiocinative, becomes redundant. The life of *Nous* is a life in relation to the One. A further step can then occur, in the desire of the Good, when the life of *Nous* is transcended in a union with the One, beyond all knowledge, in which the self is not annihilated (6.7.34 and 36; 6.9). If Plotinus' ideas, images, and terminology here are of great importance to Jewish, Islamic, and *Christian mysticism, his approach should be seen as a lived interpretation of the ascent of the soul to the Good or Beauty in Plato's *Republic*, *Symposium*, and *Phaedrus*.

(iii) In the *Republic*, the ascent to the Form of the Good is followed by a return or descent to political responsibilities, rule of the state in the light of knowledge of the Forms. A corresponding descent to political action may be indicated in 6.9.7 and may underlie the project of a Platonopolis (above, *Life*). If Plotinus' philosophy does not in principle exclude political *praxis* as the organization of material (social) existence in the light of the Good, certainly most of his writing concerns the phase of the "ascent" of the soul. In his own life Plotinus was active on the individual level, as a model and guide to his pupils.

Influence. Through the efforts of Porphyry (the edition, the *Sentences* and [lost] commentaries), Plotinus' *Enneads* were of central importance to the Neoplatonist schools of late antiquity. *Iamblichus and Proclus developed Platonism along the metaphysical lines laid out by Plotinus, even if they rejected some of his ideas and introduced elements that Plotinus could hardly have accepted (proliferating intermediary levels of reality, religious rites and doctrines). Through these schools and their scholastic heritage, Plotinus also conditioned the development of philosophy in the Byzantine, Islamic East, and early Medieval West. Outside the schools Plotinus was also widely read by leading Christian theologians, by Gregory of Nyssa, by Ambrose, and by *Augustine, who seems to have first read Plotinus in Marius Victorinus' (lost) Latin translation. If, more and more, Augustine sought to limit the place of philosophy in his thought, Plotinian ideas on central questions (the nature of God, the question of evil) have left a profound mark, particularly on his earlier works. The principal philosopher of Byzantium, Michael Psellus, appropriated large portions of the *Enneads* in his work, citing also from

Proclus' (lost) commentary on the *Enneads*. In the Islamic world Arabic paraphrases of *Enneads* 4–6 (possibly including Porphyrian material), known as the "Theology of Aristotle," were read by Al-Kindi and Al-Farabi, and other excerpts from Plotinus also circulated. The Medieval Latin West had no direct knowledge of Plotinus, but had indirect access through references and quotations in Ambrose, Augustine, and Macrobius. Plotinus only became available in the West through Marsilio Ficino's Latin translation, prepared in conjunction with his great translation of Plato and published in 1492 as part of an effort to replace Aristotelian scholasticism with a philosophy more compatible, Ficino believed, with Christian doctrine. Ficino's translation (which included a commentary) had considerable impact on Renaissance philosophers, and its influence extended to the Cambridge Platonists of the seventeenth century. In Germany, Goethe, Schelling, and Hegel took an interest in Plotinus, whose ideas sometimes seemed to anticipate theirs. Hegel's interest encouraged German scholarly work on Plotinus, and Hegel's contemporary in France, Victor Cousin, also stimulated French scholarship on Neoplatonism. More recently, Henri Bergson took a serious (critical) interest in the *Enneads*.

BIBLIOGRAPHY: Text and English tr. in A. H. Armstrong, *Plotinus*, 7 vols. (Loeb), Cambridge, MA, 1966–88 (with rev. version of the Henry-Schwyzer edition). English tr. in E. O'Brien, *The Essential Plotinus*, New York, 1964 (selection). English tr. and comm. on individual treatises: Atkinson, M., (5.1), Oxford, 1983; Fleet, B., (3.6), Oxford, 1995; Helleman-Elgersma, W., (4.3.1–8), Amsterdam, 1980; Meijer, P., (6.9), Amsterdam, 1992; Oosthout, H., (5.3), Amsterdam, 1991; Wolters, A., (3.5), Toronto, 1984. French tr. and comm.: Hadot, P. (3.5), Paris, 1990; (6.7), Paris, 1988, (6.9), Paris, 1994; Leroux, G., (6.8), Paris, 1990; Narbonne, J., (2.4), Paris, 1993. German tr. and comm.: Beierwaltes, W., (3.7), Frankfurt, 1967; (5.3), Frankfurt, 1991. Blumenthal, H. J., *Plotinus' Psychology*, The Hague, 1971; Dillon, J., *Alcinous: The Handbook of Platonism*, Oxford, 1993; Emilsson, E., *Plotinus on Sense-Perception*, Cambridge, 1988; Gerson, L., *Plotinus*, London/New York, 1994; also Gerson, ed., *The Cambridge Companion to Plotinus*, Cambridge, 1996; O'Meara, D., *Plotinus: An Introduction to the* Enneads,[2] Oxford, 1995; Rist, J., *Plotinus: The Road to Reality*, Cambridge, 1967; Sleeman, J., and G. Pollet, *Lexikon Plotinianum*, Leiden, 1980; Schwyzer, H., "Plotinos," *RE* 21. i, 471–592, 1276; supp. vol. 15, 311–28.—DOMINIC J. O'MEARA

PLUTARCH (d. at a great age, 432 C.E.), of Athens. *Neoplatonic philosopher, son of Nestorius, teacher of *Hierocles of Alexandria, *Syrianus and *Proclus. Plutarch restarted a Platonist "school" at Athens, in his own house where subsequent heads of the *"Academy" also taught.

All of Plutarch's works are lost, but we know that he wrote a *commentary on at least Book 3 of Aristotle's *De Anima*, the first since that by *Alexander of Aphrodisias. He also wrote commentaries on *Plato's *Gor-*

gias, Phaedo and *Parmenides*, the last making a significant contribution to the exegesis of that dialogue.

Plutarch's interpretation of the *De Anima* seems to have followed that of Alexander where it was possible to do so without conflict with a Neoplatonic reading of crucial passages. The commentaries by ps.-Simplicius, *Philoponus and ps.-Philoponus are probably heavily influenced by it. Like most later Platonists he was concerned to reconcile Platonic and Aristotelian texts.

BIBLIOGRAPHY: Texts and comm. in D. P. Taormina, *Plutarco di Atene: L'uno, l'anima, le forme* (= *Symbolon* 8), Catania, 1989. Beutler, R., in *RE* vol. 21.1, 1951, 962–75; Blumenthal, H. J., in *De Jamblique à Proclus* (= *Entretiens Hardt* 21), Vandoeuvres–Geneva 1975, 123–47, repr. in *Soul and Intellect*, London/Brookfield, VT, Study 12; also *Byzantion* 48, 1978, 373–75, repr. in *Soul and Intellect*, Study 18.—*H. J. BLUMENTHAL*

PLUTARCH (c. 45–125 C.E.), of Chaeronea. *Platonist philosopher, biographer, and essayist. A native of Chaeronea in Boeotia, Plutarch remained throughout his life a patriotic, if rather defensive, Boeotian. He studied in Athens and, having many friends, he travelled widely. He made several visits to Rome, but always remained faithful to Chaeronea and lived there to the end of his life, conscientiously holding local offices and gathering round him a circle of friends and disciples (who constituted a kind of mini-*Academy). His other great loyalty was to the temple of Apollo at Delphi, of which he became a priest and on whose antiquities and ceremonies he became a great authority. A considerable proportion of his essays relate to Delphi in one way or another.

Plutarch was on good terms with the Roman establishment, gaining Roman citizenship early in life. In his old age (119 C.E.) Hadrian granted him the largely honorary post of Procurator of Achaea. Some years before Trajan had granted him the *ornamenta consularia*, also a high honor.

A vast body of work by Plutarch has survived, much of which, however, has little philosophical content. An evaluation of his biographies of famous Greeks and Romans and of his nonphilosophical essays cannot be entered upon here. Of the philosophical works, we may distinguish the expository from the polemical. Many, but not all, are in the form of *dialogues, which throw some light on the life of his circle. The following are expository works: *On Isis and Osiris*; *On the E at Delphi*; *On the Oracles at Delphi*; *On the Obsolescence of Oracles*; *Is Virtue Teachable?*; *On Moral Virtue*; *On the Daemon of Socrates*; *On the Face in the Moon*; *Problems in Plato*; and *On the Creation of the Soul in the Timaeus*. In addition, remarks of interest are scattered elsewhere—for example, throughout the nine books of *Table Talk*, and indeed throughout the biographies and literary essays.

A number of treatises of a polemical nature, directed against the *Stoics or the *Epicureans, have also survived: *On the Contradictions of the Stoics*; *On "koinai ennoiai": Against the Stoics*; *That One Cannot Live Happily Following Epicurus*; *Against Colotes*; *On the Correctness of the Doctrine "lathe biôsas."*

In addition to these, we are unhappily aware from a list of his writings known as the "Catalogue of Lamprias" that many of Plutarch's most technical philosophical works have not survived. Titles such as *On What Lies in Our Power: Against the Stoics*; *Where Are the Forms?*; *The Manner of Participation of Matter in the Forms*; *What Is Understanding?*—and a number of works bearing on Academic *skepticism and the unity of the Academy—indicate a sad loss. Plutarch plainly accepted the New Academy as part of the Platonic heritage, which colors his approach to philosophy, though he is far from being a skeptic.

Plutarch was on the whole part of the mainline tradition of dogmatic Platonism. It is misleading to set him over against a supposed canon of orthodoxy, centered on an Athenian Academy, for the simple reason that there is in this period no such thing. On one issue in particular he himself is conscious of going against prevailing opinion, and that is the literal interpretation of the account of the creation of the world in the *Timaeus*. But in other areas, such as *ethics (he is strongly pro-*Peripatetic in the essay *On Moral Virtue*) or daemonology (where he seems much influenced by the theories of *Xenocrates), or in making a strong distinction between *soul and intellect (cf. *De Facie*, 943aff., and the concept of the "double death"), or, in general, in a certain degree of cosmic dualism that is apparent in his *metaphysics, there is no case for declaring him outside the pale of Platonist orthodoxy.

On this last question, the doctrines set out in the essay *On Isis and Osiris* are of particular interest. Here Plutarch is producing an *allegorical interpretation of an Egyptian myth that lends itself (with the figure of Typhon) to a dualist interpretation, and Plutarch also adduces Zoroastrian theology to buttress this (369e); but he feels that he has Platonic warrant for his position on the "evil soul" which he discerns in Book 10 of the *Laws* (896dff.) and which he equates with the disorderly principle in the *Timaeus*. Nevertheless, this has been widely viewed as an alien strand in Plutarch's Platonism, possibly betokening influence from Iran.

On the whole, however, Plutarch is thoroughly Hellenic and, despite the fact that much of his more serious philosophic works are lost, he is a major figure in the history of *Middle Platonism.

BIBLIOGRAPHY: Text of *Moralia* in Hubert, Pohlenz et al. (Teubner), Leipzig, 1925 onwards; H. Cherniss et al. (Loeb), in 15 vols. Babut, D., *Plutarque et le Stoicisme*, Paris, 1969; Dillon, J., *The Middle Platonists*, London/Ithaca, 1977, ch. 4; Jones, R.

M., *The Platonism of Plutarch*, Menasha, WI, 1916; Ziegler, K., "Ploutarchos" in *RE* 21:1.—*JOHN DILLON*

POETS, COMIC. Ancient comic poetry traditionally mocked or parodied philosophy and its practitioners. The earliest Greek comic playwright recorded, Epicharmus (6/5th cent. B.C.E.), apparently lampoons *Heraclitean notions of *change (fr.152 Olivieri) and the *cosmology of *Xenophanes, founder of the *Eleatic school (fr. 224). The art form, as it developed at Athens in the fifth century B.C.E. ("Old Comedy") featured fantasy plots about themes of civic importance; philosophers, as markedly different social types, made easy targets. In the next two centuries the form turned to milder situation-comedies, making philosophy less central. This "New Comedy" influenced the Roman dramatic comedians Plautus (d. 184? B.C.E.) and Terence (c. 190–160 B.C.E.), while Roman verse satire harked back to the social critique of Aristophanes and his contemporaries. Some of these poetic forms approached *ethical issues seriously, but comic writers of all periods distanced their wisdom from treatments of the same problems by adherents of philosophical sects.

The *Clouds* of Aristophanes (423 B.C.E.) provides the best-known caricature of a thinker, though the play's precise relation to the historical *Socrates remains problematic. Socrates in *Plato's *Apology* blamed the production for long-standing Athenian animosity towards him, even as he disavowed the interest in physical science that the comedy attributes to him. The Socrates of the *Clouds* is a mixture of *sophistic *rhetorician, cultist, experimentalist, and common thief, whose absurd investigations of celestial phenomena are associated with an idiosyncratic worship of clouds, and whose rationalist disregard of traditional divinities is tied to relativistic teaching about making the "weaker" argument appear "stronger." Elements from *Anaxagoras, *Protagoras, *Prodicus, and *Diogenes of Apollonia shape the dramatic caricature. Plato's *Symposium* depicts Aristophanes and Socrates on speaking terms; it is difficult to imagine that the playwright misunderstood Socrates; allusions to philosophic midwifery (l. 137) and to the process of *diaeresis* (l. 742) exhibit familiarity with Socrates' manner. Recent criticism has seen in the *Clouds* a critique of the actual dangers of elenctic method. The charge that Socrates "corrupted" the young finds dramatic precedent in the comedy when Socrates' instruction turns a son against his father, acerbically portrayed as a conniver who abuses Socratic "wisdom" to escape creditors.

Elsewhere in the Aristophanic corpus, philosophers and sophists are confined to allusions (e.g., Prodicus at *Birds* 692, *Gorgias *ibid.* 1701). Socrates reappears several times as a stock figure, the shabby, shoeless, hungry intellectual. More intriguing are less specific parallels: the *Ecclesiazusae* (392? B.C.E.) involves a state in which women and property are held in common, yet must predate Plato's *Republic*; the resemblance may be accidental, as utopian notions also mark Aristophanes' *Birds* and *Acharnians*, as well as the Golden Age fantasy of the *Beasts* of Crates (*Poetae Comici Graeci* [*PCG*] fr. 16).

Given the fragmentary evidence about other comedians, Aristophanes appears less unusual as critic of philosophic figures and ideas. Ameipsias in the *Konnos* mocked Socrates at the same dramatic competition in which the *Clouds* took last place (D.L. 2.27–28). Eupolis lampooned Protagoras (DK80A11) and branded Socrates a thief (*PCG* fr. 395). In the two centuries following Aristophanes, dramatic comedy continued to poke fun at *Pythagoreans (Aristophon *PCG* fr. 9–12), Plato and his disciples (Epicrates *PCG* fr. 10; Cratinus *iunior PCG* fr. 10; Alexis *PCG* fr. 247-8; cf. D.L. 3.26-28), and "sophists" *en bloc* (Antiphanes *PCG* fr. 120). On the other hand, Menander (342?–292 B.C.E.), premier poet of New Comedy and pupil of *Theophrastus (D.L. 5.36), drew on *Peripatetic ethics and *aesthetics in constructing his comedies of manners.

Nor were influences in one direction only. Plato supposedly derived his *dialogue form from a comic genre, the mimes of Sophron (D.L. 3.18). The *Symposium* with its raucous party-crashing ending is even formally like an Aristophanic play (e.g., *Wasps*). The fictitious tradition that Plato borrowed doctrine from Epicharmus (D.L. 3.9.) was already questioned in antiquity but shows that philosophy and comedy could be seen as overlapping endeavors. Plato offers several explicit reflections on the limits of comedy (at *Rep.* 395a and 606c; *Laws* 658d; *Symp.* 223d), and Aristotle wrote a full-scale analysis in the (lost) second book of the *Poetics*. *Crates, head of the *Academy in the third century B.C.E., continued the tradition (D.L. 4.23).

Nondramatic Greek poetry is little concerned with philosophy, although the *Silloi* of *Timon of Phlius (3rd cent. B.C.E.) managed to caricature all the major sects. It is in Rome that satiric poetry finds the schools a perennial interest. Varro (116–27 B.C.E.) in his *Saturae* apparently adapted the style and matter of *Menippus of Gadara, a *Cynic of the third century B.C.E. Horace (65–8 B.C.E.), who studied philosophy in Athens, acknowledges the model of Old Comedy (*Satires* 1.4.1–7) and work of the Roman poet Lucilius (d. 102 B.C.E.), who in turn had borrowed the *diatribe style of Cynic sympathizers like *Bion of Borysthenes (c. 325–255 B.C.E.). Horace's *Satires* (35–30 B.C.E.) and *Epistles* (20–15 B.C.E.) picture their author as an eclectic, often acratic, moralizer conversant with Cynicism, *Epicureanism, the *Stoicism of *Panaetius (2nd cent. B.C.E.), *Cyrenaic hedonism, and Academic doctrine. *Ep.*1.17 argues for the superiority of *Aristippus over *Diogenes of Sinope, a preference tinged with irony, as the hedonist Horace continually alludes to his own patron, the wealthy Maecenas. Similar effects occur in *Ep.* 1.1 and 1.10. The Horatian protreptic tone, anecdotal style, and ironic self-presentation recur much later in the *Consolation* of *Boethius (c. 475–525 C.E.), another inheritor of Menippean technique.

BIBLIOGRAPHY: Ambrosino, D., *Quaderni di storia* 18, 1983, 3–60; Long, A. A., *PCPS* n.s. 24, 1978, 70–72; McGann, M., *Studies in Horace's First Book of Epistles*, Brussels, 1969; Nussbaum, M. C., *YCS* 26, 1980, 43–97; O'Regan, D. E., *Rhetoric, Comedy, and the Violence of Language in Aristophanes' Clouds*, Oxford, 1992.—*RICHARD P. MARTIN*

POETS, LYRIC and ELEGIAC. The Greek philosophical poets wrote hexameter poetry, not lyric. Unlike *Parmenides, *Empedocles, and *Cleanthes, *Xenophanes of Colophon also wrote elegiacs, as did Solon and, occasionally (in his *Indalmoi*), *Timon. The point of contact between later Greek philosophy and the archaic lyric is in philosophical engagement with the moral ideas expressed in earlier poetry, but Alcman is clearly a forerunner of philosophical *cosmology. The beginning of Pindar's *Olympian* 1 ("Best is water, but fire...") has been compared with the thought of *Heraclitus. Later philosophers focussed mainly on the archaic poets' conception of *virtue (*aretê*), especially the virtue of justice. A conception of justice and the order of the natural world cohere in Solon's prayer to the Muses (fr. 13 West), which comes close to the conception of the order of nature of *Anaximander (DK12B1). Xenophanes' criticism of the value placed on athletic power is alluded to in *Plato's *Apology* 36d, and Plato subjects the concepts of justice expressed by Pindar (fr. 152 Bowra) and Simonides (*PMG* 542 Page) to criticism (and distortion) in *Gorgias* 484b, *Protagoras* 339a, and *Republic* 1, 331e. Tyrtaeus' call to valor is essential to the discussion of courage in *Laws* 1. The pithy formulations of wisdom (*gnômai*) associated with the corpus of Theognis were much cited, and the numerous quotations of lyric and elegiac poets that point a moral in *Aristotle's *Nicomachean Ethics* demonstrate how popular morality depended on archaic poetry for its articulation.

In his *Constitution of the Athenians*, Aristotle quotes extensively from Solon to illustrate Solon's political philosophy. *Epicurus depended on Solon's poetry (fr. 13 West) for his own description of justice (*Master Saying* 17). But a study of the quotations of poetry by the Greek philosophers shows that they were more attracted to tragedy than to lyric or elegy.

BIBLIOGRAPHY: Fränkel, H., *Early Greek Poetry and Philosophy*, trs. M. Hadas and J. Willis, New York/London, 1973; Snell, B., *The Discovery of the Mind*, tr. T. G. Rosenmeyer, Cambridge, MA, 1953.—*DISKIN CLAY*

POETS, TRAGIC. During the fifth and fourth centuries B.C.E., Greek tragedy stood in an oblique but significant relationship to the development of philosophy. Taking its materials from myths involving extreme situations and sufferings, tragedy broached issues of *religion, *ethics, *psychology, and *politics that impinged upon, and were sometimes influenced by, the concerns of contemporary philosophy. Philosophy correspondingly came to regard tragedy, whether favorably or adversely, as an urgent object of attention.

Reacting against an older tendency to treat the tragedians explicitly as "thinkers," modern critics have often stressed the distinction between drama and discursive thought. But this contrast in turn needs qualifying in two important respects: first, because an exclusive identification of philosophy with systematic theorizing is inappropriate for the Greek tradition; second, because Greek culture, with its notion of poets as sages and teachers, constantly looked for morally instructive meanings and normative paradigms within poetry. Debate about the degree to which determinate ideas are conveyed by the experiences of tragic agents remains delicate. We can nonetheless reasonably approach tragedy as a major manifestation of traditions of reflection that also helped to shape philosophy. Among the potentially philosophical topics with which tragedy engages are the tensions between human desire and the larger structure of reality, the psychology of human beings facing ultimate dilemmas, and the character of extreme conflicts of value. It will always, however, be problematic to try to detach such insights from the dramatic particularity in which they are embedded and which give them their vivid power. The following sketch is perforce limited to marking out some areas of special relevance.

Aeschylus (525–456 B.C.E.). Most of Aeschylus's surviving plays display stark strains between freedom and necessity, human and divine causation, and a just world order and the darker powers (inside or outside the mind) that threaten its stability. Especially Aeschylean is a sense of mental impulses working in tragically close if near-inscrutable conjunction with external forces: In Eteocles' determination to face his brother, for example, the family curse becomes inextricably entwined with the character's own fatalistic blood-lust (*Seven against Thebes* 686–718); in Agamemnon's sacrifice of Iphigeneia, a leader's fear of failure becomes a crazed wilfulness that is also the paying of a price obscurely demanded by Artemis (*Agamemnon* 205–47). Human psychology is searchingly exposed as the intersection of social, political, and personal dynamics: Xerxes' desire to enslave Greece stems from motivations that extend from the military and economic pressures of an empire to a tormented desire to emulate his father (*Persians* 197–9, 754–8). There are intimations here that could fruitfully be compared with the politico-psychological analysis in *Plato *Republic* 8–9.

Aeschylus seems often to have integrated such themes into large-scale patterns of conflict and resolution, above all through the use of connected trilogies. In the *Oresteia*, the fluctuating, irreconcilable demands of an ethic of revenge are first enacted and then transcended by the establishment of a civic justice that also reflects the harmonization of Olympian and chthonic deities within the overall will of Zeus. In the Danaid trilogy, to which *Suppliants* belonged, the Danaids' resistance to marriage with their Egyptian cousins was eventually superseded, after the murders of the second play, by a settlement embodying a sense of Aphrodite/eros as a cosmic force of attraction and union. Some of Aeschylus's work can thus be seen as driven by a momentum towards overarching unification on the level of ethics, psychology, and religion.

In this connection, Presocratic influences have sometimes been perceived in such things as the chorus's yearning invocation of Zeus as ultimate guarantor of an intelligible universe (*Agamemnon* 160–66) or the statement of a character in the lost *Heliades* that "Zeus is the air, the earth, the sky: and Zeus is everything that is greater still" (fr. 70 Radt). It cannot be wrong in principle to allow for deliberate use of philosophical materials (the "embryology" of *Eumenides* 658–66 may echo *Anaxagoras), but pursuing specific connections is not always profitable. On a larger scale, however, there is a broad parallelism between the Zeus-centred, integrative explanation of the world sometimes evoked in Aeschylus and the unificatory systems of such thinkers as *Xenophanes and *Heraclitus.

Sophocles (c. 496–406 B.C.E.). Among much else, Sophocles' work shares with Aeschylean drama a divine background that is often at least semi-opaque in its implications for humans. In one play, the *Oedipus Tyrannus*, that point is connected with a sequence of events that can be read, in part, as a symbol of the snares and delusions of a confident quest for (self-) knowledge.

The seven surviving plays suggest a cardinal interest in the ethical complexities of acute dilemmas and conflicts. In the great encounters between Antigone and Creon (*Antigone*), Electra and Clytemnestra (*Electra*), Oedipus and his sons (*Oedipus at Colonus*), the bitter contrast between Odysseus's and Agamemnon's attitudes to Ajax (*Ajax*), or young Neoptolemus's agonized wrestling with competing loyalties (*Philoctetes*), we observe feelings and arguments that project a profound awareness of the problematic standards of action, especially in relation to the fundamental yet unstable categories of "friends" and "enemies." It is not surprising that moments from such works suggested themselves to Aristotle as memorable examples of ethical subjects analyzed in his own treatises (see on Neoptolemus, *NE* 1146a19–21, 1151b18–21; on Antigone, *Rh.* 1373b9–13). The Sophoclean handling of antagonisms and intractable choices yields no reductive solutions; part of its potency stems from the way in which it compels an understanding of opposed positions. But the shape of several plays nonetheless seems to trace certain kinds of tragedy to ethical and psychological inflexibility and, correspondingly, to vindicate a capacity typified by both Odysseus in *Ajax* and Neoptolemus in *Philoctetes*: a disposition to judge particular situations with a humane suppleness that is open to the demands of compassion and pity.

As with Aeschylus, instances of direct philosophical influence on the poet's writing are contentious. One of the most widely discussed is the link between the first stasimon of *Antigone* (332–75, the so-called Ode on Man)—with its counterpoint of material progress and the problem of justice—and the *Protagorean myth of human civilization represented at Plato *Protagoras* 320c–322d. Another is the question whether the figure of Odysseus in *Philoctetes*, depicted as an amoral "technician" in argument and guile (e.g., 96–9, 407–9, 439–40), specifically evokes *sophistic relativism. Similarly, some critics have discerned in the Oedipus of *Oedipus Tyrannus* a quasi-sophistic but fatefully misplaced faith in the powers of the enquiring intellect. However conscious the interplay with contemporary ideas may be in such contexts, the effect is one not of intrusive topicality but of an expanded resonance that enhances the dramatic issues.

Euripides (c. 485–406 B.C.E.). Euripides' plays contain more passages of ostensibly philosophical speculation and theorizing than those of his predecessors. The image of Euripides as *Socratic rationalist, so familiar from Nietzsche's *Birth of Tragedy*, goes back to fifth-century perceptions of the poet, as we see from jokes in comedy (including Aristophanes, *Frogs* 1491–9). The later critical tradition connected him, often fancifully, with figures such as Anaxagoras and Protagoras. These views translate into naively biographical form features of the plays whose dramatic import is never easy to gauge. Two Euripidean traits are especially pertinent here: first, his tendency to introduce pointedly intellectual themes into his characters' utterances; second, his penchant for dramatizing the cut-and-thrust of *dialectical argument (cf. the reference at Aristophanes, *Frogs* 775, to *antilogiai*, "opposed arguments," a term that was also the title of a work by Protagoras).

When Hecuba refers to Zeus as "either the necessity of nature or the mind of mortals" (*Trojan Women* 886, cf. 988), the line echoes simultaneously a concept of presocratic *cosmology and rationalistic reinterpretations of traditional religion. The same combination appears in Teiresias's explanation of Demeter and Dionysus as embodiments of the "dry" and the "moist" in nature (*Bacchae* 274–85), a passage often linked with *Prodicus (DK84B5). Elsewhere we find clear hints of sophistic moral relativism (e.g., *Phoenissae* 499–502), and a self-consciously analytic moral psychology that can oppose reason to passion (*Medea* 1078-80) or ponder the pressures that impede people from acting on their judgment (*Hippolytus* 377–87). Although Euripides has been criticized for the supposedly gratuitous intellectualism of such passages, it is always possible to see in them something more than irrelevant allusiveness. Euripides employs philosophical motifs, as he employs other features of fifth-century culture, to produce an unsettling reworking of traditional stories in a spirit that challenges his audience to consider the relationship of mythical images to present realities. But it is not easy to identify a determinate authorial attitude behind such technique. Euripides has been dubbed both "rationalist" and "irrationalist," a product of the sophistic movement and a critic of its stratagems. Given the richness of his work and the raw antitheses that so often lie near its heart, all such descriptions are inevitably one-sided. Radical interpretive divergences bespeak, at bottom, a type of drama that provokes reflection precisely by the startling, even paradoxical, juxtaposition of ideas and actions.

Philosophical Responses. Greek philosophy typically treated tragedy as a unitary phenomenon. The concept of tragic fiction as a vehicle of nondiscursive insight may have been recognized by *Gorgias in his claim that tragedy is "a deception in which the deceiver is juster than the nondeceiver, and the deceived wiser than the undeceived" (DK82B23). Plato, however, continued and deepened an older "quarrel between philosophy and poetry" (*Rep.* 10, 607b5–6), already apparent in Xenophanes' and Heraclitus's criticisms of *Homer and other poets. Plato regards tragedy not as a formal genre but a "vision" or worldview; hence the inclusion of Homer as well as the Attic tragedians within the category (*Rep.* 10, 595c1–2, 607a3). *Republic* 10's critique of poetry culminates in the charge that tragedy induces psychological "surrender" to the displays of suffering and grief that it dramatizes: To yield to the pleasure of tragedy is to open oneself to the valuation of life, the attachment to the human world, which is seen as implicit in the behavior of tragic heroes (605c–606b). Plato thus treats tragedy as a potential *rival*, an alternative way of experiencing and construing reality: this rivalry is explicitly signalled by the idea of philosophy as "the truest tragedy" at *Laws* 7, 817b. Platonic philosophy opposes tragedy with a revaluation of human needs, a rationalistic antipathy to emotion, and a search for transcendence.

Aristotle's *Poetics* discusses tragedy principally in terms of tightly knit plots constructed around movement between extremes of prosperity and adversity. This approach presents tragedy as exploring the impingement of contingency upon, and the emergence of suffering from, chains of deliberative action. The audience's pity and fear are, *contra* Plato, an ethically valuable response, since they rest on understanding of the limitations and vulnerability of human agency; tragedy is the highest instance of poetry's quasi-philosophical capacity to convey "universals" (*Poet.* 9, 1451b5–11). The crucial condition of tragic suffering is a fallibility (*hamartia*, ch. 13) that seems to be purely human in origin, and a corollary of this is the downplaying of those religiously conceived forces that bulk so large in the tragic myths themselves. In answering Plato's strictures by making of tragedy a means of giving form and meaning to the occurrence of extreme suffering, Aristotle produces an essentially secular model of the genre.

Of post-Classical philosophers, it was the *Stoics who showed the greatest interest in tragedy. Partly under the influence of Plato's moralistic attacks on poetry, Stoics attempted to ascribe didactic value to tragedy by treating it as a reminder of the nature of life's possible misfortunes and an encouragement toward the extirpation of precisely those passions and attachments that could turn external misfortune into deep but avoidable psychological suffering (e.g., Epictetus *Discourses* 1.4.23–7, Marcus Aurelius *Meditations* 11.6). But after the intense intellectual culture of Classical Athens, the relationship between tragedy and philosophy was never again to be so important until the nineteenth century in Germany.

BIBLIOGRAPHY: Blundell, M. W., *Helping Friends and Harming Enemies: a Study in Sophocles and Greek Ethics*, Cambridge, 1989; Halliwell, S., *Aristotle's Poetics*, Chapel Hill, 1986; Nussbaum, M. C., *The Fragility of Goodness*, Cambridge, 1986; Williams, B., *Shame and Necessity*, Berkeley, 1993.—STEPHEN HALLIWELL

POLEMO (b. c. 350 B.C.E.), of Athens. Scholarch of the *Academy, 315/4–266/5. Son of the wealthy Philostratus, Polemo led a dissolute life until he was converted to the philosophic way of life while hearing *Xenocrates lecture on moderation. His nearly fifty years as head of the Academy were marked by a move away from positive *metaphysics toward moral concerns and by the development of "academic *skepticism" with his colleagues *Crantor and *Crates. Polemo is credited with having been one of the teachers of *Zeno of Citium, founder of the *Stoic school.

Our major source of information about Polemo is *Diogenes Laertius 4.3.16–20. *Lucian satirizes his youthful follies in *Bis Accusatus* 16; *Cicero cites Polemo several times. He is also noted in *Clement of Alexandria and *Plutarch.

BIBLIOGRAPHY: Texts in M. Gigante, *Polemonis Academici Fragmenta*, Naples, 1977. *RE* 21, 2524–2529; Reale, G., *The Systems of the Hellenic Age*, Albany, 1985, 79–80.—ANTHONY PREUS

POLITICAL THOUGHT, Classical. Political thought began in antiquity as the study of the *polis* (city or city-state), which the Greeks regarded as the highest form of social organization. The modern terms "political" and "politics" descend from the Greek *politikos*, that is, belonging to or pertaining to the *polis*.

There were hundreds of city-states throughout the ancient world, each of which was geographically distinct and, to a significant extent, economically self-sufficient and politically independent. Their small size and compactness made possible an unusual level of direct political participation by citizens. Because the Greeks founded many colonies and because revolutions were frequent, they had the occasion to deliberate about new constitutions. Also, because they did not draw the modern distinction between "state" and "society," they viewed the constitution as "the way of life" of the citizens. These factors contributed to the distinctive character of early political theory.

The Poets. *Homer (8th cent. B.C.E.?) had a pervasive influence over Hellenic culture through his epics, the *Iliad* and the *Odyssey*. The later Greeks took these poems to describe an earlier era when there were three social classes: kings or lords, a noble class, and commoners. Although the political relations among these groups is somewhat unclear, Homer states that "the rule of many is not good; one ruler let there be" (*Iliad* 2.204). He also contrasts the civilized life of the Greeks with that of the Cyclopes, who lived anarchically in scattered households and did not have assemblies or regulations (*Odyssey* 9.112–14). Political authority in Homer seems to depend upon the favor of the gods, and the king is supposed to be just and abide by Themis, the goddess of law and order.

*Hesiod, in his *Theogony* (c. 700 B.C.E.), treats Dikê (justice) as a goddess along with Eunomia (good law) and Eirênê (peace): They are the daughters of Zeus and Themis. Also, Hesiod's *Works and Days* advocates just conduct and condemns lawless activity (most notably that of his brother, whom he accuses of stealing his property by bribing corrupt local "kings"). Homer and Hesiod were very influential, but their concepts of justice and of political and legal institutions were not clearly defined or justified.

The Presocratic Philosophers. Although early philosophers were mainly concerned with nature, their writings reveal some political ideas. For example, *Anaximander of Miletus (c. 610–540 B.C.E.) describes the natural order as involving a process of generation and destruction in which things "make retribution and pay the penalty to one another for their injustice, according to the order of *time." He apparently means that the balance of opposites such as hot and cold, dominating each other in alternate cycles through the course of time, resembles a political order based on justice. *Pythagoras (6th cent. B.C.E.) and his followers defined "the just" as reciprocity with another. On this account what one receives must be in some sense equal to what one has done, as discussed in *Aristotle's *Nicomachean Ethics* 5.5. *Heraclitus of Ephesus (fl. c. 500 B.C.E.) seems to have held that order involves a harmony of opposed classes, with the enlightened few ruling over the benighted many. The *logos*, the principle that governs nature, is implicitly identified with *nomos* (law). Human laws are fed by the higher divine law, and law is for the *polis* what intelligence is to a human being (DK22B114). Hence, a people should fight for its law as for its wall (B44). Heraclitus here apparently anticipates the doctrines of natural law and the rule of law, although his writings are notoriously obscure.

*The *Sophists.* The most prominent early sophists included *Protagoras of Abdera (c. 485–415), *Gorgias of Leontini (c. 483–376), and *Hippias of Elis (c. 485–415). Unquestionably the most influential of them was *Protagoras, who purported to teach *virtue and pronounced that "man is the measure of all things: of things that are, that they are, and of things that are not, that they are not." As interpreted by *Plato in the *Theaetetus,* this dictum asserts that a proposition is true for someone if, and only if, he believes it, and false for that person if, and only if, he disbelieves it. The purpose of education is not to impart beliefs that are true in an absolute sense, but to persuade persons to accept thoughts that are better for them. Wise speakers substitute sound for unsound views regarding what is just. "For I maintain that whatever practices seem right and laudable to any particular city are so, for that city, so long as it holds by them" (*Tht.* 167c). Protagoras is thus a founder of the tradition of relativism in politics.

Also important was the sophists' distinction between *phusis* (nature) and *nomos* (law or convention). When one makes a moral judgment, for example, that an act is "just" or "unjust," one is only asserting that the act conforms to, or violates, certain laws or conventions that human beings have established. Protagoras and Hippias evidently believed that convention was an improvement on nature, whereas some later sophists such as *Antiphon (in his fragment *Truth*) along with Callicles and *Thrasymachus (as depicted in Plato's *Gorgias* and *Republic*) contended that conventional morality had been undermined because it was shown to be "against nature." Convention was a device by the weak to control the strong, who should defy it if they could do so with impunity.

Another sophist, Alcidamas (4th cent. B.C.E.), criticized slavery: "God set all men free. Nature has made none a slave." Lycophron drew a further corollary: The polis arises out of a contract or covenant among the citizens, and "the law is a mutual guarantee of rights" (cited by Aristotle, *Pol.* 3.9). This argument (echoed by Glaucon in Plato's *Republic* 2) is the ancestor of modern social-contract theories. The influence of the sophists is also evident in the fifth-century historians *Herodotus and *Thucydides.

Socrates. As depicted in Plato's *Apology,* Socrates (469–399 B.C.E.) devoted his life to the pursuit of wisdom and virtue by examining the opinions of others. He alleged that his habit of questioning and refuting influential persons ultimately resulted in his criminal indictment. He described his proper role as the gadfly, pestering the city with questions but otherwise eschewing politics: "The true champion of justice, if he intends to survive even for a short time, must necessarily confine himself to private life and leave politics alone." (*Ap.* 32a). Socrates was critical of Athenian democracy, although he also disobeyed the edicts and commands of the antidemocratic regime of the Thirty, which he found to be morally objectionable. Plato's *Crito* seems intended to counteract the image of Socrates as an anarchist. Here Socrates refuses to take the opportunity to escape from prison on the grounds that he has an inviolable obligation to obey the laws of Athens, because by voluntarily living in Athens he has tacitly agreed to abide by her laws and one ought always to keep one's agreements if they are justly made (i.e., not through force or fraud). Further, the laws, in overseeing his birth and upbringing, are like his parents and have analogous rights to his obedience.

Plato. The scion of a noble family in Athens, Plato (c. 429–347 B.C.E.) abandoned his early ambition to enter politics after falling under Socrates' spell and dedicated his life instead to philosophy. His early *dialogues are thought to be fairly representative of Socrates' teachings. However, the *Republic* probably expresses his own mature views, although it is open to question whether Plato himself would endorse every claim made by the character Socrates in this complex work. The opening themes of the *Republic* are the definition of justice and the issue of whether an individual benefits from being just, which leads Socrates to investigate what a fully just city would be like and then to draw parallels between the city and the individual *soul and between the virtues found in each.

Justice is defined as each part of a whole performing its proper function and not interfering with the other parts, and it is argued that the nature of a thing determines its proper function. Socrates uses this concept of justice to derive a utopian political ideal. The just city is divided into three specialized classes: workers, guardians (i.e., rulers), and their auxiliaries (i.e, soldiers). The education of the guardians is stringently regulated, and all subversive influences are prohibited. Women are educated equally with men and are to be admitted to the guardian class according to their natural merits. A communistic system is instituted for the guardian class, excluding private property and traditional family relations. Procreation is governed by a lottery system that is secretly manipulated by experts in eugenics. Finally, and most paradoxically, the rulers are philosophers: "Cities will have no respite from evil, nor will the human race, unless philosophers rule as kings in the cities, or those whom we now call kings and rulers genuinely and adequately study philosophy, until, that is, political power and philosophy coalesce" (*Rep.* 5, 473c–d). In explaining this last claim Socrates ascends to a higher philosophical level, introducing the theory of Forms, that is, of imperceptible realities to which our words ultimately refer. For example, actions and laws that we call "just" are merely particulars which participate in the Form of justice, called "the just itself," which is known by reason independently of the senses. Only philosopher-kings can contemplate these realities and thereby "establish here on earth lawful notions about things beautiful, just, and good where they need establishing, or preserve them once established" (*Rep.* 6, 484d).

The explicit aim of the *Republic* is to provide a pattern (*paradeigma*) that can be used to understand the nature of justice and its relation to *happiness and not to prove that such an ideal could exist. For it is not possible to realize everything in practice that can be formulated in speech; rather "by nature practice has less of a grasp on truth than speech (i.e., theory)" (*Rep.* 5, 472c–473a). Despite this disclaimer, the utopian ideal of the *Republic* has continued to have a powerful hold on political theorists. According to Plato's Seventh Epistle (authorship of which is disputed) he made an unsuccessful attempt to educate Dionysus of Syracuse as a philosopher-king. Perhaps chastened by this experience, Plato, in later dialogues such as the *Statesman* and *Laws*, makes greater concessions to political realities, although even these are advanced as a second-best solution, that is, the closest approximation to the political ideal under adverse circumstances.

Aristotle. For Aristotle (384–322 B.C.E.), political science is a distinct practical science, concerned with promoting good action or happiness for the polis as a whole. His *Politics* and two *ethical works (the *Nicomachean* and *Eudemian Ethics*) deal with political science in this sense.

A dominant feature of Aristotle's political theory is his naturalism. He argues that the city exists by nature, that a human being is by nature a political animal, and that the city is by nature prior to the individual (*Pol.* 1.2). This presupposes his natural teleology, the theory that human beings like all other organisms have "natural ends," that is, biologically based, internal, directive principles. Just as an acorn has as its natural end growing into a mature oak tree, a human being has as its natural end the full exercise of its rational capacities (*eudaimonia*, flourishing or happiness). The city exists by nature in a derived sense, namely, as developing out of natural social tendencies and as necessary for the attainment of human natural ends. A city is a community of human beings with a common end, and, just as an organism can be healthy or sick, a city can be in a natural or unnatural condition. A city is in a natural condition if, and only if, its members are able to cooperate for the common advantage, which requires a constitution that is correct or just.

A constitution is defined by Aristotle as an ordering of the city whereby offices are distributed and the political authority is defined with a view to a certain understanding of the end of the community (*Pol.* 4.1). He distinguishes constitutions into correct and incorrect and according to whether there is one ruler, a few, or many. The correct forms are kingship, aristocracy, and polity; the incorrect are tyranny, oligarchy, and democracy (*Pol.* 3.6; cf. Plato *Pol.* 302c–e). The correct form assigns political rights according to distributive justice, that is, on the basis of the candidate's merits. Aristotle considers three contending criteria of merit: wealth, freedom (free birth), and virtue. Aristotle defends virtue as a standard of merit against wealth and freedom, which are the basis for oligarchy and democracy respectively. Kingship would be the best and most divine constitution if there were an individual with godlike virtue. Since no such exalted individual is in evidence, the best constitution is an aristocracy governed by a small group of citizens with complete virtue and sufficient resources (*Pol.* 7–8). Aristotle criticizes the utopian elements of Plato's *Republic*, such as communism (*Pol.* 2.1–5). However, his own scheme contains repressive, paternalistic regulations and unequal social relationships, for example, natural slavery, male dominance, and political disenfranchisement of productive economic classes. He recognized that the city-states of his day were not capable of adopting his ideal constitution, because they contained opposed social classes: the rich and the poor, who favored oligarchy and democracy respectively. Hence, he developed a theory of mixed and middle constitutions, including polity, which permitted cooperation between the rich, the poor, and the middle class, where it existed, for the common advantage. He also recognized a role for the politician even in connection with inferior constitutions (*Pol.* 4.1–2). Ironically, his extant writings do not discuss the major event of his lifetime: Alexander's conquest of the Persian Empire and the creation of a new Hellenistic empire.

Hellenistic and Roman Eras. The powerful kingdoms founded by Alexander's successors eclipsed the traditional city-states, which gradually ceased to be the focus of moral and political philosophy. *Diogenes of Sinope (c. 400–c. 325 B.C.E.), founder of the *Cynics, argued that the good life involved self-sufficiency and satisfying one's natural needs in disregard of the city's laws and conventions. *Epicurus of Samos (341–270 B.C.E.) advocated hedonism: "pleasure is the beginning and end of living happily." However, true pleasure involves *ataraxia*, a state of tranquillity or freedom from disturbance. Happiness is attained not through political participation but small associations of friends. Politics is a practical necessity, in the sense argued by some sophists. For justice is "a token of that which is expedient with a view to not inflicting and not receiving injury." Justice is both "natural" in that it promotes the end of happiness and "conventional" in that it arises out of an agreement by individuals to respect one another's rights (cf. *Principal Doctrines* 37).

The *Stoics were arguably the most influential political theorists in the Hellenistic and Roman eras. Developing earlier notions of natural law, the Stoics maintained that "one eternal and immutable law will be valid for all nations and all times, and there will be one master and one ruler, that is, God over us all, for He is the author of this law, its promulgator and its enforcing judge" (Cic. *Rep.* 3.22.33). The true *polis* was the *kosmos*, the world as a whole; it was a "cosmopolis" containing all human beings as citizens, under one ruler, God, with one set of laws discoverable by "right reason in agreement with nature."

St. *Augustine, Bishop of Hippo (354–430 C.E.), was prompted by the barbarian sack of Rome in 410 to write *The City of God.* Against those who alleged that Rome fell because it forsook the pagan virtues, Augustine argued that all worldly cities are perishable because they are based on humanity's sinful nature. Politics has to be understood in terms of a theory of history based on the *Christian doctrines of original sin and salvation. Augustine contrasts the city of God based on the love of God with the earthly city of Satan based on the love of self: The citizens of the former will be saved, those of the latter damned. Neither city can be identified with historical regimes, because their respective members can only be distinguished in the last judgment. But the Christian Church is roughly the heavenly city in formation, and Augustine's two cities foreshadow the conflict of church and state in medieval history. *The City of God* is the final great work of ancient political thought, because the classical idea of the city is its starting point, but it may also be viewed as the first work of medieval political philosophy, especially insofar as it subordinates politics to theology.

BIBLIOGRAPHY: Gagarin, M. and P. Woodruff, eds., *Early Greek Political Thought from Homer to the Sophists*, Cambridge, 1995; Keyt, D. and F. D. Miller, Jr., *A Companion to Aristotle's Politics*, Oxford, 1991; Klosko, G., *The Development of Plato's Political Theory*, London/New York, 1986; Kraut, R., *Socrates and the State*, Princeton, 1984; Miller, F. D., Jr., *Nature, Justice, and Rights in Aristotle's Politics*, Oxford, 1995; Schofield, M., *The Stoic Idea of the City*, Cambridge, 1991; also Schofield and C. J. Rowe, *The Cambridge History of Ancient Political Thought*, Cambridge, 1996; Sinclair, T. A., *A History of Greek Political Thought*,[2] London, 1967.—FRED D. MILLER, JR.

POLYAENUS (c. 340s or 330s–278/277 B.C.E), of Lampsacus in Asia Minor. *Epicurean philosopher and a cofounder of the school. Originally an eminent *mathematician, Polyaenus joined the Epicurean circle at Lampsacus when *Epicurus somehow convinced him that "all geometry is false" (Cic. *Acad.* 2.106). This was in the period 310–307, before Epicurus' move from Lampsacus to Athens. Polyaenus seems subsequently to have divided his own time between the Lampsacus and Athens branches of the school. At Athens he was said to have established friendly relations with other schools, including the *Stoa. He featured prominently in later Epicurean biography, and was particularly noted for his human warmth.

The works attributed to Polyaenus include *On Definitions, On Philosophy, Against Aristo, Puzzles, On the Moon, Against the Orators,* and his collected correspondence. He also wrote on *theology, although it is not known in what work. *Puzzles (Aporiai)* seems to have been an anti-mathematical work, based at least in part on the incompatibility of traditional geometry with the Epicurean thesis of minimal magnitudes. *Against the Orators* (or perhaps *On Oratory*) apparently maintained that all *rhetoric is an expertise (*technê*). This view was sufficiently different from Epicurus' own to lead some later Epicureans to question the work's authenticity. For Polyaenus was, along with his cofounders Epicurus, *Metrodorus and *Hermarchus, considered authoritative on matters of doctrine.

BIBLIOGRAPHY: Texts, with Italian tr. and comm., in A. Tepedino Guerra, *Polieno, frammenti*, Naples, 1991; Sedley, D., *CronErc* 6, 1976, 26–54.—*DAVID N. SEDLEY*

POLYSTRATUS. *Epicurean philosopher and head of the Epicurean school in Athens after the death of *Hermarchus (who became head in 270 B.C.E.). Polystratus might have studied with *Epicurus. He is known from two tracts prerserved in the library at Herculaneum: *On Philosophy* (PHerc. 1520) and a better-preserved piece to an addressee unknown *On Irrational Contempt* (PHerc. 336/1150). The contempt in question is that of other philosophical schools for popular opinion. Polystratus makes clear reference to *Stoics and *Cynics (21.8–11). Some of his knowledge of the *logic whose hairsplitting he rejects seems to come from lectures given in the rival schools in Athens, perhaps the *Academy under *Arcesilaus (who became head in 268). The positive feature of this tract is its vindication of Epicurean *physiologia* as a means of freeing the *mind from superstitious fear and anxiety. His treatment of relativism is particularly interesting, since he defends a stable concept of noble and disgraceful action against his opponents (23–33). The treatise resembles the near contemporary Epicurean polemic of *Colotes' *Conformity to the Views of Other Philosophers Actually Makes It Impossible to Live.*

BIBLIOGRAPHY: Erler, M., in H. Flashar, ed., *Grundriss der Geschichte der Philosophie: Die Philosophie der Antike*, vol. 4, Basel, 1994, 247–250; Indelli, G., *Polistrato, Su disprezzo irrationale delle opinioni populari (La Scuola di Epicuro* 2), Naples, 1978.— *DISKIN CLAY*

PORPHYRY (234–c. 305 C.E.), of Tyre (Phoenicia). *Neoplatonist philosopher. Porphyry was educated by the *Platonist Longinus at Athens before joining in 263 *Plotinus' circle at Rome, where he became an active and prominent member, stimulating Plotinus' classes and writing and making his own written contributions. On Plotinus' advice he left Rome for Sicily in 268 for reasons of health and was absent on Plotinus' death in 270. His subsequent movements are largely unknown; he visited Tyre and may have returned to Rome. However, Plotinus' school, which had no official status, seems to have disbanded with the sickness and death of the master. Late in life Porphyry married Marcella, the widow of a friend, and c. 300 published his biography and edition (the *Enneads*) of Plotinus.

Porphyry's interests and erudition were exceptionally wide, ranging over history, literature, and comparative religion as well as philosophy, and his works were correspondingly varied and extensive. Of this, little survives, and mostly of a popularizing character: *On Abstinence* (arguments for vegetarianism), *To Marcella* (moral advice), *Life of Pythagoras* (part of a history of philosophy), *On the Cave of the Nymphs* (*allegorical exegesis of *Homer). More technical are the *Isagôgê* (a very influential introduction to *Aristotle's *Categories*), an incomplete commentary on *Ptolemy, the *Sentences* (a manuel of Plotinian *metaphysics), and of course the invaluable life and edition of Plotinus. Of the bulk of Porphyry's work, and in particular of his more advanced philosophical contributions, only some tantalizing fragments remain, from his two *commentaries on Aristotle's *Categories* and his commentaries on other parts of Aristotle's *logic and *Physics*, on *Plato's *Timaeus, Sophist, Republic, Parmenides*, and other Platonic *dialogues, from a long series of discussions of questions in metaphysics, physics, *psychology, and *ethics, from commentaries on Homer, from works concerning religious rites and doctrines (notably the *Philosophy from Oracles*, the *Letter to Anebo* and *Against the Christians*), and from other works on the relation between Plato and Aristotle and on a variety of philological, literary, and historical matters.

Made even less representative by Porphyry's erudite approach, this extremely fragmentary evidence makes difficult the reconstruction of Porphyry's own philosophical views. Only recently has a fairly complete edition of the fragments, the basis of future critical work, been published. Earlier attempts to attribute to Porphyry an intellectual evolution consisting of pre-Plotinian, Plotinian and post-Plotinian stages seem now ill-founded and premature. From being considered previously as a Plotinian rationalist who capitulated to *religions' claims to provide mankind with the way to salvation, Porphyry has more recently been championed, through P. Hadot's (contested) attribution of the palimpsest fragments of an anonymous commentary on the *Parmenides* to Porphyry, as a subtle metaphysician, source of *Christian Trinitarian speculation in Marius Victorinus and of key metaphysical distinctions transmitted by *Boethius to the Medieval West. At any rate, it seems that Porphyry took a strong interest in the claims of religion to offer to mankind in general what Platonism offered to an elite, a return of the *soul to the Good, an interest that was far from critical—witness *Iamblichus' strong reaction in *On Mysteries* to the penetrating questions put in the *Letter to Anebo* and the equally strong Christian reaction to *Against the Christians*. Porphyry also reflected systematically on the relation between Plato and Aristotle and institutionalized the study of Aristotle's logic and physics in the Neoplatonic schools, his commentaries on Aristotle and Plato providing the basis for the philosophical work of these schools. His erudite and differentiated exegesis of these texts and of Homer was also of decisive importance.

If, on joining Plotinus' group, Porphyry did not share some of Plotinus' views, he came to accept them and indeed incited elaboration of them. In publishing Plotinus some thirty years later, he can hardly have dissented much from the essentials of what he presents as the ideal of wisdom and the method for attaining the Good. The *Sentences* suggest that he sought to bring greater analytical depth and terminological precision to Plotinus' views on the relations between intelligible reality and the sensible world, between soul and body, which seems to be the case also for the relation between Intellect (*Nous*) and the One. This tendency also points the way to later Neoplatonism. It is clear then that Porphyry's historical impact was great, concerning not only the Neoplatonic schools of the Greek-speaking East but also Latin authors such as *Augustine and Boethius and Islamic philosophers to whom translations of Porphyrian texts were available.

BIBLIOGRAPHY: Texts in A. Smith, *Porphyrius Fragmenta*, Leipzig, 1993; *On Abstinence*, ed. and French tr. by J. Bouffartigue and M. Patillon, Paris, 1977–95; *Life of Pythagoras* and *Letter to Marcella*, ed. and French tr. by E. des Places, Paris, 1982; German tr. of *Letter to Marcella* by W. Pötscher, Leiden, 1969; *Letter to Anebo*, ed. and Italian tr. by A. Sodano, Naples, 1964; *On the Cave of the Nymphs*, ed. and English tr., Buffalo, 1969; *Isagôgê*, ed. A. Busse, *CAG* 4, 1, Berlin, 1895; *Porphyry Isagôgê*, English tr. by E. Warren, Toronto, 1975; comm. on Plato's *Timaeus*, ed. A. Sodano, Naples, 1964; anonymous comm. on the *Parmenides*, ed. and French tr. by P. Hadot, *Porphyre et Victorinus*, Paris, 1968; *Porphyry on Aristotle's Categories*, English tr. by S. Strange, London, 1992; *Sententiae*, ed. E. Lamberz, Leipzig, 1975; *Life of Plotinus* printed with complete editions of Plotinus and ed. with French tr. and comm. by L. Brisson et al., Paris, 1982-92; H. Dörrie, *Porphyrios' Symmikta zetemata* (miscellaneous questions on soul and body), Munich, 1959. Beutler, R., "Porphyrios," *RE* 22, 275–313; Bidez, J., *Vie de Porphyre*, Ghent, 1913; Courcelle, P., *Les Lettres grecques en Occident de Macrobe à Cassiodore*, Paris, 1948; Evangeliou, C., *Aristotle's Categories and Porphyry*, Leiden, 1988; Gersh, S., *Middle Platonism and Neoplatonism: The Latin Tradition*, Notre Dame, 1986; Girgenti, G., *Porfirio negli ultimi cinquant'anni. Bibliografia sistematica*, Milan, 1994; Lloyd, A., *The Anatomy of Neoplatonism*, Oxford, 1990; Romano, F., *Porfirio di Tiro*, Catania, 1979; also *Porfirio e la fisica aristotelica*, Catania, 1985; Smith, A., *Porphyry's Place in the Neoplatonic Tradition*, The Hague, 1974; also *ANRW* 2, 36.2, 1987, 719–73; Strange, S., *ANRW* 2, 36.2, 1987, 955–74.—DOMINIC J. O'MEARA

POSIDONIUS (c. 135–c. 51 B.C.E.), of Apamea. *Stoic philosopher, scientist, and historian. After studying in Athens under *Panaetius, Posidonius established a school of his own in Rhodes. Taking up Rhodian citizenship, he went on to hold political office and serve as ambassador to Rome in 87/6 B.C.E. With the decline of the Stoic school in Athens in the early first century B.C.E., Posidonius's school became the leading center of Stoic scholarship and instruction. Among its notable students and visitors were the founder of the Pneumatic school of *medicine, *Athenaeus of Attalia, and the Roman statesmen *Cicero and Pompey. Upon Posidonius's death his school was continued by his grandson, Jason of Nysa.

The nature and significance of Posidonius's philosophy has been subject to widely divergent interpretations. The fragmentary nature of the sources and the absence of any general characterization of his thought once led scholars to seek Posidonius behind a variety of later texts. This procedure resulted in radically different portraits, none of which gained general acceptance. In recent years more circumspect attempts to base reconstructions primarily on explicitly attributed reports has narrowed the range of proposed interpretations, but consensus remains elusive. Edelstein and Kidd's edition of fragments, rigidly limited to named reports, now defines the basis for reconstructing Posidonius's thought, while Theiler's more inclusive edition supplies additional source material for more speculative expansion and refinement. The picture that is emerging is that of an immensely learned and industrious Stoic, who made very few (albeit some important) innovations in Stoic doctrine and whose principal significance was to push the Stoic analysis of the causal mechanisms of nature to its limit, subjecting all the current sciences as well as human history to a Stoic analysis.

Posidonius's philosophical innovation is reflected in his conception of the structure of *knowledge. Whereas earlier Stoics had seen logic primarily as a means of defending Stoicism against *skeptical attacks, Posidonius, living at a time when skepticism was losing its grip on the Stoa's adversaries in the *Academy, viewed *logic as an integral part of philosophy. Logic for Posidonius was the rational mechanism whereby conclusions are derived from principles or axioms, therein constituting an aspect of both physics and *ethics. Posidonius compared philosophy to a living organism, likening logic to the skeletal structure by which the flesh and blood of physics is supported, while ethics, like the *soul, animates the whole.

Committed to philosophy as a deductive system of scientific knowledge, Posidonius defended the axiomatic method of *Euclid and traditional Greek geometry. He also collected enormous amounts of empirical scientific data to supply the phenomenal facts to be explained by philosophy and demonstrated from Stoic principles. The essence of his methodology was causal explanation (aitiology), which he sought in a combination of factors, including material substance, active force, various processes of change, and questions of value (why it is best to be so). The *Aristotelian parallels did not escape the notice of ancient readers, one of whom, *Strabo, found Posidonius's Aristotelian-style search for causes unique among Stoics.

In a series of treatises on physics Posidonius defended the traditional Stoic theory, beginning with the two principles that underlie all of nature, namely, the active cause (also identified as *logos* or god) and the passive *matter. From this starting point Posidonius explained the properties and transformations of matter, the origin and transformations of the four elements, the nature, properties and function of the *pneuma* (the warm air or "breath" that pervades everything and serves as the principal vehicle of the active power), the development, destruction, and recreation of the cosmic order, and the birth, growth, and functioning of biological organisms (see ZENO of Citium, CLEANTHES). Then, in a set of so-called meteorological treatises and in a lengthy geographical work *On the Ocean*, he applied this theory to an unprecedented range of geological, meteorological, biological, ethnographic, and geographic phenomena and facts.

Posidonius's approach to ethics and social philosophy was similarly governed by a predilection for causal explanation, which he based on two principles, the rational and the irrational factors of the soul. Following his mentor Panaetius, he rejected the original monistic *psychology of the Stoa, which regarded affections as judgments of the reason, in favor of psychological dualism, in which the irrational was assigned the status of an independent source of movement. More specifically, he adopted a Platonic tripartition of the soul into three "powers," each with its own natural object: the rational power with an affinity for wisdom and morality and two irrational powers, the competitive with an affinity for power and victory and the appetitive with an affinity for pleasure. Human action, on Posidonius's view, resulted from an internal competition between the rational power and one of the irrational powers. Victory for the rational power led to rational choice and moral action; victory for one of the irrational powers resulted in an affection and vice.

The causal analysis of actions and affections was for Posidonius the basis of his entire ethical philosophy. In his conception of moral value he followed the traditional Stoic line: Moral virtue is the only good; health, wealth, and other natural states are advantages or preferred, but morally indifferent (see ZENO of Citium). His idiosyncratic exposition of this belief in terms of a causal explanation of moral choice misled some ancient reporters into suspecting an un-Stoic elevation of health and wealth to the rank of moral goods, though today his innovation is thought to lie more in presentation than in doctrine. His suggestions for practical implementation, on the other hand, were more novel. Since he regarded affections as movements of irrational powers, he insisted that they could be controlled only by nonrational means, like music, rhythm, and habitual practice. Education for virtue required blunting the affections by discipline in addition to enhancing cognitive knowledge. Posidonius also reformulated the Stoic goal of life in terms of his novel psychology: "To live contemplating the truth and order of the universe and promoting it as much as possible, being led in no way by the irrational part of the soul."

Posidonius's innovative formulation of ethical philosophy in psychological terms was a consequence of his conception of philosophy as causal explanation. It, in turn, served as the basis for extending his aitiological project to the realm of individual human behavior and the contingent events of human history. Posidonius carried out this component of his project in his longest and probably last work, a massive history of the Mediterranean world in fifty-two books, spanning the years 145–c. 86 B.C.E.

By explaining historical events on the basis of human psychology he was able to integrate human history into his philosophy as the ultimate effect of the active cause, that is, God. Permeating the universe in the form of innate *pneuma*, God, as the divine reason of the cosmos, governs all processes and events rationally and providentially, thereby giving warrant to the science of divination as well as the science of history. The human mind, being a fragment of the divine mind, is capable of understanding the divine cosmic order and of promoting it. In all probability, Posidonius devoted most of his energies in the second half of his life to writing history precisely because he regarded an understanding of the divinely ordered causal process in history as a necessary condition for promoting the divine order, so fulfilling the goal of life.

BIBLIOGRAPHY: Texts with discussion in L. Edelstein and I. G. Kidd, eds., *Posidonius*, 2 vols., Cambridge, 1972–1988; Theiler, W., *Poseidonios: die Fragmente*, 2 vols., Berlin, 1982.—*DAVID E. HAHM*

PRISCIAN (5th to 6th cent. C.E.), of Lydia. One of the last Athenian *Neoplatonists, who went to Persia after 529 but returned shortly after. Two works survive: (i) (part of) his *Metaphrase* of *Theophrastus' *On the Soul*, itself a *"commentary" on *Aristotle's *On the Soul*, and (ii) a set of *Answers* to questions raised by King Chosroes of Persia, which survive only in Latin and are largely based on other writers. His work on Theophrastus probably also included a study of the earlier books of Theophrastus' *Physics*, of which the work on the *soul formed the central books, but none of that remains. It has been argued that he is the author

of the *Commentary* on Aristotle's *On the Soul* generally attributed to
*Simplicius, and there are many similarities. There seem, however, to be
arguments in the *Metaphrase* against views expounded by "Simplicius,"
and it is equally likely that both writers drew on *Iamblichus. Priscian is
also said to have written commentaries on *Plato.

In the *Metaphrase* Priscian quotes passages from Theophrastus that
raise questions about the interpretation of Aristotle and amplifies them
on Neoplatonist lines, drawing widely on *Iamblichus (c. 240–325), but
also using *Plutarch of Athens (d. 431/2). His is a moderate form of Neoplatonism, without the excesses of the multiplication of levels found
elsewhere. He recognises a separate intellect and an intellect in the individual and develops *psychological theories of sensation at length, much
of them on a straightforward scientific level. The end of his discussion of
imagination is lost, and he probably wrote more on intellect than survives, possibly following Theophrastus through the later chapters of
Aristotle's *On the Soul*. Several of his quotations overlap with quotations
from Theophrastus by *Themistius, and the differences are so small that
we can be sure that both authors were quoting reliably.

Since many sections of the *Answers to Chosroes* are derived from others, we cannot tell how much of what is unidentified is Priscian's own
work. The questions range from the explanation of tides to whether the
soul is immortal, and he claims to have shown that the human soul is an
incorporeal and simple substance.

BIBLIOGRAPHY: Text in I. Bywater, ed., *CAG Suppl. Arist.* I, 2, 1886. Tr. with notes
by P. M. Huby of the *Metaphrase* (volume also to contain parts of Simplicius' [?]
comm. on Aristotle's *On the Soul*), London, 1997. Steel, C., *The Divided Self*, Brussels, 1978.—*PAMELA M. HUBY*

PROCLUS (412–485 C.E.), of Constantinople. *Neoplatonist philosopher.
Proclus was trained in *rhetoric, law, and philosophy in Alexandria and
joined in 430/1 the Neoplatonic school at Athens, studying philosophy
under *Plutarch of Athens and *Syrianus, whom he succeeded as head of
the school (c. 437). Although pagan, Proclus was a respected personality
in Athens—he was obliged, however, to exile himself for a year in Lydia—and a very industrious and influential teacher.

Proclus gives systematic expression to the thought of his immediate
predecessors (his originality is difficult to determine, given the little evidence concerning the latter) in a vast body of work of which some has, in
part or in whole, survived: commentaries or essays on *Homer, *Euclid,
*Ptolemy, *Plato's *Alcibiades, Cratylus, Republic, Timaeus,* and *Parmenides,*
an important *Platonic Theology,* the *Elements of Theology, Hymns, Elements
of Physics,* treatises on providence, fate, and evil, and some excerpts and

fragments from other lost works which included *commentaries on *Aristotle, on *Plotinus and on the *Chaldaean Oracles. For Proclus, Plato was a privileged source of truths revealed also by the gods to man through oracles (notably the Chaldaean Oracles), prophets, and sages (such as Orpheus and *Pythagoras) both Greek and Barbarian. These truths teach self-knowledge, enabling a return of the *soul to its transcendent source, the Good. Theurgy prepares this return, as do such *sciences as physics and *mathematics which lead to the science of the divine (*metaphysics or *"theology") communicated in Plato's Parmenides and which itself prepares the *soul to transcend the level of discursive *knowledge. The Elements of Theology elaborates the science of the divine according the standards of strict discursive, quasi-geometrical proof, formulating a chain of propositions (each supported by demonstrative syllogisms) concerning both general principles of *being and causality (e.g., that causes are more perfect than their effects; that the more perfect a cause, the greater its power) and the particular levels of immaterial being going from the ineffable "One" or Good, source of all reality, through the "henads," entities deriving from the One and causes of the subsequent levels of intelligible and intellectual being, down to soul, all entities being arranged in mathematically inspired series in which the role of mediating terms is fundamental. A bridge to this "theology" is provided by mathematics, which Proclus interprets as dealing with concepts innate in the soul deriving from intelligible reality, which soul projects discursively in the imagination. Below mathematics is physics which Proclus, reading Plato's Timaeus, considers scientific only to the extent that the paradigms of the material world and the concepts used by the mind in judging it relate to intelligible reality. If Proclus in effect formalizes the principles of Plotinus' theory of the hierarchical derivation of all things from a unique source, he argues against Plotinus that matter is not absolute evil, but mere potentiality; evil is some privation of the good in some respect—only as such does it exist.

Proclus' work became standard in the Neoplatonist schools of Athens and Alexandria; among his pupils were his successor Marinus, *Ammonius (head of the school at Alexandria), and Isidore, Marinus' successor. Not long after, the *Christian theologian *Pseudo-Dionysius appropriated Proclus' ideas massively, but Proclus was also criticized by the Christian Alexandrian philosopher John *Philoponus. Later, however, such Christians as the Byzantine philosopher Michael Psellus and, in the Latin West, Nicholas of Cusa and Marsilio Ficino made wide use of Proclus. The Elements of Theology, in the Latin version known as the Liber de Causis, derived from an Arabic partial adaptation, was an influential source for medieval scholastic metaphysics.

See also METAPHYSICAL THOUGHT, Classical.

BIBLIOGRAPHY: Texts of the comm. on Euclid and on Plato's *Cratylus, Republic,* and *Timaeus* are published by Teubner, Leipzig, 1873 onwards; on the *Alcibiades* by L. Westerink, Amsterdam, 1954; on the *Parmenides* by V. Cousin, *Procli opera inedita,* Paris, 1864, by R. Klibansky and C. Labowsky, London, 1953, and by C. Steel (Moerbeke's Latin tr.), Louvain, 1982–85. English tr. of the comm. on Euclid by G. Morrow, Princeton,[2] 1992; on the *Alcibiades* by W. O'Neill, The Hague, 1965; on the *Parmenides* by J. Dillon and G. Morrow, Princeton, 1987. French tr. of the comm. on the *Alcibiades* by A. Segonds, Paris, 1985–86; on the *Republic* by A. Festugière, Paris, 1970; on the *Timaeus,* by A. Festugière, Paris, 1966–8. Text and French tr. of *Platonic Theology* by H. Saffrey and L. Westerink, Paris, 1968 onward; text and English tr. of *Elements of Theology,*[2] by E. Dodds, Oxford, 1963. Beierwaltes, W., *Proklos: Grundzüge seiner Metaphysik,*[2] Frankfurt, 1979; Bos, E., and P. Meijer, eds., *On Proclus and His Influence in Medieval Philosophy,* Leiden, 1992; Boss, G., and G. Seel, eds., *Proclus et son influence,* Zurich, 1987; Gersh, S., *From Iamblichus to Eriugena,* Leiden, 1978; Lloyd, A., *The Anatomy of Neoplatonism,* Oxford, 1990; Pépin, J. and H. Saffrey, eds., *Proclus lecteur et interprète des anciens,* Paris, 1987; Saffrey, H., *Recherches sur le néoplatonisme après Plotin,* Paris, 1990; Trouillard, J., *L'Un et l'âme selon Proclus,* Paris, 1972.—DOMINIC J. O'MEARA

PRODICUS (before 460–after 399 B.C.E.), of Ceos, an island near Athens. A *sophist of the fifth century. Prodicus was famous for his lectures on careful distinctions among words, which he delivered in a deep, booming voice. The *Platonic *Socrates frequently refers to Prodicus as his teacher of this subject, but his tributes to Prodicus are not without irony. Of his life we know only that he was younger than *Protagoras and still living at the time of Socrates' trial. He must have been a familiar visitor in Athens and is pictured by Plato (who likens him here to Tantalus) lecturing from his bed in the house of Callias to an attentive audience (*Prt.* 315d–e). His regular lecture on the meanings of words cost each hearer a drachma (a day's wages for a skilled man), and there are jocular references to a fifty-drachma version as well. One late source alleges that he was executed in Athens for corrupting the youth, but no modern scholars accept this story.

Prodicus was known in antiquity for his humanistic account of the origin of *religion (DK84B5) and was reputed also to have studied *astronomy, speculated about *cosmology, and investigated *medicine (B4). He is said to have written a book entitled *On Nature.* A paraphrase of his speech on the choice of Heracles survives in *Xenophon as evidence for his teaching on *ethics (B2, from a book called *Seasons*). There he presents a one-sided verbal contest between Virtue and Vice; Vice has only a catalogue of pleasures to offer, but Virtue runs through the contents of proper education or training, emphasizing the importance of service to friends, city, and the whole of Greece.

A parody of his work on language occurs in Plato's *Protagoras* 337a–c, where in the space of a few lines he distinguishes impartiality from egalitarianism, debates from quarrels, esteem from praise, and enjoyment from pleasure. This is the best evidence we have for his speaking style, pedantic as it is. He held that the proper length of a speech was "measured" and considered the writers of speeches to be on the borderline between philosophers and politicians.

Evidence for his views on the gods is scanty. His name appears on ancient lists of *atheists, and the surviving fragments suggest that he explained the origin of worship as a response to benefits received: "The sun and the moon and rivers and springs and everything else that benefits our lives were called gods by early people" (B5).

BIBLIOGRAPHY: Texts in DK84. Tr. in R. K. Sprague, *The Older Sophists*, Columbia, SC, 1972, and M. Gagarin and P. Woodruff, eds., *Early Greek Political Thought from Homer to the Sophists*, Cambridge, 1995. Guthrie, W. K. C., *The Sophists*, Cambridge, 1971; Kerferd, G. B., *The Sophistic Movement*, Cambridge, 1981; Stewart, D. J., in R. K. Sprague, *The Older Sophists*, 70–85; Untersteiner, M., *I Sofisti*, Florence, 1954.—*PAUL WOODRUFF*

PROTAGORAS (c. 485–c. 415 B.C.E.), of Abdera, on the coast of Thrace in northern Greece. First thinker to call himself a *sophist. Details of Protagoras' life are obscure; even the dates of his birth and death cannot be fixed. He had achieved eminence before the founding of Thurii in 443, for which he helped to draft the laws. He was probably a generation older than *Democritus of Abdera and therefore cannot have been the latter's pupil, as one ancient tradition alleges. We are certain that Protagoras traveled widely among Greek cities and was well paid for his teaching. In Athens he associated with Pericles and was much admired by students who followed him from city to city (Pl. *Prt.* 315a–b). Some sources tell us that Protagoras was tried in Athens and condemned for impiety, but scholars usually reject this on the basis of *Plato's testimony that Protagoras was honored to the end of his nearly seventy years (*Meno* 91e, cf. *Rep.* 600c). He was evidently an original thinker, known in antiquity for his claim that "a human being is the measure of all things," for his agnosticism about the gods, and for his method of teaching opposed speeches.

Protagoras' contemporary reputation and influence were mainly derived from his oral teaching, but he is known also to have written books, of which only a few isolated sentences survive. Plato mentions a book entitled *Truth*, to which *Sextus refers as the *Downthrowers*. The "Great Speech" known in antiquity may have been the same work and should not be confused with the long speech Protagoras makes in Plato's dialogue, *Protagoras*, often incorrectly dubbed "the Great Speech." Although the speech in Plato belongs to historical fiction, some modern scholars believe that it represents fairly accurately the thought and style of Protagoras. There was also a book known as *The Opposed Speeches* (*Antilogiai,* or *Contradictions*). Of his book about the gods we have only its first sentence. His influence on writers of his day was probably considerable, and echoes of his teaching may be speculatively identified in the work of *Sophocles, *Euripides, and *Thucydides. He is probably one of the targets of *Aristophanes' satire in the *Clouds*.

We cannot obtain a definite interpretation of Protagoras' teaching from the few fragments of text that have survived. Any account of Protagoras as a philosopher, therefore, is bound to depend on Plato's historical fiction in the *Protagoras* or his philosophical reconstruction in the *Theaetetus*, or both. Later testimony, in particular that of Sextus, may put Protagoras in a different light, but we cannot be sure that Plato was not the ultimate source for this tradition. Two pictures of Protagoras emerge: One, from the *Theaetetus* and *Cratylus*, shows a relativist so radical that he cannot consistently maintain any positive teaching, even his relativism; the other, from most other evidence, shows a positive teacher willing to criticize poets in the face of convention. Scholars have reached no consensus as to whether the two pictures can be reconciled, or which picture is to be preferred if they cannot.

Language and Oratory. In his teaching Protagoras aimed at a general education leading to good judgment (*euboulia*) and made no attempt to draw his students into a particular craft or profession. His interests touched on *epistemology and *metaphysics, but he was best known in his own day for his teaching about the use of language. There is no evidence that he conceived of his subject narrowly as the mere art of persuasion, and *rhetoric thus conceived is most likely an invention of Plato's. Correctness of diction, rather than persuasion, appears to have been the central theme of his work on language; it certainly had a uniquely Protagorean name, *orthoepeia* (*Phdr.* 267c6; cf. *Cra.* 391c3). Protagoras taught this subject by criticizing the diction of poets such as *Homer and Simonides. His concerns in this area led him to criticize conventional usage and to develop basic distinctions among kinds of speech act (Ar. *Soph. El.* 173b17 and *Poet.* 1456b15; cf. Pl. *Prt.* 338e–339a).

As a teacher of oratory, Protagoras taught the art of "opposed speeches," the title of one of his works. He is supposed to have claimed that there were opposed speeches (or arguments) on any subject (D.L. 9.51). This perhaps gave rise to the charges that his method "brought everything into dispute" (Pl. *Soph.* 232d) and "made the weaker case stronger" (Ar. *Rh.* 1402a23). Certainly his career was followed by a fashion for presenting opposed speeches in plays (such as those of Euripides) and in history (such as that of Thucydides), while the art of defending what seemed to be lost causes became central to the teaching of rhetoric. *Aristotle implies that Protagorean oratory depended on an abuse of the concept of *eikos* (reasonable expectation or probability), but we have no other evidence that Protagoras' speeches appealed to *eikos*. Later orators such as *Antiphon, however, made heavy use of the concept.

As for *logic, Protagoras is said to have invented the *Socratic style of argument and also to have denied the possibility of contradiction. This does not sit well with the tradition that he taught the art of giving opposed (i.e., contradictory) speeches or the indication that he corrected poets who appeared to contradict themselves. Many scholars believe that the difficulties may be resolved, however, by appeal to Protagoras' doctrine that a human being is the measure of all things, which implies a rejection of the law of noncontradiction (Ar. *Met.* 1007b18–25, 1062b12–a13) as well as a denial of the possibility of believing what is false.

Knowledge and Reality. About the gods, Protagoras professed that he could not know whether they exist, owing to the obscurity of the subject and the brevity of human life (DK80B4). Generally he seems to have been agnostic about what is not available to perception (Ar. *Met.* 997b35–8a4). His view that a human being is the measure of all things (B1) is presented in Plato as equivalent to the claim that perception is knowledge and also to a form of relativism: "Each thing is to me such as it appears to me, and is to you such as it appears to you" (*Tht.* 152a). Plato has Socrates continue with an elaborate reconstruction or Protagoras' theory in terms of a *Heraclitean ontology (by which all things are ceaselessly changing) and a theory of perception as interactive (sometimes known as Plato's theory of perception). Among the corollaries of the measure doctrine, as Socrates interprets it, are the relativity of moral judgments and the impossibility of authoritative teaching on justice. Socrates goes on to show that if each of us is an authority on what is true for us, we can have no reason to listen to Protagoras when he tells us so; and if he defends his view against criticism he thereby joins his critics, since his view implies that no opinion can be defended against any other (*Tht.* 171). The tables are so easily turned only on the extreme relativism attributed here to Protagoras. A less radical Protagoreanism shows up elsewhere in Plato (*Prt.* 334a–c); and one of the positions ascribed to him by Sextus Empiricus may also be immune to table-turning arguments (*P* 1.216–219).

*Ethics and *Political Theory.* The *Theaetetus* presents Protagoras as a relativist on moral questions, holding that "whatever a city judges to be just and fine, those things are just and fine for it so long as it holds that opinion." Wisdom consists not in correcting false views (since there are none), but in replacing views that are harmful (167c). The long speech of the *Protagoras* gives a different impression. Here Protagoras defends both the possibility of moral education and the democratic practices of Athens against Socrates, who had attacked both: All humans must have in some measure the virtues of justice and a sound mind if they are to survive and live together in cities; accordingly, those virtues have the status in myth of gifts from Zeus. Such virtues are universals, which it is our nature to acquire. Moral education is the responsibility of society and is as common as the teaching of Greek language to Greek children. It follows that all citizens know enough of justice to take part in public affairs. Read as the speech of a relativist, this seems a clever device to win over an audience; read in its own terms, however, the speech appears to be a sincere defense of democracy.

BIBLIOGRAPHY: Texts in DK80. Tr. in R. K. Sprague, *The Older Sophists*, Columbia, SC, 1972, and M. Gagarin and P. Woodruff, eds., *Early Greek Political Thought from Homer to the Sophists*, Cambridge, 1995. Farrar, C., *The Origins of Democratic Thinking*, Cambridge, 1988. Guthrie, W. K. C., *The Sophists*, Cambridge, 1971; Kerferd, G. B., *The Sophistic Movement*, Cambridge, 1981; Schiappa, E., *Protagoras and Logos*, Columbia, SC, 1981.—*PAUL WOODRUFF*

(PSEUDO-) DIONYSIUS the Areopagite (c. 500 C.E.). Still unidentified author of a corpus of *theological writings in Greek (the *Corpus Dionysiacum* = *CD*) consisting of four treatises (*On the Divine Names, The Mystical Theology, The Ecclesiastical Hierarchies*, and *The Celestial* [i.e., angelic] *Hierarchies*) and ten *Letters*, all fraudulently attributed to Dionysius the Areopagite, a convert of the apostle Paul in Athens (*Acts* 17).

The *CD* is the first set of writings in Byzantine *Christian history to appropriate to Christian uses the *metaphysics of Late Athenian *Neoplatonism—specifically that of the pagan *Proclus (d. 485). This is reflected in its teaching, first, of two kinds of *theology*, positive and negative, and, second, about the heavenly and ecclesiastical *hierarchies* (a term coined by Pseudo-Dionysius).

Adapting the Neoplatonic tradition, the *CD* teaches that the Christian God is a Trinity beyond existence and *being (= the Neoplatonic One), which is also the object of the "return" of all things to their cause. God produces all other beings in his "processions," described in an analysis of the divine names: a positive theology matched by a negative one. These contrasting theologies guide the *soul in its ascent to God by first positing, then negating all possible affirmations about God—who dwells in a "divine darkness" even beyond the light of Jesus.

Finally, the *CD* adopts Proclus's construction of a set of divine intermediaries between the One and our world of the senses. The angelic hierarchy (a Christian adaptation of Proclus's teaching about the henads or pagan gods), receives the souls passed up to it by the ecclesiastical hierarchy in its "mysteries" or sacraments (modelled upon the theurgy of the Neoplatonists): It describes divinely ordained acts (unifying symbols both biblical and liturgical) by divinely ordained persons (on the analogy of Jesus's descent to us in the flesh), which initiate the ascent of the soul to God.

This new Christian theology significantly influenced both the Byzantine Greek East and the Latin West. Albert the Great, for example, commented on the entire *CD*.

BIBLIOGRAPHY: Text of *CD* in B. R. Suchla, G. Heil, and A. M. Ritter, eds., *Corpus dionysiacum*, 2 vols. (of 4 planned), in K. Aland and E. Mühlenberg, eds., *Patristische Texte und Studien* 36, Berlin/New York, 1990, 1991–. Tr. by C. Luibheid and P. Rorem, *Pseudo-Dionysius: The Complete Works*, New York, 1987. Roques, R., in *Dictionnaire de spiritualité ascétique et mystique*, Paris, 1932–; Rorem, P., *Pseudo-Dionysius: A Commentary on the Texts and an Introduction to Their Influence*, New York, 1993.—*DAVID B. EVANS*

PSYCHOLOGY. See MIND, Classical Theories of.

PTOLEMY (Claudius Ptolemaeus—c. 100–175 C.E.), perhaps from Alexandria, where he did his *scientific work. *Mathematician, *astronomer, geographer, musical and optical theorist, and *epistemologist. Virtually nothing is known about Ptolemy's life. His principal works are the *Almagest* (the Arabic and conventional name of his *Mathêmatikê Syntaxis*), which is the greatest Greek contribution to astronomy; the *Tetrabiblos*, a handbook of astrology; the *Geography*, which is the most comprehensive ancient study of cartography; the *Harmonics*, a systematic treatment of the mathematics of harmony, extending (in Book 3) to correspondences between musical ratios and the parts and *virtues of the *soul and to the analogous harmony of stellar movements; and the *Optics* (surviving only in a Latin translation from an Arabic translation of the Greek original), a highly sophisticated study, recording experiments, of phenomena such as refraction. Ptolemy is also the author of other works on astronomy and of a short philosophical treatise, *On the Criterion and Commanding-faculty*, which deals with epistemology and the cognitive faculties of the *mind.

Most of Ptolemy's work belongs within fields that we today call science, as distinct from philosophy. Even within his own day, Ptolemy would have been regarded primarily as a mathematician, just as *Galen was primarily a physician. Yet, although neither of these great polymaths was formally aligned with a particular school of ancient philosophy, they both count as philosophers in the most extended sense of the Greek term *philosophia*. Like Galen, Ptolemy may justly be called an *eclectic* philosopher, and both men are of great importance to the history of Greek philosophy in later antiquity, for three principal reasons. First, their work enables us to see how philosophy could be used creatively in specialist scientific inquiry. Second, both Ptolemy and Galen frequently took up positions on issues that had been controversial in earlier philosophical discussion. Third, each of them made contributions to scientific methodology and epistemology that are of great interest in their own right.

The Almagest. The main purpose of the *Almagest* is to provide a "systematic mathematical treatment" of the observed motions of the heavenly bodies. Ptolemy drew heavily on Hellenistic astronomy, especially that of Hipparchus, but he also contributed much of his own, in trigonometry, systematic proof, new observations, and instruments. At the beginning of the work he presents himself as a philosopher in the *Aristotelian tradition of "theoretical knowledge," and his indebtedness to *Aristotle extends far beyond this preface. His basic model of the physical world is Aristotelian through and through: a spherical universe, with the fixed stars at the circumference rotating around a stationary earth at the center. Ptolemy takes over Aristotle's fifth element, the *aether*, as the material of the heavenly bodies, the Aristotelian unmoved mover as the ultimate source of motion, and the linear motions and upward or downward directionality of the four terrestrial elements, earth, air, fire, and water. He also makes extensive use of such Aristotelian concepts as form and *matter, or potentiality and actuality.

The Tetrabiblos. Here Ptolemy applies his findings about the positions of the stars in the zodiac to meteorology, ethnography, and influences on persons' temperaments, as determined by their horoscope. Drawing eclectically on Aristotelian and *Stoic *cosmology, Ptolemy seeks to demythologize astrology by explaining the terrestrial effects of the heavenly bodies in terms of heating, cooling, moistening, and drying. Through the skillful use of *a fortiori* arguments, he suggests that one cannot accept the obvious effects of the sun and moon on the earth and not also grant similar causal efficacy to the movements of the more distant stars and planets. He concedes to critics of astrology that its actual practitioners are often inept, and he also grants that the state of the heavens at birth is only the strongest of a series of necessary environmental influences none of which, taken individually, is a sufficient basis for infallible prognosis. Ptolemy's defense of astrology is more effective than anything similar that survives from classical antiquity. The work had a powerful influence on *Neoplatonism, generating lost commentaries by *Porphyry and by *Proclus.

On the Criterion and Commanding-faculty. This short work is Ptolemy's only surviving contribution to the regular agenda of philosophy in later antiquity. Starting with *Epicurus and *Zeno of Citium, philosophers other than *skeptics had made it their business to specify one or more "criteria of truth." The purpose of such criteria was to block a regress of knowledge by serving as standards for establishing evident fact. By Ptolemy's time many different candidates for such criteria had been nominated. Formal procedures had also been developed for analyzing criteria: by reference to sensory and/or intellectual faculties, and in terms of different aspects, such as "instrument" or "agent" or "mode" of judgment (cf. D.L.1.21; S.E. *M.* 7.110).

Ptolemy's work is a contribution along exactly these lines. He outlines procedures for investigating the criterion and then advances his own findings. Distinguishing between the intellect and the senses, he advances an epistemology that allows criterial force to each of these faculties according to their own functions. The senses make infallible reports about the way they are affected, and the intellect is also intrinsically reliable when making judgments about its own objects—"the same or different, the equal or unequal, the like or unlike etc." Error can arise when there is more than one perception of the same object or "when different faculties combine and join together in making judgements about objects." When the intellect concentrates only on immediate sensory input, it can never achieve more than a fallible opinion. To achieve scientific knowledge, it is necessary "to separate and combine the differences and non-differences between actual things, and to move up from particulars to universals and on to the genera and species of the objects before the intellect."

Ptolemy's epistemology borrows from all the main schools of Greek philosophy. His most obvious model is Aristotle's *De Anima* and *Posterior Analytics*, but *On the Criterion* also combines ideas from *Plato, Epicurus, and Stoicism. Unlike his *Epicurean and Stoic predecessors, he shows no interest in directly refuting skepticism. His principal aim, it seems, was to provide epistemological foundations for the studies pursued by a practising scientist. Like Galen, he expresses indifference to the terminological and conceptual distinctions that had characterized the distinctive epistemologies of the philosophical schools. What chiefly matters to both of them is a broadly based consensus concerning the methodical uses of reason and experience. Their eclecticism with respect to the philosophical tradition was a way of justifying their own science.

In the final part of *On the Criterion* (13–16) Ptolemy turns to the soul, using *hêgemonikon* ("commanding-faculty"), the term popularized by Stoics, as his name for the soul's governing principle. He sides with Plato against Aristotle and the Stoics in locating rationality in the head; yet he agrees with the latter in locating the basic principle of life in the heart. He is chiefly indebted to Plato's *Timaeus* for his view of the organs concerned with emotion and appetite, but his description of sense perception, impulse, and thought is broadly in line with Aristotle and Stoicism. As to the vexed question of the soul's *metaphysical identity, Ptolemy presents a synthesis of these earlier thinkers. He allocates the main composition of the soul, as the Stoics had done, to the elements of fire and air. But he attributes active thought to *aether*, a fascinating concession to Aristotelian cosmology.

The Harmonics. This is the most sophisticated of all Greek works on musical theory. Ptolemy begins by positing hearing and reason as the "criteria of harmony." He devotes much of his attention (in Book 1) to adjudicating between the divergent theories of the *Pythagoreans and the followers of the *Peripatetic *Aristoxenus. Ptolemy criticizes the Pythagoreans for overemphasizing reason (numerical ratios) and the Aristoxeneans for attaching too much importance to auditory experience. His aim is to develop a musical theory in which sense perception and reason reinforce one another and never conflict. This is precisely the recommendation of his work *On the Criterion.*

Of special philosophical interest is the section (Book 3.5–7) where Ptolemy draws up correspondences between parts of the soul and musical intervals. His primary inspiration here is Plato's *Republic,* but Ptolemy's classifications are strongly influenced by Stoic terminology.

Following Plato's tripartite division of the soul, he links the rational part to the octave, the spirited part to the fifth, and the appetitive part to the fourth. Ptolemy also gives musical equivalents to the soul's virtues, enumerating these according to the same list of intervals. Stoic philosophers as well as Plato would have agreed with his remark: "The whole condition of a philosopher is like the whole harmony of the complete system" (*Harmonics,* p. 97 Düring). Porphyry wrote a commentary, which is extant, on Ptolemy's *Harmonics.*

In his acumen, productivity, and influence, Ptolemy ranks with Plato, Aristotle, and Galen. His astronomy and geography were the standard treatments of their subjects throughout the Middle Ages and early Renaissance. There are partially extant commentaries on the *Almagest* by Pappus (c. 320) and by Theon of Alexandria (c. 370). In the Middle Ages the work was chiefly known in the West via a Latin translation from the Arabic made by Gerard of Cremona, completed in 1175. The Greek text of the *Almagest* did not become widely available until the sixteenth century, by which time Ptolemy's astronomy was about to be superseded by the work of Brahe and Kepler.

See also SCIENCE, Greek.

BIBLIOGRAPHY: Text of *Almagest*: in J. L. Heiberg, ed., *Claudii Ptolemaei Opera quae exstant omnia,* vol. 1, *Syntaxis Mathematica,* 2 vols., Leipzig, 1898–1903; tr. with notes and bibl. in G. J. Toomer, *Ptolemy's Almagest,* London, 1984. Text and tr. of *Tetrabiblos* in W. G. Waddell and F. E. Robins, eds., *Manetho. Ptolemy* (Loeb), London/Cambridge, MA, 1940; see also A. Bouché-Leclerck, *L'astrologie grecque,* Paris, 1899; and A. A. Long in J. Barnes et al., ed., *Science and Speculation: Studies in Hellenistic Theory and Practice,* Cambridge/Paris, 1982, 165–92. Text of *Optics* in A. Lejeune, ed., *L'optique de Claude Ptolemée dans la version latine d'après l'arabe de l'émir Eugène de Sicile,* Louvain, 1956. Text of *Harmonics* in I. Düring, ed., *Die Harmonielehre des Klaudios Ptolemaios,* Göteborg, 1930; tr. with notes in A. Barker, *Greek Musical Writings: II Harmonic and Acoustic Theory,* Cambridge, 1989. Text, tr.

and notes of *On the Criterion and Commanding-faculty* in P. Huby and G. Neale, eds., *The Criterion of Truth. Essays written in honour of George Kerferd together with a text and translation (with annotation) of Ptolemy's On the Kriterion and Hegemonikon,* Liverpool, 1989, 179–230. For a discussion of the work and of Ptolemy's background, cf. A. A. Long, in Huby and Kneale, 151–178, repr. in J. Dillon and A. A. Long, eds., *The Question of "Eclecticism": Studies in Later Greek Philosophy,* Berkeley/Los Angeles/ London, 1988, 176–207. Boll, F., *Studien über Claudius Ptolemy,* Leipzig, 1894; Lloyd, G.E.R., *Greek Science after Aristotle,* London, 1973, esp. 113–37; Toomer, G., *Ptolemy,* in *Dictionary of Scientific Biography* 11, 1975, 186–206.—*A. A. LONG*

PYRRHO (c. 360–c. 270 B.C.E), of Elis. Founder of Pyrrhonian *skepticism and **PYRRHONISM**. Pyrrho was a painter by profession. He came under the influence of three sets of philosophers: the *Megarians, the *Democriteans, and the so-called gymnosophists, the naked wise men of India whose acquaintance he made while accompanying Alexander the Great on his eastern campaigns. It has been suggested that Pyrrho's encounter with the last group was the decisive event that turned him towards the distinctive philosophical stance for which he was to become famous. Pyrrho wrote nothing, and we are indebted for what we know of him to his students, Philo of Athens, Numenius, and especially *Timon of Phlius, as well as fragments of the biography by his younger contemporary, Antigonus of Carystus. These last must be used with care, as they largely consist of anecdotes that have often been embroidered.

The predominance of anecdotal material in the tradition is not an accident, however. The great impression Pyrrho made on his contemporaries and on succeeding generations was due at least as much to his manner of life as to his teachings. His conduct displayed to an exceptional degree the then much-admired qualities of imperturbability, tranquillity, and superiority to empty verbal display. Figures like *Epicurus, *Posidonius, and *Galen, who were not in sympathy with his views, were nevertheless much impressed by his character. These qualities of character do not, however, distinguish Pyrrho's thought from that of, for example, the *Cynics and the *Stoics, who valued qualities similar to his. Hence, the first of the main difficulties a study of Pyrrho presents: Is he to be viewed primarily as a moralist or as a skeptical *epistemologist? Or if both, how are these two components of his thought related? The tendency to emphasize the epistemological significance of Pyrrho is not surprising in view of the concerns of later skeptics, whose perspective on Pyrrho has been the point of departure for both ancients and moderns curious about him. But *Cicero knows Pyrrho only as a moralist, whose position he compares with that of *Aristo of Chios, the Cynicizing Stoic who insisted on regarding everything apart from *virtue as entirely without value. Roughly speaking, the solution seems to be this: Pyrrho did subscribe to views that, like those of many of his contemporaries, set the highest value on imperturbability and indifference to what were popularly supposed to be goods and evils within the power of fortune to bestow or withhold. But he also adopted an epistemological attitude renouncing belief that, though not the same as the more sophisticated stances of the *Academy or later Pyrrhonism and without their *dialectical underpinnings, nevertheless deserves to be called skeptical. Pyrrho's distinctive achievements were to maintain that this epistemological attitude gave rise to the imperturbability and tranquillity that alone make human life happy and to illustrate by his own practice how this was accomplished.

The other issue concerning Pyrrho is whether and to what extent he was the founder of the Pyrrhonian school that flourished later in antiquity and included *Aenesidemus and *Sextus Empiricus as members. To be sure, a list of masters and pupils stretching from Pyrrho to Aenesidemus and beyond has come down to us. But Cicero and *Seneca cite Pyrrho as a perspicuous example of a once-prominent figure who was without successors or later influence. And the existence of a continuous succession was denied even within later Pyrrhonism itself. The scholarly consensus is that the Pyrrhonist school was refounded in the first century B.C.E. by Aenesidemus, a onetime Academic who reacted against what he took to be the betrayal of the Academy's skeptical heritage by Academics of his time like *Philo of Larissa. In choosing to name themselves after Pyrrho, later Pyrrhonists seem to have been primarily inspired by the model of a life of tranquillity without dogmatic belief he offered. This is not to say that later Pyrrhonists took nothing else from the tradition about Pyrrho. The ten tropes for the suspension of judgment put together by Aenesidemus and accorded a prominent place in our accounts of Pyrrhonism may owe something to such a tradition. But the Pyrrhonists' rather subtle skeptical attitude, now called suspension of judgment after the Academic model, owes more to the Academy than to Pyrrho. The vigor with which they continued to insist on the power of that attitude to produce tranquillity was their truest debt to Pyrrho.

There is an account of Pyrrhonism in *Diogenes Laertius and a far more extensive treatment in the works of Sextus Empiricus. They contain a mass of argumentative strategies, mastery of which was supposed to enable the Pyrrhonist to produce arguments of equal strength on either side of every issue. In most cases, the Pyrrhonist's dogmatic opponent will already have supplied the arguments on one side so that it is left to him to balance those arguments with an opposed case of equal strength. According to the Pyrrhonists, when confronted with considerations of equal force on either side of a question, one is led to suspend judgment. Upon universal suspension of judgment, they further maintain, follows tranquillity. Pyrrhonists, like the Academics before them, were constantly challenged to explain how any life at all, let alone a wise and happy life, was possible without judgment, that is, in some important sense, without belief. Much recent work has been devoted to the same issue, trying in particular to understand and assess the adequacy of the Pyrrhonists' answer, which depends on a distinction between belief conceived in a certain way, which they renounce, and belief understood in another way, which they allow themselves.

Interest in ancient skepticism revived during the Renaissance and grew dramatically after the works of Sextus Empiricus became widely available in Latin translation in the second half of the sixteenth century. The picture of Pyrrhonism that became widely available in this way exerted an important influence during the formative period of modern philosophy.

See also SKEPTICISM, Ancient.

BIBLIOGRAPHY: Texts in F. Decleva Caizzi, ed., *Pirrone Tesimonianze*, Naples, 1981. Bett, R., *OSAP* 12, 1994, 137–181; also *Phronesis* 39, 1994, 303–337; Burnyeat, M. F., in M. Schofield, M. Burnyeat, and J. Barnes, eds., *Doubt and Dogmatism: Studies in Hellenistic Philosophy*, Oxford, 1980, 20–53, repr. in M. Burnyeat, ed., *The Skeptical Tradition*, Berkeley, 1983, 117–48; Frede, M., in Frede, *Essays in Ancient Philosophy*, Minneapolis, 1987, 179–200; Stough, C. L., *Greek Skepticism*, Berkeley, 1969, 16ff.; von Fritz, K., "Pyrrhon," *RE* 2, 24, 1963, cols. 89–106.—*JAMES ALLEN*

PYTHAGORAS (c. 570–490 B.C.E.), of Samos. Early Greek philosopher, founder of **PYTHAGOREANISM**. Pythagoras emigrated to Croton in southern Italy c. 530 B.C.E. He established a way of life that attracted many followers who were influential in the politics of cities in southern Italy. Around 510 a conspiracy led by Cylon attacked the Pythagoreans in Croton, and Pythagoras himself took refuge in Metapontum, where he died c. 490 B.C.E. The Pythagoreans were attacked again c. 450 B.C.E. and most fled Italy. *Philolaus of Croton (470–390 B.C.E.) was the first Pythagorean to enter the main stream of Presocratic speculation on nature, and this tradition was continued by *Archytas of Tarentum (fl. 400–360) who was the first great Pythagorean *mathematician. The last followers of the Pythagorean way of life lived from 400 to 350 B.C.E., but Pythagoras himself became ever more influential as the legendary philosopher *par excellence* in the *Neopythagorean tradition.

Pseudepigrapha and Neopythagoreanism. The central problem in reconstructing Pythagoras' philosophy is that he wrote nothing. The problem is complicated yet further by a tradition, starting with *Speusippus and *Xenocrates in the early *Academy and flowering by the second century C.E. as Neopythagoreanism, that presents Pythagoras as a philosopher sage to whom the divine truth about reality was entrusted. Accordingly all true philosophy is seen as derived from Pythagoras. Thus the mature work of *Plato (the fundamental distinction between the realms of Forms and of phenomenal *change, the mathematical model of the universe in the *Timaeus*, the doctrine of the one and the indefinite dyad) comes to be treated as Pythagoras' own. Important summaries of this philosophy of "Pythagoras" appear in Alexander Polyhistor (c. 80 B.C.E.; see D.L. 8.24–33) and *Sextus Empiricus (*P* 2.248–84). He is also regarded as the master mathematician and *scientist who set in order the *quadrivium*. Some spurious documents such as the *Golden Verses* become assigned to him. A large body of pseudepigrapha forged in the names of early Pythagoreans and designed to show that they had anticipated the central ideas of Plato and *Aristotle had developed by the first century B.C.E. Many fragments and some complete treatises survive, most notably the treatise by Timaeus of Locrus that is supposed to be the original of Plato's *Timaeus* and Ocellus' *On the Nature of the Universe*.

*Cicero reports that Nigidius Figulus revived Pythagoreanism in the first century B.C.E., and Moderatus of Gades (50–100 C.E.) and *Numenius of Apamea (2nd cent. C.E.) were also important figures. Some Neopythagoreans emulated Pythagoras' role as a wonder-working sage. Apollonius of Tyana (first century C.E.), as presented in *Philostratus' *Life of Apollonius*, is the most important figure in this tradition. *Nicomachus (c. 50–150 C.E.) in his *Introduction to Arithmetic* provides clear examples of the tendency to treat *Platonism as if it were in fact Pythagoreanism. He also illustrated Neopythagorean interest in numerology, especially in connection with the gods in a work that is one of the major sources of the anonymous text (sometimes ascribed to *Iamblichus) known as the *Theology of Arithmetic*. Most important of all was the Neoplatonist Iamblichus (c. 250–325 C.E.), who composed a ten-volume work *On Pythagorean Doctrine*, which influenced later Neoplatonists such as *Proclus and *Syrianus (5th cent. C.E.). The first volume of Iamblichus' work, *On the Pythagorean Life*, along with the third-century lives of Pythagoras by *Diogenes Laertius and the Neoplatonist *Porphyry, are the oldest complete works on Pythagoras to survive and have thus exercised the greatest influence on the common picture of Pythagoras from the Renaissance to the present day.

Many Neopythagorean writings, notably the pseudepigrapha, present no arguments for their doctrines and are products of faith in the great Pythagoras rather than philosophical reasoning. This strain of Pythagoreanism appears in the writings of a number of syncretic religious traditions during the Roman empire (e.g., the *Chaldaean Oracles*) and may have had influence on religious ideas such as the return of the *soul to the stars upon death (astral immortality), although again Platonic ideas ascribed to Pythagoras are dominant. On the other hand, figures such as Moderatus and Numenius played an important role in the development of Neoplatonism both by handing on the Platonic doctrine of the one and the indefinite dyad as ultimate principles and by developing it in ways that anticipate *Plotinus. However, in order to understand Pythagoras himself it is necessary to get behind this Neopythagorean picture and see what the earliest evidence tells us.

The Early Evidence. Pythagoras had more impact on Greek society than any other Presocratic philosopher. Plato says that even in his day, people who followed the Pythagorean way stood out in society (*Rep.* 600b). In this same passage, the only Platonic reference to Pythagoras, Pythagoras' greatness is said to lie in his role as a leader of education and in the impact of personal contact with him. Plato's contemporary *Isocrates says that Pythagoras "exceeded others so much in reputation that all the young wanted to be his pupils and parents were happier seeing their children associate with him than attending to the affairs of the household" (*Busiris* 29). In his extant works Aristotle, like Plato, says nothing about specific contributions of Pythagoras to theoretical philosophy. His discussion of Pythagoreanism always refers to "the so-called Pythagoreans" of the fifth century B.C.E., an expression probably used to distance the Pythagoreanism of Philolaus, who is Aristotle's primary source, from Pythagoras himself.

The earliest sources present Pythagoras in very general terms as a wise man, but whenever any specifics are given they portray him as an expert on religious ritual and the fate of the soul after death and thus suggest that the Pythagorean way of life was directed at purification and training of the soul. It is certain that Pythagoras taught the doctrine of metempsychosis, that the human soul is reborn into other human and animal bodies after death. *Xenophanes, a contemporary of Pythagoras, mocks this view, saying that Pythagoras once begged a man to stop beating a puppy, saying, "It is the soul of a friend of mine, I recognized his voice" (DK21B7). Another contemporary, *Heraclitus, criticizes him, along with *Hesiod, Xenophanes, and *Hecataeus, for his polymathy (DK22B40) and as being the "chief of swindlers" whose wisdom was an "evil trickery" (B81, 129). Heraclitus' language is vague enough to have led to controversy as to whether he sees Pythagoras as a figure like Hesiod, who claims special knowledge about the gods, or as a practitioner of the more rational Ionian *historia* (inquiry) like Hecataeus and Xenophanes.

However, *Herodotus introduces Pythagoras in contexts that imply his expertise on religious ritual and on the afterlife. He says that the practice of not burying the dead with wool garments is often said to be Orphic and Bacchic, but is in reality Egyptian and Pythagorean (2.81). Isocrates supports this picture of Pythagoras when he reports that he became a pupil of the Egyptians and "was more conspicuous than others in his interest in sacrifices and rites in temples" (*Busiris* 28). Ion of Chios (b. 490 B.C.E.) says that Pythagoras ascribed some of his own poems to Orpheus. The connection with Orphism, which promulgated a theogony in connection with a belief about the fate of the soul, again points to Pythagoras' reputation for expertise in these areas.

Although Xenophanes and Heraclitus were critical of Pythagoras, *Empedocles (b. 490) is all praise when he describes Pythagoras as "a man knowing exceptional things who possessed the greatest wealth of wisdom, master of all sorts of wise works, for whenever he would reach out with all his intellect he easily beheld each of all the things that are in ten and even twenty generations of men" (DK31B129). The emphasis on "wise works" and on wisdom that spans many generations of men certainly fits someone who gave advice on what to do to ensure the best fate for the soul through the generations of rebirth. It is also significant that *Democritus' book on Pythagoras was classified by *Thrasyllus with the *ethical works rather than the physical or mathematical works (D.L. 9.46).

The fragments of Aristotle's special works on the Pythagoreans support and expand this picture of Pythagoras. Miraculous deeds were part of his persona. He was seen in both Metapontum and Croton at the same time, was called the Hyperborean Apollo by the citizens of Croton, and once while sitting in a theater revealed that he had a golden thigh, probably a sign of special initiation into divine rites (Ar. fr. 191 [Rose]). Again Aristotle reports a number of *acusmata* ("things heard") and *symbola* ("signs") that seem closely tied to the Pythagorean way of life, although none are explicitly assigned to Pythagoras himself. These are short maxims often of ritual or ethical content. Some are injunctions against certain actions such as jumping over a scale or stirring a fire, others make statements about the natural world such as that "the sea is the tear of Kronos" (Ar. fr. 196, 197). There are also dietary prohibitions that forbid the eating of parts of animals such as the heart, but most famous of all was the prohibition against eating beans (a type of European vetch that does in fact cause digestive problems; Ar. fr. 195). It is controversial whether or not Pythagoras urged vegetarianism. Metempsychosis would seem to demand it, and it is supported by many aspects of the ancient tradition (e.g., Empedocles espoused it [DK31B136]), but other authors deny it (*Aristoxenus [D.L. 8.20]), and the fact that the acusmata ban certain types of animals and certain parts of animals suggests that total vegetarianism was not practiced.

The most authoritative treatment of Pythagoras in this century, that of Walter Burkert, regards him as analogous to a shaman, a figure first studied in regard to tribes in Siberia. A shaman has the ability to enter into an ecstatic state in order to make contact with gods and spirits and in particular to travel to the beyond (e.g., the underworld) to bring back health for the community. Few scholars would agree that Pythagoras was literally a shaman, and it is important to note that Burkert himself presents it only as an analogy. Some scholars argue that in light of Pythagoras' great impact on society and the fact that he grew up on the island of Samos next door to Miletus, the home of Ionian rationalism, he must be something more than a wonder-working sage. However, mere proximity to and knowledge of the Ionian tradition in no way necessitates participation in that tradition, and it is not clear why a Presocratic writer on nature should be supposed to have more impact on society than someone who is an expert on the fate of the soul. Again, it might seem that there must be some truth to the later tradition's presentation of Pythagoras as a natural philosopher and mathematician and that the burden of proof is on anyone who would deny it. However, since there is a consensus that the later tradition is full of misrepresentations, the only way to evaluate it is in light of the early evidence.

Pythagoras as a Mathematician and Writer on Nature. The argument from silence is always problematic, but it is striking that no source up to and including Plato and Aristotle assigns any significant mathematical discoveries to Pythagoras or portrays him as a writer on nature. The only early evidence for his connection to mathematics and natural science are acusmata such as "number is the wisest thing" and "the planets are the hounds of Persephone." The later tradition reports that his followers took oaths by "he who handed down the tetraktys to our generation" (S.E. *M* 7.94). The tetraktys, or "group of four," refers to the first four numbers whose sum is ten, the perfect number for the Pythagoreans. It is mentioned in some of the acusmata and might go back to Pythagoras himself, although some parts of the oath are clearly later. The later tradition makes Pythagoras the discoverer of the fact that the harmonic intervals of the octave, fourth, and fifth are governed by the whole number ratios 1:2, 3:4, 2:3. However, none of the stories about how Pythagoras made this discovery are scientifically plausible. Stories about the discovery by Lasus in the late sixth century and the Pythagorean Hippasus in the fifth century make more sense. Pythagoras may have known of the intervals without discovering them himself.

The same seems to be true about the famous "Pythagorean theorem." Knowledge of the formula embodied in the theorem goes back to the Babylonians, and the history of Greek geometry makes it very unlikely that the set of elements necessary for the proof of the theorem was available until several generations after Pythagoras. The reports of his connection to the theorem are all very late and in fact may have been more important for the debate on Pythagoras' supposed vegetarianism, since they assert that when he found the theorem he sacrificed an ox. The emphasis in the story seems to be on the importance Pythagoras assigned to the truth of this theorem. Indeed, the early evidence is most convincingly interpreted as showing Pythagoras as someone impressed with discoveries of others that show the importance of the first four numbers in musical harmony and in mathematical relations. The famous doctrine of the harmony of the spheres, the idea that the planets are ordered according to number and accordingly produce a harmonious music by their movements, might then go back to Pythagoras. However, the idea that Pythagoras was a serious mathematician or that he was primarily interested in explaining the natural world like other Presocratic philosophers is not supported by the early evidence.

The Pythagorean Way of Life. The earliest evidence gives little detail about the Pythagorean way of life, and consequently every aspect of that way of life is beset with controversy. Most of the evidence comes from authors of the third and fourth centuries C.E., such as Iamblichus, although these later accounts are primarily based on authors of the late fourth century B.C.E. such as Aristoxenus, *Dicaearchus, and the historian of southern Italy, Timaeus. Some scholars believe that the whole notion of a Pythagorean community based on any sort of strict "rule" is an anachronism read back onto the early period by Neopythagoreans. Yet, Plato's assertion of the importance and longevity of the Pythagorean way of life suggests a distinctive and durable structure of some sort. There were grades of Pythagoreans. The most important split is described in a report that goes back to Aristotle (Iamblichus *On General Mathematical Science* 76.19). The *acusmatici*, who are clearly tied to the acusmata, claim that another group, the *mathematici* are really followers of Hippasus (fl. 500–450 B.C.E.?) and not Pythagoras. The *mathematici* accept the *acusmatici* as genuine Pythagoreans, but regard them as those who only wanted to know how to act without understanding the underlying reasons for the actions. The evidence does suggest that Hippasus is the first Pythagorean to have some connection to mathematics and speculation on nature, although he wrote nothing.

The later tradition reports secrecy about aspects of Pythagorean doctrine, and it is a priori likely that a movement like Pythagoreanism should have secrets. Some acusmata may have been secret, and Aristotle is given as the source for the assertion that one of their very secret doctrines was that "of rational beings one is divine, one is human, and one is like Pythagoras" (Iamblicus *On the Pythagorean Life* 31). However, neither Plato nor Aristotle seems to have any problem discussing the philosophy of the Pythagoreans of the fifth century. Later traditions that the discoverer of irrational magnitudes or the first person to construct the dodecahedron was punished by drowning for revealing the discovery to the masses are very suspect since such mathematical discoveries are too technical to be of concern to the public at large. Related to the issue of secrecy and perhaps behind the later traditions concerning it is the issue of Pythagorean silence. Timaeus reports that there was a five year novitiate that enjoined silence.

There was a strong emphasis on friendship in the Pythagorean community. Timaeus suggests that, in accordance with the maxim that "friends have all things in common," Pythagoras urged some sort of communal property. Pythagoras is presented as emphasizing the virtues of frugality and modesty and urging training of the memory. It is most probable that the Pythagoreans exercised political influence through the prominence of individual members rather than as an organized political party.

Conclusion. Pythagoras is remarkable as the first Greek philosopher to propose a detailed and systematic regimen of life that applied not just to special religious occasions but to all aspects of life and that appealed not just to a handful of philosophers but to a broader spectrum of society. This way of life was likely to be based on a general notion of the order of the cosmos including special knowledge about religious ritual and the fate of the soul after death. The philosophy of nature developed by Philolaus and Archytas had influence on Plato; but, in the search for semidivine figures as sources for revealed truth that develops in the first centuries C.E., it is once again Pythagoras himself who becomes the central figure.

See also PHILOLAUS and ARCHYTAS.

BIBLIOGRAPHY: Texts in DK14. Burkert, W., *Lore and Science in Ancient Pythagoreanism*, tr. by E. Minar, Cambridge, MA, 1972; Dillon, J., *The Middle Platonists*, London, 1977; Dillon, J., and J. Hershbell, intro. to *Iamblichus: On the Pythagorean Way of Life. Text, Translation and Notes*, Atlanta, 1991; Guthrie, W. K. C., *A History of Greek Philosophy*, vol. 1, Cambridge, 1962, 146–340; Kahn, C., in A. P. D. Mourelatos, ed., *The Pre-socratics*, New York, 1974, 161–85; O'Meara, D., *Pythagoras Revived*, Oxford, 1989; Thesleff, H., *An Introduction to the Pythagorean Texts of the Hellenistic Period*, Abo, 1961; also *Pythagorean Texts of the Hellenistic Period*, Abo, 1965.—CARL A. HUFFMAN

R

RELIGION, Classical. See THEISM and ATHEISM.

RHETORIC, Greek and Roman, the art of persuasion through extended discourse; conceived through much of the classical era as the counterpart of *dialectic and the basis of an educational program alternative to that provided by philosophy.

Although sensitivities to the forms and functions of speaking may be noted in archaic literature, including the poems of *Homer and *Hesiod, the earliest conceptualization of rhetoric as the theory of speaking almost certainly arose in Sicily around mid-fifth century B.C.E. Here Corax and Tisias taught the use of speech parts—proem, narration, argument, and epilogue—as well as the utility of probable reasoning in practical speechmaking. These advancements were soon adopted as mainstays in the educational curricula of the *sophists, who otherwise offered instruction in expression and *logic. Among the sophists, it was not uncommon to refer to the theory of speaking as a *technê* or art (e.g., Gorgias *Encomium to Helen* 13; *Dissoi Logoi* 8). Consistent with this practice, a number of sophists composed "arts" or treatises dealing with the subject.

Early in the fourth century B.C.E., the theoretical activities of the sophists received criticism from *Isocrates, who rebuked some for writing "arts" limited to legal speaking and others for failing to realize that political speaking did not constitute a fixed art or science, but a creative practice (*Against the Sophists* 12, 19). Still, Isocrates recognized the theory of speaking as an art and placed it at the center of his own *philosophia*, an educational program designed to inculcate right action and speech in public contexts. Isocrates' response to the sophists did not long stand before his critique was enlarged with less sympathy by *Plato. In the *Gorgias*, Plato dismissed the rhetoric of his day as a forensic knack and not an art, because it ignored the nature and benefit of its object, the *soul, and had no account to give of its methods (*Grg.* 465). In his later work, the *Phaedrus*, Plato presented a new conception of rhetoric based on adaptation of discourses to types of souls (*Phdr.* 271). Within the *Phaedrus*, rhetoric was now an art, one which concerned itself with soul-leading in private as well as public contexts (261); moreover, it used dialectic—particularly collection and division—as the means of discovering and arranging discourse materials (264–66).

The philosophical legitimacy afforded rhetoric by Plato's *Phaedrus* was consolidated in *Aristotle's *Rhetoric*. Aristotle accepted Plato's association of *psychology and dialectic with rhetoric; he also conceived of rhetoric as an art. But Aristotle maintained a certain distance from Plato's view. For Aristotle, rhetoric was an art because the processes of successful speaking could be observed and reduced to a system (*Rh.* 1.1, 1354a6–11). Psychology was germane to rhetoric since audiences were persuaded to judgment through argument and character, arriving at different judgments depending upon their emotional states (1.2, 1356a5–20). Dialectic and rhetoric were alike, because both were concerned with proof of opposites on any subject using heuristic topics (1.1, 1355a24–b17; 1.2, 1358a2–32). Moreover, both employed deductive and inductive argument forms; just as dialectic used syllogism and epagoge, rhetoric used enthymeme and example (1.2, 1356a35–b10). Aristotle also adapted certain elements from earlier rhetorical theories, including the character of the speaker, probability, and preexisting material as sources of proof; the four-part arrangement of speeches; and a particular focus on public discourse, though he may have been the first to divide rhetorical speeches into three genera—deliberative, forensic, and epideictic (1.3, 1358b6–8). In the end, however, Aristotle's theory reconceptualized rhetoric in two ways that would influence most subsequent thinking on the subject. On one hand, he expanded the conceptual resources of rhetoric by organizing his theory with reference to functional activities of speakers—finding proofs, expression, delivery, and arrangement of speech parts (3.1, 1403b6–27). On the other hand, he constricted the scope of rhetoric by limiting its application to just those matters of uncertainty that fell outside the boundaries of other arts (1.2, 1357a1–7).

From the final quarter of the fourth century through the first half of the second, rhetorical theory continued to develop, though largely along established lines and more in philosophical than in rhetorical schools. In the school of *Nausiphanes, for instance, the traditional interest of rhetoricians in public affairs emerged in a linkage of rhetoric with statesmanship, both of which were to arise in philosophers with mastery of *phusiologia* or the theory of Nature (Philod. *On Rhetoric*, PHerc. 1015/ 832 col. 38 Sudhaus). Among the *Peripatetics, *Theophrastus elaborated Aristotle's nascent theories of expression and delivery, the former by isolating a canon of expressive qualities—correctness, clarity, aptness, and ornament—the latter by adding an account of gesture to Aristotle's account of voice. Other Peripatetics joined in similar studies, including *Demetrius of Phalerum and *Hieronymus of Rhodes; this research almost certainly developed a theory of stylistic types, an eventual outcome of which was the theory of four characters of style—plain, grand, elegant, and forceful (Demetrius *On Style* 36). Within the *Stoic school, *Cleanthes and *Chrysippus both wrote rhetorical arts and these arts may have envisioned the rhetorical treatment of general themes, unlimited by any reference to specific persons and circumstances (Cic. *Fin.* 4.6–7). In other respects, Stoic theories apparently resembled the Peripatetic account (D.L. 7.41–43), but with a crucial restriction that the speaker not create emotional disturbance (Cic. *Or.* 1.228). At the *Academy, we have indications of interest in rhetoric by *Speusippus, *Xenocrates, and *Heraclides of Pontus (D.L. 4.5, 5.88; S.E. *M* 2.6, 61), but there is no evidence for systematic study of the subject before the first century B.C.E. Of course, it may not be assumed that all philosophers who attended to rhetoric were concerned with its advancement. We have evidence for a work entitled *Against the Rhetoricians* by the Peripatetic, *Aristo of Ceos (D.L. 7.163), and we know that *Diogenes of Babylon claimed only the Stoic "wise man" could be a rhetor (Philod. *Rh.*, PHerc. 1004 col. 47 Sudhaus). Moreover, for nearly two centuries after Aristotle, the *Epicureans stood in opposition to rhetoric and its apologists, insisting that rhetoric was inartistic, because its success at persuasion was unsure, and useless for practical speaking, because audiences would not endure contrived speeches when serious matters were at stake (see, e.g., Philod. *Rh.* 2, PHerc. 1674 cols. 54–56 Longo; *Rh.* 3, PHerc. 1426 cols. 3a–5a Hammerstaedt).

Around mid-second century B.C.E., relations between philosophical and rhetorical schools became strained, not least on account of competition for students. A particular focus for the hostilities was Hermagoras' *Rhetorical Arts*, which offered a new conceptual scheme for analyzing rhetorical problems. As elements of this scheme Hermagoras insisted that rhetoric was concerned entirely with political questions and that, among such questions, rhetoric handled particular questions (hypotheses) that were limited by reference to specific persons and circumstances, alongside general questions (theses) that were not limited in this way. This position aroused considerable philosophical criticism. Some philosophical schools had long-standing views that political understanding did not come from rhetoric (on Stoics and Epicureans, see Philod. *Rh.* 3,

PHerc. 1506 col. 14 Sudhaus, col. 44 Hammerstaedt), and such views were brought to bear against the stance (Cic. *Or.* 1.85). Likewise, Hermagoras' position was attacked for allocating general questions to rhetoric, since these themes were outside its disciplinary boundaries (Cic. *Or.* 1.56, 85). Besides these particular complaints, more general arguments also arose, for the Academy and Peripatos joined the Garden in claiming that rhetoric was not an art. The main substance of the arguments was that rhetoric dealt in uncertainty, was not a reliable guide to success at persuading, and was useless to speakers as well as their constituencies (see, e.g., S.E. *M* 2.12–42). The rhetoricians, for their part, returned fire, rebutting arguments that their discipline was distinct from statesmanship and constrained to particular questions (Cic. *Or.* 1.47–57, 85-88); they also added arguments that philosophy had no practical utility, treated unimportant matters, and did not promote the good life or provide ultimate mastery of discourse (Philod. *Rh.*, PHerc. 1078/1080, 1669 *passim* Sudhaus, Ferrario).

By early first century B.C.E., both camps were showing signs of adaptation to the other's views. For example, in *Cicero's De Inventione we have express denial that rhetorical competence includes facility in political science (1.6) and even a refutation of Hermagoras' inclusion of general questions within the scope of rhetoric (1.8). Likewise, among philosophers, *Philo of Larissa introduced rhetoric in the Academy as an instructional subject (Cic. *TD* 2.9), while *Zeno of Sidon and *Philodemus argued that sophistic (or epideictic) rhetoric was an art according to the masters of the Epicurean school (Philod. *Rh.* 2, PHerc. 1674 cols. 43–44, 49 Longo). Still, hostilities continued, for we know that *Posidonius delivered a lecture opposing Hermagoras on general questions as late as 62 (Plut. *Life of Pompey* 42). It is not surprising, then, that in 55 Cicero composed his *De Oratore* partly as a response to the philosophers. Within this work, Cicero shifted theoretical focus away from the rhetorical discipline and onto the qualifications of the rhetorical speaker. Insisting that the complete speaker must know all important matters and arts, Cicero admitted the orator's need for philosophy, but asserted the orator's superiority over the philosopher, inasmuch as the orator added the ability for persuasive expression to the philosopher's theoretical knowledge (3.143).

Cicero's view was influential at least through the next century. Its polemical value was exploited by Quintilian, who extended dispute with philosophers by claiming for oratory what Cicero had secured for the orator, namely, all the subjects of philosophy (*Institutio Oratoria* 1.pr.16–17, 2.21.13). Working along more general lines, Tacitus adopted Cicero's view as a description of the philosophical education that made eloquence possible among the "ancients" (*Dialogus* 30.2–32.7). Tacitus' appreciation for philosophy was shared by many teachers and practitioners of rhetoric, including the younger *Seneca (*Epistle* 90.1–3) and Dio Chrysostom (*Oration* 70.7). Despite isolated attempts to place rhetoric and philosophy at odds (as in Aristides *To Plato on Rhetoric* and S.E. *M* 2), the two arts became increasingly difficult to separate in the literary activities of intellectuals. From the second century C.E. through the end of antiquity we commonly find mention of philosophical sophistication in rhetoricians such as Favorinus (Philos. *VS* 489) and Cassius Longinus (Eunapius *Lives of the Sophists* 455–56). Likewise, there is ample evidence of theoretical attention to rhetoric by philosophers, for example, the *Neoplatonic *commentaries of *Porphyry in Minucian's *Rhetorical Art* (Sopater *Ad Hermog. Stat.* 5:9 Walz) and *Syrianus in Hermogenes' *On Staseis* (*Syriani in Hermogenem Commentaria* 2, Rabe).

BIBLIOGRAPHY: IJsseling, S., *Retoriek en filosofie: wat gebeurt er wanneer er gesproken wordt?* Bilthoven, 1975; Kennedy, G., *The Art of Persuasion in Greece*, Princeton, 1963; also *The Art of Rhetoric in the Roman World: 300 B.C.–300 A.D.*, Princeton, 1972; Kroll, W., "Rhetorik" in *RE* supp. 7; Vickers, B., *In Defence of Rhetoric*, Oxford, 1988: von Arnim, H., *Leben und Werke des Dio von Prusa. Mit einer Einleitung: Sophistik, Rhetorik, Philosophie in ihrem Kampf um die Jugendbildung*, Berlin, 1898.— ROBERT N. GAINES

S

SCIENCE, Greek. The distinction between "science" and "philosophy" is not to be found in Classical Greece. Nevertheless, by the end of the fourth century B.C.E., disciplines such as geometry, arithmetic, harmonics, optics, *astronomy, zoology, botany, and meteorology were distinguishable both from each other and from *dialectic (*Plato) and first philosophy (*Aristotle). They were also being distinguished from "the crafts," which included *medicine. In the following discussion, however, medicine will be included among the "sciences," for three reasons: First, medicine became increasingly dependent on comparative anatomy as it developed, and thus closely associated in its methods with zoology. Second, the method of experimental verification of theory originates in medicine. And finally, the long-standing debate over the roles of "theory" and "observation" in science has its origins in Greek medicine.

Plato and Aristotle refer to a distinct group of predecessors as "investigators of nature," the earliest of whom (*Thales, *Anaximander, and *Anaximenes) disseminated their views from Miletus in the early to middle sixth century B.C.E. We have no manuscripts of their written work, few and fragmentary direct quotations from them, and a tradition of stories about their ideas and activities stretching from Plato, *Herodotus, Aristotle, and *Theophrastus through the later Greek *commentaries on Aristotle a millennium after their deaths. Extreme caution must be used, then, in attributing ideas to these early thinkers based on such reports. For example, about Thales' view of the soul, Aristotle says, "Thales, *judging by what they report, seems to have believed* that the soul was something which produces motion, *inasmuch as he said* that the magnet has a soul because it moves iron" (*DA* 1, 411a7–8). Not only are Thales' beliefs about soul based on the reports of others, those others apparently *inferred* his beliefs from something he said about magnets!

Our sources, such as they are, ascribe to these thinkers speculations about the stars and their movements, the general structure of the earth and cosmos, about an "origin" or "origins" for all things, including life, and occasionally remark on their geometric talents. Thus, while not practicing what Plato or Aristotle would call "geometry" or "astronomy," they were asking a distinctive set of questions and answering them in characteristic ways. They sought explanations for observed phenomena by drawing inferences from observations to their "origins" or "causes." But in common with *Hesiod, particular interest is shown in the origins of the cosmos and of life and in the nature and causes of portentous events such as lunar and solar periods, eclipses, rainbows and violent storms.

The *Hippocratic medical writings, some of which are certainly from the fifth century B.C.E., are our earliest nonfragmentary evidence of scientific specialization. A number of these documents show clear dependence, in style of argumentation and substantive doctrine, on the tradition of natural inquiry begun in Ionia. *On Ancient Medicine*, for example, is critical of attempts to derive all diseases from hypothetical first principles such as hot, cold, moist, and dry; while the insistence in *On the Sacred Disease* that all diseases have a natural source discoverable by rational inquiry affirms the fundamental premise of Ionian natural inquiry.

These treatises represent an array of positions, both in theory and in practice, on the role of experience and theory in science. The explanation for epileptic seizures in *On the Sacred Disease*, while ingenious, is based on a prior commitment to a humoral theory and to a theory of respiration and the vascular system that is entirely without a basis in dissection or experimentation. On the other hand, works like *Fractures*, *Epidemics*, and a *Regimen for Health* evidence respect for careful observation and accumulated experience, while being relatively free of attempts at systematic theory. *On Ancient Medicine* defends the patient accumulation of medical experience as the starting point for the discovery of new treatments. As we will see, this document prefigures a central debate in Hellenistic medicine over the role of experience and theory in the advance of medicine.

Our earliest nonfragmentary, systematic investigations of nature outside of medicine are Plato's *Timaeus* and the many treatises of Aristotle in this category. Aristotle and his younger colleague Theophrastus initiate the first systematic investigations of animals and plants, respectively. Roughly one quarter of Aristotle's extant writings are devoted to zoology, and we have three books of Theophrastus devoted to botany.

These works originate the science of biology and will be discussed briefly below.

Many passages in the writings of Plato and Aristotle also provide tantalizing hints regarding the practices of arithmetic, geometry, solid geometry, astronomy, optics, harmonics, and mechanics in the early to middle fourth century B.C.E. Plato's *Republic*, books 6–7 and *Timaeus* 30–39, and Aristotle's *De Caelo* and *Metaphysics* 12.8, make it clear that a form of astronomy had been developed in the fourth century that attempted to explain the observed movements of the fixed stars, sun, moon, Mercury, Venus, Mars, Jupiter, and Saturn by appeal to geometric models conceiving of a spherical earth, an outer sphere of fixed stars, and the sun, moon, and planets circling the earth at varying distances and speeds at an angle to the celestial equator referred to as the ecliptic. Aristotle discusses explicitly the views of *Eudoxus and Callippus in *Metaphysics* 12.8.

In the *Republic's* discussion of the divided line (509d–511e) and the education of the guardians (522c–531c), there are brief discussions of arithmetic, geometry, solid geometry, astronomy, and harmonics. (Plato here tells us, approvingly, that the latter two are considered by the *Pythagoreans to be sister sciences.) Though it is clear that Plato is in part criticizing current practice and recommending reforms, one can learn a good deal about the practice itself by attending to what is being criticized. For example, we are told of an astronomy useful for agriculture and navigation that allows one "to be able to tell accurately the times of the month and year" (527d). And Plato criticizes practitioners of astronomy and harmonics for relying too heavily on perception and manipulation rather than proceeding, "as we do in geometry, by means of problems" which, applied to harmonic science, would involve "inquiring which numbers are inherently consonant and which not, and why" (530b, 531c). At *Gorgias* 451c Socrates defines astronomy as concerned with the relative speeds of the movements of the stars, sun, and moon. Timaeus' final description of the movements of the world soul refers to "circles that move in opposites senses to one another; while in speed three should be similar, but the other four should differ in speed from one another and from the three, though moving according to a ratio" (36d).

Clearly, then, by the early fourth century, and perhaps earlier, a number of investigations of natural phenomena—the movements of the planets (with which the Greeks include sun and moon) and the fixed stars, sound, reflective and refractive phenomena—were thought of as amenable to *mathematical description and proof. This raised any number of philosophical questions. There were numerous disagreements among the practitioners themselves over the proper principles and methods of investigation to be used in these studies.

Plato focuses on the questionable *epistemological status of the assumed starting points of these sciences, the ontological status of mathematical objects, and the use of observation, construction, and diagrams in these sciences. He argues that these starting points must be grounded in the results of dialectical inquiry, which will discover that the true objects of mathematics are formal entities existing entirely apart from their confusing representations in the natural world. According to the view expressed in the *Republic*, the use of empirical methods and mechanical techniques in these sciences distracts the inquirer from pursuing the real objects of mathematics. In the *Timaeus* and *Philebus*, however, Plato seems to be exploring the idea that the physical world is mathematically structured and thus open to understanding for the properly trained philosopher.

In the *Posterior Analytics* 1.13, *Physics* 2.2, *Meteorology* 3.2–6, and *Metaphysics* 12.8 and 13.3, Aristotle discusses these same disciplines as involving mathematical first principles, though the phenomena are investigated and organized like other natural phenomena. In the *Physics* Aristotle describes these as "the branches of mathematics nearest to nature" (194a7–9), while in the *Analytics* he presents a somewhat different picture, of two sciences related in a quasi-deductive manner—astronomy, optics, and mechanics to geometry, harmonics to arithmetic (78b32–79a16). On this picture a part of *natural* inquiry observes and organizes the explananda, while a part of the relevant branch of *mathematics* provides the principles that explain *why* the phenomena are as they are. A brief sketch of such explanations in harmonics may be reconstructed from *APo.* 2.2, 90a18–22; more helpful is the detailed use of geometric proof in his explanations of rainbows and haloes at *Meteorology* 3.2–5.

Regarding the fourth century, then, it is only with medicine, zoology, botany, and meteorology that we have entire treatises to guide us in knowing what these studies entailed. However, besides the reflections on the mathematical sciences found in Plato and Aristotle, works from the third century by *Aristoxenus (*Elementis Harmonica*), *Euclid (*Phaenomena, Elements, Sectio Canonis*), *Aristarchus (*On the Sizes of the Sun and Moon*), and *Archimedes (*The Method, The Sand-reckoner, On the Sphere and Cylinder, On Spirals, On Floating Bodies*) give us some idea of earlier achievements.

In what follows, attention will be given to two sets of questions of more general philosophical importance, to indicate briefly how familiarity with Greek science aids in the exploration of these philosopical questions.

The first set of questions involves the nature of *epistêmê*, variously rendered "knowledge," "scientific knowledge," or "understanding." Does knowledge involve definition, and if so, what *are* definitions? How are they grounded, and what role do they play in science? Does knowledge involve explanation? If so, what form do explanations take, and what grounds explanation? Are all explanations causal? If so, what are causes? If not, what else besides a thing's cause might explain it? Do ideal explanations render their conclusions necessarily true? If so, how is this accomplished? What counts as an ideal explanation, and under what conditions is such an ideal achieved? How are perception, experience, belief, and knowledge related? Are they different ways in which knowers are related to the same thing, or do they represent relationships to different things?

Such questions are often raised in Platonic *dialogues like the *Meno, Phaedo, Theaetetus, Republic, Timaeus, Philebus,* and *Laws,* as a result of reflection on natural inquiry and/or mathematics. Similarly, Aristotle's investigation of these questions in the *Posterior Analytics* draws richly on examples from geometry, arithmetic, astronomy, meteorology, botany, zoology, and harmonics. In addition, he discusses, both in the *Analytics* and elsewhere, how natural sciences that use mathematical demonstration do so. The philosophical introduction to the study of animals, *Parts of Animals* 1, consistently compares and contrasts zoological investigations with those of mathematical astronomy (e.g., at 639b8–12, 639b22–640a8, and 644b22–645a10; with which cf. *Meteorology* 1.1, 339a6–9).

A second, closely related set of questions concerns the roles of reason and experience in science. Must science be limited to what is directly given in experience? Can inference take us beyond the given, and if so, how? Are there truths of reason than can be known independently of experience? Perhaps the most productive ground for exploring these issues in the Hellenistic period is in the debate between medical writers of empiricist and rationalist persuasions.

Of the many fruitful interactions between philosophy and the sciences in the Classical and Hellenistic periods, the following are of particular interest: (i) Aristotle's zoology; (ii) the medical debate, reported in *Galen, between "Rationalists" and "Empiricists" (see also MEDICINE, Ancient Theories of); and (iii) the remarks of *Ptolemy about the nature of astronomy in the introduction to the *Almagest.* (see also PTOLEMY).

(i) The first book of Aristotle's *Parts of Animals* is actually an introduction to the theoretical investigation of animals. Such a science is unprecedented, and it is clear that Aristotle is self-consciously defending the validity of such a science, as well as laying out the appropriate principles and standards for its practice. In his *Metaphysics,* animals are paradigmatic examples of natural substance, and *Physics* 2 makes it clear that a central domain of "natural philosophy" will be the study of animals. They are, after all, his principal example of form organizing materials for the sake of self-maintenance and self-replication. This helps explain why between a quarter and a third of Aristotle's extant writings (depending on whether one includes the *De Anima*, *Parva Naturalia* and *Meteorology* 4) are works of zoology, the most substantial being *Parts of Animals* (four books), *Generation of Animals* (five books), and *History of Animals* (ten books). Remarkable achievements in their own right, they gain significantly in interest because of the light they throw on such central philosophical concepts as being, nature, *matter, form, potentiality, actuality, necessity, and cause. Further, as these works report a systematic scientific study by the author of the *Topics* and *Analytics*, they also shed light on his understanding of dialectic, demonstration, definition, and induction. Of particular interest for students of the *Analytics* is the self-conscious separation of the organization of zoological data (in the *History of Animals*) from the causal explanations of those data (particularly in the *Parts* and *Generation of Animals*). Theophrastus' *History of Plants* and *On the Causes of Plants* self-consciously reflect this organization. Their influence, both scientific and philosophical, stretches well into the eighteenth century.

In Aristotle's zoology one has a rare opportunity to observe a philosopher of science not merely practicing a science, but essentially creating it *de novo*. There is little doubt that his philosophical principles played a crucial role in this creation.

(ii) As mentioned above, in the Hippocratic writings the question is already raised of the relative importance of experience and theory in advancing the art of medicine. This question becomes more acute as the practice of anatomical dissection becomes a central part of medical education in Alexandria in the third century B.C.E. Whether or not, as *Celsus reports, *Herophilus and *Erasistratus "laid open men while alive and while still breathing," it is certain that human corpses were dissected. Theoretically this practice rested on the claim that, in order to discover new treatments for disease, it was necessary to understand how the parts functioned naturally, how they were systematically connected, and how they looked, felt, and malfunctioned during sickness. Treatment required knowledge of the causes of disease and of the effects of those causes on the human body. Thus, from this "Rationalist" viewpoint, the systematic development of medicine depends on inferences from experience to causal agents and their influences. Galen is perhaps our best source of evidence that the systematic use of experimental testing of theoretical claims developed within this school of medicine. Theoretical claims made about the function of specific organs had implications for what should happen under certain contrived conditions. Critics could then test the cogency of the theoretical claim by subjecting a test organism to those conditions.

In opposition to this viewpoint, medical Empiricists claimed that no such speculation is necessary, or even beneficial, to medicine. Rather, the art advances by accumulating experiences of treatments that have been correlated with the curing of various diseases. These are formulated by the physician in theorems and are passed on as "history" to others. Medicine advances both on the trial-and-error accumulation of such experience and on the deliberate trying of treatments on similar diseases or similar treatments on the same diseases when necessary. The art of medicine is the accumulation of such theorems.

As Galen (129–200 C.E.) reports it, this debate was not about how to administer treatment, but over how best to discover new treatments. In *An Outline of Empiricism*, Galen indicates that the Empiricists depended for their attack on the Rationalists on *skeptical arguments developed by *Pyrrhoneans; and *Sextus Empiricus was both a leading skeptic and a medical practitioner of the Empiricist school. On both sides, however, the issues at stake were the validity of various forms of inference and the epistemological status of causal laws and claims about unobservables. It is still unclear to what extent the philosophical development of skepticism was influenced by the medical debates and to what extent the philosophical views of *Stoics and Skeptics shaped those debates. That there was some sort of interplay seems beyond question.

While Galen reports this debate fairly, there seems little doubt from his own work that he is on the Rationalist side on most issues. Works such as *On the Natural Faculties* and *On the Uses of the Parts* treat the human body as a teleologically organized system, each of the parts fulfilling various nutritive, cognitive and locomotive functions by means of various "powers." Their claims are based on detailed anatomical dissection, and the claims of others are challenged by experimental inference. Further, *On Therapeutic Method* defends the logical method of definition by division, just the sort of thing Empiricists would have found useless, at best.

(iii) Ptolemy (100–175 C.E.), a rough contemporary of Galen's, lived and worked in Alexandria. The *Almagest* was probably written about midway through the second century C.E. and stands as the ultimate achievement of Greek astronomy. It remained astonomy's central text until the seventeenth century. It begins with an attempt to place astronomy within the theoretical sciences, understood, after Aristotle, *Metaphysics* 6.1, to be physics, *theology, and mathematics. But his epistemological attitude to each of these is quite unlike Aristotle's. It is Ptolemy's view that "the first two divisions of theoretical philosophy [physics and theology] should be called guesswork rather than knowledge, theology because of its completely invisible and ungraspable nature, physics because of the unstable and unclear nature of matter"; and that "only mathematics can provide sure and unshakable knowledge to its devo-tees" (Heiberg, p. 6; Toomer tr.). Ptolemy goes on to argue that in so far as one can move beyond guesswork in the other two subjects, it is through the application of mathematics to their quantifiable features. In-deed, the implication seems to be that astronomy is the application of geometry to the eternal and unchanging attributes of the heavenly bod-ies. Here again philosophical reflection on the nature of astronomy leads to a new understanding of the relationship between the various branches of "philosophy."

Recent scholarship (see bibliography) has shown the fruitfulness of paying careful attention to the actual issues debated within the sciences and medicine, which clearly form the backdrop to many of the philo-sophical debates of classical Greece. New studies challenge a long-stand-ing division of scholarly labor between "Greek science" and "Greek phi-losophy," a division that the ancient thinkers would not have under-stood. The dividing line between classical philosophy and classical sci-ence is nebulous at best; at the most it distinguishes works primarily de-voted to an investigation of nature and those primarily reflecting on the nature of that investigation. If this is true, the study of such "philosophi-cal" work should be thoroughly informed by the investigations upon which it reflects.

BIBLIOGRAPHY: Barnes, J., J. Brunschwig, M. Burnyeat, and M. Schofield, eds., *Science and Speculation*, Cambridge, 1982; Barnes, T., ed., *The Sciences in Greco-Ro-man Antiquity*, Edmonton, 1995; Bowen, A. C., ed., *Science and Philosophy in Clas-sical Greece*, New York, 1991; Gotthelf, A., and J. G. Lennox, eds., *Philosophical Is-sues in Aristotle's Biology*, Cambridge, 1987; Hankinson, R. J., ed., *Method, Medicine, and Metaphysics: Studies in the Philosophy of Ancient Science*, Edmonton, 1986; Lloyd, G. E. R., *Magic, Reason and Experience: Studies in the Origins and Development of Greek Science*, Cambridge, 1979; also *Methods and Problems in Greek Science*, Cambridge, 1990.—JAMES G. LENNOX

SECOND SOPHISTIC. See SOPHISTS, The.

SENECA, Lucius Annaeus (c. 1 B.C.E.–65 C.E.), of Rome (often distin-guished from his namesake and uncle, the *rhetorician L. Annaeus Seneca, by being called "the younger"). *Stoic philosopher, politician, and poet. Seneca was tutor to the young Nero, then advisor to the em-peror Nero until increasingly strained relations with Nero prompted him to withdraw from politics in 62. Suspected by Nero of plotting against him, Seneca was forced to commit suicide in 65.

Seneca's philosophical writings consist of numerous essays and let-ters on *ethical topics and a physical treatise, *Natural Inquiries*. His philo-sophical originality lies in adapting Stoic philosophy to Roman politics. Seneca modified Stoic theory by blending in some *Platonic *psychology and some *Epicurean ethics, and Roman values. He wrote in an ornate style, studded with pointed sentences and historical examples. This style was designed to impel the reader to the emulation of *virtue. Seneca's main achievement is perhaps the development of a humanistic ideal. Committed to traditional values, Seneca yet sought to embrace all humans, including slaves, in a vision of the nobility of every individual. He believed that it was the task of every human being to free himself or herself from petty concerns and disturbing emotions, so as to attain the goal of a serene philosophical enlightenment. Although often condemned for hypocrisy and pomposity, Seneca had a deep understanding of ethical issues and a broad sympathy for moral predicaments. This accounts for his profound influence on ethical thought in the Middle Ages, the Renaissance, and the modern period.

Seneca's essays and letters offer a personal reponse to Stoic ethics. They provide much information about earlier Stoic thought, which Seneca studied carefully. Their chief importance, however, lies in Seneca's own forging of an ethics that takes into account the political and social circumstances of Romans such as himself. Although Seneca was well acquainted with Stoic *logic, *epistemology, and literary theory, he rebuked the Stoics for giving too much attention to trivial theoretical refinements. Scholarly interests and theoretical analysis, he believed, should be firmly subordinated to the practice of virtue. Stoic ethics was traditionally reputed to be inflexible, harsh, and impracticable. Seneca tried, with all the persuasive means of his considerable rhetorical powers, to make it attractive to the Romans. He softened the paradoxes, and he invested the goal of perfect virtue with a joyfulness that owes much to the Epicurean notion of *happiness. Seneca's concept of the supreme *good is based on an acute awareness of the hardships and struggles of life—the cruelty of an unpredictable fortune, the trials of everyday existence, the devastation inflicted by power. He calls upon his fellow Romans to overcome adversity in a continuous effort to attain the serenity of moral goodness. Virtue allows a person not only to turn aside the blows of fortune, but even to turn them to one's benefit. It is ironic (though entirely understandable) that Seneca, who enjoyed a position of power, should feel so vulnerable. His writings are an intriguing counterpoise to the lectures of *Epictetus, a former slave, who attained a tranquillity that escaped Seneca.

Among Seneca's moral essays, *On Clemency* (or *On Mercy, De Clementia*) is addressed to the eighteen-year-old Nero near the beginning of his reign (late 55 or early 56). It is an extremely adroit plea to Nero not to abuse his power. Seneca argues that clemency is a virtue by distinguishing it from the emotions of pity and pardon, which are reprehensible. Clemency falls within a juridical area in which a judge may practice the discretion of issuing a milder or harsher punishment. Seneca goes to great lengths to praise Nero for the mildness he has shown so far in his exercise of absolute power. At the same, the treatise hints at a worry about the future, prompted perhaps by the ill-disguised murder of Nero's stepbrother Britannicus early in the year 55. *On Anger* depicts in harrowing detail the ravages caused by anger. As a Stoic, Seneca attempts to show that anger should be eliminated altogether. His longest ethical work, *On Benefits*, treats with great subtlety the exchange of gifts and favors. Based on Seneca's own extensive experience, it is a fascinating guide on how to make deals in politics and business. *On the Happy Life* is a defence of wealth. In response to accusations that he profited flagrantly from his imperial connections, Seneca defends the use of wealth by the philosopher. His *Consolation to Helvia* is ostensibly a consolation to his mother on his own exile. Seneca had been exiled by the Emperor Claudius to the island of Corsica on a charge of adultery. The address to his mother gives Seneca ample opportunity to plead with Claudius for his return. *Consolation to Polybius* is a plea to Claudius' powerful freedman, Polybius, for a pardon for the same offence. Under the pretext of consoling Polybius for the death of his brother, Seneca mounts a case for his return from exile. *Consolation to Marcia* urges the addressee to end her long mourning for her son. *On the Briefness of Life* is a general treatise of consolation. *On Providence* defends the Stoic notion that everything in the world is arranged in accordance with a benevolent divine will. *On the Tranquillity of the Soul* and *On Constancy* celebrate the equanimity of the wise person. *On leisure* deals with the problem of whether a philosopher should retire from public life. It depicts Seneca's own moral dilemma as a philosopher to whom life at the court of Nero has become unbearable.

In the *Letters to Lucilius*, addressed to a young friend, Seneca gathers moral thoughts and sayings from many sources, primarily *Epicurus, and blends them into a personal philosophy that combines Stoic morality with Epicurean contentment. Composed mostly toward the end of his life, the *Letters* are a distillation of Seneca's manifold reflections on human life. Written in a more casual and succinct style than the essays, they get to the point quickly and incisively. They offer advice on a great variety of subjects, including slavery (admonishing slave-owners to respect slaves as fellow human beings), the liberal arts (on behalf of a liberal education), human progress (arguing for less technical and more moral progress), illness and death, what to read and how to write, and, most of all, how to practice philosophy.

Natural Inquiries (*Naturales Quaestiones*) deals with meteorology, *astronomy, and geology. It rounds out Seneca's philosophical writings by treating an area of physics that touches on theology.

BIBLIOGRAPHY: Texts and trs. in var. eds., *Seneca*, 10 vols, (Loeb), London/ Cambridge, MA, 1917–1972; also L. D. Reynolds, *Dialogoi*, Oxford, 1977. Cooper, J. M. and J. F. Procopé, eds. and trs., *Seneca: Moral and Political Essays*, Cambridge, 1995; Griffin, M. T., *Seneca, A Philosopher in Politics*, Oxford, 1976; Sørenson, V., *Seneca the Humanist at the Court of Nero*, tr. G. Jones, Chicago, 1984.—*ELIZABETH ASMIS*

SEVEN SAGES (*hoi hepta sophoi*), legendary wise men, some later called philosophers, who lived about 600 B.C.E. Although their *acme* (585/584 B.C.E.) was widely used by chronologists, it—like much about them—is semifictional. Individual sages appear early, but whether they were grouped before *Plato (*Prt.* 343) is disputed. Most lore comes from *Diogenes Laertius 1.22–122 (c. 200 C.E.). Seventeen names are associated with the group; the canonical list comprises *Thales of Miletus (c. 624–545); Solon, chief archon of Athens in 594; Chilon, Spartan ephor in 565; Pittacus, tyrant of Mytilene (c. 650–570); Bias of Priene; Cleobulus of Lindos; and Periander, tyrant of Corinth from 625–585. Other figures sometimes substituted include Anacharsis the Scythian, Myson of Chen, (whom Plato preferred over Periander), *Pherecydes of Syros, and Epimenides of Crete. An inscription found in 1966 at Ai-Khanum shows that a list of 147 "Sayings of the Seven Sages" was already current in the third century B.C.E. and was thought to be an exact copy, by the *Peripatetic Clearchus of Soli, of an original from Delphi. Plato alludes to the sages' dedication there of laconic sayings, including "know thyself" and "nothing in excess"; specific attributions vary widely. Another collegial enterprise, the story of the sages' tripod, may have arisen in the clash of propaganda from competing archaic Apolline sites. Of the two major versions, one claimed that each sage, instructed to give this treasure to the wisest, passed it to the next sage, until Solon dedicated it at Delphi. Another version said an Arcadian left at his death a bowl to be given to one who had done most good by his wisdom; Thales ultimately dedicated it at Didyma, the Ionian oracle.

Though probably fictional, such representations allow us to reconstruct a context in which the existence of an idealized society of Seven Sages, even before being attested as such, makes sense. The tripod stories follow models of Greek gift-exchange already archaic by Classical times. Furthermore, the three most commonly shared traits in accounts of the sages—work as poets, involvement in politics, and aptitude for public performance—exhibit a concern for self-presentation, style, and power befitting an agonistic group context.

The sages may owe something to Babylonian traditions mentioned as early as *Gilgamesh*. Early Sanskrit texts frequently mention seven seers who are also poets, sacrificers, and forms of the Pleiades. Given parallels with religious activities of the Greek sages, the concept may be a survival of an archaic Indo-European tradition. In later Greek tradition, the Sages are chiefly remembered for inventions, predictions (e.g., Thales and the eclipse of 585 B.C.E.), and pithy sayings.

BIBLIOGRAPHY: Fehling, D., *Die sieben Weisen und die frühgriechische Chronologie: eine traditionsgeschichtliche Studie*, Bern, 1985; Martin, R., in C. Dougherty and L. Kurke, eds., *Cultural Poetics of Archaic Greece*, Cambridge, 1993, 108–128; Snell, B., *Leben und Meinungen der Sieben Weisen*,[4] Munich, 1971.—*RICHARD P. MARTIN*

SEXTUS EMPIRICUS (2nd cent. C.E.). *Pyrrhonian *skeptic. Sextus Empiricus is usually thought to have flourished in the latter part of the second century C.E., though a later date has also been argued for. Sextus is included in the succession-list of Pyrrhonists preserved by *Diogenes Laertius, where he is the last named but one. The author of this list thought the amount and quality of Sextus' writings worthy of comment, and his subsequent reputation rests on the extensive body of work that has survived.

The works that have come down to us are The *Outlines of Pyrrhonism* (*HP*) in three books and *Against the Mathematicians* (*M*) in eleven books. The first book of the *Outlines* (i) explains the Pyrrhonists' own skeptical attitude and way of life; (ii) expounds the argumentative strategies or tropes for the suspension of judgments organized by earlier Pyrrhonists like *Aenesidemus; (iii) explains how the skeptical formulae such as "all things are undetermined" are to be understood as expressions of the Pyrrhonist's own skeptical attitude rather than dogmatic pronouncements about the unknowable nature of the world; and (iv) compares Pyrrhonism with and carefully distinguishes it from other schools with which it has certain affinities. *HP* 2 and 3 provide an outline of the Pyrrhonists' skeptical case against the teachings of the dogmatists, divided conventionally into *logic, physics, and *ethics. *M* 7–11 cover the same ground as these last two books, but in more detail. The reference back to a discussion of Pyrrhonism itself with which they begin is usually taken to refer to *HP* 1, but it has been suggested that it refers to another treatment of the subject now lost. *M* 1–6 form a distinct work devoted to the skeptical examination of the six arts, *grammar, *rhetoric, geometry, arithmetic, *astronomy, and music. There is no reason why they could not have appeared after *M* 7–11. Indeed the only recent attempt to discover the chronology of Sextus' writings has concluded that they were composed in the order: *HP* 1–3, *M* 7–11, *M* 1–6. Sextus also refers to his works on Empirical *medicine and the *soul, which have not survived.

The received view is that Sextus' writings do not reveal an original philosophical intelligence at work and that the material he puts at our disposal is drawn chiefly from the works of earlier Pyrrhonists, of whom Aenesidemus was presumably the most important. Some scholars have maintained that Sextus failed to understand much of the material he took from elsewhere; others regard him as highly competent and careful. To be sure, it cannot be denied that Sextus sometimes fails to understand the views and arguments he preserves, but his misunderstandings are comparatively rare and usually concern rather subtle points. There is no reason not to credit him with a high level of competence and perhaps some original touches as well.

As a Pyrrhonian skeptic, Sextus maintains that a life of tranquillity follows on the suspension of judgment about all matters. It is to help others reach this happy state that he has put together the enormous mass of arguments against dogmatic positions offered in his books. He is careful to give an account of these positions, and his books are consequently of great use to historians of philosophy and logic interested in other ancient schools. He also furnishes us with our fullest account of the Pyrhonists' answer to the charge brought against all ancient skeptics, namely, that far from rendering life tranquil and happy, universal suspension of judgment makes it impossible. According to Sextus, despite suspending judgment about everything, the Pyrrhonist is able to live a full and active life. He is guided by the Pyrrhonian criterion, the apparent, which Sextus further elaborates into four divisions: the guidance of nature, the compulsion exerted by the affections, the tradition of laws and customs, and the instruction of the arts.

Sextus illustrated the Pyrrhonists' commitment to an active life himself. He was a physician in the Empirical school; his surname "Empiricus" means "the Empiricist." On closer inspection, it is clear that the relation between Pyrhonism and medical Empiricism was close and of long standing. Six of the eight figures in the list of Pyrrhonists after Aenesidemus were also medical Empiricists. It seems, then, that we should look to the Pyrrhonists' practice of Empirical medicine for illumination if we wish to understand how suspension of judgment can be combined with an active life. Yet when Sextus takes up the relation between Pyrhonism and medical Empiricism in the section of *HP* 1 that compares Pyrhonism with other schools, he inveighs against the dogmatic way in which Empiricists renounce knowledge of the nonevident matters and suggests that a Pyrrhonist interested in a medical career might do better to practice as a member of the competing Methodist school of medicine. Nonetheless, it is probably a mistake to suppose that Sextus or Pyrrhonism established links with Methodism. His remarks are directed against a dogmatic tendency in Empirical medicine, rather than Empirical medicine as a whole. Nondogmatic forms of Empiricism that escape Pyrhonism's skeptical strictures against dogmatism remain a fruitful subject of study and are likely to throw light on the Pyrrhonists' conception of their skeptical way of life.

We are indebted to Sextus for most of our knowledge of Pyrrhonian skepticism. His works became widely available in Latin translation in the latter half of the sixteenth century and engaged the attention of a wide range of thinkers in the formative period of modern philosophy.

BIBLIOGRAPHY: Texts in R. G. Bury, ed. and tr., *Sextus Empiricus: Works*, 4 vols. (Loeb), London/Cambridge, MA, 1933–49; and H. Mutschmann and J. Mau, eds., *Sexti Empirici Opera*, 3 vols., Leipzig, 1914–58; vol. 4, K. Janácek, Indices, Leipzig, 1962. Allen, J., *ANRW* 2, 36.4, 1990, 2582–2607; Annas, J., and J. Barnes, trs., *Sextus Empiricus: Outlines of Scepticism*, Cambridge, 1994; Voelke, A.-J., ed., *Le Scepticisme Antique, Perspectives historiques et systematiques; Actes du Colloque International sur le scepticismen antique* (= *Cahiers de la Revue de Theologie et de Philosophie* 15), Lausanne, 1990.—*JAMES ALLEN*

SIMPLICIUS (c. 490–560 C.E.), native of Cilicia in Asia Minor. *Neoplatonist philosopher, disciple of *Ammonius (d. c. 517) in Alexandria and of *Damascius (d. after 538) in Athens. We possess Simplicius' *commentaries on *Epictetus' *Handbook* and on *Aristotle's *Categories, De Caelo, De Anima*, and *Physics*. His commentaries on the first book of *Euclid's *Elements*, Aristotle's *Meteorologica* and *Metaphysics*, on *Iamblichus' writings on the *Pythagorean sect, and on *Plato's *Phaedo*, as well as his *Summary* of *Theophrastus' *Physics*, are lost.

According to Agathias (*History* 2.30.3ff.) Simplicius took refuge in Persia along with a group of pagan Greek philosophers led by his teacher Damascius, in the wake of measures taken by Justinian in 529 against pagans and other heretics. There they stayed until a peace treaty was signed (in 531) between Justinian and the Persian king Chosroes. At the latter's initiative, the treaty contained a provision permitting the philosophers to return to the Byzantine empire and to live there undisturbed. Recent work by Tardieu (see bibliography) has enabled us to identify Simplicius' place of residence after 531 as Harran (Carrhae), a city located on the Persian border and within Persian sphere of influence. It was there that Simplicius wrote all of his commentaries.

All of Simplicius' work bears the stamp of the philosophical system of his teacher Damascius, from whom he only rarely distances himself. Hence Simplicius' philosophy, even in his commentary on Epictetus' *Handbook*, is representative of Greek Neoplatonism in its final, most sophisticated stage of development. Damascius had made the already very complex ontological system of *Proclus even more complicated by moving closer at many points to the philosophy of Iamblichus, but he made constant use of the works of Proclus—by criticizing them—as the point of departure for his own philosophy. We do not have any work by Simplicius like Damascius' commentary on Plato's *Parmenides*—the subject of which made possible a detailed presentation of his ontological system—but we can recognize in Simplicius' various commentaries scattered developments that make clear that he adhered to Damascius' system and borrowed the latter's peculiar philosophical terminology. We should also not hesitate to attribute to Damascius' influence Simplicius' tendency to follow very closely in his own commentaries (*In Cat.* and *In De Anima*) those of Iamblichus when these were extant.

Simplicius' various commentaries, each conceived of as a spiritual exercise, are inscribed in the pedagogical program established by the Neoplatonists for the study of philosophy and adapt themselves, each in a strict manner, to a specific level of knowledge attained by students. The commentaries on the treatises of Aristotle interpret these works from a typically Neoplatonic perspective in that they assume a fundamental unity in the philosophies of Aristotle and Plato, all the while affirming the superiority of the latter over the former. His commentary on Epictetus' *Handbook* is propaedeutic in character. Philosophical studies proper started with Aristotle's *Categories*, and the commentary on that work is explicitly addressed to beginners. The Aristotelian treatises, *De Caelo*, and *De Anima* as well as *Physics*, fall under the category of "Physical Writings" within the group of "Theoretical Writings," and Simplicius' commentaries on them would thus be geared to a sufficiently advanced level of knowledge on the part of the students. Discussion of *theological problems must commence with the commentary on Aristotle's *Metaphysics* (of which we have only a few fragments), but could only take its full scope in the Platonic cycle of studies with the commentary on the *Parmenides*. For these reasons we should not expect to find a complete unfolding of Simplicius' system of *metaphysics in his commentary on the *Categories*, his propaedeutic commentary, or even in his other commentaries that have come down to us, although in the latter we shall find many more details that bear on this system.

It is impossible to determine whether Simplicius' thought underwent an evolution. That would only be possible if we had several commentaries of his on the same treatises conceived at different times. For the vocabulary as well as the problems raised were determined on the one hand by the content of the treatise being commented on, and on the other by the pedagogical concerns of the late Neoplatonists who assigned to each treatise a specific purpose that determined the framework of its interpretation.

BIBLIOGRAPHY: Texts in I. Hadot, ed., *Simplicius: Commentaire sur le Manuel d'Épictète, Introduction et édition critique du texte grec*, Leiden, 1996; *In Cat.* in *CAG* vol. 8; *In De Caelo* in *CAG* vol. 7; *In De Anima* in *CAG* vol. 11; *In Phys.* in *CAG* vols. 9 and 10. Hadot, I., in R. Sorabji, ed., *Aristotle Transformed*, London, 1990, 275–303; also *Le problème du néoplatonisme alexandrin: Hiéroclès et Simplicius*, Paris, 1978; also *Simplicius, Commentaire sur les Catégories*, fasc. 1, Leiden, 1990 and fasc. 3 (by C. Luna), 1990 (fasc. 4, Paris, 1997); also *Simplicius, Commentaire sur le Manuel d'Epictète*, Leiden, 1996; also in H. J. Blumenthal, ed., *Soul and the Structure of Being in*

Late Neoplatonism, Liverpool, 1982, 46–70; M. Tardieu, *Les paysages reliques*, Louvain/Paris, 1990; also in Hadot, ed., *Simplicius: Sa vie, son œuvre, sa survie*, Paris 1987, 40–57.—*ILSETRAUT HADOT*

SKEPTICISM, Ancient. Two schools or movements in Greek philosophy are commonly referred to by the title "skepticism": (i) *Academic Skepticism, whose most prominent members are *Arcesilaus (c. 315–240 B.C.E.) and *Carneades (214–129/8 B.C.E.), and (ii) *Pyrrhonian Skepticism, which originated in the ideas and activities of *Pyrrho of Elis (c. 360–270 B.C.E.), but which became a recognizable philosophical tradition only when *Aenesidemus (1st cent. B.C.E.) initiated a method of thought claiming Pyrrho as its inspiration. The best-known member of this later Pyrrhonist tradition and the only skeptic of whom we have works surviving intact is *Sextus Empiricus (probably 2nd cent. C.E.). The term "skeptic" itself seems to have arisen in the later Pyrrhonian period. But already in antiquity it was also applied to the Academics, and there is enough in common between the two movements to justify this usage. Skepticism, in the ancient context, consists in suspension of judgment (*epochê*), that is, in a withdrawal from all beliefs. There is room for debate about how strongly the notion of belief is to be understood here, and the answer may well vary from one skeptic to another. But on any reading, it is important to distinguish this from skepticism in the modern sense, which is usually taken to consist in a *denial* of the possibility of knowledge in some domain. For the ancients, the latter position would be classified as "negative dogmatism" rather than skepticism; an ancient skeptic refuses to "dogmatize," or to subscribe to definite commitments, positively or negatively. (Instead, according to Sextus, he continues to investigate all possibilities, hence the term "skeptic"—literally, "inquirer.") By the same token, those Greek thinkers prior to the official skeptical movements who seem to have doubted or denied the possibility of knowledge, at least in certain domains—most obviously *Xenophanes, *Democritus, *Socrates, and the *Cyrenaics—should not be regarded as forerunners of ancient skepticism in any strict sense. Several of the skeptics later showed a good deal of interest in them; but this may be explained primarily by their usefulness as counterweights to the "positive" dogmatism of the majority of philosophers, rather than by their having properly exemplified the skeptical outlook.

Pyrrho is traditionally regarded as the first skeptic. There is considerable debate, however, over the exact character of his philosophy and even over whether the term "skeptic," as normally understood, applies to him. He wrote nothing, and the evidence for his ideas is scarce. The most important text relating to his general philosophical attitudes (*Aristocles, cited in Eus. *PE* 14.18.1–5) has been read both as expressing the standard skeptical *epochê* and as advancing a *metaphysical thesis to the effect that things are by nature radically indeterminate. In the latter case it is less obvious why the later Pyrrhonians would have seen him as a forerunner. However, in either case the passage makes clear that Pyrrho did not trust "sensations or opinions" to reveal the way things really are, and that from ceasing to trust them he derived an attitude of "freedom from disturbance" (*ataraxia*); the distinctive combination of these two points may well have been enough for Aenesidemus and his successors to have viewed Pyrrho as a kindred spirit. Other biographical anecdotes from *Diogenes Laertius and elsewhere confirm that his imperturbability was extraordinary, and several fragments of his disciple *Timon praise Pyrrho for not inquiring into, or otherwise concerning himself about, physical or other theoretical matters. It is possible that, as Diogenes implies (9.61), Pyrrho was influenced by the "naked philosophers" whom he encountered while traveling in India with Alexander the Great's campaigns; but this is far from certain, since his ideas also appear to have numerous points of contact with earlier Greek philosophy.

Pyrrho seems to have had no immediate successors beyond Timon. Skepticism next appears in the Academy under Arcesilaus. He too wrote nothing, as did Carneades. He is said to have declared that nothing can be known, which may sound like "negative dogmatism." But we are also told that he practiced *epochê* "because of the oppositions of arguments" (D.L. 4.28) and that he regularly brought about such oppositions by arguing against whatever thesis anyone might propose. His most prominent opponent was the *Stoic *Zeno of Citium, and the claim that nothing can be known should probably be understood as a rejoinder, in this spirit, to Zeno's views concerning the "cognitive impression." According to Sextus (*HP* 1.232–233), Arcesilaus proclaimed, with dubious consistency, that *epochê* was good and that it was the end (*telos*). This may be a misinterpretation, but *Cicero also suggests (*Acad.* 2.77) that his enthusiasm for *epochê* was exceptional. Yet neither Arcesilaus nor any other Academic suggests that the result of *epochê* is *ataraxia*, or any other desirable state of mind; this is perhaps the point at which Academics and Pyrrhonians most clearly diverge. Nonetheless, it was important for Arcesilaus, as for any other ancient skeptic, to show that living a life while suspending judgment was at least possible. And in response to the charge, probably from the Stoics, that *epochê* ruled out rational choice, and indeed action of any kind, Arcesilaus argued that one can direct one's actions by reference to "the reasonable" (*eulogon*), rather than on the basis of any supposed "cognitive impressions," and that, contrary to the Stoic contention, action does not require assent—that is, commitment to the truth of some proposition—and hence is compatible with *epochê*.

Arcesilaus' skepticism marked a major change of direction for the Academy. Nonetheless, as was noticed in antiquity, some antecedents for the skeptical stance can certainly be found in *Plato, and it is not unlikely that these influenced Arcesilaus. It is also possible that Arcesilaus received some inspiration from Pyrrho; at any rate, this is implied by both Timon and the contemporary Stoic *Aristo of Chios.

Little is known about the Academy between Arcesilaus and Carneades, though it may be assumed that a generally skeptical orientation was maintained. Carneades' outlook parallels that of Arcesilaus in many ways, though the evidence suggests that it was developed with greater sophistication and with greater awareness of possible or sometimes actual objections; he also seems to have tackled a greater range of subjects, and to have directed his arguments against a wider range of "dogmatic" philosophers. A major focus of his attention, however, was the criterion of truth, and he argued in detail that there was no such thing. Again, this need not be seen as "negative dogmatism"; it may be read either as designed to be juxtaposed with positive arguments (primarily Stoic ones), the intended result being *epochê*, or as a purely *ad hominem* argument, designed to show the Stoics the unwelcome consequences to which *they* are committed, given certain premises which they accept. Some of Carneades' successors in the Academy interpreted him as saying that it is permissible to hold opinions. But *Clitomachus, the student whom he himself declared to have understood him best, denied that he permitted this deviation from *epochê*—instead, he "rid our minds of assent" (Cic. *Acad.* 2.108)—and this testimony should be preferred. There is, however, scarcely any explicit mention by Carneades of *epochê* or its merits; this reticence may be designed to avoid the criticism of self-refutation to which Arcesilaus may have been liable (see above). In answer to the question how choices can be made and a recognizably human life lived, in the absence of a criterion of truth, Carneades offered an elaborate account of rational choice centered around the notion of the "convincing impression" (*pithanê phatasia*); in answer to the question how action is possible at all without belief, he argued that one can "approve" or "follow" an impression—that is, let oneself be guided by it for the purposes of action—without committing oneself to its truth.

Clitomachus continued Carneades' skeptical position and wrote a large number of books explaining it. But others in the Academy following Carneades ceased to maintain a strict *epochê*; *Metrodorus of Stratonicea and *Philo of Larissa allowed the holding of opinions, provided one admitted their status as mere opinions (and also, as noted above, claimed that Carneades had allowed this). At some point in the first century B.C.E. Aenesidemus initiated a new skeptical movement, purporting to follow in the footsteps of Pyrrho and setting itself against the increasingly nonskeptical Academy. It has generally been thought that Aenesidemus was himself originally a member of the Academy, but this has recently been challenged. The evidence for Aenesidemus' own position is sparse and somewhat confusing. We are told by Photius, in a passage summarizing Aenesidemus' *Pyrrhôneioi logoi* (*Bibliotheca* 169b18–170b3), that he described the Pyrrhonists as "free from all dogma," and to have said that the Pyrrhonist "determines nothing." But the same passage also seems to suggest that he asserted a form of relativism which Sextus, at least according to his official presentation of Pyrrhonism (at the beginning of *HP* 1), would have repudiated as dogmatic. Moreover, numerous references in Sextus suggest that Aenesidemus, at least at some point in his life, was in some sense a follower of *Heraclitus. However, in common with both Pyrrho and Sextus, he did identify *ataraxia* as the outcome of his purported lack of dogma; and he was the originator of two of the sets of Modes, or standardized forms of skeptical argumentation, which figure prominently in Sextus' introduction to Pyrrhonism.

It is doubtful whether the later Pyrrhonists were either numerous enough or sufficiently united in time, place, and outlook, to be considered a "school"; few Pyrrhonists besides Aenesidemus and Sextus are known to us even by name, and Sextus' works seem to draw largely on sources from the first century B.C.E. or earlier. There does appear, however, to have been a substantial connection between Pyrrhonism and the school of Medical Empiricism. According to Diogenes (9.116), Sextus taught a Pyrrhonist called Saturninus; but it is not clear how far into late antiquity Pyrrhonism survived as a live philosophical option.

Sextus' surviving writings are voluminous (fourteen books). A large proportion of them consists of summaries of earlier philosophies, and for this reason Sextus is often a valuable source of evidence for thinkers from Presocratic to Hellenistic times. His aim, however, is not neutral reporting. Rather, he assembles these extensive arrays of conflicting positions on the same topic, often supplemented by his own arguments calling into question the very concepts or the very existence of the objects with which they deal (for example, *time, place, or the criterion of truth), in order to produce a situation of what he calls "equal strength" (*isostheneia*), that is, a situation in which many incompatible views on the same subject strike one as equally plausible. The effect of this, he claims, will be *epochê*, followed by *ataraxia*. The same result is achieved by the various sets of Modes, which provide schemes for generating opposing impressions or arguments on a very wide range of subjects. Unlike Aenesidemus and Pyrrho (as far as we can tell), Sextus explains *why epochê* produces *ataraxia*; his main point is that only through *epochê* is one rid of the belief that some things are good and other things bad, and that this belief brings with it untold worries about getting or keeping the good things and avoiding the bad. As for the recurring question how the skeptic can live without beliefs, Sextus answers that this can be done by "following appearances"; it is a matter of some dispute how this is to be interpreted and whether this procedure is ultimately sustainable.

It should be clear from the foregoing that ancient skepticism, in both its Academic and its later Pyrrhonian forms, is not a conclusion but an attitude of mind; the skeptic is led to suspend judgment, but does not argue (at least, if he is being consistent) that *one ought to* suspend judgment. And it is an attitude that requires ongoing intellectual activity to maintain. To be a skeptic, then, is a long-term project—a project that, according to the Pyrrhonians, actually improved the quality of one's life, but that, according to the Academics as well, at least needed to be incorporated into one's life.

BIBLIOGRAPHY: Annas, J., and J. Barnes, *The Modes of Scepticism*, Cambridge, 1985; Brochard, V., *Les Sceptiques grecs*,[2] Paris, 1923; Burnyeat, M., ed., *The Skeptical Tradition*, Berkeley, 1983; Decleva Caizzi, F., *Pirrone testimonianze*, Naples, 1981; Ioppolo, A. M., *Opinione e Scienza: il dibattito tra Stoici e Accademici nel III e nel II secolo a. C.*, Naples, 1986; Janácek, K., *Sextus Empiricus' Sceptical Methods*, Prague, 1972; Stough, C., *Greek Skepticism*, Berkeley, 1969.—RICHARD BETT

SOCRATES (469–399 B.C.E.). Athenian philosopher. Socrates was born in Alopeke, one of the demes of Attica, in 469. His father, Sophroniscus, was probably a stonemason; his mother, Phaenarete, may have been a midwife. Nothing is known of Socrates' youth, but it is likely that he was schooled in his father's trade. At some point, Socrates married Xanthippe, whose name suggests that she was from an aristocratic family. *Plato says little about their relationship, although *Xenophon indicates that Xanthippe was quarrelsome and that the marriage was not a happy one. Socrates had three sons, two of whom were still youths and one an infant at the time of his death, all presumably with Xanthippe. Whether Socrates was married more than once, as some later biographers claim, cannot be known, though the silence of Plato and Xenophon on this point seems telling.

Socrates' physical appearance made him easily recognized on the streets of Athens. His snub nose, bulging eyes, massive forehead, and protuberant stomach combined to make him strikingly unattractive. He may also have had a peculiar gait and a disconcerting habit of darting his eyes back and forth. Showing no concern for his manner of dress, Socrates often walked the streets barefoot, wearing the same cloak. Wealth was of little or no concern to Socrates, and his poverty is often underscored by ancient writers. Nowhere is he described as engaged in gainful work. From the fact that he served in the hoplite ranks during the Peloponnesian War, however, one can infer that Socrates was probably not destitute.

According to Plato, Socrates was a model soldier, serving at Potidaea shortly after the outbreak of the war and later at Delion and Amphipolis. If Plato's remarks are to be believed, Socrates distinguished himself by his quiet endurance and courage in the most hostile circumstances.

Though unconcerned with either wealth or power, Socrates seems to have been on friendly terms with some of Athens' most influential citizens. He was also regularly accompanied in public by wealthy young men, who, according to Plato, enjoyed Socrates' trenchant refutations of the views of others. It is likely that Socrates developed an intimate relationship with at least one of his followers, the notorious Alcibiades, though the exact nature of the relationship, how long it lasted, and why it ended cannot be determined. At some point, Socrates' admirers probably included *Critias and Charmides, men who would lead the Thirty Tyrants during their murderous reign in Athens immediately after the end of the war.

Just when Socrates began to concern himself with philosophical questions cannot be known. In the *Phaedo* (96a6ff.), Plato writes that as a "young man" Socrates was interested in "inquiry about nature" and the causes of change and permanence, but soon abandoned such investigations because they failed to explain why things are the way they are. Although commentators mostly agree that the references made in this passage to the theory of Forms cannot represent the views of the historical Socrates, they are divided over whether or not the historical Socrates ever had a serious interest in natural *science. Be that as it may, it is very likely that he had a considerable reputation as an intellectual by the time he was in his mid-forties. Otherwise, *Aristophanes' *Clouds*, first produced in 423, could not have used a character named "Socrates" to lampoon the "new intellectualism" that was by then well entrenched in Athens.

For Socrates, philosophy was not solely a matter of refuting the views of others and showing thereby that they were not really wise. Ancient sources agree that Socrates had definite philosophical views of his own, many of which conflicted with commonly received opinion. There is, however, no reason to think that Socrates made acceptance of any of his views a condition of carrying on discussion with him. Thus, although he had a band of loyal followers, it would be misleading to say that he had "students" or that he and his admirers constituted a school. His discussions were conducted informally, often in public settings such as the agora.

Plato cites two instances in which Socrates, at great risk to his personal safety, defied those in power. The first occurred when popular sentiment called for the ten generals who managed the Athenian victory at the Arginusian islands to be tried as a group for dereliction. Socrates, who happened to be presiding over the Council at the time, refused to participate, believing that such a trial was illegal. The second occurred when Socrates refused an order by the Thirty Tyrants to participate in what he considered to be the wrongful arrest of one Leon of Salamis. Socrates was not arrested himself, presumably because shortly after his defiance, the Thirty were overthrown and the democracy restored.

In 399, three years after the democracy was restored, Socrates was placed on trial in a Heliastic court for violating the law proscribing impiety. Why Socrates was prosecuted at this particular time is not clear. *Diogenes Laertius reports that Favorinus claims to have seen the specific charges, sworn against Socrates by one Meletus, recorded in the Metroon: "Socrates is guilty of not believing in the gods the city believes in, and of introducing other, new divinities; and he is guilty of corrupting the youth. The penalty is death." Plato, Xenophon, and perhaps others wrote speeches that purport to be what Socrates said in his defense. Commentators have usually held that of the two extant versions, Plato's and Xenophon's, the former is more likely to be closer to what Socrates actually said at his trial. It is perhaps significant that Plato claims to have been present, whereas Xenophon was in Asia Minor and hence knew about the speech only secondhand.

Xenophon comments that the speech Socrates gave in his defense was characterized by "boastfulness" (*megalêgoria*), which Xenophon explains by claiming that Socrates simply did not wish to live any longer. Although Plato's version does not explicitly address the question of why Socrates gave the kind of speech he did, many commentators have argued that Plato shares Xenophon's view that Socrates simply did not make any serious attempt to persuade the jury to release him. Recently, however, this reading of Plato's version of the speech has been vigorously challenged, principally on the ground that some of Socrates' most basic commitments require that he do everything in his power, consistent with his other principles, to persuade the jury to allow him to continue what he calls his "mission" on behalf of the god.

Although the actual charges brought against Socrates pertained to his alleged violation of religious standards, some scholars have argued that the principal motive for prosecuting Socrates was to punish him for his pro-oligarchic sentiments, charges that the prosecution would have been prevented from advancing by the conditions of the amnesty passed in 403. These same scholars tend to argue that Socrates refused to respond to any distinctly political accusations against him because he was in fact guilty and had no defense. A number of recent studies have shown, however, that there is no credible evidence that the motivation behind Socrates' trial was in any sense political. Socrates was apparently surprised by the closeness of the vote to convict him. When it came time to propose a counter-penalty to Meletus' proposal that he be put to death, Socrates eschewed several penalties, including exile, that the jury might well have accepted and proposed instead a fine of thirty minae, to be paid with the assistance of his friends. Contrary to what is often written about Socrates' proposed fine, it was, in fact, a considerable sum of money. But in light of Socrates' vow to return to the streets of Athens to carry on his philosophical examinations, the very thing for which he had been convicted, it is not surprising that the jury rejected his proposal. Socrates was led away to the prison of the Eleven, where, again according to Plato, a month after his conviction he was executed by drinking a poison extracted from hemlock.

Sources. The difficulty of arriving at any fuller view of the historical Socrates has become known as the "Socratic problem." Because Socrates himself wrote nothing—or, at any rate, nothing that has survived—any adequate account of his life and thought must rely on the reports of those who actually knew him or who were in a position to write knowledgeably about him. Apparently, "*Sokratikoi logoi*," or writings involving Socrates, were not uncommon in the years following his death. But much of what was written has been lost, and works by later authors such as Diodorus Siculus (c. 40 C.E.), *Plutarch (c. 50 C.E.), and Diogenes Laertius (c. 200–250 C.E.) are of doubtful accuracy. Their reports, though interesting, are likely to be infected with apocrypha, developed over many years, about the life and views of such a notorious figure in Athenian history. Substantial writings by three of Socrates' contemporaries, Aristophanes, Xenophon, and Plato, have survived the ages, however. Commentators agree that it is with their testimony, if anywhere, that the search for the historical Socrates must begin. Unfortunately, when taken together, the Socratic writings of these three contemporaries hardly form a consistent picture of the man or his thought.

The "Socrates" of Aristophanes' *Clouds* is the self-aggrandizing, amoral proprietor of a "think-shop," where gullible students pay to listen to ridiculous quibbles and pseudo-scientific speculations. Until recently, commentators have dismissed Aristophanes' character as a source of information about the historical Socrates on the ground that his "Socrates" is a composite of many thinkers in what is obviously a lampoon of the "new intellectualism." A number of contemporary commentators have challenged the traditional assessment, pointing out that even if the character is a composite, no comedic effect could have been achieved if the character's challenge to traditional Athenian values did not bear some, even if exaggerated, resemblance to to that of the historical Socrates. Indeed, recent scholarship has demonstrated the many similarities between Aristophanes' character and the person described in the pages of Plato and Xenophon.

Also problematic as reliable sources are the four works purporting to be about the historical Socrates by Xenophon: *Memorabilia, Oeconomicus, Symposium*, and *Apology of Socrates*. The fact that Xenophon's Socratic writings are transparently apologetic calls into question the objectivity of their reporting. Moreover, many aspects of Xenophon's accounts simply fail to square with important, well-established facts about Socrates' life. First, Xenophon's Socrates is so dull and innocuous that it is impossible to see either why any bright, serious, philosophically minded person such as Plato would have been attracted to Socrates or why an Athenian jury eventually found it necessary to convict him of serious crimes. Not only does Xenophon's Socrates mouth commonly held moral and religious precepts, but he often dispenses advice on such mundane matters as the maintenance of one's property. When Xenophon's Socrates does propound a philosophical argument, it is rarely interesting or subtle. Occasionally, Xenophon's Socrates attacks democratic institutions, but his criticisms hardly constitute evidence that Socrates was a danger to the city's democratic regime.

Many contemporary scholars accept two independent theses regarding Plato's early *dialogues: First, the "Socrates" who appears in Plato's early dialogues (in alphabetical order: *Apology, Charmides, Crito, Euthydemus, Euthyphro, Gorgias, Hippias Major, Hippias Minor, Ion, Laches, Lysis, Menexenus, Protagoras*, and *Republic* 1, with the *Meno* counting as a transition to the middle-period dialogues) represents a substantially different philosophy and philosophical style than we find expressed by the "Socrates" in Plato's middle and late periods. Second, Plato's early dialogues constitute the solution to the "Socratic problem." The "Socrates" of the middle and late period, on the other hand, expresses Plato's own views, many of which—for example, the theory of separated Forms—simply had not occurred to the historical Socrates.

Like Xenophon's, the Socrates of Plato's early dialogues is portrayed as being far more concerned than his fellow citizens about moral *virtue and the care of the *soul. But Plato's Socrates is strikingly different from Xenophon's in several important ways: First, Plato's Socrates is concerned, almost exclusively, with moral questions. Second, Plato's Socrates often gives disingenuously unfavorable assessments of his own abilities and disingenuously favorable assessments of the abilities of his interlocutors. Third, Plato's Socrates typically makes his points by means of well-crafted arguments and insists that his interlocutors do the same. Finally, according to Xenophon but not to Plato, the foundation of Socrates' conception of virtue is *enkrateia*, self-mastery.

Commentators who take the Socrates of Plato's early dialogues to be the solution to the "Socratic problem" can point to the fact that Plato's characterization explains precisely what Xenophon's characterization cannot: why other serious philosophers were attracted to Socrates and why Socrates was tried and put to death for his philosophical activities. If Plato's characterization is at all accurate, the historical Socrates was not merely adept at pointing out the foibles of those who pretended to know what they did not, but he was also working on a coherent moral philosophy that wove together powerful and novel theories of virtue, moral *psychology, moral *epistemology, and moral methodology. But because his activities were at odds with the unreflective moral education of the day, his philosophizing appeared to threaten the established values.

The same commentators are apt to point to Aristotle as corroborating the view that the Socrates of the early dialogues represents the historical Socrates. Aristotle frequently seems to distinguish between the views of the historical Socrates and those of Plato, and references to the former fit well with the views defended by the Socrates of the early dialogues. Using Aristotle's testimony in this way, however, requires that the assumption that Aristotle was in a position to know the difference between what Socrates believed and what Plato believed. Not all commentators have been willing to make this assumption, however, believing instead that Aristotle relied exclusively on Plato's early dialogues for his evidence about what the historical Socrates believed. If so, even if Aristotle sincerely believed he was reporting what the historical Socrates thought, he may, in fact, only have been reporting Plato's own developing views, views Plato put into the mouth of a highly fictionalized character he called "Socrates."

Method and Teaching. Taking Plato as our principal authority, we discover that Socrates was a man with a moral mission, which he supposed was given him through an oracle given by the god (Apollo) at Delphi, who answered "no" to (his friend) Chaerephon's question, "Is anyone wiser than Socrates?" (*Ap.* 20e8–21a7). On learning the news, Socrates was astonished; he was unaware of having any wisdom of any kind (*Ap.* 21b4–5). Investigating the meaning of the oracle, he discovered by questioning those who had a reputation for wisdom that, indeed, none were wiser than he: Either they had no wisdom of any kind, or they had some modest forms but were ignorant of other, more important things, and (worse) were also ignorant of their ignorance. Believing that the god led him to this realization, Socrates concluded that the god had actually given him a mission: He must examine people relentlessly, demonstrating their ignorance to them and encouraging them to care more for virtue than for the reputation and wealth they so prized (*Ap.* 29d7–e3). Above all, he saw his mission to require him to exhort all to open their lives to examination, for "the unexamined life is not worth living for human beings" (*Ap.* 38a5–6).

Socrates performed his examinations and his exhortations through what has come to be known as the *elenchus*, or "elenctic method," by which Socrates would demonstrate the inherent absurdities or incoherencies in his interlocutors' thoughts on *ethical subjects. Typically, these demonstrations would begin when the interlocutor explicitly expressed, or in some other way betrayed, a point of view Socrates would target as suspect. By patiently eliciting premises from among what he insisted must be his interlocutor's other sincerely held views, Socrates would show how the targeted view did not cohere with the interlocutor's other views. The results of these demonstrations were not always what Socrates sought: Sometimes his interlocutors did give up their incoherent positions; often, however, they ended up unrepentant and annoyed, thinking that some kind of trick had been played on them.

Although one often hears of the "Socratic method" of teaching, there are a number of reasons to wonder whether Socrates thought of himself either as a teacher or as employing anything like a "method" in his elenctic philosophizing. He explicitly and repeatedly denies being a teacher in the *Apology*, for example (at 19d8–20c3, 33a5–b6); and even when he is seen as a teacher in more friendly circumstances, he invariably denies it (see, e.g., *Chrm.* 165b5–c1, 167b6–7, 169a7–8, 175e5–176a5; *La.* 186a3–c5, 186d8–e3), on the grounds that he has no wisdom to offer through teaching. He often claims not to know the answers to his own questions (e.g., at *Chrm.* 165b5–c1; *Rep.* 1.337e4–6, 354c1–3, and esp. *Hp. Mi.* 372a6–e6, 376b8–c6). Those who use the "Socratic method" typically do know the answers to their leading questions. Moreover, since Socrates always insists that the interlocutor answer with only the interlocutor's own sincerely held opinions, Socrates can hardly work his way through arguments in some methodical way. He must always improvise, always argue *ad hominem*. Experience in such arguments no doubt made Socrates into a remarkably versatile and adept arguer, but his deftness seems unlikely to have resulted from anything that could count as a "method."

There is much discussion in the literature about how much positive philosophical doctrine, if any, Socrates thinks he can derive from elenctic argument. What has come to be known as "the problem of the *elenchus*" is that Socrates often acts and speaks as if he has proved something in an elenctic argument, though the form of the argument seems to warrant only the conclusion that some one or more of the premises Socrates elicits from his interlocutor conflict with the proposition originally targeted for "examination."

Some scholars have attempted explanations according to which Socrates' arguments may be seen as deriving from unstated and very powerful assumptions that would secure his conclusions as having been proven by the arguments. These theories have not been met with general acceptance. Other, far more negative assessments have insisted that Socrates did not seek to generate positive doctrinal results at all; but these approaches seem to underestimate the degree to which Socrates' own expressions of confidence in certain issues seem to derive from his experiences in elenctic argumentation. More likely, perhaps, are views that allow Socrates to gain increasing confidence in his conclusions as his *ad hominem* examinations always seem to yield the same results, no matter what premises his interlocutors seem prepared to accept—certain points of view, that is, begin to reveal themselves as untenable no matter what one's other positions seem to be (see *Grg.* 508e6–509a7). Still, no matter how much he may think he gains in philosophical insight from elenctic argument, it is also clear that he does not regard it as a path to the wisdom he persistently disclaims having. After all, though an exemplar of the "examined life" he exhorts his fellow Athenians to live, he none the less continues to confess his ignorance even in his old age.

Knowledge and Wisdom. It has puzzled many commentators, however, that Socrates could so persistently profess his own ignorance but nonetheless occasionally make knowledge claims of his own and also grant such claims to others. On the one hand, he claims, on the authority of the Delphic oracle, to be the wisest of men, but then shows that the substance of his wisdom is only that he alone recognizes that he is "in truth worth nothing in respect to wisdom" (*Ap.* 20e8–23b4). But if the best one can hope to achieve is knowledge of one's own ignorance, why is it that we find Socrates also willing to say that he knows various things, including some things that must surely count as significant moral truths (see, e.g. *Ap.* 29b6–9, 37b2–8; *Euthyd.* 293b7–8, 297a1)? Moreover, Socrates sometimes seems prepared to concede that others, too, have knowledge (see, e.g. *Ap.* 22c9–d4; *Grg.* 512b1–2; *Ion* 532d8–e3). Some scholars have tried to downplay the apparent conflict in such claims by claiming (contrary to what he explicitly says) that when Socrates makes and grants knowledge claims, he *really* means only to claim something like *true belief*, which falls short of knowledge. More sophisticated and promising interpretations have tried to offer ways in which Socrates could mean different things by "knowledge" when he disclaims it, on the one hand, and claims and grants it to others, on the other. One influential argument had held that Socrates distinguishes between certain knowledge and elenctic knowledge, where the warrants for the former are infallible and those for the latter are only elenctic and fallible. But it remains a problem for those inclined to this view that, in fact, none of the knowledge claims Socrates makes or grants to others are tied in any of the early dialogues to elenctic arguments. There must be one or more other sources of knowledge, for Socrates.

It does seem likely, however, that Socrates did hold some view that would distinguish between kinds of knowledge, only some (or just one) of which would qualify as the wisdom he disclaims. Other sorts of knowledge certainly are available to human beings, including the knowledge had by craftsmen (see *Ap.* 22c9–d4), the knowledge involved in perfectly ordinary skills, such as swimming (*Grg.* 511c4–5), perhaps something like "common knowledge" (see *Ion* 532d8–e3), and possibly other sorts, as well. But none of these sorts of knowledge are what Socrates disclaims when he makes his famous confession of ignorance. Scholars have distinguished between expert and nonexpert knowledge, but what appears to be at the heart of the important distinction is whatever qualifies some instance of knowledge as an instance of, or as deriving from, *wisdom*. Often enough, this is explicitly the sort of knowledge Socrates says he lacks. It is fair to say that he would not regard any of the less distinguished sorts of knowledge as the kind of wisdom no human being seems to have. Only "the god," he says, "is truly wise" (*Ap.* 23a5–6).

Ethics. There is general agreement among scholars that Socrates embraces "eudaimonism," the view that something is good only in so far as it makes its possessor better off with respect to *happiness (*eudaimonia*). Thus, when Socrates says that one should always pursue virtue (*Ap.* 28b5–9), he is prepared to defend his claim on the ground that virtue is always a good. Scholars continue to dispute, however, about Socrates' conception of the relationship between virtue and happiness and about whether virtue in some way guarantees happiness. Citing Socrates' remarks about pleasure and the good in the *Protagoras* (351b3ff.), some commentators argue that the dialogue reveals that Socrates actually embraces hedonism and, thus, takes virtue to be of instrumental value only. The prevailing view among commentators, however, is that this is a misguided reading of the *Protagoras*, for in the *Gorgias* (495e1–499b3), Socrates quite explicitly rejects hedonism. But if Socrates of the early dialogues does not endorse hedonism, many commentators argue, he must think that that virtue is either the sole constituent of *eudaimonia* or that it is such a dominant constituent that anyone who possessed moral virtue must be happy.

Counting against the constitutive view of the value of virtue is the comparison Socrates frequently draws between virtue and various crafts, or *technai*, bodies of knowledge through which their possessors are able to produce *erga*, or products. Since all crafts owe their identification and their value to the *erga* they produce, any successful account of the relationship between happiness and virtue must show what the *ergon* of the *technê* of virtue is, how that product is related to happiness, and how the value of virtue is derivative from its product.

In *Republic* 1 (353d2–354a2), Socrates comments that the function of the soul is "management, rule, deliberation, and life" and that virtue enables the soul to perform its function well. Although he does not say just what the soul manages and rules, it is reasonable to think that Socrates has in mind the way a person lives. If so, and since Socrates sometimes identifies right action with "living well" (*eu zên*) and "acting well" (*eu prattein*; *Cri.* 48b5, *Grg.* 507c1–5) and "living well" and "acting well" with *eudaimonia* (e.g., *Cri.* 48b5, *Rep.* 1, 354a1–2), Socrates must take happiness to be the product of the *technê* of virtue and virtue itself to be the knowledge of how to produce that product. Understanding Socrates' conception of happiness as right activity produced by the *technê* of virtue also allows for an explanation of Socrates' claims that there can be goods, such as health and wealth, in addition to virtue (*Euthyd.* 279a1ff.), and that there can be evils, such as chronic disease and poverty, in addition to vice (*Grg.* 477c1–2, 512a2–b2, *Cri.* 47e3–5). Though goods other than virtue are not always good, when they are led by virtue, they invariably facilitate right activity (*Euthyd.* 281a6–b4), whereas the evils other than vice can make such activity either exceedingly difficult or impossible.

Socrates' apparent acceptance of evils other than vice presents a problem for the widely accepted view that he thinks virtue is actually sufficient for happiness. The sufficiency of virtue for happiness has been taken to be a direct implication of the famous remarks attributed to Socrates in Plato's *Apology* that "a better man cannot be harmed by a worse" (30c8–d4) and that "no evil comes to a good man in life or in death" (41d1–2). Both the *Crito* (47e3–5) and the *Gorgias* (512a2–b2), however, make clear that at least one nonmoral evil, disease, can actually make one's life not worth living. Since one could retain moral goodness and yet have one's life rendered not worth living by disease, the possession of virtue alone cannot guarantee *eudaimonia*. When Socrates says that a good man cannot be harmed or that a good person cannot be harmed by a worse person, he probably means that in so far as a person retains moral goodness, that person cannot be made vicious. The possession of moral goodness insulates one from suffering the one thing that is always evil and evil in virtue of nothing but itself.

The attribution to Socrates of the view that virtue is necessary for *eudaimonia* is also problematic. Scholars generally agree that, in spite of its material simplicity, Socrates counts his life as happy, for, as noted above, he equates happiness with right activity, and he regards himself as having scrupulously avoided injustice throughout his life (cf. *Ap.* 41c9–d2). But though he considers himself to be morally good, Socrates also he sees himself as lacking the very sort of moral knowledge required for virtue (*Ap.* 21b1–d7, *Euth.* 5a3–c7, *La.* 186b8–c5, *Grg.* 509c4–7). Moreover, if Socrates does not regard himself as happy, even though he thinks that his life is blameless, then he must also think that *eudaimonia* is simply out of the reach of human beings, a consequence it is doubtful Socrates could have accepted. One possibility is that Socrates distinguishes the sort of moral goodness he possesses from moral virtue and regards only the former as necessary for happiness.

Room for the distinction between moral goodness and moral virtue is created by Socrates' conviction that moral virtue is like a *technê*. If the virtuous are like true craftsmen in the relevant ways, they would be able to produce the moral *ergon* uniquely and unerringly. Moreover, a craftsman of virtue would be able both to give an account of how the moral *ergon* is produced and to produce that same knowledge in others. Socrates' goodness, of course, enables him to avoid the commission of most evils. But unlike someone with the craft of virtue, whose moral knowledge enables the production of a noble product without fail and who could teach others the moral craft, Socrates, guided only by his imperfect method of elenctic testing and the occasional help he receives from his *daimonion* (*Ap.* 31c7–d4, 40a4–6), can only see himself as extraordinarily fortunate to have avoided the commission of evils so consistently.

One of the most vexing features of Socrates' moral philosophy is his view of how the moral virtues are related to one another. It is uncontroversial that he holds the paradoxical view that the virtues always formed a unity at least in the sense that anyone who possessed one of the moral virtues also possessed each of the others. In the *Protagoras* (331a6ff.), however, Plato's Socrates suggests that in fact the virtues are "one thing," a claim that has led many commentators to the conclusion that Socrates believed that each of the virtue names—"justice," "courage," "temperance," "piety,' and "wisdom"—are really different names for the same power of the soul and that this power is knowledge of good and evil. The attribution of such a theory of the unity of the virtues to Socrates is complicated by Socrates' assertions in other dialogues (e.g., *La.* 190c8–d5, *Euth.* 11e7–12e2,) that the individual virtues, such as piety or courage, are proper parts of the whole of virtue and even proper parts of other individual virtues.

Attempts to reconcile these apparently incompatible views of how the virtues are related have generally taken the position that wisdom is, for Socrates, the preeminent virtue and that each of the other virtues must be understood as instances of wisdom. Some commentators are skeptical about whether reconciliation is possible, since a successful account must meet two seemingly incompatible conditions: It must show how the same cognitive condition (wisdom) can be identical with the whole of virtue and how the individual virtues can have *different* definitions that capture the essential properties of the individual virtues.

A second paradox associated with Socratic ethics is his rejection of *akrasia*, the moral failing of doing other than what one recognizes to be good for one. Socrates is driven to deny the existence of *akrasia* by his conviction that all action is motivated by desire aiming at and only at what the agent takes to be good or beneficial for the agent. What is crucial, then, to the explanation of why one action is chosen in preference to another is how the agent conceives of the two actions. As Socrates points out in the *Meno* (77d4–e4), agents frequently do what is in fact bad, or detrimental, to themselves, but no one does what is evil believing that what he or she is doing is bad for them. In light of Socrates' view about the nature of desire, and given his conviction that injustice is a great evil, it is clear why he insists, as he does in the *Gorgias*, that in acting unjustly the tyrant does not do what he really wants to do (468c4–e6).

Contrary to what is sometimes claimed, in denying the possibility of *akrasia* Socrates is not simply denying that *knowledge* of what is good can never be overcome by a desire for pleasure. Given his view that the single aim of all desire is the good of the agent and, thus, that there simply cannot be competing desires aimed at incommensurable goals, Socrates is equally committed to the view that one could never act for the sake of pleasure contrary to one's *belief* that such is not the better course of action. Socrates' conviction that *akrasia* never really occurs could be undone by a successful account of how desire can aim at an end other than what the agent takes to be good. Socrates' reply, however, would no doubt cite the fact that his interlocutors unfailingly assert that their own happiness is their only ultimate goal and that therefore they cannot desire anything which they know or believe will undermine their happiness.

Politics. In Plato's *Apology* (31c4–e1), Socrates explains that he has not participated in the political institutions of the city—his "divine sign" opposed such activity, and, he has decided, it is a good thing that it did, for had he done so, he would have perished and, thus, would have benefitted neither his fellow citizens nor himself. This remark stands in sharp contrast to the claim made in the *Gorgias* that Socrates regards himself as the only person who "tries to practice the true political craft" (521d1–8). Socrates justifies both claims on the ground that conventional politics, in which he refuses to participate, aims only at pleasing public audiences, whereas the "true political craft," which he tries to practice, "aims at improving the souls of citizens." In this sense, then, Socrates' philosophical "mission" is quintessentially political in so far as it consists in exhorting his fellow citizens to care most for "wisdom, truth and the perfection of their souls" (*Ap.* 29e1–2).

Although Socrates finds politics as it is usually practiced to be often harmful, commentators have often disputed which of the two competing political systems of his time, democracy and oligarchy, he favors. As

Xenophon portrays him, Socrates is often overtly hostile to democracy (*Mem.* 2.2.26, 3.1.4, 3.7.5–9, and 3.9.10). Commentators, however, have usually dismissed this aspect of Xenophon's portrait of Socrates on the ground that it is obviously colored by Xenophon's own antipathy for rule by the *demos*. But, citing the trenchant criticisms of the judgment of *hoi polloi* (e.g., *Ap.* 24e4–25c1, 31e1–32a3, *Cri.* 47a2–48c6, 49c10–d5, *Grg.* 471e2–472d1), his caustic remarks about famous democratic politicians (e.g., *Meno* 92d7–94e2, *Grg.* 515c4–517a6), and his apparent friendship with Critias and Charmides, some scholars have concluded that Plato's Socrates is also fundamentally antidemocratic.

The fact that Plato's Socrates criticizes democracy and democratic institutions is not evidence that he actually favored oligarchy, however. First, nowhere among his criticisms of democracy in Plato's dialogues does Socrates praise oligarchs or oligarchy. On the contrary, he is depicted just as often as showing contempt for oligarchic leaders. Moreover, whatever friendship may have existed between Socrates and Critias and Charmides, there is no evidence whatever that Socrates admired them for their political commitments, nor is there any evidence that a friendship continued after the Thirty began their violent campaigns at the end of the century. Indeed, as was noted above, on one occasion Socrates, no doubt at great risk to his own life, defied their orders. Moreover, one of his principal criticisms of democracy applies equally well to oligarchic forms of government. One of the basic features of Athenian democracy was the assumption that any citizen was suitable for holding office. Against this, Socrates frequently points out that one should always defer to expert opinion even if the vast majority of nonexperts oppose it. Since oligarchy is based on the principle that governing should be limited to "the few" who possess wealth and since the possession of wealth does not make one a political expert, Socrates is equally opposed to limiting governing to those who possess wealth.

In fact, there is at least some reason to think that Socrates favored democracy over oligarchy after all. He obviously believes that the regular practice of philosophical examination improves its practitioners and that the practice of philosophy is possible only if one is free to engage others in conversation and question whatever values are put forward, regardless of how precious those values are to those in power. But the right of free expression was fundamental to Athenian democracy. Indeed, he tells the jury at his trial that he is nowhere freer to engage in his customary pursuits than in Athens (*Ap.* 37c7–d2), which explains why of all the legal systems he could have lived under he chose the Athenian (*Cri.* 52e3–53a4).

Socrates' criticisms of democracy notwithstanding, in Plato's *Crito* Socrates argues that he has a moral obligation to abide by the conditions laid down by Athens' legal system. He imagines the personified laws of Athens declaring that if he escapes from prison he will be trying to destroy the laws and the entire city (51b1–2). His argument hinges on at least two points: (i) he has benefitted from living under the laws of Athens, and he was not coerced to live under the laws of Athens, and (ii) he was free to leave at any time during his seventy years there. By benefitting and not leaving, the laws argue, he has entered into a tacit agreement: "You must either persuade your country or do whatever it orders and submit to any punishment that it imposes ... in war, in court, and everywhere, you must do what the city and country commands, or you must persuade it as to what is really just" (*Cri.* 51b3–c1). It appears to follow from this agreement that were Socrates neither to obey nor persuade the laws to alter their commands, he would be guilty of trying to harm the city.

Commentators have often argued that if Socrates' position in the *Crito* requires that he obey the law if he fails to persuade, then he contradicts himself in two different ways: First, since it is possible that the laws could order that philosophy not be practiced in Athens and Socrates could fail to persuade the laws of the injustice of their command, he contradicts his vow made in the *Apology* (29c5–d6) never to abandon his mission to practice philosophy and, second, he contradicts his commitment, expressed earlier in the *Crito*, never to do what it is unjust.

The concerns about inconsistency may, however, be misplaced. First, the jury at Socrates' trial did not have the legal authority to forbid Socrates from engaging in philosophy as a condition of his release. Thus, any order by the jury to do so would itself have been illegal. Moreover, at least in Socrates' eyes, any law the Assembly might pass forbidding the practice of philosophy would contradict the law forbidding impiety, since Socrates believes that his philosophizing has been commanded by the god. Were such a situation to arise, Socrates obviously could not have obeyed one law without disobeying another. Perhaps it is (just barely) conceivable that the Athenian Assembly could rescind the law forbidding impiety and pass a law proscribing philosophy. It is important to notice, however, in order to generate a contradiction between the *Apology* and the *Crito* regarding disobedience of the law one is required to decide what Socrates would have done in such a far-fetched hypothetical situation, very far removed from the actual situation he faced at his trial and very far from the one in which he found himself in the *Crito*.

Finally, regarding the alleged contradiction within the *Crito* itself, it is important to bear in mind that the laws never claim that they are infallible. On the contrary, they recognize that there can be genuine disputes about what justice requires, and they encourage the citizen to show them when they are mistaken (51e7–52a2). When Socrates says that the city simply cannot survive if the citizen feels free to disobey the laws' commands, his point is that the very existence of the city requires that there be an *authoritative* adjudication of such disputes. Socrates' point seems to be that justice never requires of the individual citizen that he or she act contrary to an authoritative judgment of what is just. If so, there is a straightforward sense in which the citizen who fails to persuade the laws to rescind a command he or she thinks is unjust nevertheless fails to act unjustly in carrying out the laws' command—even if, in fact, the dissenting citizen's judgment of what justice requires is correct and the civic authority's is incorrect. Socrates' political philosophy may well have been more defensible had he made room for a theory of justified disobedience to legal authority. But in not doing so, he was not guilty of contradiction.

Religion. A number of aspects of Socrates' religious views have aroused scholarly interest. But what has perhaps puzzled interpreters the most is what appears to contemporary philosophical readers to be an obvious tension between Socrates' relentless appeal to reason, together with his expressed trust and belief in what seem obviously to be various extrarational, religious phenomena. On the one hand, he proclaims himself to be "the sort of man who is persuaded by nothing but the reason (**logos*) that seems best to me when I consider it" (*Cri.* 46b4–6). On the other, he talks of obedience to "oracles and dreams and every way in which any divinity has ever commanded a human being to do anything whatsoever" (*Ap.* 33c4–7). Contemporary scholars have found it impossible to accept that Socrates could ever count things like "oracles and dreams" as "reason(s) that seem best" to him, and hence they have made strenuous efforts to reinterpret Socrates' professed religious commitments in what they regard as more rationalistic ways. Whether or not such attempts can provide plausible interpretations of all of Socrates' religious proclamations remains to be seen. At any rate, there appears to be a fairly substantial variety of religious views that will require appropriate interpretation.

Regarding piety, it seems obvious, from Socrates' own contributions to the discussion in the *Euthyphro* and from the arguments he offers in his own defense in the *Apology*, that he regards philosophizing as an exemplar of pious activity. Given Socrates' view that philosophizing, for him, is a religious "mission" (see, e.g., *Ap.* 22a7, 23c1, 30a6–7, 33c4–7), it seems clear at least in this case that Socrates sees no tension between his religious and his rational commitments. Moreover, the precise way in which Socrates characterizes his own coming to understand the Delphic oracle as giving him a mission reflects a process that is carried out through repeated elenctic practices.

Perhaps more difficult to reconcile with a modern conception of rationality is Socrates' conviction that he has a certain "divine something" (*daimonion ti*: see *Ap.* 31c8–d2, 40a4–6; *Euth.* 3b5–7; *Phdr.* 242b8–9), which he sometimes calls a "divine sign" (*sêmeion*: *Ap.* 40c3–4, 41d6; *Euthyd.* 272e4; *Rep.* 6, 496c4; *Phdr.* 242b8–9), or "voice" (*phônê*, *Ap.* 31d3; *Phdr.* 242c2). Though a few scholars have dismissed Socrates' references to his *daimonion* as requiring nothing more exotic than some form of rational intuition, such interpretations cannot stand up to the unanimity of the ancients' perception of Socrates' "sign" as an uncanny religious phenomenon. Indeed, both of our most proximate sources (Plato and Xenophon) make it plain that Socrates' talk about his *daimonion* was the source of the claim that he "invented new divinities"—one of the three specifications of the charge of impiety, for which he was convicted and sentenced to death (see Pl. *Ap.* 31c8–d2, *Euth.* 3b5–7; Xen., *Ap.* 12).

In Plato's dialogues, Socrates characterizes his *daimonion* as functioning only to stop him when he is about to do something wrong. In Xenophon, we find the *daimonion* sometimes offers positive advice, as well. Ps.-Plato's *Theages* also depicts a more positive role played by the *daimonion* in Socrates' decisions. In each of these sources, in any case, Socrates may be seen to rely on the monitions of the *daimonion* with a trust that exceeds his trust in his own ratiocinations. For example, he makes clear (at *Ap.* 40a2–c3) that he takes the inaction of his *daimonion* to be a "great proof" that he has done nothing wrong or bad for him in his preparation for, or speeches at, his trial. Plainly, it follows from the fact that such activity *could* have occurred that the *daimonion* could oppose Socrates when he is acting in a deliberate way. And we never find any examples of Socrates ignoring or disobeying his *daimonion*. No doubt another such example appears at *Ap.* 31c7–d5, where Socrates says his *daimonion* opposed his engaging in politics. We should not assume that Socrates would undertake to engage in politics without prior deliberation as to how, when, and why he would do so. But his *daimonion* opposed him, and so Socrates desisted from politics, despite whatever reasons he may have taken himself to have for pursuing such activity. Later on, Socrates comes to understand why his *daimonion*'s promptings in this case were right (see *Ap.* 31d5–6).

Socrates' views of the afterlife have also been matters of considerable debate. On the one hand, it is clear that he regards anyone who would claim to know what death might be like to be guilty of "the most disgraceful sort of ignorance" (see *Ap.* 29a4–b6). On the other hand, he seems to regard two of the accounts he has heard as the most likely (see *Ap.* 40c4ff.)—either death is like an endless sleep or else it is a migration to some other place where the dead are judged by "true judges" (*Ap.* 40e7–41a3). In the *Apology*, Socrates betrays no obvious preference for either of these two alternatives, but in the *Crito* and the *Gorgias* the migration option is the only one Socrates seems to take seriously (see *Cri.*

54c6–7; *Grg.* 523a1–527a4). It is a matter of dispute among scholars whether the accounts in the *Apology, Crito,* and *Gorgias* are consistent.

BIBLIOGRAPHY: Benson, H. H., ed., *Essays on the Philosophy of Socrates,* New York/Oxford, 1992; also "The Problem of the Elenchus Reconsidered," *AP* 7, 1987, 67–85; also "The Priority of Definition and the Socratic *Elenchos,*" *OSAP* 8, 1990, 19–65; Boudouris, K. J., ed., *The Philosophy of Socrates,* Athens, 1991; Brickhouse, T. C. and N. D. Smith, *Socrates on Trial,* Princeton/Oxford, 1989; also *Plato's Socrates,* New York/Oxford, 1994; Devereux, D. T., "The Unity of the Virtues," *PR* 102, 1993, 765–789; also "Socrates' Kantian Conception of Virtue," *JHP* 33, 1995, 381–408; Guthrie, W. K. C., *Socrates,* Cambridge, 1971; Irwin, T. H., *Plato's Ethics,* Oxford, 1995; Kraut, R., *Socrates and the State,* Princeton, 1983; McPherran, M., "Socratic Piety in the *Euthyphro,*" *JHP* 23, 1985, 283–309; also "Socratic Reason and Socratic Revelation," *JHP* 29, 1991, 345–73; also "Socrates and the Immortality of the Soul," *JHP* 32, 1994, 1–22; Nails, D., *Agora and Academy: An Alternative Approach to the Socratic Problem* (diss.: University of Witwatersrand, South Africa), 1993; Penner, T., "The Unity of Virtue," *PR* 82, 1973, 35–68, repr. in H. H. Benson, ed., *Essays;* also "What Laches and Nicias Miss—And Whether Socrates Thinks Courage Is Merely a Part of Virtue," *AP* 12, 1992, 1–27; Rudebusch, G., "Death Is One of Two Things," *AP* 11, 1991, 35–45; Santas, G. X., *Socrates: Philosophy in Plato's Early Dialogues,* London/Boston, 1982; Seeskin, K., *Dialogue and Discovery: A Study in Socratic Method,* Albany, 1987; Stokes, M., *Plato's Socratic Conversations: Drama and Dialectic in Three Dialogues,* Baltimore, 1986; Teloh, H., *Socratic Education in Plato's Early Dialogues,* South Bend, 1986; Vlastos, G., *Socrates: Ironist and Moral Philosopher,* Ithaca and Cambridge, 1991; also *Socratic Studies* ed. M. Burnyeat, Cambridge, 1994; Woodruff, P., "Expert Knowledge in the *Apology* and *Laches*: What a General Should Know," in J. Cleary, ed., *PBACAP,* vol. 3, Lanham/New York/and London, 1987, 79–115; also "Plato's Early Theory of Knowledge," in S. Everson, ed., *Companions to Ancient Thought I: Epistemology,* Cambridge, 1990; Woozley, A. D., *Law and Obedience: The Arguments of Plato's Crito,* Chapel Hill, 1979; Zeyl, D., "Socratic Virtue and Happiness," *AGP* 64, 1982, 225–38.—*THOMAS C. BRICKHOUSE and NICHOLAS D. SMITH*

SOCRATIC CIRCLE. Ancient authors usually referred to the Socratic circle by the expression *"hoi peri ton Sokratên,"* "the people around *Socrates," or *"hoi Sokratikoi,"* "the Socratics." The former could indicate only those who knew Socrates in person and were his close associates, while the latter applied both to the members of Socrates' entourage and to the members of the so-called Socratic schools, each of which claimed to be the true heir of the Socratic spirit. These schools were in existence up to one and a half centuries after Socrates' death (399 B.C.E.).

The sources list several people as the intimate associates of Socrates, but relatively few of them are known except by their names. Aside from *Plato, who probably did not occupy among the Socratics as important a position as his subsequent philosophical development would suggest, there was a wide variety of other members. *Xenophon the Athenian was

Plato's exact contemporary. After a military career outside Athens, he retired to his private estate, pursued his interests in history, political and
military leadership, household management, and horsemanship and
wrote some forty books including his memoirs of Socrates. *Antisthenes
developed an anti-intellectual streak in Socratic *ethics and also treated
and taught a variety of subjects such as *logic and *metaphysics, *grammar, literature, *rhetoric, *political philosophy, and *religion. *Aristippus
of Cyrene was interested primarily in practical ethics but also in familiar
topics of the Greek intellectual tradition such as rhetoric, linguistic morphology and semantics, history and, perhaps, literature. He is mentioned
in the *Phaedo* alongside Cleombrotus (59c), who is otherwise almost unknown. *Euclides of Megara was an ethical monist whose logical method
betrayed the influence of *Eleatic arguments and opposed Socratic
*dialectic in that it rejected arguments from parallel cases. *Aeschines the
Athenian, an accomplished writer of Socratic discourses, was nevertheless accused of plagiarizing Socrates and of borrowing heavily from the
works of his fellow Socratics. He was also a successful composer of
forensic speeches. Aeschines' fragments contain sour comments on three
other Socratics, namely, Callias, Hermogenes, and Critoboulus. These
last two, as well as the Athenians Apollodorus, Epigenes, and Menexenus, were present during Socrates' last hours, according to Plato's
Phaedo (59b). *Phaedo of Elis (or, conceivably, of Melos), an ethicist who
discussed themes of the *sophistic tradition, emphasized the educational
and reformatory power of philosophy and, perhaps, reexamined the role
of pleasure in the virtuous life. Crito the Athenian, a wealthy gentleman
with a deep affection for Socrates and, if we trust the *Crito*, not without
philosophical abilities, was the author of seventeen Socratic *dialogues
concerning ethics, *epistemology, religion, poetry, and literature. Simon,
an Athenian cobbler who made notes from memory of the conversations
that Socrates and his friends held in his workshop, had an important role
in the emergence of Socratic discourses as a literary genre. He was the
author of several dialogues on ethical and epistemological subjects and
of a dialogue on number. Chairephon was an active democrat exiled by
the Thirty. His devotion to Socrates famously brought him to the Dephic
oracle and was caricatured by *Aristophanes. *Critias, a brilliant intellectual and orator, is a protagonist in the *Charmides* and one of the few Platonic interlocutors able to hold his own ground against Socrates. His
participation in the tyranny of the Thirty proved a great liability at
Socrates' trial. Charmides was allegedly encouraged to take up a political
career by Socrates, who was impressed by the modesty and sweetness of
his character and by his intellectual gifts. Alcibiades was a ward of Pericles and undoubtedly the strongest personality of the Peloponnesian
war. He appears as the main character in Plato's eponymous dialogue

and as subject of one of the finest portraits in the *Symposium*. He availed himself of all the help that Socrates could give him, and yet he led Athens and himself to disaster in the closing stages of the Peloponnesian war. Of the Thebans Simmias, Cebes, and Phaedondes, the first two carry much of the burden of the discussion in the *Phaedo*, although no theory discussed in it can be attributed to them. Simmias was probably more active than Cebes as a writer, since he is credited with twenty-three dialogues on ethical, political, educational, and literary subjects, whereas only three dialogues are attributed to Cebes, whose titles reveal little about their contents. Terpsion of Megara is barely known except as a minor character in Plato. Glaucon the Athenian, author of nine dialogues, may be identical with Plato's brother Glaucon, a principal interlocutor in the *Republic*. It is possible that *Theaetetus the geometer joined the Socratic circle briefly before Socrates' death. In Plato's *Laches*, the Athenian general Nicias declares that he is accustomed to conversing with Socrates, a familiarity that enables him to give an artful account of Socrates' method and of the way in which he treats his interlocutors. He, too, is likely to have been involved in the Socratic circle.

These Socratics are not a homogeneous group. Some of them had their own pupils and eventually founded the so-called Minor Socratic schools. Antisthenes' followers were identified as a separate sect, the Antisthenians, and their leader was considered, in some senses, the founder of the *Cynic movement. According to the *doxographers, Aristippus was the founder of the *Cyrenaic school, Euclides of the *Megarian school, and Phaedo of the school of Elis, which, from *Menedemus onwards, was known as the Eretrian school. On the other hand, thinkers such as Xenophon and Aeschines, who by no means lacked philosophical capacities, left no disciples.

Differences in origin, social status, education, political opinions, and financial capacity marked them deeply. Many of them were Athenians, but Aristippus came from Libya. Plato, Critias, Charmides, and Alcibiades belonged to powerful Athenian aristocratic families but associated with Antisthenes, the son of a Thracian slave, and Phaedo, an ex-slave perhaps forced into prostitution. Plato had a splendid curricular education and so did Alcibiades, whereas this is unlikely to have been true of Simon the cobbler or of Aeschines, the son of a sausage-maker. Chairephon was a democrat, Xenophon an oligarch. Both Critias and Charmides died defending tyranny. While most Socratics had strong political views, they tolerated Antisthenes' political indifference and Aristippus' cosmopolitanism. Differences in situation and in temperament may be the motives of personal aversions or attachments. For example, Aeschines became attached to Aristippus, and probably neither of them was in sympathy with Plato. In some cases, there are family connections between the Socratics: Crito is the father of Critoboulus, Critias and Charmides are first cousins, and Plato is the nephew of both. But there are also Socratics who kept apart from one another, as apparently Plato and Xenophon did.

Despite these differences, at least some of the Socratics conceived of themselves as one circle or group: In the *Crito*, Socrates refers to a consensus on key moral tenets achieved in past discussions between himself and others including Crito (46b–e, 49a–b). Already in the fourth century, the assumption that they constituted a circle appears in the title of a book by the *Peripatetic Phanias (*On the Socratics*) and marks the history of philosophy from *Panaetius onward.

In conclusion, it seems that we are justified in speaking of "a Socratic circle," a relatively cohesive philosophical group animated by Socrates himself. All Socratics had a lively interest in philosophy, regardless of their other interests and occupations. All of them explored ethical topics, although not all devoted their philosophical activity exclusively to that task. Their sets of beliefs, particularly their moral beliefs, usually present family resemblances. For example, Antisthenes' views on moderation in pleasure are similar to those of the Platonic and of the Xenophontic Socrates and considerably different from those of Phaedo and of Aristippus. Aristippus' detachment from the bonds of citizenship is shared by Antisthenes, and the positions of both differ from Plato's and Xenophon's civic commitment. However, there are a few opinions that all Socratics held in common, at least for part of their lives, for example, the importance of virtue for happiness, the educational role of philosophy in moral life, and the importance of self-examination and of assessing critically the values and habits of ordinary life.

BIBLIOGRAPHY: Texts in *SSR*. Humbert, J., *Socrate et les petits Socratiques*, Paris, 1967; Grote, G., *Plato and the Other Companions of Socrates*, London, 1875; Vander Waerdt, P. A., ed., *The Socratic Movement*, Ithaca, 1994.—*VOULA TSOUNA-McKIRAHAN*

SOPHISTS. The "older sophists" were travelling teachers of the fifth century B.C.E. The "second sophistic" refers to a renaissance of the teaching of *rhetoric in the first through third centuries C.E.

The older Sophists travelled among Greek cities teaching a variety of subjects to adult or young adult students for substantial fees, bringing with them the sort of intellectual excitement that is evident in the opening of *Plato's *Protagoras*. All of them represented the spirit of inquiry that grew in Greece during the fifth century and has been called the Greek enlightenment or the new learning. They were most famous for their study of language and their teaching of what has come to be known as rhetoric. They are known to us mainly through the historical fictions of Plato, who was probably the first to consider them as a group and to separate them as sophists from other intellectuals of the period. In their own time they were not clearly identified as a group or with a single intellectual movement, but showed considerable diversity in ideas and interests. The word *sophistês* in its earliest uses referred to wise men such as poets and still occurred in the fourth century as a general term for philosophers and orators, but soon came, under Plato's influence, to refer to the teachers of the new learning, whom he wished to distinguish from philosophers.

Among the subjects taught by sophists were the art of words, *ethics, *political theory, law, history, mnemonics, literature, *mathematics, and *astronomy. Some sophists dealt also with *metaphysics and *epistemology. Others pursued an anthropological interest in the origins of human culture through learning and invention. The idea that learning leads to progress, associated with some sophists, fueled the demand for teachers.

Little of the many books and speeches produced by sophists has survived. We can be certain that the sophists included highly original and influential thinkers, but on points of doctrine we are often left to draw speculative conclusions from exiguous evidence. Much of this evidence is derived from Plato, who is on the whole an unfriendly witness. He is critical of sophists in general for presenting themselves as teachers of subjects he did not think they properly understood. *Socrates (as Plato portrays him) challenges various sophists to defend their claims to knowledge and teaching ability while disclaiming such things for his own part. Though Plato seems to treat a few of them with respect, he shows a number of sophists being refuted by Socrates or held up to ridicule. Some of these appear to use fallacies deliberately to dazzle an audience; others claim to be able to win over audiences by the power of rhetoric on any subject, whether or not they are expert on that in their own right. Plato's portrayal of sophists has given us the term "sophistical" for devious argumentation, and *Aristophanes' satire on the new learning in the *Clouds* has given the sophists a reputation for teaching students to use rhetoric in defense of unjust causes. Following leads in Hegel, the British scholar George Grote gave a powerful defense of the sophists in his *History*, and most modern scholars of the new learning have attempted to separate their subject from the negative image it has carried through most of the history of philosophy.

Principal Figures. The first and most successful sophist was *Protagoras, who was also the first teacher to call himself a sophist. Like most of those who followed him, Protagoras had interests in a variety of subjects, only one of which could be called rhetoric. His profession, as he defined it, was to improve his students by imparting to them the *virtue of good judgment (*euboulia*), which, he said, would make them highly capable or powerful in public life as well as in managing their own households.

Roughly contemporary with him was *Gorgias, who was primarily a teacher of public speaking and made no claim to improve his students in other ways.

Protagoras' success as a teacher and Gorgias' fame as a speaker paved the way for the next generation of sophists. We have evidence bearing on the teachings of *Prodicus, *Hippias, *Antiphon, *Critias, Evenus, *Euthydemus, *Thrasymachus, Alcidamas, and Lycophron. The *Anonymus Iamblichi (an unknown writer quoted by *Iamblichus) and the author of *Dissoi Logoi are also considered sophists. Views related to those of the sophists appear in Plato's Republic 358e–359b (on the social contract) and Gorgias 483a–484c (Callicles on the conflict between law and nature).

Socrates appears as the principal teacher of the new learning in *Aristophanes' Clouds (surviving version, 420 B.C.E.), giving lessons in natural science and the sort of public speaking taught by the sophists. In fact, Socrates has much in common with the sophists. He shares their interests in ethics and adopts some of their ideas and methods. His theory of punishment is close to that of Protagoras, and his method of questioning is a variation on a sophistic practice. His interest in defining concepts such as justice is related to sophists' work on the correctness of words. He differs from most sophists, however, in not travelling and in not accepting fees for teaching. On matters of doctrine he differs from individual sophists on various points, as individual sophists differed from each other.

The Art of Words. The first known teachers of the art of words were Corax and Tisias in Sicily. These are usually not listed as sophists, however; and the first teacher of oratory to be called a sophist was Gorgias, who took Athens by storm on his visit from Leontini in 427 B.C.E. and who was the major influence on the next generation of sophists who taught oratory. This was evidently the most popular of the subjects offered by sophists. The advent of democracy in Athens and Sicily during the fifth century had given new powers to strong speakers in law courts and assemblies, but the art of words was not an invention of fifth-century teachers. Greeks had been fascinated by displays of public speaking as early as *Homer and had always honored those who succeeded in contests of speeches. Statesmen such as Themistocles owed their success to oratory long before sophists came on the scene, and set speeches were a feature of the earliest Greek plays.

The tradition in philosophy of construing rhetoric narrowly as the art of persuasion is largely due to Plato (see Cole). The art of words most sophists taught was not limited to persuasion, but covered such topics as correct use of words, distinctions among speech acts, and types of argument.

"Correctness of words" was the title for a variety of teachings by a number of sophists, but we know only in a few cases what this meant. Protagoras argued, for example, that "wrath" in the first line of the *Iliad* (a feminine noun in conventional Greek) should be understood as masculine in gender. He also sought to correct poets who appeared to contradict themselves in their verses. Prodicus argued for the precise use of words, making careful distinctions between such pairs as "pleasure" and "enjoyment." Both evidently sought greater precision with words than conventional usage allowed.

Argument schemes taught by sophists had practical applications, especially in deliberative or forensic oratory. The most common of these is appeal to reasonable expectation (*eikos*), of which there are good examples in the *Defense* and *Tetralogies* of Antiphon. A rich man accused of stealing a cloak, for example, could appeal to the expectation that a rich man would not bother to steal a cloak. Speakers generally turn to *eikos* when eyewitness testimony is lacking. *Thucydides employs the method in investigating early Greek history, and his speakers use it frequently in debate. Such reasoning is what modern logicians call *defeasible*; it holds only for normal conditions and is defeated by unexpected abnormalities. Plato wrongly treats *eikos* as a value offered by sophists in place of truth (*Phdr.* 267a); in actual usage, *eikos* is an admittedly risky method for exploring truth when the available evidence will not support more reliable conclusions. As such, the concept of *eikos* depends on that of truth. Defeasible reasoning is often the best one can do (as in the case of most medical diagnosis). Its disadvantage, however, is that different appeals to *eikos* can lead to opposite results. If there is no witness to settle the matter, a contest of speeches appealing to *eikos* appears to be merely a contest between the persuasive powers of the two speakers, independently of the facts; and one speaker can argue as well on side of an issue as he can on the other if he is trained to do so.

Protagoras and other sophists taught the art of opposed speeches—of giving arguments on both sides of an issue, such as we find in the *Tetralogies* of Antiphon and the *Dissoi Logoi*, as well as in the *History* of Thucydides and the plays of *Euripides and Aristophanes. This art is closely related to "making the weaker argument stronger," which, given the ambiguity of the Greek words, meant also "making the wrong argument right." The idea that oratorical might makes right was disturbing to the Greeks of the period, as Aristophanes' *Clouds* testifies. It was part of the unspoken charge against Socrates and was held against Protagoras as well. Gorgias' surviving display speeches illustrate how clever argument can strengthen a weak case, as does the startling speech of Lysias in Plato's *Phaedrus*.

Gorgias' art of words depends on the concept of *kairos*—saying the appropriate thing at the right time. He celebrates the power of language to deceive in the *Encomium to Helen* and in a few surviving sentences on literature; but he appears to assert that we cannot communicate the truth at all in his essay *On That Which Is Not*.

Playfulness abounds in early Greek speeches. The use of absurd fallacies, such as the ones that made Euthydemus famous, is more suited to to dazzle an audience than to hoodwink or persuade it against its will. On the whole, however, the art of words was intended for serious purposes and commanded serious fees. In democratic cities, demagogues used the art of speaking to influence policy, but Greek history does not support the idea that the power of oratory was overwhelming in politics, or even that it provided a secure defense in courts of law. Pericles, the most able speaker of his day, was unable to defend himself in court; and Antiphon's speech in his own defense a generation later, though a success among intellectuals, did not save the speaker from execution.

Politics and Ethics. An important issue of the age of sophists was the contest among constitutions—Athenian democracy, Spartan traditional government, monarchy or tyranny, and oligarchy (government by the few and the rich); but sophists as a group did not express a preference for any particular form of government. Although sophists and their new ideas appear to have been more welcome in democratic cities than in oligarchies, they came to teach students who were generally rich or wellborn and frequently opposed to democracy. There seem to have been sophists on both sides of the issue between democracy and oligarchy. The long speech of Protagoras in Plato's dialogue of that name supports democracy, while Antiphon was a leader of an oligarchic coup in Athens. (Some scholars make a distinction between Antiphon the sophist and Antiphon the politician; see ANTIPHON.)

Sophists generally presented themselves as teachers of virtue (Pl. *Meno* 95c). Protagoras proclaimed his ability to make his pupils better each day and spoke also of the importance of justice and respect to the survival of the human species. In a speech reconstructed by Plato (*Prt.* 320d–328d) he says that unless such virtues are universally distributed, people will not be able to form cities, and without cities they will be destroyed by their enemies; everyone must acquire such virtues through education and training. We also have a paraphrase of a speech by Prodicus (the "Choice of Heracles") that emphasizes the education of young people to serve the interests of society construed beyond conventional limits. Of Hippias' moral teaching we know only that it existed and that he was not permitted to bring it to the youth of Sparta, a city that was famously conservative on education.

Plato represents Protagoras in the *Theaetetus* as a relativist on moral and all other questions. Plato's view has been influential, but other evidence counts against the attribution of moral relativism to Protagoras or to any other sophist who expressed moral views. A relativist would hold that the conventions of each city are right for it and that there is no external basis in truth or nature for defending or criticizing a city's customs. But in the *Protagoras* Plato shows Protagoras defending morality not by appeal to relativism, but by putting justice among the natural necessities of human life. Similarly, sophists who criticize conventional morality tend to do so by appealing to a nature-based concept of what is right or necessary. Relativism, however, would bar any appeal to nature and is therefore at odds with the tenor of sophistic work in ethics.

Most criticism of conventional morality from sophists aims to achieve what they see as reform. Some sophists probably questioned conventional notions about slavery and the place of women in society. A few second-generation sophists hold that *phusis* (nature) is poles apart from *nomos* ("law," "convention," or "custom"). Plato's Callicles attacks conventional justice on the grounds that it interferes with nature, while the law of nature in his view commands that the strong should be free to satisfy their greatest desires. Other sophists who attack convention or appeal to nature do so for less self-seeking ends. Hippias appeals to *phusis* to defend his view of the natural kinship of humankind (or at least of the wise), who are divided by the mere conventions of national difference. Thrasymachus rejects conventional justice because, he claims, it serves only the interests of the rulers who make the laws; in view of DK85B8 this is implicitly a complaint against the unfairness of such arrangements. Like Thucydides (8.97), Thrasymachus seems to favor government that is efficient and serves no special group.

Science and Technology. Hippias had the widest range of interests and is the only sophist with a claim to have made an advance in science (the invention of the curve known as "quadratrix"). He was known also for his work in astronomy. A number of sophists, along with like-minded poets and historians, were interested in accounting for the origins of society and culture. Although perhaps sparked by *Democritus, the anthropology that developed was mainly associated with the sophists. Common to most of the sophists' or sophist-influenced anthropologies is the idea of progress through combined technological and political advances, in contrast to *Hesiod's view that the rise of technology comes after a decline in morals. In spite of their respect for technology, most sophists taught only subjects suitable to the leisure class, although Hippias actually practiced and taught a number of crafts.

Knowledge and Reality. Plato thinks most sophists value persuasion over truth. He blames them for presenting themselves as moral teachers when their knowledge amounts (in his view) to little more than an ability to pretend, to mimic experts. The charge is unfair, in that any normal human teacher would fail to meet Plato's high standards for knowledge; but it is fair in that some sophists seem to hold views inconsistent with their being teachers of any subject other than rhetoric. Many sophists are interested primarily in teaching persuasive speech, and at least one has a negative theory that does not seem to allow him to claim any other expertise: Gorgias appears to have denied either the existence of reality or the possibility of knowing or saying what it is. Any of these denials would imply that speakers can aspire no higher than to persuade their hearers. Persuasion would then be the only criterion of success for an orator. (Such a claim resembles *skepticism, but ancient skepticism made no claims, not even negative ones.) Gorgias was probably the only sophist to take this negative line; most others, as we have seen, claimed to teach a range of subjects, and many of them also appealed to natural reality in their arguments against convention.

Relativism. Relativism is any view that allows conflicting judgments to be equally true for the people who believe them. Forms of relativism were under discussion in Greece several generations before sophists took up the theme. It is misleading to say that all the sophists were relativists. There were, however, ideas commonly held by sophists that resemble relativism or are as unsettling to traditionalists as relativism has been. Most important of these is the view that traditional morality is arbitrary because it rests only on custom.

The power of custom (*nomos*) was recognized before the sophists and was celebrated in the often-quoted line of Pindar, "Nomos is king" (S 169). As early as 500 B.C.E., *Xenophanes challenged conventional *religious ideas by calling attention to the different ways cultures represented the gods (DK21B15, 16). *Herodotus observes how customary notions of right and wrong vary across cultural boundaries (3.38); and, as travelling teachers, some sophists developed an interest in comparing ethical, political, and religious ideas in various cultures. Such comparisons are not necessarily relativistic, since they are compatible with the view, held by many sophists, that there is a natural basis for right and wrong distinct from all of the different conventions. Still, research of this kind tends to make people think of traditional values as arbitrary, and defenders of tradition in the later fifth century had reason to feel threatened by the new learning. Even conservative, antidemocratic sophists (such as Thrasymachus probably was) could be critical of what was currently regarded as tradition.

A form of relativism shows up in the work of *Heraclitus (521–487 B.C.E.), whose views imply that conflicting human opinions are equally supported by the balance of shifting opposites in the world, although they are false when contrasted with those of a god: "To god all things are beautiful and good and just, but human beings have taken some things to be unjust and others just" (DK22B102).

Like Heraclitus (B61), Protagoras probably held that the same thing could be good for one species and bad for another (Plato *Prt.* 334a–c). On this view, conflicting opinions about the healthfulness of a certain oil would be equally true, depending on whether the oil was to be taken internally or externally. Such relativism does not threaten us with contradiction, but it may have furthered in some minds the more radical idea that there is no such thing as an absolute good or an absolute evil.

In the *Theaetetus* Plato attributes to Protagoras a more radical form of relativism. "A human being is measure of all things," wrote Protagoras (probably in a book called *Truth*), "of those things that are that they are, and of those things that are not that they are not." By this he meant, according to Plato, that each thing is to me such as it appears to me to be, while to you it is such as it appears to you to be (152a). In its initial context this seems to apply only to perception, but Plato seems to extend it to opinion in general. On Plato's understanding, Protagoras intends to claim that no opinion is ever false and that every opinion is true for the person whose opinion it is. Plato treats as a consequence of this doctrine the related (but different) view that justice in a given city is exactly what the city judges it to be (167c). It follows from the measure doctrine that no one's opinion counts more than another's, a consequence that threatens to undermine Protagoras' claim to be a teacher, as Plato shows. Plato supposes that Protagoras advances this relativism as a denial of the existence of a single stable underlying reality, but there is some evidence to suggest that Protagoras believed in a single reality that is complex enough to support all of our various opinions about it. In any case, Protagoras was not a consistent relativist; his interests in correcting conventional word usage and in a number of other topics will not allow us to attribute to him a thorough-going relativism.

The Second Sophistic. The expression was coined by *Philostratus (c. 170–245 C.E.) in his *Lives of the Sophists*. Peace and prosperity in the Greek near east under Roman imperial rule were favorable to a restoration of classical culture that promoted education through the study of rhetoric. The second sophistic influenced literature, both poetry and prose, and came to be seen as a conduit of classical culture to the Byzantine period. Like the fifth-century sophists whom they emulated, the sophists of the Roman period were celebrated as performers for public occasions. Unlike their forbears, however, most were primarily teachers of rhetoric, and they modelled themselves more on Gorgias than on Protagoras. Many were rich and well-connected, vying with each other for the attentions of the imperial court. What Plato does for the older sophists, by identifying them as a group, Philostratus does for the second sophistic; but though Philostratus is a supporter of the movement he defines, he shows little interest in the intellectual content of his subjects' teaching. Through collecting gossip and anecdote, he tells the lives of some thirty sophists and mentions others he deems less worthy. The movement begins in the first century C.E. with Nicetas of Smyrna, whom Nero admired, and Isaeus of Syria, who was celebrated by Pliny for his happy life teaching rhetoric in schools. A considerable body of work (five Loeb volumes) has survived from Dio of Prusa (Dio Chrysostom), also of the first century C.E.; his writing testifies to the versatitlity of intellectuals of this period. The main figures of the movement were Polemo and Herodes Atticus, both of whom flourished under imperial patronage in the second century C.E.. Rome drew the most successful sophists to the splendors of its court, while the centers in Greece for the teaching of the second sophistic were Smyrna, Athens, and Ephesus. Roman-period sophists travelled widely, the best of them either with or under the protection of the emperor. Polemo and his descendants had the right of free travel granted them by Hadrian. Third-century emperors were less interested in supporting the sophists, but the schools continued to flourish through the fourth century. For this later period our main source is Libanius, who taught with great success in Constantinople and was supported by the pagan emperor Julian, himself an accomplished sophist. *Themistius, a fourth-century sophist, was also a statesman and eclectic philosopher, serving in the senate in Constantinople and writing *commentaries on *Aristotle. In this period there were both *Christian and pagan sophists, as well as those like Themistius who attempted to combine the two. We cannot define an end for the second sophistic; its last historian is the fourth- and fifth-century sophist *Eunapius, who taught at Athens.

BIBLIOGRAPHY: *The Older Sophists:* Tr. in R. K. Sprague, *The Older Sophists,* Columbia, SC, 1972, and M. Gagarin and P. Woodruff, eds., *Early Greek Political Thought from Homer to the Sophists,* Cambridge, 1995. Classen, C. J., *Sophistik,* Darmstadt, 1976; Cole, T., *The Origins of Rhetoric in Ancient Greece,* Baltimore, 1991; Grote, G., *A History of Greece,*[6] London, 1888; Guthrie, W. K. C., *The Sophists,* Cambridge, 1971; Kerferd, G. B., *The Sophistic Movement,* Cambridge, 1981; Romilly, J. de., *The Great Sophists in Periclean Athens,* Oxford, 1992; Solmsen, F., *Intellectual Experiments of the Greek Enlightenment,* Princeton, 1975; Untersteiner, M. *The Sophists,* tr. by K. Freeman, Oxford, 1954. *The Second Sophistic:* Anderson, G., *The Second Sophistic,* London, 1993; Bowersock, G. W., *Greek Sophists and the Roman Empire,* Oxford, 1969; also Bowersock, ed., *Approaches to the Second Sophistic: Papers presented to the 105th Annual Meeting of the American Philological Association,* University Park, PA, 1974; Reardon, B. P., *Courants littéraires grecs des IIe et IIIe siècles après J.-C.,* Paris, 1971.—*PAUL WOODRUFF*

SOPHOCLES. See POETS, TRAGIC.

SOTION (c. 200–170 B.C.E.), of Alexandria. *Peripatetic author of *Diadochai*, or *Successions (of Philosophers)*. Sotion's history of philosophy appears to have been the first to attempt to place as many philosophers as possible in teacher–student "successions," especially within a given school; philosophers were discussed chronologically within a series, systematically from one series to the next. This structure was later used by *Diogenes Laertius, who ultimately owes much else besides to Sotion. Sotion is cited twenty-one times in the *Lives*, not as often as three or four other historians, but still rather frequently.

Sotion probably contributed to the notion that Greek philosophy (perhaps philosophy in general) began with *Thales; he appears to have taken Thales as "founder" of the Milesian school, although he seems to have had (as Diogenes does) an introductory chapter on the contributions of "barbarian" nations to the history of philosophy. Sotion also seems to have been the source of the idea that the roots of the *Stoic school can be traced back to *Socrates via the *Cynics.

BIBLIOGRAPHY: Texts in Wehrli supp. vol. 2: *Sotion*. Aronadio, F., *Elenchos* 11.2, 1990, 203–255.—*ANTHONY PREUS*

SOUL. See MIND, Classical Theories of.

SPEUSIPPUS (c. 410–339 B.C.E.), of Athens. *Plato's nephew, head of the *Academy after Plato's death. Speusippus succeeded Plato in 348/347, remained head of the Academy for eight years, and died an old man (D.L. 4.1–3). *Diogenes Laertius (4.4–5) gives a bibliography with thirty-odd titles; nothing has survived and fragments are rare.

Reconstruction of Speusippus' *metaphysics proceeds from two texts in which *Aristotle names Speusippus, chaining from these to others that can plausibly be taken to concern him. One is in *Iamblichus; the ascription to Speusippus, here taken as correct, is controversial (see Merlan, Tarán, Dancy).

In *Metaphysics* 7.2 (*T1*) Aristotle tells us that, whereas Plato thought there were three types of substances: Forms, *mathematical objects, and perceptible objects, "Speusippus, having started from the one, thinks there are even more substances, and principles for each substance: a principle for numbers, another for magnitudes, then for soul; and in this way he extends the substances." And (*T2*) in *Metaphysics* 12.7, after arguing that there is an eternal principle, the unmoved mover, for this universe, which is also eternal, Aristotle says: "Those who suppose, with the *Pythagoreans and Speusippus, that the most beautiful and best is not in the principle, because of the fact that whereas the principles for plants and animals are causes, the beautiful and the complete are in the things that derive from these, do not think rightly. For seed or sperm is from prior complete organisms, and what is primary is not a seed, but the complete organism."

Speusippus' universe has distinct principles at each level (*T1*); this makes it plausible to suppose that it is a view of Speusippus' about which Aristotle is complaining in 12.10, where he says that it makes the universe "episodic"; the absence of Forms from and prominence of numbers in *T1* also fits this passage, where the view is identified as that of those who put mathematical number first. The complaint of disjointedness and the primacy of mathematical number both surface again in 14.3; the detachment of goodness from principles and the analogy with organisms in *T2* together with the primacy of mathematical numbers and the episodic universe run through a view being criticized throughout 14.4–5, and these parallels lead in turn to Iamblichus, *De Communi Mathematica Scientia* 4.

The resulting picture has Speusippus rejecting Plato's Forms together with a view of causality that comes with them: Forms caused other things to have the features they do by possessing those features preeminently and transmitting them to those others. Speusippus' universe starts from the one, which is not itself one of the beings in that universe: "The principle is not yet of the same kind as the things whose principle it is," so the cause of all beings cannot itself be a being.

Mathematical numbers are "generated" from the one and another principle, plurality. At the next level geometrical magnitudes are similarly "generated" from the point, which somehow represents the one at this level, and another principle that parallels plurality. In both cases the generation is metaphorical: It has to do with existential, not temporal, priority. The next level contains *souls, and at the bottom there are perceptible objects. There is a causal relation between the principles at each level and the rest of the entities at that level, but if Aristotle's repeated complaint about Speusippus' episodic universe is just, none between one level and the next.

Speusippus apparently thought that in mathematics the proper method was axiomatic, starting from principles that recommend themselves to the soul and proceeding systematically from there (Ar. *Met.* 14.3, Proclus *In Eucl.* 178–179). And, although he supposed that perceptible things were in some sense knowable (S.E. *M* 7.145–146 has him speaking of "epistemonic" or "knowledge-attaining" perception), he argued for the existence of mathematical objects on the basis of the claim that mathematics was not about perceptible things.

Speusippus was also a radical wholist about *knowledge: It is impossible to know anything without knowing its likenesses with and differences from everything else (Ar. *APo.* 2.13 with the anonymous commentary *ad loc.*; cf. Pl. *Phil.* 18c). He appears to have arrived at this view from consideration of the Platonic "method of division," which he employed in investigations in biology (referred to frequently in Athenaeus' *Deipnosophistae*) and in semantics (Simplicius *In Cat.* 38.19–24).

*Clement (*Stromata* 2.22) ascribes to him the goal of unperturbedness (*aochlêsia*: cf. the standard goal in Hellenistic *ethics of undisturbedness, *ataraxia*). This must have included freedom, not merely from pain, but from pleasure as well, which, he appears to have argued, *contra* *Eudoxus, was an evil (*Phil.* 44a–50e attacks a view at least related to this—see Schofield).

BIBLIOGRAPHY: Texts in P. Lang, *De Speusippi Academici Scriptis*, Bonn, 1911; repr. Hildesheim, 1965; M. Isnardi Parente, *Speusippo: Frammenti*, Naples, 1980; L. Tarán, *Speusippus of Athens*, Leiden, 1981. Dancy, R. M., *AP* 9, 1989, 207–243, revised in *Two Studies in the Early Academy*, Albany, 1991, 63–119 and 146–178; Merlan, P., *From Platonism to Neoplatonism*, The Hague, 1953, 1960, 1968; Schofield, M., *Mus. Helv.* 28, 1971, 2–20, 181.—R. M. DANCY

SPHAERUS (c. 285–after 222 B.C.E.), of Bosporos (or Borysthenes). Student of *Zeno of Citium and *Cleanthes. Sphaerus was the tutor of Cleomenes III, king of Sparta, and supported his revolutionary program of reform. He probably followed Cleomenes during his exile in Egypt (222) to the court of Ptolemy III Euergetes and Ptolemy IV Philopator.

Sphaerus concerned himself with *logic, physics, and *ethics. A list of thirty-two titles is transmitted by *Diogenes Laertius (7.178). We know practically nothing of his thought. Only one fragment of *On Seed* and two testimonies are preserved: In one he asserts that darkness is visible, while in the other he gives various definitions of fortitude. His work *On the Spartan Constitution* would have been of particular interest in connection with the reforms planned by Cleomenes and with the meaning of the myth of Sparta in the Old *Stoa. In an anecdote reported by Diogenes Laertius and Athenaeus, Sphaerus resorts to the notion of the *eulogon* (reasonable) to defend himself against the *Academics from the charge of having lapsed into error because of a case of indistinguishability among presentations.

BIBLIOGRAPHY: Texts in *SVF* 1, Frs. 620–630. Hobein, H., "Sphairos," in *RE* 3A.2, 1929, 1683–1693.—*TIZIANO DORANDI*

STILPO (c. 360–c. 280 B.C.E.), of Megara. According to *Diogenes Laertius (2.113; cf. *Suda*, s.v. "Stilpo"), Stilpo studied with *Diogenes of Sinope and with various *Megarians, in one report including *Euclides himself, but the chronology makes this improbable. He wrote "no fewer than twenty dialogues" (*Suda*); Diogenes mentions nine extant ones (2.120), but elsewhere reports that he wrote nothing (1.16). He is mentioned as upholding static monism (see EUCLIDES).

*Simplicius (*In Phys.* 120.12–17) ascribes to the Megarians an argument to the effect that since things are different of which there are different accounts (*logoi) and Socrates considered as something educated has a different account from Socrates considered as a white thing, Socrates will be separated from himself. This appears to connect with *Plutarch *Against Colotes* 22–23 (1119c–1120b), where *Colotes is made to attack as Stilpo's the view that we cannot call a man good or a general, but can only call a man a man, a good a good, and a general a general (for an antecedent to this, see Pl. *Soph.* 251a-c). (Plutarch himself, *contra* Colotes, reads Stilpo as merely propounding a *dialectical puzzle, but he is unconvincing.)

Stilpo seems to have espoused an ideal of passionlessness (*apatheia* or *aochlêsia*, Seneca *Epistula* 9.1–3; Alexander *De Anima* 150.34–35, etc.), alongside the *Cynics and later the *Stoics.

Diogenes (2.113) says that "he exceeded the rest in verbal invention and sophistry by so much that almost all Greece was drawn to him to Megarize (*Megarizein*)"; Diogenes (2.113–114) lists a number of students of Stilpo who had defected from other schools, among them *Zeno of Citium (see also D.L. 7.2, 24), who later founded the Stoa. So it is unfortunate that we know next to nothing about what his views were; it is impossible to avoid the impression that he may have had more style than substance.

BIBLIOGRAPHY: See under MEGARIAN SCHOOL.—R. M. DANCY

STOA, The, and **STOICISM.** The Stoa, founded by *Zeno of Citium c. 301 B.C.E., was the fourth and last of the major schools of philosophy to appear in classical Athens. Zeno's fascination with *Socrates led him to study philosophy in Athens and to emulate Socrates in his own career. Study with representatives of the *Cynic, *Academic, *Megarian, and *Dialectical traditions exposed him to the rich diversity of the Socratic heritage. At last, convinced that he alone understood Socrates and his call to *virtuous living, Zeno set out to follow in his footsteps by instructing students as an independent teacher in the Painted Stoa in the Athenian marketplace.

Zeno's appearance in the marketplace turned Athenian philosophy and education in a new direction. In the late fourth century B.C.E. education was carried out principally in the three *gymnasia of Athens (the Academy, *Lyceum, and *Cynosarges), which furnished not only athletic training and competition, but also opportunities for regular instruction by an array of teachers of *grammar, literature, *mathematics, *rhetoric, and philosophy. *Plato and *Aristotle were among those who contributed to it by teaching philosophy in the Academy and Lyceum respectively. By teaching in the marketplace instead of in a gymnasium,

Zeno had the opportunity to reach a wider cross-section of the popula-
tion, in geographical distribution and in social rank. By offering instruction not only in philosophy but across a broad range of subjects, from
grammar, composition, and literature to rhetoric and philosophy, Zeno
appealed to a wider range of ages and interests. His iconoclastic entry
into the philosophical scene profoundly shaped the nature and destiny of
the school.

The Hellenistic School in Athens. The school that emerged from Zeno's
initiative was characterized by a broad scope of subject matter, high
moral aims, missionary zeal, and loose institutional structure. Many, if
not most, of its students in the early years were adolescents seeking a
general liberal arts education prior to a career in public life. Some stayed
on or joined the school as young men for more technical, philosophical
education. A few remained indefinitely, committing themselves to a life
of philosophy and over time developing individual specialities and divergent opinions. These permanent associates debated with each other
and with other philosophers, wrote books, and sometimes taught students of their own at various locations, including the gymnasia and the
Odeon. The Stoic school thus became a loose association of Stoic
philosophers and teachers, committed to common goals and acknowledging a single leader (scholarch), who held office for life.

Long-term affiliation with the school typically brought prestige and
public recognition. Scholarchs and associates were often invited by rulers
and governments around the world to serve as teachers, advisors,
diplomats, public officials, or government agents. For services rendered
to Athenian education some were offered citizenship and civic honors.

The vigorous, complex philosophical life of the Stoa during the two
centuries that it was centered in Athens may be surveyed from four
points of view: (i) *Defining the Scope and Nature of the Movement.* Zeno's
primary aim was to change the way people thought and lived, rather
than to solve philosophical puzzles or establish the credibility of a philosophical system. He seems to have made no effort to promote uniformity
of teaching or lifestyle among his followers. Since he wrote little and left
many issues unsettled, his students and associates followed their own
lights in developing his philosophy and implementing the life of virtue.

Some, like *Aristo of Chios and *Herillus, pushed the Socratic principle of virtue as the only good to its limit. They rejected the study of
physics and *logic and sought a basis for moral action in an intuitive, direct apprehension of the *good, rejecting Zeno's efforts to establish differences in value among indifferents. Others, such as *Persaeus, explored
the social and political implications of Zeno's teaching and leapt at the
opportunity to put their theory into practice in the service of the Macedonian king. Finally, there were those (e.g., *Cleanthes, *Sphaerus, and

*Chrysippus) who were committed to preserving the full panoply of themes that Zeno had found in the Socratic tradition, specifically, an uncompromising commitment to virtue as the only good, discrimination of natural differences in value among indifferents, a science of nature to support their worldview and value system, serious study of *dialectic and logic to defend their position, and finally a commitment to apply their principles to achieve *happiness (*eudaimonia*) and improve the social and political order.

While these differences in emphasis were not incompatible, they strained the unity of the movement and for a time resulted in three separate philosophical circles, meeting regularly at different locations, each named after its leading teacher, "Zenonians," "Aristonians," and "Herillans." The crisis of identity was resolved in the late third century B.C.E. by Chrysippus, a Zenonian, who overwhelmed his opponents with a massive barrage of arguments. After Chrysippus's refutation we hear no more of Aristoneans or Herillans, and the name "Stoic" comes into common use in place of the sectarian titles.

(ii) *Defending the Faith*. Even before the Stoics had settled this issue, they were confronted by assaults from other schools. *Epicurean *atomists attacked the physical and ethical premises of the Stoics, forcing Cleanthes, Sphaerus, and Chrysippus to engage in an intense polemical campaign in defense of their beliefs. Even more serious was a confrontation with the Academy, which under *Arcesilaus in the third century pushed the Socratic tradition of questioning assumptions to its logical limit. *Skeptical of any dogmatic knowledge, Arcesilaus challenged Zeno's interpretation of Socrates and Greek culture, as well as the basis of his ethics and knowledge of nature. Arcesilaus' attack initiated a two-century-long sustained argument between the Academics and the Stoics, pitting Arcesilaus, and later *Carneades, against a succession of Stoics, including Zeno, Persaeus, Aristo, Cleanthes, Chrysippus, and *Antipater of Tarsus. At stake was the Stoic claim that sensation was capable of yielding trustworthy information about the world, a claim that the Academics vehemently rejected. The dispute ended in a draw, though the practical victory went to the Stoics when the Academic *Antiochus of Ascalon returned to a dogmatic position in the first century B.C.E.

These polemical engagements taught the Stoics the importance of logic and dialectic, forced them to develop a carefully articulated *epistemology and theory of action, and provoked repeated revisions in their physical and ethical theories. Among the beliefs subjected to revision were the criterion of truth, the goal of life, the precise nature of virtue and vice, the seat of sensation, the eternity of the world, the validity of divination, and the unity of the *soul.

(iii) *Expansion and Consolidation.* The flexibility and comprehensive scope of Zeno's philosophical vision encouraged his followers to expand Stoicism's range of applications. Zeno's students, Cleanthes and Sphaerus, began the process by expanding on Zeno's physical philosophy and reacting to new scientific theories. In the next generation Chrysippus carried the expansion of physical philosophy even further and developed dialectic and logic to a comparable degree, devoting nearly half of his enormous literary output to the new Stoic logic of propositions. By the end of the third century the school had a carefully articulated and rigorously argued position in the three traditional fields of philosophy: logic, physics, and ethics.

In the second century B.C.E. the Stoics had to face up to the challenge of consolidating the rich and diverse heritage of the previous century. The leading Stoics, *Diogenes of Seleucia, Antipater of Tarsus, and *Apollodorus of Seleucia, devoted much or their energy to writing introductions, summaries, textbooks, and reference works. This enterprise was not without philosophical import, since it forced the Stoics to grapple with the problems of how to divide and systematize philosophy and how to construe discrepancies and disputes among their predecessors, such as the much-publicized disagreements between Chrysippus and Cleanthes.

The process of extending the application of Stoicism continued in the second and first centuries B.C.E. Language and literature were now subjected to a Stoic analysis on a grand scale by Diogenes of Seleucia, *Crates of Mallos, and *Apollodorus of Athens. Around the end of the second century B.C.E. Stoic scholars extended the application of Stoic analysis to additional scientific fields, Dionysius of Cyrene to *mathematics, and *Posidonius to geology, meteorology, geography, and ethnology. In the first century Posidonius's student, *Athenaeus of Attaleia, applied Stoic physical principles to *medicine and laid the foundations for the so-called Pneumatic school of medicine. Finally, history and political events began receiving serious attention, first from *Panaetius and then from Posidonius. By the first century B.C.E. Stoics had applied their specific form of analysis to virtually every field of study.

(iv) *The Challenge of Practical Application.* Zeno did not shrink from spelling out the radical implications, individual and social, of his commitment to virtue as the only good and a sufficient basis for happiness. As a paradigm of virtue he painted a portrait of the perfect wise man, living the totally rational, harmonious life, however paradoxical such a state might seem and however unachievable it might be for ordinary people. In his *Republic* he portrayed a utopian, harmonious society composed of such truly wise men.

Zeno himself eschewed practical politics. Some of his followers placed more hope in the political process. Though the school itself seems to have had no specific political agenda, its adherents found its principles supportive of the whole spectrum of contemporary political programs, including the Macedonian monarchy, the Roman aristocracy, and democratic reforms at Sparta and Rome.

The ethical implications were also creatively refashioned after Zeno. In the second half of the second century B.C.E. Antipater of Tarsus and his followers adopted a new strategy for calling people to a life of virtue. Whereas earlier Stoics had held up the Stoic wise man as a paradigm of perfect virtue, decisively differentiated from ordinary people, Antipater, Panaetius, *Hecato, and Posidonius shifted their attention to the process by which an ordinary individual advances toward that perfection. At the same time they gave greater articulation and emphasis to morality in the social and political context, thereby increasing the relevance of Stoicism for politically active Greeks and Romans.

In the late second century B.C.E. the Stoics decisively rejected the Cynic strain in Stoicism. By this time the traditional Stoic sympathy for Cynicism and its unconventional, even antisocial, behavior had become an embarrassment to the school. Stoic authors went so far as to rewrite their own history to distance their school from the Cynic movement. About the same time comprehensive standards of doctrinal orthodoxy began to be drawn up in the form of brief, synthetic *doxographies, such as the one handed down in *Diogenes Laertius 7. This doxography validated a wide variety of Stoic physical and ethical beliefs, while decisively rejecting all Cynic-style ideas and any earlier Stoics who were thought to have advocated such, for example, Aristo and Herillus. The effect was to consolidate the Stoic position in ethics firmly on the side of the highest conventional moral values without aligning it with any particular political agenda or diminishing its utility for moral education. This revisionist portrayal of Stoicism, disseminated by *Apollonius of Tyre, remained the accepted view for the rest of the history of the school.

From its inception the Stoic approach to philosophy and life had a broad appeal that carried it beyond the city of Athens to centers of power and culture around the Mediterranean. Foreign students of the Stoa, returning home, created a demand for general education as taught by the Stoics. Associates of the school willingly accepted invitations of foreign rulers to establish schools first in the capitols of the Macedonian, Ptolemaic, and Seleucid empires, then also in the rising kingdom of Pergamum and the commercial center of Rhodes.

The one major city that did not become the site of a satellite school of Stoic philosophy was Rome. Members of the Roman ruling class were either indifferent or openly hostile to Greek philosophy prior to the middle of the second century B.C.E. Panaetius, who lived in Rome for an extended period of time, was the first to spark an interest in Stoic philosophy among Roman nobles. More importantly, he became the prototype of a new kind of Stoic teacher, the house philosopher, supported by and responsible to a single aristocratic patron. Thus Panaetius paved the way to a mobile Stoic "school," tied neither to the parent institution in Athens nor to a single location.

This happened just as loyalty to philosophical schools as corporate institutions was breaking down and being replaced by loyalty to the founder of the movement and as the very concept of school was changing from a localized community of scholars with shared convictions to an ideological position or school of thought, defined by a historical tradition. Symptomatic of this development among the Stoics were attempts to define doctrinal identity by means of doxographies and to document Stoic history and its relationship to other schools.

Sometime during the first quarter of the first century B.C.E. the Stoic school in Athens effectively disappeared as a corporate institution. The last attested teachers in continuous succession from Zeno were *Mnesarchus and *Dardanus of Athens, ironically the first native Athenians to achieve prominence in the Stoic school. The cause of the disintegration is not clear. The revolt of Athens against Roman rule in 88 B.C.E. may have been a factor in forcing supporters of Rome to leave. At any rate, when *Cicero visited in 79 B.C.E., he reported no Stoics actively teaching in Athens.

Stoicism as a Greco-Roman School of Thought. The emancipation of Stoicism from its institutional origins altered its nature and development. Once commitment became a purely mental act, people could study philosophy as an intellectual discipline without making a commitment to a particular school of thought or to its way of life. *Seneca and *Epictetus both complain about students who have become skilled interpreters of Stoic doctrine with no noticeable effect on their attitudes or behavior. Committed followers could change schools or even subscribe to doctrines from competing schools simultaneously. Some philosophers, including some Stoics, deliberately synthesized the teaching of several schools of thought, blurring the lines between the schools.

Teachers of philosophy, now free agents supported by student fees, were even less bound to a given locality than in earlier centuries. None of the Stoics known in the last half of the first century B.C.E. worked in Athens. Those who are known changed residences, sometimes more than once, usually to follow a wealthy patron. The result was the further spread of Stoic education. Casual references to the teaching of the four schools or sects in various cities in the second century C.E. suggest that by this time Stoic teachers were widely distributed and that anyone who could afford it could get at least an elementary Stoic education in any country or province. The advanced study of Stoic logic, physics, and ethics, now based chiefly on the study of classic Stoic texts by Chrysippus, Antipater, and *Archedemus, was available from a limited number of teachers in a few major cites, notably Rome. Some Stoics became itinerant street preachers, rejecting material possessions in Cynic fashion and emphasizing the possibility of virtue and happiness regardless of external circumstances.

Though Stoic teachers could be found in many cities, Rome became the center of Stoic education in the early first century C.E. Despite its earlier hostility to Greek philosophy, Rome began attracting Stoic philosophers in the mid-first century B.C.E., when a few prominent Republican leaders, like Cato and Cicero, brought Stoic philosophers into their homes. On the whole, however, Stoicism held less appeal for Romans in the Republican era than did the other schools, perhaps because of the deliberately rough, "natural" rhetorical style of the Stoics.

Augustus continued the practice of supporting philosophers of various persuasions in his home, including at least one Stoic, *Athenodorus Calvus, thereby bringing philosophy under imperial patronage. The Stoics, with a philosophical stance supportive of the old Roman virtues promoted by Augustus and now less handicapped by their rhetorical style in the changed political climate, found increasing favor among upper-class Romans.

In the first century C.E. Stoic teachers, like Attalus and *Cornutus, flourished. Before long a group of outspoken Stoics came to dominate Roman intellectual life and imperial adminstration, including the poets Persius and Lucan, the philosopher-statesman *Seneca, and a number of imperial officials, such as Thrasea Paetus, Barea Soranus, and Helvidius Priscus. All were persuaded that Stoicism had something to say to the Roman people and their ruler. Their criticism of Nero's excesses resulted in imperial hostility, periodic exile, and in some cases death.

The oppressive regimes of the second half of the first century C.E. did not, however, deter the Stoics. A new generation of teachers arose, among them *Musonius Rufus and his pupil Epictetus. Adopting the firm moral stance of their predecessors, they too were persecuted and forced to pursue their teaching in exile, as was Musonius's student, the orator Dio Chrysostom, when he involved himself in Roman politics.

The attempts of the Roman Stoics to play the role of moral conscience for the Roman empire in the first century C.E. was not without philosophical consequence. Their inability to achieve any significant political impact turned many Roman Stoics toward a more private and internal type of Stoicism, directed at personal salvation from the vicissitudes of fortune and emphasizing simple living, self-sufficiency, detachment, and inner freedom.

The imperial repression lasted on and off until the end of the first century. In the second century the Roman emperors were friendly to philosophers and to the Stoics in particular. The emperor Marcus *Aurelius (161–80 C.E.) himself became a Stoic, published a journal of his philosophical ruminations, and seriously tried to live and rule by Stoic principles. In 176 C.E. he promoted the teaching of philosophy by establishing four professorships in Athens, one in each of the four schools of thought. This imperial endowment of private teachers gave financial security to at least one philosopher of each philosophical sect.

Unlike their educational and political activities, the more technical philosophical activities of the imperial Stoics are not well documented. There are a few clues, however, that Stoic philosophical discussion, as distinct from Stoic education, did not diminish as much as the surviving Roman literature might suggest. When Seneca was forced to retire from politics, he devoted his time to serious exploration of ethical issues and geological and meteorological phenomena. The intensive anti-Stoic polemics of the *Platonist *Plutarch and the *Peripatetic *Alexander of Aphrodisias indicate that Stoic epistemology, physics, and *metaphysics continued to find articulate defenders and interpreters down through the second century C.E. *Cleomedes' *On the Circular Motion of the Heavens* and *Hierocles' *Exposition of the Elements of Ethics* give us a taste of the serious, creative philosophical analysis that continued alongside the practical ethical and social applications dominating the surviving Roman literature.

Stoicism as a defined school of thought came to an end around the middle of the third century C.E. A number of names are known from the first half of the third century, but none later. No ancient source explains why. Modern speculation points to the social and economic disintegration that set in in the third century. Some observe that popular culture and the emerging world views of *Neoplatonism and *Christianity shared a belief in transcendent, immaterial reality and a hope for personal immortality, with the suggestion that such beliefs may have been more appealing under the circumstances than the worldly materialism of the Stoa.

The disappearance of Stoic teachers and self-confessed Stoics did not spell the end of the Stoic tradition, however. The detachment of Stoic teaching from any corporate institution had accelerated the circulation of its ideas outside the Stoic sect and even outside philosophical circles altogether. The Stoic way of thinking had already begun to affect non-Stoic scholarly and scientific literature in the first century B.C.E. Stoic contributions to grammar, geography, meteorology, and *astronomy carried Stoic conceptions and methods into these disciplines. In medicine the Stoic-influenced pneumatic theory, combined with discussions by other doctors who had studied Stoicism (e.g., *Galen), left a permanent imprint on the field. When the Alexandrian Jewish writer *Philo used Stoic and Platonic concepts to interpret Jewish sacred texts, he introduced Stoicism into theology. *Clement and *Origen of Alexandria continued to draw on Stoicism along with Platonism to expound Christian theology. Finally, Platonism itself had absorbed much from Stoicism since the first century B.C.E. In the third century C.E. *Plotinus brought Stoic and Peripatetic ideas together with Platonic philosophy to create Neoplatonism, the philosophical system that, with Christianity, was to replace Stoicism as the dominant worldview. Stoicism thus did not die out even after its professed proponents did. It was rather transformed once again, this time from a philosophical school of thought to an integral component of the culture of late antiquity.

BIBLIOGRAPHY: Texts and translations in LS. Erskine, A., *The Hellenistic Stoa: Political Thought and Action*, Ithaca, 1990; Griffin, M., and J. Barnes, eds., *Philosophia Togata: Essays on Philosophy and Roman Society*, Oxford, 1989; Long, A. A., *Hellenistic Philosophy: Stoics, Epicureans, and Sceptics,*[2] Berkeley, 1986; Pohlenz, M., *Die Stoa: Geschichte einer geistigen Bewegung,*[4] 2 vols., Göttingen, 1949; Sandbach, F. H., *The Stoics*, London, 1975.—DAVID E. HAHM

STOBAEUS, Ioannes (John of Stobi—fl. early 5th cent. C.E.). Anthologer and educator. An immensely learned non-Christian scholar of the early fifth century C.E., Stobaeus compiled a massive anthology of "excerpts, sayings, and admonitions" to educate his son Septimius. His anthology originally contained excerpts of varying lengths from more than five hundred Greek poets, philosophers, orators, historians, and previous anthologers, ranging in time from *Homer to *Themistius. These were organized under more than two hundred headings, in four long books. Beginning with selections in praise of philosophy, Stobaeus surveyed *mathematics, *theology, and physical philosophy (Book 1), *epistemology, *logic, *rhetoric, language, the art of poetry (beginning of Book 2), *ethics (rest of Book 2 and Book 3), and *political theory and practice, followed by a host of practical subjects, concluding with death and burial (Book 4). The arrangement suggests that Stobaeus saw his anthology as a comprehensive, systematic textbook designed to instruct in all branches of learning, but aimed primarily at moral improvement and instruction in practical living.

Stobaeus' work caps a long tradition of collecting pithy sayings (gnomes) and literary quotations for educational purposes. It so far surpassed its predecessors that it became the most popular anthology in the Middle Ages and the principal source of classical quotations for later anthologers and scholiasts. Sometime after the ninth century the work was substantially abridged. By the eleventh century it was circulating as two separate works, the severely abridged Books 1 and 2, *Selections of Physical Opinions* (*Eclogae*), and the more popular and less severely abridged Books 3 and 4, *Anthology* (*Florilegium*). It remains an invaluable source of quotations of lost works and an important independent witness to the Greek text of surviving works.

BIBLIOGRAPHY: Texts in C. Wachsmuth, ed., *Ioannis Stobaei Anthologii libri duo priores*, 2 vols., Berlin, 1884; O. Hense, ed., *Ioannis Stobaei Anthologii libri duo posteriores*, 3 vols., Berlin, 1894–1912. Hense, O., *RE* 9.2, cols. 2549–86; Chadwick, H., *Reallexikon fur Antike und Christentum* 7, Stuttgart, 1964, 1131–59.—*DAVID E. HAHM*

STRABO (64/63 B.C.E.–c. 25 C.E.), of Amasia, a city near the Black Sea coast of eastern Turkey. A *Stoic geographer and historian, whose one surviving work, the *Geography*, was composed as a follow-up to a long historical treatise, the *Historical Recollections*, now lost. Strabo came from a prominent family of mixed Greek and Asiatic lineage and was educated by the noted *Aristotelians Xenarchus and Tyrannio and the Stoic *Athenodorus. A late source reports that he was also tutored by *Posidonius (who was still alive during Strabo's youth), but Strabo himself never mentions any such relationship to his great predecessor. In any case the *Geography* has little of the scientific ambition of Posidonius' *Histories* and does not apply Stoic principles to the study of the earth in any consistent or thoroughgoing way (as does the Roman work that followed it by half a century, *Seneca's *Natural Questions*). However Strabo apparently considered himself a more faithful Stoic than Posidonius, since he compares his own rejection of causal explanations with the "Aristotlizing" of the elder scientist (2.3.8).

Strabo also contrasts his own Stoic beliefs with the eclecticism of *Eratosthenes, the third century B.C.E. geographer and scholar whom he regarded as chief adversary on a number of issues. Strabo rebukes Eratosthenes for having deserted the teachings of *Zeno of Citium, principally in the area of literary criticism: Whereas Stoic dogma demanded that poetry have a useful and instructive purpose, Eratosthenes had dared to suggest that it aimed instead at *psuchagogia,* entertainment or aesthetic pleasure. This fundamental difference in outlook led to opposing interpretations of poems like *Homer's *Odyssey*, a text that Strabo debates at length in Book 1 of the *Geography*. Homer knew all about the structure of the earth, claims Strabo, and wrote the *Odyssey* to convey that knowledge; his poem conforms to Stoic ideas about pragmatism and instruction, not to the Eratosthenic goal of *psuchagogia*.

Elsewhere in the *Geography*, Strabo muses vaguely about the nature of divinity or the role of Forethought in shaping the earth, but in general he should be seen as a redactor and raconteur with philosophic pretensions rather than as a true philosopher. His work is more noted for what it preserves of the lost writings of Eratosthenes, Posidonius and others than for its own scientific achievements.

BIBLIOGRAPHY: Texts in H. L. Jones, *The Geography of Strabo*, 8 vols. (Loeb), London, 1917–24. Aujac, G., *Strabon et la science de son temps*, Paris, 1966; Bunbury, E. H., *A History of Ancient Geography* vol. 2, London, 1879, chs. 21–2; Hamilton, H. C., and W. Falconer, *The Geography of Strabo*, 3 vols., London, 1854–7; Tozer, H. F., *Selections from Strabo*, Oxford, 1893.—*JAMES ROMM*

STRATO (d. c. 268 B.C.E.), of Lampsacus in Mysia on the Hellespont. Head of the *Peripatos after *Theophrastus. Having earlier been tutor to Ptolemy Philadelphus of Egypt, Strato succeeded Theophrastus in about 286 and was in turn succeeded by *Lyco. Among his students was the astronomer *Aristarchus, and he influenced the physician *Erasistratus.

*Diogenes Laertius lists some forty-seven works by Strato (5.59–60), all now lost, though fragments remain. Some works now falsely attributed to *Aristotle may be by him, such as *On Things Heard* and the *Mechanics*. Opinions differ, but he was probably largely an orthodox *Aristotelian, improving on rather than rejecting Aristotle's teachings, but also reacting to contemporary *Stoics and *Epicureans. Later writers probably distorted his teachings and picked out only points where he differed form others; and many of them used handbooks of opinions that had already classified him, perhaps inadequately. Much of our evidence comes from *Cicero, *Sextus Empiricus, and Tertullian. Repici's study (see bibliography) shows how much more is needed to interpret such evidence.

Polybius says that Strato was better at refuting the arguments of others than at setting out his own views. Evidence suggests that he was also a keen *scientific observer and an innovator in the use of experiments, which justifies his epithet "the scientist." Evidence about his theory of the *void comes from the works of the engineer Hero of Alexandria. Whereas Aristotle had denied the existence of any kind of void, and the *atomists had postulated void on a large scale, Strato argued for the existence of microvoids, bubbles in *matter, as it were: Air was a body, and there were microvoids existing naturally in matter, whereas large-scale voids existed only unnaturally. Opinions differ about how far he is responsible for the apparatus described by Hero to show the compressibility of air, but he probably used the existence of compressibility to show the existence of microvoids. He abandoned Aristotle's theory of natural place and said that all matter has weight. He also criticized Aristotle's account of *time as the number of movement and gave a new account of it as the measure of movement and rest.

The evidence concerning Strato's *psychology is controversial. He followed Aristotle generally, but he argued that perception is impossible without some kind of thought; for example, we are aware of the distance from us to a heard sound, which must be by some kind of calculation. Even the activity of intellect involves movement, and so he may have provided as much an analysis of the concept of movement as a piece of psychology. He believed that the *soul was unitary and used the analogy of a flute to explain its workings. He developed aspects of Aristotle that are downplayed by modern philosophers, like that of the *pneuma* as the basis of the activities of the soul. He explained sleep as the segregation of the vital *pneuma* (the complete departure of which results in death), and dreams (though the textual evidence is uncertain here) by the activity of thought (*dianoia*). He denied that sound is the result of air being given a shape, and he may be responsible for the theory in *On Things Heard* that air is affected by blows and so travels outwards.

Strato defined *being as "the cause of permanence." He somehow identified God and nature, though his account of the workings of the universe seems to have excluded the influence of God and steered a course between the Stoics and the Epicureans, arguing that nature acted without reason but spontaneously. *Olympiodorus reproduces his arguments against the proofs of the immortality of the soul in Plato's *Phaedo*: three against anamnesis and twenty-one against the various arguments from the opposites. These are short and varied, some giving counter-examples (e.g., old men do not become young), and others being more philosophical (e.g., the relevant identity might be formal, not numerical; or, we must distinguish between immortality and indestructibility).

Strato wrote on the same *ethical subjects as his predecessors, but little is known of his views, except that the *good is what perfects potentiality into actuality. He followed his predecessors' views in *logic, but little of his work in this area has survived.

Strato's successors in the Peripatos are shadowy, but some works in the Aristotelian Corpus have been attributed to his pupils, including the *Mechanics* and some of the *Problems*. *Problems* 4 and 9 have been attributed to a medical associate of his, and many parts of this varied collection probably come from his associates. Erasistratus seems to have applied his theory of microvoids to physiology. His pupil Aristarchus developed the heliocentric theory of the universe, perhaps as a hypothesis only. This might have been influenced by Strato's antitheological approach to nature.

BIBLIOGRAPHY: Texts in Wehrli 5; Gottschalk, H. B., ed., *Strato of Lampsacus: Some Texts*, Leeds, 1965 (additions to Wehrli). Furley, D., in J. Wiesner, ed., *Aristoteles, Werk und Wirkung*, Berlin, 1985; Repici, L., *La Natura e L'Anima Saggi su Stratone di Lampsaco*, Turin, 1988.—PAMELA M. HUBY

SYRIANUS (d. c. 437 C.E.). *Neoplatonist, head of the *Academy from 432, student of *Plutarch of Athens and teacher of *Proclus. Little biographical information is available, and most of his work is lost. There remains a *commentary on Books 2, 4, 13 and 14 of *Aristotle's *Metaphysics*, in which Syrianus defends the theory of Forms against Aristotle's critique, and commentaries on two *rhetorical works of Hermogenes. Hermias' commentary on *Plato's *Phaedrus* is believed to be a fairly close account of Syrianus' lectures on that dialogue.

His philosophy is of the late Neoplatonic type that began with *Iamblichus, characterised by a high level of realism that led to the multiplication of intelligible entities. He seems to have had a strong inclination to *Pythagoreanism and numerology, manifested by the composition of ten books on the agreement of Orpheus, *Pythagoras, and Plato, as well as a special interest in the role of Monad and Indefinite Dyad in the constitution of the world. Pending further work on the excavation of his doctrines his significance lies primarily in his apparently considerable influence on Proclus, at Athens, and also, through Hermeias, on *Ammonius, the inaugurator of the Aristotle-exposition industry at Alexandria.

BIBLIOGRAPHY: Texts in W. Kroll, ed., *CAG* vol. 6.1, Berlin, 1902; Rabe, H., *Syriani in Hermogenem Commentaria*, 2 vols., Berlin, 1892, 1893; Cardullo, R. L., *Siriano Esegeta di Aristotele: I Frammenti e testimonianze dei commentari all'* Organon, Florence, 1995. Cardullo, R. L., *Siculorum Gymnasium* n.s. 40, 1987, 71–182; Sheppard, A. D. R., in H. J. Blumenthal and A. C. Lloyd, eds., *Soul and the Structure of Being in Late Neoplatonism*, Liverpool, 1982, 1–14.—*H. J. BLUMENTHAL*

THALES (early 6th cent. B.C.E.), of Miletus, known only through reports by various authors from *Herodotus onward: If Thales wrote anything—and this was disputed in antiquity—nothing survives even in quotations. *Diogenes Laertius asserts that he was the son of Examyes and Cleobuline and that whereas some (perhaps following Herodotus) claim that Thales was of Phoenician descent, most maintain that he was a true-born Milesian.

Herodotus, the earliest extant source of reports about Thales, mentions him in connection with a solar eclipse that purportedly occurred during a battle between the Medes and Lydians. This report, which apparently sealed Thales' renown as an *astronomer, is puzzling and subject to divergent interpretations. First, did an eclipse actually take place? In the ancient world, solar eclipses were ominous events; and it is clear in later texts that such eclipses were sometimes affirmed for literary effect when none had in fact occurred. Accordingly, modern calculations that a solar eclipse took place in 585/4 B.C.E. may well be beside the point, especially given the range of dates assigned the battle in antiquity. Next, what does Herodotus mean in saying that Thales had told the Ionians that this solar eclipse was going to occur, setting as a limit the year in which the eclipse took place? The assumption that Thales foretold the particular eclipse on the basis of Babylonian observational records is certainly naive and ill-informed, and there is no need to ascribe it to Herodotus. Indeed, if Herodotus supposed that Thales relied on Babylonian celestial science, his meaning would more likely be that Thales had proclaimed the *possibility* of a solar eclipse during the given year. Later writers such as Diogenes Laertius, who cites *Eudemus' *History of*

Astronomy, maintain that Thales predicted the particular eclipse that occurred; but, though the idea of stating in advance the date of a solar eclipse visible at a given location is attested in Greco-Latin literature of the first century B.C.E., this was beyond the Babylonians at any period, and it is not clear that even the astronomical treatises written by *Ptolemy would equip one to do this. Other writers, such as Pliny, the anonymous scholiast on Homer, *Odyssey* 20, and *Theon of Smyrna (who cites Dercyllides again citing Eudemus' *History*), attribute to Thales a causal account of solar eclipses. In effect, they take Herodotus to mean that Thales had announced that the sort of eclipse observed during the battle occurs only at certain moments during the Sun's annual course—that is, when its conjunctions with the Moon meet certain requirements.

Herodotus also credits Thales with expertise in political affairs and mentions a story accepted in his time about Thales' prowess in military affairs. By the fourth century B.C.E., Thales' reputation as one of the *Seven Sages (*sophoi*) was well established. Indeed, no ancient list of these Sages fails to include his name. Such popularity as an intellectual type may underlie the anecdotes told of Thales as well as the ascription to him of numerous maxims and gnomic assertions including "Know Thyself." *Plato (*Tht.* 174a–b), however, is the first to present Thales as a philosopher rather than just as a Sage, albeit he does so in a story to illustrate the philosopher's inevitable, but not necessarily innate, incompetence in practical matters, a theme amplified later in anecdotes of Thales' business acumen. *Aristotle likewise characterizes Thales as a philosopher, but his account is significant for making Thales the first *phusikos*, that is, the first of those philosophical inquirers into the nature of things as whole who posited *matter of some sort as the ultimate, invariant principle underlying all *change. Beyond asserting that Thales posited water as the single, fundamental principle of all things, Aristotle's remarks about Thales lack detail and seem guarded, indicating perhaps that Aristotle was sifting through what was by his time largely a literary fiction. Later writers are less scrupulous and confidently assign to Thales ideas that Aristotle had ascribed tentatively, namely, that the cosmos is full of gods, that some things commonly considered inanimate have *soul, and that the earth floats on water.

The earliest extant reports that Thales discovered some elementary geometrical theorems date from the first century C.E. Such reports, combined with Herodotus' contention that the Greeks got geometry from the Egyptians and Thales' reputation as a Sage, may be the warrant for the thesis first attested a century later that Thales was responsible for introducing geometry to the Greeks.

BIBLIOGRAPHY: Testimonia in DK11; cf. also DK10. Aaboe, A., *Journal for the History of Astronomy* 3, 1972, 105–118; Bowen, A. C. and Goldstein, B. R., *Physis* 31.3, 1994, 689–729.—*ALAN C. BOWEN*

THEAETETUS and **THEODORUS**, *mathematicians. The evidence for Theodorus of Cyrene (5th–4th cent. B.C.E.) and Theaetetus of Athens (c. 414–369 B.C.E.) comes principally from *Plato's *Theaetetus*. Theodorus was a friend of *Protagoras (a *Pythagoraean, according to *Iamblichus), whom Plato may have visited in Cyrene (D.L. 3.6). Theaetetus studied with Theodorus. Taking the mathematics of *Theaetetus* 147d–148b seriously enables conjectural reconstructions of their mathematics based principally on (i) the *dialogue; (ii) *Proclus *Commentary on Euclid's Elements* 1, on the eminence of Theodorus in geometry (cf. Iamblichus *On Common Mathematical Science*) and the relation of Theaetetus' work to *Eudoxus' work; (iii) *Eudemus' claim (4th cent. B.C.E.) that Theaetetus developed three classifications of irrationals as three kinds of means (cf. Pappus *Commentary* 1.1, 2.17–20); (iv) scholia to *Elements* 10.9 and 13 that 10.9 and the constructions of the octahedron and icosohedron are due to Theaetetus (all five solids according to the late *Suda*); (v) traces of early proportion theory in Aristotle *Topics* 158b29–35; and (vi) *Euclid's heterogeneous treatise, the *Elements*, especially 2, 7, 10, and 13. Our investigation is ultimately an archeology of Euclid's *Elements*.

Prior to the discussion of the *Theaetetus*, Theodorus had proved that a three-square-foot power (*dunamis*) or square (Knorr followed by Burnyeat), up to a 17-square-foot-power is or is not commensurable in length with a square foot (i.e., the sides of the squares with a foot length), but stopped for some reason at 17. Why? If we seek a mathematical reason— it makes little sense otherwise—Theodorus would have got stuck either on 17 or on 19, since 18 is trivial on almost any account and may be skipped. Of the latter sort some reconstructions use continued fractions, the Euclidean algorithm for finding greatest common measures (*antuphairesis*): for two magnitudes A>B one finds $C_1 = A - n_1 B < B$, and then with this remainder one finds $C_2 = B - n_2 C_1 < C_1$, and so forth. A and B are commensurable iff the sequence ends ($C_i = 0$). Knorr has Theodorus get stuck on 17, which fits Plato's text best. Here Theodorus looks at right triangles with hypotenuse and one leg commensurable and proves them incommensurable with the other if, when hypothesized numerical ratios of the sides get divided out by twos, the integer associated with one leg must be both odd and even. The method fails if the ratios of the sides are $\sqrt{17}$:8:9.

Building on the work of Theodorus, Theaetetus, in the dialogue, states a general theory of squares and cubes. Let X~Y mean that magnitudes X, Y are commensurable, and A≈B that lines A, B are commensurable only in power ($A^2{\sim}B^2$, but not $A{\sim}B$), and let F be some measure, and n, m integers. Theaetetus classifies numbers as either square or oblong and a line A, where $A^2{=}nF^2$, as length if n is square and as power if n is oblong. He claims for such lines, $A{\sim}F$ iff A is a length, and likewise where $A^3{=}nF^3$, $A{\sim}F$ iff $\exists m(n{=}m^3)$. The historical Theaetetus proved at least the generalizations, $A{\sim}B$ iff $\exists n,m(A{:}B{=}n{:}m)$ and $A{\sim}B$ iff $\exists n,m(A^2{:}B^2{=}n^2{:}m^2)$ (*Elements* 10.5–9), probably using continued fractions (cf. 7.1–3, 10.2–6, Aristotle's *Topics*). He defines a line A as rational iff $A^2{\sim}F^2$ (note that this is not the modern notion) and derives three classes of irrationals. Let A, C be rational, but $A{\approx}C$, and $A{>}C$. Following Pappus,

The medial B is a geometric mean A:B=B:C.

The binomial (in Euclid A+C) is an additive mean, $B{=}\dfrac{A+C}{2}$.

The apotome (in Euclid A–C) is a harmonic mean. The harmonic proportion is A-B:B-C=A:C. Hence (A+C)B=2AC. Since AC is a medial area (i.e. the square of a medial), so is (A+C)B. But since A+C is binomial and (A+C)B is medial, B=D-E, where A:C=D:E and $A{\sim}D$ (modify *Elements* 10.112).

Analysis of a pentagon inscribed in a circle (*Elements* 13.11) for the construction of the icosohedron shows this system to be incomplete and leads to the complete system of *Elements* 10.

BIBLIOGRAPHY: Text of *Theaetetus* in J. Burnet, ed., *Platonis Opera*, vol. 1, Oxford, 1900. Becker, O., *Quellen und Studien zur Geschichte der Mathematik, Astronomie und Physik*, Abt. B, 2, 1933, 311–333; Burnyeat, M., *Isis* 69, 1978, 489–513; also exchange with Knorr, *Isis* 70, 1979, 565–70; Euclid, *The Elements of Euclid*, T. L. Heath, tr., Cambridge, 1926; Fowler, D. H., *The Mathematics of Plato's Academy*, Oxford, 1987; Knorr, W. R., *The Evolution of the Euclidean Elements*, Dordrecht, 1975; Mueller, I., *Philosophy of Mathematics and Deductive Structure in Euclid's Elements*, Cambridge, 1981; Pappus, *The Commentary of Pappus on Book 10 of Euclid's Elements*, W. Thomson, tr., Cambridge, 1930.—HENRY MENDELL

THEAETETUS, **Anonymous Commentator on Plato's**. *Middle Platonist philosopher, whose commentary on the *Theaetetus*, partially preserved in an Egyptian papyrus, is probably our earliest specimen of philosophical commentary. He is datable between c. 50 B.C.E. and c. 150 C.E., when the actual copy was written. The original editors, Diels and Schubart (*Berliner Klassikertexte* 2, 1905), associated the author with the so-called school of Gaius at the end of that period, but recent opinion veers towards its earlier part. The author, who refers to commentaries of his own on *Symposium*, *Phaedo* and *Timaeus*, remains unidentified. He is hostile towards the *Stoics, but recruits *Aristotle as an ally, using his *Topics* as a methodological handbook. The surviving seventy-five columns cover *Theaetetus* 147–153 and 157. Championing a doctrinal brand of *Platonism, he repeatedly resists the Hellenistic *Academy's *skeptical interpretation of the *Theaetetus*: rather, the *dialogue is a piece of midwifery, which at its close leaves the reader on the brink of the correct definition of knowledge, namely, that found at *Meno* 98a.

BIBLIOGRAPHY: Text, Italian tr. and comm. by G. Bastianini and D. Sedley in *Corpus dei papiri filosofici greci e latini* pt. 3, Florence, 1995. Tarrant, H., *CQ* 33, 1983, 161–87.—*DAVID N. SEDLEY*

THEISM and ATHEISM. The Greek noun *theos* or "god" stands roughly for some superhuman power or being. The attribute that was thought to belong most appropriately to a god was immortality, perhaps because it was that which humans most keenly felt the lack of in themselves. Personal attributes such as thinking, will, desire, and so on were widely, but not universally, associated with gods. The word *atheos*, literally "without god," is an adjective referring to someone who rejects some particular entrenched conception of a god and that god's attributes. Eventually, the term was used for those who rejected the existence of gods unqualifiedly.

A convenient way to begin to understand ancient philosophical approaches to the divine is to follow a division of theology that is likely *Stoic in origin. According to this division, there are three types of theology: (i) civic, (ii) mythical, and (iii) philosophical, wherein (i) refers to the uncritical beliefs embodied in the cultic practices of political or ethnic groups; (ii) refers to the stories of the poets *Homer and *Hesiod and others that comprised the common patrimony of all Greeks as well as those who were deeply influenced by Greek culture, such as the Romans; and (iii) refers to the arguments of philosophers regarding the existence and nature of divinities. These last were frequently advanced in conscious opposition to (i) and (ii).

Amidst a welter of contradictory and unsupported popular beliefs, the earliest Greek philosophers reasoned that the study of the divine should employ the same methodology by which we seek to understand the causes of phenomena generally. Thus a philosopher, like the Presocratic *Xenophanes, could argue against what he took to be gratuitously anthropomorphized deities and for "one god, greatest among gods and men, and in no way similar to mortals either in body or in thought" (DK21B23). This "one god" is evidently an explanatory cause, part of a larger framework of scientific explanation. It is like a neutrino or the unconscious or other postulated entities in various versions of scientific realism. It is a philosopher's god, considerably removed from any religious context, personal or social. Xenophanes explicitly does not deny the existence of other gods, but he sets them aside as irrelevant to the context of philosophical theology. A large part of the story of theism and atheism in ancient Greek philosophy is the development of philosophical theology and its interaction with popular belief, first in the form of the various pagan religions, and then in the forms of Judaism and early *Christianity. Since this form of theology both consists of arguments with premises drawn from the natural world and aims thereby to arrive at an understanding of nature, it is sometimes called "natural" theology.

By contrast with Xenophanes, there were some true atheists, such as *Prodicus of Ceos, Diagoras of Melos, and *Theodorus the *Cyrenaic, whose critical analysis of the mythical deities was not in aid of a reconstructed philosophical theology. And there were others, like the *sophist *Protagoras, who arrived at the position of agnosticism, denying that he had any means of knowing whether or not the gods exist. Protagoras was perhaps one of the first to make agnosticism a part of a more general *skeptical argument regarding the possibility of knowledge.

Among the Presocratics, *Parmenides stands out as one who attempts to attach the putatively divine characteristics of immortality, unchangeability, and perfection to impersonal being. We might say that he seeks to detach *metaphysics not just from civic and mythical theology, but even from any philosophical theology that insists on the relevance of the personal to *cosmological explanation. Revealingly, Parmenides has his argument for *being as the subject of authentic thinking revealed to him by a goddess. Mythical theology is thus reduced to a literary device now put into the service of philosophy.

The theology of *Plato represents a rich source of philosophical thinking in relation to traditional beliefs about the gods that we possess from antiquity. Plato does not repudiate myth altogether in the representation of the divine. Rather, he argues for a use of myth controlled by philosophical argument. Thus, in the *Euthyphro* he has *Socrates argue that the gods love something because it is pious, not that it is pious because the gods love it (10a–11b). If this is so, our understanding of our relations to the gods is based not on discerning an inscrutable divine mind but on philosophical knowledge of piety and the other virtues. The popular gods here are accepted as a part of the universe but are excluded from a role in ultimate philosophical explanations. In Plato's great work, the *Republic*, the ultimate explanatory entity is said to be the Form of the Good (505a–509c; 523a–534c). This Form was assumed by later commentators in antiquity obviously to be divine owing to its role at the pinnacle of an intelligible universe, but it possesses no personal attributes.

Plato's theology changes along with the development of his thinking about the nature of reality and *knowledge and the human person. In his most influential work, the *Timaeus*, he argues that a contingent world must have a maker (28a–c). This maker he calls "Demiurge" (Gk. *dêmiourgos*, "handicraftsman"). Identifying its creative activity as essentially good, he says that the Demiurge was ungrudging in making the world as good as possible. The traditional mythical deities are not here repudiated, but rather demoted to the position of subordinates to the Demiurge and set apart as mostly unknowable through philosophy. It is the figure of an omnibenevolent, eternal, and omniscient *mind that is at the center of Plato's most mature thinking regarding the divine. Plato, however, denies that the Demiurge is omnipotent. The Demiurge is constrained in his construction of the sensible world by "necessity," which represents basically an element of unintelligibility in a contingent universe. Such a constraint does not entail a similar constraint in knowledge. The Demiurge apparently knows all that is knowable.

In Plato's last work, the *Laws*, he lays down the principles of a state religion based upon his arguments concerning the existence and nature of the divine (Book 10). Plato proposes a rational basis for the extirpation of atheism from his proposed state. According to Plato, an atheist holds one of the following propositions: (i) the gods do not exist; (ii) the gods are indifferent to human concerns; or (iii) the gods can be bribed by prayer and sacrifice. To counter atheism and to establish the contradictories of the above three propositions, Plato has recourse to a lengthy argument striving to show that everything in the universe in motion must ultimately be caused by something that moves itself, namely, a *soul. Thus, Plato's proof for the existence of a god is a proof for the cosmic priority of soul. Whether there are many or only one soul governing the universe seems to be a question of secondary importance to Plato.

*Aristotle, in his early philosophical *dialogues, now extant only in fragmentary form, shows a strong interest in drawing out the *ethical consequences of a conception of the gods very much like that which is evident in the *Laws*. In his later more technical writings, however, Aristotle begins to focus on a more rigorously philosophical understanding of theology. He agrees with Plato that things that are moved do not explain their own motion. He denies, though, that the explanation is to be found in a self-mover. Rather, he argues that god must cause things to move as an unmoved mover. In the *Metaphysics*, god does this by being a final cause, an object of desire (1072a26ff.). In addition, this unmoved mover, identified by Aristotle with perfectly actual form, must be unique. Thus Aristotle is a more philosophically scrupulous monotheist than Plato, but at the same time he is led to posit a god who can have only a special type of effect on things here below and no interest in them whatsoever. It should be added, however, that in many passages Aristotle shows a sincere respect for popular theological beliefs. There is no way of knowing how Aristotle supposed these beliefs to cohere with his own more austere philosophical conclusions.

Aristotle describes god as pure thinking thinking about itself. Its complete self-absorption makes it impossible for it to be related to anything in the universe except as an ideal life to be emulated. For Aristotle, the science of being qua being or metaphysics is ultimately identical with theology (though it is not easy to see how this is so). Aristotle thought that theology was actually the most noble and satisfying activity for human beings. But this was not because one could thereby enter into some sort of personal relationship with the divine.

*Epicurus is a philosopher who holds an extreme version of the position, implicit in Aristotle, that the divine is unrelated to human affairs. For Epicurus, god or the gods, being blissfully happy by definition, care nothing at all for their inferiors, we human beings among them. Of course, someone who holds that gods are happy and even that this is obvious to us cannot be said to be an atheist in the sense of one who denies the existence of the gods. Nevertheless, Epicurus was reviled in antiquity as an atheist for his denial of divine providence. Like the *atomists before him, upon whose physical theories he relied, he believed that the category of divinity was simply irrelevant to scientific explanation.

Just as Epicurean theism was taken to be a kind of atheism for its denial of providence, so *Stoic theism was taken to be a kind of atheism for its denial of the existence of independent immaterial entities. For the Stoics, god was identical with a material principle that pervades the intelligible universe. The existence of god is therefore inferable from the presence of design in the universe because god is virtually identical with that which makes a design rational. In addition, the uniqueness of god is directly deducible from the uniqueness of the universe. But the Stoic god is radically impersonal. Whereas the Epicureans rejected providence altogether, the Stoics identified it with the causally determined order of events. And whereas *Parmenides held a metaphysics without theology, the Stoics, as thoroughgoing materialists, held a theology without metaphysics.

The period known as *Middle Platonism includes a number of philosophers who attempted to meld *Platonic, *Peripatetic, and Stoic theological positions with various degrees of acuity and plausibility. It is difficult to know if *Albinus (perhaps to be identified with *Alcinous), for example, believed that Aristotle and Plato actually held the same doctrine about god or whether Albinus intentionally thought he was constructing a theology that united the most defensible features of each. Albinus held that Platonic Forms exist and that they are identical with thoughts in the mind of god who is, following Aristotle, an unmoved mover, causing motion as object of desire. Albinus further enriched the concept of god with the attributes of will and efficient causal activity, much as the Demiurge of Plato. God becomes for Albinus the paradigm of goodness.

A different and enormously influential type of syncretic theology is found in *Philo of Alexandria, a Hellenized Jew who tried to incorporate what he took to be the best of Greek philosophy into his own understanding of the revealed religion of the Old Testament. Whereas the Greek philosophers already mentioned viewed philosophical theology as superior to other types of theology owing to its rational nature, Philo argued that philosophical theology was itself properly subjected to the control of revelation. Accordingly, he could use the Biblical picture of God as a criterion for evaluating competing philosophical conceptions. In particular, he found in a combination of Platonism and Stoicism the most satisfying rational explanations of the divine. For Philo, God is both the ultimate immutable principle of cosmic rationality and a loving person.

The importance of theology to Greek philosophy generally can be gauged from the attention *Skeptics paid to the refutation of the possibility of theological argument. As *Sextus Empiricus put it, "if we can show the doubtfulness of inquiry concerning the gods, then we will have virtually shown that neither is wisdom the knowledge of divine and human things, nor philosophy the practice of wisdom" (P 1.13). The basic strategy employed by Sextus, a strategy that very likely reflects earlier skeptical argument, is to show that the existence of nonevident deities cannot be inferred from anything evident, such as our own sense-experience. And given the fact that people differ in their conceptions of the gods and some even deny their existence, one can hardly say that it is evident that they exist. Therefore, there is no rational basis for holding that gods exist or that they possess the attributes traditionally assigned to them, such as being providential. A thoroughgoing skeptic, however, will allow that there is equally no rational basis for a dogmatic assertion that the gods do not exist.

The *Neoplatonist *Plotinus brought not only Platonic but also Peripatetic, Stoic, and Middle Platonic ideas to his remarkably original systematic philosophy that is at its base theological. For Plotinus, god is unique and the cause of the being of everything in the universe. Owing to the necessary simplicity of god, it is more accurate to speak of god negatively than positively. We can also speak of god analogously, saying, for instance, that god has a sort of will and a sort of intellect, and so on. Plotinus believed that he could prove the existence and uniqueness of a perfectly simple cause of everything. He also believed that the perfectly simple first principle of all must be identified with the paradigms of personal attributes such as will and intellection. But the manner in which these are present in god is literally incomprehensible. In a way, Plotinus' god is even further removed from this world than is the god of Aristotle and even more intimately connected with it than the god of Plato.

After Plotinus, Greek philosophers found themselves increasingly in opposition to *Christianity. Since Christian theology was itself in the process of development at this time, there occurred numerous disputes regarding the principles and conclusion each camp could and could not accept from the other. As Christianity began to dominate the ancient intellectual world, Christian theologians found themselves as often as not employing Greek theological arguments to attack the remnants of paganism. In this milieu, atheism came to be identified with the rejection of the Christian doctrines regarding the divine. The Christian theologians Justin Martyr and *Clement of Alexandria are two good examples of those steeped in Greek philosophy who tried to sift out of it what was in harmony with Biblical teaching (see also CHRISTIANITY).

BIBLIOGRAPHY: Arnou, R., *Le Désir de Dieu dans la philosophie du Plotin,*[2] Rome, 1967; Bodeüs, R., *Aristote et la théologie des vivants immortels,* St. Laurent, Que., 1992; Burkert, W., *Greek Religion,* Cambridge, MA, 1985, ch. 7, "Philosophical Religion." Dragona-Monachou, M., *The Stoic Arguments for the Existence and the Providence of God,* Athens, 1976; Fahr, W., *Theous Nomizein,* Hildesheim/New York, 1969; Gerson, L. P., *God and Greek Philosophy: Studies in the Early History of Natural Theology,* London/ New York, 1990; Jaeger, W., *The Theology of the Early Greek Philosophers,* Oxford, 1947; Pépin, J., *Idées grecques sur l'homme et sur Dieu,* Paris, 1971.—LLOYD P. GERSON

THEMISTIUS (c. 317–388 C.E.), of Paphlagonia. Statesman, orator, and *Peripatetic *commentator on *Aristotle and contemporary of *Iamblichus but outside the prevailing *Neoplatonic tradition. Like others who did philosophy in the Byzantine world, he had a career in politics, but unlike them his philosophical output was confined to an early period of his career. About that we have more information (from his public speeches) than for any other philosopher of the Imperial period, with the possible exception of *Plotinus.

Themistius' extant philosophical works are paraphrase commentaries on Aristotle's *Posterior Analytics, Physics,* and *De Anima* and in Hebrew versions of Arabic translations *De Caelo* and *Metaphysics* 12: We do not know whether he wrote a complete commentary on the *Metaphysics.* There are also references to commentaries on the *Categories, Prior Analytics, De Generatione et Corruptione,* and at least some of the *Nicomachean Ethics.* What may at first sight look like a reference in Photius to commentaries of the standard type can be shown not to be so, and there is no other evidence that Themistius wrote commentaries of a type other than the paraphrases we have. Themistius will, however, abandon the paraphrase style for more prolonged discussion on certain points of major importance such as the meaning of *De Anima* 3.5. He himself describes his aim in writing the paraphrases as extracting Aristotle's meaning and setting it out concisely.

When Themistius wrote, Neoplatonism was already the dominant philosophy and was to influence all philosophical work till the end of classical antiquity. Themistius is conspicuous by his adherence in general to Peripatetic principles, though he does occasionally adopt *Platonist views; and there are some possible parallels with the writings of Plotinus: On the basis of these it has even been argued that he is a Platonist. In much of his exposition he follows *Alexander of Aphrodisias, with whom the Platonist commentators frequently disagreed: This can be seen even where Alexander's work is lost, as in references to his *Physics* commentary by the sixth-century commentator *Simplicius. Important pointers to his standpoint are the absence of Platonist intelligible hierarchies or any division of the Platonic type into intelligible and sensible reality with the intelligible having an independent and prior existence of its own. Notably *soul is the form of the body and his interpretation of the "active intellect" of the *De Anima*, which he probably holds to be identical with the lowest level of Aristotle's unmoved movers, is closely argued from the text of Aristotle and makes it less transcendent than did Alexander. Themistius' account of this part of Aristotle's *psychology was to be extremely influential in the Arabic and Western Medieval traditions, since Alexander's lost commentary and Themistius' paraphrase were the main Greek sources for Averroes' much used *Commentarium Magnum* on the *De Anima*, while Themistius' commentary was one of the works translated into Latin for Aquinas.

BIBLIOGRAPHY: Texts in *CAG* vols. 5.1, 5.2, 5.4, 5.5, and 5.8; H. Schenkl et al., *Themistii Orationes Quae Supersunt*, 3 vols., Leipzig, 1965, 1971, 1974. Blumenthal, H. J., in R. Sorabji, ed., *Aristotle Transformed*, London, 1990, 113–23; Dagron, G., in *Travaux et mémoires* 3. Centre de recherche d'histoire et civilization byzantines, Paris, 1968, 1–240. Vanderspoel, J., *Themistius and the Imperial Court: Oratory, Civic Duty and* Paideia *from Constantius to Theodosius*, Ann Arbor, 1995.—H. J. BLUMENTHAL

THEODORUS of Cyrene. See THEAETETUS and THEODORUS.

THEODORUS (Cyrenaic). See CYRENAIC PHILOSOPHY.

THEODOSIUS (2nd or 1st cent. B.C.E.), of Bithynia. Geometer and *astronomer. Besides two minor works, the *De Habitationibus* and the *De Diebus et Noctibus*, Theodosius' principal work is the *Sphaerica*, a treatise in three books on the elements of spherical geometry. Book 1 examines general properties of the sphere, for example, that the section of the sphere by a plane is a circle (1.1). The first half of Book 2 examines how circles on the sphere intersect each other or are tangent or parallel to each other. The second half, together with Book 3, treats of configurations specifically pertinent to geometrical astronomy, although still couched in the idiom of pure geometry.

Theodosius' treatise—indeed, one might say the entire ancient discipline of "spherics"—inhabits a sort of twilight zone between formal geometry and astronomy. While the field has obvious bearing for astronomy (cf. the astronomical terminology of *Euclid's *Phaenomena*), works like Theodosius' seem to camouflage this link. On the other hand, what is actually required for astronomy—the equivalent of identities for solving spherical triangles and the trigonometrical apparatus to compute their values—are developed only later, by Hipparchus (late 2nd cent. B.C.E.) and *Menelaus (early 2nd cent. C.E.). At best Theodosius' treatise provides only preliminary and partial results toward these ends.

On this account, as noted by some modern critics, the older contributions to spherics are little needed and less cited by *Ptolemy in the *Syntaxis* (mid 2nd cent. C.E.). Nevertheless, Theodosius was frequently cited for general results on the sphere among scholiasts of treatises in stereometry and optics and was studied and commented on in the later schools, most notably by Pappus. The popularity of the *Sphaerica* within the *mathematical curriculum continued through translations into Arabic, Hebrew, and Latin in the Middle Ages and through editions of the Greek and new Latin translations in the sixteenth and seventeenth centuries.

BIBLIOGRAPHY: Texts in J. L. Heiberg, ed., *Sphaerica*; Fecht, R., ed., *De Habitationibus* and *De Diebus et Noctibus*, both in *Abh. Gesell. Wissen. zu Göttingen,* vol. 19, pts. 3–4, 1927. Heath, T. L., *A History of Greek Mathematics,* vol. 2, Oxford, 1921, 245–252; Neugebauer, O., *A History of Ancient Mathematical Astronomy,* Berlin/Heidelberg/New York, 1975, 748–767.—*WILBUR R. KNORR*

THEOLOGY. See THEISM and ATHEISM; also METAPHYSICAL THOUGHT, Classical.

THEON (2nd cent. C.E.), of Smyrna (Izmir, Turkey), author of the *Exposition of Mathematics Useful for Reading Plato,* which sets out a great deal of elementary *"mathematics" based on the assumption that *Plato is a *Pythagoreanizer for whom mathematics provides the fundamental key to unlocking the secrets of the universe. Despite its frequent murkiness and the fact that it does not develop the conception in detail, the *Exposition* provides a good introduction to this view of Plato. Among the topics covered are "Pythagorean" figurate numbers, arithmetical harmonics, the *tetraktys,* the harmony of the spheres, and the epicyclic and eccentric theories of planetary motion. Theon preserves material of some interest by *Eratosthenes, *Thrasyllus, Dercyllides, and Adrastus of Aphrodisias.

BIBLIOGRAPHY: Text in E. Hiller, ed., *Theonis Smyrnaei Philosophi Platonici Expositio Rerum Mathematicarum ad Legendum Platonem Utilium* (Teubner), Leipzig, 1878. von Fritz, K., "Theon [14]," in *RE* 2.5, cols. 2067–2075.—*IAN MUELLER*

THEOPHRASTUS (372/1 or 371/0–288/7 or 287/6 B.C.E.), of Eresus on Lesbos. *Periptatetic philosopher; colleague and successor of *Aristotle. Theophrastus is said to have studied first at Eresus under Alcippus and then at Athens under *Plato. The latter report is problematic; but if true, it would explain an early association with Aristotle. After the death of Plato (347), it is likely that Theophrastus joined Aristotle in Asia Minor. He probably influenced Aristotle's move to Mytilene on Lesbos (345/4); and when Aristotle was called by Philip to be the tutor of Alexander (343/2), Theophrastus very likely accompanied his mentor to Macedonia. Eight years later the two returned to Athens, where Aristotle founded the *Peripatetic school (335). For the next thirteen years Aristotle and Theophrastus were colleagues. After the death of Alexander, anti-Macedonian feeling forced Aristotle to leave Athens for Chalcis where he died. Theophrastus remained in Athens and took over the school, which he directed for thirty-six years.

*Diogenes Laertius preserves a list of some 225 titles. There are duplications, but the number of titles fairly represents Theophrastus's extraordinary productivity. The surviving works include two extensive botanical treatises, *Research on Plants* and *Plant Explanations*, a short treatise on *metaphysics, a *doxographical work recording earlier views on sense perception (probably part of a larger work on tenets in natural philosophy), three opuscula on human physiology, one on fish and others on odors (originally part of the larger work *Plant Explanations*), fire, winds, and stones. There is also the well-known *Characters*. The lost works contained much of interest for the history of philosophy and related disciplines. References to the lost material are scattered throughout both ancient and medieval literature. The latter includes Arabic as well as Greek and Latin sources.

Logic. Theophrastus continued Aristotle's work on logic, making improvements, but also important modifications. Regarding statements, he distinguished between those that are singular and those that are particular, maintaining that the former are definite and the latter indefinite. Affirmations with a privative predicate he called *ek metatheseôs*. In regard to the categorical syllogism, Theophrastus added five moods to the canonical four of the first figure. The five are those of the indirect first figure, which is equivalent to the later fourth figure. They are neither perfect nor undemonstrated and are mentioned by Aristotle only in passing. Theophrastus also held that the first mood of the third figure has two different forms. In the same figure he proposed another order of the moods based on the directness of their proofs. In modal logic, Theophrastus maintained against Aristotle that the universal negative problematic premise (that of one-sided possibility) converts just as do the assertoric universal negative and the necessary. In the case of syllogisms constructed from premises of different modalities, he held that the conclusion in every case follows the weaker premise (*peiorem*-rule), while according to Aristotle it follows the major premise. In connection with the

*Academic search for *eidê*, Theophrastus developed a special logical form, the prosleptic syllogism, which cannot be reduced to a categorical syllogism. One proposition contains potentially a third term, which is made explicit in a second proposition; and the two propositions together yield a conclusion. Theophrastus also did more systematic research in hypothetical syllogistic than Aristotle, and almost certainly influenced the *Stoics. But he remained an *Aristotelian, concerning himself mainly with the logic of terms and not that of propositions.

Physics and Metaphysics. Theophrastus recognized the need to justify the assumption that natural science involves principles, causes, and elements. He also warned against inquiring into the cause of everything. Nevertheless, his physics is in large measure an attempt to trace observed phenomena back to principles of order and determination. He believed in the divinity of the heavens and the eternity of the universe and held that the heavenly bodies possess regularity in the highest degree. However, he denied a clean break between the heavenly and sublunary spheres, holding that the universe is a single system in which the same physical laws apply to all its parts. Theophrastus considered the possibility that the sun might be a form of fire, but the discussion is aporetic and not proof that Theophrastus rejected Aristotle's fifth element, aether, as *Strato did. Theophrastus does, however, appear to depart from Aristotle by analyzing place in terms of arrangement and position with reference to the whole universe.

Academic discussion and Aristotle's postulation of an unmoved mover form the background to Theophrastus's treatise on metaphysics. Many of the views discussed are considered plausible, but often we do not know what Theophrastus accepted as part of his own theory. It is probable that Theophrastus rejected Aristotle's unmoved mover and laid greater emphasis on the limits of teleological explanation. Like both Plato and Aristotle, he held that the study of first principles is more definite and ordered than the study of nature. Intelligible and physical entities are related as prior and posterior, but further specification of the relationship is not clearly provided. Most likely Theophrastus posited an unbroken causal series, for he requires continual explanation of all phenomena.

*Epistemology and *Psychology.* In Theophrastus's theory of principles there is a shift towards epistemology; appropriate method is a major concern. Analogy and the different forms it takes in research are stressed. Theophrastus investigated the relationship between sense perception and intellectual activity, arguing that they provide knowledge that is self-evident and indemonstrable. Imagination is thought to play an important part in linking them. Sense-perception is said to provide us with the differentiae and causes of observed phenomena; at the higher level of thought and knowledge we are concerned with the question of how observed differences and stated causes can be traced back to identical rules and more general principles.

Like Aristotle, Theophrastus held that the *soul has nutritive, sensitive, and intellectual capacities. He maintained the lower division of Aristotle's *scala naturae*, that between plants and animals, but appears to question the upper division between animals and human beings. He dealt with the physiological aspects of sensation, extending the doctrine of the intermediate to sound and smell. Desires, appetites, and feeling of emotion were said to be bodily motions. In regard to intellect, Theophrastus appears to have started from Aristotle, accepting the idea of intellect coming from without and likening it qua potentiality to a tablet devoid of writing. According to some reports, Theophrastus argued that the intellect is receptive of abstract form, just as *matter is receptive of form. Whatever the meaning of this analogy, Theophrastus does not ascribe a material nature to intellect. He construes its passive character in terms of activity (*energeia*).

Human Physiology, Zoology and Botany. Theophrastus followed Aristotle in making the heart the seat of all psychic functions; also in recognizing four fundamental qualities—hot, dry, cold, and moist—and in emphasizing the importance of proper blending. He was interested in a wide variety of physiological processes and wrote short treatises on paralysis, fainting, vertigo, tiredness, and sweat. These *opuscula* reveal an interest in both general theory and individual problems, the latter providing a close connection with the ps.-Aristotelian *Problems*. Theophrastus lays stress on the role of breath (*pneuma*), which is extended throughout the body. This may mark a move away from Aristotle and toward Strato, but the position of the former is problematic.

As part of the division of research within the Peripatos, Aristotle wrote at length on zoology and Theophrastus on botany. Nevertheless, Theophrastus took an interest in animal behavior and considered explaining the same phenomena in different ways. He is more prepared than Aristotle to credit animals with intelligent behavior and appears to anticipate Strato in assigning intellect to animals. But the sources can be read in more than one way. In any case, Theophrastus tells us that animals do many things for which we lack an explanation.

In botany, Theophrastus' method, like that of Aristotle in zoology, is first to observe the facts and then to offer theories that are based on and explain the facts. He distinguishes large classes of plants (tree, shrub, under-shrub, herb) and thinks exact classification practically impossible. He is concerned with the formation of botanical concepts that contain a well-defined core but form a continuous transition from one to another. Morphological research is carried out with exactitude. Interest is shown in the generation and habits of plants, the effects of environment and cultivation, and plant geography. Spontaneous generation is not rejected, but Theophrastus is careful to take note of cases that only appear spontaneous. Characteristically he concludes that the matter needs further investigation.

*Ethics, *Religion, and *Politics. Like Aristotle, Theophrastus recognized that virtuous behavior is often a matter of correct emotional response. He also held that the moral *virtues (êthikai aretai) are mean dispositions between two opposed vices and subordinated practical wisdom (phronêsis) to theoretical wisdom (sophia). He thus recognized the primacy of contemplation, regarding it as similar to the life of the gods. Theophrastus is said to have been involved in controversy with *Dicaearchus, who championed the practical life over that of leisured study. Whether the two Peripatetics criticized each other directly may be questioned; in any case, we should not infer that Theophrastus recognized no independent value in political and social activity.

Theophrastus followed Aristotle in distinguishing between friendship based on virtue, on pleasure, and on utility. Like *Eudemus, he recognized friendship involving superiority within each of the three kinds. Our source makes explicit reference to friendships between husband and wife. That is important; for according to St. Jerome, Theophrastus wrote a work on marriage, asked whether the wise man should marry, and presented arguments against marriage in which the wife is characterized as an intolerable nuisance. The text of Jerome is highly polemical; it may well be drawn from a *rhetorical excercise, for elsewhere Theophrastus not only recognizes that wives can be virtuous but also recommends that they be treated with care, for they will return kindness. This recommendation is part of a larger concern with maintaining appropriate relationships. The concern extends to caring for parents and to worshipping the gods. In the latter case, Theophrastus recognizes that sacrifices need not be large, only frequent, and that the sacrifice of animals is unacceptable. Theophrastus's argument against animal sacrifice was later embraced by *Porphyry as part of an attack on eating meat, but there is little to suggest that Theophrastus made the connection. Rather his argument is based on a natural relationship (oikeiotês, not to be confused with Stoic oikeiôsis) between all creatures endowed with sensation. Most striking, Theophrastus recognizes that men can and do treat animals unjustly.

In personal relationships like friendship, Theophrastus recognized the importance of the particular situation, for example, when a friend is in great danger, helping him contrary to the law may be justified. Similarly in political activity, he emphasized the present cirumstances. He wrote multiple books on politics with a view to the critical moment (kairos) and gave examples of well-regarded politicians. His work On

Laws in Alphabetical Order was of considerable length; it reflects the division of labor within the Peripatos. Aristotle supervised the collection and organization of material concerning constitutions, while Theophrastus did the same for laws, non-Greek as well as Greek. The sources preserve interesting material on legal procedures like those of impeachment, retrial, and ostracism. Regulations concerning property and commerce also received attention.

Rhetoric, Poetics, and Music. Theophrastus discussed rhetorical argument and appears to have been especially influential through his work on style. He expanded Aristotle's tripartite virtue of style into four qualities, shared an interest in metaphor, and discussed prose rhythm. He adopted a more positive attitude toward delivery and extended discussion of the subject to include gesture as well as voice. No source tells us explicitly how Theophrastus treated character in a rhetorical context, but it is significant that later rhetoricians made use of the *Characters* for instruction in the schools.

It is also possible that Theophrastus referred to the *Characters* when lecturing on poetics. Many of the sketches have a direct relationship to the stage-figures of New *Comedy, whose most famous playwright, Menander, was a pupil of the Eresian. In his work *On Comedy*, Theophrastus is said to have related a story concerning the Tirynthians, who tried to rid themselves of an excessive propensity toward laughter. The story may have been used to illustrate comic plot; possibly Theophrastus introduced it while recommending a catharsis of laughter. A cathartic effect was also assigned to music. According to several sources, the *aulos* could relieve and even cure sciatica and epilepsy, but the value of these reports is debatable. It is certain that Theophrastus considered music from the standpoint of virtue and education. He rejected the idea that pitch is a quantitative property of sound—an idea common to the *Pythagoreans, *Platonists, and Peripatetics including Aristotle—and argued that differences in pitch are essentially qualitative.

BIBLIOGRAPHY: Texts in S. Amiques, ed., *Research on Plants*, 5 vols. with tr. (Budé), Paris, 1988– (in progress); Coutant, V., ed., *On Fire*, with tr., Assen, 1971; Coutant, V., and V. Eichenlaub, eds., *On Winds*, with tr., Notre Dame, 1975; Eichholz, D., ed., *On Stones*, with tr., Oxford, 1965; Eigler, U., and G. Wöhrle, eds., *On Odors*, with tr. (Teubner), Leipzig, 1993; Einarson, B., and G. Link, eds., *Plant Explanations*, 3 vols. with tr. (Loeb), 1976–1990; Fortenbaugh, W., ed., *On Sweats*, with tr., forthcoming in *RUSCH*; Hort, A., ed., *On Signs* (spurious), with tr. (Loeb), 1916; Laks, A., and G. Most, eds., *Metaphysics*, with tr. (Budé), Paris, 1993; Rusten, J., ed., *Characters*, with tr. (Loeb), London, 1992; Sharples, R., ed., *On Fish*, with tr., in *RUSCH* 5; also *On Vertigo*, with tr., forthcoming in *RUSCH*; Sollenberger, M., ed., *On Tiredness*; with tr., forthcoming in *RUSCH*; Steinmetz, P., ed., *Characters*, 2 vols. with tr., Munich, 1960–62; Stratton, G., ed., *On Sensations*, with tr., London, 1917; van Raalte, M., ed., *Metaphysics*, with tr., Leiden, 1993; *Fragments and Re-*

ports in FHS&G. General Studies in F. Wehrli, in H. Flashar, ed., *Grundriss der Geschichte der Philosophie*, vol. 3, Basel 1983; Regenbogen, O., *RE* supp. 7, 1354–1562; *RUSCH*, esp. vols. 2, 3, 5, 8; see also vols. 4, 6, 7; Commentaries on FHS&G: R. Sharples, vol. 5, Leiden, 1995; other vols. forthcoming. Topical Studies: (i) *Logic:* Bochenski, I., *La logique de Theophrastus*, Fribourg, 1947; Repici, L., *La logica di Teofrasto*, Bologna, 1977. (ii) *Metaphysics:* Reale, G., *Teofrasto e la su aporetica metafisica*, Brescia, 1964, Eng. tr. 1980. (iii) *Physics:* Sharples, R., "Theophrastus on the Heavens," in J. Wiesener, ed., *Aristoteles: Werk und Wirkung*, vol. 1, Berlin, 1985; Steinmetz, P., *Die Physik des Theophrastus*, Bad Homburg, 1964. (iv) *Doxography—Sense Perception:* Diels, H., ed., *Opinions of the Natural Philosophers*, Reimer, 1879; Mansfeld, J., in *RUSCH* 5; Baltussen, H., *Theophrastus on Theories of Perception*, Utrecht, 1993. (v) *Biology and Botany:* Wöhrle, G., *Theophrasts Methode in seinen botanischen Schriften*, Amsterdam, 1985. (vi) *Ethics:* Fortenbaugh, W., *Rh. Mus.* 118, 1975, 62–82; also *Quellen zur Ethik Theophrasts*, Amsterdam, 1984. (vii) *Religion:* Bernays, J., *Theophrastos' Schrift über Frömmigkeit*, Breslau, 1866; Pötscher, W., *Theophrastos:* Peri Eusebeias, Leiden, 1964. (viii) *Politics:* Szegedy-Maszak, A., *The Nomoi of Theophrastus*, Arno, 1981. (ix) *Rhetoric:* Stroux, J., *De Theophrasti virtutibus dicendi*, 1912; Solmsen, F., *Hermes* 66, 1931, 241–67; Kennedy, G.. *HSCP* 62, 1957, 94–104. (x) *Poetics:* Dosi, A., *Rendiconti: Instit. Lombardo di scienze e lettere* 94, 1960, 599–672; Fortenbaugh, W., *Rh. Mus.* 124, 1981, 245–60. (xi) *Music:* Barker, A., *Greek Musical Writings*, 2 vols., Cambridge, 1984, 1989, 1.186–9 and 2.110–18.—*WILLIAM W. FORTENBAUGH and JOSIP TALANGA*

THRASYLLUS (d. 36 C.E.). Polymath of uncertain origin and friend of the emperor Tiberius, since before the latter's accession in 14 C.E. He taught Tiberius astrology, and left his mark upon the astrological tradition. He organized the *Platonic corpus and the *Democritean corpus in tetralogies. While the originality of these arrangements in *Diogenes Laertius 3 and 9 has been disputed, it cannot be proved that they antedated him. He introduced the system of double titles for Plato's *dialogues and influenced subsequent Platonic corpus-theory.

Thrasyllus is mentioned alongside the Platonizing *Pythagoreans Moderatus, *Numenius, and Cronius as writers who gave accounts of the first principles of *Pythagoras and Plato. As such he foreshadowed the work of *Plotinus (Longinus in Porphyry *Life of Plotinus* 20–21). He also set Democritus in the Pythagorean tradition. Thrasyllus influenced the harmonic theory of *Theon of Smyrna and of *Porphyry, the latter of whom also used an interesting *logos-theory that derives from Thrasyllus and has affinities to *Philo of Alexandria.

BIBLIOGRAPHY: Tarrant, H., *Thrasyllan Platonism*, Ithaca, 1993.—*HAROLD A. S. TARRANT*

THRASYMACHUS (2nd half of 5th cent. B.C.E.), of Chalcedon, a Greek colony on the Bosporus. An orator or *sophist known in antiquity mainly as a stylist but to readers of *Plato for the role he is given in the *Republic*.

He is said to have had the power to raise and quell emotions by oratory and is listed as a successor of Tisias and inventor of the "middle" style. Only one long quotation from his works survives, the opening of a conservative and antidemocratic speech that he wrote for a young Athenian politician to deliver. Another brief fragment or paraphrase complains that the gods overlook people's neglect of justice, which he calls the greatest human *good (DK85B8). Neither this nor the other evidence prepares us for the brilliant attack on *Socrates we read in Book 1 of Plato's *Republic*. There Thrasymachus blames Socrates for defining justice as beneficial without saying who it is that justice benefits. Evidently referring to conventional justice, Thrasymachus insists that justice is "the advantage of the stronger" and as such benefits the rulers at the expense of the ruled. He later confuses the issue by adding that doing justice always benefits someone else.

BIBLIOGRAPHY: Texts in DK85. Tr. in R. K. Sprague, *The Older Sophists*, Columbia, SC, 1972, and M. Gagarin and P. Woodruff, eds., *Early Greek Political Thought from Homer to the Sophists*, Cambridge, 1995. Guthrie, W. K. C., *The Sophists*, Cambridge, 1971; Kerferd, G. B., *The Sophistic Movement*, Cambridge, 1981.—PAUL WOODRUFF

THUCYDIDES (5th cent. B.C.E.), of Athens. Historian of the Peloponnesian War between Athens and Sparta (431–404 B.C.E.). Thucydides was born between 460 and 455. He was an Athenian general in 424, lost an important city to Sparta, and was exiled from Athens. He died early in the fourth century, before completing his book.

Thucydides' *History* covers the period 431–411, explaining the major decisions of the war through reconstructed speeches and debates that present at least two sides on each issue. Educated by various *sophists, he had a philosophical interest in human nature and the conflict between justice and the interests of an imperial state such as Athens. Human nature, in Thucydides' view, turns bad when not controlled by law. The chief factors in human motivation are fear, ambition, and avarice. These, for example, cause the expansion of the Athenian Empire, which frightens the Spartans into making war. Radical democracy leads to lawlessness (3.84); Athens functions best when it is a monarchy in all but name under Pericles (2.65). The best government is "a moderate blending of the interests of the few and many," in which neither party pursues its interests at the expense of the other (8.97).

In describing the plague at Athens and in recounting the civil war on Corcyra, Thucydides shows how badly people behave when they no longer feel the constraints of law. City-states behave no better: Both Athens and Sparta disregard justice toward their neighbor states. The Athenians choose not to execute the rebellious people of Mytilene merely from a calculation of their own advantage; a similar calculation leads them to destroy the people of Melos, since justice (in their view) is irrelevant to the stronger party in a dispute (5.89). Spartans appeal to justice against Athens (1.86) but are not held back by justice from killing the Plataeans (3.68).

Thucydides' reconstruction of Pericles' funeral oration has been an important model for public speaking. Other speeches reconstructed by Thucydides illustrate reasoning of the sort taught by sophists. Speakers tend to appeal to necessity (*anankê*) or to reasonable expectation (*eikos*), but are often refuted by events or countered by other speakers whose arguments are equally strong on the other side.

BIBLIOGRAPHY: Text in H. S. Jones and J. E. Powell, eds., *Thucydides*, Oxford, 1942. Comm. by S. Hornblower, Oxford, 1991–. Connor, W. R., *Thucydides*, Princeton, 1984; Farrar, C., *The Origins of Democratic Thinking*, Cambridge, 1988; Hornblower, S., *Thucydides*, London, 1987; Orwin, C., *The Humanity of Thucydides*, Princeton, 1994.—*PAUL WOODRUFF*

TIME, Ancient Theories of. Ancient investigations into the nature of time focussed on three, not always distinct, sets of questions: ontological, mereological, and topological. Questions concerning the ontology of time include: What is time? Is the existence of time contingent on the existence of anything else? Are there different "kinds" of time? Questions concerning the mereology of time include: What are the proper parts of time? Out of what is time composed? How are "nows" related to each other? Questions concerning the topology of time include: Has there been an *infinite past? Will there be an infinite future? Might time have a cyclical structure? Of course answers to one or more of these questions may affect answers to others. For instance, if one thinks that time requires orderly motion (as *Plato, *Aristotle, and many others seem to have thought), then one could not conceive of an infinite past if orderly motion had come into being.

The Presocratic period is not particularly rich in theories concerning time. *Pherecydes in the sixth century B.C.E. was perhaps the first clearly to think that time was uncreated (see D.L. 1.119; Damascius *De Principiis* 124). There is some evidence that *Pythagoras and *Empedocles believed in the everlasting recurrence of events, yet this need not entail the (perhaps incoherent) notion of the recurrence of times. Time plays a role in the thought of both *Anaximander (see DK12A9 = Simplicius *In Phys.* 24, 13, on "the assessment of time," and DK12A10 = ps.-Plutarch *Stomata* 2, where we find perhaps the earliest philosophical use of *aïdios* "eternal," or "everlasting") and *Parmenides. Neither thinker, however, can be said to have a *theory* of time, or to have explicitly discussed any of its features. With *Zeno of Elea's "Arrow paradox," we find perhaps the first argument directly bearing on the structure of time (namely that it is composed of "nows"), yet here too our sources are so condensed that it is difficult to attribute any clear cut views about time to Zeno.

Plato is the first to develop an articulated position concerning time (*Timaeus* 37c–39e). Time is held in opposition to eternity, which is said to be that "in which" the model of the universe exists (eternal existence is some sort of atemporal existence). Time is "a moving likeness of eternity," which came to be along with the heavens. Moreover, time is dependent on the existence and movement of the heavens. The parts of time are said to be days, nights, months, and years. "Was" and "shall be," on the other hand, are said to be forms of time that come to be along with time (that is, when the heavens were created and put into regular motion).

That time is dependent on the regular, circular, clocklike motion of the heavens and is, in some sense, a measure of this motion, is commonplace in Greek thought. Time is thought to exist only if orderly motion exists, and the regular circular motion of the stars and planets is taken by many, including Plato, to be paradigmatic of such orderly motion. That it is *circular* motion that time measures for Plato and many others tempts some (including *Proclus *In Tim.* 36e, etc.) to think that Plato thought time itself to be cyclical. The evidence is inconclusive and complicated by the fact that it is often unclear whether a given thinker distinguishes clearly the notion of the repetition of *events*, or positions of the heavens, from the repetition of *time* or times.

It also became commonplace to distinguish time and things which exist in time, from eternity and things that exist atemporally. It is difficult to describe what sort of existence atemporal existence is, except negatively. Plato and others, possibly influenced by Parmenides, argue that there must be some such existence. On at least one plausible reconstruction, Parmenides claimed that what is must "be" in a manner that precludes all *change, coming to be, destruction, and even the attribution of "did exist" and "will exist" to it (see especially DK28B8). For Plato, Forms and the Demiurge enjoy such existence.

A related problem for Plato's *cosmology is that he talks of a period of chaos *prior* to the creation of the heavens and so *prior* to the creation of time. Part of the inconsistency in such a view is no doubt due to the great difficulty we have in talking about atemporal entities and the deep-seated pull to conceive of time, or something timelike, as having to have existed infinitely into the past and infinitely into the future.

Aristotle shaped the direction of subsequent theorizing concerning the nature of time primarily by means of two paradoxes found at the beginning of his extended investigation into time (*Phys.* 4.10–14). Both seem to demonstrate the unreality of time. The first (217b33–218a9) attempts to do so by claiming that none of the parts of time exist. The past no longer exists, the future does not yet exist, and "the now," being a sizeless instant, is not a part of time but the terminus of extended periods of time. The second (218a8f.) assumes that the present is always different, and so asks when it ceases to exist. It cannot cease to exist when it exists, nor in the next instant (for there is no next instant), or at some arbitrary later instant, for then one instant would exist for a stretch of time and so for an infinity of instants. There is much controversy as to how, or if, Aristotle offers a satisfactory solution to these paradoxes. What is clear is that they exercised many subsequent thinkers who pondered the nature of time, especially the *Neoplatonists.

As for the "structural" features of time, Aristotle, like Plato, thought that time is dependent on change and, in particular, that time is the measure of motion. But unlike Plato, he also thought that both the past and future are infinite, so that there always has been, and always will be, change.

Paradoxes such as those mentioned above convinced the *Stoics to downgrade the existence of time, placing it in the category of things that merely subsist. However, one should note that there is disagreement among various Stoics concerning the status of time, in particular present time. (See Stobaeus 1.105.17f. for the accounts of *Apollodorus of Seleucia, *Posidonius, and *Chrysippus). The Stoics seem to agree that time is the measure of motion, many making it the measure of the world's motion.

A live question concerning the Stoics is whether some of them may have conceived of time as circular. It is difficult to formulate this doctrine in a precise way. To claim that the same time may happen again seems incoherent, because what could "again" mean, other than at a different time? Perhaps the closest one can come to a coherent description of a closed topology for time is to say that if time is closed, then given any two events, each lies in the absolute past and absolute future of the other. The Stoics may have conceived of time as having such a topology since some Stoics seem to have thought that there is a recurrence of numerically identical events. However, there is some confusion on this issue, since both orthodox Stoics and Posidonius hold that the past and future are infinite—a view hard to square with the recurrence of time.

An important innovation in the theory of time is the *Epicurean notion of the *atomic structure of time. In *Physics* 6.1 Aristotle argued that an atomist must be committed to postulating the atomic nature of magnitude, motion, *and* time (231b18). Only then, according to Aristotle, could one consistently uphold the atomic character of *matter. In addition, only such "global" atomism can "solve" Zeno's paradoxes of motion. *Epicurus took all this to heart.

St. *Augustine developed a unique response to the paradox of the parts of time in Book 11 of his *Confessions*. He claimed that the parts of time should be viewed as mental states, and so the past, present, and future can all coexist in the mind. In *City of God* 12.16 this is related in an unexpected way to the question of whether time requires change or motion, by having time depend on the mental motion of angels, who existed *before* the heavens (of whose motion time is usually thought to be a measure) were created.

Many other discussions of time exist in antiquity—most notably, perhaps, that of the *Neoplatonist *Iamblichus, who in response to the paradox of the parts of time distinguished between a static and a flowing time. Only flowing time is dependent on the existence of change. The Neoplatonists also have lengthy discussions on the nature of eternity and, in general, on temporal versus atemporal existence.

BIBLIOGRAPHY: Cornford, F. M., *Plato's Cosmology*, London, 1937; Goldschmidt, V., *Le Systeme stoicien et l'idee de temps*, Paris, 1953; KRS; LS; Owen, G. E. L., in P. Machamer and R. Turnbull, eds., *Motion and Time, Space and Matter*, Columbus, 1976, repr. in M. C. Nussbaum, ed., *Logic, Science and Dialectic*, Ithaca, 1986, 295–314; Sorabji, R., *Time, Creation and the Continuum*, Ithaca, 1983.—ERIC LEWIS

TIMON (c. 325–c. 235 B.C.E.), of Phlius. Satirical poet and follower of *Pyrrho. In the course of his ninety years, Timon plied a variety of trades, having been at one time or another a dancer on the stage, an author of tragic, comic, and epic verse and, though it is not clear what this involved, a *sophist. He is best known, however, for his verses celebrating Pyrrho of Elis, from whom Pyrrhonian *skepticism took its name, and mocking the vain pretensions of other philosophers. These were the *Silloi* (*Lampoons*) and the *Indalmoi* (*Images*), fragments of which have survived. We also know of prose works including the *Pytho*, a *dialogue that seems to have been Timon's first work on Pyrrho, books against the physicists and concerning the senses and a work, *The Funeral Feast of Arcesilaus*, in which he is said to have praised *Arcesilaus, who was, along with Pyrrho, the figure most responsible for initiating the skeptical turn in Hellenistic philosophy.

Pyrrho was not Timon's first philosophical teacher. He came to him only after having spent time with *Stilpo of Megara. He also felt a strong but qualified admiration for the Presocratic *Xenophanes of Colophon. The verses in which Xenophanes mocked, for example, the anthropomorphic gods of *Homer, were the model and inspiration for Timon's own satirical verses, where he appears as Timon's spokesman in the second two books of the *Silloi*. But Xenophanes erred, according to Timon, by replacing the Homeric and popular view of the gods that he had satirized so effectively with a positive conception of his own. For this reason, he criticized Xenophanes as half-conceited or semi-vain, reserving for

Pyrrho alone the honor of being entirely free from conceit. In Pyrrho Timon had found his true philosophical master. His attitude towards him was very much like that of *Lucretius towards *Epicurus: He hails him as a godlike man who alone has found the way to *happiness for human beings.

In antiquity Timon was most important as a source of information about Pyrrho. It is very doubtful whether there was a continuous Pyrrhonian tradition connecting Pyrrho with *Aenesidemus, who seems to have founded a new Pyrrhonian school in the first century B.C.E. Much of what later Pyrrhonists knew of the figure after whom they had chosen to name their school must have reached them via Timon. And Antigonus of Carystus probably drew heavily on Timon in his influential biography of Pyrrho as well. The fragments of Timon are a boon to modern scholarship because of the view of Pyrrho they afford—uncorrupted by later Pyrrhonian tradition, in which there is a considerable admixture of *Academic skepticism.

BIBLIOGRAPHY: Texts in H. Diels, *Poetarum Philosophorum Fragmenta*, Berlin, 1901, 173–206; Lloyd-Jones, H., and P. Parsons, eds., *Supplementum Hellenisticum*, Berlin, 1983, 368–395. Burnyeat, M. F., *CQ* n.s. 30, 1980, 86–93; Long, A. A., *PCPS* n.s. 24, 1978, 68–91.—*JAMES ALLEN*

V

VIRTUE, EXCELLENCE (*ARETÊ*). See ETHICAL THOUGHT, Classical.

VOID, Theories of the. The concept of void played an important role in many ancient natural philosophies. Its existence was thought necessary by some (particularly the Presocratic *atomists and *Epicureans) in order to account for motion and *change. For *Aristotle and later *Aristotelians the existence of void was anathema, and so a physics had to be developed which did not rely on the void. For others, such as the *Stoics, the void played primarily a *cosmological role.

What is the void? From at least the time of *Homer onward, Greek had the concept of, and terms for expressing, "the empty." However "the empty" is a relative notion. An empty cup contains no liquid, an empty fuel tank contains no fuel. Such empty cups and tanks are not thought to contain a void. Indeed, both *Anaxagoras and *Empedocles, according to Aristotle, proved that such "empty" containers are not truly empty. "They show that air is something" (Ar. *Phys.* 213a22f.), by experimenting with clepsydras and inflated wineskins. (See also Empedocles' account of respiration, DK31B100).

Precisely what a void is, then, is difficult to say. Two possible characterizations come to mind: void as unoccupied space and void as a special kind of space occupant. (Those characterizations of void as simply space, and so the notion of a "filled void" will be ignored in this discussion, as will Aristotle's arguments against the possibility of place being a three-dimensional extension.) Both these characterizations employ the notion of space, yet it would be false to assume that a well-formed notion of space preceded the development of some sort of theory of the void. It is for this reason that the conception of void as a space occupant is actually conceptually more primitive than that of void as unoccupied space. This is because conceiving of the void as the former commits one to claiming only that there can be "void here," or, say, *"matter here"—that the universe is tiled in, so to speak, by two or more things, one of them being void. No questions as to *what* is being tiled need be asked. Conceiving of the void as an unoccupied something, say space, does seem to require some sort of theory as to what it is that is unoccupied.

Some see the void playing a role in *Pythagorean cosmology, although the reports, the earliest being from Aristotle, seem dubious. It is therefore *Melissus who first clearly employs the notion of the void in an argument of great influence. (The adjective *keneon*, "empty," is employed by Empedocles [DK31B13].) Aristotle reports that both Empedocles and Anaxagoras proved that air is something, but none of these cases require the concept of a void to have been in play. In addition, Xuthus, perhaps a Phythagorean to whom Aristotle refers (*Phys.* 216b22f.), need not predate Melissus; and, in any case, it is unclear whether Aristotle means to attribute to Xuthus any more than the claim that the universe swells like a sea.) In DK30B7 Melissus argues that void, "the empty," is a necessary precondition for motion. Since Melissus also thinks that the void does not exist (since what is empty is nothing, and what is nothing cannot exist), he concludes that there is no motion.

The Presocratic *atomists, *Democritus and *Leucippus, take up Melissus' challenge. They accept both the characterization of the void as "what is not" (*mêden* —a name the atomists give to the void), claiming that "what is not exists no less than what is" (Ar. *Met.* 985b4f.), and the claim that motion requires void. Since the atomists take it to be empirically given that there is motion, they conclude that the void must exist (see Ar. *GC* 325a23–32). *Epicurus also accepts this argument for the existence of the void (*Letter to Herodotus* 40).

*Plato's views on the void are far from clear. The void does not play any obvious role in his cosmology. It is with Aristotle that we find a systematic attack of far-ranging influence on the possibility of the existence of void.

Aristotle objects to both cosmic and extracosmic void. That is, he denies both that the ordered cosmos contains any empty regions and that the finite ordered cosmos itself is surrounded by empty place or space. His objections to both types of void were to be extremely influential. His main objection to extracosmic void is based on defining void as that in which it is possible that there comes to be body. Since he argues that it is impossible for there to be extracosmic body, he concludes that extracosmic void is impossible (see *DC* 1.7–1.9). The most famous and influential argument in favor of the existence of extracosmic void or space was produced by the Pythagorean *Archytas, a near contemporary of Plato, who, according to *Eudemus of Rhodes, argues that upon approaching the edge of the cosmos one must either be able to stretch out beyond it or not. That one could not is absurd, and so the fact that one can shows that there must be place (or body) beyond the cosmos (see Simplicius *In Phys.* 467, 26–32). One should also note the telling objections to Aristotle's position raised by the Stoic *Cleomedes and the arguments supporting Aristotle against Archytas by *Alexander of Aphrodisias (*Quaestiones* 3.12, 106, 35–107, 4).

The vast majority of Aristotle's arguments against the existence of the void bear directly on the atomist's insistence that the void is a necessary prerequisite for motion. Aristotle argues that, far from making motion possible, motion through a void would be impossible. *Phys.* 4.6–9 is devoted to discussing the views of his predecessors on the void (4.6), defining the void (4.7), and then refuting its existence (4.7–9). He argues in general that the void cannot be the cause of the natural motion of the elements (*Phys.* 214b12–17). One reason is that there could be no difference of direction in a void (no up and down), upon which natural motion depends (*Phys.* 215a1–14). Since for Aristotle all motion depends on natural motion, a refutation of the possibility of natural motion given the existence of void is also a demonstration of the incompatibility between motion in general and the void. In related arguments, Aristotle thinks that in a void a body would have no reason to move one way rather than another. The conclusion is that bodies in a void must rest, or, absurdly, either explode or move as an intact unit, in all directions. Similarly, were a body to be moving through a void, it would have no reason to come to rest here rather than there (*Phys.* 214b17–215a24).

Aristotle also raises objections based on the role media play in motion. If the resistance which a medium offers against something moving through it were to go to zero (as it would with motion through a void), then the velocity of the object through this medium would be *infinite. Such infinite velocity Aristotle finds absurd, and so motion through a void is ruled out (*Phys.* 215b22–216a4).

Aristotle's account of projectile motion is also incompatible with motion through a void. For Aristotle, if I throw a ball, the initial impulse I give to the ball via my hand is not enough to keep the ball in motion after it leaves my hand. The air surrounding the ball must do the work which my hand did. This is accomplished by the air behind the ball pushing the ball along, a power that the air somehow takes on due to the initial movement of my hand (*Phys.* 266b27–267a20). Obviously this cannot be accomplished in a void. This theory of projectile motion became a major stumbling block for the development of modern dynamics and the notion of inertia.

All of Aristotle' arguments were to exert enormous influence. Some of them are best seen as directed against the possibility of extracosmic void, while others seem also to be directed against motion through pockets of intracosmic void. The Stoics postulated extracosmic void, and the Epicureans postulated pockets of void scattered throughout the cosmos, so both had to—and did—respond to Aristotle's arguments.

The Stoics accounted for there being objective directions in a cosmos surrounded by void by claiming (with Aristotle) that down is toward the center of the ordered cosmos, and that everything has a natural tendency to move toward this center (see Plut. *SR* 1054B–1055C; Cleomedes 10.24f.; Stobaeus 1.166, 4f., etc.). Against Aristotle, they accounted for the coherence of the cosmos even though it was surround by void by postulating a holding power (*hexis*). This holding power is a power of the *pneuma* that permeates the whole ordered cosmos.

Epicurus' position concerning the role the void plays in motion is uncertain. He may have accepted the claim that motion through a void is instantaneous, since he characterizes the velocity of atoms through the void as being "quick as thought" (*Letter to Herodotus* 61). Alternatively, his atomism may entail that nothing in fact ever *is* moving, and so the effect the void might play on something in motion is rendered a nonissue. He believed that there is a preferred direction "down," even though the cosmos is infinite, this being the direction from our head to our feet.

It is primarily via the Greek, Latin, and Arabic *commentaries on Aristotle (especially those on the *Physics* and *De Caelo*) that the Aristotelian legacy is passed on to the Latin West. The famous scholastic saying that "nature abhors a vacuum" can be traced back to Alexander of Aphrodisias, Averroes, and the Greek pneumaticist Philo of Byzantium. Many of the issues concerning the void that were discussed in antiquity continue to trouble philosophers in the Latin West and in the Islamic tradition.

BIBLIOGRAPHY: Furley, D. J., *Two Studies in the Greek Atomists*, Princeton, 1967; Grant, E., *Much Ado About Nothing*, Cambridge, 1981; KRS; LS; Sedley, D., *Phronesis* 27, 1982, 175–193; Sorabji, R., *Matter, Space and Motion*, Ithaca, 1988.—*ERIC LEWIS*

XENOCRATES (396/395–314/313 B.C.E.), of Chalcedon. Student in
*Plato's *Academy and its third head. *Diogenes Laertius (4.14) relates
that Xenocrates became head of the Academy after *Speusippus in
339/338, held that position for twenty-five years and died at the age of
eighty-two. On the death of Plato, Xenocrates and *Aristotle apparently
left Athens together, and Xenocrates returned, apparently at Speusippus'
request, to succeed him (D.L. 4.3). The *Academicorum Index Herculanensis*
(cols. 6–7, ed. Mekler, 38–39) suggests that the younger members of the
Academy voted on this question and confirmed Xenocrates by a narrow
margin.

Diogenes' bibliography (4.11–14) lists over seventy titles; nothing
whatever has survived, even in the form of identifiable quotations in
other authors.

*Sextus Empiricus (*M* 7.16) relates that Xenocrates was explicit about
the division of philosophical topics implicit in Plato into "physics,"
*"ethics," and *"logic"; this became the norm in *Stoicism and Hellenistic
philosophy in general. Here we should have to include *epistemology
under "logic" and *metaphysics under "physics."

Nothing is reported about what we would think of as pure logic;
Sextus (*M* 7.147–149) gives us a scrap about epistemology. Xenocrates is
supposed to have divided the substances or entities into three groups:
perceptible, intelligible, and believable (also referred to as "composite"
and "mixed"). The intelligible ones were objects of knowledge, which
Xenocrates apparently spoke of as "epistemonic *logos*" or "knowing account," and were "located" outside the heavens. The perceptible ones
were objects of perception, which was capable of attaining truth about

them but nothing that counted as knowledge; they were within the heavens. The composite ones were the heavenly objects themselves and objects of belief, which is sometimes true and sometimes false.

Putting flesh on these bones is difficult, but (i) the scheme is a descendant of that in Plato *Republic* 6 *ad fin.*; (ii) the tripartite division of objects looks like that in Aristotle *Metaphysics* 12.1; and (iii) the phrase "epistemonic *logos*" is one Sextus also assigns to Speusippus (*M* 7.145), as well as recalling discussions in Aristotle (e.g., *Met.* 7.15) and the end of Plato's *Theaetetus*; (iv) the intelligible domain must have included form-numbers (see below); and (v) the special place for the heavens accords with the fact that one of the items in Diogenes' bibliography is "*On Astronomy*, six books."

It is not much help when Sextus tells us (149) that Xenocrates associated the three fates with his three groups of substances: Atropos with the intelligible ones, Clotho with the perceptible ones, and Lachesis with the believable ones. But it has a Xenocratean ring: It connects with the interpretation of Plato (see *Rep.* 10, 620d–e) and takes mythology very seriously.

Most of what we can reconstruct about Xenocrates' "physics" pertains to his metaphysics. This is done largely by identifying views of his that appear in Aristotle's criticisms and linking together with these other texts that can plausibly be taken as dealing with his views. In *Metaphysics* 7.2, Aristotle tells us that Plato accepted three sorts of entities: Forms, mathematicals, and perceptibles, and goes on to mention a view according to which the "Forms and numbers have the same nature." Asclepius (comm. *ad loc.*) relates that the reference is to Xenocrates. Passages in *Metaphysics* 12–14 can then be associated with Xenocrates: he will be saying that the distinction between Forms and mathematicals is unnecessary. One of the differences between Form-numbers and mathematical numbers in Aristotle's discussions is that Form-numbers are composed of units that cannot be detached from the number and added to units detached from another number; mathematical numbers, by contrast, are composed of undifferentiated units. It is the latter, then, that makes "2+3=5" true. Xenocrates, it appears, is assimilating mathematical numbers to Form-numbers, and Aristotle is then able to complain that he has no way of handling addition (see, e.g., *Met.* 13.6, 1080b28–30). These Form-numbers are construed as Platonic Forms, and Xenocrates provided a definition of "form" that was intended to capture Plato's notion: a Form or "Idea" is "a paradigmatic cause of the things that are always constituted according to nature" (Proclus *In Parm.* 888.15–19; cf. Pl. *Parm.* 132d).

In parallel with Speusippus and Plato (as Aristotle reports Plato), Xenocrates operated with a scheme in which two principles—the One and something called any or all of "the everflowing," "plurality" (Aëtius 1.3.23), or "the Indefinite Dyad" (Theophr. *Met.* 6)—generate these Form-numbers, and then, in turn, lines, planes, solids, and perceptible things. Here, "generate" is not to be understood literally: the question is what depends for its existence on what, and Xenocrates lays it out as if it were a temporal process only to make it easier to understand. Xenocrates extended his own nonliteral use of talk about generation in time to the interpretation of the creation story in the *Timaeus*: It, too, was not to be taken literally, but as a didactic device used as *mathematicians use constructions in time to describe the eternal. Aristotle argues against this interpretation (*DC* 1.10 with Simplicius' comm. *ad loc.*).

Simplicius relates that Xenocrates objected to Aristotle's list of ten categories as too long: He thought all that was needed was the distinction, visible in Plato, between things that are "by virtue of themselves" and things that are "relative to something." Additionally, a text preserved in Arabic (see Pines) has *Alexander of Aphrodisias criticizing Xenocrates for saying that the (less general) species is prior to the (more general) genus because the latter is part of the former.

Xenocrates accepted the existence of *daimones*, beings intermediate between gods and men, as isosceles triangles are intermediate between equilateral and scalene ones (Plut. *Mor.* 416c–d); they come in good and bad varieties (*ibid.* 360d–f, 417b), and Xenocrates apparently ascribed some bizarre traditional cult-practices to their influence. He also accepted the existence of indivisible lines on the basis of *Zenonian (of Elea) arguments (see especially *Porphyry, cited in Simplicius *In Phys.* 140.6ff.) and may well be the target of the pseudo-Aristotelian *On Indivisible Lines*. Xenocrates is also responsible for an opaque definition of soul recorded by Aristotle (*DA* 408b32–33): It is a self-moving number.

*Plutarch claims (*Mor.* 1069e–f) that Xenocrates made *happiness turn on living in accordance with nature; since this may derive from *Antiochus of Ascalon, whose project it was to assimilate the Academy to Stoicism, it is suspect. *Clement (*Stromateis* 2.22) ascribes to him the view that happiness is the possession of one's own excellence in the soul, a view very like Aristotle's. Similarly, Xenocrates evaluates philosophical activity as "stopping the disturbance of the affairs of life" (ps.-Galen *Historia Philosophiae* 8); its negative emphasis sounds like a step in the direction of the Hellenistic goal of undisturbedness.

BIBLIOGRAPHY: Texts in R. Heinze, *Xenocrates* (Teubner), Stuttgart, 1892; repr. Hildesheim, 1965; M. Isnardi Parente, *Senocrate—Ermodoro: Frammenti*, Naples, 1982. Pines, S., *TAPA* 51, 1961, 3–34.—*R. M. DANCY*

XENOPHANES (?570–?478 B.C.E.), of Colophon. Presocratic philosopher. Some ancient sources set Xenophanes' year of birth as early as 620, and others as late as 540 B.C.E., but since he spoke of himself as having lived for ninety-three years (DK21B8) and was reported by the historian Timaeus (A8) to have lived in Syracuse during the reign of Hieron (478–467), the dates of 570–478 can be accepted as approximately correct. The reference in B7 to one who recognized the *soul of a friend in the cry of a puppy reveals an awareness of *Pythagorean doctrines and other fragments discuss natural phenomena studied by the Ionian philosopher-*scientists, but there is no firm evidence of any formal affiliation. In antiquity Xenophanes was known primarily as a rhapsode and a critic of the poetry of *Homer and *Hesiod. There are forty-three surviving fragments of his poetry, in elegiacs and hexameters, with B14 a combination of iambic trimeter and hexameter.

Many of the surviving poem-fragments deal with the usual topics of ancient symposiac poetry: how the feast has been prepared, how the wine should be mixed, what one ought to discuss during dinner, and the like. But even when his topic is a conventional one, Xenophanes' remarks are often original and controversial. In B1, for example, he criticizes the telling of the old tales of conflict among the gods and calls for more socially beneficial forms of poetic expression. B2 criticizes the special treatment accorded to victorious athletes, and B3 reminds his audience of the disaster that befell the citizens of old Colophon when they pursued wealth and useless luxury. Although these poems do not raise distinctly philosophical questions (Greek moral philosophy was largely the result of the challenges raised by the *sophists of mid-fifth century Athens) Xenophanes was nevertheless assuming the role of social gadfly later played by *Heraclitus and *Socrates, and many of his normative views foreshadow those expressed by *Plato in the *Republic*.

Xenophanes is perhaps best remembered for his critique of anthropomorphism in *religion and an advance toward monotheism. B16 (as reconstructed by Diels) notes that Thracian gods resemble Thracians and Ethiopian gods resemble Ethiopians, and B15 conjectures that if horses and oxen had hands and could paint pictures of their gods they would look remarkably like horses and oxen. By contrast, in B23 Xenophanes maintains that "one god is greatest, not at all like mortals in body and thought," and B24–26 speak of a god of maximal power, able to see, hear, and think "as a whole" and to "shake all things" by the exercise of his thought alone. On one traditional account, Xenophanes' "one greatest god" was the physical (spherical) universe, but this interpretation rests largely on loosely phrased remarks of *Aristotle and the tendency of later writers to conflate Xenophanes' doctrines with those of *Parmenides. A spherical universe would have been inconsistent with the assertion of B28 that the earth extends downward without limit, and the purity of Xenophanes' monotheism (or monism) is compromised by repeated references to plural gods (e.g., in B1 when he urges his dinner companions to "honor the gods (*theôn*) always").

Xenophanes' idea of a supreme divinity isolated from all human affairs dovetails neatly with his demythologized view of nature. B27–33 and B37 present straightforward factual accounts of the earth, sea, sun, rainbow, and underground waters; and *testimonia* A1, A32–33, and A36–48 credit Xenophanes with views that make use of strictly natural forces and substances. The assertion (in B32) that "she whom they call Iris (rainbow), this too is by nature a cloud, purple, red, and greenish-yellow to behold" typifies the approach: The popular view of this natural marvel must give way to understanding and defining it in terms of its observable properties. Similarly, B18 favors "seeking" over intimations from the gods. A33 (from *Hippolytus) reports that Xenophanes' theory of periodic flooding was based on discoveries (perhaps made by others) of fossilized remains of sea creatures at inland locations. His chief scientific innovations were a somewhat simplistic "cloud-based" physics and a dualist (earth *and* water) reply to the "basic substance" question posed by the Milesians. But unlike many early thinkers Xenophanes did not embrace a principle of "cosmic justice," nor did he hold that nature operated according to what is best.

*Pyrrho's student *Timon spoke of Xenophanes as a fledgling *skeptic (A35), and the famous opening line of B34, "... the clear and certain truth (*to saphes*) no man has seen" lends some credence to that assessment. But given that Xenophanes' subject was "the gods and what I say about all things" (e.g., that "all things ... are earth and water") and that other writers of his era linked knowing *to saphes* with having firsthand information (cf. Herodotus 2.44; Thucydides 1.22.4, Alcmaeon DK24B1), the point of B34 was probably that since speculations about the gods and basic natural causes cannot be confirmed on the basis of direct observation, certain knowledge concerning such matters is not possible. Xenophanes' allusion in B37 to "however many things they [presumably: the gods] have made evident for mortals to look at" and his positive support for inquiry in B18 suggest that he thought that human beings can aspire to some knowledge—concerning whatever the gods bring directly before them—but beyond the small circle of what they can experience for themselves lies only conjecture (cf. B34.4: "opinion is allotted to all").

Both Plato (*Soph.* 242c–d) and Aristotle (*Met.* 1.5, 986b18ff.) characterized Xenophanes as a founder of *Eleatic philosophy, a view perpetuated by the pseudo-Aristotelian treatise *de Melisso Xenophane Gorgia* and in many later *doxographical summaries. But this tradition may rest on no more than the fact that Xenophanes inquired into "all things" and affirmed "one" being (namely, the "one greatest god" of B23). Scholars have generally discounted the probative value of the later summaries in light of the practice of crediting the founder of a movement with doctrines developed by his followers. The Xenophanes who appears in the surviving fragments of his poems fully qualifies as a thoughtful social critic and inquirer into nature in the tradition of the first philosopher-scientists of Miletus.

BIBLIOGRAPHY: Texts in DK21; texts, tr. and comm. in J. H. Lesher, *Xenophanes of Colophon—Fragments: A Text and Translation with Commentary*, Toronto, 1992; see also KRS. Guthrie, W. K. C., *A History of Greek Philosophy*, vol. 1, Cambridge, 1962, 360–402.—*J. H. LESHER*

XENOPHON (c. 430–after 355 B.C.E.). Successful Athenian general, prolific and innovative author, and follower of *Socrates. During his youth Xenophon came under the spell of Socrates. In 401 B.C.E. he joined Greek mercenaries on an expedition to overthrow the ruler of Persia. The expedition failed, and he played a chief role leading the Greek troops on a retreat to the sea. His *Anabasis* recounts his experiences. He later served with the Spartan king Agesilaus II. About 394, perhaps because of his pro-Spartan activities, Xenophon was banished from Athens. He retired to an estate given to him by Agesilaus, where he led the life of a country gentleman, farming, hunting, and also writing.

Xenophon wrote an *Apology of Socrates*, and three Socratic *dialogues: the *Memorabilia* or *Recollections of Socrates*, *Symposium*, and *Oeconomicus*. His chief work of political theory is the *Cyropaedia*. Two shorter works are the *Agesilaus* and *Hiero*. He also wrote history and treatises on economic and technical subjects.

The greatest area of controversy concerning Xenophon's philosophical writings is the reliability of his testimony concerning Socrates. His portrait of Socrates was quite influential in antiquity. Over the last two centuries, some scholars have argued that Xenophon is our best source for the historical Socrates, since *Plato was too creative to be a good historian, and *Aristophanes falsified his portrait for comic effect. Others have argued that Xenophon's portrait is confused and misleading, since he was too unphilosophical to understand the real Socrates. "The problem of the the historical Socrates," as it is known, remains the object of vigorous scholarly debate.

The *Memorabilia*, or *Recollections of Socrates*, is Xenophon's major Socratic work. *Memorabilia* 1.1–2 are a defense of Socrates against the accusations made by Anytus at his trial. These chapters are a revised and expanded version of Xenophon's *Apology of Socrates*. The rest of the *Memorabilia* is devoted to continuing this defense by showing that Socrates' words and deeds were beneficial to his companions and to Athens. The *Memorabilia* is a rich and episodic work that contains a great deal of valuable evidence concerning the philosophical activity of Socrates and his followers.

According to Xenophon, the foundation of Socrates' *virtue is in self-control and not (as in Plato) in knowledge of his own ignorance. Xenophon portrays Socrates as being useful to those around him through concrete advice and moral example, as well as by philosophical argument and discussion. Xenophon's Socrates identifies the good with the beneficial, and the just with the law-abiding. He argues that *cosmological speculation is useless and foolish, whereas rational investigation of *ethical and *political topics is both possible and necessary.

The *Symposium*, or *Dinner Party*, is Xenophon's most elegant and humorous Socratic work. It is less grand and magnificent than Plato's work of the same name, but it is still a serious work of philosophy. Xenophon's *Symposium*, like Plato's, stresses the importance of loving individuals, not for their external beauty or wealth, but for their virtue, or potential for virtue. The identification of the beautiful with the good, and the good with the useful, is brought out by Socrates' argument that he should win a beauty contest on the grounds that his flaring nostrils are more useful at catching odors.

The *Oeconomicus* or *Estate Manager* is a dialogue about household or estate management. The household or estate was the level of social organization intermediate between the individual and the city/state. The *Oeconomicus* was quite influential in the Renaissance, which recognized it as the earliest systematic treatment of a major branch of social philosophy. The role of women in the household is a major topic of discussion, and the views presented are subtle and complex. The country gentleman Ischomachus rules the household and trains his wife in her duties, but the woman is given some autonomy and is portrayed as superior to her husband in important areas of knowledge.

A fundamental question of political philosophy is what is the art of ruling. In the *Oeconomicus* Xenophon presents the view that that the art of ruling oneself, the art of ruling a household, and the art of ruling a city are the same.

The *Cyropaedia* or "Education of Cyrus" is Xenophon's longest and most comprehensive work. It is written in the form of a historical novel about Cyrus the Great. Historical accuracy is not, however, Xenophon's aim; rather, he presents an idealized portrait of a great leader. Cyrus has an unlimited desire to rule over others, which leads him to acquire an empire. He is successful at this because he is pious, disciplined, and beneficent. Although ambitious for power, Cyrus is not a tyrant, since he aims to rule over willing subjects in accord with law. Xenophon recognizes that the goodness of a ruler is not the goodness of a saint: Cyrus' beneficence is tempered by manipulation, deceit, and ruthlessness.

Like Plato, Xenophon is hostile to democracy. At the beginning of the *Cyropaedia* he remarks that a central problem of politics is instability. Democracies are notoriously unstable. Xenophon's recommended alternative is a talented and beneficent monarch like Cyrus. But, as he shows through the breakup of Cyrus' empire immediately after his death, this alternative is dangerously dependent on an individual personality.

The *Agesilaus* is a short speech in praise of Xenophon's friend and patron. The speech portrays an idealized portrait of constitutional and beneficent rule. The *Hiero* is a dialogue between Hiero, tyrant of Syracuse, and the poet Simonides. A repeated theme of Xenophon's political writings is that good regimes are bound by laws and rule over willing subjects. The alternative is tyranny, which produces a miserable life for both the ruler and the ruled. The topic of the *Hiero* is whether the tyrant's life is miserable or happy.

Xenophon was not a professional philosopher in the sense that Plato was. Nonetheless, he was an intelligent, subtle writer who was keenly interested in many of the moral and political questions raised by Socrates. He made important original contributions to social and political thought.

See also SOCRATES.

BIBLIOGRAPHY: Texts in E. C. Marchant, *Xenophontis Opera*, Oxford, 1900–1904. Breitenbach, H. R., *Xenophon von Athen*, Stuttgart, 1966 (= *RE* 9.A2, 1967); Strauss, L., *Xenophon's Socrates*, Ithaca, 1972; Vander Waerdt, P., ed., *The Socratic Movement*, Ithaca, 1994.—*DONALD R. MORRISON*

Z

ZENO (c. 334/3–262/1 B.C.E.), of Citium on Cyprus. Founder of the *Stoa. Zeno laid the foundations of a powerful and coherent system that became immensely influential in antiquity and beyond.

Having come to Athens as a young man, Zeno is said to have studied with a variety of philosophers: the *Cynic *Crates of Thebes, the *Academic scholarch *Polemo, *Stilpo of the *Megarian school, and the *dialecticians *Diodorus Cronus and *Philo. About 300 B.C.E. he set up as a philosopher in his own right, lecturing near the Athenian agora in the *Stoa poikilê* ("Painted Colonnade"), from which the name of his school and its adherents is derived. Zeno's pupils included *Cleanthes of Assos, his successor as head of the school, *Persaeus, *Sphaerus, *Herillus of Carthage, and *Aristo of Chios. Unlike some of his pupils, Zeno abstained from political activity. He was highly esteemed for his sober and consistent demeanor and wholesome influence on the city's youth. Both during his lifetime and posthumously he received official distinctions.

Writings. *Diogenes Laertius (7.4) provides an incomplete list of Zeno's writings, illustrating the scope of his concerns: the *Republic*; *On Life according to Nature*; *On Impulse*, or *On the Nature of Man*; *On Passions*; *On Appropriate Action*; *On Law*; *On Greek Culture*; *On Vision*; *On the Universe*; *On Signs*; *Pythagorean Questions*; *Universals* (? *Katholika*); *On Modes of Speech*; *Homeric Problems*; *On Reading Poetry*; *The Art* (of Dialectic? Rhetoric?); *Solutions*; *Refutations, Memories of Crates*; *Ethics*. Other extant titles are *Conversations (Diatribai)*, *On Nature*, *On Reason (Peri Logou)*, *On Substance (Peri Ousias)*. Of these treatises none has survived. A handful of quotations in later authors afford glimpses of the contents of a few of them.

Logic. Zeno propagated the notion of philosophy as a system, treating logic as one of its "parts," alongside *ethics and physics (D.L. 7.39). Ancient sources commonly regard Stoic logic as largely *Chrysippus' achievement and offer little information about its Zenonian stage (cf. Cic. *Fin.* 4.9). *Plutarch (*SR* 1034E) suggests that Zeno was interested in *dialectic mainly as a tool for solving fallacies (cf. his *Solutions*), which seems to imply a restricted, rather defensive view of logic. Closer consideration of the evidence, however, reveals a more extensive concern with logic. Zeno accepted the methods of definition and division, presumably under the influence of the Academy. But his idea of proof is based on the propositional logic of Diodorus Cronus. Zeno's syllogisms prove dogmas such as that of God's existence from two agreed premises, reflecting both a characteristic stress on brevity and the more traditional view of dialectic as proceeding by question and answer. Zeno rejected universals, positing the logical and ontological priority of particulars. In the linguistic part of logic, he subscribed to the natural origin of language and accepted etymology.

Ontology and Natural Philosophy. Taking the power to act or be acted upon as the criterion of *being, Zeno held that this is satisfied by corporeal entities alone (cf. Pl. *Soph.* 247e). By the same criterion he denied existence to universals (i.e., to separate or inherent "forms"), whose only function, he held, is to classify reality. Within reality he distinguished two principles, separable in thought but not in fact. The passive principle, or *matter, is the inexhaustible substrate of all *change and lacks qualities of its own, though existing always in a particular form. The active principle or cause informing all matter is called *Logos or "Reason." Other designations are: God, Providence, Fate, Cause, and (cosmic) Nature. Its physical vehicle is the creative Fire, conceived as a psychic and rational power. There is one cosmos, surrounded by infinite *void and going through an eternal cycle punctuated by periodical conflagrations. Each conflagration marks the supreme dominance of the divine Fire, which contains the "spermatic formula" for each new world-order and proceeds to create this by differentiating the physical elements, water, air, earth, and (ordinary destructive) fire. Given God's perfection and omnipotence, each successive cosmic period is repeated in precisely the same way down to the smallest details. Zeno postulates an inexorable chain of cause and effect, that is, God in his aspect of Fate, legitimizing divination.

Physical processes are based on the continous transformation of the four elements into one another, an idea that owes something to *Aristotle. But unlike Aristotle, Zeno accepts the total interblending of substances, which is crucial to his doctrine of divine Fire permeating the whole cosmos and that of the corporeal *soul pervading the body as psychic *pneuma* (i.e., fiery breath). The soul in its more specific sense, that is, as responsible for the higher functions, has eight distinct parts. Its ruling part (*hêgemonikon*), or *mind, is the central organ of ratiocination, perception, and volition. From it five rays of *pneuma* operate the senses, while two further parts extend to the reproductive and speech organs. The ruling part is wholly rational; there are no irreducibly nonrational powers in the soul.

Epistemology. Zeno distinguished the reception of sense-perception, causing an imprint in the pneumatic soul, from an active response whereby the mind accords or denies assent (*sunkatathesis*) to the received impression. The mind contains no innate ideas. It generates universal concepts and ideas about nonperceptible entities on the basis of perceptions that are retained in the memory. Zeno took one class of impressions to represent objects as they really are and to command assent directly. These so-called cognitive ("cataleptic") impressions are accorded the status of criterion of truth. Assent to a cognitive impression is called cognition (*katalêpsis*). Cognition is common to both knowledge and opinion, which are sharply differentiated in all other respects. Knowledge consists of a stable system of cognitions uncontrovertible by argument, whereas opinion is a mixed bag of cognition and incorrect beliefs marked by instability and inconsistency. Zeno's theory is original in several aspects, notably the idea of assent.

*Ethical and *Political Thought*. Taking his lead from the Socratic and Cynic traditions, Zeno taught the self-sufficiency of *virtue for *happiness, viewing virtue as the perfection of man's rational nature (i.e., knowledge) and defining happiness as a "smooth flow of life." The life according to virtue is identical with that according to nature, as it is described in Zeno's formula of the human goal or fulfilment (*telos*). Alternatively, he spoke of living consistently (*homologoumenôs*) *tout court*. The good resides in virtue and virtuous action alone; evil consists in moral badness (i.e., an ignorant and passionate state of mind). Bodily and external things are indifferent (*adiaphora*) yet represent value in another, not strictly moral sense: Zeno distinguished between "preferred" (*proêgmena*) and "relegated" (*apoproêgmena*) things: life vs. death, wealth vs. poverty, honor vs. disrepute, health vs. illness, and so on. Man exhibits a pattern of responses or impulses (*hormai*) towards or away from these things, depending on their being conducive or detrimental to his nature as a human being. This concerns not only the things directly related to our physical well-being (the "first things according to nature") but also those belonging to the rational and social behavior typical of adult humans. The actions consistent with one's nature have "a well-reasoned justification" and are called *kathêkonta* ("appropriate actions"). Zeno appears to have seen virtuous actions as a special class of appropriate actions, namely, those that result from a perfectly rational mental disposition and thus exhibit the highest degree of consistency.

Zeno accepted the traditional quartet of cardinal virtues with the qualification that temperance, courage and justice are forms of practical knowledge (*phronêsis*) applied to different spheres of action, for example, courage is "knowledge of what is to be endured and what is not." Hence all virtues presuppose one another. Strictly, souls are either good or bad, either wise or ignorant; there are no gradations between the two states. From his absolute division of mankind Zeno developed his famous "paradoxes," identifying the sage as the only one to whom predicates like "happy," "strong," "king," and the like, apply. Likewise, the common run, or "fools," are "miserable," "weak," "slaves," and so on.

Passions are unnatural or excessive impulses triggered by faulty judgements concerning the value of indifferent things. The correct attitude consists in a certain detachment vis-à-vis external and bodily valuables, which after all cannot be securely controlled given the preordained course of events and our ignorance of the future. Accordingly, virtue as one's inner disposition rather than the effects of our actions constitutes the locus of moral responsibility. Man's freedom lies in his capacity to grasp his role in the divine plan, not in the possibility of effecting any change in it.

The *Republic* was notorious for its abolition of conventional institutions such as marriage and traditional religion. Zeno envisaged a community in the ordinary sense of the word, but one bound together by love and perfected by its communist institutions and the moral virtue of its citizens. Modelling his ideal state in many respects on historical Sparta, he continued the tradition and style of political theorizing familiar from Plato's *Republic*, setting simplicity and concord against the latter's elaborate proposals.

BIBLIOGRAPHY: Texts in *SVF* 1, nos. 1–332; A. C. Pearson, *The Fragments of Zeno and Cleanthes*, London, 1891; see also T. Dorandi, ed., *Filodemo, Storia dei filosofi: La stoà da Zenone a Panezio* (PHerc. 1018). Graeser, A., *Zenon von Kition. Positionen und Probleme*, Berlin, 1975; with J. Mansfeld, *Mnemosyne* 31, 1978, 134–78; Mansfeld, J., *Elenchos* 7, 1986, 295–382, esp. 317ff.; Pohlenz, M., in *Nachricht. der Akad. der Wiss. Göttingen*, phil.-hist. Kl. 1, 2.9, 1938, 173–210; Schofield, M., *Phronesis* 28, 1983, 31–58; also *The Stoic Idea of the City*, Cambridge, 1991; von Fritz, K., in *RE* 10A, cols. 83–121.—*TEUN L. TIELEMAN*

ZENO (b. c. 490 B.C.E.), of Elea in Southern Italy. *Eleatic philosopher, student of *Parmenides. Little is known of Zeno's life. In the *Parmenides*, *Plato reports that Parmenides and Zeno came to Athens for the great Panathenaic festival when Zeno was about forty years old. The internal evidence of the *Parmenides* places the date of the visit in about 450 B.C.E., thus suggesting c. 490 for Zeno's birth. The chronology of post-Parmenidean philosophy is very difficult to fix, but Zeno was probably a contemporary of *Anaxagoras, *Empedocles, and possibly *Leucippus. Ancient sources report that Zeno was a loyal citizen of Elea, tortured for his part in a plot against a tyrant. *Aristotle called Zeno "the Father of *Dialectic."

In the *Parmenides* Plato suggests that Zeno wrote only one book, a defense of Parmenides against those who ridiculed his views, and this is repeated in *Simplicius. The *Suda* mentions four works, *Disputations*, *Against the Philosophers*, *On Nature*, and a *Commentary on Empedocles*. Only the *Suda* mentions the latter; it is probably spurious, and the first three may be alternate titles for a single work. The evidence of the *Parmenides* suggests that Zeno's work was a series of arguments all beginning with the hypothesis, "If there is a many" and deriving contradictions from the hypothesis. *Proclus suggests that there were forty of these arguments (although some commentators have suggested that Proclus had access to a different work of Zeno's). Only the argument at *Parmenides* 127e1–128a1 and one quoted by Simplicius (DK29B3) survive in this form. If this was the nature of Zeno's treatise, it is not clear how the arguments against motion reported by Aristotle fit into the overall scheme.

It is likely that Plato is correct in his assessment of the targets of Zeno's arguments. There is little textual support for the view (originating with Paul Tannery—see Owen) that Zeno intended to undermine certain supposed assumptions of early *Pythagorean *mathematics. Moreover, despite several attempts to find an overall structure to the arguments, the surviving texts are inconclusive. Zeno's treatise seems rather to have been a collection of arguments taking on both theoretical and common-sense views about plurality, space, and *time that were, in his view, at odds with Parmenides' arguments.

There is little scholarly agreement about either the exact details or the import of the surviving arguments. There are a number of arguments against plurality and four arguments against motion. In addition there is the report of an argument against place and the so-called millet-seed argument.

Arguments against Plurality. Simplicius (*in Phys.* 97.12–13) quotes *Eudemus' report that "They say that Zeno said that if someone would give him an account of what in the world the one is, he would be able to explain the *beings." Thus, a plurality might be possible if it were grounded in a one (or ones) that were coherent entities. But Zeno's arguments purport to show that no such one is possible. The arguments against plurality all show that assuming plurality results in a contradiction in the description of the entities. The argument at *Parmenides* 127e1ff. claims that if there is a plurality, things must be both like and unlike and this is impossible. B1 and B2 contain a report by Simplicius of an argument that shows that if there is a many, things must be both so small as to have no magnitude (and thus could not even be at all) and so large as to be unlimited. Thus, there cannot be a many. Simplicius reports that Zeno first shows that "each of the many is the same as itself and one." It seems that magnitude, solidity, and bulk are incompatible with a thing being the same as itself and one, since these would imply parts that would make the thing different from itself and not one. Simplicius then relates the result: What has no magnitude, solidity, or bulk cannot be at all, for when added it adds nothing and when subtracted it takes away nothing. The second part of the argument shows that anything that is must have magnitude and, indeed, unlimited magnitude. If something has magnitude one part can be distinguished from another. But that part must have magnitude as well, and thus a further part that can be distinguished, and so on. The assumption here is apparently that an unlimited number of parts, each with magnitude, can be generated and that the sum of these parts will yield an unlimitedly large thing. B3 yields yet another argument against plurality: "If there is a many, the same things are both limited and unlimited." The first arm of the antinomy asserts that the things that are are just as many as they are, and so limited; the assumption is that there is a definite number and so a limit to the things that are. The second arm claims that if there is a many, the many things can be differentiated from each other, and "there are always others between the things that are" that serve to differentiate. But these others must be differentiated from the first things, and so there are yet others between, and so on. Thus, there is no limit to the things that are.

Arguments against Motion. The four attacks on motion are the most controversial of Zeno's arguments. We have no direct textual evidence for them, only short reports of or references to them in Aristotle (who clearly expected his hearers to be familiar with them), with expanded explanations and elucidations in the *Aristotelian commentators. The four arguments show that motions can be neither completed (the stadium or the dichotomy) nor begun (the Achilles), involve contradictions (the moving blocks), or are simply impossible (the arrow).

The "Dichotomy" paradox (*Phys.* 239b11–13) asserts that a runner can never complete a run in a stadium. There are two ways of reading Aristotle's account of the argument. First, the runner must first pass a halfway mark, and to do that he must complete half of the run to the halfway mark. But there is a halfway mark in this part of the run as well, and so, indefinitely. On the second reading, having reached a halfway point, the runner still has half the distance to the end to go. But having reached this, there is yet another halfway point, and so on. There is always some distance left to go, and so the run cannot be completed. The argument assumes that it is impossible to pass or touch an *infinite number of points in a finite time, and so the runner cannot complete the motion. Aristotle first criticizes the argument (at *Phys.* 233a21–31) by denying the assumption. According to Aristotle, like a finite length, a finite time is infinitely divisible, and so the task can be completed. At *Physics* 263a15ff. Aristotle revises his criticism. The earlier will do *ad hominem*, but if the time or distance is actually rather than only potentially infinite, the task is indeed impossible. The "Achilles" (*Phys.* 239b14ff.) follows the same pattern, with the same assumptions, but with division into proportions other than halves. It shows that a faster runner can never overtake a slower who has a head start. The faster must first reach the spot where the slower was when the faster began. During that time the slower has moved on, and the faster must now reach that spot. But when he does, the slower has again moved, leaving yet another gap that must be made up, and so on.

The "Arrow" paradox purports to show the impossibility of motion. Aristotle gives a brief reference to it at *Physics* 239b5–7, and both the text and the proper interpretation of Aristotle's analysis of the argument are uncertain and controversial. Zeno is supposed to have claimed that at each instant of its flight the arrow occupies a proper place, namely, a space equal to itself. But anything in a proper place is at rest. So at each instant or moment of its flight the arrow is at rest. Thus, the arrow does not move. Aristotle's objection to the argument is to deny that time is composed of discrete instants. According to Aristotle, time is continuous, and thus Zeno's argument fails.

The paradox of the "Moving Rows" in a stadium is supposed to show that the assumption that motion is possible leads to contradictory results. Aristotle offers a summary and an analysis (at *Phys.* 239b33–240a18). Introducing the paradox, he says that it involves equal bodies moving past equal bodies in the opposite direction, at the same speed. This, according to Aristotle's report, shows that "half the time is equal to the double." Simplicius provided the following diagram of the starting positions (Diels attributed the diagram to *Alexander, but it is not clear that this is correct). D marks the beginning of the stadium, E marks the end:

$$
\begin{array}{ccc}
 & \text{AAAA} & \\
\text{D} & \text{BBBB} \rightarrow & \text{E} \\
 & \leftarrow \text{CCCC} &
\end{array}
$$

When the motion is completed, according to Aristotle, the blocks will be lined up together:

$$
\begin{array}{c}
\text{AAAA} \\
\text{BBBB} \\
\text{CCCC}
\end{array}
$$

The leading B will have passed all four C's but only two A's, just as the leading C will have passed all four B's but only two A's. From this, according to Aristotle, Zeno concluded that the transition from the first state to the final state takes both a period of time and half that period of time, which is impossible. Zeno apparently assumed that it always takes the same amount of time for one block to pass another block. Aristotle rejects Zeno's assumption on the grounds that bodies moving in opposite directions (the B's and C's) move past each other with a relative speed that is greater than the speed at which they move past something that is stationary (the A's).

Paradoxes of Place and the Millet Seed. In the paradox of place (DK29 A24) Zeno notes that every existing thing exists somewhere. Whatever exists somewhere must exist in something else, namely, in a place. But a place is an existing thing and must exist in something other than itself. Therefore, a place must be in a place; this second place is itself an existing thing that must be in a place. This goes on without limit, which is impossible, so there is no such thing as the single place where a thing is. The paradox of the millet seed (DK29A29) attacks the assumption that things are composed of parts. A single millet seed does not make a noise when it falls. Yet a bushel of seed does make a noise. But because there is a ratio between the single millet seed (the part) and the bushel (the whole), there should be a similar ratio between the sound of a single seed and the sound of the bushel. The seed both does and does not make a noise when it falls. Thus it is unintelligible to think of a thing as composed of parts that are in a certain ratio with the whole. The argument is sometimes also taken as an attack on sense perception.

Zeno's arguments influenced later Presocratic thought and, as Aristotle realized, raised serious difficulties about the nature of space, time, continuity, and infinite divisibility. Although the arguments have sometimes been dismissed as fallacious, many philosophers have shown that their resolution demands the investigation of profound questions about the nature of infinity, space, time, and the adequacy of quantitative analysis for describing and understanding natural phenomena. Recent philosophers have argued that Zeno's arguments succeed, but only because they describe tasks it is logically impossible to perform.

BIBLIOGRAPHY: Texts in DK29. Furley, D., in A. P. D. Mourelatos, ed., *The Pre-Socratics*, Princeton, 1993, 353–367; Grünbaum, A., *Modern Science and Zeno's Paradoxes*, London, 1968; Lee, H. D. P., *Zeno of Elea: A Text with Translation and Notes*, Cambridge, 1936; repr. Adolf M. Hakkert, Amsterdam, 1967; Owen, G. E. L., in Owen, *Logic, Science and Dialectic: Collected Papers in Greek Philosophy*, Ithaca, 1986, 45–61; Salmon, W., ed., *Zeno's Paradoxes*, Indianapolis, 1970; Solmsen, F., in Mourelatos, *Pre-Socratics*, 368–393; Vlastos, G., in P. Edwards, ed., *The Encyclopedia of Philosophy*, New York, 1967, vol. 8, 369–379.—*PATRICIA CURD*

ZENO (b. c. 150, active in Athens in 79/78 B.C.E.), of Sidon. *Epicurean philosopher and head of the Epicurean community after the death of Apollodorus, Kepotyrannos. Zeno was succeeded by *Phaedrus of Athens. His philosophical interests were broad. He engaged in a controversy with the *Stoics over the nature of signs (*sêmeia*) and empirical inference, lectured on *ethics, and offered a criticism of *Euclidean geometry. There are no remains, but two writings of his pupil *Philodemus of Gadara are identified by their titles as derived from his lectures (PHerc. 1289 and 1471). Philodemus wrote a pamphlet on his lectures (PHerc. 1003), and his *On Methods of Inference* seems to be in his debt. Explicit references in the full title of Philodemus' *On Plain Speaking* and in Book 5 of his *On Poets* also reveal a considerable debt. *Proclus' *Commentary on the First Book of Euclid's Elements* contains the evidence for his criticism of Euclid (214–218 Friedlein).

BIBLIOGRAPHY: Texts in A. Angeli and M. Colaizzo, eds., "I frammenti di Zenone Sidonio," *CronErc* 9, 1979, 47–133. Erler, M., in H. Flashar, ed., *Grundriss der Geschichte der Philosophie: Die Philosophie der Antike*, vol. 4, Basel, 1994, 268–272; Vlastos, G., in L. Wallach, ed., *The Classical Tradition: Literary and Historical Studies in Honor of Harry Caplan*, Ithaca, 1966, 148–159, repr. in D. W. Graham, ed., *Studies in Greek Philosophy*, vol. 2, Princeton, 1995, 315–324.—*DISKIN CLAY*

ZENO (fl. c. 210 B.C.E.), of Tarsus. *Stoic philosopher, son of Dioscorides, student of *Chrysippus. Zeno of Tarsus was the fourth head of the Stoic school, succeeding his teacher Chrysippus. *Diogenes Laertius (7.35) claims that he wrote few works, but had many students. Many of Zeno's predecessors held that *ethics, physics, and *logic were the three parts of philosophical *discourse* (*logos*). Zeno, by contrast, thought they were parts of philosophy *itself* (D.L. 7.41). He agreed with Chrysippus, *Posidonius, and others in dividing the ethical part of philosophy into seven topics, concerning (i) impulse, (ii) good and bad things, (iii) the passions, (iv) *virtue, (v) the end, (vi) primary value and actions, and (vii) encouragements and discouragements in acting (D.L. 7.84). Zeno also held in doubt (or "suspended judgment on," *epischein*) the Stoic views about the conflagration of the world (Arius Didymus cited in Eus. *PE* 15.18.2).

BIBLIOGRAPHY: Texts in *SVF* 3, 209.—*IAKOVOS VASILIOU*

A Chronological Outline of Classical Philosophy

The historical progression of the course of Greek and Roman philosophy may usefully be divided into the following stages or moments: (i) Presocratic philosophy, (ii) the Sophists and Socrates, (iii) Plato and the Academy, (iv) Aristotle and the Lyceum, (v) Hellenistic philosophy; (vi) Roman philosophy, and (vii) the philosophy of late antiquity.

Presocratic Philosophy: Sixth and Fifth Centuries B.C.E. The traditional date that marks the beginning of the period of Greek and Roman philosophy is 585/4 B.C.E., the year in which an eclipse, reportedly predicted by *Thales, is supposed to have occurred (see THALES and the cautions expressed there). Since *Aristotle names Thales as "the founder of this sort of philosophy" (*Met.* 1.3, 983b20–1), that is, of inquiry into the causes of natural phenomena, Thales has been taken to stand at the head of a tradition called "Presocratic" philosophy. The term is something of a misnomer: Strictly speaking, it should refer only to Greek philosophy prior to *Socrates. In fact, however, it more usually refers to a tradition of theorizing about the origin, causes and constituent principle(s) of the natural world (as well as a tradition of theorizing about such theorizing). That tradition continues well into the second half of the fifth century B.C.E. and beyond. *Democritus, by many accounts among the greatest of the "Presocratic" philosophers, outlived Socrates, perhaps by as much as forty years.

The sixth-century Presocratic philosophers represented in this w~ include Thales, *Anaximander and *Anaximenes (called the "Miles because ~~ey were native to the city of Miletus, or "the Ionians" ~

Miletus is situated in Ionia, the central region along the Asia Minor coast); *Pythagoras, *Alcmaeon, and *Xenophanes. *Heraclitus and *Parmenides are the major figures straddling the two centuries, and much of fifth century Presocratic thought is forged in more or less conscious response to Parmenides' arguments. The major fifth-century Presocratic thinkers include *Empedocles, *Anaxagoras, *Archelaus, *Zeno of Elea, *Melissus, *Diogenes of Apollonia *Philolaus and *Democritus.

The Sophists and Socrates: Second half of Fifth Century B.C.E. Social and political developments in Athens brought with them a need for a broadly based education, and training in public debate. That need was supplied by the sophists, professional teachers who traveled throughout the Greek world and taught for a fee (see SOPHISTS). Prominent among them were *Protagoras *Gorgias, *Hippias *Antiphon and *Prodicus.

Whether *Socrates, their contemporary, should be reckoned among the sophists is a matter of debate. *Plato emphasizes that he neither traveled nor taught for a fee; on the other hand, his interest in ethics and his style of critical questioning has much in common with theirs. Socrates' brilliance and no doubt the force of his personality and way of life attracted a number of young admirers and devotees (see SOCRATES; SOCRATIC CIRCLE).

Plato and the Academy: First Half of Fourth Century B.C.E. After the death of Socrates in 399 B.C.E. several of his followers went on to pursue philosophy and found associations or schools of their own (see SOCRATIC CIRCLE). By far the most preeminent of these was Plato, who founded the *Academy in 387 (see ACADEMY; PLATO). Plato remained head of the Academy until his death in 347. Prominent thinkers affiliated with Plato in the Academy included *Eudoxus, *Xenocrates, *Speusippus and *Aristotle.

Aristotle and the Lyceum: Middle Decades of Fourth Century B.C.E. Aristotle had joined the Academy in 367 B.C.E. but shortly after Plato's death broke with the Academy and left Athens. Returning to Athens in 335 after an absence of twelve years, Aristotle founded the *Lyceum, a school with different intellectual interests from those of the Academy. His best known student and associate was *Theophrastus. Other notable figures included *Aristoxenus and *Dicaearchus.

Hellenistic Philosophy: 323–31 B.C.E. The "Hellenistic age" of Graeco-Roman civilization denominates a period, beginning with the death of Alexander the Great, in which Greek civilization came to permeate the ntire Mediterranean world. The philosophy of this period is marked by foundation of two highly influential philosophical traditions, *Stoi- and *Epicureanism. The major figures in each of these traditions are merous to mention here (see STOA, the, and STOICISM; EPI- NISM). These schools interacted with each other as well as with the Academy (which, after a turn to *skepticism in the third century B.C.E. seems to have returned to a Stoicized *Platonism in the first century B.C.E.) and the Lyceum, the home of *Aristotelianism until its demise early in the first century B.C.E. In addition to the emergence of the new schools a tradition of skepticism unrelated to that of the Academy and descending from *Pyrrho also figured prominently in the period.

The destruction of Athens in 86 B.C.E. at the hands of the Roman general Sulla led to the decline of Athens as the intellectual center of the world. Although the city remained a leading center for philosophy in the ancient world, many other centers of learning rose to prominence throughout the Mediterranean world, and among these, Alexandria in Egypt with its museum and library attained preeminence by the close of the Hellenistic period.

Roman Philosophy: First Century B.C.E. to Second Century C.E. The year 31 C.E. witnessed the victory of Octavian over Mark Antony at the battle of Actium, an event usually taken to mark the transition of Rome from republic to empire. Rome had already welcomed the Hellenistic philosophical schools more than a century earlier, when an embassy of philosophers from Athens, consisting of the Stoic *Diogenes of Seleucia, the Academic *Carneades and the *Peripatetic *Critolaus, visited Rome in 155/6 B.C.E. The Roman writers *Lucretius and *Cicero, both writing during the Roman republic, are two of our most important sources for Hellenistic philosophy.

The period of the Roman empire saw the continuation of all the schools of Hellenistic philosophy. Stoicism especially had a strong appeal during the imperial period (see STOA, the, and STOICISM).

Philosophy of Late Antiquity: Third to Sixth Centuries C.E. This final stage in the history of Graeco-Roman philosophy is marked by the dominance of a revived Platonism. As was noted above, the Academy came to abandon skepticism and return to a "dogmatic" position in the first century B.C.E. This return inaugurated a tradition known as Middle Platonism (see PLATONISM) which developed in the latter half of the first century B.C.E. and was based in Alexandria. In the mid-third century C.E. Platonism came to philosophical prominence when *Plotinus founded a school in Rome. Plotinus' Platonism, synthesized with elements of Aristotelian and Stoic ideas, eventually constituted the most definitive philosophical system antiquity has bequeathed to us. Neoplatonism, as the system was called, replaced Stoicism as the dominant world view, and maintained its dominance well beyond the close of the Graeco-Roman period.

A Guide to Bibliography

The sheer volume of publications of newly edited texts and of scholarly books and periodical articles in the field of Classical Philosophy is immense and continues to accelerate. This note is intended as a guide to recently published bibliographies that, though not exhaustive, are extremely useful and should be consulted to supplement the bibliographies given under the individual articles.

The Presocratics

Kirk, G. S., J. E. Raven, and M. Schofield, *The Presocratic Philosophers: A Critical History with a Selection of Texts*, 2nd ed., Cambridge, 1983 (=KRS), 453–460.

Barnes, J., *The Presocratic Philosophers*, 2 vols., London, 1979 (in 1 vol., revised, 1982.), 647–675 (in revised volume).

McKirahan, R. D., Jr., *Philosophy before Socrates*, Indianapolis/Cambridge MA, 1994, 414–420.

Guthrie, W. K. C., *A History of Greek Philosophy*, Cambridge, vol. 1, 493–503; vol. 2, 508–522.

Socrates

Benson, H. H., ed., *Essays on the Philosophy of Socrates*, Oxford, 1992, 317–339.

Brickhouse, T. C. and N. D. Smith, *Plato's Socrates*, Oxford, 1994, 213–219.

Plato (incl. Socrates)

Kraut, R., ed., *The Cambridge Companion to Plato*, Cambridge, 1992, 493–521.

Complete bibliographies for Plato for the years indicated are given in:

Brisson, L., *Lustrum*, 1977, for 1958–75.
Cherniss, H., *Lustrum*, 1959, 1960, for 1950–57.
McKirahan, R. D., Jr., *Plato and Socrates: A Comprehensive Bibliography, 1958–1973*, New York, 1978.

Bibliographies for recent (1992–1994, 1994–1996) and current work on Plato are being compiled and published by L. Brisson and F. Plin, CNRS, Paris.

Aristotle

Barnes, J., ed., *The Cambridge Companion to Aristotle*, Cambridge, 1995, 295–384 (important update of earlier bibliographies, incl. that in Barnes, et al., *Articles on Aristotle*, London, 1975).

Hellenistic Philosophy

Barnes, J, et al., *The Cambridge History of Hellenistic Philosophy*, Cambridge, 1997, forthcoming.
Long, A. A. and D. N. Sedley, eds. and trs., *The Hellenistic Philosophers* (= LS), vol. 2, Cambridge, 476–512.

Plotinus and Later Platonism

Blumenthal, H., "Plotinus in the Light of Twenty Years' Scholarship, 1951–1971," and K. Corrigan and P. O'Cleirich, "The Course of Plotinian Scholarship from 1971 to 1986," *ANRW* 2, 36.1, 528–623.
Gerson, L. P., *Plotinus*, London, 1994, 294–316.

Topical:

Everson, S., *Companions to Ancient Thought 1: Epistemology*, Cambridge, 1990, 251–272.
_____, *Companions to Ancient Thought 2: Psychology*, Cambridge, 1991, 218–252.

_____, *Companions to Ancient thought 3: Language*, Cambridge, 1994, 237–263.

Additionally, exhaustive year-by-year bibliographical data are provided for publications in philosophy by *The Philosopher's Index* (Philosophy Documentation Center), Bowling Green, Ohio, 1967–, and for publications in classics, by J. Marouzeau, *L'Année Philologique*, Paris, 1924/6–.

Computer Resources:

A database in various aspects of Classical studies, including Classical Philosophy, is available on CD-ROM and the Internet. It is *Perseus 2.0* and is published by the Perseus Project located at the department of Classics, Tufts University. It may be accessed at:
                    http://www.perseus.tufts.edu

A new database in Classical Philosophy, named *Archelogos* (Theodore Scaltsas, Project Director) is currently being developed for CD-ROM and the Internet. It may be accessed at:
                    http://www.archelogos.phil.ed.ac.uk.

Index

Main entries and page numbers are indicated in boldface type

List of Contributors

James Allen, Associate Professor of Philosophy, University of Pittsburgh, USA (*Aenesidemus, Agrippa, Arcesilaus, Lacydes, Pyrrho and Pyrrhonism, Sextus Empiricus, Timon*)

David Armstrong, Professor of Classics, The University of Texas at Austin, USA (*Manichaeanism*)

Elizabeth Asmis, Professor of Classics, The University of Chicago, USA (*Epictetus, Epicurus, Panaetius, Philodemus, Seneca*)

Andrew Barker, Reader in Classics, University of Birmingham, UK (*Aristoxenus, Damon*)

Richard Bett, Associate Professor of Philosophy, Johns Hopkins University, USA (*Carneades, Clitomachus, Skepticism*)

D. L. Blank, Professor of Classics, University of California at Los Angeles, USA (*Diogenes of Seleucia, Grammar*)

H. J. Blumenthal, Reader in Greek, University of Liverpool, UK (*Ammonius, Plutarch of Athens, Syrianus, Themistius*)

István Bodnár, Associate Professor of the History of Philosophy, Eötvös University, Budapest, Hungary (*Anaximander, Anaximenes*)

Abraham P. Bos, Professor of Ancient and Patristic Philosophy, Free University, Amsterdam, The Netherlands (*Christianity*)

Alan C. Bowen, Institute for Research in Classical Philosophy and Science, Princeton, USA (*Oenopides, Thales*)

R. Bracht Branham, Associate Professor of Classics and Comparative Literature, Emory University, USA (*Lucian*)

Thomas C. Brickhouse, Professor of Philosophy, Lynchburg College, USA (*Socrates*)

Diskin Clay, R. J. R. Nabisco Professor of Classical Studies, Duke University, USA (*Greek Dialogue, Latin Dialogue, Diogenes of Oeno-*

anda, Lyric and Elegaic Poets, Phaedrus of Athens, Polystratus, Zeno of Sidon)

Alan D. Code, Steve R. & Sarah E. O'Donnell Professor of Philosophy, The Ohio State University, USA (*Aristotle*)

Patricia Curd, Associate Professor of Philosophy, Purdue University, USA (*Eleatic School, Melissus, Zeno of Elea*)

R. M. Dancy, Professor of Philosophy, Florida State University, USA (*Academy, Euclides, Eudemus, Eudoxus, Megarian School, Speusippus, Stilpo, Xenocrates*)

Joseph G. DeFilippo, Assistant Professor of Classics and Philosophy, University of North Dakota, USA (*Apuleius, Aspasius, Callipho, Chaldean Oracles, Cicero*)

Daniel T. Devereux, Professor of Philosophy, University of Virginia, USA. Associate Editor

John Dillon, Regius Professor of Greek, Trinity College, Dublin, Ireland (*Calcidius, Eudorus, Gnosticism, Origen of Alexandria, Philo of Alexandria, Platonism, Plutarch*)

Tiziano Dorandi, Research Fellow, Centre National de la Recherche Scientifique, Paris, France (*Anaxarchus, Archedemus, Boethus, Dardanus, Diocles, Hecataeus, Hecato, Mnesarchus, Sphaerus*)

Walter G. Englert, Professor of Classics and Humanities, Reed College, USA (*Herillus, Lucretius, Metrodorus of Stratonicea, Monimus*)

David B. Evans, Associate Professor Emeritus, St. John's University, USA (*[Pseudo-] Dionysius*)

Andrew Ford, Associate Professor of Classics, Princeton University, USA (*Aesthetics, Critias*)

William W. Fortenbaugh, Professor II, Classics, Rutgers University, USA (*Aristo of Ceos, Demetrius of Phalerum, Dicaearchus, Theophrastus*)

Dorothea Frede, Professor of Philosophy, Philosophisches Seminar, University of Hamburg, Germany (*Alexander of Aphrodisias, Aristocles*)

Robert N. Gaines, Associate Professor of Speech Communication, University of Maryland at College Park, USA (*Rhetoric*)

Lloyd P. Gerson, Professor of Philosophy, University of Toronto, Canada (*Theism and Atheism*)

Christopher Gill, Reader in Ancient Thought, University of Exeter, UK (*Ethical Thought*)

Mary Louise Gill, Professor of Classics and Philosophy, University of Pittsburgh, USA (*Matter*)

Pamela Gordon, Associate Professor of Classics, University of Kansas, USA (*Epicureanism*)

H. B. Gottschalk, Reader in Classics Emeritus, The University of Leeds, UK (*Aristotelianism, Dionysius, Heraclides of Pontus*)

Daniel W. Graham, Professor of Philosophy, Brigham Young University, USA (*Change*)

Ilsetraut Hadot, Director of Research, Centre National de la Recherche Scientifique, Paris, France (*Hierocles of Alexandria, Simplicius*)

David E. Hahm, Professor of Classics, Ohio State University, USA (*Aelian, Antisthenes of Rhodes, Apollonius of Tyre, Arius Didymus, Eunapius, Posidonius, Stoa and Stoicism, Stobaeus*)

Stephen Halliwell, Professor of Greek, University of St. Andrews, UK (*Tragic Poets*)

Jürgen Hammerstaedt, Research Associate in Papyrology, University of Cologne, Germany (*Maximus, Oenomaus*)

R. J. Hankinson, Professor of Philosophy, The University of Texas at Austin, USA (*Galen, Theories of Medicine*)

Pamela M. Huby, Honorary Senior Fellow, University of Liverpool, UK (*Peripatetic School, Priscian, Strato*)

Carl A. Huffman, Professor of Classics, DePauw University, USA (*Archytas, Philolaus, Pythagoras and Pythagoreanism*)

Brad Inwood, Professor of Classics, University of Toronto, Canada (*Empedocles*)

Karsten Friis Johansen, Professor of Ancient and Medieval Philosophy, University of Copenhagen, Denmark (*Logos*)

G. B. Kerferd, Professor of Greek Emeritus, University of Manchester, USA (*Antiphon, Dissoi Logoi, Gorgias, Hippias*)

Wilbur R. Knorr, Professor of the History and Philosophy of Science, Stanford University, USA (*Archimedes, Menelaus, Theodosius*)

David Konstan, Professor of Classics, Brown University, USA (*Infinite, Nausiphanes*)

Richard Kraut, Professor of Philosophy, Northwestern University, USA (*Plato*)

André Laks, Professor of Ancient Philosophy, Université Charles De Gaulle–Lille III, France (*Diogenes of Apollonia, Hippo*)

Robert Lamberton, Associate Professor of Classics, Washington University in St. Louis, USA (*Allegory, Cornutus, Hesiod, Pherecydes*)

James G. Lennox, Professor of History and Philosophy of Science, University of Pittsburgh, USA (*Greek Science*)

J. H. Lesher, Professor of Philosophy and Classics, University of Maryland, USA (*Theories of Knowledge, Xenophanes*)

Eric Lewis, Associate Professor of Philosophy, McGill University, Canada (*Andronicus, Time, Void*)

A. A. Long, Irving Stone Professor of Literature, University of California at Berkeley, USA (*Hierocles, Ptolemy*)

T. J. Luce, Professor of Classics Emeritus, Princeton University, USA (*Herodotus*)

John Patrick Lynch, Professor of Classics, University of California at Santa Cruz, USA (*Gymnasium, Lyceum*)

Arthur Madigan, S. J., Associate Professor of Philosophy, Boston College, USA (*Aristotelian Commentators*)

Richard P. Martin, Professor of Classics, Princeton University, USA (*Comic Poets, Homer, Seven Sages*)

Gareth B. Matthews, Professor of Philosophy, University of Massachusetts at Amherst, USA (*Augustine*)

Jørgen Mejer, Reader in Classics, University of Copenhagen, Denmark (*Aëtius, Apollodorus of Athens, Diogenes Laertius, Doxography, Philostratus*)

Henry Mendell, Associate Professor of Philosophy, California State University at Los Angeles, USA (*Aristarchus, Nicomachus, Theaetetus and Theodorus*)

Stephen P. Menn, Associate Professor of Philosophy, McGill University, Canada (*Metaphysical Thought*)

Fred D. Miller, Jr., Professor of Philosophy and Executive Director, Social Philosophy and Policy Center, Bowling Green State University, USA (*Political Thought*)

Phillip T. Mitsis, Professor of Classics and Director of the Alexander Onassis Center, New York University, USA. Associate Editor

Deborah K. W. Modrak, Professor of Philosophy, University of Rochester, USA (*Theories of Mind*)

John L. Moles, Professor of Classics, University of Durham, UK (*Crates of Thebes, Cynics and Cynicism, Demonax, Diogenes of Sinope, Hipparchia, Hypatia, Menedemus of Lampsacus, Menippus, Musonius Rufus*)

Donald R. Morrison, Associate Professor of Philosophy, Rice University, USA (*Xenophon*)

Alexander P. D. Mourelatos, Roy Allison Vaughan Centennial Professor in Philosophy, The University of Texas at Austin, USA (*Parmenides*)

Ian Mueller, Professor of Philosophy, The University of Chicago, USA (*Bryson, Clement of Alexandria, Early Greek Mathematics, Euclid, Hippolytus, Nemesius, Theon*)

David K. O'Connor, Associate Professor of Philosophy, University of Notre Dame, USA (*Aeschines, Antisthenes*)

Dominic J. O'Meara, Professor of Philosophy, Chair of Ancient Philosophy, University of Fribourg, Switzerland (*Amelius, Ammonius Saccas, *Damascius, Dexippus, Iamblichus, Numenius, Origen [pagan], Plotinus, Porphyry, Proclus*)

Anthony Preus, Professor of Philosophy, Binghamton University (SUNY), USA (*Hermetica, Polemo, Sotion*)

Jeffrey S. Purinton, Lecturer in Philosophy, University of Oklahoma, USA (*Demetrius of Laconia, Democritus, Leucippus, Metrodorus of Chios*)

Mark T. Riley, Professor of Classics, California State University at Sacramento, USA (*Manilius*)

T. M. Robinson, Professor of Philosophy, University of Toronto, Canada (*Cosmology, Cratylus, Heraclitus*)

James Romm, Assistant Professor of Classics, Bard College, USA (*Eratosthenes, Strabo*)

R. B. Rutherford, Tutor in Greek and Latin Literature, Christ Church, Oxford, UK (*Marcus Aurelius*)

Edward Schiappa, Associate Professor of Communication, University of Minesota , USA (*Isocrates*)

Malcolm Schofield, Reader in Ancient Philosophy and Fellow of St. John's College, University of Cambridge, UK (*Alexinus, Anaxagoras, Archelaus, Aristo of Chios, Bion, Cassius, Persaeus*)

Lawrence P. Schrenk, unaffiliated scholar (*Philoponus*)

David N. Sedley, Reader in Ancient Philosophy and Fellow of Christ's College, University of Cambridge, UK (*Colotes, Hermarchus, Metrodorus of Lampsacus, Polyaenus, Anon. Comm. on* Theaetetus)

Nicholas D. Smith, Professor of Philosophy, Michigan State University, USA (*Socrates*)

Robin Smith, Professor of Philosophy, Texas A & M University, USA (*Dialectic, Logic*)

Eleonore Stump, Robert J. Henle Professor of Philosophy, St. Louis University, USA (*Boethius*)

Josip Talanga, Fellow of the Institute of Philosophy, University of Zagreb, Croatia (*Theophrastus*)

Harold A. S. Tarrant, Professor of Classics, University of Newcastle, NSW, Australia (*Albinus, Alcinous, Antiochus, Crantor, Crates of Athens, Olympiodorus, Philo of Larissa, Thrasyllus*)

Teun L. Tieleman, Lecturer in Ancient Philosophy, Catholic University of Nijmegen, The Netherlands (*Chrysippus, Cleanthes, Zeno of Citium*)

Robert B. Todd, Professor of Classics, University of British Columbia, Canada (*Cleomedes, Geminus*)

Voula Tsouna-McKirahan, Assistant Professor of Classics and Philosophy, Pomona College, USA (*Aristippus, Cyrenaic Philosophy, Phaedo, Phaedrus, Socratic Circle*)

Iakovos Vasiliou, Assistant Professor of Philosophy, Georgia State University, USA (*Athenodorus of Tarsus, Diogenes of Ptolemais, Eudromus, Panthoides, Zeno of Tarsus*)

Heinrich von Staden, Professor of Classics and Comparative Literature, Yale University, USA (*Alcmaeon, Athenaeus, Celsus, Erastistratus, Heraclides of Tarentum, Herophilus, Hippocrates and the Hippocratic Corpus*)

Barbara Price Wallach, Associate Professor of Classical Studies, University of Missouri at Columbia, USA (*Diatribe*)

Michael J. White, Professor of Philosophy, Arizona State University, USA (*Dialectical School, Diodorus Cronus, Philo the Dialectician*)

Stephen A. White, Associate Professor of Classics, The University of Texas at Austin, USA (*Antipater of Tarsus, Antipater of Tyre, Apollodorus of Seleucia, Critolaus, Diogenes of Tarsus, Hieronymus, Lyco, Menedemus of Eretria*)

Paul Woodruff, Professor of Philosophy and Thompson Professor in the Humanities, The University of Texas at Austin, USA (*Anonymus Iamblichi, Euthydemus, "Old Oligarch," Prodicus, Protagoras, Sophists, Thrasymachus, Thucydides*)

Donald J. Zeyl, Professor of Philosophy, University of Rhode Island, USA. Editor

ISBN 0-313-28775-9

90000>

EAN

9 780313 287756

HARDCOVER BAR CODE